Isabel the Queen

Life and Times

REVISED EDITION

Peggy K. Liss

PENN

University of Pennsylvania Press
Philadelphia

THE MIDDLE AGES SERIES

Ruth Mazo Karras, Series Editor
Edward Peters, Founding Editor

A complete list of books in the series is available from the publisher.

Publication of this volume was assisted by a grant from the Program for Cultural Cooperation between Spain's Ministry of Culture and United States Universities.

Originally published 1992 by Oxford University Press

Revised edition published 2004 by the University of Pennsylvania Press
Printed in the United States of America on acid-free paper

10   9   8   7   6   5   4   3   2   1

Published by
University of Pennsylvania Press
Philadelphia, Pennsylvania 19104-4011

Library of Congress Cataloging-in-Publication Data

Liss, Peggy K.
    Isabel the Queen : life and times / Peggy K. Liss.—Rev. ed.
        p.   cm.—(Middle Ages series)
    Includes bibliographical references and index.
    ISBN 0-8122-1897-3 (cloth : alk. paper)
    1. Isabella I, Queen of Spain, 1451–1504.   2. Spain—History—Ferdinand and Isabella,
1479–1516.   3. Queens—Spain—Biography.   I. Title.   II. Series.
DP163.L48   2004
946'.03'092—dc22
[B]

                                                                2004043084

Frontispiece: Master of the Magdalen Legend, Portrait of Isabel la Católica, 1492. Prado, Madrid.

To Peter.

Some things never change.

Contents

Illustrations

Preface to the Revised Edition

Anniversaries, like family gatherings, have a way of exploding conventional truths. This book originally appeared in 1992, during the quincentenary of Christopher Columbus's arrival in America on a voyage commissioned by Isabel. By that year's end, Columbus had been demoted from discoverer to invader, his future status in the history books under siege.

And now in 2004, what of Isabel, on this, the five hundredth anniversary of her death? I can only conclude that, whatever the fate of Columbus, Isabel stands firm; she is a major historical figure of the Western world. Her sponsoring of a voyage linking Europe and America and setting the initial nature of encounter remains one reason why. Another is that her stature has never been based solely upon a positive assessment of what she did and why she did it. Within Western history, she has no pedestal to crash down from.

Nonetheless, Isabel was a force, personally and politically: she threaded her way through conspiracies, faced down adversaries, triumphed in a civil conflict and then in a religious war. She gained the crown on her own terms, surrounded herself with able administrators, evoked awed respect from her subjects, and forged powerful alliances. She built a state and led her country into international preeminence and toward world empire. She was also fortunate in that she shared a remarkable lifelong love and working partnership with an equally strong king, Fernando of Aragón, whom she had married sight unseen and whose temperament and skills complemented hers. A reigning queen, she was the mother of notable queens, as well as of a unified Spain. That said, there remains the infamous Isabel who instituted the Spanish Inquisition and gave Jews and Muslims the choice of conversion or expulsion from their native land.

The original edition of this book pried apart the jointness of the dual reign of Fernando and Isabel and established the authority and something of the personality of Isabel. At the time, I was swimming against a tide of interest in social and regional Spanish history by choosing to take a new look at a political figure. Nonetheless, reconsidering a ruling queen provided new insight into social and cultural matters: for instance, shedding light on the importance of the royal role—Isabel's role—in the Inquisition and in promoting or inhibiting violent outbreaks against Jews, as well as in orchestrating the lead-up to their expulsion. I also then sought to overturn two dismissive verdicts on Isabel, to establish that she was neither simply a woman of saintly piety nor a religious fanatic. In the doing, the range of imagery and symbols she employed to advertise herself and her program became apparent and highly important. Yet questions have lingered: Her ideology unpacked, how effective was it? How much of it did she herself take to heart? And how did an intrepid but obscure young princess become so formidable a monarch? This edition responds to those questions. It looks harder at Isabel's character and her acute sense of what was expected of her as a Spanish ruler, as well as at her determination to meet the highest of those expectations. It more clearly charts the evolution of her personality, intellect, and goals in interaction with events. The revision and rearrangement of certain chapters, builds on what was initially presented as background information in discussing how importantly history and tradition figured in her thinking and self-representation. In this edition, too, my sources are much more fully documented.

Reflection has confirmed that Isabel was highly intelligent, courageous, and politically astute. Developed and underscored here is her demonstration of several outstanding traits: she was possessed of great moral conviction, she was ambitious, and she was literal minded. Isabel had a strong sense of reality, and her own reality included a huge legacy of myth interwoven with sacrosanct tradition and construed as divinely inspired history. Upon gaining the crown, she committed herself wholeheartedly to fulfilling the traditional aspirations of her nation and its greatest rulers as she understood them. Isabel believed fervently that Spain's ruler was preeminent on Earth and divinely charged with leading an ongoing Spanish mission that in time was to culminate universal history, and that central to that mission was Christian advance against infidel and heretic. She was now that ruler. Moreover, she recognized that to reign successfully the monarch must be seen as imbued with virtues considered royal, the foremost of them being prudence, and she strove both to cultivate and personify those virtues.

This book tells how Isabel, displaying moral conviction and unflinching moral certitude, turning an imagined future into Spanish destiny, gained immense popularity. It looks at how she and her adherents widely disseminated her stance through chronicles, architecture, and iconography, drama, poems, and ballads, and songs and sermons. And it traces how what she stood for struck responsive chords in popular belief. Clearly, however disparate her policies, in carrying them out she translated aspirations commonly understood as Spanish ideals into anticipated reality; and her policies gained cohesion through each being presented as furthering the national mission. It shows how Isabel, both behaving as an absolute monarch and firmly believing in the propaganda she engendered, successfully presented centralizing innovation as continuity and reform as renovation. In the doing, she seamlessly linked religion and politics. So, for example, she rationalized the Inquisition and the expulsions of Jews and Muslims as the eradication of impurities or stains from the social fabric.

A principal criticism of the original edition was that it relied too strongly on the writings of Isabel's chroniclers and courtiers. Since then, work in various fields of history has confirmed that such accounts, beyond being many and rich and pleasurable, can be read to provide invaluable insights into the context and narrative of a royal life and into ideologies speaking to systems of cultural belief as well. To a generation wise in the art of the spin, it is far easier to accept that Isabelline chroniclers both attest to the gap between historical reality and operative myth and to their symbiosis. The decade or so since that first edition appeared has reconfirmed that how Isabel and her publicists presented her can yield crucial evidence regarding her character, convictions, and purposes, as well as the ideational, religious, and political contexts of her times. Those chronicling contemporaries of hers—along with the rhetoric she and they employed and other conduits of her symbolic imagery—reveal just how Isabel appealed to, and stimulated, an ingrained militant religious faith and a belief in national mission. Moreover, she did so with telling effect on Spanish, Western, and indeed world history. The historian José Manuel Nieto Soria, who has done much in the past dozen years to trace the two-way flow of political theology in Isabel's Spain, has put it this way: "At the end of the fifteenth century, the ideological foundations and the practice of propaganda that were consubstantial were not secondary aspects of ruling, but essential dimensions of it, in a context more or less generalized in the West and that Machiavelli left accurately defined in asserting that *to govern is to make to believe.*"

In the years since 1992, Isabel's historical stature has if anything increased, as is reflected in a stream of Isabelline studies. This new edition has benefited from recent scholarship as well as my own further research and reconsiderations. New monographs and the resurgence of scholarly interest in Spanish political history and in royal figures have served to confirm Isabel's power and effectiveness, illuminate her personality, times, and governance, and affirm her place as a mover and shaker in Western history. That historians have become more concerned with religious influences on politics has served to enhance the prominence of a queen who provides a stellar instance of counting on the interplay of the religious and the political to achieve maximum cultural impact. Citations to a number of their newer works and others appear in the endnotes here. Throughout, I have restored annotations omitted from the first edition and corrected errors and misprints.

*   *   *

My appreciation to everyone who offered help, advice, and criticism, who in one way or another kept me at it: to Barbara Abrash, Jonathan Brown, Bill Christian, Tom Colchie, Vicenta Cortés, Kathleen Deagan, John Elliott, Leslie Freeman, Susan T. Freeman, Michael Gill, Annette Gordon, David Henige, Carole Horn, Richard Kagan, Ronda Kasl, Peter Korn, Sabine MacCormack, Angus Mackay, Linda Martz, Helen Nader, Joseph O'Callaghan, Beatrice Patt, William Phillips, Jack Pole, Jim Saksteder, Joyce Seltzer, Matias Verna, Jake Viebrock, Stephen Weissman, and Sara Wolper; to Miguel Angel Ladero Quesada for his careful reading of the entire penultimate draft; to Sandra Sider while at the Hispanic Society of America, to Everette Larsen, Georgette Dorn, and the late Dolores Martin at the Library of Congress; to those who helped at the Archivo General de Simancas, the Biblioteca Nacional, the British Library, the Fitzwilliam Museum Library, the Fundación Lázaro Galdiano, the Morgan Library, the Newberry Library, the New York Public Library; and the many others over the years. I particularly want to thank the John Simon Guggenheim Memorial Foundation for a fellowship spurring completion of this book. In addition to my initial acknowledgments, for advice and help directly and indirectly bearing on this edition, I am indebted to Dave Kelly at the Library of Congress for unfailingly finding supposedly lost books and answers to hard questions. It has been a pleasure to work with Jerry Singerman, Erica Ginsburg, and Christine L. Sweeney at the University of Pennsylvania Press. And once again, my gratitude to Inés Azar, who produced a superb Spanish translation of the original edition and has continued to do her best to keep me from wild surmise and to textual accuracy.

THE ROYAL RELATIONSHIPS OF ISABEL OF CASTILE

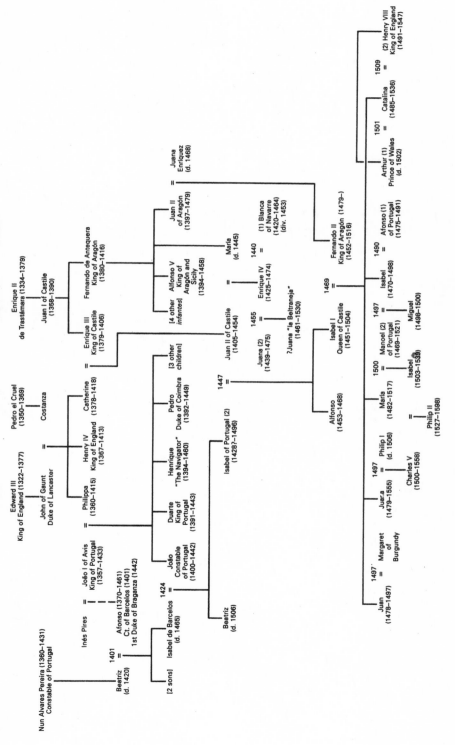

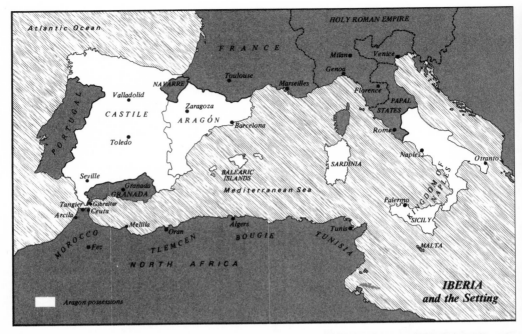

IBERIA
and the Setting

Aragon possessions

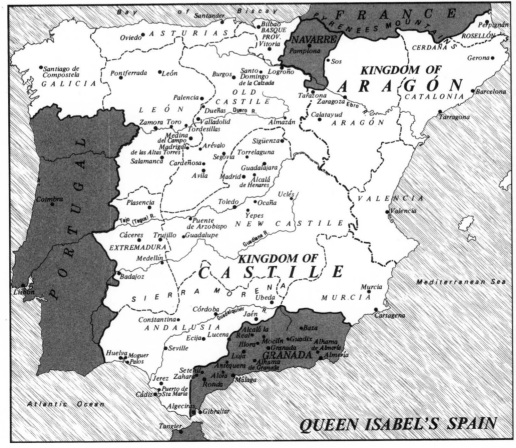

QUEEN ISABEL'S SPAIN

Cosa fué por cierto maravillosa, que lo que muchos hombres y grandes seño-res no se acordaron de hazer en muchos años, solo una muger, con su trabajo y gouernación lo hizo en poco tiempo.

It was certainly a thing most marvelous, that what many men and great lords did not manage to do in many years, a single woman did in a short time through work and governance.

—Hernando del Pulgar, Las coplas de Mingo Revulgo, *ed. Domínguez Bordona, gloss on copla 21, p. 224*

An Embassy to Egypt: 1502

On return to Spain from an embassy to Egypt in September of 1502, Pedro Mártir exulted in having reached once more the most secure port of all, the Queen. Where, he asked a friend, could be found among the ancients, "among the queens and the powerful, such a one, who does not lack either the valor to undertake great endeavors, or the constancy to carry them through, or the enchantment of honesty?" She was a woman "stronger than a strong man, more constant than any human soul, a marvelous example of honesty and virtue; Nature has made no other woman like her."[1]

Nor was he alone in his opinion. A consensus existed among her contemporaries that the queen of Castile was an extraordinary woman who was also an extraordinary monarch, one of the most powerful the world had ever known. Truly extraordinary still is the extent to which Isabel's powerful intellect and powerful will interacted with her will to power in enabling her to become the monarch she sought to be. Europe had no queen as great until the advent of England's Elizabeth I.

Yet unlike Elizabeth, Isabel was no virgin queen, but is generally remembered as half of a royal couple who ruled jointly and forged a nation of the medieval kingdoms comprising Spain. She alone was proprietary queen of Castile, he king of Aragón, smaller in territory and one-fifth as populous. From those two disparate realms arose modern Spain. The power she and Fernando exercised was seen as so seamlessly joint and the great harmony that existed between them was perceived as so complete, that Hernando del Pulgar, her most astute chronicler, could not, on Isabel's having given birth, resist commenting that "the King and Queen had been delivered of a daughter." That lifelong facade of shared power was imposed by Isabel. It has continued to confound some people who should know better. Thus, the British Library in its subject catalogue as late as 1985 listed her as "Isabella. Queen. Consort of Ferdinand V of Spain."

Still, there are other reasons for her relative obscurity. Until recently, biographers have preferred to take on subjects more exemplary than not, and Isabel presents a hopeless amalgam of qualities, some worthy of admiration, some deplorable. And, while making possible Spanish unity and international standing, she was also responsible for some of Western history's low points.

She it was who introduced the Spanish Inquisition, who made war on the emirate of Granada, and who expelled Spain's Muslims and Jews. And today descendants of peoples then inhabiting America and many others place in the same condemnatory category her backing of Christopher Columbus.

*   *   *

Pietro Martire d'Anghiera, a native of Milan and a humanist, a teacher of the liberal arts, came to Spain to tutor noble boys and stayed, to become known there as Pedro Mártir de Anglería.[2] He sponged up the atmosphere and the news at court and recorded it all in the form of several hundred letters addressed to friends and benefactors. His arrival in Spain in 1487 had coincided with the royal siege of the kingdom of Granada's principal port, Málaga; he writes of being dazzled by the ability and resolve of the king and queen and was instantly caught up in the prevailing spirit of militantly high-minded endeavor, so caught up that he became a soldier. Mártir exudes continual delight in being close to great personages impelling great events. He exulted in an atmosphere charged with the energetic and effective pursuit of religious idealism, and in the aura of power and glory emanating from its pursuers.

Mártir was especially devoted to the queen and went to Egypt principally on behalf of her Castile. His account of his mission to Egypt chiefly as her emissary reveals his ardent seconding of her goals, as well as something of their scope and context. His message to the sultan of Egypt, then, yields insight into the queen he served—into how Isabel's mind worked, her projection of her self-image, what she wanted for her realm, and how she went about attaining it.

*   *   *

On February 2, 1502, al-Ashrāf Qānsūh al-Ghawrī, sultan of Babylon, lord of Egypt, Syria, and Palestine, summoned the recently arrived Spanish envoy into his presence—with great secrecy so that the many and influential Muslims and Jews in Cairo who had fled or been expelled from Spain would not hear of it.

In effect, Mártir had been sent to dissuade the sultan from carrying out his threat to treat Christians in his domains as the rulers of Spain were treating Muslims in theirs. Yet at the same time, since the sultan held Jerusalem, Mártir was also instructed to dissuade him from withdrawing his protection from its Christian holy places. We have his report of that interview.

The sultan's immediate response to that request was not auspicious. Why, he asked, should he not retaliate? For the Spanish rulers had not only seized Muslim Granada, but after agreeing that its people might stay and keep their religion they had instead forced them to become Christians. And why had they expelled the Jews?[3]

Mártir replied that he had not been sent to render account, and that his monarchs were so powerful they feared no lord or king, for their empire extended from the pillars of Hercules to the sultan's own coasts; still, he would satisfy his curiosity. That explanation took the form of a history lesson. Centuries before, when the Visigoths ruled Spain, a count named Julian, to avenge "an affront" that Rodrigo, the Visigoth king, had inflicted on his daughter, had sought the help of African Muslims. Those Moors had swept through all Iberia, up to the forbidding northern mountains of the kingdom of Asturias. There, however, a small group of Christians, led by one Pelayo, besieged in a mountain cave, turned the tide. Thirty men and women, hurling stones and shooting arrows, drove back the attackers. And from then on, over centuries, the land was regained, until the present monarchs completed its reconquest. And so they had injured no one, for they had but retaken from cruel usurpers what their ancestors had lost. Mártir gave the sultan a version of the accepted view of Spanish history, although diplomatically omitting certain traditional parts, such as that Spain had been lost because of divine anger at the sins of its Christians and their kings, or that Pelayo and his small band, restored to God's good graces, had withstood several hundred thousand Muslims, or that the Lord had seen to it that 124,000 of those Ishmaelites somehow died in battle and another 63,000 hurtled to their deaths in a divinely generated earthquake. "He who parted the waters of the Red Sea so that the children of Israel might cross," as one chronicler told it, "also crushed, with an immense mass of mountain, the Arabs who were persecuting the church of God."[4]

As for his monarchs' going back on their word, Mártir continued, it was not so. They had permitted many Muslims and Jews to leave Spain rather than forcing them to turn Christian, and in doing so had emulated Christ, who spurned force. Even when the entire kingdom of Granada had revolted, its Muslims killing many Christians and deserving death, the monarchs had shown mercy, allowing them to become Christian or providing ships for those who preferred to go to Africa. And in two of their highnesses' many kingdoms, Aragón and Valencia, there yet resided many more thousands of Muslims than Christians. They lived in peace, with no less liberty than anyone else and protected by law. They might freely attend their mosques, ride horses, possess arms, build houses, cultivate fields, and own cattle. What he said was true, as far as it went. What he did not say was that those Muslims were productive farmers, artisans, and laborers, highly useful to local nobles and protected by them so that royal disruption of those arrangements would prove extremely impolitic. Mártir had carefully drawn a parallel closely corresponding to the sultan's policies regarding Christians. The Jews, however, were another matter, one of far less moment to the sultan.

As to the Jews, Mártir explained, his monarchs had expelled them because they were "a putrid pestilence," infecting Christians and breeding heresy, and if the sultan but knew the contagion they spread, he would again throw them out of Egypt as had the pharaohs, for they dirtied what they touched, corrupted what they looked upon, disrupted the divine and the human, and destroyed everything by their words. Merely to expel such abominable people had been mild and merciful.

Here Mártir freely relayed the current and official attitude in Spain. He reported following faithfully the detailed royal instructions he had received, and also indicated that those instructions were remarkably accurate in forecasting the issues the sultan raised and suggesting how he should respond to them effectively.[5] His report and the royal instructions in turn sheds light on opinions then widespread in Isabel's Spain. Together, they disclose a vision of reality that the queen nurtured in her country and exported abroad, and in which there existed a certain amount of historical distortion. Mártir relies on the accepted Spanish view of history and attests to its fostering by the royal court. How that mix of myth and history came to define Spain and its people, and how the long-standing royal role in promoting it affected the ongoing present and the subsequent course of that history, are essential aspects of Isabel's story. So is another and less celebrated topic raised by Mártir.

Changing tack, he next proposed to the sultan an alliance with Spain's rulers. They were mindful, he said, that, although Mameluke Egypt was Muslim, it stood in effect as a bulwark against their common enemy, the Ottoman Turks, who threatened both Egypt and Europe. And he reminded the sultan of another shared interest, in the vital trading routes linking Europe, Africa, and Asia, the mercantile network connecting the Indian Sea with the Mediterranean and through it with the Atlantic Ocean. Between them, Mártir observed, Spain and Egypt controlled those great hubs of a single commercial system, the port cities at either end of the Mediterranean Sea: Seville, Valencia, Barcelona, and Sicily in the West, and Alexandria in the East, with its further connections to Asia. Both men were aware that, even while warring against the Muslims of Granada, Spaniards had traded in Alexandria, and that a favorable balance of trade, involving a continuing flow of gold from Muslim Africa, had contributed to Spanish victory. Mindful of mutual military and economic interests, the sultan was won over. He expressed his great admiration for the power of the Spanish sovereigns and recognized their value as allies against a mutual adversary. He would do all they asked, but now their envoy must leave at once and as he came, secretly. And so Mártir returned, as he put it, to the most secure port of all, the queen, Isabel.

*   *   *

Today, medieval Spain generally calls to mind a kingdom closed in on itself, much like a large crusader fortress. How was it, then, that it lay so open to trade, including with the avowed religious enemy? Or that numerous Muslims and Jews had lived within its borders for centuries when, in 1451, a princess was born? Moreover, how did it turn out that, against all odds, that princess, Isabel of Castile, became one of Spain's most notable rulers and had a world-wide impact?

Mártir's account and opinions convey some answers. One is an aware-ness, common to the sultan and his sovereigns, of the political efficacy at home of religious warfare and its usefulness to people in power. Mártir affirms that the crusades had demonstrated to Western rulers the popular appeal and uni-fying qualities of holy war and that Spanish kings had long represented them-selves as committed to crusading against the religious enemy and to regaining territory within the Iberian peninsula, that they had made it a policy to show that they were, to coin a phrase, homeland crusaders. By Isabel's time, the greatest kings were remembered as those who had fought the Moors and won battles and land. Mártir's account also attests to a wide consensus that to be Spanish, and particularly to be a Spanish ruler, was to share a history strongly driven by holy war.

What he did not say to the sultan was that Spain's rulers were not expected, and themselves did not expect, to stop at its borders. Rather, as a medieval prophecy popular in court circles and among royal subjects alike foretold, a Spanish leader was one day to regain Jerusalem and the holy places and so usher in the world's final, golden messianic age, and that allied with that Christian ruler would be Babylon-Egypt.[6]

In the interim, as royal tradition endorsed and Mártir's embassy corrobo-rated, avowed devotion to what is now known as the reconquest of Spain did not preclude Spanish monarchs from quietly making advantageous alliances with Muslim heads of state. Nor, until Isabel and Fernando, had it stopped any of them from supporting religious coexistence within Spain and asserting their own authority over each religious group.[7] Yet for centuries religious antipathies had smoldered, deeply embedded in popular Christian culture and ready, like live coals, to burst into flame when stirred—as happened sporadi-cally until Jews and Muslims were expelled.

The questions remain: How and why then did a queen tap into this kingly crusading tradition, and how did she come to turn her back on another position taken by her royal predecessors and to destroy a religious arrangement so long useful to them? Those questions and others—how to interpret her reputation for piety? how to evaluate the extent of her power? how to begin to assess what impelled her massively inhumane policies?— have gone far to shape and direct my search for Isabel. The short answer to them all is that while she operated on certain fundamental convictions, quite frequently throughout her life one thing led to another. An old Spanish ballad announces, *Yo no digo esta canción / sino a quien conmigo va*—"I will not tell this song except to those who go with me." Isabel is to be found in her unfolding story.

I

Princess

Chapter 1
Walls and Gates: Castile, 1451

On Thursday, April 22, at four and two-thirds hours after midday in the year of our Lord 1451 was born the Holy Catholic Queen, Doña Isabel, daughter of the King, Don Juan II, and of the Queen, Doña Isabel, his second wife.
—*Cronicón de Valladolid*[1]

The Queen, Our Lady, from childhood was without a father, and we can even say a mother. . . . She had work and cares, and an extreme lack of necessary things.
—*Hernando del Pulgar*[2]

In 1451 the town council of Murcia heard from the king of Castile, Juan II, of the birth on April 22 of an *infante*. An *infante* could be male or female, but the more specific term for a princess other than the heir presumptive is *infanta*. Such recourse to ambiguity, while undoubtedly cleared up by the royal messenger, carried notice that the king and his queen consort, Isabel of Portugal, had had a child who could inherit the crown of Castile. This *infante* was indeed an *infanta*, and was given the name of Isabel. At birth she was second in line of royal succession after her half-brother, Enrique, King Juan's son by his first queen, María of Aragón. And Enrique, although twenty-six years old and married for quite a while, remained childless, making Isabel's succession a possibility.

Murcia's councilors quickly organized a procession and a mass of thanksgiving for the arrival of the royal child and the health of the queen. They took longer to comply with the order accompanying the king's announcement that they honor the occasion with a gift to a certain royal secretary and treasurer. Faced with what to give and how to pay for it, the town fathers found 10,000 *maravedís* through mortgaging the income on municipal sales taxes on meat and fish, then decided that a fitting present to the royal functionary would be an *esclava mora,* a female Muslim slave. When the woman selected died of plague, Murcia's *corregidor*—the royal official imposed on most municipal councils to oversee and expedite their business—simply appropriated another woman. Immediately, an irate couple appeared before the council complaining that their Miriem had been seized against her will. There is no record that Miriem was ever consulted, even when at length her masters agreed to sell her for the 10,000 *maravedís* budgeted by the council and paid to them through Abraham de Aloxas and Mose Axarques, Jews who either managed the public funds or advanced the sum against future repayment. With so much invested in their gift, the councilmen also hired a man and a mule to deliver Miriem to the house of her new owner.[3]

*   *   *

Plague and Muslims were facts of life in this town near the western edge of the Mediterranean Sea and had long represented a twin-pronged threat to Europe. In 1451, the year of Isabel's birth, the most dreaded Muslims were the Ottoman Turks who, under the Grand Turk Mehmet II, began moving westward in earnest, and two years later would conquer Constantinople. Bubonic plague had arrived in Europe from the eastern Mediterranean a century earlier. Thousands, perhaps hundreds of thousands, of people had died of it, among them the king of Castile, Alfonso XI, in 1350, while besieging Muslim Gibraltar. His death had triggered a series of events leading to the reign of a new royal dynasty, the Trastámara, which was Isabel's. Now, in the mid-fifteenth century, at Isabel's birth, the devastated populace and economy were recovering, but epidemics still occurred sporadically. The death of her younger brother, Alfonso, purportedly caused by bubonic plague, would open for Isabel the way to the crown. And during her reign, those metaphors for evil, terms of pestilence and defilement, would proliferate, including in diatribes against Jews similar to the one Pedro Mártir delivered to the sultan of Egypt. But that is getting ahead of the story.

Madrigal de las Altas Torres

Isabel was born far inland, behind the lofty walls of Madrigal de las Altas Torres—Madrigal of the High Towers—in the heart of the *meseta*, the flat tableland at the heart of Castile. The forty-eight *altas torres* rising along the forty-foot-high walls ringing the town spoke of safety in a world geared to war, particularly war between Christian inhabitants and Muslim raiders. But those walls also spoke of paradox: made of brick and rubble, materials typical to *mudéjar* construction, they revealed an origin or an inspiration unequivocally Arabic.[4] Madrigal, like other places on Spain's central plateau, had been alternately occupied by Christians and Muslims until well into the eleventh century, and it was home to some inhabitants of Muslim culture afterward. In Madrigal too, in the great house abutting those walls called the royal palace,

Isabel toddled under intricately worked wooden ceilings, *artesonados,* carved by *mudéjares,* Muslim subjects of Castile's king. And tradition has it that she was baptized in Madrigal's church of San Nicolás, in its baptismal font thickly encrusted with gold from Muslim Africa.

✳   ✳   ✳

The red-brown soil around Madrigal is fertile, in the summer a landscape of wheat, grapevines, and Mediterranean light, irrigated by the Zapardiel River to the east, and by the Trabancas to the west. In 1451, Madrigal was essentially an agricultural town, with roughly nine hundred *vecinos,* or householders, translatable as between three thousand and forty-five hundred inhabitants. Outside its four gates, the land had been worked in concentric circles of garden plots, vineyards, and fields of grain; beyond lay deep woods. The forests provided firewood and game—with the help of Madrigal, it was said, "the king's table held many partridges"—as well as acorns to feed pigs and cattle and to sustain the numerous herds of sheep that wintered in the area until their annual trek northward to spring and summer pasture. The vineyards yielded Madrigal's white wine, "renowned for its good bouquet and better taste," famed in Castile and sought after abroad, so celebrated that the poet Jorge Manrique could have a drunk in a tavern make the irreverent toast, "*O, Beata Madrigal / ora pro nobis a Dios!*"—"O blessed Madrigal, pray for us to God," in a play on the words of the Ave María.[5]

Darkness and Light

Only an occasional reference sheds light on Isabel's childhood. At seventeen, she wrote to her half-brother, the king Enrique IV, accusing him of having treated her badly, representing herself as a semi-orphan raised in obscurity and kept in want by him. Her court chronicler, Hernando del Pulgar, was to state that her early years were spent "in extreme lack of necessary things," and that she was without a father and "we can even say a mother."[6]

Isabel was three when her father, Juan II of Castile, died. He had doted on her mother, Isabel of Portugal, his young second wife, and, rumor had it, come to resent the control exerted over him by his longtime mentor, Alvaro de Luna, who sought to regulate the king's conjugal visits to his queen. What is indisputable is that shortly after Isabel's birth, Luna was beheaded at Juan's order. Within a year, Juan, whether through regret or because Luna's restraining hand was gone, grew immoderate, it was said, in the pleasures of love and table, fell ill of quartanary fevers, and although believing prophecies that he would live to be ninety, died on July 21, 1454, and the crown passed to his elder son, Enrique. Juan was forty-nine years old, the longest-lived king of his dynasty in five generations.

Enrique IV was then thirty. He had had no children with his first wife, Blanca of Navarre, and his second, Juana of Portugal, would have none until Isabel was ten; until then Isabel grew up seeing her younger brother, Alfonso—born in November 1453 when she was two—as heir apparent to Castile's crown and herself as second in line, as her father's last will had stipulated. To the childless Enrique, the two children represented family and dynastic continuity, but also a potential threat. As for Isabel, after the death of her father, her circumstances were none too secure on several other counts she did not mention in that letter.

Her mother, the young dowager queen, Isabel of Portugal, who was twenty-seven years old at her husband's death, then took the two children to live in Arévalo, a royal town consigned to her in Juan's will. Shortly thereafter, according to the chronicler Alonso de Palencia, Enrique called on her accompanied by a favorite of his, Pedro Girón, the master of the military order of Calatrava; Girón immediately "made some indecent suggestions" that shocked the recent widow. Palencia, who is generally vitriolic about both Enrique and Girón, went on to assert that the importuning by this overhasty, unwelcome (and, patently, not sufficiently noble) suitor threw Isabel of Portugal into a profound sadness and horror of the outside world, that she then "closed herself into a dark room, self-condemned to silence, and dominated by such depression that it degenerated into a form of madness."[7]

Another chronicler, who was more in touch with events at the time, confirms the reclusiveness of Isabel's mother but dates it earlier, from her daughter's birth. Whatever the cause or date, young Isabel grew up with a deeply disturbed mother. The child may well have dreaded becoming like her, and suffered tension between affection and fear. Surely too she was aware that her own birth was among the causes mentioned for her mother's madness. It is tempting to conjecture that qualities that Isabel displayed as an adult—love of order and the striving for it; a no-nonsense, highly rational stance; and a sharply defined personality, were honed in reaction to her mother's condition, and even to think that her desire for light in all its forms, and especially in its religious associations—her abhorrence of the forces of darkness, her determination to cleanse the body politic of impurities—was not unrelated to the circumstances of her childhood.

Isabel grew up, then, in several sorts of obscurity, her childhood a sort of purgatory and a test of moral fiber she passed magnificently. Such was long the accepted version of her early years; it was her own version. It is neither strictly accurate nor complete.

Arévalo, fifteen miles from Madrigal and like it a market town, is remembered as the best fortified of royal towns. There, her mother's condition notwithstanding, Isabel spent her early years in great stability and familial warmth. For when she was two and her mother again pregnant, her widowed grandmother, Isabel de Barcelos, arrived from Portugal. Tellingly, when first mentioned in the chronicles Isabel de Barcelos is in her forties and sitting, at King Juan's request, in his privy council. Contemporaries, among them the chronicler Diego de Valera, recognized in her "a notable woman of great counsel." Valera affirmed that after the death of the king, Isabel de Barcelos "was of great help and consolation to the widowed queen, her daughter"; and he commented that her death, in 1466, "was very harmful."[8] Pulgar adds that Isabel missed her grandmother sorely. Surely Isabel de Barcelos ran her daughter's household. And she it doubtlessly was whom the child Isabel took as model. It is revealing that later, as queen, Isabel of Castile enjoyed keeping about her elderly women of good repute and good family.

From all accounts, Isabel de Barcelos was a formidable lady of formidable lineage. She came of royal Portuguese stock with a history of going for the throne and of doing it with claims far weaker than would be those of her Castilian grandchild. Daughter of the first duke of Braganza, Portugal's most powerful noble and an illegitimate son of the king, João I, she had married her uncle, Prince João, one of five sons João I had with Philippa, his queen consort. Philippa too came of redoubtable stock. Her father was John of Gaunt, the English king-making duke of Lancaster, and her mother, Costanza, was a Castilian *infanta*. This lineage meant that young Isabel carried in her veins the royal blood of Castile, Portugal, and England. Doubtlessly too, she took dynastic pride in her own name, Isabel, repeated through seven generations of royal women and originating in her ancestor Saint Isabel, the thirteenth-century Portuguese queen canonized for her good works and miracles.

Isabel's *aya*, or nurse-governess, in Arévalo was also Portuguese. She was Clara Alvarnáez, married to Gonzalo Chacón, to whom Juan II had consigned his children's education. Chacón was also the dowager queen's *camerero,* the administrator of her household. Oddly enough, Chacón had earlier filled the same post for Álvaro de Luna, Juan II's former favorite. Even so, Chacón and Clara Alvarnáez remained close to Isabel throughout their lifetimes. Yet at the same time, Chacón, who had stayed loyal to Luna while he lived, continued to venerate Luna's memory: attributed to Gonzalo Chacón is a chronicle written during Isabel's early years. Chacón focused on Luna, and on Luna's own emphasis on absolute royal authority.[9] The subsequent behavior of Chacón's young royal charges, Isabel and Alfonso, amply demonstrated that, whatever the source, they shared those lofty views on royal power.

Between her grandmother and Chacón, Isabel was raised in an ambience conducive to generating in her a sense of self-esteem bound up with her high station in life, and also a firm belief in her own royal lineage as worthy of a crown, an ambience sustaining a vision of that crown gleaming with the luster of divinely favored monarchy. Moreover, the circumstances of her childhood were such as later to lead Isabel away from unhappy memories of death and madness into imagining her royal parents in their prime, as she would have them sculpted on their tombs in the Charterhouse at Miraflores, where they lay side by side, resplendent in full regalia amid symbols of worldly power and divine majesty. Nonetheless, over that stable household and over its affirmation of her self-worth hovered the shadow of her mother's illness, and beyond that familial circle lay the uncertainty of how she would be received in a wider world known to be treacherous for *infantes*.

Visitors and Others

A child growing up in that *meseta* town of Arévalo would learn that many things were more complex than they appeared. The town's size did not equal its strategic importance. He who wants to be lord of Castile, it was said, had to hold Arévalo. And Arévalo provided a number of lessons in what mattered in Spanish history. It took pride in being a scene of Castile's glorious past and host to some biblical and classical greats. Arévalo remembered the apostle Saint James, patron saint of all Spain, as having preached there. Hercules himself, *el gran Hércules,* had come from the east through Africa bringing Egyptians and Chaldeans to settle Arévalo; he had founded Segovia, Avila, and Salamanca as well, and had left as memorials to his achievements the arches of the Segovian aqueduct (in fact Roman in origin), some statues of himself, and great bulls carved of stone recalling those he had bested in Libya. In 1454, Arévalo had at least two such *toros,* and in its churches were to be seen some ancient caskets of hewn stone, revered as "caves of Hercules." That designation surely referred to the variant legend that Spain had been destroyed by Muslim invaders not because the Visigothic king, Rodrigo, had raped Count Julian's daughter, but rather because Rodrigo had opened a forbidden casket hidden in a cave dug by Hercules beneath the Visigoth capital, Toledo. And just outside Arévalo's walls stood a circle of arched boulders where, as everyone knew, Hercules, that demigod, claimed as illustrious ancestor by Castile's kings and nobles, had revealed the secrets of the movement of the stars and their influence on the world below.[10] The area around Arévalo had also attracted the noble Visigoths, as evidenced by the name, Palacio de Goda, of a nearby hamlet. Moreover, Arévalo's device was an armed knight sallying forth from a castle, meant to commemorate its men who had followed the great king Alfonso VIII into battle at Las Navas de Tolosa in 1212, to achieve the victory against the Moors that had opened Andalusia to Castile. Arévalo offered two lessons that Isabel later demonstrated she had learned well: that size does not necessarily equate with strategic importance and that community rests on nothing more strongly than on pride in a shared past.

More immediately, and although Isabel did not live at court after her father's death, her isolation was relative, for court figures came to Arévalo—relatives of hers who would in one way or another play significant roles in her life. Shortly after her father died Isabel's aunt, his sister María, queen of Aragón, arrived, visibly saddened. María was powerful in her own right; for nearly twenty years she had effectively ruled the kingdom of Aragón while her husband its king, Alfonso V, known as the Magnanimous, held court in Naples. María, *infanta* of Castile and queen of Aragón, had at crucial junctures mediated in the turbulent relations between the two kingdoms. In her peacemaking, she was joined by another María, an *infanta* of Aragón and the first wife of Juan II of Castile. Those two queens, cousins married to cousins, had interceded to avert war between brothers, husbands, and a son—Enrique, then prince of Castile. At the time it was said that if the queen of Castile were its king, there would be peace and well-being in the realm. In Arévalo in 1454, Aragón's queen stayed on to negotiate with her nephew, the new king Enrique IV, on behalf of her brother-in-law Juan, the king of Navarre. It was agreed that Juan make formal renunciation of some Castilian lands he claimed in return for 3.5 million *maravedís* annually.[11] It would be the last of María's many good offices, for she died the next year. Enrique never paid. In 1459, Juan of Navarre succeeded to the crown of Aragón; he would more than compensate for his losses in Castile, dynastically, through the marriage of his son, Fernando, to its future queen, Isabel.

Isabel's half-brother and Castile's new king, Enrique IV, and his court had arrived in Arévalo in September of 1454; they would stay until January of 1455. It was from Arévalo during that time that Enrique proclaimed war against the Muslim emirate of Granada. In 1451, the year Isabel was born, the Ottoman sultan, Murad II, had just died and his son and successor, Mehmet II, known as the Terror of Europe, had taken up Murad's westward campaign, heeding old prophecies that Constantinople would fall and then Rome: *Constantina cadent et alta palatia Romae.* Christians too knew that prophecy, and through Italy the terror-inducing words *Constantina cadent* then "ran from mouth to mouth."[12] When, in May of 1453, Mehmet II took Constantinople, European opinion swelled for a crusade against the Turk. For, as a Spaniard put it, to Christians "Noble Constantinople . . . [was] the second Jerusalem."[13] Jerusalem, the core of Christendom long held captive by Muslims, was the lodestar of crusading impetus, chivalric ideals, and messianic hope, and the ultimate goal of Spanish reconquest. In Castile, the liberation of Jerusalem's holy places was coupled in prophecies and sermons with Spain's future greatness, even with achievement of world empire. Jerusalem's restoration to Christian rule was believed an obligation laid by God upon Castile's monarch, and the driving of Muslims from Spain was viewed as a necessary step in that direction. That holy endeavor had lagged for some time; now Enrique announced it was to be resumed.

Among his first acts as king, "Enrique ordered the members of his council and his *contadores mayores* to Arévalo," wrote the chronicler Valera, his prose reflecting an expectancy in the air, "because there would be drawn up the list of lands, privileges, stipends, alms, and other payments to nobles for bringing their armies to war, and of wages for the people . . . who have to recover the lands that the Moors have usurped in Spain."[14] Whatever those preparations for war that winter meant to a three-year-old, warfare would recur throughout Isabel's youth, eventually to become a way of life. But she would not again see it directed against Muslims until she herself took up the reconquest.[15]

The royal court and the household of the dowager queen arrived in Aré-valo at about the same time, and certainly their members had contact, for it was around then that Enrique and Pedro Girón made that devastating visit to the young and recent widow. It may have been that Girón aspired to gain control of the *infantes* through their mother; or perhaps Enrique was heedful of Juan's last will, which left to his wife a stipulated allowance and several towns, including Madrigal and Arévalo, as well as the custody of the children, but with the proviso only "as long as she remained chaste."[16] Girón was clearly proposing she not do so. That encounter could have done nothing to endear Enrique to Isabel's mother and grandmother, nor to alter their refusal to allow the children to join Enrique's court.

An Education

Isabel of Portugal was devout. Although unable to conceive a child in the early years of her marriage, she did so shortly after making a vow to Holy Mary, which she fulfilled by a barefoot pilgrimage to the shrine of Nuestra Señora de la Vega outside the town of Toro; that child was Isabel of Castile.[17] In Arévalo, the dowager's household had contact with Franciscans whose convent stood just beyond the town's walls and who belonged to the austere Observant branch of that religious order. Tradition has it that those friars had a reputation for sanctity and learning and a hand in Isabel's education, and that the convent had a fine library for, Franciscan vows not to own anything notwithstanding, one Gonzalo de Madrigal, a teacher of theology, had collected the books, then solicited and received from the pope an order against that library ever being broken up.[18] There too Alonso de Madrigal, known as *El Tostado*—a counselor of Juan II, teacher of theology at the University of Salamanca, and widely celebrated in Castile as a model of spirituality and erudition—had begun his own career as a student, and there his death in 1455 was surely mourned; years later Isabel supported publication of his writings.[19] As queen, she also reportedly sent gifts to at least one of that convent's friars, "whom she had known well when she was growing up in Arévalo,"[20] Whatever the extent of her contact with those Franciscans, she was always supportive of that religious order, although not exclusively. She was, as she instructed in her will, buried in Franciscan habit, although most probably because it was a shroud much favored by royalty and thought to facilitate entry into heaven.

Another sort of churchman, an esteemed confessor and advisor of her father's, Lope de Barrientos, bishop of Cuenca, came to the royal court while in Arévalo. King Juan's will had entrusted the education of Isabel and Alfonso to him. Whatever the extent to which Barrientos took up that charge, Isabel came to share an unusual antipathy with him; she would own a copy of his authoritative treaty condemning black magic and would herself become noted for detesting divination.[21] And, like both Barrientos and another mentor of hers, Gonzalo Chacón, she would assume Divine Providence to be directly active in human affairs. Isabel would also exhibit fervent belief in both the power of God and the efficacy of a disciplined and free human will, in both God's power and human initiative. As queen, she would be prone to moralizing and partial to Aesop's moralizing fables; and, among the points the Christian version of Aesop made, one in particular surely struck a responsive chord: "God helps him who helps himself."

In Arévalo with the royal court that fall of 1454 was Rodrigo Sánchez de Arévalo, diplomat, writer, priest, and Enrique's counselor and secretary. Although his name suggests a family connection to the town, Sánchez de Arévalo was accustomed to living in Burgos and at the courts of France and the papacy, and he did not much enjoy wintering in what he wrote of as *"esta desierto villa de Arévalo,"* "this deserted small town of Arévalo." His impression of the place has contributed to the view of Isabel's childhood as isolated and lonely. That cosmopolite, faced with enforced country life, passed the time, as a Florentine in the same predicament would later, by writing down his views on politics and on the education of the prince. And if Sánchez de Arévalo interested himself in the education of the royal children he encountered there, his ideas and his own experience surely lent support to schooling for Isabel; he himself had attended an elementary school for both boys and girls, the free school of the Dominicans at Santa María de Nieva, whose patron was Isabel's paternal grandmother, queen Catalina, yet another reputedly formidable forebear of hers.

Sánchez de Arévalo is also known to have highly esteemed one woman in particular, Joan of Arc, known in Castile as *la poucella,* the virgin; he had been in France during her meteoric career. His admiration was shared by Chacón; Luna's chronicle views that French warrior-saint as inspired by God. Its author recalls glowingly the grand reception accorded her envoys by Juan II of Castile;

and reports Luna was so taken by Joan's valorous deeds that he carried about with him a letter from her, showed it around the court, and treated it like a holy relic.[22] All in all, it is unlikely that as a child, Isabel, although hearing tales of those more usual exemplars for girls, nonviolent women saints, yet did not learn, as she later demonstrated, to admire a strong, assertive will and to appreciate in particular the militant deeds of that devout and intrepid woman warrior, Joan of Arc.

Just what Isabel was formally taught is unknown; if the story of her sewing Fernando's shirts is to be believed, she received the usual female training in domestic arts. She surely too learned the Portuguese spoken at home, and she reportedly rode well. The upbringing of her younger brother, Alfonso, is more easily retrieved, from a description of the essentially chivalric education customary at the time for highborn Castilian boys that appears in the chronicle of Pero Niño, count of Buelna. Before the age of fourteen Pero Niño had learned from the *ayo* provided him by the king that "knights have not been chosen to ride an ass or mule." Rather, they were *cabelleros*—horsemen—and had to excel in jousting, be courteous and well spoken, and, preferably, well built and well dressed, indeed the model of fashion. A knight had to know all about armor, saddles, and horses, and to shine with sword, lance, and bow, as well as at games of darts, bowls, discs, and stones. He was to avoid women and greed, be sober, think before speaking, trust to experience, and value good advice and friends. Above all, he had to master himself: "Plato says we should go against our appetites," the soul restrain the body. All extremes were evil. His heart was to be governed by the Christian virtues. A knight had to have great faith in God and uphold Holy Mother Church. He was not to believe in the false prophecies of Merlin and others like him and he was to beware of alchemists. He might though see in Hercules a paragon of knightly virtue.[23] However closely Alfonso may have striven to follow those injunctions, Isabel's behavior would come to confirm that she herself subscribed to many of those chivalric precepts.

For six or seven years, during most of her childhood, Isabel lived in Arévalo. It was the longest she was ever to stay in any one place. Whatever her formal education there, children in fifteenth-century Europe were seldom sheltered from any aspect of life. And Isabel, highly intelligent, curious, and observant, was undoubtedly aware of whatever could be understood of the world from Arévalo outward, and in that understanding, religion played a central role.

In that upcountry town, as everywhere in Europe, the Roman Catholic religion, its holy days, its ceremony and ritual, marked time and events and the cycles of the year. It profoundly affected behavior, intellect, and emotions, and it explained human relationships, the natural world, and the universe. All acceptable varieties of knowledge and speculation came filtered through faith.

Isabel—living in a pious household, in contact with devout friars, very familiar with worship in Arévalo's churches, the hours of her days tolled by their bells—grew up fully immersed in the Christianity of that time and place.

It was no secret that Arévalo's parish church, San Miguel, was built on the remains of a mosque, reflecting a time-honored practice in Castile of reconsecrating mosques as churches and often dedicating them to Saint Michael, the militant serpent-slaying archangel. Often too, they were dedicated, as was another in the town, to Santa María de la Encarnación, to Holy Mary of the Incarnation, for the doctrine of the Incarnation—of God become flesh—since hated by Muslims, signaled Christian triumph over the infidel. Isabel would see to it that Granada's mosques came to bear those same holy names, and she would not forget those particular cults in her own devotions.

Yet even while becoming steeped in a Roman Catholicism militantly opposed to Islam, the royal child became accustomed to a Christianity borrowing culturally and materially from Muslims. For Arévalo was among the most *mudéjar* of Castilian towns. Its substantial churches, its walls and towers, its bridges and houses, and the porticoed arches over its streets had all been constructed of *ladrillo*, bricks and rubble, in *mudéjar* style. Examples familiar to Isabel are still to be seen in Arévalo, among them the church of San Juan adjoining the site of the royal palace (no longer extant), the Muslim-inspired belltower of the church of San Nicolás, and the church of San Martín with its two *mudéjar* Romanesque towers.

Isabel was also accustomed to the physical presence in the town of people of Muslim culture and of Jews, to people of other customs and religions, thought of as alien and different and looked down upon, but there, a fact of daily life. In the 1450s, among Arévalo's inhabitants were *mudéjares*, a small commuity yet one of the largest in Castile. There was also a Jewish *aljama* or community, whose rabbi, Tsaddic of Arévalo (who died in 1454), and his historian son Josef were highly respected by their coreligionists for their learning.[24] In Castilian towns at that time Muslims and Jews sometimes lived not in closed-off precincts but alongside Christians. Yet while the young *infanta* became accustomed to the polycultural life of Castile, it was most likely at a distance. For although she may have seen and observed them, and been served by some of them, it is unlikely that she mingled with Muslims, or with Jews, or for that matter with any of the other townspeople.

That was not necessarily true in regard to the highborn Granadans who came to Arévalo as honored guests at the Castilian court. In Isabel's childhood, an embassy had arrived in Castile led by Abū'-l Ḥasan 'Alī, the son of Granada's king, Abū Nasr Sa'd. Juan II and then Enrique IV enjoyed watching the prince and his retinue riding Moorish fashion, *a la jineta*, on low saddles, short-stirruped, knees high, on small fast horses, a manner preferred by Enrique and many other Castilians as well.[25] Enrique also had Muslims among his guards. Reputedly a splendid rider herself, did Isabel watch too? However that may be, and although she had firsthand experience of the reality of the mixed population of Iberia and possibly also of the elegance and chivalric reputation of Muslim knights, she nonetheless encountered, very close to home, constant reminders that the first obligation of a Spanish monarch was Christian reconquest.

*   *   *

Enrique had, immediately after his father died, ostensibly "to prevent rumblings and all suspicion," asked the archbishop of Toledo, Alfonso Carrillo, to persuade the dowager queen to come to court, but in vain. While acknowledging herself and her children in the king's power and subject to his will, Isabel of Portugal stoutly refused. Her determination, or perhaps her mother's, won out and, instead, Enrique, upon departure, left posted in Arévalo two hundred men to guard his stepmother and her children, that is, both to keep them safe and maintain control of them.

Thereafter, while Enrique went on three annual campaigns against Muslim Granada, the children's proximate world included those guards, and among them were old border fighters, undoubtedly with inflated memories of exploits during earlier expeditions against Granada. One, Fernando de Villasaña, had raided Granadan border forts and been with a force succoring the Christian outpost of Huelma, whose conquest fifteen years earlier was still celebrated. Such bygone campaigns remained alive in the popular imagination through ballads and legends commemorating the feats of Christian knights and becoming ever more fashionable at court. Part of the experience of growing up for a Castilian child were such spoken or sung poems and veterans' tales of glorious frontier exploits, *hazañas*, against the infidel. The ballads or *romances*, the legends, the reminiscences all imparted a nostalgia for more heroic times, a bygone dedication to high purpose, and a tendency to see Muslim knights as both customary and worthy adversaries. While in Arévalo too, Isabel literally bought into the reconquest-as-holy-war. It is documented that, in 1458, the *infanta* Isabel, aged seven, received a bull of indulgence for her contribution of two hundred *maravedís* to that year's Granadan campaign.[26]

A young captain of the Arévalo garrison, Pedro Puertocarrero, a grandson of the lord of Moguer, represented another facet of the multifaceted Castilian reconquest.[27] Moguer was a thriving port of Andalusia whose seamen would one day join those of nearby Palos on an Atlantic expedition sponsored by Isabel and entrusted to one of the Genoese so familiar in southern Spanish ports, Christopher Columbus. Indeed, the heritage of Andalusians included Atlantic venturing and religious warfare waged at sea; well remembered were the great battles Christian ships had fought against Muslims in the Strait of

Gibraltar. Moreover, while Isabel was growing up in Arévalo, Andalusians were known to be audaciously, and often extralegally, gaining a foothold in North Africa, venturing out into the Atlantic, and raiding and trading along the West African coast. Ships out of Andalusian ports sometimes competed, sometimes cooperated with the Portuguese in sailing to African coasts and seeking to profit from cargos of African slaves and, even more, from African gold. Such activity was explained as Christian advance toward regaining parts of Africa once held by the Visigoths.

Isabel de Barcelos would surely have concurred in having a different, a Portuguese, version of Christian reconquest, one not focused on taking Granada but directly on expansion overseas. Her father-in-law, João I of Portugal, had led expeditions against the strategic city of Ceuta opposite Gibraltar. In a North African mosque converted into a church he had knighted his sons, one of whom, his namesake, João, she was to marry. Another of them, Henrique, known to history as Henry the Navigator and as devoted to both chivalry and crusade, during Isabel's childhood gained renown for avidly promoting Portuguese exploration along African coasts. Henrique put it about that, according to his horoscope, destiny called him to discover hidden secrets, and he proposed to contact the legendary rich and powerful Christian priest-emperor Prester John (myth located his kingdoms in Africa, India, or Asia and declared them reachable by sea from the Atlantic) and possibly even, by thus outflanking Islamic lands, to open a route to Jerusalem.[28] Years later, Isabel would sponsor such an exploratory venture.

Isabel, it is well to remember, had not only a Spanish but also a Portuguese heritage. To her mother, her grandmother, her great-uncle, Henrique, and to her *aya*, Clara Alvarnáez, belonged a vision of reconquest more ample than the Spanish. To the Portuguese, who no longer shared a land border with Muslims, reconquest had become an aggressive campaign against Islam at sea and overseas, one for Christianity and for commerce, ever more focused on the Atlantic Ocean; rumor ran of their accruing greater and greater wealth in gold and slaves. Theirs was an enterprise directed to far lands. Henrique spoke of strange and hostile peoples encountered by voyagers as *homines silvestri,* and thought of them as noble savages, worthy adversaries for Christian knights, and apt for conversion. Be that as it may, all such Portuguese enterprise was ultimately claimed to center on reaching and regaining the old crusading goal of Jerusalem. It was a vision of extensive Christian reconquest with which Isabel was to demonstrate great familiarity.

Did she hear when she was seven of the Portuguese campaign to conquer Morocco, to which Dom Henrique had persuaded his admiring nephew, Portugal's new king Afonso V? And did Isabel de Barcelos tell her grandchildren of the pilgrimages her father and her brother had made to Jerusalem itself? Or of the fabled travels of her brother-in-law, Dom Pedro, another son of João

I? Did Isabel and Alfonso hear of Dom Pedro's encounters with marvels and monsters, and with Amazons of India, widows of a band of Goths and subjects of Prester John? Did they hear about the letter from Prester John that Pedro reputedly brought back to their father, Juan of Castile? Did young Isabel catch the excitement aroused by such searches for unknown—"hidden"—lands and their mythical wealth?[29] If so, it could help to explain her later interest in Africa, the Atlantic, the East, and Jerusalem, and her inclination against much learned opinion to back Columbus. Whether or no, throughout her life, Portugal was important to her: sometimes enemy, sometimes competitor, always family.

Impressions

Enrique too was family, and with him Isabel had a familial quarrel. Isabel remained in the Arévalo household until she was ten, and then lived at his court. At seventeen, she wrote a letter to the king accusing him of having treated her badly, inferring that he had strapped her mother, her brother, and herself by not honoring the provisions Juan II had made for them—which was true, but whether through design or sloppy management is hard to tell. In his relations with his half-sister as in much else, Enrique vacillated, surely exasperating decisive, straight-arrow Isabel. And Enrique was by all accounts devious, a trait particularly unsettling in so powerful a person. A letter he wrote to her in 1463 is very warm—"you do not have any one in this world who loves you as much as I do"—but those words could also be construed as a threat, warning against listening to his enemies.[30] Elsewhere, the terms of affection with which he addressed her were largely formulaic, yet even formula had basis in the strong sense of familial attachment current among the powerful in fifteenth-century Castile, and she and Alfonso were after all the king's closest relatives, which of course cut two ways. Still, Enrique's most sympathetic chronicler, Diego Enríquez del Castillo, sounds defensive in stating that "the King always treated them [Isabel and Alfonso] with much love and great honor, and showed no less to the Queen their mother"; and goes on to say that he *held* them in safe places.[31] Moreover, unless Enrique made unrecorded trips to Arévalo, after his initial stay there he saw little of them, for he is known to have returned only five years later, in the summer of 1459 and then again the following April. When, probably in 1461, he did bring Isabel and her younger brother to court, it was, as shall be seen, not through unalloyed family feeling.

Yet whatever Enrique's sentiments, that Isabel's story is one of a Cinderella-like transformation, that Isabel somehow metamorphosed from a neglected, deprived child to powerful—indeed brilliant—monarch, is clearly not the case. Isabel's childhood, if relatively austere by later fifteenth-century aristocratic standards, was no more than that. Why has it been thought otherwise? The chronicler Pulgar admired Isabel enormously and, even when critical of her policies, such as the workings of the Inquisition, he defended her as well intentioned. He shared her reliance on religious truth as the infallible source of rightmindedness, and he tended to equate display of firm moral conviction with strength of character. It was in considering the formation of her character that he mentioned her early years, leaving the impression that solely through great inner strength and firm faith did this neglected child develop into a peerless monarch. In jointly depicting her childhood as unrelievedly dismal, Isabel and her major chronicler indicated that adversity, when surmounted through self-discipline, was the nursery of great rulers, just as it assuredly was for saints and knights; theirs was an age and a faith that construed suffering and tribulation as a rite of passage attesting to God's special attention and his favor.[32]

Thus, the impression conveyed of young Isabel as poor shunted-aside orphan was an image superimposed on reality; while not completely false, neither was it true. What is true, and of great importance to her later life, is that she herself came to view her childhood that way; she represented herself as someone who had early and resolutely triumphed over adversity. Early too, and certainly in writing that letter at seventeen, she had come to understand well the political value of both showing herself as possessing great fortitude and claiming the moral high ground. It is true, too, that latter-day celebrants of her life have tended to take her moral certainty—visible when princess and heightened in a queen appropriating royal traditions of being divinely directed—for religious piety.

In point of fact, that early self-image of hers, of misfortune overcome through her own efforts, owed much to the concept of ideal monarch given cogency during her father's reign. Luna—in today's terms an expert spinmaster—had seen to it that the king be represented as elected by God and as wielding absolute power. At the same time, Isabel's mentor Chacón and other men close to Juan II had exposed the fissure between royal ideal and that king's behavior. They had criticized her father severely, both to his face and in writing, for shirking responsibility and lacking moral fiber. Isabel's contemporary chroniclers—Valera who spanned the reigns, caustic Palencia, and astute Pulgar—wrote of her in implicit contrast, attributing to Isabel the desirable royal qualities Juan had lacked, qualities long associated with the good ruler who exercised strong personal monarchy, and did so within a universe in which God had made much depend on the crowned head of Castile. Isabel comes to us through those chroniclers as possessing traits consonant with the qualities Castilians had come to endorse as properly kingly, traits she demonstrated repeatedly as queen, among them moral certitude, decisiveness, ambition, mental acuity, political savvy, piety, prudence, and a firm sense of both royal prerogative and royal obligation; all of them had firm basis in the world of her youth.[33] She comes to us as a heaven-sent corrective, to her father and also to her half-brother Enrique, and there is good evidence, as we shall see, that she saw herself in the same light.

Unquestionably then, Arévalo's isolation was relative. And there Isabel learned a good deal about what was expected of the ruler of Castile, including that the otherwise distinct communities of Christians, Muslims, and Jews were united in having the same political head, that a ruler was expected to develop and display a character in accord with traditional concepts of good kingship, and that it was encumbent upon the monarch to carry out the reconquest. Nor is it surprising that, as queen, her public image and her own vision of herself, including of her childhood, would come to coincide remarkably.

Growing up in Arévalo, she assuredly gained a pride in royal lineage, a sense of both royal entitlement and responsibility, and a certainty regarding right and wrong, good and evil, as inseparable from religious faith and ruling well. During her first ten years, before Enrique had her brought to court, she had a more intimate family life, more stability of people and place, and more direct contact with men and women politically astute, than most royal children ever experienced. In her veins, she had learned, ran the blood of warriors, of heroic Goths and Moor fighters, of monarchs and saints, of powerful men and women; she had learned that hers was a heritage for a queen.

God's Design

Isabel's childhood initiated a defining of self, a self formed through discovering moral imperatives—among them ideals of royalty and chivalry and values considered character building—and through taking pride in one's genealogy and the dictates of Spanish history. Above all, her very being had to do with God's design, much of it still hidden, yet to be brought to light.

Light was tenuous. For there was darkness, manifest in the internal war of the soul, and the stain of original sin that was especially onerous for women, the daughters of Eve. Light was Eve's counterpart, Holy Mary. Light was Christ. Darkness was ever present in the tricks and enticements of Lucifer, in the threat of Antichrist and of descent into the abyss. Darkness was to be headed off only by militant vigilance and unrelenting personal effort. The battle between the forces of God and the devil was being waged in this world, eternally. The stark contrast of good and evil was frightening and yet exciting, and it provided high relief, and boundaries, shaping and ordering a cosmos and endowing it with parameters and the certitudes, ultimately comforting, of God's providence.

At some point Chacón took Isabel and Alfonso to Toledo, the city at the heart of Castile's history; Toledo evoked memories of the mighty Visigoths and the exploits of El Cid. They visited the cathedral and, in it, "the rich and marvelous chapel" where Álvaro de Luna lay entombed. Some of the decorations in that chapel might well have attracted a child's attention. A neighboring tomb is ringed with a frieze of *salvajes,* wild men totally naked except for the turbans on their heads.[34] Such savages were highly symbolic, favorite aristocratic motifs, and Castilians like Chacón and the children were expected to grasp their several meanings. Among other things, they stood for those imagined inhabitants of Prester John's kingdom, who, much like admired Muslim warriors, were considered to be innately chivalrous by Dom Henrique and by many Castilians as well. And without turbans they might represent noble savages, people who, like Hercules, somehow naturally possessed Christian strength and virtues. They also called to mind *salvajes* believed to inhabit far lands as yet hidden in darkness whose revelation would lead to the final universal triumph of Christendom.[35]

More marvels were to be seen outside the chapel. Encircling the choir, fifty-eight scenes carved in wood a half century earlier presented a vision of the universe—of God's design and of paradise lost and the promise of redemption. Mirroring the stuff of liturgical plays and countless sermons, those carvings made graphic a common fund of belief. There were (and still are) to be seen there, among other scenes, the separation of darkness and light with which the Book of Genesis begins, Adam and Eve in the Garden of Eden, the adoration of the law received by Moses, and numerous prophecies drawn from everywhere: the Bible, the apocrypha, pronouncements of Roman sybils, legend, and the Jewish cabala and haggadah.

What was to be made of it all? A boy being educated as a knight, and his observant older sister, would know. Castilians were in the habit of seeing events construed as biblical as their own ancient history, and prophecies as the expected future. The royal children would know of the Creation, original sin, and Lucifer, the angel who fell from heaven into hell. God it is, they would learn as had Pero Niño, "who frees us and takes us from the power of the Devil." A *caballero* though had to do his utmost: fight for the law and the faith, heed the poor, and follow the example of Santiago who, although his members were cut off one by one, never denied Jesus Christ. Both the boy and his sister were to show themselves resolved to do their utmost.

Chapter 2

The Wrong King: 1461–1467

It is bittersweet to reign.
—Motto of Enrique IV[1]

At ten, in late 1461, Isabel was at court; her mother and grandmother remained in Arévalo. However Enrique had managed it, Isabel and Alfonso had joined the royal household. Quite possibly their living elsewhere had become too risky for a king feeling increasingly uneasy about dissident nobles and their foreign allies, particularly Juan II of Aragón.[2] For Enrique was supporting a faction of rebellious Catalans against his cousin Juan, and Juan was in turn busy fomenting trouble for Enrique. When, in Castile, noble factions had battled for control of the king and his largesse during the reign of his father, Enrique as prince had participated in the cabals and plots, and so had Juan of Aragón, who was born in Castile and had extensive property interests there. Juan, however, engaged seemingly enthusiastically and with great skill in such contests; Enrique strove to avoid them.

*　　*　　*

At his accession in 1454, Enrique IV was considered "a most powerful king," among Europe's most opulent.[3] The Castile he governed included four and a half million people, two-thirds of the population of the Iberian peninsula, as well as over two-thirds of its territory. Enrique had inherited a royal fortune—one swelled by income from taxes on an expanding economy, the tremendous wealth reclaimed from the fallen favorite Luna, and a stake in the great revenues of the military orders of Santiago and Alcántara. Yet in the 1460s an economic downturn occurred after a decade of prosperity, bringing inflation, devaluation, and greater noble pressure on the lands of smaller holders and in urban affairs. Infighting among factions supporting or opposing the king escalated. The royal response was to print more money and to reward the loyal and placate critics alike with gifts—*mercedes*—of royal lands and revenues.[4]

Throughout Europe at the time, a particularly strong and aggressive generation of kings were intent upon tightening their control, especially over justice and revenue, two spheres tradition and law assigned to them. They also strove to become more efficient, and to show themselves proficient, in a third, the business of waging war. They were, that is, moving into what is known as modernity, and their successes resulted in consolidating their own power and transforming their kingdoms into nation-states manned by bureaucracies directly responsible to their royal selves. These rearrangements required adroit handling of the nobility even while undercutting its power; it was a process often involving a show by the king of customary behavior while undertaking a redefining of the very concept of nobility so as to shift its basis from birth and military prowess to talent and service to the crown. As to the ruler, traditional expectations of him intensified: he was expected to possess a dominant personality, an impressive bearing, an ability to expand the realm and its wealth, and to have whatever it took to convince people it was in their own best interests to follow him. Accordingly, European monarchs and their publicists worked to project throughout their realms and beyond a powerful royal image by means of the available media—through the language of their public decrees, visually in art and architecture, and through the written word, ritual, and ceremony—a majestic, heroic, and absolutist image that would inspire subjects with love and fear of the royal self.[5] In this pursuit kings also relied strongly on the support of the clergy and the concept of the sacredness of the royal role.

In hindsight, Enrique IV of Castile seems to have undertaken modernizing steps that, however, came to appear then and thereafter as a truncated and maladroit version of what his fellow rulers in France, Burgundy, and England were about. In seeking to bypass the old nobility, Enrique flatfootedly elevated men who caught his eye to high social and political positions. And, unaware or uncaring, rather than claim continuity for his innovations he baldly flouted any number of hallowed traditions. However worthy his intentions, his policies and demeanor—as generally perceived, or as wilfully misinterpreted by his opponents—would open for Isabel a path to the crown and as queen provide her with both modernizing precedent and an example of how not to go about making changes. Both in proposed reforms and as a cautionary example of pitfalls to avoid, Enrique and his reign greatly influenced her own.[6]

The surviving contemporary accounts, some but not all written or revised in Isabel's reign, indicate Enrique had neither the qualities necessary to rule successfully nor the acuity to develop them. Taking into account what even his friendly commentators say, Enrique was perhaps his own worst enemy. Plainly, from his youth on, his character did not inspire confidence. He was a difficult child, the despair of his tutor, Barrientos, and often at odds with his equally difficult father the king. The vituperative chronicler Palencia, however, is alone in insinuating that Enrique's paternity was questionable, in stating that Juan II of Castile was believed by some to be the father of Enrique IV but by all of Alfonso and Isabel.

Enrique was married young but possibly introduced to homosexual activity even younger, reputedly at Álvaro de Luna's instigation, to keep him tractable through creating a dependency on favorites, the chief of them being Luna's nephew, Juan Pacheco. Whatever their relations, among the earliest of the prince's intimates was Pacheco, whose advice continued to sway him and whose displeasure continued to distress him. Even so, Enrique as king proved stronger-willed and wilier than his father. He made sporadic attempts to stand up to Pacheco as Juan never had to Luna, or to offset Pacheco's influence by turning to other favorites, men of small social stature reliant solely on himself, but none of them outlasted Pacheco. Moreover, Pacheco, playing balance of power, saw to it that Enrique's advancing of those others to power was taken as a provocative slight by some of the more powerful nobles, the magnates who would soon be termed *grandes*.

Enrique seems to have paid more attention to governing than did Juan II of Castile, but not much more. Certainly he preferred the pleasures of music, hunting in the forests of Segovia and Madrid, and collecting a zoo, and he sought the company of men who were not nobles of first rank as well as that of visiting Granadan Moors. Nor could Barrientos or other concerned advisors get him to act as expected of a good and proper prince.[7] Certainly his physical attributes were far from kingly. His official and friendliest chronicler, Diego Enríquez del Castillo, who held the important post of royal secretary, describes Enrique as tall and corpulent with very large hands, red eyelids, and jutting chin. Palencia, who plainly despised him, states that Enrique's aspect was dissolute, his skin white, his hair red, and that he had a hangdog, disheveled look about him, dressed carelessly, displayed no emblem of royal distinction, and wore common stockings, coarse leggings, and inappropriate shoes, his attire mirroring his generally melancholic state of mind. Even so, Palencia goes on, Enrique's eyes were fierce, never still, having a hunted look. Several scholars, in view of this comment, suggest Palencia was inferring that Enrique was on drugs, or drugged; it is a charge impossible to assess at this distance.[8]

Palencia had not finished with Enrique, for he then added the detail he meant as metaphor for Enrique's character: Enrique hated agreeable odors, but he enjoyed the smells of heads cut from horses and burnt leather and other emanations of "the fetidness of corruption."[9] Palencia's was in effect a portrayal of an anti-king, a description drawn with implicit parallels to notions of Antichrist. Conversely, there is a complete absence of the usual royal eulogies. Enrique, however, had greater problems than bad press.

Just before coming to the throne, he had put aside his wife of thirteen years, Blanca, the daughter of the queen of Navarre and its king consort, who subsequently became Juan II of Aragón. The papal annulment stated that

Enrique and Blanca had never had sexual intercourse, not through any fault of either but because their union was bewitched by a demonic spell. Blanca, it said, had been medically examined and declared capable of childbearing; further, several women had testified that Enrique had had sexual intercourse with them.[10] Thus such was the papal finding as to conclude that while the marriage was unconsummated, both were free to remarry with a hope of producing a child.[11] Shortly after the divorce, in May of 1455, Enrique wed Juana, the sister of Afonso, king of Portugal.

The chronicles tell of lavish wedding festivities in Córdoba, the high-spirited, sixteen-year-old bride and her women both dazzling and scandalizing Castilians, for they dressed in the outlandish and gaudy style of a Portuguese court newly prospering from trade in African gold and slaves. Juana and her women reportedly powdered their bodies white and bared much of their breasts, the women flirting unabashedly. Equally shocking, if very different, was the attire of the bridegroom, for Enrique appeared in dingy clothes of poor quality and wore a broad-brimmed black hat "that no one ever saw him take off." The morning after their wedding, says the chronicler Valera, although the king and queen had shared one bed, to everyone's chagrin the queen remained as virginal as she had arrived; the customary bedsheet with the expected stain was not publicly displayed. Then too a story went around that a wit of Seville was heard to say that first among those things he would not bother stooping to pick up if he saw it laying in the street was Enrique's virility.[12]

Seven years later, Juana of Portugal gave birth to a daughter, also named Juana. The question continuing to tantalize scholars throughout the intervening centuries has been Was the child Enrique's? Because if so, she might supersede Isabel and everyone else in line of succession. While the line of succession in Castile was not fixed legally, custom conferred the crown on a child of the royal incumbent, usually but not always on a male child. The question of Juana's paternity, as we shall see, was to surface publicly, raised by Enrique's opponents. It hinged on two further questions: Could Enrique have the ordinary form of sexual intercourse and, more basic, was his sperm fertile? Pulgar insists that "the impotence of the King to engender was notorious."[13] But he gives no evidence. Enríquez del Castillo and even the hostile Palencia cite the testimony of two women who swore to having sexual relations with Enrique. Yet while those women had been examined by physicians, ostensibly immediately after the fact, Enrique never was.

Years later, Hieronymus Münzer, a German physician who visited Spain during Isabel's reign, wrote of having talked at length with court figures while there and been informed of the generally accepted medical verdict that Enrique's "member was thin and weak at the base but large at the head, so that he could not have an erection," and that accordingly doctors, undaunted, had made a golden tube and placing it in the queen's vagina, introduced his semen, but to no effect, for the king's semen was watery and sterile.[14] Those findings were taken to indicate that Juana was not Enrique's child. Whatever the truth of the matter, it was a verdict that served to confirm the legality of Isabel's rule.

While the entire issue has remained in the realm of high speculation, some sort of sexual inadequacy existed that did nothing for Enrique's public image nor his self-image. Clearly Enrique had physical cause for unhappiness. Whatever the problem, problem there was, surely complicating an already complex personality. His lack, first of any heir at all and then of a male heir, troubled his adherents and provided ammunition to his opponents.

Enrique was perceived as having yet a further failing, made visible at the outset of his reign and most serious to Castilians. It was his idiosyncratic way of carrying on the reconquest of Spain, and it proved a costly mistake whose lessons would not be lost on Isabel.

Reviving Reconquest

Among Enrique's first acts as king was to respond to a papal call—following the fall of Constantinople to the Ottoman Turks—for a European revival of crusading, and to do so in Spanish fashion through waging war within Iberia. So it was that during his stay in Arévalo there went out the summons to "a cleansing war" against the Muslims of the kingdom of Granada. It was a timely and popular summons to a war considered both defensive and holy, long urged by loyal critics of Juan II and all proponents of strong monarchy; and it was a summons welcomed by Castile's magnates as the right thing to do and as promising employ, honor, and great profit. Indeed, some among them had suggested the campaign in the first place.[15]

War also promised to profit the royal treasury. It brought in subsidies from the Cortes, a form of parliament, then consisting of the compliant representatives of seventeen royal towns called at the king's pleasure. Contributions came too from towns and clergy and religious establishments, as did payments of levied wartime assessments. And the king also got from the pope, Calixtus III—who was a Valencian, Alfonso de Borja—three concessions: a share of Castilian contributions for reconquering Constantinople; the grant of indulgences remitting punishment for sins, of the sort customarily granted or sold to crusaders, for Castile's men-at-arms fighting the Moors of Granada; and the further right to sell such indulgences to other Castilians to help finance this crusade within Spain. Indulgences known as Bulls of Crusade, such as young Isabel had bought, promised spiritual relief and also had the patriotic appeal of war bonds.

Enrique sent Sánchez de Arevalo to make the financial arrangements with Rome, while at home his *contador mayor,* or chief comptroller, Diego Arias, set up the profitable indulgence business; and when after two campaigns the papacy approved Arias' suggestion that those soul-redeeming licenses be extended to cover the dead in purgatory as well as the living, the royal treasury did even better. So did everyone involved in their sale. The king also got from the pope the lucrative right to appoint proxies to the masterships of the military orders of Santiago, Calatrava, and Alcántara, and thus gained greater control over the power and wealth stemming from their knights and from their holdings of towns and lands and vast herds of wool-bearing sheep.[16]

Enrique raised an army. His chancery having made all arrangements while in Arévalo, in April of 1455 and in three subsequent years he led south a host largely composed of the *mesnadas,* or private forces, of the Castilian nobility. Valera recounts that, in the campaign of that year, nobles marvelled because the king would order no sieges or battles.[17] (Marvel would be a favorite word of Isabel's, for unpleasant surprises.) Enrique, Valera says further, had in fact allowed such destruction and had himself participated in skirmishes in a first incursion, but in a second that year when briefly encamped before Málaga he permitted no skirmishes and no laying waste to the countryside, causing the nobles to suspect he had made a secret treaty with the Moors.[18]

Palencia was as usual yet more critical, writing that for four years in a row, the army saw the king turn that holy war into feints and cattle raids. Enrique, Palencia claims, was generally loath to destroy olive groves and vineyards, and decreed that any man who cut down even one fruit tree—"so slow to take root and grow, so quick to die,"—would lose an ear, and some did. At one point, the chronicler states, the King sat the army down within view of Granada, supplies and funds dwindling, while he refused battle and lectured his men on the preciousness of each life.[19] Although he assuredly faced what is today known as a hostile press, nonetheless the impression emerges that Enrique, while he may have been an early environmentalist, was no devotee of the traditions of the Spanish reconquest.

It seems likely that the campaigns were adequately waged and provisioned, but barely, and that while Enrique in fact sought to pursue more than a token war, a principal royal goal was to make money. In this he relied on time-honored methods, retaining funds raised for fighting the Moor as well as harassing the enemy into renewing customary tribute payments, while seeking not to destroy his resources wholly. That may well be the explanation of Enrique's forbearance at Málaga.

Sánchez de Arévalo, when in Seville with Enrique in 1456, followed another tradition in presenting the king with a treatise in effect lecturing him on royal qualities and behavior. That worthy, in the fashion of the esteemed counselors of Juan II who had been his own mentors, reminded his prince of the great realm entrusted to him—that Castile was head of the five kingdoms of *la nación española,* and that Enrique as its king was obliged to regain the lands once held by the Goths: "May your kingdom expand over infidel barbarians and to the Great Ocean and the Mediterranean Sea, your virtue not rest until your name and power spread to the darkest parts of Africa and your money is coined [in those places] and you recover these provinces which . . . your progenitors . . . possessed in peace." Enrique must "change dishonest peace into . . . praiseworthy war," for kingship comes from heaven and war against the infidel is not only just but a divine obligation. The king is God's instrument.[20]

Then he got to the sore point. While the hunting and music to which Enrique devoted himself were suitable royal pastimes, the one "which will excite hearts and acts of virtue . . . the primary royal exercise or sport, is the magnificent pursuit of military glory"; the best royal sport was war against the Moors.[21] Enrique, that is, had to get serious about that war. Enrique was being told that, whatever his inclinations, it was extremely impolitic to be seen by Castilians as belittling their hallowed concepts of how to wage war, and unwise to show himself as a king without interest in distinguishing himself in arms or appreciation of the intense commitment of young nobles to sacrosounct spanish traditions and chivalric values—values essentially medieval but, as in the case of Sánchez de Arévalo, then becoming reinforced by Renaissance emphasis on the classical desiderata of fame, honor, and glory.

Certainly traditional knightly ways of warfare were then becoming outmoded; as shown at Agincourt, where French heavy cavalry and affinity for single combat had proved inadequate against English longbows. Enrique in fact knew the advantages of riding with light armor and arms, for he himself rode in Muslim fashion, *a la jineta,* in a low saddle, short-stirruped, knees high, on small fast horses. Where Enrique came acropper was, once again, not through trying to keep up with changing times but through demonstrably taking pleasure in making light of values held dear by his most powerful subjects. In refusing to besiege a town or join battle without adequate explanation, he ran counter to the grain of the society he governed. In shucking customary ways, rather than introducing change as renovation as was customary, he offered no good reason and provided no acceptable example.

Enrique was, on occasion, seen to assert his authority strongly, but in ways appearing arbitrary and chimerical. *Caballeros*—knights—felt his rage, wrote Palencia, when, counter to his orders, they responded to challenges to single combat by Granadans. When through doing so the very noble youth Garcilaso de la Vega fought and killed a Muslim horseman before Málaga, it was especially galling to all the young nobles to see Enrique award the Moor's charger not to the victor as customary but to a lowborn current favorite. And Enrique incurred yet greater wrath when, on campaign two years later, Garcilaso having died of a poisoned arrow in the neck, the king again outraged tradition and its adherents by giving the rents of an *encomienda,* a royal grant Garcilaso held of certain lands and villages, to that same favorite's brother, rather than, as was customary, to Garcilaso's son. Incensed, Rodrigo Manrique, the renowned Moor fighter who was Garcilaso's uncle, together with Garcilaso's cousins of the powerful Mendoza clan, then protested— vehemently but futilely.[22] To look ahead, Enrique was to find Manrique and his very numerous noble relatives among the leaders of a revolt. The Mendozas would remain loyal much longer, yet in the end their support would be decisive in Isabel's attaining the crown.

*   *   *

Year after year, the king returned north in the fall with a surplus of treasure, some from royal taxes collected on the huge amount of provisions the campaign required, some from Muslims grateful for his having spared towns and crops, and with valuable gifts from the king of Granada as well and treaties with him promising yet more gold in tribute. But no one else except the favored recipients of royal largesse made expenses. There were few customary spoils of victory for the nobles and their men, few reputation-enhancing deeds permitted to their *caballero* sons. Those dismayed aristocrats repeatedly saw Enrique divert war funds and present *mercedes*—the royal offices, titles, money, towns and villages, and rights to royal taxes and customs—that is, all the entrees to wealth and power, to his companions of inferior birth; so to the upstart Pedro Girón went the captaincy of the entire Muslim frontier. And they fumed at Enrique elevating to high office recent converts from Judaism such as his treasurer Diego Arías, or lavishing gifts and attention on his personal guard of Moors, three hundred strong, who went richly dressed and magnificently horsed while the Christian rank and file grumbled about scarcity of necessities.[23]

Enrique would continue to antagonize many of his barons in one way or another to the point of open revolt, and then seek to avoid armed conflict through mollifying the disaffected with large gifts of jurisdictions, rents, and honors, so that a dance of rebellion and reconciliation, rather than reward for steady loyal service and valor shown against the Moor, became recognized as the most certain route to wealth and influence at court. That Enrique was suggestible and volatile both deepened a growing atmosphere of insecurity fed by economic woes and heartened opportunists of the sort observed during Juan II's lifetime, of whom it was said that "it no doubt pleased them to have such a king, because in turbulent and disordered times, it is in the troubled river that rich fisherman are made."[24]

Nor was it just that Enrique did not heed convention in campaigning against the Moor. Fueling much of the criticism of him at the time was high irritation at his demonstrations of capriciousness, a mordant playfulness that delighted in defying convention as such. In Andalusia, while his knights chafed at being restrained from doing battle, he was seen to encourage his queen and her ladies to stand on the battlements and pretend to shoot arrows at the foe. Palencia viewed the episode probably much as did disgruntled young bloods, as indicative of Enrique's near profanation of the serious, indeed sacrosanct, enterprise of war against the Moor. And an extended practical joke played on the archbishop of Toledo, Carrillo, helps to explain why he—"the second person in Spain after the king, not only in dignity but in vassals," who held hundreds of cities, towns, villages, and castles, enjoyed huge revenues, and had at his call an army—became the soul of the rising opposition to Enrique that was ultimately responsible for Isabel's succession.

The archbishop, known to be "of tenacious character and robust temperament"—imperious and obstinate—although left by Enrique during his initial foray south as a viceroy to oversee the royal chancery in Valladolid, repeatedly saw his decisions overridden by royal directives. A principal advocate of regaining Spain and converting all Muslims, Carrillo also complained of Enrique's lackluster campaigning; and in 1457 Carrillo protested against Enrique's misuse of funds from the sale of Bulls of Crusade. The archbishop smarted too from the king's having undercut his authority in Toledo and generally chipped away at ecclesiastical immunities and privileges, which Enrique had been heard to refer to as "sheepskins and goatskins, witnesses to the ridiculous."[25]

The archbishop, never known to suffer in silence—"he was a man of great heart and his principal desire was to do great things and to have great standing, fame, and renown"[26]—made known his unhappiness to the extent that Enrique, at Pacheco's suggestion, resolved to get Carrillo away on the pretext of having him lead a campaign to retake the Muslim-held towns of Baza and Guadix, Granadan strongholds claimed by the see of Toledo, as well as Málaga, Granada's second city and major seaport, and the king added the offer of an advance of monies from the sale of indulgences. Of course, if the archbishop did not take those towns he was to return the money, and Enrique knew full well that on such short notice their conquest was impossible. Carrillo, bellicose by nature, together with Rodrigo Manrique and the count of Alba, rode south immediately, to Ecija, where Pacheco met them. The game was joined. It was early September. First Pacheco must go scout out Málaga; he would return shortly. Weeks passed. Carrillo awaited him, impatience mounting. Near the end of the month, Enrique arrived from Córdoba. Besiege Málaga? Alas, it was too late and too cold and too few provisions remained. Carrillo, Manrique, and Alba must come with him to Jaén. They went, arguing for the siege, and the game continued in Jaén, until, well into October, three furious nobles realized they had been had, and concluded that "the king would not war on Muslims but on his vassals, good customs, and the old laws."[27]

Shortly thereafter Carrillo, with Manrique's support, formed a league to consolidate their own power and to curb Enrique's. Juan Pacheco connived with the league on and off, for Pacheco intensely disliked the competition he met in the king's newer favorites, especially the latest one, the dashing Beltrán de la Cueva.

At Court

It is now that Isabel enters this picture. Enrique wished to counter the weight of those nobles, or anyway to neutralize their not-so-secret ally, Juan of Aragón. In 1457, accompanied by his queen, Enrique conferred with Juan, who was then Aragón's regent and heir to its crown, and his second wife, Juana Enríquez, the daughter of the admiral of Castile, and a double wedding was arranged. Isabel and her brother, Alfonso, were to marry Fernando and Juana, the regent's children.[28] But when in 1460 Carrillo established a coalition of nobles intent on getting control of the royal council and having young Alfonso proclaimed heir to Castile, and Juan, then king of Aragón, supported those dissidents, Enrique offered Isabel in marriage to Juan's elder son, Carlos of Viana, who had joined Catalans at odds with his father. In response, Carlos sent an envoy to Arévalo seeking Isabel's hand; he reported back that the *infanta* was very content with the prospect of marrying the heir to Aragón. Its king, Juan, far less content, detained Carlos' subsequent emissaries. On September 23, 1461, Carlos died suddenly, rumor had it poisoned by his stepmother, Juana Enríquez, in order to clear the way to the crown of Aragón for her own son, Fernando. If so, Carlos's engagement to Isabel was a contributory factor in his death.

From then on, Enrique kept the Catalans stirred up against his Uncle Juan, now their king. Enrique had bestowed on Juan Pacheco the marquesado de Villena, which contained much of Juan of Aragón's former inheritance in Castile. Pacheco prodded and abetted Enrique in inciting the rebellious Catalans, while he simultaneously negotiated with Juan for the marriage of Fernando to one of his own daughters. Although Fernando got away, Pacheco's machinations did at length achieve what was undoubtedly his great goal: advantageous marriages for his ten children—four sons, six daughters—assuring his family an ongoing powerful position within the interlocking directorate that constituted Castile's high nobility.

In 1461, Juana, Enrique's queen consort, was pregnant. Enrique, having reconciled with Carrillo, at his urging and that of Pacheco then brought the *infantes* Isabel and Alfonso to live at court. Seemingly the move was arranged through Carrillo, who on occasion could display an exquisite sense of the apposite, as he did in reportedly arguing that the *infantes* had to come to court "because there they will be better raised and learn more virtuous customs."[29]

Isabel was in Queen Juana's entourage when on February 28, 1462, Juana went into labor, an event attended by the great nobles and much of the court. The queen, supported by the conde de Alba de Liste, squatted, the customary position for giving birth; she was flanked on one side by, in strict order of rank, the king, the marqués de Villena, the commander of a military order, and a royal secretary, and on the other by the archbishop of Toledo and two other dignitaries. After a hard labor the queen gave birth to a daughter. The child, also named Juana, was baptized by Carrillo, who was assisted by the bishop of Calahorra, Pedro González de Mendoza, whose rise at court had begun. The *infanta* Isabel, now eleven, was godmother to her niece.[30]

The Sunday following, Enrique elevated his *mayordomo,* Beltrán de la Cueva, to conde de Ledesma. Beltrán, it was later widely rumored, was the child's true father and had been urged upon the initially recalcitrant queen by Enrique himself. Whether or no, Enrique celebrated the birth royally. On April 12 fifteen bulls were run and on May 6 a joust was held (in which one knight died). Valera recalled Enrique being as happy as though the child were indeed his daughter. Nor is it certain she was not, although she has come into history as *Juana la Beltraneja.* At court, Isabel's education was proceeding apace.

Isabel stayed in the town of Aranda with the queen and the newborn infant from February until at least July. She and Alfonso were both present in Madrid on May 9 when Enrique had the nobles, some of them very reluctantly, take the customary oath to the infant Juana as princess of Asturias, heir apparent to the throne; in July in Toledo the children heard the delegates to the Cortes repeat that pledge. Afterward they traveled with the court to Guadalajara, the seat of the Mendozas, to celebrate Beltran's wedding to Mencia de Mendoza, granddaughter of Iñigo de Mendoza, marqués de Santillana, eminent poet, Moor fighter, and advisor to Juan II. That marriage signaled the rise at court of a new faction, its true head the bride's uncle, the bishop Pedro González de Mendoza, who was Santillana's ninth and most remarkable child and who had recently entered the Royal Council. Although Santillana, who died in 1458, had been a critic of his government, Enrique sought in the powerful Mendoza family, in their numbers, their talent, and their widespread domains, a counterweight to Carrillo and the nimble Pacheco. And well he might, for Juana's birth had escalated tensions and the coalition supporting Alfonso swelled. Those dissidents ever more stridently asserted Alfonso's right to the succession. And Pacheco was more than ever determined to topple Beltrán.

During the next few years, Isabel remained in the queen's suite and resided principally in Segovia. Its *alcázar* was the grandest of royal residences in northern Castile, described by a traveler as "a most elegant palace adorned in gold, silver, and the heavenly color called azure, and with floors of alabaster." Lining its great hall was the collective majesty of Castile, as represented in the larger than life statues of its kings, forty-two of them—all those who had ruled Castile and León "after the destruction of Spain," beginning with the near-legendary Pelayo and ending with Enrique himself, and among them also were El Cid and Castile's founder, Count Fernán Gonzalez, "because they were such noble knights and did such great deeds." All the figures were seated on thrones and held scepters and orbs, and all, it was said, were made of pure gold. They were in fact of wood, carved and polychrome, painted in silver and gold. Enrique had added ten of the most recent, including his Trastámara forebears. Castile's seven proprietary queens, however, he placed behind and to the side of their substituted husbands.[31] Whatever Isabel's reaction to that positioning, those splendid kings and queens evoking Castile's mighty past could only have been taken to represent her own direct line and legacy. She would know the histories of the mightiest, so often told and retold and to be found in the royal library by a young woman fond of reading. And the frequent sight of those numerous, illustrious, indeed resplendent, royal progenitors had to point up the contrast with the all too human qualities displayed by the current monarch, her half-brother, Enrique. All that said, he and she had happy moments together; sometimes, it is said, Isabel danced and Enrique sang.

While at court, Isabel had as well other sorts of experiences significant for her own reign. In late 1463, the royal family attended a series of sermons preached by Franciscan friars about "how in these kingdoms there is great heresy by those who judaize, keep Jewish rites, and give children Christian names." One friar, Alonso de Espina, a confessor of Enrique's, vowed he could produce one hundred foreskins of circumcised sons of highly placed *conversos*. His point was that no *converso* was to be trusted to be a sincere Christian.

There was precedent in that fourteen years earlier a ground-breaking statute of the Toledo council denied public office to all converts and raised the question if any of them could ever be wholly Christian. One response, based on the erroneous idea that the Jews constituted a race apart, was no, for their blood was forever tainted. Another was yes, many *conversos* were sincerely Christian and should not be differentiated from others, that Christ came to redeem everyone, that all the faithful formed a single mystical body in Christ. And one commentator then pointed out a practical difficulty in separating new from old Christians in that some of the most powerful Old Christian families had *converso* forebears. Yet that was not to be the end of the matter.

In 1463, Enrique, annoyed—perhaps bored with Espina's harangue, perhaps amusing himself, even possibly concerned with the issue, and certainly seizing an opportunity to assert royal authority in religious matters—told

Espina such allegations against Christians were a grave insult to the faith, one it was up to the king to punish. He demanded to see the foreskins and to know whose they were; the evidence was not forthcoming. Enrique, though aligning with anti-*converso* exponents when it suited his purposes, was sufficiently non-doctrinaire to resist propagandists who condemned all New Christians of Jewish lineage and, accordingly, he invited the highly respected Hieronymite friar, Alfonso de Oropesa, the prior of Guadalupe, to come preach at court against such sweeping allegations.

Oropesa had written a tract distinguishing between true converts and heretics, defending the majority of *conversos* as sincere Christians, and urging a union among all Christians whatever their origins. At the same time he had condemned Jews for resisting the grace of God in Christ, for "using all their astuteness and diabolic means to corrupt Christians," and for causing suspicion of all people belonging to what he spoke of as the Jewish *raza*. (The term *raza* has a meaning midway between "lineage" and "race.") He had a different sort of separation to suggest. His solution was that New Christians and Jews should be kept apart, and Jews induced to become Christian, if possible through 'love,' if not through whatever coercion was necessary.[32] Enrique, approving, urged Oropesa to take charge of the traditional process of having the bishops institute an inquiry or inquisition in order to root out and punish heretics and apostates and exonerate true converts. Although civil war and perhaps Enrique's aversion to consistency intervened, the case for an inquisition had been made, and at a court wherein resided a girl who would one day implement that proposal on the basis of those same arguments, but in a revolutionary new fashion. At the time, one of the principal advocates of an inquisition was Carrillo, to whom Oropesa dedicated his treatise, and who would soon become a most influential mentor to Isabel.[33]

Propositions

After the death of Carlos of Viana, a party of Catalans had proposed to Enrique that he, rather than Juan of Aragón, rule them and he had accepted. Pacheco, playing a double game and fearing that if Enrique waged war with Juan he might win, had talked him into foregoing the expense of armed combat by having Louis XI of France, whose reputation for guile should have deterred Enrique, mediate the matter. When, in April of 1462, Louis did not decide Catalonia should be his, Enrique quickly realized that Pacheco had not only lost him territory and standing, but that, through secret negotiations with Louis XI and Juana Enríquez, he had arranged to keep power in precarious balance requiring Pacheco's own services. Enrique realized too that although Louis could keep Juan busy protecting Aragón's borders with France, and although France was a traditional ally of Castile, yet Louis was not to be trusted, and from 1463 he moved closer to England, leading to a treaty of alliance in 1467 that enabled Castile to attain new heights of trade. Even so, Enrique's offer of Isabel's hand to Edward IV was refused; instead the English king married an English commoner. It was a slight Isabel would not forget.

By 1464 Enrique had decided to marry Isabel elsewhere, to the recently widowed Afonso of Portugal, who was thirty-two years old, and whose revenues and prestige were continuing to swell from trade in the gold and slaves of Africa. The Portuguese king, having taken tiny Alcázar-Seguer in Africa in 1458, was thereafter known as Afonso the African. From Enrique's standpoint it was a fine match: it would remove Isabel from the kingdom permanently, and Afonso already had a son and heir, virtually precluding that any child of hers wearing Portugal's crown would ever muddy dynastic arrangements in Castile.

In April he took his queen and Isabel, just thirteen, to Puente de Arzobispo to meet Afonso, who arrived wreathed in the glory of having laid siege to Tangiers and was en route to the shrine of the Virgin of Guadalupe to fulfill a vow. He was much taken with Isabel and said he would consult his nobles on the marriage. Although Pulgar had it that Afonso suggested they become engaged and she replied that the laws of Castile said she must first consult its great lords, Palencia is probably closer to what occurred in stating that "under the Queen's seductive influence" Isabel was ready to accept Afonso; moreover, her mother had told her always to prefer a Portuguese marriage.[34] And from what is known of Isabel later, surely she was impressed by Afonso's African exploits. However that may be, when Carrillo and Pacheco learned of the meeting only afterward, they laid having been kept in the dark to the Mendozas—that is, to Pedro González de Mendoza and Beltrán de la Cueva—and, on May 16, they and Pedro Girón, now both master of Calatrava and captain general of Andalusia, signed an accord, their stated purpose "to ensure the security of Alfonso and Isabel," because "some persons of damnable intent" had gained control of the *infantes* and were planning to kill Alfonso and have Isabel marry "where she ought not; nor as complying with the good and honor of the royal crown of these kingdoms and without the accord and consent of the *grandes* following custom. . . . all this to the end of giving succession in these realms to [one] to whom by right it does not belong."[35] They meant the princess, Juana; they also had a silent partner, Juan of Aragón.

The court went on to Madrid where Enrique, sensing something was afoot, lodged Alfonso and Isabel in the alcázar's keep, the *torre de homenaje*. Shortly thereafter, his guards drove off armed men attempting to break into the royal residence to seize the king and the *infantes*. Enrique, well aware that they had been hired by Pacheco and not amused when that master of dissimulation urged him to find the unknown assailants and avenge the insult, is said to have responded in exasperation: "Does what has been done to my doors, Marqués, seem good to you? Be assured that this is no time for much patience."[36] Even so, when the court moved on to Segovia, Pacheco went along, now insisting to the king that the mastership of Santiago belonged to Alfonso, not Beltrán, to whom Enrique had given it. And one night, while Pacheco himself was in the royal apartments conversing with Isabel, another plot to seize king and *infantes* was averted, only just in time. In so bizarre a series of events, the most incomprehensible is their upshot—that Enrique, to placate the dissidents, capitulated to Pacheco, recognized Alfonso as his heir, and agreed to hand the boy over into his keeping. On September 6, two days after the king and the coalition of nobles had signed an agreement, yet a third attempt was made to seize Enrique. This one was foiled by archers of the *hermandad*, or brotherhood, local vigilantes, dedicated to upholding law and order, who were funded by towns and notoriously loyal to the crown.[37] Isabel would build on those propensities.

Two Kings for Castile

From at least 1457, Enrique had been criticized widely for moral and religious failures by preachers espousing traditional concepts of good kingship. And in a letter of 1462, Diego de Valera, as ever doing his duty as he saw it, informed this king that the greater parts of the three estates of the realm were discontented—with his having ceased to war on Muslims, giving high office to unworthy men, even selling offices, and being hard of access, paying badly, and not doing justice. Valera warned that a number of kings in the past had been deposed and killed, and appealed to Enrique to "guard these kingdoms that God has commended to you."[38]

Nor did it help Enrique's standing when Gibraltar was taken from the Muslims that year by Andalusian nobles rather than by the king. Sánchez de Arévalo then conveyed widespread elation in writing to the pope, Pius II, that "in the west the sun of justice and faith has risen." In the doing, he had chosen a well-known metaphor carrying dual allusion. It signified that in conquering Gibraltar the Castilians were offsetting Christian losses to Muslim Turks in the East.[39] It also alluded to prophecies that Spaniards had long associated with war against the Moor, prophecies foreseeing Christian advance westward as a millennial sign and as being accomplished by a messianic Spanish king; in short, that royal secretary was doing his best to keep his king in the picture. Even so, that heralded feat by others put Enrique on the spot at home for having desisted from his obligation to lead Spanish armies against Muslim Granada. An observant young woman living in the royal household at the time would never afterward underestimate the political power of prophecy, nor the efficacy of a war both acquisitive and holy, nor the mischief Andalusian nobles could make for the crown.

More immediately, worse was in store for Enrique. On September 28, 1464, the leagued dissidents, having done much to feed discontent and bent on young Alfonso's succession, sent a circular letter throughout the kingdom. In it they expressed shock and dismay at Enrique's perversion (implied was homosexuality) and at his consorting with Jews and Muslims and mocking the reconquest. They claimed as Alfonso's by right the mastership of Santiago, held by Beltrán, whom they accused of controlling the king and the *infantes* against the public good. And now they explicitly declared that young Juana was not Enrique's child, and they demanded that Enrique and his partisans— they meant the Mendozas—be brought to account, and that the king convoke a *cortes* to take the oath to Alfonso as heir to the crown.[40]

Although the aged Barrientos, now high chancellor, urged Enrique to fight fire with fire, he again temporized.[41] In November he gave Pacheco custody of Alfonso and a seat on the royal council, that out-of-favor favorite having assured him that in exchange there would be peace. It was also agreed that Alfonso was to receive the administration of the Order of Santiago, which Pacheco as his *mayordomo* would exercise for him, and that Alfonso was to marry the princess Juana—an arrangement that would ensure crowns to them both. As for Isabel, she was not to marry without the consent of the three estates, nor was she to be considered as promised to anyone. Her mother was to send her five or six ladies of good reputation; she was to have her own household and the king was to maintain her in proper state. Beltrán and his people were to quit the court. As agreed, too, a commission of arbitration was set up and ordered to make recommendations for reform of the kingdom. Each side appointed two members and jointly agreed on the fifth—the Hieronymite prior, Alonso de Oropesa. And it was now, for the first time, that Enrique, surely seeking to protect Juana's right to the crown and his own honor, presented sworn medical testimony to his ability to father a child.[42]

On January 16, 1465, the arbitral commission made its report, a long one, known as the *sentencia* of Medina del Campo. Enrique had it circulated throughout Castile. Its 129 clauses addressed the full range of complaints against his government and prescribed remedies, often radical, and, while in the main consistent with the demands of his opponents, they tell much about current conditions. Among them, royal judges and officials should be curbed, the clergy freed of restrictions, finances put right, and nobles tried by peers. Enrique's intervention in Catalonia was illegal and must end. There were to be free elections to the Cortes and no taxation without its consent. Offices were not to be inherited. Men-at-arms directly under the king were to be reduced from three thousand to six hundred lances—a lance signifying an armed knight and his attendants. The Royal Council should be made up of three

nobles, three bishops, and three representatives of the towns. In sum, government should be overhauled so as to vest power in the king's council,
strengthen the Cortes, reinforce the power of nobles and clergy, and generally
circumscribe royal authority.[43] While many of those proposed reforms fell by
the way, the *sentencia* of 1465 in declaring a religious exclusivism foreshadowed
things to come. It presented Enrique's tolerant attitude as sinful and stated
that Muslims and Jews must be expelled from the kingdom, their property
confiscated, and an inquisition established.

Finally, the *sentencia* was much concerned with the *infanta* Isabel: she was
not to marry the Portuguese king without the consent of the Cortes. She was
in fact the subject of the very first clause; it substantially reiterated Enrique's
November agreement with Pacheco. Her mother was to chose five or six
women to attend her. Isabel should have her own household, and should
reside wherever her mother and grandmother were until she married; and
while those arrangements were being made, she was immediately to be sent to
a separate residence in Segovia accompanied by her ladies "and two or three
honest men." Enrique was to pay her maintenance as stated in Juan II's will.

The implication was that the court was no fit place for a young *infanta*,
such was the behavior of the king and the queen, and other sources corroborate that view. The queen's ladies were portrayed as laughing and gossiping
amid the constant comings and goings of go-betweens carrying indecent messages, and as "devoured night and day by a restless craving" more common to
brothels.[44] While those comments come from the very biased Palencia, they
had some basis in fact. At least one of those ladies, Mencia de Lemos, was
known to have formed an illicit liaison; she would have two sons with a man
in holy orders, Pedro González de Mendoza.

Moreover, poets familiar with life at court reveal ferocious undercurrents
and pressure to conform to a lax morality. One produced satiric verses
acknowledging both the courtiers' scandal-evoking attire and behavior and the
converso issue when he suggested: Circumcise the gallants and the pages, but
do not circumcise the clothing worn at court, it is so short already.[45] Isabel
had, since September, been with the queen at Segovia. Whatever her exposure
at the time, she was very careful to exemplify decorum ever after.

*   *   *

It was quickly obvious that neither the rebels nor Enrique would honor any
accord. In December, after Pacheco's promise of peace and while the *sentencia*
was being drawn up, a document ostensibly made up of petitions from high
clergy, nobles, and knights had circulated, reiterating the rebel league's September charges, then going on to condemn the reign in the blackest terms possible as godless.[46] A month later, within two weeks after having the *sentencia*

circulated, Enrique revoked it. Ever since the commission first met, he had been ordering loyal nobles, forts, and town militias to ready for combat; now he renounced Alfonso as his heir and commanded Beltrán to prepare for battle. It was civil war.

On June 5, 1465, Carrillo, Pacheco, Rodrigo Manrique, and other insurgents assembled by Avila's stern walls. There they drew upon a melange of tradition that included the old Visigothic practice of notables choosing a king, the popular rite of acclamation, and political theory claiming it the right of the political community to depose a tyrant; above all, they invoked their own right, as the nobility of Castile and spokesmen for the body politic, to elect and depose kings. Against those walls a platform was hastily constructed, and from it Enrique was declared an unfit ruler and deposed in effigy: a straw figure was stripped of royal regalia and thrown to the ground, and an assembled crowd acclaimed the eleven-year-old boy, Enrique's half-brother, as King Alfonso XII. Palencia claims to have personally dissuaded Pacheco and Girón from charging Enrique then and there with heresy by reminding them that, once the quarrel was on religious grounds, Enrique had more money for bribes for Rome.[47]

In referring to Visigothic precedent the assembled nobles felt on firmer ground. At least one insurgent, Rodrigo Manrique, claimed actual descent from the king-electing Goths. Manrique devices reflected this pride in lineage and view of kingship: "We are not descended from kings, but kings from us," and "Manrique, blood of Goths, defense of Christians and terror of pagans."[48] Rodrigo Manrique, glorying in his reputation as another Rodrigo, El Cid, looked backward nostalgically to a more militant, more kinglike king, one who would smile on barons such as himself.

In marked contrast, Manrique's cousin Pedro González de Mendoza appealed to Alfonso's adherents for reconciliation, his argument couched in terms of what was best for Castile as a whole. He did not try to defend the current king but instead argued that when the body politic finds itself sick, it is not wise to try and cure it by cutting off its head. Mendoza, priest and lawyer, stated the case for kingly power then currently being made by European courts. Kings are anointed by God, he reminded them, and not subject to human justice. The Scriptures warn that a divided kingdom is worse than a bad monarch; if the rebels were well-intentioned they would not put up an eleven-year-old boy as king. Rather, they showed a prime concern with their own interests and not with the common good; and if indeed their cause were just they would pursue it by juridical means.[49]

Pedro González de Mendoza, bishop of Calahorra, the son of the marqués de Santillana, the renowned poet and royal hairshirt, had been educated in canon and civil law at the University of Salamanca, and he combined current European regalist concepts of royal authority with traditional Castilian theory of strong monarchy. He drew largely on the latter in invoking the Holy Scriptures as decreeing kings must be obeyed; those who did not obey the king were schismatics. This was to fight fire with fire, for here he too alluded to the Visigoths, but to the authority of Isidore of Seville and his invoking of biblical support for Visigothic monarchy. Nonetheless, the fused national and religious grounds on which this noble prelate chose to stand in 1465 were at once doctrinal and rooted in Spanish interpretations of imperial Roman law. He and they both would enjoy long and powerful influence in Spain.

The opposition, in much preferring its own interpretation of political tradition and its own king, also relied strongly on religion to make its case and gain popular adhesion. Immediately, circular letters full of moral outrage went out under Alfonso's signature; they were to be the first of many. On July 6, an order signed by Alfonso XII instructed the count of Arcos to take the oath of homage to him; that order contained a litany of Enrique's sins, its tenor being that as the count well knew, "the great evils and harms all these my kingdoms and their three estates have continued to receive" have come "from my predecessor [Enrique], in whose time the holy Catholic faith of our savior and redeemer Jesus Christ" has received unprecedented detriment.[50] A long list of accusations followed, detailing how Enrique had brought God's wrath upon the land: he had attacked the immunities of the church, dishonored knights, robbed citizens and peasants, violated privileges of towns and cities, and rather than doing justice had sold it. His crimes and excesses were termed notorious. The enormous and ugly impieties occurring in his palace were certain to ruin the kingdom, and Alfonso now detailed them. Enrique had evilly given Doña Juana, called his wife, to Beltrán de la Cueva, and made a daughter of hers heir to the kingdoms rightfully belonging to himself, Alfonso, as son of King Juan; implicit here is a questioning of Enrique's own legitimacy.[51] A war of political theologies had begun, one clearly intended to capture the hearts and minds of ordinary Castilians.

More explicit now was that order's new insistence on Enrique's impotence as notorious and his intent toward the *infantes* as evil. Enrique had, it said, given Alfonso and his sister Isabel into the hands of the queen and the traitor Beltrán, their plight denounced by many prelates and lords. A circular letter of August 2 to the city of Palencia added the charges that Enrique had no will of his own, and that he sustained Muslim enemies of the holy faith, even to having them guard his palace and giving them double pay. In yet another letter, to the council of Burgos on July 22, Alfonso spoke of his intent to expel Enrique from the kingdom and to redeem his sister Isabel, in manner and in language more usually used when referring to Christians held captive by Muslims.[52]

Alfonso was fighting his own version of holy war. A variant on the manifesto of August 2 going out in his name promised that he would uproot and destroy "the sins of heresy, sodomy, and blasphemy, which were prevalent, as is notorious, in the reign of my predecessor Enrique."[53] Enrique, it stated, was willfully bringing on the destruction of Spain; Alfonso's charge was to save the realm. At bottom, Alfonso's stance was militantly apocalyptic; and it was highly effective. A foreign traveler then observed that most of the ordinary people he encountered were partial to the young king because of his greater inclination to the Christians, and everyone believed that he would triumph completely.[54]

*   *   *

Behind this demonizing of Enrique lay some long-standing criticism. His reign, begun with the rosy hope that beginnings tend to engender, had soon drawn censure even from men whose opinion he valued and who advised Enrique to embrace and demonstrate a political morality and concept of kingship as set out in the legal code, the *Siete Partidas,* and echoed in books of advice to princes. The king, they reminded him, was head of the body politic, his conscience the conduit of God's will; the health of the realm depended on his good government. The highest of royal purposes must be war against the Moor. Such rebuke we have seen came from earnest advisors seeking to set Enrique on the right path, from Barrientos and Valera, and from Sánchez de Arévalo and Mendoza, both of whom were protégés of Juan II's counselors, the marqués de Santillana and the bishop of Burgos and legal scholar, Alonso de Cartagena. Harsher criticism of Enrique came from other disciples of theirs, followers of Alfonso, such as the chronicler Palencia and Gómez Manrique, who was Mendoza's cousin and Rodrigo Manrique's brother. Yet after Avila, while the propagandists of both sides spoke of Castile as defiled and sinful, Alfonso's polemicists insisted much of the blame lay with Enrique, while Enrique's advisors then blamed the entire body politic.

Anonymous, biting, thinly veiled satirical poems also took up the attack on Enrique. In one, the *Coplas de Mingo Revulgo,* the people have lost the four cardinal virtues—justice, fortitude, prudence, and temperance—the four dogs who had guarded the flock, and Enrique is the bad shepherd who then lets the wolves—the nobles—devour his sheep.[55] In another, the *Coplas del Provincial,* the superior of the corrupt monastery that is Castile reports on the previous nine years—that is, Enrique's reign—and describes various of Castile's mighty: the men are incestuous and sodomites, cuckolds, and Jews, and the women are adulterous and devoid of virtue. *Conversos* are particularly vilified: Diego Arias, the royal comptroller, when asked why his coat of arms bears not a foreskin but a cross, is said to reply that it is because he was at the crucifixion and put Christ on the cross. Homosexuality is given the full religious weight of an abominable sin, a violence against God, rather than, as was at the time often the case, viewed leniently.[56] The author of those verses and the manifestos of Alfonso's supporters could also count upon homosexuality being widely interpreted as a sign of the dreadful times prophesied to precede the last days. Thus, Enrique is blamed for bringing on a second destruction of Spain—an event signifying the end of the world. And as the antithesis of the Good Shepherd he is Antichrist. *Mingo Revulgo* too played on that apocalyptical theme among others and employed devices of apocalyptic prophecy, such as animal allegories and disaster foretold on the basis of astrological predictions and revelations in a dream.

Strong criticisms of society as a whole were also leveled in signed verses that were couched as timely warnings of catastrophe in a world turned upside down. *"Mundo ciego, mundo ciego"*—"blind world, blind world"—lamented Hernán Mexía, a municipal councilor of Jaén; for such was Enrique's realm, embroiled in discord and tyranny.[57] What had become, Mexía asked, of the virtues and of good men, of the worthy governors, the priests, the *caballeros*, and the *letrados? Ubi sunt?* The sins of the powerful infected the entire body politic. It was, he said, like the fall of Rome or the dreaded coming of Antichrist. Mexía and the other poets who told of evil abroad and predicted disastrous consequences in scriptural terms were by and large *conversos,* their verses distilling a mounting insecurity, intensified by their own precarious situations.

Yet their anguished vision was not far from that of Alfonso's devoted Old Christian follower, Gómez Manrique, in whose poems, although the chivalric convention of courtly love dominated, grim realities intruded. "The immense turbulence of this Castilian kingdom makes my hand heavy . . . ," Manrique wrote.[58] For, though the world itself was "quicker to change than February," though fame was "fleeting as brandy flame," yet conditions in Castile went beyond the usual ups and downs of the world, and he painted a world turned completely topsy-turvy in revelatory stanzas: "In a village where a Moor is stupidly made mayor, iron will be worth more than gold, and silver given away."[59]

Nor was Enrique's camp immune from expressing such sentiments of disorder, of upended morality having become a plague on the land. In March of 1466, his chronicler and secretary, Enríquez del Castillo, writing in Enrique's name to the urban militias, the *hermandades,* commended all those towns and cities forming such brotherhoods as inspired by God, for now robbery and murder were commonplace, and no road or house was safe. Certainly, in the years of escalating jockeying for power and warring over jurisdictions, ordinary peoples' lives and livelihoods became ever more hazardous: towns endured siege, highwaymen proliferated, crops and herds were lost, and law and order belonged to the strong; ordinary people suffered most. Now at last Enrique was calling up the *hermandades,* urging them to act for the common good, to free the land, for "the glory and crown of Spain is in your hands."

The dreadful state of the realm, Enríquez del Castillo stated, "has come among us for our sins," employing the collective, not the royal, we. Hellfire threatened; and he appealed to the clemency and grace of God, cited David and Jeremiah, and made the familiar comparison of "the destruction of Jerusalem to the destruction of our afflicted Spain."[60]

Plainly, Enrique's partisans, as well as Alfonso's publicists, favored the apocalyptic imperative. By 1466, both sides proclaimed crisis, God's wrath having descended, and both claimed it their sacred duty to cleanse the land of defilement, while each side declared the other responsible. That language proved highly effective in sanctioning civil strife as just and holy war. Moreover, the widespread and increasing sense of anarchy and immorality chroniclers report existing under Enrique IV and the apocalyptic terms in which they were expressed were not, as is sometimes asserted, manufactured subsequently by Isabel and her apologists. Whatever the extent to which chronicles may later have been doctored, Enrique's reign inspired contemporaries with increasingly less confidence in it.

Civil War

For four months after Avila, the two sides clashed in armed combat, *guerra guerreada*. It was a war waged on small villages, on crops and cattle, and through fear, its principal zone the *meseta*. Enrique, offering a general pardon on July 12, bitterly noted that not withstanding the *mercedes* he had granted, "*los cavalleros mis rebeldes*" were "so numerous they could not be counted."[61] All Castile then felt the effect of lack of strong central authority: it reverberated in bandits and guerillas and forts seized or besieged in local contests, *guerras chicas,* waged ferociously.

Isabel by then had from Enrique the semblance of her own household, with Gonzalo Chacón as her *mayordomo mayor* and an income derived from *juros*—royal bonds—and rents from certain jurisdictions. Enrique also named her *señora* of the towns of Trujillo and Casarrubios del Monte and so entitled to revenues from them, and he was still determined she marry Afonso of Portugal; Queen Juana was making the arrangements with her brother.[62] Even so, in April of 1466, he received an offer from Pedro Girón, who was then a forty-three-year-old widower, made with the support of Pacheco, to provide Enrique with men and money—three thousand horse and sixty thousand gold doubloons—and to turn over Alfonso in exchange for permission to marry Isabel. Enrique told Girón to come quickly and take her, and as a precaution he yet again dismissed Beltrán and Mendoza from court. Immediately, Girón set out from Almagro, his stronghold in Extremadura, "with great power, in men as in money," and bringing finery for the wedding and the customary tourneys accompanying it.[63]

On being told just beforehand of his imminent arrival and why he was coming, Isabel for a day and night neither ate nor slept, but prayed to God, says Valera, that he kill either one or the other of them in order to stop the wedding. When Girón, suddenly stricken with what is referred to as quinsy or croup, died on the way, how could she not think that heaven had answered her prayers? While the later celebrants of her piety do not date it from that deliverance, they make much of its efficacy in that crisis. And, with Girón seemingly having been struck down so fortuitously, as though by God's hand, it is highly unlikely that, however devout she may have been before, she was any less so afterward. As for her chroniclers, they emphasized not simply divine action but its interplay with a commendable exercise of free will on her part; that is, they adjudged her reprieve to have been "a victory wrested from fortune by patience and fortitude."[64] The chances are good that someone poisoned Girón, and the people with most to gain from his death were themselves at odds. They were Juan of Aragón and the Mendozas.

The contest dragged on. The Mendozas returned to royal favor, and the princess Juana, again heir apparent, was given into their keeping in August of 1467, chiefly as a hostage against Enrique's vacillation. Enrique also promised them to make no accords with Alfonso's followers for at least three months, nor to turn over the queen or Isabel to anyone. He accepted the suggestion of the papal legate, made earlier by Pedro González de Mendoza, that Juana be betrothed to Alfonso. He also renewed the offer of Isabel's hand to Afonso of Portugal, now in exchange for military aid. It was too late. For on September 15, with the help of Pedro Arías, a son of the royal comptroller, who in 1466 had lost an eye during an attempt made on his life by Pacheco with Enrique's complicity, Alfonso's partisans occupied Segovia and, while the queen fled, Isabel stayed, to be reunited with Alfonso and to celebrate his fourteenth birthday.[65]

At Isabel's request, Gómez Manrique wrote a *momo*, a masque, for the occasion, full of classical allusion and moral injunction, its theme good kingship. In it, Isabel and seven of her ladies performed as muses bearing gifts, and Isabel, in the role of Fortune, pronounced to her brother predictions of greatness such as were once made to their father, Juan II.[66] Alfonso's birthday presents were virtues, skills, and a glorious future: he would be liberal and just, a Hercules in strength, yet a gentle knight, well loved and well feared. As climax, Isabel promised him triumphs and victories, glories both earthly and celestial. And as in so much else, she showed consistency in continuing to commission *momos* to celebrate family occasions, in relying on Gómez Manrique to write

Figure 1. Isabel at prayer (c. 1521). Felipe Bigarny. Royal Chapel, Granada.

them, in her penchant for political theater, and in her sense of dynastic expectations.

Isabel and Alfonso rode back to Arévalo and their mother, but not before Isabel got a document from Alfonso and his supporters stating that she would not be forced to marry against her will. They were there on December 7, when

Alfonso presented his sister with the jurisdiction and estimable rents of Medina del Campo and so of its great trade fairs that attracted merchants from all Spain and abroad and that neither side in that civil war wanted to close down.[67]

For Isabel life at Enrique's court had been far from secure, her position uncertain, the times turbulent, and events potentially overwhelming. Still, the impression is left that she remained self-possessed, even self-contained, and from the outset she evinced a quiet firmness and a moral certainty. To whatever extent she may have enjoyed life at court, and there are indications it was not all bleak, what comes through is that she was astute enough to make the most of her surroundings, and that those formative years were such that the patience and forbearance she later displayed, whether or not innate, were self-protective qualities she assiduously cultivated.

From all appearances, Isabel had arrived at court feeling not so much a poor relation as an outsider, one already possessing a distinctly different, and superior, moral code, which she retained. Still, she also demonstrated the wisdom to take on the protective coloration necessary for survival. She seems to have got on well with the king, the two enjoying happy moments together, even while learning from his example how not to rule. At the same time, she gravitated toward the dissidents, who courted her, and, whatever their motives, whose cause bound her brother and herself to them. She herself would never, though, employ the impassioned apocalyptic rhetoric they favored, the sort going out under Alfonso's signature. Isabel was no hothead. Her style would be exactly antithetical, that of a monarch determined to act sensibly: her tone highly rational, if also self-righteous and imperious. At the same time, she knew the value of doomsday rhetoric when wielded in support of a reign, and of its traditional role in enhancing the royal image. She recognized its appeal, particularly in wartime, and most of her life, from early childhood on, was lived in times of war.

Isabel's years at Enrique's court were those of a growing demand for social and religious order. Subsequently, she would display a penchant for order, a faith involving a direct relationship with an ordering, just God, and a firm belief in the efficacy of prayer, especially that of God's delegates who ruled Spain.

Chapter 3
The Right Marriage: 1467–1469

It has to be he and absolutely no other.
—*Isabel*[1]

Alfonso was fourteen years old, and he was upright and vengeful. Three stories are told of him: Alfonso saying he would suffer what he must patiently until he was of an age to punish injustices; Alfonso responding angrily to a request from men in Toledo for authority to take the posts and property of *conversos* and to exile them; and Alfonso concerned about the effect on Isabel of the immodest dress and behavior of Juana's women; "although he well knew her great virtue and honesty, he would have enjoyed seeing her leave such company."[2] An impression builds of dogmatic chivalry. Yet there is something else, a vindictiveness, evident in his slaughter of the animals Enrique had collected and cherished in Segovia: deer, bear cubs, leopards, and ocelots; Pacheco got him to spare one huge mountain goat, "knowing Enrique loved it."[3]

Palencia provides extenuating circumstance, if in his best overripe prose. Enrique, he says, had kept the boy confined for some time in the *alcázar* of Segovia, where "Alfonso, wrenched from his mother's arms, existed as though buried . . . exposed to perversity and in danger of a very cruel death."[4] (By perversity he meant homosexual enticement.) And, he went on, it was said that while Alfonso was jailed in the tower the queen often tried to poison him with herbs but the keeper of the *alcázar* prevented it, until Enrique at length freed him. Whether or not accurate, Alfonso most probably believed it. Moreover, his father (and Isabel's) reportedly had a cruel and vengeful streak, but in his case along with insufficient spirit to do much harm. And many years later, a great-niece of Alfonso's who also felt persecuted when young would, forcefully, wreak sufficient vengeance to become known as Bloody Mary. Her reign, too, would be truncated.

*   *   *

In March of 1468, when Gonzalo Chacón encountered resistance in taking possession of Medina del Campo for Isabel, it was symptomatic of a wider movement. In the constant oscillations of rival urban factions seeking outside support against one another, towns that had gone over to Alfonso, among them Burgos and Toledo, were returning to Enrique. In Toledo, Alfonso, who despite his protestations had lost the support of the *converso* faction on the rumor that he was disposed to persecute such New Christians, subsequently lost the backing of the opposing faction when he would not agree to removing *conversos* from the town council. Enrique, more obliging, did some fishing of his own in troubled waters and won back Toledo; on June 16, 1468 he issued a general amnesty, and on July 3 he abolished the city council seats held by *conversos*.[5] Trouble had begun in Toledo in 1467 between *conversos* and Jews competing to farm taxes. Feeding into it was a contest between the cathedral council and the principal royal official there, the *alcalde,* between, that is, Carrillo, Toledo's archbishop, who supported Alfonso, and Enrique IV. Subsequently, *conversos* in Toledo were attacked, robbed, and killed. It was an example of a religious issue put to use for other purposes, and there would be more such incidents.

At the end of June, Alfonso, with Pacheco and Carrillo and a number of his people, set out from Arévalo to besiege and regain Toledo. Alfonso had accompanied Isabel to Medina del Campo in May when she had expressed a wish to go to the fair and now she rode with him. On July 2, at Cardeñosa near Avila, Alfonso fell ill. Within three days he was dead, purportedly of bubonic plague. Palencia says he collapsed immediately after lunching on a trout *empanada* and asserts that he was poisoned by Pacheco.[6] However that may be, in the preceding weeks, Pacheco had raided the treasury: Alfonso had signed an unusual number of *mercedes* to him and his family and, on April 14, an oddly belated order to the *contadores mayores* to reimburse Pacheco for expenses incurred in liberating himself and Isabel.[7]

Palencia also averred that Alfonso, ever since he had been proclaimed king at Avila, had tried to get Carrillo to discuss in council the need for "reforming palace life," and the chronicler recalled that he himself had been approached by the boy-king for help in escaping Pacheco's care, for Alfonso could not tolerate the *hombres infames* Pacheco had surrounded him with, the same sort of men (snorts Palencia) who had been introduced to rouse Enrique to licentiousness, to make him effeminate and thus to dominate him.

Juan Pacheco, marqués de Villena, had a dynasty of his own to establish, a purpose generally counter to the interests of Alfonso and Isabel. Pacheco strove to be mayor of the palace in the tradition of Charles Martel or the powerful Abd-al-Rahman of al-Andalus or like his mentor, Alvaro de Luna. His early plan seems to have been to join the dissidents, gain Alfonso the succession, then having seen to it that aspersions on Juana's paternity ensured that she was not a desirable match for royalty, have her marry a son of his, then again switch sides and restore her good name and standing. It was not beyond him. He had secretly agreed with Louis of France that Juana was to wed one of his, Pacheco's, sons.[8] And in June of 1467, Pacheco was negotiating for his daughter Beatriz to marry Fernando of Aragón. While Alfonso lived, it appears, Isabel was only Juan of Aragón's second choice for his son Fernando. Still, by August of that year, Pacheco had decided Alfonso XII of Castile would be a preferable match for his own daughter Beatriz.

Plainly, however, there was little congenial in the natures of the suave marqués and the young martinet. And Alfonso had become ever more truculent. Now, with the boy gone and Pacheco making certain that Isabel married out of the kingdom, it was possible that one of his brood might both marry Fernando and wear the crown of Castile; for, barring Isabel, and with Juana's paternity discredited, the prince of Aragón and his father were as closely related to Enrique as was anyone: Juan I was their common progenitor. So matters stood when Alfonso fell mortally ill.

Princess

A letter to the kingdom under Isabel's name went out from Cardeñosa on July 4, 1468, while Alfonso still lingered. A copy directed to Murcia survives, stating that should Alfonso die, Isabel was his legitimate heir, and that the city should be held in her name as its rightful lady, its *señora natural,* and deputies be readied to take the oath to her in Cortes. The following day she signed another, announcing Alfonso's death that very afternoon: "at three, it pleased Our Lord, for the sins of these kingdoms, to take from this present life the lord king my brother."[9] That explanation, customary in epidemics of plague, also suggested that Alfonso XII's demise was both a sacrifice for the realm and a sign of God's displeasure with its condition. In years to come, Isabel would hold to the view of God she expressed that day, a stern judge, personally meting out merited punishment, and reward, to the monarch who personified the nation, and not only through plague, although doubtlessly part of the virulence of that punitive concept of divinity had to do with the persistence of plague.

There is no way of knowing how Isabel felt at the time. She spoke of founding a convent in her younger brother's memory at the place he died. Although she never did, she did have him sculpted, in a wall niche by their parents' tombs in the charterhouse of Miraflores, as youthful promise personified, and blighted. His adherents, who were now hers, lamented Alfonso's death in similar terms. Jorge Manríque, Rodrigo's son, saw it as a blow of fortune, leaving unfulfilled a promise of justice and virtue.[10] And Gómez Manrique, reiterating the themes of Alfonso's birthday masque, eulogized him as a young Caesar who, had he lived, would have conquered barbarous nations and established an empire overseas.[11] Palencia went yet further, or perhaps higher, in speaking of Alfonso as "that monarch born in the old age of his father to give hope to the people," and in presenting him as another young Isaac, and even as Christlike, as "the holy boy" who had given up "his immaculate soul."[12] And Valera reported that as Alfonso lay dying, in many places of Avila and Segovia other people on their deathbeds and especially children spoke of going to glory in the company of the blessed king *don Alfonso*.[13] Even so, the strongest impression conveyed by the niche at Miraflores and those laudatory chroniclers is one of Alfonso as a harbinger, such as an angel with a trumpet, announcing the reign that would be Isabel's.

Isabel was not present when Alfonso's body was interred, on the night of his death, in the convent of San Francisco at Arévalo. Carrillo and Pacheco had taken her to Ávila, where they squabbled over what to do next. Pacheco insisted that she declare herself not Alfonso's heir but Enrique's, not queen but princess. Carrillo wanted her immediately proclaimed queen as Alfonso's successor, arguing that he did not trust Enrique: had he not put her in his wife's care so that she would grow up unfit to rule? Pacheco then insisted that she marry Afonso of Portugal. Carrillo, equally adamant, insisted she should wed Fernando of Aragón. Pacheco threatened to carry her off bodily. Carrillo retorted he assuredly would not, for the garrison of Ávila was his. Pacheco pleaded the presence of plague. And Carrillo assured him that it only attacked boys.[14]

Two weeks later, Isabel signed a letter to Chacón, "Isabel, by Grace of God Princess and legitimate hereditary successor to these kingdoms of Castile and León."[15] She would be Enrique's heir. With disagreement between her mentors the decision had been hers. At court, within the Royal Council there was recognition that she herself had made the choice and that she was extremely astute, that for an unmarried seventeen-year-old *infanta* to have claimed the crown would have been foolhardy.[16] Too, everyone knew that support for Alfonso and his faction had eroded, that nobles and towns had deserted to the extent that strong backing remained only in Extremadura and Andalusia, whose great lords were always quick to acknowledge the least constraining superior authority. Enrique, that is, could not be dislodged. Yet there was very broad consensus that since Enrique must have a successor, a woman of marriageable age, Isabel, was preferable to a young girl, Juana. As for Enrique, however he had felt about Alfonso, he interpreted his death as a prospect for peace. The great nobles were tired of civil war. Queen Juana was in disgrace, having had a son by her keeper. So it was that Isabel and Enrique jointly signed a document on September 18, stating that it had become publicly manifest that for the past year "*la reina doña Juana* had not used her person cleanly as complies with the service of the King nor her own," and that the king had been informed "that he was not, and is not, legitimately married to her."[17] It was a roundabout and conditional disclaimer of her daughter's legitimacy.

King and rebels reconciled, meeting in an open field in Avila's countryside, beside a Hieronymite monastery in a place known as Toros de Guisando. Isabel arrived on a mule with Carrillo walking beside her, holding its reins, a gesture an archbishop would only make for the highest dignitary in the land. He had come reluctantly and he refused to kiss Enrique's hand as a sign of obedience until after the rebels had been forgiven and Isabel promised succession. The promise was given, and she in turn pledged to marry no one without the king's consent. The papal envoy absolved everyone of the oath taken to young Juana.[18]

Mute witnesses to this reconciliation, which would not last, there stand to this day the Toros de Guisando, a row of stone bulls hewn ages ago, similar to the ones that once stood in Arévalo and were attributed to Hercules. If, as learned opinion has it, they were set up initially to delineate cattle paths and ensure fertility, their primordial symbolism retained its potency that day. Although it was Isabel who proffered homage to Enrique, it was at bottom her victory: for hers was the inherent power of youth and fertility. She was soon, too, to concern herself with delineation of other boundaries, to push against limits in exercising her new authority as princess. As heir presumptive to the crown of Castile, she would in the months to come receive her own council, jurisdictions, and household. She would be introduced to governing and receive her own sources of income. And it was imperative she marry.

For the next nine months, Isabel was in Ocaña, where Enrique too spent much of his time. Ocaña was a stronghold of Pacheco, who again dominated the Royal Council; the Mendoza had gone home to Guadalajara, but not without having received custody of Queen Juana and her daughter. Isabel now lived in the house of Gutierre de Cárdenas, Chacón's cousin, whom she made her *maestresala,* in charge of her household, and who, like Chacón, she named to her privy council. Cárdenas had been in Carrillo's household—"he was with Carrillo for a great while, with no more than a mule"[19]—and both he and Chacón had adhered to the dissident league, worked with Pacheco, followed Alfonso, and now gave to Isabel a primary loyalty, never to be withdrawn.

At Ocaña, with her people around her and Carrillo nearby in Yepes, she organized a staff and began to enjoy the stature and power of princess of Asturias, heir to the crown. Enrique granted her the jurisdiction and revenues of Medina del Campo, as Alfonso had, and other towns as well, and he assigned to her all royal authority over the mint at Avila. She bestowed *mercedes* and she engaged in another politic occupation, writing innumerable letters to nobles, high clergy, urban councils, and religious houses, couched as keeping

Castilians informed of her situation and consulted regarding whom she should marry. She thereby tested the temper of the realm, strengthened her own position within it, and showed herself aware of the potency of public opinion and adroit at shaping it.

Some advice she had not solicited also came to her, on or about her seventeenth birthday, in the form of a guide for young ladies, a *Garden of Noble Maidens*. Its author was Martín de Córdoba, an Augustinian friar and renowned preacher who had been a preceptor to Alfonso. That treatise, while mentioning some qualities commonly attributed to good monarchs, chiefly urged upon her the usual maidenly desiderata—chastity, modesty, a sense of shame, and a guarded tongue. While obviously a manful attempt to put the best face possible on expectation of a woman ruler, its litany of ideal feminine attributes had little to do with the qualities shown by the remarkably strong women who had recently been queens consort and regents in Spain. At bottom, it was an extensive Augustinian essay on original sin and on the descent of women from the original sinner, Eve, the product of Adam's rib (the friar went into a learned disquisition on just which rib), who was also held up as the source of all feminine weakness and inferiority. That is, Isabel was informed that she was among the best of the worst and must work very hard to be virtuous, since, having high position, she would be an exemplar to other women. Even should she become queen, the author did not expect the queen to be the one who ruled. In the event, he was dead wrong. Yet his advice had some resonance, for as queen Isabel would deport herself with modesty even while ruling powerfully.

Martín de Córdoba clearly did not have Isabel or any woman in mind as ever actually reigning when he wrote that God had put the seat of the king of Spain in the West, "wherefore it appears he is sharing the reign of earth with our king."[20] Here he relied on the commonplace prophecy alluded to by Sánchez de Arévalo a few years earlier, that a final millennial kingdom would arise in the West. Whatever she made of the friar's platitudes, Isabel would adapt that prophecy to her own purposes. Other, more practical, but not completely dissimilar birthday wishes came from the faithful Gómez Manrique, who, after wishing her happiness, added a hope "that God will give you a king for a husband."[21]

Suitors

Isabel, who throughout her life was indeed mindful of the wisdom of displaying among other qualities those of an exemplary woman, while in Ocaña did guard her tongue. And there was dissimulation in the letters she sent out, for she had already chosen a husband, possibly even before meeting Enrique at

Toros de Guisando. She had resolved to wed Fernando, prince of Aragón, whose father had in June enhanced his son's stature with an additional title, king of Sicily. Immediately after Alfonso's death, that old fox Juan of Aragón had broken off negotiations for Fernando to marry Beatriz Pacheco and intensified his concurrent campaign for Isabel. Through a combination of deft diplomacy, promises of greater position and power to influential Castilians, and well-placed applications of Aragonese gold in Castile, he had gained sufficient acceptance for that match among Castilian nobles and ecclesiastics; importantly, in May he got from the Mendoza a secret promise not to obstruct Isabel's inheriting the crown. Juan's chief allies in those negotiations were his father-in-law, Fadrique Enríquez, Castile's admiral, and Carrillo, who in turn worked closely with Rodrigo Manrique, that stalwart of the old nobility.[22]

Other suitors as well were seeking out Isabel now that she might well bring Castile in her dowry. Louis XI of France requested her hand for his brother and heir presumptive, Charles, duke of Berry and Guienne. Although Edward IV of England had married elsewhere, one of his brothers, possibly the future Richard III, was another candidate. And Afonso of Portugal now demanded she marry him as recompense for the affront suffered by his niece, young Juana. Pacheco had come to support the Portuguese match vigorously: not only would it leave Fernando free to marry his daughter Beatriz, but the new king of Sicily who had his own good claim to the Castilian crown might well be a far more acceptable ruler to Castilians than a queen married to the powerful king of Portugal. With Pacheco back at his side, Enrique, shortly after reconciling with Isabel but without her permission and seemingly belying any renunciation of the queen's child, again accepted Afonso of Portugal for Isabel, and Afonso's promising son, João, heir to Portugal, for young Juana, and an embassy from Lisbon arrived at Ocaña to make arrangements.

Amid those formal negotiations, messages flew back and forth from Isabel's household to Carrillo at Yepes. "All the exquisite vigilance of the Master"—Enrique had confirmed Pacheco as master of Santiago—"was ineffective," says Palencia, then a secretary of Isabel's, to avoid envoys secretly entering Ocaña and talking quietly to her.[23] The necessary preliminary documents for her marriage to Fernando were signed secretly in January of 1469. That same month Isabel affirmed to her trusted retainers that she would marry only "the king of Sicily," that "it has to be he and absolutely no other."[24]

It is in recounting those events that Pulgar argues the decision was hers to make since she was in effect an orphan, and he then adds that she also believed that if she did not marry Fernando, Enrique would ultimately choose him for Juana and disinherit her. She then, as arranged by Carrillo in close accord with Chacón and Cárdenas, formally consented to marry Aragón's prince and Sicily's king before witnesses and with a proxy, Carrillo's son, Troilos, standing in for the groom.[25] Juan of Aragón promised her an engagement gift of forty thousand gold florins; and since she and Fernando were second cousins, a dispensation was secured for marrying within the third degree of consanguinity, not from the pope but from the bishop of Segovia, Juan Arías, issued on the basis of a supposed papal bull that Aragón's king represented as having been received during earlier wedding negotiations. Juan had most likely forged it.[26]

The complicated arrangements necessary to clearing the way for a surreptitious royal wedding progressed. Pacheco, it was surmised, knew of them and was planning to spring a trap. With Carrillo was Pierres de Peralta, Juan of Aragón's trusted counselor and constable, who informed his king in cipher that Pacheco was increasingly unpopular and that "when he decides to jump, [everything is ready] to jump ahead of him."[27] Enrique, at Ocaña on and off that spring, was uneasy, as well he might be, for in the streets children playing at being knights on stick horses were chanting "*Flores de Aragón / dentro en Castilla son, / Flores de Aragón / dentro en Castilla son*"; ("Flowers of Aragón are inside Castile, Flowers of Aragón are inside Castile") and then, laughing and waving small banners, they would shout "*¡Péndon de Aragón, Péndon de Aragón!*" ("banner of Aragón! banner of Aragón!").[28] There was no doubt that the populace preferred an Aragonese king to a Portuguese one, and especially a young and robust one.

When Enrique, ever more suspicious, had a nobleman threaten Isabel with arrest should she not leave the decision of her marriage to him, she broke into tears. Enrique, unswayed, had the Portuguese emissaries swear to use force if necessary to see to it that she married their king. And he did not, although he had promised he would, declare her his heir in the rump Cortes, of ten cities only, he then convoked at Ocaña. Later Isabel accused him of having had even those docile delegates intimidated into agreeing to the Portuguese marriage. He was arranging to have her taken to the *alcázar* of Madrid, when, threatened with Carrillo's sending troops to her rescue, he desisted, only to find that the hubbub his plans for her had created throughout the town had caused the Portuguese envoys to decamp.

And so matters stood when, on Pacheco's advice, Enrique went south to reassert royal authority in rebellious Andalusia. Isabel excused herself from accompanying him on the grounds of having to stay to escort Alfonso's body from Arévalo to permanent interment in Avila. Before he left on May 7, Enrique had her swear she "would make no innovations concerning her marriage." Leaving her behind on oath was Pacheco's idea, thinking it should flush out her intentions. He had also arranged for her to be watched closely and left his nephew, Luis de Acuña, bishop of Burgos, to keep an eye on her. He was confident he had convinced her ladies, Beatríz de Bobadilla and Mencia de la Torre, of the folly of the Aragonese suit, and he had placed on alert his ally, Alfonso de Fonseca, archbishop of Seville, who stood ready with a large garrison at the nearby castle of Coca. Although it was a fine point, since Isabel had previously vowed to wed Fernando, she could construe plans forwarding the Aragonese match as not being innovations.

She left, as planned, for Arévalo. Once there, she further proposed to reclaim the town for her mother, for Enrique had granted it to the count of Plasencia, Álvaro de Stúñiga. Her intent suspected, at Arévalo's gates Stúñiga's lieutenant turned her away in no uncertain terms, an insult that rankled and that would be avenged, for Isabel did not easily forgive. She nonetheless collected Alfonso's body from the Franciscan convent outside the walls, saw it safely to Avila, and then went on visit her mother, who was at Madrigal. There in late July she received an envoy from France, sent on by Enrique.

Louis XI, hoping to encircle Aragón and concerned about Castile's pact with England and with Enrique's discouraging Castilian merchants from trading with France, had sent the cardinal of Albi to him in Andalusia in order to renew friendly relations and the suit of the duke of Guienne, his brother and heir apparent, for Isabel's hand. Enrique obligingly broke the pact with England and signed one with France, but, unable to get the *grandes* to support the French marriage and anxious to get rid of the long-winded cardinal, had suggested he go to convince Isabel herself of the advantages of the French connection. The princess heard him out and then gave her stock time-buying response to such unwelcome overtures. According to Pulgar, she told him "she waited for God to show His will, and would do that which was to His service and the good of these kingdoms . . . and nothing without the advice of the *grandes* and knights. . . ."[29] Most of the great nobles, of course, were known to be opposed to the match. Patently, she had learned to say no while seeming to say perhaps.[30]

She had reason to put off the French. Palencia mentions that she had recently sent her chaplain, on the pretext of business, both to France to look over Charles and to Aragón to observe Fernando. The man had reported that in all excellence the prince far exceeded the duke, for the prince of Aragón was very gallant and he was handsome in countenance, body, and person; he was of noble air and very disposed to all she would wish, while the duke was soft and effeminate, with spindly legs and watery half-blind eyes, so that before long he would have more need of someone to support him than of horse and arms for knightly endeavor. Moreover, her envoy reminded her, the customs of the French were repugnant to Castilian gravity. Isabel was delighted with his report.[31]

She had had a letter from Fernando; her reply survives. Addressed "to the Lord my cousin, King of Sicily" and carried to Fernando by Peralta, it guardedly expresses her commitment:

Lord cousin, since the Constable is going there, there is no need for me to write at greater length, except to ask your pardon for so late a reply. And the reason for the delay, the Constable will explain to Your Mercy. I beg you to trust him and to say what you wish me to do, for that I must do. And the reason I must do that today more than ever you will know from the Constable, because it is not to be written. From the hand that will do as you may order, *La princesa.*[32]

It is an early instance of the mix of courteous formality and heartfelt sincerity that she would retain in writing to him, and she would continue to make similar avowals of service and obedience, formal usages to be understood in chivalric terms. She would also, maddingly, often refer him to the messenger for specifics. Yet beneath her seemingly deferential demeanor is discernible, and imparted, her own sense of self-worth, indeed of how fortunate he is that it is she who addresses him so. That style of hers has been well described as "meek grandeur."

Far less meek was a letter she wrote several months later to Enrique, an open one expected to be widely circulated, explaining her recent behavior—for she had bolted—and justifying it as response to his bad faith. While in Madrigal, she began, she had discovered that he had ordered the town council to keep her there forcibly. And while the town fathers had wavered, she had found that some of her women and servants had also been suborned and set to spy on her, even that her ladies, Beatriz de Bobadilla and Mencia de la Torre, had left her and gone to Coca, and that its lord, Fonseca, on Pacheco's orders, was to arrive within six days to seize her. It was then she found it necessary, she informed him, to send for her uncles, Carrillo, and the admiral.[33] She did not mention that her emissary, who was her confessor, Alonso de Burgos, had so insolently demanded their help that Carrillo nearly did not come. Moreover, it would be surprising if her seemingly disaffected ladies with whom she soon reconciled were not in reality her spies.

Arriving with six hundred horse, the archbishop and the admiral had proposed to escort her out of Madrigal in order, she informed Enrique, to quit the fears of the townspeople. She had left with them (she omitted that she had first gleefully said goodbye to Pacheco's factotum, the bishop of Burgos, telling him she was going where she wished). It is recorded that she then rode off in that company "with great joy and to the sound of many trumpets and kettle-drums," first to Fontiveros, where the people feared the king's wrath, then to her city of Avila, where they found that pestilence was growing worse daily, and so finally to Valladolid, which was healthy and secure and adhered to the admiral. She had, as Juan of Aragón was informed, taken the leap.

That she had not simply acted impulsively is manifest in her having, prodded by Chacón and Cárdenas, insisted that before committing herself decisively she receive, as earnest of Fernando's intent, the forty thousand gold florins promised in January. Palencia, sent by Carrillo to fetch them, had instead returned with some pieces of gold and a gold necklace inlaid with pearls and large spinel rubies that had belonged to Aragón's queens and was worth, said Palencia, the forty thousand florins. Just before coming to escort her out of Madrigal, Carrillo sent it to her together with eight thousand florins in cash, with which, said Palencia disapprovingly, she had been prodigal, in giving two thousand each to Chacón and Cárdenas, and another one thousand to Clara Alvarnáez, "as her most obedient servants." Palencia notwithstanding, her confidence would prove well placed.

In Valladolid she stayed in the house of Juan de Vivero. His wife was María de Acuña, whose father, the count of Buendía, was Carrillo's brother, and whose mother was Fernando's maternal aunt. From Valladolid on September 8 she wrote Enrique that long open letter. In it she also reminded him of her moderation on Alfonso's death in refusing the title of queen, indicated that it was he who had broken their agreement at Toros de Guisando in arranging a marriage for her against her will, and complained of his insisting she marry the king of Portugal and of threats made to her and to the delegates to the Cortes of Ocaña should they not comply with that decision of his. The tone she took in writing—bordering on righteous indignation, hovering between disappointment in him and recrimination, certain of her own moral position—she would resort to frequently and in a wide variety of communiqués and situations. She chastised Enrique for following bad advice and declared her own decision to be based upon the collective will and best interests of the kingdom. She reminded him that, when faced with the Portuguese marriage, he had, "condescending to the will of some individuals," decided she be forced to consent. Then, "I, alone and deprived of my just and proper liberty and the exercise of free will that in marital negotiations after the grace of God is the principal requisite, secretly made inquiry of the *grandes*, prelates, and *caballeros*, your subjects, concerning their opinion."

They responded, she went on, that the Portuguese marriage "in no manner complied to the good of your kingdoms." As for the French marriage, his subjects desired she should not wed in parts so far from her own land and customs, and they believed that alliance would turn his kingdoms into dependencies, allowing France to accrete power, take Aragón and so neighbor Castile, and "to occupy the lordly domains *[senoríos]* of our close relatives." But "all praised and approved the marriage with the Prince of Aragón, King of Sicily." That union, she assured him, would add to the glory of his realm.

Throughout, Isabel played on the consanguinity making her heir apparent, repeatedly reminding him that their differences were a family matter: so she spoke of Alfonso as "our brother," of Afonso of Portugal as "my cousin," alluded to their mutual royal progenitors, and referred to the kings of Aragón as "your near relatives." She then listed the benefits of an Aragonese union, and recalled that their common grandfather, Enrique III, in his will had counseled his descendants to it. Throughout, she presented herself as "a younger sister desirous of your service and the peace and tranquility of these your kingdoms," implying contrast to his nonrelated and sinister advisors who had little interest in the welfare of the realm. She was right about public opinion concerning France and Portugal, but she did overstate the popularity of the Aragonese match.

From Valladolid, Palencia and Cárdenas were dispatched in haste to Aragón, to escort Fernando to Castile before Enrique and Pacheco returned to the *meseta*. They soon sent Isabel disconcerting news, that many of the Castilian clergy and nobles they had been counting on for assistance along the way had changed sides and, worst of all, that the Mendozas, from whom they had expected neutrality, had gone over to Enrique, so that their great castles and forts along the entire frontier from Almazán to Guadalajara stood threatingly between Fernando and Valladolid. Cárdenas voiced concern that Fernando would not attempt the trip; Palencia was certain he would. He had been with Fernando in Valencia, he explained, while Fernando was getting the ruby necklace for Isabel out of pawn, and had then to dissuade him from setting off with it immediately to come to her rescue.[34]

The Prince of Aragón and King of Sicily

Palencia and Cárdenas reached Zaragoza at the end of September and there, in great secrecy, they rendezvoused with the prince of Aragón and king of Sicily in a secluded cell of the Franciscan convent. The seventeen-year-old they encountered was of medium stature, with bright, smiling eyes, straight dark brown hair, and "he had so singular a grace that everyone who talked to him wanted to serve him." Although twice deathly ill as a child, Fernando was now strong and fit, having "been raised at war and endured many hardships and dangers."[35]

Fernando was born on March 10, 1452 in the village of Sos in Aragón. His mother, Juana Enríquez, had come there from Navarre expressly to establish her child's claim to the kingdom his father might well inherit. Fernando had grown up close to this strong, indeed headstrong mother, whom her much older husband—in 1452 she was twenty-eight, he was fifty-four—loved and indulged. She brought up her son to succeed to Aragon's crown, beginning by putting off his baptism for nearly a year, until Juan was regent in Aragón and it could be held in the cathedral in Zaragoza. There, with royal magnificence, the child was named for his paternal grandfather, Fernando de Antequera, a king of Aragón who was as well the foremost Castilian hero of the wars against the Moors in recent memory.

Fernando was five when his father, becoming Aragón's king, became immediately immersed in wars. Juan waged them personally, even though he was half blind from cataracts until 1466, when he became completely blind; but three years later, always a risk taker, Juan underwent an operation performed by a Jewish doctor, and regained his sight. Juan fought the French, who were encroaching on Aragon's borders; and from his accession he was faced with civil war, waged chiefly with the Catalans.

Catalonia, with Barcelona at its heart, Aragón's largest and wealthiest province, had fallen far from its golden age of trade and undergone related economic woes and suffered recurrent plague. Propertied Catalans had been unsympathetic to the dynastic and imperial adventures in the Mediterranean of Juan's brother and predecessor, Alfonso V (known to history as the Magnanimous), and they did not trust Juan from his regency on. In Barcelona, while artisans and guilds looked to him for economic redress and for support against proprietors and landlords, proprietors and landlords wanted to take charge of stabilizing conditions themselves. Moreover, in the countryside Aragonese peasants, suffering from plague and hard times, opposed nobles who were seeking to extract more work from fewer laborers and to renew lapsed señorial dues. Particularly onerous was the *remensa,* a money recompense exacted from peasants by a lord should they leave his lands. Peasants under the *remensa* system rebelled; their landlords raised armies against them. When such people appealed for relief to the new king, he, in trying to steer a moderate course, pleased no one.

As to the Catalans, in rising against Juan they chose as their king his elder son, Carlos of Viana, and when Carlos died in 1461 they claimed that the queen, Juana Enríquez, had had him poisoned. Juan, busy rebuffing French attempts to seize territory, did not soothe them when he immediately convoked Aragón's parliament, the Corts, and appointed Fernando, then nine years old, his lieutenant governor in Catalonia, delegating that authority to the queen. The Catalans soon declared her arrogant and intrusive in their affairs, forced her to leave Barcelona, and renounced Fernando as governor; it was then they appealed to Enrique IV of Castile. As for Juana Enríquez, she retreated with her son to Gerona, where she directed the repulse of a Catalan siege. Three years later, at age twelve, Fernando, at the head of royal forces, squared accounts with the Catalans in defeating them on the battlefield. Subsequently, Juan, without calling the Corts, named Fernando lieutenant-general of the realm. The civil war wore on.

When the Corts was at length convened, at Zaragoza on February 6, 1468, Juana Enríquez, afflicted by a cancer of the breast and neck, was too sick to preside. Fernando did so instead; he was sixteen years old. Two weeks later she died; Valera insists that a wonderful odor arose from her corpse, implying she was a saint, which was unlikely. The king was as usual then battling the French in the north, and it was Fernando who saw to his mother's funeral. Then, in faction-torn Valencia, addressing the city's notables with tears streaming down his face, he paid her a tribute she would have appreciated: "Lords: You all know with what hardships my lady mother has sustained the war to keep Catalonia within the house of Aragón. I see my lord father old and myself very young. Therefore I commend myself to you and place myself in your hands and ask you to please consider me as a son." The town councilors responded satisfactorily, promising a truce to factional strife there until the war's end and donating to the crown the proceeds from Valencian taxes on bread and wine. "And so console yourself," they told their prince, "because we have confidence in Our Lord, and that you will recover your lands."[36]

The Valencians had lionized Fernando ever since his victory over the Catalans, their arch economic rivals. With Barcelona in revolt, Valencia was thriving as Aragón's chief port, and it stood to benefit further from a marriage ensuring freer interchange with Castile. So it was that in July of 1469 the Valencian authorities, with exuberant pomp and ceremony, presented Fernando with the ruby necklace so that he might give it to Isabel, overlooking its being held as surety for a loan made to the king his father. They also advanced him thirty thousand *sueldos* to pay for his wedding, for Juan's wars with the French and his greasing of Castilian palms to make the marriage had exhausted the Aragonese treasury.

*   *   *

Somehow, Fernando had received an education in other than military leadership. He had been raised, as royal children often were not, in the parental household. By ten, when he was given his own staff, he had received the initial training in letters, arms, and horsemanship usual to the education of noble boys. If the exigencies of war had brought him more experience in the saddle, in siege warfare, and in council than familiarity with arts and letters, yet his innate intelligence and curiosity ensured a lifelong respect for knowledge and those who possessed it. Among his preceptors was Alfonso de la Torre, who wrote Dantesque and erotic verse but who at Juan's request had produced didactic poems for Fernando's instruction; another was Joan Margarit, bishop of Gerona, some of whose advice he seems to have taken to heart. Margarit advocated the unity of Spain. He also told his pupil that the administration of a kingdom required exercise of prudence rather than an unbending morality: the prince might, he conceded, choose his moment for revealing truth, and he might make promises in war he need not fulfill. Fernando, as observed by Pulgar, who knew him later, displayed the princely virtue of seeking out good counsel and the gift of listening. "He was a man of truth, although the great need in which wars put him made him sometimes deviate."[37] Pulgar, incidentally, says much the same of Isabel.

By 1469, this dashing young hero-prince displayed yet another propensity Pulgar mentions: "he gave himself to women." That year he fathered two children (their mothers unrecorded): Alfonso of Aragón, born in 1470 "*de un virgen generosa*," who would become bishop of Zaragoza, and Juana of Aragón, born in 1469, whom Isabel would one day welcome to her court and whom she would marry to Bernardino Fernández de Velasco, constable of Castile. Two more daughters of his born later would be less welcome to her, and would become nuns.[38]

Now in the fall of 1469, Fernando was resolved to marry the princess of Castile. He immediately left for Valladolid with Cárdenas and Palencia, accompanied only by a few retainers. Riding mules, the small band traversed hostile countryside disguised as merchants and their servants. Wherever they stopped, Fernando, playing the servant, served supper and curried the mules. Along the way, the riders were much cheered when Palencia spotted a good omen, a pair of eagles, soaring high. At the border town of Burgo de Osma they found Gómez Manrique waiting; Isabel had sent him with a squadron as escort.

On October 9, in Valladolid, she received Palencia and Cárdenas, who had ridden ahead to let her know that Fernando had arrived at nearby Dueñas, had been royally received by Buendía, Carrillo's brother, and the countess, Fernando's aunt, and that he was safe and on his way. Her happiness was intense, recounts Palencia, not least because while waiting she had had to cope with arguments against the wedding put to her by envoys of Pacheco and Queen Juana, both of whom by then knew something was in the wind. Isabel had to fend off as well some of her own courtiers, who insisted that the dignity of the royal house of Castile and the excellence of the princess far exceeded that of the king of Sicily and prince of Aragón, and it was unfitting that, through being male, he should enjoy any advantage whatsoever over his spouse.

On October 12, Isabel wrote to Enrique: "By my letters and messengers I now notify Your Highness of my determined will concerning my marriage," which at her age she adjudged to be a very reasonable event. In view of who she was, she went on, and whose daughter and whose sister, she had made the most suitable match possible, after having consulted the principal people of the realm. She wrote only now because she had been informed that Enrique, "following the counsel of some," had sought to intercept Fernando, who, she wanted him to know, had arrived at Dueñas. Have him as a good vassal, she urged Enrique, and approve her intention. Then came that frustrating phrase that occurs so often: Her secretary who was bringing that letter would inform him further.[39]

Figure 2. Fernando and Isabel. Carta de Privilegio al Colegio de Santa Cruz, Valladolid (1484).

To Wed

Two days later, she and Fernando met for the first time. He came to Valladolid from Dueñas, secretly, with only three retainers, in the middle of the night, and entered the house by a postern gate. Carrillo greeted him—the archbishop tried to kiss his hand but Fernando instead embraced him—and led him inside to meet Isabel. As they entered the room, Cárdenas excitedly pointed him out to her: ¡*ése es, ése es*!—that is he, that is he! Cárdenas, as authorized by Isabel, ever after proudly bore two *ss* emblazoned on his coat of arms.

Isabel was eighteen, auburn haired and comely, her blue-green eyes steady. From all indications she was tall and stately, her bearing regal. (Her surviving portraits show only a much older and ill queen). She saw enter the room a gallant youth, eyes sparkling, taut with energy, a cousin, and a very welcome one.[40] She and he talked for two hours. "The presence of the Archbishop repressed the amorous impulses of the lovers," according to Palencia, "though they soon enjoyed the licit joys of matrimony."[41] By all accounts, theirs was an instant attraction, and, remarkably, it proved a passionate and long-lasting love.

A notary took down their formal promises to marry. Fernando gave Isabel customary, if unspecified, gifts and that night he returned to Dueñas.

Through the formality of that first meeting is discernible mutual delight and the sense of a triumphal and momentous encounter, of danger and complicity heightening emotions. There is about that meeting too something calling to mind the chivalric and religious feat, St. George slaying the dragon and rescuing the maiden, a favorite in Catalan art. Even so, this was not simply a romantic encounter. It was a formal meeting of state concerning the union of Castile's princess with Aragon's prince and Sicily's king. There were final contractual stipulations to be considered and there remained to be decided the many questions of protocol so vitally important to the rites of royalty.

Fernando returned on the eighteenth, this time riding into Valladolid with a company of knights. At dusk, surrounded by a large group of well-wishers in Vivero's great hall, Isabel and Fernando heard the archbishop read out first the bull dispensing with the impediment of consanguinity and then the marriage agreement signed by Fernando and his father. They may have secretly wed that night. One scholar states that for royalty and nobility to marry at the time, it was only necessary for the couple to consummate the marriage before eye witnesses, preferably notaries; he also states that is what happened in this case.[42] Whether or no, that night Fernando went to stay with the archbishop. The next morning they wed publicly, in the same hall, the admiral, Fernando's grandfather, and María de Acuña standing with them. The faithful were there in force: the Enríquez, Manriques, and other lords, and knights, royal justices, priests, and, say the chronicles, two thousand people of all estates. Carrillo assisted a priest, one Pero López de Alcalá, who the previous January had heard Isabel's promise to wed and who now performed the ceremony. The couple presented him with the dispensation of consanguinity and asked him to marry them. He read it aloud and declared them absolved; then, having said mass, he gave the nuptial blessings.

Public festivities went on all day. The chronicles say the marriage was officially consummated thereafter. Immediately upon that event, it is reported, witnesses, waiting at the door of the bridal chamber, entered, and then, to the fanfare of trumpets and flutes and the roll of kettledrums, they reappeared to display the customary stained bedsheet to the throng waiting expectantly in the hall below. Valera adds that those witnesses surveyed the bridal bedroom as well, suggesting it was to make certain they were not being duped. Celebration went on for a week. At its end the prince and princess of Aragón and king and queen of Sicily attended mass, said by Carrillo, and received his benediction. Still, their standing in Castile was unclear. Enrique arrived back in Segovia by October 20, a storm cloud. Pacheco, reportedly ill with a quartanary fever made worse by the news, retreated to Ocaña.[43]

The terms of that marriage read out by Carrillo on its eve had been agreed upon nearly a year beforehand, on January 7, 1469. Those terms appeared in a *capitulación*, not within a contract signed by both parties but as a formal offer by one of them based upon a previous mutual agreement. In this case it was Fernando who with his father, Juan II of Aragón, promised certain things to Isabel. He would, it was stated, behave himself fittingly, obey Castile's king, observe Castile's laws and customs, respect its *grandes,* appoint only Castilians to office there, and live in those kingdoms; furthermore, he would not take Isabel out of them nor any of their children, the arrival of children being "no less than should be expected."[44] Neither of the pair were to make *merced* of any city without the other's consent. They would sign everything jointly and share all titles. Fernando promised to honor Isabel's appointments of officials, to respect her grants of lordships, and to make "no movement" or any war or confederation in Castile without her counsel and consent. Fernando was to inherit his father's realms, and Isabel to rule in them should he die before her, but in lifetime tenancy, redounding to his heirs. Everything his aunt, María, regent of Aragón, and his mother, Juana Enríquez, had held as dowry should belong to Isabel. When she and he had in their joint power those kingdoms, they would be obliged to war against the Moors, enemies of the holy Catholic faith, as other Catholic kings, their predecessors, had done.

The *capitulación* employed the royal plural, accentuating the joint nature of this arrangement and tending to obfuscate just who was being referred to in a given instance, whether it was Fernando himself employing the royal we or he and Isabel jointly. What emerges more clearly is the expectation that Fernando was thereby empowered to join Isabel in her inheritance, to take charge in Castile if observing certain stipulations. In this document, Juan had hit upon an arrangement satisfactory to her partisans, still nervous about his claims within Castile, and first among the eminences whose honors and pre-rogatives the *capitulación* promised to respect was "the archbishop of Toledo, primate of Spain, *chanciller mayor* of Castile and our dear and very loved uncle." Carrillo was after all the Castilian who, together with Juan of Aragón, had masterminded the match.

While allaying fears of an Aragonese takeover or any attempt to settle old scores, this document, the closest thing they had to a marriage contract, was not so much about Isabel's exercise of authority as about Fernando's gain of it. Her envoys had additionally extracted a last minute oath from him before leaving Zaragoza, that he would never make a *merced* in Castile without her assent. For all that, he could still envision himself as becoming, at Enrique's death, the actual ruler of Castile. He did not yet know Isabel.

Chapter 4
To the Crown: 1469–1474

¡Castilla, Castilla, Castilla, por la muy alta poderosa Princesa e Señora, nuestra Señora la Reyna Doña Isabel, y por el muy alto e muy poderoso Príncipe Rey e Señor, nuestro Señor el Rey Don Fernando como su legítimo marido!

—Acclamation, Segovia 1474[1]

Immediately after the wedding, Isabel and Fernando went to work, in concert. Together, on October 22, they held the first formal meeting of a council of state incorporating their chief advisors, then dispatched letters to elicit support from everywhere and everyone that mattered. A conciliatory embassy to Enrique reiterated their loyalty, informing him they had married on the advice of the kingdom's prelates and great lords, and asking that he receive them as his true children; the approach was one of correcting a family misunderstanding; Isabel was relying on her standing as designated heir. They also decided to send an envoy to Rome to obtain papal dispensation for their marriage; there is no record of when Isabel found out that none existed. And Palencia was dispatched with a request for one thousand lances to Juan of Aragón, who, ever hard pressed by the French and the Catalans and penniless, could send back only advice: Fernando should listen to his grandfather, the admiral, and especially to Carrillo.[2]

Carrillo and the Aragonese Peralta thrashed out the details of their formal relationship, while they themselves established a more personal one. They discovered immediate affinity in working together. Cousins, both of them born and bred Trastámara, while sharing that dynastic frame of reference, nevertheless also had temperaments that, while very different, were remarkably complementary. By then, Isabel had shown herself decisive, indeed resolute to the point of intransigence, and very serious, if with a gift for irony; she gave her trust sparingly but when she did, wholeheartedly. Fernando had demonstrated he was deft of mind, affable, and cocksure. Now his gallantry softened her edges, and won over his wife and the Castilians. Her earnestness reinforced an intensity latent in him. Both of them were quick to take a stand; and both had the gift of self-monitoring, curbing impetuosity, and especially they both exhibited the capacity to reassess whatever the other thought unreasonable. Above all, nothing in Isabel's remarkable life is more remarkable than the love and respect she and Fernando demonstrated mutually, immediately, and ever after.

From the first, they were passionately attracted to one another. While they were often apart in those early years, Fernando repeatedly braved danger in order to return to her, as Palencia puts it, "in visiting his most beloved wife obeying impulses of duty and desire."[3] And Fernando himself later wrote Isabel of looking forward to being with her and promising that "some day we will return to our first love."[4]

Their initial devotion, coupled with a mutual trust, mitigated the problems arising from their sharing power and overcame the divisive schemes to empower one or the other repeatedly hatched among their counselors. Fortunately, Fernando had become accustomed to making decisions of state together with a stong-willed woman, his mother. And Isabel, although very much in love and although always careful to employ the rhetoric of wifely subservience, stood by her punctilious sense of royal prerogative and asserted what she considered her rights as heir to Castile and now as queen of Sicily. She could anger him with her stubborness; yet when, as happened more than once, he became so exasperated with her and her counselors that he threatened to leave, she would disarm him by dissolving in tears. The images that have come down of the stoic queen and Machiavellian king are stick figures not drawn from life.[5]

In February of 1470, having heard nothing from Enrique since Isabel had informed him of their wedding plans, they wrote to him jointly. They presented their union as a fait accompli, recalled Isabel's right to succession as having been sworn to at Toros de Guisando, respectfully informed him that they could not be denied justice for—and here came a threat, or an appeal to his more responsible counselors—great turmoil would result, irreparably harming the realm, even most of Christendom. They asked that a conclave of great lords and high clergy adjudicate, and should it not reach a decision, a commission be appointed made up of the priors of the religious orders—the Franciscans, Dominicans, Hieronymites, and Cistercians. Enrique replied only that he would take it up with his council. By June, having heard nothing more, they wrote again, warning him against bad advisors and against putting "enemies of nature above dutiful and loving children" to such a point that they might have to seek violent means to resist such minions.[6]

They had, in fact, embarked on a war of words. Those letters, conveying their own sense of solidarity achieved, they caused to be circulated throughout Castile and abroad. Isabel courted public opinion to an extent not seen in Castile since the first Trastámara, Enrique II, had done so while fighting *his* half-brother, Pedro I, for the crown a century ago. They appealed to the nobles, the clergy, and the towns; and although, unlike that founder of the dynasty, Isabel sought to be recognized not as monarch but as heir apparent, the line was thin and the parallel plain.

Enrique's immediate response to the marriage was indirect but pointed: he formally granted to the count of Plasencia Isabel's mother's town of Aré- valo, with its million *maravedís* of annual revenue, while his powerful sup- porter, the count of Benavente, secured Valladolid. In September, Fernando set off with two hundred lances to regain that key city, but had to desist, for Enrique was riding to defend it with one thousand armed knights. By then the young couple retained only Medina del Campo, held for them by Gonzalo Chacón, and Avila, by Chacón's son, Juan. Both towns, fortunately, produced substantial rents.[7]

Still, it was a bleak winter. They retreated to safe but dismal Dueñas. Tempers grew frayed. Carrillo having told Fernando that he was a youngster needing to be directed, Fernando responded pointedly that he did not intend to be governed by anyone, for that was how many of Castile's kings had come to grief.[8] Relations between them were patched up, and thereafter it was more frequently Carrillo and Isabel who were at odds. The plan to seek a papal dis- pensation was dropped, for they well knew that there was truth in the saying that in Rome the victors are crowned and the vanquished excommunicated.[9] Nor did they want their adversaries to take up the issue of the legality of their marriage, especially under the circumstances.

For Isabel was with child, and their brightest hope lay in offering Castili- ans what Enrique had not, a male heir who would provide stability promising continuity. On October 2, in Dueñas, Isabel gave birth to a daughter. Her letter of announcement, recalling that of her own birth, spoke ambiguously of the arrival of an *infante*.[10] The child, as customary in her maternal line, was named Isabel, and, if her mother was initially disappointed in her sex, she yet cher- ished her greatly. And certainly that birth signified, to Isabel and everyone else, that more children could be expected. Still, the strain told on eighteen-year- old Fernando, the sex of his child disappointing, and the place confining and dreary. He refused to hear out his advisors, insisted on making all decisions on his own, and took to jousting furiously. Soon after the birth he fell ill, developing so high a fever that Isabel feared for his life, as did his physician, who attributed his illness to too many falls from horses. Whatever the cause, he rallied quickly; within days he informed his father that he had dressed and attended mass.[11]

A Cold Winter

That the child was female delighted the opposition. Now Medina del Campo went over to Enrique, and a conspiracy developed in Avila. Enrique sent throughout the kingdom a manifesto disinheriting Isabel and once again naming "Juana, his beloved daughter" as his heir. The proclamation declared Isabel a dissolute woman who, acting without the king's counsel and flouting Castile's laws, had lost her shame and coupled with Fernando, prince of Aragón, who was so closely related they could not wed without papal dispensation, which she had scorned. She had consorted with an enemy for the perdition of Castile; she was no wife, but a concubine. Juana, he declared, was to wed the duke of Berry and Guienne, heir to the crown of France. He signed that proclamation together with the queen, the felt need to present the child as their joint progeny outweighing her indiscretion in having had by then two sons known not to be Enrique's. On November 26, 1470, in a reversal of Toros de Guisando, with the queen and young Juana attending, Enrique repeated the substance of that manifesto in a solemn ceremony; and a papal bull (probably forged) was read aloud, releasing all those present from the oath to Isabel.[12] No one there was aware that the duke of Guienne had died three days earlier, in a tourney celebrating his engagement to Juana. His death, however, in leaving her a single, unaffianced woman, weakened her position in relation to that of Isabel.

Isabel waited until early spring. In March of 1471 she circulated a rejoinder, her prose riper than it would ever be again, fueled with moral indignation and a sense of righteousness that she would continue to express, but in more restrained fashion. She immediately established her own reaction as outrage and moral indignation against false accusation. "Without doubt, I can say with *Santa Susana* that I am greatly anguished, because I can not remain silent without offense or harm to myself, nor speak without offending and displeasing the king, my brother, and both [courses] are very grievous to me."[13] She and Alfonso—and here she reproached Enrique more strongly than she ever had before, and in language Alfonso had used—had been wrested from their mother's arms and brought to court. Once there, she claimed, "I remained in my palace in order to be rid of your immorality, taking care for my honor and fearing for my life . . . [persevering] through the grace of God, which was for me greater protection than I had in the King, and in the Queen." She once more recounted Enrique's failure to keep their pact at Guisando, by not divorcing his wife and in attempting to force her, Isabel, to marry against her will. She had kept her word. She had wed Fernando, prince of Aragón, with the advice and consent of the greatest and most rational of the kingdom's great nobles. The king accused her of marrying without papal dispensation; she had satisfied her own conscience and in time would be able to show the approval of the Catholic Church. Assuredly, Fernando would bring Castile prosperity—a thinly veiled reference to his masculinity while Enrique's own impotence was notorious. Moreover, Enrique had previously sworn to the queen's brazenness, so that his measures—disinheriting her and reinstating Juana as his heir—were clearly illegal.[14]

Her heated prose undoubtedly owed something to her circumstances. At year's end, in what was a breach with Carrillo, Isabel and Fernando had left Dueñas, to spend much of the next year, 1471, in Medina del Rioseco, the stronghold of Fernando's grandfather, Fadrique Enríquez, the admiral of Castile. Gruff, clannish, small of stature but great of heart, the admiral exhibited a deep love of family. And his family was extensive, embracing Mendozas and Manriques and most of the high nobility of Castile, for he had nine sisters, all of whom had married well. Equally strongly, he hated his enemies: it was said that Fadrique Enríquez would gladly lose an eye to ensure that Juan de Vivero would lose both of his. Revelatory of the admiral's great impatience, high sense of moral rectitude, and deep respect for tradition as he construed it, was a knuckle-rapping letter he wrote to Pacheco and his cohorts. Why, he inquired, do you want to set so bad an example for all nobles that we [Spanish] may lose our souls forever and our fame in the chronicles? And so that we will suffer worse destruction in our time than did Spain's Visigoths? And so that greed and upstarts may destroy the most honorable reputation that a Christian kingdom could ever have?[15] Clearly, Isabel and he were kindred spirits. The admiral, undoubtedly influential in the tenor of that letter of hers to Enrique, died within a few years, but not before receiving good indication of having been instrumental in assuring a bright future for his grandson and his grandson's wife.

Enrique, buying loyalty and time, continuing to court powerful allies by giving away much of what remained in royal domain, courted disaster. For not only had he increasingly less to give, but his prodigality was interpreted as weakness. At the same time, those concessions brought changes in lordship that continued to exacerbate urban factionalism and economic malaise. Lawlessness and local warfare flourished. Rival magnates battled over control of Seville and, in Extremadura, contended for the mastership of the military order of Alcántara. Factions in Salamanca fought one another even while united in opposition to the lord to whom Enrique had granted the town. In Avila where one faction supported Enrique, the other Isabel and Fernando, Valera reports the townswomen fighting in the streets *virilmente* beside the men. Pulgar lamented, "If there were more of Castile, there would be more wars."[16]

Slowly but ineluctably, the tide turned, toward Isabel, fueled by the prospect of the better times the young and vital couple appeared to represent. Basque mountaineers and seamen who felt threatened by Enrique's friendship with France and prohibition of trade with England came over, as did the port town of Bilbao. Other towns announced for her and Fernando, much as they had in 1465 for Alfonso, in protest against a dominating noble or against the imposition by Enrique of a royal overseer, a *corregidor,* over the municipal council. With those municipalities came their valuable militias, the *hermandades.* Very heartening was the declaration for Isabel by Sepúlveda, a gateway between Castile and Andalusia, and a recent *merced* of Enrique's to Pacheco; Sepúlveda rose against its new lord in mid-February of 1472. Pacheco's greed and power, coupled with his intrusiveness in local affairs, were also inclining powerful Andalusians to Isabel and Fernando, or to playing a double game. And Enrique's new *mercedes* did more than escalate rivalries and shift allegiances: Pedro Fajardo, lord of Murcia, seized the opportunity to declare against any king whomsoever.[17]

Enrique having allied with France, Isabel and Fernando, as monarchs of Sicily, made alliances with Burgundy and with England.[18] They thereby both abetted the France-encircling policy of Juan of Aragón and demonstrated that they had sovereign standing in their own right in international affairs. So matters stood when, in late February 1472, Fernando left for Aragón, responding to an appeal from his father for help in laying siege to rebellious Barcelona. Isabel had resolved differences with Carrillo and was established with her small daughter and her small but growing court in his archepiscopal palace at Alcalá de Hénares.

It would be the first of many separations. Fernando returned only in time for Christmas, having entreated leave of his father through, says Palencia, "employing the most efficient solicitude to return to his conjugal marriage bed."[19] That in the interim he may well have had sexual relations with other women was within the mores of the time. When Pulgar observed that, "although he loved the queen his wife greatly, he gave himself to other women," it was a statement of fact, one Pulgar made frequently of notable male contemporaries. Be that as it may, when Fernando left again the following May, Gómez Manrique, in a plaintive poem, told of how

In looking at the royal face of the Princess of Spain which is sad, beautiful, and honest,
we feel an almost pleasurable grief.
She flees the meadows like a turtledove.
She is undone by her desire. . . .
The music which used to be her greatest joy
is now her worry
Because the melody adds troubles to the troubled one.
The great sadness which sickened Diana
Saddens and worries all of us
Enough to say right now
The ladies-in-waiting and the lady herself
are as lonely as the empty city where no one dwells.[20]

Queen of Sicily

In Aragón that year of 1472, Fernando was hailed by its official chronicler, Fabricio Gauberto de Vagad, in terms recalling popular prophecies of a Spanish redeemer-king; he was The Prince awaited by the Spanish kingdoms.[21] Fernando had become a charismatic young paragon as well to many Castilians, who were caught up in a seemingly eternal shortage of food, law, order, and heroes. Isabel, then less known, was generally thought of as that gallant's wife and lady, much as Manrique then portrayed her. Yet Castilians did not lose sight of the fact that it was Isabel who was Castilian born. And she herself never forgot that, though lady and wife, hers was the claim to the crown of Castile, nor that, by the terms of her marriage, she was entitled to jurisdiction in her own right over some regions of Sicily.

Certainly Juan of Aragón had come to appreciate the qualities of his daughter-in-law, and to know her persistence at firsthand. Immediately after the wedding, she had requested that he turn over to her as promised the Cámara de la Reina in Sicily, a rich revenue-yielding area centered on Syracuse, and he had said he would, in a document of May 1470. He then went on to extol her "virtue and incredible constancy," maintained through wars, revolts, and misfortune, and to laud her resistance to contrary counsel and pressures. Hers, he told her, were liberality, integrity of customs, decorum, prudence, magnanimity, composure, and perfect beauty. No doubt he admired her; no doubt too he meant to keep his own administrator in that Sicilian region. For, when that July Juan de Cárdenas, Gutierre's son, en route to Sicily to complete the transfer, stopped in Aragón to receive from its king the necessary executive order, he had to first guarantee he would not take over as governor for Isabel; even so, once in Sicily he did just that. As a foreigner imposing a new stringency, however, he soon angered the Syracusans, and that provoked a battle of wills, conducted in more or less measured tones, between Juan and Isabel. Upon sending Cárdenas, Isabel had written to Juan sternly that she expected him to fulfill the contract without any change whatsoever— "*sin mudar una sola jota.*" In November 1470, she temporized to the extent of ratifying Syracuse's privileges, but insisted that Cárdenas remain in his post. In January of 1471, in what was becoming a battle of wills, Juan annulled his appointment. She would not have it, and, by June, she had obliged her father-in-law to revoke that order and to reinstate his prior agreement. The following year, in July of 1472, she wrote in courteous salutation that she kissed his hands, but regarding Sicily requested that from then on he do nothing without her knowledge and that he allow her to act as she would in what he gave her and to do what it seemed to her she should do, "for it is certain I will do nothing unless it is just."[22] The queen of Sicily was clearly confidant that, as was said of Spanish rulers, her heart was in the hands of the Lord. The king of Aragón, while unused to being bested, was assured he had a daughter-in-law of royal caliber.

As the balance of power within Castile shifted favorably, Isabel took care to assert her proprietary rights there as well. Devoted to Fernando, she was yet

mindful of her advisors' worries about his growing popularity, his own hereditary rights, and his giving every indication of equaling in strength a father who,
among his considerable achievements, was semi-legendary for his penchant for
making mischief in Castile. Thus when the town of Aranda, exhausted by
bloody factional warfare exacerbated by an official imposed by Queen Juana,
recalled that by hereditary right it belonged to the king of Aragón and declared
for the young couple, it was, pointedly, Isabel who sent a garrison to claim it
in her name alone.

Isabel, instinctively wise in the ways princes were evaluated and in the
usages of symbols of position and power, had understood from the outset the
value of courting the populace and impressing all who saw her. She was well
aware of the power and authority implicit in the display of regal splendor.
Thus, while she was at Alcalá, ambassadors from Burgundy came seeking an
alliance in the late spring of 1472, and again a year later. On one of those visits,
she was described as welcoming them in velvets, satins, and jewels. Then, when
holding audience surrounded by her ladies and courtiers, she was dressed yet
more elegantly and expensively, and around her neck gleamed the great ruby
necklace. She entertained the Burgundians equally sumptuously, with drinking
and dancing, though she herself never touched wine, and, as was customary
when Fernando was absent, she danced only with her ladies. As their visit wore
on her finery mounted, seemingly no matter the occasion. Thus, when she
arrived on horseback at a bullfight held in their honor, she wore a cape of
pleated satin, a crimson dress, its skirt stylishly hooped on the outside in cir-
clets of gold, a gold necklace, and on her head a great crown, "a closed imperial crown" encrusted with jewels. Her horse's harness was of gilded silver; the
Burgundians estimated its weight as over 120 marks. Even for envoys of
Europe's most splendid court, they were sufficiently impressed to conclude
that she was a great lady of highest rank.[23] Nor would her stay with the extravagant Carrillo have done anything to diminish her penchant for lavish display
when the occasion presented itself.

Carrillo had lived in Italy, from 1423 to 1439, and had returned to Castile
with a taste for intrigue and warfare, a proclivity to magnificence, and a thirst
for grandeur and fame. As was the style in Italian courts, including that of
the papacy, the archbishop became a patron of both arms and letters. He was
especially drawn to those aspects of Italian classicism and learning that reinforced his own stature and his view of the world, which was centered upon
Spain and the prospect of its Christian reconquest. To anyone living in the
archepiscopal palace those interests and attitudes were inescapable.

At Alcalá during Isabel's two-year stay was Gómez Manrique, for Carrillo,
like great princes, adorned his court with poets, who, however, tended to do
double duty; so Manrique, as Carrillo's *mayordomo*, captained the fifty knights
escorting the Burgundian envoys up to the archepiscopal palace and into its

great hall hung with cloth of gold and fine silks. The *mayordomo*-poet also exchanged verses with another resident, Pero Guillén de Segovia, who doubled as an accountant, and whom Carrillo had commissioned to chronicle his own valorous deeds in battling in behalf of Alfonso and Isabel. Guillén's encomium said little of Carrillo being an ecclesiastic but made many flattering comparisons of the archbishop to militant heroes of classical history.[24]

Manrique and Guillén shared an admiration for the versifying moralists of Isabel's father's court, whose advocacy of strong personal monarchy and the royal obligation to go against the Moors they transferred to Isabel and Fernando. Manrique, who had repeatedly voiced nostalgia for older aristocratic values lost under Enrique, now found them embodied in the young pair, who seemed to him sprung from chivalric romance. The company of those articulate, informed, and admiring courtiers could only have broadened Isabel's horizons as well as reinforced values she had already displayed. Nor were they alone in their admiration for her and her cause.

It was perhaps inevitable that Isabel would evoke comparison to another heroine projecting a clear national vision and single-minded purpose and held to be divinely inspired, one who battled mightily in just cause against great odds—Joan of Arc, the Maid of Orleans. Isabel possessed a chronicle of the warrior maiden, dedicated to her by an author whose identity is unknown. It spoke of Joan as directed by heaven, and it dwelled upon her chivalric ethic and rock-ribbed sense of morality. The Maid had redeemed and restored the crown, ran the dedication to Isabel, so it was not so incredulous that a powerful and excellent queen might recover these lost kingdoms, for the most difficult things are possible to God. In the greatness of Isabel's own will, it went on, was known to reside the desire not only to recover what was hers but to make large inroads into the lands of "the damned sect"—the Muslims—so that in her time all faith and law would be one.[25] It was a point of view also in keeping with that of an archbishop who saw himself as warlord and king-maker, or queen-maker, and who advocated regaining Muslim Granada and supported an inquisition. It was also one that Isabel, his young guest, would implement.

The Cardinal and the Bishop

After calling on Isabel, in June of 1472, the Burgundian envoys sought out Fernando in Tarragona, their mission to have the princes of Castile and Aragón and *reyes* of Sicily join the alliance of Charles the Bold, Edward IV of England, and Juan of Aragón against Louis XI of France.[26] The king and queen of Sicily figured importantly too in the policy of the new pope, Sixtus IV, who was sending legates throughout Europe to arouse enthusiasm and raise funds for a renewed crusade against the Turk. It was known that Isabel and Fernando were drawing closer to Genoa and Venice to counter Turkish advance; and that with Mehmed II threatening the Balkans, Sicily's position, wheat, and revenues were of great consequence. The papal envoy sent to Spain on that business was a native Valencian, the cardinal Rodrigo Borja (in Italian, Borgia), who arrived at that port on June 18 with two galleys and a retinue of bishops, all of them greedy, insists Palencia, and aware that Spaniards would spend freely for honors. Borja himself Palencia describes as insolent and given to pomp, luxury, "and other unbraked passions," and notes that he freely advertised his delegated faculties of papal investment and dispensation and his stock of papal bulls: "he held the nets to catch many fish."[27] Later, Borja would pursue much the same business on his own behalf, as Pope Alexander VI. Borja also brought the desired bull absolving Isabel and Fernando for marrying without papal dispensation; reassuringly, it referred to Isabel as "Princesa of Castile."[28] Palencia aside, Borja was both fisherman and prize catch.

Isabel, who had moved to Torrelaguna on report of plague in Alcalá, kept informed of Borja's talks with Fernando and Juan; she learned he and Fernando had met again in Valencia, in mid-September, and that joining them was Pedro González de Mendoza, then the bishop of Sigüenza. Indeed, Torrelaguna lay within that bishopric, indicating a reapproachment with the Mendozas. Pedro González, sent to greet the papal envoy by Enrique, nevertheless had his own agenda: the bishop wanted a cardinal's hat. Fernando wanted both his support and Borja's. Borja wanted both men in his debt, the promising young king of Sicily and prince of Aragón who aspired to the crown of Castile, and the bishop who was among Spain's most powerful nobles and who was distinguishing himself as also among its most perspicacious.

Borja's ceremonial entry into his native city was brilliant. It was eclipsed by Mendoza's. Pedro González de Mendoza rode in—on the afternoon of October 20, 1472, the eve of the feast of St. Ursula—on the customary episcopal mule but, commented an eyewitness, "with more entourage than common to kings," and with trumpets blaring and drums rolling.[29] Two imposing blacks beating kettle drums preceded him on horseback. Thirty knights flanked him, among whom were two of his brothers and various nephews; all were richly attired, chains of heavy gold gleaming about their necks. Behind them rode two hundred light cavalry and a veritable army of falconers and huntsmen, then came a stream of foot soldiers and servants, and a long mule train heaped with baggage. Fernando and Mendoza met, bargaining counters already in play. Fernando had from his father Juan a promise that Mendoza's brother, the second marqués de Santillana, might keep what had been a great chunk of Juan's Castilian inheritance, and Mendoza had written Fernando a few days beforehand that he would support Isabel as Enrique's successor.[30]

Five days after his arrival, Borja, who was not of a disposition to be outdone by a bishop, entertained Fernando, Mendoza and his clan, eight visiting bishops, and the notables of the city at an extravagant feast. The banquet hall was hung with damasks and silks. A huge centerpiece of sweet-smelling herbs spelled out *"Ave María, gratia plena"*—"Hail Mary, full of grace"—which Mendoza had taken as his motto. Each dignitary was brought a large gilded silver basin for washing hands. The courses were many and calculated to impress: there were peacocks with golden heads—cooked and then reconstituted, and with the Borja coat of arms hung about their necks. There were pies of fowl, veal, kid, and bacon, accompanied by sauces. Then came more peacocks, with perfumed water spouting from their mouths, and, finally, condiments and sweets were served.

Yet, impressive as it all was, the occasion belonged neither to Mendoza nor Borja, but, despite his relatively small retinue and extremely small resources, to Fernando. For word had arrived two days beforehand that the king of Aragón had at last entered Barcelona, in triumph, and Valencia had erupted in a week-long celebration, which centered on its prince. On departing the banquet, Borja's satiated guests could pass only with great difficulty through streets filled with jubilant crowds, singing and dancing, ecstatic when catching a glimpse of their prince. Such was the joy of the city fathers, who also anticipated increased Flemish trade as a result of Juan's recent treaty with Burgundy, that unsolicited they voted Fernando eighteen thousand *sueldos* and lent him another thirty thousand. By November, when Borja and Mendoza left together for Castile, a secret three-way bargain had been struck, of great consequence for Isabel.

Isabel had written immediately to congratulate her father-in-law, saying she was certain that taking Barcelona brought him great happiness, for the great honor and service he derived from it, and for "the revenge that you can have because of it on all those who did not want the prosperity and augment [of power] of Your Majesty; undoubtedly it is for them a defeat."[31] Here was an early but not isolated display of an assumption of hers that would receive substantial application, that vengeance was an expected and estimable motive. Her mother had taken revenge on Luna, who tried to regulate her relations with her husband. Juan of Castile too had a reputation for being vindictive. His son, her brother Alfonso, had viewed vengeance as a knightly quality, and, in the predominating medieval tradition, the God of the Old Testament was strongly disposed to wreak vengeance. Vengeance was considered by Isabel and many of her contemporaries to be another face of fairness and justice, of recovering one's own, of restoring balance to the world.

At the same time, Isabel indicated something of what was to be a preferred modus operandi. Immediately, she pushed her advantage in writing to the chastened council of Barcelona demanding that it turn over to her the Catalan places promised in her dowry; she had no way of knowing that at the moment those places were highly sensitive issues in dispute between Juan and the city. So on December 29, having been reunited with Fernando and undoubtedly apprised of that situation, she wrote again to those councilors, but now she graciously felicitated them for some matter or other. Then, having allowed time to smooth over her gaffe, on February 2, 1473 she again insisted on her dower rights.[32]

She was in Carrillo's Alcalá when Borja visited her at the end of February. He stayed three weeks and came away favorably impressed with her; but she had formed no high opinion of him, nor would she ever. Nor would she then agree, as Borja urged her to do, to put herself completely in the hands of the Mendozas and accept their hospitality in Guadalajara, even though he promised that if she and Fernando did so he would support them and arrange that they be given charge of young Juana. Not only was Carrillo dead set against Borja's proposal, but the deciding factor was that since the untrustworthy Pacheco currently had custody of Juana and so must be involved in the plan, it might very well be a trap. Still, word of papal warming toward herself and Fernando, as well as the overtures of the Mendozas, were welcome both in themselves and as reflecting the couple's increasing standing among Castilians.[33]

Fernando again left for Aragón in late April of 1473. Isabel agreed he must go when word came that Juan, immediately Barcelona was secured, had gone to retrieve Rosellón and Cerdaña, Aragonese provinces held by Louis XI as surety for a debt, and that, having taken Perpignan, was now under siege there by the French. Isabel wrote to her father-in-law on April 29 to say that Fernando was about to depart; she added that she felt such great anguish at the news of the new French invasion that, if affairs allowed, she would come with the prince to his aid, for the journey would be less onerous than the separation; still, she had great consolation and hope in the Lord and his blessed mother that Fernando's journey would go well and result in glorious victory.[34]

That invocation, an early and characteristic expression of her piety, was less a supplication than an expectation, that heaven was with them and abetting their armies. And so it was. The French, on hearing that Fernando was coming with a sizable force, decamped. As a result, he was welcomed handsomely in Barcelona, and in an anonymous poem was again identified as the object of a hallowed prophecy: he was the Bat, the hidden one now revealed as divinely called to universal monarchy.[35] Yet, from August through October, Fernando's mortality was all too apparent: for he came down with a fever and lay gravely ill. Then, barely recovered, he received a message from Isabel urging him to hurry back to Castile. Obtaining Juan's permission to go, he left his sister, Juana, as royal lieutenant in Barcelona in his stead. On December 1 he informed Isabel of political matters and his imminent departure, and in a handwritten note lamented that "for three years, I have not been with Your

Highness for seven months in a row."[36] In June he had had from her a highly confidential message, interpretable as "all the business of Castile is in the hand of its princes."[37] By the time he took to the road, the meaning of that message had become clear to everyone in Castile.

Reconciling

When Pedro González de Mendoza received from the pope his cardinal's hat in the previous spring of 1473, it was celebrated by a procession through the streets of Segovia and a mass in its cathedral, and that hat was carried by Andrés de Cabrera. Cabrera, who as Enrique's *mayordomo mayor* held the *alcázar* of Segovia and the royal treasury it housed, was also a leader of Segovia's *conversos*. He had been with Pacheco at the symbolic dethroning of Enrique at Avila, but had subsequently broken with him over his double-dealing. So it was that when the following year, Pacheco incited "a great uproar in the city and factions [clashed] in the streets," as a preliminary to his attempt on the *alcázar* and its treasure, it was Cabrera who, warned by Santillana, had closed the city to the inveterate troublemaker and calmed the populace. As a result, Pacheco had withdrawn to Madrid, where he planned to execute the same maneuver: to incite townspeople against Jews and *conversos,* then come to restore order and so take control of the town. From the trouble in Toledo in 1449, he or his cohorts had had a hand in provoking most major anti-*converso* groundswells. (An exception was Valladolid, where an adherent of Isabel's, employing the same tactics, had set in motion an anti-*converso* uprising resulting in a slaughter that she and Fernando condemned but could not stop.)[38]

Cabrera, who had also been influential in reconciling Isabel and Enrique after Alfonso's death, had recently married Isabel's longtime favorite lady-in-waiting, Beatriz de Bobadilla.[39] On June 15, Isabel signed an accord with Cabrera, promising to name him marqués of Moya, a town near Cuenca, his birthplace, in return for making Segovia hers and seeking reconciliation between herself and Enrique. Involved in those negotiations, too, was Beatriz de Bobadilla, who was also somehow on intimate terms—*muy de gracia,* as Palencia put it—with both Cardinal Mendoza and the powerful count of Benavente. Subsequently, the Cabreras discussed the question of the succession at length with Alfonso de Quintanilla, Isabel's *contador mayor,* and Quintanilla made thirty-six trips between Segovia and Alcalá to arrange matters between the king and his sister. Such was the context of Isabel's letter to Fernando of that June.[40]

Throughout 1473, amid unrelenting civil strife, towns and cities had continued to come over to Isabel. All the great nobles had come to favor that reconciliation with the exception of Pacheco and Alvaro de Stúñiga, the new duke of Arévalo. So matters stood when, on November 4, Isabel signed an agreement with Benavente: she would meet Enrique in Segovia to resolve their differences with the understanding that she would succeed him; she then notified Fernando to hurry home. He joined her in Aranda at Christmas time. Beatriz de Bobadilla and Carrillo came to fetch her the evening of December 27th. They rode through the night, and Isabel entered the *alcázar* of Segovia on December 28. For Pacheco had just arrived, but, still remained outside its walls, having been forbidden entry to the city by the Cabreras. Isabel had won the race to reach the king; Pacheco decamped. Enrique was terrified of Pacheco's anger, but now Pacheco was not there, and Enrique was being bolstered by Benavente, Cardinal Mendoza, and Beltrán de la Cueva.[41]

It was all very festive: Isabel and Enrique were delighted to see one another. They talked a good deal and attended a banquet the next day. Isabel danced and Enrique sang, as they used to do, and they rode through the city together so that people might see them reconciled. Enrique requested that Fernando come immediately; he arrived on New Year's Day and after dinner Enrique came to call. They had never met but got on well. On January 9, all three of them rode through the city together and then dined with the Cabreras.[42]

Cabrera had sworn that if Enrique did not fulfill the compact he made at Guisando he would immediately turn over to Isabel and Fernando the *alcázar*, the treasury, and the keys to the city gates. Now Benavente and Mendoza convinced Beatriz, who convinced her husband, to ask a surety of the young couple: custody of the *infanta* Isabel and of the fortress of Avila, and she did so. Isabel resisted; she did not want to give over her daughter as a hostage and she was indignant that her word would not suffice. Cabrera, trying to persuade her otherwise, held his temper with difficulty, but Carrillo, incensed at her jeopardizing everything, reminded her of the danger and sacrifice he himself had endured in her cause, and how much he had spent on men-at-arms. Fernando, inclined to meet the conditions, told her she was being obstinate.[43] By January 11 she had yielded, reluctantly, and all was seemingly agreed.

Then occurred one of Palencia's many fortuitous accidents. He had entered Segovia secretly—he was persona non grata to Enrique—to deliver a message to Fernando and Isabel from Fernando's uncle, Alfonso Enríquez, now admiral of Castile, urging them to be wary. Somehow, while preparing to sleep in a small bedroom, he heard just outside the voices of Benavente "and two other men" conspiring to seize Fernando, Isabel, and their child. Immediately he informed *los principes* and suggested, as he tells it, that Fernando leave; Isabel would be safe in Segovia since she was viewed as only half the problem. Palencia thought Benavente was in league with Mendoza. Other accounts say that the cardinal, when he became aware of the plot, warned Enrique that the kingdom so strongly believed the couple to be rightfully his legitimate successors that to seize them might endanger his own life.[44]

However that may be, Isabel too advised Fernando to go, but she insisted on staying. She had made the decision to face danger for high stakes, possibly trusting to her own influence on Enrique—while with him, anyway. So Fernando left, on January 16, on the pretext of going hunting, and immediately transferred their daughter from Aranda to Sepúlveda, secure under the admiral. Enrique, with no stomach for such business, indeed suffering from an intestinal ailment since the day of the Cabreras' banquet, left for Madrid. Isabel herself was running a small fever. She stayed and put herself and the city under heavy guard; she was in possession of Segovia. At bottom, it was a coup, and a victory for her strength of will and her ability to elicit loyalty. There would be many more.

The Princess in Segovia

Fernando returned soon after, says Palencia, for "he could not resist the desire to visit Isabel," then left again quickly, to stay in the village of Turégano, several hours' ride away. Isabel, for her part, resolved he come to take part in a tourney despite the risk and although it was held on a day prohibited by the church, Passion Sunday.[45] And with Segovia hers, Isabel increasingly relied on Mendoza, to Carrillo's mounting chagrin. Her affection for her longtime protector and her sense of indebtedness to him had been eroded by his intransigence, his lack of political vision, and his increasing involvement with other worlds. For the archbishop of Toledo, primate of Spain, had come under the influence of an alchemist, one Fernando de Alarcón, an unsavory adventurer, who, says Palencia, had travelled in Sicily, Rhodes, and Cyprus, had everywhere married, and who in Barcelona and Valencia "had corrupted nuns to incest and all sorts of obscenities." This unscrupulous necromancer had convinced Carrillo that he, Alarcón, could fly through the air and, most compelling, that he knew the secrets of the philosopher's stone and could produce for him mountains of gold. The archbishop, in thirsting to possess the greatest splendor and wealth in Castile, spent most of his huge rents—Palencia avers that "his natural largesse reached prodigality"—on Alarcón's attempts to manufacture for him yet more wealth. In seeking to make gold of iron, it was said, he made iron of gold. Pulgar, ever more circumspect, speaks rather of Carrillo's pleasure in knowing the properties of waters and herbs and other secrets of nature, and of his desire for gold for alms; he also says that Alarcón was a creature of Pacheco.[46]

Isabel, while at Alcalá, had encountered the alchemist and had—her chroniclers say—reluctantly, to please Carrillo, granted him five hundred Aragonese florins on the rents of Sicily and daily entrée to her on a par with members of her council. Was she intrigued by his rooms full of arcane equipment and his visions of far places, terrestrial and heavenly, and of mountainous riches? Years later, in 1492, she would respond cautiously but more positively to another visionary seeking to make a marvelous discovery. Yet she expressed herself on principle strongly opposed to superstition and magic, and from the outset Alarcón encountered a formidable and voluble opponent in her confessor, the blunt and forthright fray Alonso de Burgos. In Segovia, the halls rang with arguments between the friar and Alarcón, at one point they went at each other with staves. At length Isabel—Palencia says she was bored with him—threw Alarcón out of the palace. Even so, at bottom Carrillo's infatuation with magic and alchemy was less damning than that he looked backward, to ecclesiastical and baronial autonomy and to king-making and other moribund medieval practices. Mendoza, in contrast, faced forward, to a future as first minister atop the expanding bureaucracy of an emerging nation-state.

Carrillo left Segovia. He broke with Isabel and he convinced Enrique, who was considering calling the Cortes to recognize her, to remain loyal to Juana. Mendoza, becoming archbishop of Seville that May of 1474, within the month declared himself in suggesting to the duke of Alba and the admiral that they join him against the coalition of Stúñiga, Benavente, Pacheco, and quite possibly Carrillo. Again it was civil war, between factions adhering either to Enrique and Juana or to Isabel and Fernando. In June, Isabel actively enlisted military support, promising *mercedes*. When that month the French again invaded Rosellón, Fernando again left for Aragón. Yet there in September he demonstrated that he shared with Isabel a primary interest in Castile in refusing Juan's appeal for Castilian participation in an offensive against Castile's traditional ally, France. For Isabel now sought French support, sending an envoy to Louis XI suggesting that his newborn heir Charles and her daughter Isabel marry. Juan of Aragón, unfazed, offered to mediate within Castile.

So matters stood when, on October 4, Juan Pacheco died, of the same catch in the throat, it was said, that had borne off his brother, Girón. The news was slow to get out, for only servants were with him at the time; they immediately stole as much as they could, threw his body in a wine vat, and ran off. Neither Carrillo nor anyone else of note showed interest in attending the eventual funeral.

The realm (God pardon it), Gutierre de Cárdenas wrote Fernando in Barcelona, looked on the death of the master of Santiago as a happy miracle. Isabel, he related, showed a little sentiment, as was fitting in being rid of an enemy, hers and everyone's, although recently they had been becoming more friendly, as at first. The king had taken it harder than he had ever taken anything, saying he had lost a father, that Pacheco had been as a father to him since he was very young. And Cárdenas went on to intimate that great things were about to happen. All the world was pregnant he said, and pressing to give birth, and it would not wait nine months: "I believe that there will be very grand and new happenings in these realms in which I expect Your Lordship and the Lady Princess will be well served."[47]

However much grieved at Pacheco's death, Isabel immediately wrote Fernando proposing they get papal bulls vesting the now vacant mastership of Santiago in the crown, and that, meanwhile, she would show benevolence to those great lords who asked her support in seeking it but make them no promises. Enrique, less wise in view of the numerous disappointed aspirants thereby created, bestowed that mastership instantly on the late Juan Pacheco's son and heir, Diego, the new marqués de Villena, and so swelled adherence to Fernando and Isabel among the disappointed contenders.

"The king," recounted Palencia, "who before had suffered some intestinal attacks, began to weaken with his repeated excesses; he was incontinent in eating as in all else, only obeying his caprice and never the dictates of reason."[48] Enrique would not consult doctors, considering them inept and capricious. "When sick he cared only for purges." Ill since January, he increasingly vomited blood and suffered bloody stools. His health worsened in late November, and on December first he attempted to ride to a favorite hunting lodge outside Madrid but collapsed on the way and died there.

At the end, Enrique neither requested last rites nor made a will, and while debate continues as to whether or not he named Juana his successor at the last, no one says he named Isabel. Palencia states that when the physician who had been called in told him he had only a few hours to live, Enrique said, "I declare my daughter heiress of these kingdoms," even though a priest had arrived and tried to dissuade him. Was it proof she was indeed his, or a last stab at dignity and dynasty? We do not know. That he was fond of the child comes through letters he wrote to the Mendozas in 1470, solicitous for her health: they should attend to the princess's diet; she should not have fruit nor anything made from milk. At his deathbed were Cardinal Mendoza, Benavente, young Pacheco, and other council and household members.[49]

Enrique IV died in Madrid sometime during the night of December 11, 1474. He was forty-nine years of age and had reigned nineteen years and five months. As he requested, the cardinal had his body carried to the shrine of Mary at Guadalupe, where his mother was interred. He had a proper but miserably attended funeral service. As the news went out, one of Fernando's counselors wrote to Juan of Aragón of how remarkable it was that "the deaths of the Master and then the King, obstacles of that succession, had occurred in such a short space of time."[50]

La Reyna Doña Isabel

In Segovia, Isabel had received word of Enrique's death by the evening of December 12. She cried, dressed in mourning, began sending out letters to the realm, and called together her council.[51] Only Cabrera, Cárdenas, and a few others were in the city. They urged her to act without delay, that awaiting the *grandes* was like bestowing on them what was owed only to God and nature; Isabel, her political theory obviously having altered greatly, agreed. The next day, dressed in mourning, she went on horseback to the church of San Miguel, where Enrique's standards and those of the city had been lowered and draped in black. There she attended the customary mass and rites for the dead and then returned to the palace. Shortly after, to the roll of kettledrums and to resounding trumpets and clarinets, she reappeared, in the *plaza mayor,* now richly, dazzlingly dressed, jewelry of gold and precious stones "accentuating her singular beauty."[52] And there, in the portico of the church of San Miguel, on a hastily constructed platform covered with brocade, she was raised to the throne as queen of Castile and León.

A notary—one of those scribes indispensable to putting an official seal on events—set down the details of the ceremony. He recorded that present were the papal legate, some nobles and knights, a number of Franciscans and Dominicans, the notables of Segovia, and a crowd of townspeople. The cry went up: "The king is dead!" A *letrado* of Isabel's council on behalf, as he announced, of all her subjects informed her that by law the succession and inheritance and right to reign were hers; that she had been recognized by the previous ruler in September of 1468 and been sworn to by the realm. Placing her right hand on the Bible, she then swore by God and the sign of the cross and the words of the holy evangel that she would obey the commandments of the Holy Church. She would honor its prelates and ministers, defend the churches, look to the common good of the realm and to the good of its royal crown, and do her utmost to aggrandize those kingdoms and maintain her subjects in justice, as best given her to understand her duty; and, in accord with the custom of her glorious progenitors, she would respect and guard the privileges and liberties and exemptions of the *hidalgos*—the nobles, and the municipalities.[53]

The clergy, the nobles, the knights, and her councilors kneeled before her and, speaking both for themselves and in the name of Castile's kingdoms, they took an oath to her as their queen and the proprietary *señora natural* of the kingdoms and to "the king don Fernando, her legitimate husband." Segovia's notables repeated the oath, then handed their staffs of office to her; she gave them to Cabrera, who returned them to the officials. Cabrera then turned over to her the keys of the *alcázar* and the royal treasury and she returned them into his keeping as her *alcaide.* He in turn swore homage to her, placing his hands between those of Gonzalo Chácon. Her daughter, Princess Isabel, now four, was lifted up, and heralds made the awaited proclamation "Castile for . . . our Lady and Queen, Isabel, and for . . . our Lord and King, Fernando, as her legitimate husband!"[54] Castile's monarchs were customarily considered as installed by acclamation rather than by the act of being crowned. Even so, that defining moment was recorded for her as proclamation, not acclamation, and it can be interpreted as a form of another Spanish tradition, the royal one of self-coronation. Her royal standard was raised and music swelled. Isabel descended, entered the church of San Miguel, prayed before its main altar, and then, taking up a royal banner hanging on a lance and placing it in the hands of a priest, she thus offered it to God.[55]

She emerged from the church. A procession formed. Isabel on horseback was surrounded by nobles on foot, some carrying the canopy of state sheltering her and others holding the train of her gown. Segovia's dignitaries (dressed as fittingly as possible on such short notice) marched behind, and a throng followed after. Ahead of everyone rode a single horseman, Gutierre de Cárdenas, in his right hand a naked sword, held by the point, pummel up "as in Spanish usage," so all could see even at a distance that the bearer of royal authority who could punish the guilty was approaching. "And that night the Queen slept in her palace."[56]

Palencia writes of murmuring at the insolence of a woman appropriating attributes rightfully belonging to her husband, but that it ceased "before the adulation of those who proclaimed that the inheritance of the kingdoms in no way belonged to don Fernando, but legally exclusively to the Queen." Here, adds Palencia, was the origin of more of those contests so enjoyed by the *grandes*.[57]

*   *   *

Three things, ran a Castilian saying, maintain the kingdom: the king, the law, and the sword.[58] In a later guide to princes dedicated to Isabel, a favorite poet and courtier of hers, fray Iñigo de Mendoza, in declaring that she had come by grace of God to do justice, fight tyranny, and kill the corrupt few in order to save the kingdom as a whole, made extended use of the sword as metaphor for both justice and armed might. There was as well Isabel's chivalric bent, the memory of the sword-bearing Joan of Arc, and the popularity of sword-filled Arthurian romance. Her brother, Alfonso, had ordered coins, *alfonsíes,* minted depicting him on horseback wearing a crown, and with a naked sword in his hand. And there had been prophecies at her father's birth envisioning Juan of Castile as a redeemer-king who came bearing a sword.

Still, in Castile traditionally the monarch's symbol was a scepter bearing a gold orb topped by a golden cross and held in the left hand; Enrique IV had referred to the scepter as the symbol of justice at the cortes of Ocaña in 1469, and so had Gómez Manrique in his *Regimen for Princes*. The tomb effigy of Juan II, commissioned by Isabel, holds a scepter. What Isabel chose to do at her accession, then, was to revive an earlier and more militant usage. In 1484, a traveler, seeing Isabel and Fernando riding in the annual Christmas Eve procession in Seville in remembrance of its reconquest, was surprised to see a small, age-blackened sword being carried pummel up before them. When he asked the reason, he was told that it symbolized justice.[59] Yet the symbolism went deeper, for carried that way it looked like a cross. Plainly it alluded to a militant justice and to a militant faith, for that was the hallowed sword of Fernando III, San Fernando, celebrated as the greatest hero of the holy war that was Spain's reconquest. That sword had also been carried, as a talisman and with symbolic intent, by a namesake of his, Fernando de Antequera, both while on campaign against the Moors and in his own ceremonial entry into Seville. Isabel's appropriation of all that symbolism spoke to hallowed tradition, yet it presciently looked forward as well.

Over a century later, the imagery of the sword would be unsheathed on behalf of another queen, Elizabeth I of England, in a yet more explicit reference to the old prophecy that in the last days the greatest of all rulers, an emperor, was to take up "a responsibility for supporting the entry of Christ into the world with the sword of justice," and that through that messianic agent justice would flow from God to the world.[60] Elizabeth was also held to personify a prophecy found in Virgil's fourth *Eclogue*, that a golden age was about to return, heralded by a virgin, who had been conflated by Dante with Astraea, Ovid's personification of justice. As adapted into Christian prophecy, the return of Justice signified the second coming of Christ, the Messiah. There were those among Isabel's people who knew their Virgil, Ovid, and Dante, and some years later Isabel would, well before Elizabeth but like her, be hailed as Astraea, the personification of justice returning to the earth.

That was later. The sword borne aloft in Segovia represented intent and commitment rather than achievement: it spoke of Castile's new queen as promising to restore and uphold the great, potent, and awe-full medieval principle of Justice. That particular sword announced too that this queen was the heir proper of those Castilian hero-kings dedicated to reconquest. Yet even so, it also spoke of this woman as having a powerful male consort, yet another Fernando, at her side. Still, it was surely more than coincidence that among her large and splendid tapestries would be one of Fame showing a queen holding a sword.

*   *   *

Highly significant too, and undoubtedly indicative of the reception of the new queen in towns friendly to her, is a surviving account of how the populace of

Avila celebrated her accession. On Saturday, December 17, municipal officials and her *corregidor,* Juan Chacón, gathered in the choir of the church of San Juan at the toll of its bell as was customary, to hear read a letter from Isabel requesting their oath. They promptly proposed to accede to her request; it took much longer to agree on how to finance the usual ceremonies. That problem resolved, the following day they attended a requiem mass for Enrique, while "all the Jewish and Muslim men and women made their laments amid the crowd" of *los enjergados*—mourners, dressed in serge—gathered outside the church.[61] The notables emerged and raised the cry, given at Segovia and here undoubtedly orchestrated by Juan Chacón, for Castile, the queen, and the king her husband. Thereupon a procession formed, while canons sang the Te Deum and resident Muslims performed *momos* and sword dances. Then it advanced, with trumpets and timbrels resounding and a standard-bearer on horseback holding aloft the royal banner. Among the townspeople falling in were Jews carrying two Torahs. Traversing the town, wending through the fish market, it came to a halt at the gate of the *alcázar,* where everyone watched while Chacón and Avila's worthies affixed Isabel's banner to the top of the tower. Then from the tower the acclamation came again, and the populace below took it up. On January 9, the town council convened and formally took the oath to Isabel and Fernando.

When the same letter from Isabel arrived in Zamora, the response was more complicated, for the city was split between old partisans of Enrique and those of Enrique Enríquez, the count of Alba de Liste, who was Fernando's uncle. The count, along with his brother, the admiral, disapproved of Isabel's solo accession; their position was that Juana was indeed Enrique's daughter but that women could not succeed to the throne, so that, since Fernando descended in male line from Juan I of Castile, the crown most properly belonged to him. Although no one mentioned it, it was an argument making the succession in Castile of Juan of Aragón even more legitimate. Here then is one explanation of Isabel's decision to take the crown quickly and alone. Yet also valid is the rationale she later gave to Fernando, that since they had but one child, who was female, her own accession could set precedent highly important to their daughter. In view of what was to come, she made an astute decision.

Arriving in Segovia a few days after the ceremonies were the cardinal and his brothers, and the admiral, the constable, Beltrán, Carrillo, and now Benavente, to kiss their queen's hand and take the oath of allegiance. Many other nobles and knights came on the same errand, and yet others sent deputies. Isabel heard nothing, however, from Stúñiga or Diego de Pacheco or young Rodrigo Girón. Nor did Pacheco's Madrid or Stúñiga's Plasencia recognize her; but neither was there any mention of Juana.

* * *

So began the reign of Isabel I of Castile. Once queen, what she did and why she did it have mystified generations of subsequent commentators. Her contemporaries though understood it all quite well. That is because they shared with her similar expectations of Castile's ruler and found them embedded in common cultural memory. The best place to begin the story of her reign, accordingly, is with some relevant cultural assumptions, in themselves made up of the history, legend, and myth, that formed the world as she knew it and went far to shape her outlook and her policies.

Chapter 5
A Royal Heritage: Perception and Reality

I'm the king . . . when I pray God answers.
—Henry VIII in Maxwell Anderson, Anne of the Thousand Days

The king's heart is in the hand of the Lord.
—Prov. 21:1, glossed in Las Siete Partidas, pt. 2, tít. 2, ley 3

Isabel would keep her word. She would keep the pledge given in her oath of accession. She would do her best to be an exemplary ruler, as she understood it, "in emulation of my glorious progenitors," kings of Castile. She would attend, as she promised, to the common good of the realm and to the good of its royal crown, and do her utmost to aggrandize those kingdoms and maintain her subjects in justice. She would, up to a point, guard the privileges and liberties and exemptions of the nobles and the municipalities. And to her mind, all of those obligations interlocked with her pledge to obey the commandments of Holy Church, not necessarily as they were relayed to her by popes and bishops, but as her predecessors had been expected to do.

Assuredly, the key to the enigma that has been Isabel for five centuries lies in her taking to heart from the outset those royal traditions that defined her realm and instructed her in how to rule it. As has been said, the stories people believe about what happened in the past will often govern the way they lead their lives. Many of those stories, much of the history, that Isabel knew had been shaped in an interplay among royal ideology, religious views, and principles and popular sentiment and beliefs. The result had become widely accepted as Spain's story; and that nation-making history did not necessarily conform to reality. It was, moreover, a history with prophetic overtones, a history not confined to the past, a history driving the present and going somewhere splendid, outward and upward; it included history as prophecy, as an unfolding revelation of God's power and providence. And within it, Spain and its queen had an important assignment.

Figure 3. Regalia: Isabel's crown, scepter, and sword. Royal Chapel, Granada.

Walls and Gates Revisited

As a child living in Madrigal and Arévalo, Isabel would not have escaped celebration of the Spanish past. The walls of Madrigal and Arévalo's castle spoke
proudly of a militant society. So did the device on Arévalo's official seal showing a knight riding out of one of Arévalo's gates. Walls, castle, and seal conveyed communal pride in town origins during the centuries of Christian
reconquest, and in knights who sallied forth to confront and drive back the
Muslim enemy. So Arévalo represented itself as an outpost within a society
geared for war. Moreover, it is often said that Isabel's childhood was spent in
isolated places. Both assertions are far from the whole story.

Isabel's Arévalo and Madrigal de los Altos Torres—Madrigal of the High
Towers—were among the many towns dotting the rich farmlands of the central *meseta* that appeared at a distance closed in on themselves by turreted
walls, yet that on coming closer revealed wide gates. Occasionally, inhabitants
would see local knights ride out to do battle through those gates. They might
even see kings and queens with their armed retinues come and go, for Madrigal and Arévalo were royal towns and sometime residences of the itinerant
court. Yet—and most frequent but least mentioned—those gates opened daily
to a flow of cattle, sheep, and produce, and to a wide variety of people.

The fortified places Isabel first lived in lay athwart well-traveled trade
routes, close to Medina del Campo, the site of one of Europe's greatest semi-
annual fairs, which she much enjoyed attending. Those routes connected *meseta* towns to others throughout Castile and to the wider world: to the west,

with Portugal; to the north through the mercantile center of Burgos to the Cantabrian coast; to the east with the Mediterranean world through the ports of Aragonese-held Valencia and Murcian Cartagena; and to the south through Seville and its subsidiary Andalusian ports and so with Mediterranean and Atlantic ports, and with Africa. Everywhere in this network cultural, technological, and commercial exchange were facts of life. A royal household would reflect the resulting exchange of goods and conception of the wider world.[1]

Yet, despite the fact that town gates opened on that wider world and high walls encircled culturally and religiously diverse inhabitants, in those places of Isabel's childhood communal pride and sense of identity were plainly bound up exclusively with an essentially militant tradition of Spanish cultural and religious distinction. No matter that for centuries Isabel's royal predecessors had ruled over a mix of peoples and faiths, or implemented such far-flung exchange as she herself was to do in sending Pedro Mártir to Egypt.[2] For the accepted ideology—shared by every strata of the dominant Christian society including townspeople, kings, and a particular queen—of who Castilians were focused solely on a population of brave warriors and divinely guided rulers.[3] Yet if their history as they envisioned it was not exactly true to life, it was truly manufactured in Spain. The evolution of that sense of history—the history of that history—that surrounded Isabel in her formative years is a crucial element in her view of her job description and the responsibilities she would assume on taking the crown.

Spain Imagined and Remembered

Regarding Spain's past, what can be ascertained is this. A cavalcade of Mediterranean peoples, as well as Celts from the north, settled in certain areas of the Iberian peninsula, followed later by Roman legions who superimposed Roman law and administration. Eventually, Rome introduced Christianity. Yet as the Roman Empire disintegrated in the West, Visigoths arrived and imposed their authority. Their elected kings governed from Toledo, accepted Roman Catholicism, and relied heavily on the administrative system already in place at the local level, that of the ecclesiastical hierarchy; it proved a mutually supportive arrangement. Goth kings also turned to leading clergy for advice. Most influential among them, during his lifetime and thereafter, was Isidore, bishop of Seville (d. 636), who wrote down his thoughts on Spain's exceptional history and on the divine calling of kings. The Visigoths soon disappeared, but Isidore's vision of Spain survived for a thousand years, as cultural memory, as the bedrock of Spain's history. His history of the Goths transformed the Roman province of Hispania into a special place, an eternal heaven-blessed nation, a veritable earthly paradise housing an exceptional people: "Of all lands from the West to India, you are the most beautiful, O Spain, sacred and ever-blessed mother of princes and peoples . . . glory and ornament of the earth, home of the famed and gloriously fecund Goths."⁴ By Isabel's time all of Spanish history had become the ongoing story of Isidore's eternal and blessed Spain and its Goths, although having been briefly and lamentably interrupted.

For in 711 Arabs and Berbers had crossed the Strait of Gibraltar from Africa to Spain, and—the account by Pedro Mártir to the sultan of fierce resistance notwithstanding—thereafter "the conquest of Spain appears to have been a gradual walk-through . . . Muslim columns followed the Roman roads, obtaining the surrenders of key towns, and in many cases leaving Jewish garrisons behind."⁵ Remnants of the Visigothic aristocracy retreated into the mountains of Asturias in Cantabria in the far north, and, whatever the truth of Pelayo's stand, from there Christian chieftains did slowly push southward. Over centuries, they led raids for booty into Muslim-held territory and they encouraged settlement along frontiers, first in the no-man's-land north of the Duero River, then across it, founding fortified towns such as Madrigal and Arévalo. That moving frontier created Christian kingdoms from Asturias to León, to Castile, and then, under its kings, Castile moved into La Mancha, Extremadura, and Andalusia.⁶ From the eighth century on, moreover, royal decrees and royal chronicles presented this movement as the regaining of a lost Spain, and as a religious mission. With the advent of European-wide crusades in the eleventh century, crusading within Spain was urged by clergy and kings as divinely impelled; in Spain the project of holy war unified kings, nobles, clergy, and commoners in a defining mission promising reward on earth and in heaven.⁷

Especially did kings, their courts, and clergy play on and promote a communal purpose as revealed in history, a history that encompassed the future. So the *Prophetic Chronicle* written at the court of Alfonso III of Asturias-León looked ahead, to assume that Alfonso, as heir to Pelayo, was to take the lead in recovering the realm of the Goths from the Moors. And, in envisioning that historical future, its anonymous author looked back; he relied on the authority of prophecies found in the Old Testament and in the Book of Revelation (or the Apocalypse) of John the Evangelist. In particular, the chronicler drew on predictions in the Books of Daniel and Ezekiel to identify Muslim-held Iberia, al-Andalus, with the biblical land of Gog and Magog, and Gog and Magog with giants who were to conquer the world as the Last Judgement neared, but who would in turn be defeated by a messianic warrior-king who would usher in a final universal age of peace and plenty. Now the reign of Gog and Magog was ending; in Spain, the chronicler stated, Alfonso III would soon free the subjugated lands and restore the Gothic kingdom.⁸ It was a prediction taken up in turn by publicists for subsequent kings, a mission clamped on the Spanish, and a conception of history centered on Spain. It was a vision encompassing the past, the present, and the prophetic future, a vision identifying Spanish Christians with biblical Israel as God's elect, endowing Spain with a historical task of universal importance, and assigning to Spanish kings a providential and even messianic role.

From its founding, the kingdom of Castile and its society originated, evolved, organized, and defined itself within that militantly Christian ideational context, and as dedicated in the first instance to peninsular reconquest. Nobles were defined by owning horses and armor; Castilian peasants were relatively free to take advantage of moving frontiers and expected to defend themselves along them; and kings enjoyed combined civil, military, and religious authority. Kings were chief justices, civil administrators, and above all war leaders of the armed host. They were God's champions against an enemy whom medieval Spanish Christians tended to identify with the forces of Antichrist.[9]

A band of Christians in ninth-century Muslim Córdoba had identified Antichrist with Muhammad; one such *mozárabe*—a Christian living in Muslim territory—had taken that notion north, inserting it within the *Prophetic Chronicle* he produced at Alfonso III's court; another identified the beast of ten horns, described in both Daniel and the Apocalypse, with Antichrist, Satan, and their Muslim cohorts. Lucifer, the fallen angel become the devil, was a central figure in the medieval European imagination. The devil waged a ceaseless contest for human souls with God; the world was their battleground. An early church council in Toledo described him as "a large, black, monstrous apparition with horns on his head, cloven hooves, ass's ears, claws, fiery eyes, gnashing teeth, a huge phallus and a sulphurous smell."[10] All sinners aided him, belonged to him. He too, like Christ, had a mystical body; sinners were its limbs and heretics were literally his members. He was also Antichrist, or Antichrist was his lieutenant on Earth, his son by the Jewish whore of Babylon. The original sin of Adam and Eve had put humanity in the devil's power; Christ had come to free those who would follow him. People had to choose, and the Devil was wily; they had to beware, always. Demons were everywhere. Antichrist, the deceiver, might soon reveal himself in the guise of the messianic king of the Last Days, or as the Messiah himself. God the Father was envisioned as remote—old and bearded, stern, moody, and terrible in his wrath. Such was the ideational world of medieval Spain.

Accordingly, the war defining Spanish society was a holy war of universal importance. Against infidel and demons Isabel's predecessors had raised the banner of Santiago Matamoros, Saint James the Moorslayer. It was said that Santiago, the patron saint of Spain, had appeared miraculously during more than one battle to ensure Christian victory. And, as Castilians advanced into

Andalusia, they unfurled beside Santiago's standard that of Holy Mary, Protectress of the Armies.

Seldom was it remembered that Christian advance was largely a conquest of space, that war, waged only sporadically against Muslims, had allowed communities to form, towns to grow, and a complex relationship between Christians and Muslims to evolve. That Christians sometimes fought Christians as well as Moors or made alliances across religious lines is revealed in epic poetry and those popular ballads known as *romances*. The actions and values of Rodrigo de Vivar, El Cid, are at once entrancing to latter-day readers and jarring to their preconceptions, for in the *Poema del Cid* he does not behave as we expect of an epic hero. Although a Christian considering himself a loyal vassal of the king of Castile, El Cid hires out as military chief to Muslim lords. He takes Valencia as his own domain, and, says the poet, he leads his men in exploits both highly valorous and part of a day's work "to obtain one's bread," "*ganarse el pan.*" Wealth, as Rodrigo says to his wife, Jimena, "marvelous and grand wealth, is what comes to us" through warfare; and it is to be spent on dowering their daughters, that is, on aggrandizing family and enhancing lineage. (They had no sons.) Like El Cid, later nobles maintained private armies and expected subsidy for them from the king, yet on occasion allied with Muslims and saw no disloyalty in accruing as much independent power of their own as possible. For Isabel herself, however troublesome her nobles, El Cid nonetheless exemplified heroism; he belonged to Spain's pantheon. Isabel had encountered his statue set among those of kings in the great hall at Segovia. She would honor the town of Vivar as his birthplace and, in referring to Valencia, which he had governed, take obvious pleasure in speaking of it as "Valencia del Cid." And, like his daughters, she too came into an inheritance in the absence of a male heir. El Cid was for her a romantic hero, a chivalric figure of strong character. Those qualities endeared him to her, but, as the history she knew related, a ruler of Spain had specific obligations to fulfill. And history as she knew came down to her principally as filtered through earlier court chronicles that in turn built on their predecessors.

Castilians of Isabel's day tended not to recall that El Cid's king, Alfonso VI, who gained Toledo in 1085, did so not by waging war but through peaceful transfer from his erstwhile Muslim ally, al-Qadir, who found Christian control preferable to that by internal enemies. Nor, as one scholar observes, did Alfonso make major changes: "The new *pobladores* came to bathe in the old Muslim public baths, and to bake their bread in the old ovens."[11] Still, it was no part of the accepted historical canon that under Christian domination Toledo remained a city culturally and religiously mixed. It was from Toledo that Isabel's birthplace, Madrigal, was established permanently, on a site repeatedly occupied and destroyed alternately by Muslims and Christians. Its eleventh-century founders received a royal charter, built a church dedicated to Holy Mary on the foundations of an old Muslim fortress, and organized a governing council. On this new frontier between the Duero and Tajo Rivers, Madrigal and other places were relatively self-governing and had fewer priests, monks, and lords than to the north. Even so, in common with northern places, the more powerful inhabitants soon came to dominate the towns and their councils. And settling before long in Madrigal, as in Arévalo, were Muslims and Jews. Nonetheless and as we have seen, those towns remembered their origins as wholly military, carved out in the armed combat attendant upon regaining Spain.

Although remembered otherwise, some Christians lived alongside Muslims and Jews, who, while themselves not always living in segregated enclaves, were legally considered members of largely self-governing religiously defined communities retaining their own laws and customs, and were considered directly subject to royal authority. Perception of social arrangements diverged appreciably from the complex reality. So Murcia at Isabel's birth and other places had both Muslim slaves and Muslim communities.[12] El Cid, who fought both for and against Muslims, in the poem both borrows money from Jews and prides himself on cheating them. German travelers in Isabel's youth also reported that large stretches of the *meseta* were inhabited by *infieles,* infidels— that is, people seeming to them not Christianized.[13] From the outset, a gap yawned between the perception of Castile as a militantly advancing Christian frontier and the reality of Castile as a land where at least three cultures lived. That gap, one of several between what was and what was said to be, was a paradox bequeathed to Isabel, who would demonstrate little tolerance for paradox, unless it proved extremely useful.

Such paradox had typified her predecessors, among them Fernando III. That revered conqueror had led Spanish armies into Andalusia, conquered Muslim Seville in 1248, reputedly hanged many people, and boiled many in cauldrons for heresy. Yet, the loss and disruption caused by an attempt to expel so large and productive a population soon caused a tactical change. So inscribed on his sumptuous tomb in Seville's cathedral are eulogies of him in Hebrew, Arabic, Latin, and Castilian, or Spanish. Clearly, it was extremely politic to indicate such inclusivity, to have it declared that Castile's king stood as the political head to each community. That inscription did bridge those several cultures, but its purpose was to cast Fernando III as both Christian conqueror and highest authority over each one of them. It celebrated the extent of his conquests: as Fernando is said on his deathbed to have told his son, Alfonso, "I leave you the whole realm from the sea hither that the Moors won from Rodrigo, king of Spain."[14] And histories written during Fernando's reign concentrated on his role in Christian advance.

Visions of Monarchy

Fernando III's son, Alfonso X, was faced with imposing his authority over vast stretches of land, and with governing a greatly expanded and heterogenous populace, although in 1265, following a rebellion, many of Andalusia's Muslims emigrated; still, Alfonso too failed in an attempt to expel them en masse.[15] Alfonso was also bent on establishing for himself a preeminent position among Spain's kings. Some consequent activities of his would have lasting impact, particularly on how Castilian monarchy was viewed and conducted— not necessarily the same thing.

While Alfonso X vowed to drive the Muslims into the sea and to pursue them into North Africa, he is now best remembered otherwise, as Alfonso *el Sabio,* the Learned, who, impelled by love of knowledge, surrounded himself with Muslim and Jewish scholars and translators to bring Western and Eastern learning into a synthesis, one particularly Spanish and still potent in Isabel's day. Still, there were more pragmatic reasons for his intellectual pursuits. Alfonso, perched on a frontier of many sorts—geographical, cultural, and spiritual—felt the tension between the attraction of the complex civilization he found in al-Andalus and its threat to Christians. He sought, as a nephew of his put it, to know the great errors of Islam and Judaism. He also recognized how badly educated were the Castilian clergy and how wretched their Latin. Moreover, his delving into Islamic science, history, morality, legend, and lore, and into Arabic astronomy and astrology, culling them all for moral wisdom and the secrets of the universe, was thought of as an accepted way to fathom and so carry out the divine plan. Consequently, his learning responded to a happy combination of religious imperative, intellectual interest, and royal empowerment. It also reflected an awareness of the international prestige accreting to a learned monarch and a cultured court and clergy.

Alfonso founded the University of Salamanca for the same purposes, but also to train men in canon and civil law that, derived from Roman imperial codes, stated kingly authority was near absolute; Salamanca was to produce *letrados* who would staff and strengthen royal government. Similarly inspired, he set jurists to countering the jumble of Castilian law and custom so supportive of local autonomy by drawing up a uniform royal law code, the *Fuero Real,* and he personally oversaw the compiling of an encyclopedic treatise on law and government, the *Siete Partidas,* or *Seven Divisions.* The *Partidas,* owing much to the jurisprudence of imperial Rome and to concepts of social order associated with Roman Catholicism as well, presented an ideal of community as normal social reality. That treatise supposed a well-ordered earthly kingdom, at its head the near-absolute king who was a paragon of virtue, devoted to justice. "Kings," the *Partidas* stated, "are vicars of God, each put in his kingdom over its people to maintain them in justice and in truth in temporal matters, just as an emperor in his empire." According to the *Partidas,* the king was to guide the people as the head does the body; the king should be elegant; the king is the soul of the people. He had been designated by God as his alter ego on earth, his viceroy, his mirror image. The king's heart was in the hand of the Lord.[16] The king's conscience, synonymous with his heart, was expected to perceive the will of God. Isabel possessed at least six copies of the *Partidas,* one having a silver cover etched with a Y for Isabel and an F for Fernando.[17] She would heartily endorse those principles, extend them to include herself, and do everything in her power to establish them as commonplace and the *Partidas* as law of the land.

Castile's clergy could be counted on to disseminate the royal views on the intimate relationship between ruler and God. Traditionally, the church in Spain was strongly national, and many of the clergy served as royal administrators. The clergy also sanctified and promoted as religious imperative the regaining of Spain from the Moors and reinforced the fusing of religious faith and national identity. Conversely, kings often behaved much like high priests. Alfonso X, particularly devoted to Holy Mary, carried her standard into battle, endowed her cult, and served as her troubadour. In his *Cantigas de Santa María—Songs of Holy Mary,* over four hundred of them—he praised the Virgin Mary and celebrated her miracles, which in the *Cantigas* are often performed in favor of kings. Isabel owned a sumptuously illuminated manuscript of the *Cantigas;* she esteemed and supported the cult of Mary, and she would show a particular devotion to Mary of the Armies.

Yet it was still another of *el Sabio*'s activities that surely most influenced Isabel's sense of Spain and her own identity as a Spanish ruler. Alfonso either wrote or more likely sponsored two histories: one of the entire world, the other of Spain, both presenting the land and people as had Isidore of Seville, but with embellishments. In Isabel's library were six manuscript copies of Alfonso's *General estoria,* or *General History,* and seven of his *Primera crónica general,* or *History of Spain.*[18] Both chronicles represented Spain and Castile's monarchy as culminating a universal history unfolding in accord with God's design. Both told of all past history as leading up to Alfonso's reign and looked forward to Spain fulfilling a great and cosmic destiny. They assumed Castile exercised hegemony over all Spain and they provided Spain with several founding myths. One, connecting Spain to classical antiquity through the demigod Hercules, told of Hercules as coming from Troy, conquering Africa, landing at Cádiz, setting up the pillars that bear his name, then traveling through the peninsula and founding Seville and a number of other cities; Isabel's Arévalo claimed to be one of them. Among numerous feats, Hercules vanquished Penthesileia, the queen of the Amazons, women warriors whom some Castilian chronicles identified as the widows of a band of slain Goths, thus making of those warrior women Spanish progenitors.[19]

Hercules became a great prince and lord who, having conquered much of Iberia, made his nephew, Hispalis, Spain's first king; from Hispalis and the line of Hercules, succession had come down uninterruptedly to the present through native *Hispani* rulers and Visigothic kings, down to Alfonso X himself.[20] Descent from Hercules in turn put Spain in the forefront of a broader Mediterranean tradition, so the Spanish stemmed from Troy as had the Romans, yet they possessed an even more prestigious origin, for Alfonso's Hercules was also a descendant of Noah. Alfonso's histories gave to Spaniards and their rulers an antiquity of their own, at once classical and biblical. They described Visigothic Spain as a golden age of simple virtues and natural morality. The Visigoths had been noble barbarians pure in spirit; they too had descended from Noah and they had vanquished the Roman Empire.[21] It was not unrelated that Alfonso sought to become Holy Roman Emperor, a title carrying universal connotation.

While it was Alfonso X's accounts of history and kingship that took a cultural fix, defining Spain, its kings, and what it meant to be Spanish, still Isabel particularly admired another Alfonso, Alfonso XI, for several reasons. In the early fourteenth century, Alfonso XI had announced God's commending to him of sovereignty and his consequent debt to no earthly power by having himself crowned by the moving arm of a statue of Santiago. Then as king, having shown himself a mighty warrior in turning back the last Muslim expedition from Africa in winning the battle of Salado, this Alfonso fulfilled a battlefield vow by endowing the then inconsequential shrine of Holy Mary at Guadalupe; Guadalupe would be Isabel's favorite retreat. Moreover, by 1350, when he died of the black plague while besieging Gibraltar, Alfonso XI had sired ten children, only one of them, Pedro, by his queen. One of the others, Enrique de Trastámara, rebelled against Pedro, who is known to history as *el Cruel* and who had had murdered Enrique's mother, his brothers, his friends, and even some strangers. Enrique at length killed Pedro and took the crown as Enrique II, and so this son of Alfonso XI began a new dynasty, the Trastámara, which was Isabel's.

Both Alfonsos also commissioned guides to princes instructing their sons on how to rule; Isabel appears to have taken some of that advice to heart. She possessed, too, a book that Alfonso X had ordered translated from Arabic, *The Secret of Secrets,* supposedly a collection of the deepest mysteries revealed by the sage Aristotle to his pupil, Alexander the Great; aside from imparting occult knowledge, it placed practical wisdom above virtue, although it advised the prince to appear virtuous. A century later Alfonso XI, perhaps aware of his heir's proclivities, had commissioned a more orthodox guide for young Pedro. Isabel owned a copy of it as well. Adapted from a Latin *Mirror for Princes,* it advised the prince to exercise self-control and free will, to form his character through meditation and good habits, and to maintain a right relationship with

God. It counseled demonstrably strong, personal, virtuous rule, consonant with the idea of Christian kingship that comes through the *Partidas* and royal chronicles. By Isabel's time, Spanish books of advice to princes were a common literary genre; she owned several, and others were written for her.[22] In general, they viewed the good ruler as a divine instrument, a leader in war, an even-handed dispenser of justice, and as dedicated to recovering Spain from the Muslims.

Reconquest, Prophecy, and Monarchy

Isidore of Seville and the histories of Alfonso X simply assumed the prophesied future was part of God's design for history, and that the future belonged to Spain. History was neither haphazard nor open-ended, it had a clear trajectory through time. History was divinely prepackaged, and Spanish rulers had a central role to play in it, as past events and prophecies of the future corroborated. Within this divinely established trajectory, Christian Spain was destined to regain the peninsula, but once accomplished and as Alfonso X construed it, the Spanish mission extended overseas. In the divine scheme, Iberian reconquest was a step toward the great crusading goal of retaking Jerusalem.

In medieval Europe, various Christian kings and their publicists staked competing claims to be chosen by heaven as leader of that final crusade, and they often did so through appropriating a popular prophecy concerning a final world emperor, a prediction frequently attributed to an ancient sibyl or to a seer imported from Britain, Merlin.[23] Continental compilations of prophecies that were ascribed to Merlin linked royal aspirations, chivalric values attributed to the Round Table, and revealed religion in its apocalyptic reaches. In Castile, an anonymous epic poem thought to have been written by a monk about 1260, incorporating learned and popular elements, and celebrating Castile's founder, Fernán González, cited Merlin as prophesying that a king of Castile, called the Crowned Lion, would emerge from the cave of Hercules and overcome the ruler of Granada, whom it called the Dragon. The Lion King's sons would conquer Africa, Asia, and Jerusalem. The poet relied on lost epics and battle songs, wrote in the vernacular, and took an Isidorian pride in Spain. In *The Poem of Fernán González*, Spain itself becomes a type of Israel; the Castilians are God's chosen people—God, as everyone knew, had sent St. James to aid and honor those most powerful warriors, the Spanish—and Castile is another Jerusalem. In turn, an epic *poema de Alfonso XI* drew both on *Fernán González* and on prophecies of the Lion King attributed to Merlin.[24] Merlin—a prescient standby in France and Germany, whose warring rulers outdid one another in being hailed as the prophesied Last Emperor—in Castile wrapped its kings in a divine mantle and announced them to be in international competition for primary position among Europe's crowned heads.[25]

In the mid-fourteenth century, the prophecy of a final world emperor became attached to Enrique de Trastámara during his protracted struggle with Pedro *el Cruel* for the Castilian crown. A prediction then circulated that represented Enrique as being called to loftier endeavors once he won the unsavory civil war he was then engaged in. Enrique, it foretold, was destined, as king of Castile, to gather Christian warriors and overcome barbarous nations. He was to be the long-prophesied Lion King and stretch his tail to the ends of the earth. He would be lord of all Spain, standard-bearer of the church; his sons would subject Africa, Asia, and the Holy Land. That prophecy of the Lion King was recycled for subsequent Spanish kings. In some Aragonese versions, the messianic world emperor was called the Bat, as when applied to Fernando.[26] In some others, he was *el Encubierto*—the Hidden One. He was a variety of anti-Antichrist, soon to reveal himself. The Bat like the Lion was to emerge from a dark cave. Such forecasts, blending religion and politics, circulated by word of mouth and were occasionally compiled.

In medieval Spain and throughout Europe, prophecy was, in short, considered eminently respectable, a part of knowledge, among the most reliable of guides to the future, pointing to truths unknowable by rational means, to matters hidden within the divine design. And while, according to church doctrine anyone at all might be a true prophet, it was an unwise claim for an individual to make. Far safer was adapting an old prophecy ascribed to a recognized authority. The danger was that prophecy paralleled and sometimes merged with unsanctioned routes to hidden secrets, the occult sciences among them. Suspect but not forbidden was a blend of astronomy and astrology; it was viewed as a way of predicting the future based upon the influence of the movement of forms and images in the heavens. Isabel dismissed outright soothsaying and black magic, but not learned prophecy based on the authority of the Bible or Spanish history. Moreover, astronomical indications, Merlin, and biblical allusion had come together in a spate of prophecies at the birth of Isabel's father, Juan II, in 1405 and again at his accession in 1419. The strands of prophetic tradition converged on that none-too-promising Trastámara, who was, however, the great dynastic hope. For his royal predecessors had been short-lived, his father known as Enrique the Ailing, and the holy war against the Moor largely neglected. Royal authority needed all the buoying it could get.[27]

At Juan's birth, prophesying court poets expiated on the mysteries of Scripture and claimed inspiration by the Holy Ghost. One also declared Fortune and the seven planets had invested this prince with world empire and crowned him with all the virtues—theological, cardinal, and moral. Juan would be as strong and constant as Hercules. He would hold the sword of justice in his right hand and, in his left, the crown of world empire. He would be like Alexander and Julius Caesar when they conquered the world. During Juan's minority, another declared the prince to be the strong lion predicted by Merlin and that, following Scripture, in the Last Days he would bring the world to one faith under one divinely designated ruler. Upon Juan's becoming king, verses announced that now the angry lion of Spain was emerging from his cave to pursue reconquest and to cleanse the seas of Muslims. He would surely have his throne in Jerusalem, be crowned high emperor, and fulfill all prophecy.

In much the same vein, young Juan's tutor, the bishop Pablo de Santa María, wrote for him a historical summary in verse called *The Seven Ages of the World*.[28] That long poem presented the universal past as a continuous unfolding of God's will and design and all history as culminating in Spain, its people, and its king. King and people were one in the Old Testament sense, and Castile was a nation synonymous with Spain. Castile had been prefigured in the Jewish and Roman monarchies; its royal house descended from King David, Roman emperors, Goth kings, and medieval emperors. Everything that had happened in the world had been leading up to the current reign. And, citing the Bible, the old chronicles, and Merlin alike, Santa María restated as historical fact not only the legendary past but the prophesied future.

The bishop's dedication to young Juan informs the prince, echoing St. Paul, that "we are those in whom the end of all the centuries is now come."[29] Merlin and the Books of Daniel and Revelation all point to Spain as the final empire. The bishop makes explicit what others had implied: he weaves the Lion King, Nebuchadnezzar's dream of four empires as interpreted by Daniel, and the vision in Revelation of the opening of the seven seals into a progression to be completed by the Spanish Trastámaras. Juan has a millennial role to play. The poem's final stanzas compare the prince to "our Lord in his coming," all Castilians to be liberated by his birth.[30] As Christ fulfilled the Old Testament promise, so Juan will complete human history.

It should be mentioned that Santa María and many of those court poets were *conversos,* steeped in the Old Testament and the sense of a chosen people, its kings in contact with God, and that they patterned history as did the prophet Jeremiah, centering on an elect nation, ending in the universal recovery of a lost Eden, but requiring fortitude, faith, and morality along the way. From the early years of the fifteenth century, such New Christians, who had gained entrée into Christian society, to the court, and some into royal confidence, were also among the foremost proponents of absolute monarchy. As for Santa María, he had been a renowned rabbi, then studied Christian theology at the University of Paris; he was also well versed in the Spanish chronicles and royal ideology, and he was a principal advisor to Juan's father, Enrique III.

Santa María understood the efficacy of political theology when put to political purposes.

It was not necessary, however, to have come from a Jewish milieu to write of Spain's history in those messianic terms, for that sort of rhetorical strategy had become traditional. Even so, Santa María and other *conversos* brought to standard formulations a newly intense religious approach having a considerable impact on established ideology, endowing it with great and imperative moral conviction and a sharpened and more urgent militant and messianic outlook.

Circumstances, and other figures as well, contributed to disseminating that message and impressing on individual Spaniards that they had a crucial personal as well as communal stake in the common mission. Then best situated to drive home that connection of the private and public, the religious and political, were the clergy, and especially those itinerant friars who traveled widely, preaching in towns and villages to large crowds. Clergy had long served as two-way conduits between court and realm, including in bringing popular and royal views into harmony with one another. Preaching friars put intimacy, cajoling, and threat into that tradition; they effectively delivered highly personalized messages and presented themselves as messengers arriving just ahead of the storm.

The Dominican friar Vicente Ferrer was Europe's most renowned preacher. A wielder of prophecies of Armageddon as imminent, he traveled through Spain during the minority of Juan II. Ferrer, initially invited by Santa María, drew crowds everywhere and held them spellbound with his sermons, all of them riveting interpretations of apocalyptic prophecies found in the Books of Daniel and Revelation. Time was short, he warned. Sinners must repent and nonbelievers must see the light. Everyone's soul was at stake, for Last Judgment loomed. If Jews and Muslims would not be baptized they must be isolated at once, for that sign of the End, Antichrist, whom they followed, was abroad.

Ferrer relentlessly coupled the looming end of the world and the need for immediate and total conversion of its inhabitants; the forces of Antichrist must disappear. Among them, Jews in particular posed a multiple threat. They awaited Antichrist as their messiah; they stole Christian children; like demons, they tempted people to sin; and their refusal to recognize the Messiah blocked the way to the brief but happy final time of one flock. Jews must convert or otherwise vanish, and quickly. To kill a man, Ferrer also said, was a mortal sin, but if God commanded it, it was not sin but virtue.[31] Mobs often attacked Jews after his sermons. An anonymous author of a manuscript written about 1500 told of hearing from his grandfather of how Ferrer's preaching had incited the slaughter of nineteen of Toledo's most eminent Jewish families—men, women, and children—who were beheaded and thrown into a mill-run; it was "a thing sad to see, the wheel turned human blood instead of water."[32]

Shortly after Ferrer was invited to preach at court the royal regents decreed that Jews be segregated and circumscribed in their activities. Those *conversos* who had accepted Christianity were not yet considered problematic: that would come—with political turmoil in Toledo in 1449, and Espina's preaching at court during Isabel's early years. Espina was in the rhetorical tradition of Ferrer, and Isabel would encounter many more such friars. She would, on occasion, count on such people to broadcast her own messages in popular terms.

Among the traditions Isabel would take up was reading the popular temper and playing upon popular belief and sentiment so as to couch and disseminate royal desiderata effectively. In the doing, she would avail herself of the many conduits of contact—written, visual, and oral, the last including sermons, hymns, prophecies, and the popular poems, songs, and *romances*.[33]

Juan II and Alvaro de Luna

Isabel, basing her right to the crown on being the heir of her father, Juan II, sought not to emulate him but to adhere to certain principles underscored during his reign. By her father's time, Spain's king was claimed to be divinely elected, a claim avowedly based on the combined authority of the Bible, the church fathers, prophecy and its interpretation, history as recorded in Spanish chronicles, and the two laws, canon and civil, both derived from imperial Rome. Restrictions on royal power were held to exist only in custom, in the king's conscience, in the length of the royal reach, and in the strength of the nobility. The chief theoretical limitation on monarchy in late medieval Europe, that the king owed his authority to the community, surfaced rarely; it helped that most people found the nobles closer and more oppressive. The king possessed an aura of holiness, an aura that the royal court was instrumental in cultivating. and that increased markedly during the reign of that weak king, due largely to his favorite, Luna.

At six, Juan II had been given as his page Álvaro de Luna, who came of an obscure but well-connected Aragonese family, who was some years older than himself, and from whom the boy soon refused to be separated. Luna became his *privado*, his most intimate friend and advisor, and after Juan came of age he appointed Luna constable of Castile and largely left all governance in his hands. Luna, relying as little as possible on other nobles, thereafter acted like a king in the name of the king and himself became the wealthiest and most powerful of lords, an effective (if avaricious) administrator who established a governing apparatus dedicated to centralizing power. To staff it, he chose able men, many of them *conversos,* and allowed them sufficient latitude to run Castile for royal benefit and his own. He enlarged the royal chancery and its staff of *letrados.* He relied on men who knew, as he did, that their own standing, wealth, and power were dependent on the prestige of the monarchy. Thus it was that during the reign of so ineffective a king as Juan II, the principles and apparatus of absolute monarchy nevertheless received tremendous impulse. Under Luna's direction, chancery documents ceaselessly referred to royal prerogatives in the most absolute terms, and to the king as patently above the civil law. And some of those same *letrados,* so assiduous in producing absolutist documents under Juan II, would compile or find law, equally regalist, for Isabel. During Juan's reign too, deputies of the Cortes, who were drawn from royal towns and generally desirous of limiting the grasp of the nobility, also linked royal power to furthering the common good.

Letrados of the royal chancery that Luna built up eventually, on Juan's orders, put their experience to finding law to support the king's right to move against their mentor, Luna—to justify indicting and executing so great and powerful a noble and confiscating most of his estate. In the process, the regalism of the *Partidas,* the ideals of the mirrors for princes, the precedent of biblical kingship, and the general belief that nothing could deceive the heart of the well-intended monarch, were further advanced as operative principles.

Thus in 1453, in the order Juan signed for Luna's arrest, the king reminded his subjects of "the place of God which I hold on earth, with regard to justice, in order to administer and exercise it as properly and principally as every Christian Catholic king must do who wants to pay his dues and discharge his conscience." A decree of the Cortes sitting at Burgos that same year backed him up: the king, as head to the body that was the kingdom, was above all a judge who might pass judgment on the other parts of that body. A letter Juan signed stated it most simply: that to serve the king is to please God.[34]

Yet for thirty-odd years Juan had stayed clear of governance and instead devoted himself to hunting, music, tourneys, and other pleasures of court life. Says Palencia, Juan "gave himself up to unrestrained sensuality." Another contemporary states he was greedy, luxury loving, cruel, and vindictive, but without sufficient spirit to carry anything out.[35] Like his Trastámara predecessors, Juan preferred the *meseta,* where he lived as honored guest of great nobles or in the various large royal houses called palaces, and he enjoyed reading and having about him wise and educated men. Still, some of those he welcomed at court were nonetheless highly critical of his neglect of personal rule and lectured him roundly.

Around the time of Isabel's birth and as Luna's star waned, a coterie of powerful and highly respected men, *letrados* and nobles, bureaucrats and poets, laymen and high clergy, voicing ever more vehemently the pressing need to stem civil strife, remedy communal misery, and redeem Castile through moral regeneration, prodded Juan to exert strong personal monarchy. Among the most powerful and persistent of those critics was Iñigo López de Mendoza, marqués de Santillana, who hated Luna. Santillana's fortune had been assured when his uncle, (an earlier) Pedro González de Mendoza, perished in the battle of Aljubarrota against Portugal in 1385, having given his horse to the king. Santillana himself had gained a reputation for valor in service on the Muslim frontier and during Juan II's few forays against the Moors. He further distinguished himself in letters: he is remembered as among the century's foremost poets. Still, Santillana chose prose to voice "a lamentation made in prophecy of the second destruction of Spain." Turning to familiar history, he drew the usual analogy to the Muslim conquest—the first destruction of Spain; he invoked the august heritage of the Goths, and saw Spaniards as a chosen people being punished by an angry God—the implication being because of Luna's abuse of power and Juan II's inactivity. That remarkable diatribe of scriptural cadence, reminiscent of the prophet Jeremiah's lament for Jerusalem, indeed seeing Spain as an analogue of Jerusalem, represents the rhetoric and spirit of a generation of worried but loyal counselors, who concluded in common that national deliverance lay in the king rousing himself and leading his people against the Muslims.

In that lament Santillana pronounced their shared verdict, that Spain, having lost all sense of national purpose, was about to be destroyed again as in 711. "How great can be your blindness," he asked the personified nation, thus indirectly addressing the king.

How can you not see the terrible destruction and harm that are coming upon you . . . and the ferocious divine fires that will burn you? How can you not see your people turned against one another, brother against brother, parent against child, and all manner of discord and evil around you, as all peace, love, truth, and security are fleeing from you? I see your people as sheep without a shepherd. I see your churches turned into stables of infidels, and the cursed name of Muhammad exalted, and the banner of Christ fallen in the dust. . . . And I see the Trojan fires consuming the walls of your cities.[36]

The people, Santillana lamented, had fallen into avarice and luxury. God, the great sovereign, was full of vengeance. And Santillana entreated Juan to bestir himself and exercise his will, to govern righteously and to go against the Moor. While Juan did none of those things, his daughter would take to heart such advice and be far more successful in achieving those goals, and to do so she would rely heavily on Santillana's son, another Pedro González de Mendoza.

Isabel would rely too on Juan's hairshirt extraordinary, Diego de Valera—knight-errant, scholar, poet, chronicler, royal counselor, and *converso*—who, perhaps because his father had been royal physician, was remarkably at ease with kings and felt impelled to prescribe for the common good of wretched

Spain. "Try to remember," Valera lectured Juan, "that you are king . . . that you reign in God's stead on Earth."[37] Valera would continue to offer advice to kings, and, to greater effect to a queen, for another thirty-odd years.

The grandiose vision, long inflated by royal panegyrists, of the Lion King from Spain who would regain Jerusalem, spilled into imperative with a renewed Turkish advance. Spain must have a strong ruler. Juan de Mena, poet and royal secretary, put the appeal to Juan within the context of opposing forces of good and evil, heaven and hell. He laid the civil strife then so endemic and so deplored to disloyal and greedy nobles, sin, and black magic. Mena, resorting to earlier prophecies delivered in court, but changing them from celebratory salutations to injunctions akin to those of the friars, declared there was chaos in Castile caused by the minions of Antichrist, demons; Muslims were their instruments. Against that evil lot, said Mena, stood Christian dedication to regaining the land, divine providence, loyal counselors, the spur of fame, and, ideally, the king. Mena exhorted Juan to show strength and courage, "for you were made king on earth by the King of Heaven /. . . . Thus you who are in command, / turn your wrath, turn your wrath against the Moors." (The Spanish verses, staccato, rise to a crescendo: "¡por ende, vosotros, essos que mandades, / la yra, la yra bolued en los moros!")[38]

Isabel, born into a world newly dreading the Muslim advance that might bring on its end, and into a Spain internally chaotic and feeling unprotected in lacking a strong, decisive, and militant ruler, in coming to the crown in 1475 had a clear path laid out for her—by her own experience to date, current circumstances, Spanish history as Castilians saw it, and one thing more, her own moral conviction.

From the outset, she would rule as she thought she should, in accord with royal traditions and in the world as she knew it. Central to her perception of that world and its traditions was the waging of war deemed holy against religious enemies. The new queen had known war firsthand and for much of her life to date, and she was to know much more of it. War was to her a fact of life, but wars covered a moral range, and the best war was directed to that prime goal of Spanish kings, completing the reconquest—to crusading, holy, war. Her immediate predecessors gave lip service to regaining Spain but were adjudged to have neglected that all-important royal obligation with grim results. She would pursue it wholeheartedly. It was not that she did not concern herself with other aspects of governance, but that she understood such religious warfare as her highest duty. In 1475, Spain's crusading mission in world history and the leading role of its ruler were at the core of royal ideology and known to constitute an article of faith for royal subjects. They did so for Castile's new queen as well.

Pursuing reconquest, fusing religion and politics, Isabel—perhaps corroborating the prime indication of the sword borne before her—was resolved to take up a mission come to define Castilian society as a whole, and she understood that society as a body politic ruled by its head, whose own heart was in the hands of the Lord. In 1475, moreover, it was clear that nothing would so get powerful Castilians behind her nor win public approval as for a queen and her king to return to the enterprise of driving out the Moor. But first, she had to wage another sort of war, one to secure her crown. And most immediately, there was domestic crisis.

II

La Reina

Chapter 6
Contests: 1475

Between the King and Queen there was no discord . . . they ate together in the public hall, talking of pleasant things as is done at table, and they slept together.

Where affection, bravery, and gentileza *are found, they are always more pleasing to the god of love than to [the God] of heaven.*
—*Crónica incompleta*[1]

To Fernando, at Zaragoza presiding over the Corts of Aragón, Isabel sent a concise message: Enrique had died; Fernando's presence would not be useless but he should do what he thought best, considering circumstances in Aragón. He had already had the news, for Carrillo's messenger had outsped Isabel's. Castile's new king left for Segovia immediately, and on the second day en route received additional letters from Isabel and also one from Gutierre de Cárdenas describing in detail Isabel's taking the crown and making much of his own role in having ridden before her with upraised sword.

Fernando—says Palencia, who was with him—was surprised at not hearing of that ceremony from Isabel and amazed at it having taken place. When before, he wondered, had a queen ever been preceded by a symbol threatening her vassals with punishment? It was a rite of kings; he knew of no queen who would have usurped that male prerogative.[2] Neither Palencia nor another companion on that ride, the lawyer Caballería, had heard of it. Caballería, concerned, had immediately advised Juan II that he, as he alone could, should do his best to enamor Fernando and Isabel of their union and of concord and its benefits, that it was very necessary, for the situation in Castile "was not without suspicion of something sinister," and that Castilians were acceding to the succession only because they could do nothing else, but were ready to take advantage of any discord between the king and queen.[3]

Fernando was confidant. He confided, says Palencia, "in conquering with patience and felt certain he would triumph through satisfying assiduously the demands of conjugal love, with which he could easily soften the intransigence that bad advisors had planted in his wife's mind." He rode into Castile and to

Segovia in high spirits, banners flying and trumpets proclaiming the presence of royal majesty "so that vassals might know it was their king who was in the land." And although he continued to marvel at Isabel's behavior, still he did not expect that she would hold him rigidly to the terms of the prenuptial *capitulación.*[4]

On January 2, 1475 he entered Segovia, kingly indeed in a flowing coat of cloth-of-gold lined in Russian marten fur, to be met by Mendoza and Carrillo, a host of dignitaries, clergy bearing crosses, and a great throng of townspeople. Before the portico of the church of San Miguel, where Isabel had stood two weeks earlier, a formal ceremony of accession again took place, but with a difference. Would he, Fernando was asked, reign in those kingdoms as the legitimate husband of the queen? Yes, he responded graciously, he would. Thereupon Segovia's councilmen swore that "they would obey and receive His Highness as legitimate husband of Our Lady the Queen for their King and Lord."[5] Their language was construable as relegating Fernando to king consort and revelatory of the stance being taken by Isabel and her counselors. Theirs was an interpretation of her authority in Castile in relation to his that was at great variance with what had been anticipated by the Aragonese. For in Aragón women could not succeed to the crown; nor in Castile had any woman reigned in her own right in several hundred years.

And Isabel? Afterward, when the procession arrived by torchlight at the *alcázar,* the queen greeted the king just inside the gates, in the patio, with great formality. The message was clear: it was she who was proprietary ruler. Pulgar, finding precedent in the old chronicles, produces a long list of women who had governed Castile and its parent kingdoms of León and Asturias. He begins with Ormisinda, daughter of Pelayo (whom he refers to as king of León); since Pelayo had no son Ormisinda had inherited León and the man she married had become its king, Alfonso I *el Católico.* Odisina, sister of Froyla, king of León, succeeded as queen in the same situation. Doña Sancha, sister of King Bermudo, also succeeded in León and her husband became King Fernando the Great. Doña Elvira, queen of Navarre, succeeded in Castile, then a county, and her son, Fernando, became its first king. Urraca, the daughter of Alfonso VI, married to Count Ramón de Tolosa, succeeded in Castile and León, and, after the count died, Urraca married Alfonso, king of Aragón, known as the Battler, yet it was she who continued to rule Castile and her son, Alfonso VII, succeeded her. Similarly, Berenguela, mother of Fernando III, married to Alfonso, king of León, the kingdoms now separate, ruled Castile. Never, Pulgar states, when there was a legitimate daughter descended by direct line should a male born into the transveral line—the reference to Juan of Aragón is implicit—inherit the crown. Beyond dispute, the government of the kingdom belonged to the queen; she was its legitimate proprietress.

All this, Pulgar continues, Isabel explained to Fernando, assuring him that what he commanded as the queen's husband must be done in Castile; and that afterward, pleasing God, those kingdoms would go to their children, his and hers. God until then had given them no other heir except Princess Isabel; after their days, therefore, "should a male come descended from the royal house of Castile claiming the kingdom by the transverse line, or should the Princess Isabel marry a foreign prince who wants to take over Castile's fortresses and royal patrimony, the kingdom would come into the power of a foreign dynasty, "which would weigh heavily on their consciences and be a disservice to God."[6] For those reasons, she had taken the crown alone.

Fernando's adherents argued angrily against her assertion of sole proprietorship and against succession passing not to him but to a child of theirs. Agreeing, Palencia stated their position: by natural, statutory, and divine law, the man holds the prerogative and should have precedence, as was customary in those kingdoms and elsewhere. Further, there existed an old Castilian law stating "that in the marriage of a female heir to the kingdom, although her husband may be of lesser rank he is jointly to wield the scepter and is to have the name of king and to receive the other distinctions given the man everywhere." Moreover, Fernando's was the better claim to the crown, through the male line of the royal house, and certainly Fernando was the legitimate heir to Castile and León should his wife die.[7] Be that as it may, in view of the numerous deaths without which she would not have come to the crown, it is understandable that Isabel's supporters would frown on Fernando's gaining the crown in his own right as an outcome of her death.

Palencia, himself fanning discord, warned Fernando that "the Cardinal and other principal caballeros ceaselessly fomented in the womanly mind of the Queen the petulance that had begun to form there," that fawning courtiers insisted she defend her hereditary rights and that she avoid the conjugal yoke that the king would try to impose upon Castilian necks. Yet he also reports that, while swayed by such advice, the queen, "a woman after all," had made the distinction that the rights of matrimony had no bearing on those of lordship and royal power.

With grudging admiration, Palencia reported that Isabel immediately sought to change the opinion of the many who saw her as overbearing and arrogant. And nothing was more effective in that direction than her demonstrated ability to put out of her mind, as her religious advisors urged she do, all such talk and insinuation "when receiving her husband," her ability "to proceed to all conjugal concord" and only elsewhere to speak with Fernando of the conditions of governing, "which from the most remote centuries have favored the man."[8] Confessor to them both was Alonso de Burgos, whom Isabel and Fernando would reward for his great services, surely that welcome advice among them. Alonso de Burgos, he who tangled with Carrillo and his magician Alarcón, has been described as coarse and immoral. Still, it is worth speculating what brakes on passion the more austere confessors who followed him might have counseled, and the consequences for that marriage, and for Spanish history.

Somehow, Isabel asserted her political supremacy while not challenging the commonplace assumption that the male was by nature dominant in marriage. And her personal relationship with Fernando did parallel the known philosophy of one churchman. A treatise (probably wrongly) attributed to *El Tostado* had proposed that, since a man could not escape love's trammels, he had best find one good woman, that, most deeply, love and friendship linked individuals to one another and to God, and that "to love is to have a friend who is another who is oneself."[9] Castile's queen would manage to maintain a semblance of traditional wifely role and to be seen working as an equal with her husband in public life. Fortunately, such was his own familial experience given his strong-willed mother and aunts that Fernando would go along with good grace.

The upshot was that Isabel and Fernando agreed to leave the working out of an agreement on their respective authority and functions to their arbitrators, and "between the King and Queen there was no discord . . . they ate together in the public hall, talking of pleasant things as is done at table, and they slept together," the only friction occurring when one would want to do something for a loyal adherent, but usually "their wills coincided through intimacy born of love."[10] Moreover, both undoubtedly realized that separately neither would be very powerful, that neither of them alone could rule in Castile. Ambition there was, and passion, and something more: as Pulgar puts it, "love held their wills joined."[11] It is, after all, the soundest explanation. And its course did not run smoothly.

Initially, they left settling the terms of their respective roles to Carrillo and Mendoza. But Fernando was put on guard when the archbishop warned him his own people were losing out to the "evil *grandes*," as Palencia puts it, and to "the instilled pride of the Queen." In those circumstances, when Fernando discovered that the chancery had returned letters of homage to Seville for correction because they named the king before the queen, he informed Isabel that he was deeply offended in honor and reputation, that people saw his virility being undercut, and that he was leaving for Aragón. She, "protesting that she would never for any reason have wanted to cause the least setback to her most beloved consort, for whose happiness and honor she would sacrifice willingly not only the crown but her very health," insisted that it was all a formal legal matter. And she pleaded with him passionately "not to leave his beloved wife, for she would not or could not live separated from him." Fernando stayed.[12]

It was Caballería and Mendoza, seconded by the *letrado*, Rodrigo Maldonado de Talavera, who produced a formal accord, signed on January 15 by Isabel and Fernando and ratified by the great lords then at court. The *capitulación* signed by Juan and Fernando in 1469 had envisioned Isabel as adjunct, Fernando exercising rule. This accord of Segovia, while permitting him wide powers, reversed the balance. It firmly established that proprietorship of the crown was Isabel's alone. They might jointly issue documents, coins, and stamps: the king's name was to precede the queen's, but her coat of arms was to come first; homage was to be sworn exclusively to the queen, as it had been up until then; she would appoint all Castile's treasurers and other officials, although the king might also apportion revenues. She would concede *mercedes* and posts; both of them could propose appointments to masterships and church offices but at her volition. The castles were to be obedient to the queen. She was to name governors of castles and forts, but the king was to distribute garrisons and, because of his skill in war, "since accustomed to bearing arms from his youth," he would have supreme command of the armies. Orders of the king alone referring to war, crime, and authorizing expeditions were also valid, but not those treating of other affairs, particularly the collection of revenue. They would administer justice when together and each might do so when apart, always mindful of the Royal Council. Revenues of Castile, Sicily, and Aragón were to pay the expenses of the realm, any surplus to be distributed by joint accord. They were jointly entitled *reyes*—that is, dual monarchs—of Castile, León, and Sicily, and *principes* of Aragón. The order of succession was fixed so that the princess Isabel might inherit the crown.[13] Remarkably, nothing was said of foreign affairs.

Fernando, although he signed it, was so irritated by the arrangement that he again threatened to leave. And it was now that Carrillo performed his last great service: he angrily berated them both. Isabel, once alone with Fernando, sobbed: all the dissension had been Carrillo's fault; Fernando must not go. She would have the terms modified. As Palencia tells it: "The love *(cariño)* of his wife, whom he loved *(amaba)* deeply, calmed the king's ire and, obeying his feelings, he assented with good grace to his wife's entreaties."[14] Some adjustments concerning collecting rents, doing justice, and rewarding services ensued; Fernando and Isabel agreed to use one seal, join coats of arms, and have both their portraits on the coinage. And so it was that their coins showed the two of them, their shared coat of arms, and such mottos as "whom God has joined let no man separate."[15]

Jointly, they set up a traditional royal household staff, appointing chaplains, an armorer, a chief barber, a quilt maker, jewelers and silversmiths, a foundryman, a butler, and a first huntsman. They confirmed the cardinal, Mendoza, as chancellor of the secret seal, the post he had risen to under Enrique. They named Gonzalo Chácon *contador mayor,* or principal comptroller, Gutierre de Cárdenas second *contador,* and Rodrigo de Ulloa, who had been a *contador* of Enrique's, a third; Gabriel Sánchez was charged with household finances. Sánchez alone was Aragonese, and he was a *converso*, as were many, perhaps most, of the administrators and the jurists who increasingly predominated (where nobles once had) in the Royal Council and the Chancery.[16] Even so, the cardinal, the duke of Alba, and the admiral dominated the council.

Isabel and Fernando also retained many of Enrique's appointees, and they confirmed many *mercedes* he had made, although not that of Arévalo to Stúñiga, and not Pacheco's having invested in his son, Diego, the *marquesado* of Villena. For once again those powerful magnates, Stúñiga, young Pacheco, and his twin cousins, Rodrigo Téllez Girón and Juan Téllez Girón, were conspiring. Stúñiga would not relinquish Arévalo, and he dominated a vast expanse of northern Extremadura. Pacheco held the *marquesado* of Villena and the Giróns had extensive domains in Andalusia, the mastership of military order of Calatrava, and the county of Urueña, near Valladolid. All of them commanded formidable resources, private armies, and dense networks of relatives and retainers.

Rumblings

Isabel and Fernando postponed convoking Cortes, although Isabel had initially spoken of doing it as soon as possible. Rather, on January 18 they held a full council meeting. Then immediately, invoking the royal responsibility to mete out "Justice, to which—as an anonymous chronicler puts it—more than any other principle they were inclined,"[17] they called to court outstanding legists, who, conscious of setting tone, sentenced a number of reachable mid-level malefactors of the previous reign swiftly and harshly. And in towns and villages, royal overseers, *corregidores,* although their own previous behavior might not bear examination, sniffed the wind and emulated the court's draconian measures. The imposition of royal law and peaceful order, however, was hampered when Carrillo, in withdrawing from court on February 20, signaled a return to factional conflict, which one observer laid to "our sins growing greater."[18] Certainly the time of troubles was not over; heaven was not yet smiling on Castile.

Carrillo, although his influence and revenues had both depleted, could still take with him into the opposition a great chunk of the kingdom's central places and their rents. And Diego Pacheco had custody of Juana, now thirteen years old. He and Stúñiga now took up her claim to the crown. She would marry her uncle, Afonso, king of Portugal; he must come claim her and the kingdom.[19] The stage was again set for civil war in Castile, and for war with Portugal as well, but now Castile's crowned heads were a close-knit pair, dominated by no one, but advised primarily by a lawyer, cleric, and statesman, the worldly and astute Pedro González de Mendoza, a man as bent on promoting royal authority as was Luna, but one who possessed a well-established power base of his own, greater and more far-seeing vision, and, as he had already demonstrated, a devotion not to party but to country.

Recently Afonso of Portugal had become wealthier than ever. In 1471 his Portuguese had conquered Arcilla, in Fez, a terminal of the Saharan gold route, and eight days later he himself had taken Tangier. Portuguese ships too had reached Atlantic coasts under Africa's hump. Fernão Gómez, whom Afonso had licensed in 1469 to explore one hundred leagues of coast each year in the area referred to as Guinea and who paid the crown handsomely for the privilege, had arrived at the Costa da Mina, the Gold Coast, and there the Portuguese were advantageously exchanging trinkets, old clothes, and the conch shells of the Canary Islands for enslaved Africans or potential slaves and, most profitably, for gold. Having taken Ceuta in 1415, they had diverted gold there from the old hubs of exchange along the Mediterranean coast of North Africa and now they were exporting it from the Guinea coast as well. In the process, they had disorganized Catalan trading patterns with Egypt and North Africa; they were also affecting the gold flow into Castile and challenging Castilian seamen. Conversely, Aragón and Castile in concert posed a threat to Portugal in Africa and the Atlantic.[20]

None of this was lost on the king of France. And though one historian has overstated in saying "Afonso V of Portugal was a peon in the hands of Louis XI," yet nothing could suit Louis better than that his ally Portugal take on Aragón's new ally, Castile, and he relentlessly pressured Afonso to enter Castile.[21] Although in January Isabel and Fernando had promised Juan of Aragón two thousand lances for defense of Perpignan against the French, on hearing rumblings from Portugal they sent an embassy of friendship to France, a traditional ally of Castile and important to their control of Sicily.[22] The lances never left; in February Fernando explained to his father it was because of Carrillo's defection and the threat of civil war. Implied was *los reyes'* acceptance that Perpignan would again fall to the French—as it would do in March—and that the primary and immediate concern of them both lay not in Aragón but in Castile, although that Aragón retain the contested provinces of Cerdania and Rosellón was to Castile's interest. Even so, that spring Isabel offered, in response to Louis's claim to Rosellón, to sell it to him; she had sent Pulgar to France and instructed him to discuss the transaction. Louis's response to her was that there had been few cases of offers by individuals of sale of things jointly held, but how much did she want for it? She should send *grandes* to negotiate. By then, however, Pulgar had discerned that the French king, while signing an agreement of friendship that March, was playing for time while preparing to support an invasion of Castile by Afonso of Portugal.[23]

In that situation Fernando, more experienced than Isabel in international relations, told her that they both should sign international agreements and urged that she understand them thoroughly, especially the one pending with Louis.[24] Thereafter foreign affairs remained a sphere of joint competency, and Isabel learned quickly. She continued to tread carefully between Louis XI and her father-in-law, to whom she wrote regularly, and, together with Fernando, she also exchanged formal promises of friendship with Edward IV of England. Behind this diplomacy lay royal interest in Castile's burgeoning commerce, for despite unstable conditions within Castile the export of wool had climbed from the 1460s on; so had long-distance trade—in the produce of Andalusia, the iron of Bilbao (especially sought after in London), and the exchange in precious metals, all designedly swelling royal income through customs receipts and sales taxes; the retrieval of those revenues by the crown, however, was dependent on regaining grants made by Enrique as well as ending outright siphonings. It depended that is, on imposing and enforcing royal authority.

The Knight and His Lady

In late January, Isabel and Fernando had sent an embassy to Afonso, hoping to dissuade him and offering him the hand of Fernando's sister Juana, but to no avail. They then sent a second, instructed to say that the contemplated war was unjust and Enrique's purported daughter Juana illegitimate and that Enrique's impotence and his queen's lewdness were common knowledge, and they reminded Afonso of a difficulty that lay ahead for him should he cross the border: the ancient hatred of the Castilians for the Portuguese. Bitterly remembered in Castile was the war fought between them nearly a century before, in which, at the battle of Aljubarrota in 1385, Castile had suffered great losses of men and many noble lines were extinguished. The ambassadors to Lisbon were two friars, a Franciscan and a Dominican, their vocation adding religious weight to a political argument itself steeped in religion. They claimed, says Pulgar, that their sovereigns possessed the realm by the grace and will of God and by the right of succession belonging to the queen, Isabel; they also, alluding to the medieval belief in trial by combat, said they prayed that God would show where justice lay through granting them victory.[25]

The choice of such emissaries was astute, for word came from Portugal that Afonso was equally certain that the Lord was with him and his people, that he had avowed he was impelled by destiny. He had, it was said, convinced himself that prophecies of the church fathers revealed that Spain was to obey the king of Portugal, and that his conquest of Castile would be just, glorious, and preliminary to waging war against the kingdom of Granada. The kings of Portugal relied on variations of Iberian history and the mission it sanctified. More concrete, Afonso told his council that he had received guarantees of support signed by many Castilian *grandes* and sealed with their secret seals, and that the papacy would provide, for a sum, the dispensation he needed to marry his niece, Juana. He expected too that Louis XI of France, who had suggested the project to him in the first place, would be a powerful ally.

Isabel and Fernando went on royal progress in mid-March. Alba turned over to them Medina del Campo and its fortress of La Mota. Benavente gave up to them the great house in Valladolid in which they were wed. They reconfirmed the privileges of the cities but they did not call Cortes. Stúñiga and Pacheco announced their support for Juana and so their opposition to the couple as usurpers. And they heard from Afonso: he would marry Juana and reclaim Castile on her behalf.

On April 3, although war loomed, Pedro de Velasco, lord of Haro, held a lavish spring tournament in Valladolid. Fernando jousted. From a throne on a raised dais, Isabel presided, elegantly attired and wearing a crown; her fourteen ladies-in-waiting all wore coronets. Isabel had arrived on horseback, the harness of her mount trimmed in silver and adorned with flowers of gold. The nobles attending had spent prodigiously in vying with one another in rich attire and in the size and magnificence of retinues, down to dressing their pages in embroidered cloth of gold trimmed with furs of marten and sable.[26] Beginnings are wonderful and that handsome and vibrant young couple exuded hope and promise commensurate with the season, and not least because Isabel was again pregnant. "It seemed," an onlooker would recall, "that God had come to the world to entertain us lavishly."[27]

All the *caballeros* jousted prodigiously, mindful of evoking the knights of the Round Table, responding to the dual imperatives of chivalry and courtly love, and despite being at odds with religious obligations. It was after all Eastertime, but the attitude was plainly "where affection, bravery, and *gentileza* are found, they always are more pleasing to the god of love than to [the God] of heaven." No heed was paid to such censure as the poet Iñigo de Mendoza addressed to troubadours for invoking the god of love for the service of the devil. Each contestant so gloried, an anonymous chronicler says, in seeking to serve his lady that, covered in sweat and although receiving great blows, none felt much pain.

Isabel was married to such a knight, whose gallantries survive in his letters to her, their phrases of devotion more usually found in love letters directed to an *amiga* than to a wife. Fernando jousted with distinction that day, and throughout April he continued to participate in jousts and tourneys, prodded by companions who, deriding the Portuguese, assured him that Afonso would never dare to enter Castile. There was criticism: "These ridiculous inventions, jousts," snorts Palencia, who thought Fernando lured into them by nobles who did not want to see him put his mind to governance and so exert authority.[28] But tourneys were also war games and political theater wherein to demonstrate strength, magnificence, and disdain for opponents, as well as to make known the proud and confident temper of both Castile and its new monarchs: "And there was shown how little was thought of the king of Portugal and his cohorts. . . ."[29] And especially did tourneys provide opportunity for displays of calculated self-representation.

Fernando's chivalric device at Valladolid was an anvil, *un yunque,* its first letter the Y of *Ysabel.* It also stood for his current motto: "Like an anvil I keep silent and endure, because of the times." It signified physical strength and fortitude, and could be taken as combining comment on impending civil war, his lingering unhappiness with the extent of his authority in Castile, and even a current inability to counter Louis XI in Aragón. Silence and endurance were also aspects of his father's favorite virtue, the most royal one, prudence. The anvil called to mind as well the blacksmith who forged and shaped strong weapons of war. Yet its message was scarcely inspiring, and he would soon exchange that device for another also beginning with Y, a *yugo,* or oxen yoke, a double yoke most patently emblematic of their joint power through working in harness; moreover, a yoke of oxen was known to signify the worldly riches of love.

Isabel's own device remained a bundle of arrows, *flechas,* which returned the compliment in beginning with an F.[30] Arrows were prime missiles of war and the execution of justice: in Castile common criminals were traditionally dispatched with bow and arrow. Her arrows, gathered together and bound, resembled as well Ceres' bundle of wheat, and so fertility. That neat bundle conveyed too Isabel's love of imposed order, and her readiness for war as well. Isabel and Fernando would throughout their lives continue to employ the celebratory and ceremonial appeal of those and other chivalric usages and to advertise their particular fusion of love and war; and war there would be.

As Afonso's forces gathered on the border, Castile's queen and king mobilized. On April 28, they granted a general pardon for past crimes to all volunteers and, realizing they would have to work apart, Isabel in effect modified the arrangement agreed upon in January, in yielding to Fernando powers "to provide for, decree, make, and organize" all he saw as necessary and complying with the interests of them both and the welfare and defense of their kingdoms. He might make *mercedes* of cities, villages, and forts, or name officials to them. His authority in all matters was to be joint with hers.[31] It was not a full equality, for she remained sole proprietary ruler of Castile, but an indication of increased necessity and also of deepened trust; they would work in tandem, although often separated, and they would keep in constant touch by fast couriers.

Isabel, unfortunately for us, favored verbal communication. Thus, in a letter of May 16, Fernando, who was at Tordesillas, chided her roundly, and archly: although, he says, messengers come and go between them, she does not write to him, "not for lack of paper and not for not knowing how to write but for insufficient love and haughtiness, and because you are in Toledo and I in the provinces," and it was then that came the courtly coup de grace: "but someday we shall return to our first love." And he closes: "If you do not want to make me kill myself, you should write and tell me how you are."[32] Here was a playful intimacy, bespeaking a mutual consent to his cutting through her natural reserve by teasingly pointing it up.

On May 25, Isabel had war proclaimed throughout the land.[33] At about the same time, Afonso entered Castile with a formidable army. He came across the border into Albuquerque with 3,600 to 3,700 horse, 8,000 to 10,000 foot, 200 carts of provisions, heavy artillery, some smaller cannon and large cannon-lombards, and, as Fernando informed his father, with gold and silver crosses gleaming aloft and hymns resounding in praise of the God of Armies. Afonso brought, too, much engraved silver plate and gold and silver coin. His lords and knights were sumptuously equipped. That the wherewithal for that splendid entry came of exploration and trade was not lost on his opponents. The treasures of Guinea, says Palencia, had turned the old pride of the Portuguese into a great display of unbridled arrogance.[34] It was also reported that Afonso was being carried in a litter, perhaps because of a complaint of the liver but more likely in order to have his arrival comply—if by a stretch—with a well-known prophecy of the coming of the messiah-king. The hidden one, *El Encubierto,* was to arrive carried on a horse of wood; and it was said he would then sweep Spain clean of Jews, locusts, bloodsuckers, robber-wolves, and the friar-cats who are the *conversos. El Encubierto* was the messianic designation favored in Portuguese prophecy and roughly synonymous with the Bat and the Lion King; Afonso was announcing just where God's favor lay.[35]

Afonso, joined by Pacheco and Stúñiga in Extremadura, tarried there while proclaiming Juana legitimate queen—Afonso claimed the Cortes had sworn fealty only to her and that Isabel and Fernando had poisoned Enrique—and he lavishly celebrated his engagement to the lady Isabel now referred to as La Beltraneja, the daughter of Beltrán de la Cueva, thus giving Isabel and Fernando crucial time to prepare. They held a council of war and afterward Isabel rushed to Tordesillas with reinforcements for its garrison, certain that Afonso must come to neighboring Arévalo, held by Stúñiga. Tordesillas would be her principal base for much of the next two years, and there her penchant for meticulous detail would manifest itself. Nor would it show up only in organizing and deploying men and materiél; for surviving from that period is a directive of hers to the Clares, nuns attached to the Franciscan order whose convent abutted the royal residence: Would they be so good as to clear their courtyard of dung?[36]

Isabel stayed in the *mudéjar* palace housing both the royal quarters and the convent of Clares. Alfonso XI had had it built with booty taken at Salado and by Andalusian workmen who had brought from their homeland its tiles, its gilded *artesonado* ceilings, and its traditional baths. In the vestibule of that palace a mermaid, a siren, still evokes a Muslim fable of the sea; and etched on the facade is the Muslim motif of the keys to paradise.[37] Isabel, amid one war, had a foretaste of the more exquisite spoils of another. But at the moment her mind was on other things.

Tirelessly, she garrisoned and readied other *meseta* towns, while Fernando secured Salamanca, Zamora, and Toro, or so he thought, by confirming in their positions the men who held those places and their forts. Embassies arrived, from England and France, Brittany and Burgundy; the French dissimulated; the others promised support. Castile's great lords were sent home to gather their *mesnadas,* and the Cabreras were reminded of their promise to turn over the royal treasure they guarded in the *alcázar* of Segovia. They complied, but only after finally being given custody of the child princess, Isabel.

Isabel proposed to visit Carrillo, who was thought to be sulking in Alcalá, hurt particularly by her lack of gratitude. Accordingly, she wrote to him on May 10 that the queen of Castile would much appreciate the pleasure of dining in the archbishop's company. He responded, irony palpable in his mimicking of the royal tone, that should the queen enter Alcalá by one gate the archbishop would leave by another. It had become a hopeless clash of imperious temperaments. Thoroughly convinced of his defection, she hastened to the core of his archbishopric, Toledo, and arriving on May 20 to a reassuringly hearty welcome, she made certain of the loyalty of its key administrators. But the strain told, and on May 31, en route to Avila, she miscarried; the stillborn child was male.[38]

She remained in Avila for several weeks, recuperating. Too, Àvila possessed a mint and it was her town. Then she sent word to Fernando, who was in Burgos, thinking Afonso would attack there in an attempt to open the road to France and so to link up with Louis XI. She would, she said, come confer with him if he thought it essential. On June 12 he responded: "To me it seems that it is very necessary and that Your Ladyship ought to come, because in getting together we help each other more than anything in life, and now is the time that all our power should be jointly exerted."[39] They got together, in Valladolid, on June 25. Three days later, Isabel skirted the enemy rearguard to reinforce Madrigal and then rode on the same mission to Medina del Campo. By July 9 she was again in Tordesillas.

Adversaries

Afonso was in Arévalo; he had arrived with his fiancée on the first of June. When the news came that Enrique IV's widow, Juana, had died in Madrid on

June 13, it evoked no show of mourning from her brother or her daughter or anyone else; indeed, it was widely rumored that Afonso, embarrassed by her defying of convention, had had her given poison, *hierbas*. Afonso, says Palencia, was certain that he would meet no resistance on the Castilian *meseta*, that Fernando had lost the opportunity to ready for combat by frittering time away in vain distractions. Moreover, while Burgos had proclaimed for Isabel, Stúñiga's son Juan held the fortress towering over it, his huge lombards firing at will into the city. As for Isabel and Fernando, they now had the treasury of Segovia. Isabel, in Tordesillas, awaited the results of having sent the admiral to rally the nobles and their men, and of having called on the towns to confront the traditional enemy for the common good and the glory of Castile.

By July 12, most of the great lords bound by oath to the crown had brought their squadrons into the royal encampment outside Tordesillas—Palencia says afraid not to and although having accepted much money from Portugal—because the cause was so popular. Preachers had inspired large numbers of volunteers and the general pardon brought in others. From the mountains of Asturias, and from Vizcaya, famed for its archers, came over twenty thousand men, the bulk of the infantry. Beatriz de Bobadilla arrived from Segovia with one hundred lances and one thousand foot.[40] Even so, that army was ill-trained and it was ill-coordinated, each lord independently commanding his own men. And numbers proved a mixed blessing, for so great was the host that expenses quickly outran resources. Isabel arranged for the Segovia treasure to be coined, but it could not be done rapidly enough, so that men had to be paid with small bits of silver cups, or so says Palencia.[41]

It was a blow when the news came that the Portuguese had left Arévalo where food had become scarce for strategically vital Toro. The town, although considered impregnable atop an escarpment, had been turned over to Afonso by its *corregidor*, Juan de Ulloa; and the Portuguese were besieging Toro's fortress, held by Aldonza de Castilla, the wife of its *alcaide*, the *contador* Rodrigo de Ulloa, who, although he was the traitor's brother, rode with Fernando. In council *los reyes* resolved that Fernando should lead their armies to the relief of Toro's *alcázar*, and they hoped to bring the Portuguese king to a decisive battle.

Yet they delayed, awaiting with some anxiety Benavente and the Mendozas under Santillana and Beltrán de la Cueva with their large complements of heavy cavalry. They were not yet certain of the loyalty of those *grandes*, who possessed much of the former domain claimed by Juan of Aragón and his family. During that wait and preparing for battle, Fernando made a will; its provisions open a window on his sentiments and policies. In them, he affirms Isabel's sole right to the crown of Castile. He commends to her together with his father the raising of his natural children, Alfonso and Juana, as well as the care of their mothers. He calls upon, as his special patrons, the Virgin Mary and St. John the Baptist, and he makes the sort of charitable bequests customarily associated with saving one's soul: he designates five hundred thousand *maravedís* for redemption of Christians held captive by Muslims and an equal sum to dower poor orphaned girls for marriage or nunnery. And he states that he must be buried wherever Isabel chooses for her own tomb: "I very much desire that as we were united by marriage and singular love in life, that we may not be parted in death."[42] His daughter Isabel is to be his successor in Aragón and Sicily, notwithstanding any impediment in Aragonese law; he requests his father arrange matters. He designates her his heir, he states, not through ambition, but because he loves her as much as could possibly be, "especially for being the daughter of so excellent a queen and mother"; and because he foresees the great good, "the public good," that will result through the unity of Aragón with Castile and León. To draw up that document he chose a Hieronymite, Hernando de Talavera, despite that friar having recently scolded him for falling short of "the perfection and excellence obligatory for a prince."[43]

On July 15, Santillana arrived with three of his brothers, Beltrán, and their *mesnadas.* Fernando set out for Toro the next day, although he and Isabel were still uneasy about Benavente who, if he chose, could tilt the balance of power toward Portugal. With the king went a large army, an estimated two thousand heavy cavalry, six thousand light horsemen, *jinetes,* and twenty thousand foot. The night before he had written Isabel a note; she was in the palace, he in camp across the Duero River. "God knows it weighs on me that I will not see Your Ladyship tomorrow, for I swear by your life and mine that never have I so loved you."[44]

He was wrong about one thing. For that morning Isabel appeared in camp, spoke in council, and went among the men as they readied, "with heartening words and cheerful face." Then from atop a hill she watched them move off: the great lords on horseback at the head of their hundreds-strong squadrons of cavalry and infantry; Pedro de Manrique, count of Treviño, leading thousands of Asturian foot and Biscayan archers; then the recruits come in from the cities; and she recognized her own guards, bearing her banner embroidered with bundled arrows. She distinguished the great lords in brilliant brocades and velvets, their gold and silver ornaments gleaming. Watching those thousands wend their way alongside the Duero River and disappear over the horizon, "the Queen saw herself *señora* of this powerful fighting force." She had been dissuaded only through much effort on the part of the king and the magnates from riding with them.[45]

Next day, Isabel received worrying word that Zamora, key to provisioning the army at Toro, had defected. Then, shortly thereafter, Benavente at last arrived, magnificently accoutered, on a mount equally resplendent in armor of silver platelets, and bringing eighteen hundred lances, largely light cavalry. Isabel hid her unhappiness at Zamora's loss, greeted him warmly, and flattered him extravagantly. He was so welcome, so great a lord, so young yet so renowned for bravery and virtue; he was grand even among the *grandes,* and highly important to the service of God and the good of the kingdom. And she confided to him how great was her own suffering and shame at the Portuguese presence in Castile and entreated him to lift her grief—"waiting every hour to be avenged"—and to go where his valorous heart might have a chance to outdo itself. She then made him munificent *mercedes* for the numerous excellent people he had brought to serve her, and, within the hour, he found himself again in the saddle at the head of his *mesnada,* on the way to report to Fernando.[46]

Toro was a disaster. Afonso would not come out to fight. Fernando sent Gómez Manrique, twice, to remind the Portuguese king that he had declared he would engage in personal combat. On the second try, Afonso accepted the challenge, on condition that the *grandes* hold Juana and Isabel as hostages during the contest. Manrique refused, stating that the two women were not of equal stature nor legitimacy, and that Isabel possessed realms and a superior army.

That army, however, proved overlarge and unruly; funds and provisions ran out, and success was out of reach with loss of Zamora; there was, too, suspicion that the nobles were reluctant to have Fernando emerge as the hero of that contest. Accordingly, on July 23, the king and his council lifted the siege, although not before Fernando had formally elevated the head of the Mendoza clan, Diego Hurtado de Mendoza, the second marqués de Santillana, to duke of Infantado. The retreat was disorderly; the troops drifted away. Isabel, riding out from Tordesillas, encountered an army greatly diminished and in disarray, one far different from the proud host of two weeks before. She accosted its captains, as the anonymous chronicler tells it, insisting they return at once to Toro, to no avail; then in Tordesillas, all through that night she furiously berated the *grandes* for serving her badly, "and she spoke to the King with audacity, her words fitting her state of mind; and that night no council met because of the anger of the Queen."[47] And when it did convene next day, she was there to address it.

A Debate

"Her womanly nature did not allow her to hide her anguish" at the army returning without glory writes Palencia, with most uncharacteristic restraint.[48] For that morning at Tordesillas, the twenty-four-year-old queen delivered an impassioned harangue. And if an anonymous chronicler took license in setting it down verbatim, the gist appears to accord with what else is known of that event and its participants. Although, Isabel began, it may be that women lack discretion to know and strength to dare, and even language to speak—thus did she perfunctorily dispense with rhetorical protestations of modesty—yet she had found that they have eyes to see. Certainly, she had seen a great host depart from Tordesillas. And what greater honor, what greater benefit, what greater service to God could there be than joining battle? "If you say to me that women, since they do not face such dangers, ought not speak of them . . . to this I say that I do not know who ventures more than I do, for I risked my King and lord, whom I love above all else in the world, and I risked so many and such noble *caballeros,* and so many men and riches that, they lost, what more could I have to lose?"[49] Woman she may be, but she was also Castile's queen, delivering to her subjects, as she thought, a deserved tongue-lashing.

"I would wish," she continued at full tilt, "to pursue uncertain danger rather than certain shame. . . . There must first be a battle in order to have a victory." Never would Hannibal, the famed general, have crossed the frozen Alps nor won the great battle of Cannae if his heart had deferred to the weak advice of his brain. Some see as best the rules of philosophy and others those of the sword, she admonished them, but in the highest affairs it is impossible to have compass or measure, but only to take risks boldly and let God guide as he will. War wants more advice from audacity and less from *letrados,* "so that we may commit ourselves to doing things that afterward the brain may marvel at in contemplating"; and it may still find impossible after the deed that which, if judged rationally beforehand, we would never have dared to do. "For that which seems most difficult the hands and heart may accomplish, and especially kings and their people in defending their land."

As an example to those knights, she held out her own anguished introspection:

I find myself in my palace, with angry heart, gnashing my teeth and clenching my fists, as if, seeking revenge, I am fighting with myself, and if, *caballeros,* you took unto yourselves such anxiety, the greatest danger from your enemies would be less than that from yourselves. Of my fury, being a woman, and of your patience, being men, I marvel. And excellent King, My Lord, and virtuous knights: if I have extended my words more than I reasonably ought, may your virtue pardon such an error, for with daring to complain I have quieted the passion that naturally grows in the hearts of women.

If the chronicler is to be believed, and even allowing for rhetorical convention, that morning in Tordesillas her impetuosity and emotion overstepped the propriety usually ascribed to her. Yet this was not the first nor the last time she voiced impassioned sentiments, a strong will, even wilfulness, a call for vengeance, a certainty regarding right and wrong, or a plumbing of her own conscience to ascertain divine intent.

Following much discussion among those assembled about who should reply to the queen, all agreed it must be the king, as most credible since best informed about why they had retreated from Toro. So Fernando is said to have responded, and with equal conviction: "*La gracia* with which, *Señora,* you complain to us and the sweetness of how you say it, may make the very just feel very guilty, and though we were right in the doing we may lack in the telling. If you have been maliciously informed, hear the truth, and then we want you to judge." The adversary, he explained, had equal numbers of men and sat atop a high palisade, its sheer sides impossible to scale; the enemy had artillery to defend that fortress and hoists and blankets and provisions that her army did not have. Those who have to gain honor, said Fernando, have to undertake things in which they are equal to their opponents, and although they may see some disadvantage, "it can not be so great as to be so hopeless that God may have to open the sea to the width of twelve carts in order to save them." Strength and time gain victory, he told her, madness hinders it. As Hannibal had crossed the Alps, so he himself would cross mountains although even more frozen, if Hannibal's enemy, snow, was the only danger. And as Hannibal won the battle of Cannae, so he would win, or at least fight, if his adversary would come out into the field. Now he urged:

Señora, give repose to the anxieties of your heart, for in the days to come we will bring you such victories, that even if they were to defeat us this time, with a thousand won you will pardon this one. . . . I had believed that returning in despair I would hear from your tongue words of consolation and encouragement. . . . Women are always malcontent; and you especially, *Señora,* by being who you are could content us. It is the accusation in the recesses of your will that makes you feel shame; but I and these *caballeros* are well satisfied in our own wills, and no blame hidden in our souls cries out, nor are we shamefaced. No one is as obliged to content women or to benefit the world as to look to his own honor.

The time was past, he went on, when a battle might be won by walls falling to Earth, as they did for Joshua at Jericho, after he said prayers and took seven turns around a besieged town and the sun had turned back twenty-four hours; rather, "today one conquers with strength, diligence, and men. . . . In equal affairs we ask God's help, but without expecting a return to the marvels of the Old Testament." She must not think that with many men one performs great deeds, but with few, acting in concert. "Prudence is the God of the battles; and, above all let us trust ourselves to that high Judge, without whom, as San Juan said, nothing is done. . . . And he in manner least expected will give us vengeance, as a just Judge. . . ." God was humbling them, Fernando concluded, but also charging them to persevere and to show piety.

In his emphasis on prudence, Fernando was his father's son. In his reliance on the God of Battles and on judgment from on high, he touched on traditional royal themes that he and Isabel had taken as their own. Vengeance too was important to them both. Yet his words conveyed a sentiment of incipient modernity: he expected no miracles. And it is noteworthy that it was in his mouth, not Isabel's, that the well-informed chronicler who wrote for his own contemporaries put expressions of piety. The time had not yet arrived to fashion Isabel as stolid and pious, nor Fernando as devious and Machiavellian. Rather, in the spring of 1475 the chronicler had described them with reason as lord and lady of chivalry, and their verbal interchange after Toro was also a variant on the genre of courtly love, wherein passion and reason are perpetually at war.

The worst was yet to come. In August Toro's fortress fell to Afonso, and Carrillo swore homage to him and Juana as king and queen of Castile. The archbishop declared he had raised Isabel from the distaff and he was going to send her back to it. Spirits lifted, however, when Enrique Enríquez, conde de Alba de Liste, who was Fernando's uncle, came riding from Andalusia with fresh and experienced troops. Isabel had sent emissaries to Seville in February to see to collection of its sizeable revenues and to extract funds from its wealthy, including resident Italian merchants, but nothing had as yet come. And, desperate for money, rather than take Juan of Aragón's advice to give *mercedes* on expected income, she instead followed the counsel of Cardinal Mendoza and her new confessor, Hernando de Talavera—Alfonso de Burgos having been elevated to bishop of Córdoba—in appropriating from the churches half of their silver and the revenues from lands donated to maintain them, and promising to repay everything within three years.[50] There was precedent: her father, or Luna, had done the same thing when preparing a campaign against Granada.

She had the silver minted into coins that affirmed and disseminated a dedication to a joint royal mission: the silver *reales* then coined at Toledo bore a crown under intertwined Fs and Ys and the legend: "The Lord is my help and I do not fear what men may do to me." Other coins depicted on one side Isabel and Fernando, wearing crowns, facing each other, and, on the other, the arms of Castile and León, Aragón, and Sicily under the outspread wings of the great eagle of John the Evangelist and bearing the legend: "Under the shade of your wings protect us, Lord."[51] Both mottos suited the metal's provenance at least as well as its purpose.

A war of royal titles ensued: Afonso styled himself ruler of Castile and León, Fernando and Isabel appropriated to themselves Portugal and the Algarves—including the African algarve, or littoral, of Tangiers and Arcila—places also claimed by earlier Spanish rulers, a claim they would not forget. At the same time, both sides further reinforced their *meseta* garrisons, and Burgos was now clearly seen by both as the key to victory.

Chapter 7
Resolutions: 1475–1477

See, Your Majesty, to what you are obliged, and why you were placed on the peak of honors and sublime dignities.
—Hernando de Talavera[1]

Lady, I swear to you by Jesus Christ . . . you cannot spur your horse in that posture, you must take one leg and put it over the saddle bow.
—William Marshal[2]

In August and September of 1475, Isabel reinforced garrisons important to the defense of Burgos while Fernando laid siege to its fortress. Afonso of Portugal left Toro on September 17, with Carrillo, Diego Pacheco, Stúñiga, and Rodrigo Girón, ostensibly for Burgos, only to hear on reaching Peñafiel that the road to the north was closed, that Isabel and the cardinal had got to Palencia ahead of them with reinforcements, blocking the way. Afonso returned to Toro, and in October moved to Zamora, to lay over for the winter.

Meeting in November in Dueñas, Isabel and Fernando determined to regain Zamora by burrowing from within, having heard that its inhabitants had rediscovered a love of country on rumor that Afonso would expel them all and resettle the town with Portuguese.[3] Then, while Fernando returned to Burgos, Isabel went to Valladolid, from where she dispatched troops to him, detailed others to end Portuguese depredations on the *meseta*, and yet others to Rodrigo Manrique who was attacking the strongholds of Pacheco and the Giróns in Extremadura.

So matters stood when Isabel sent word to Fernando that entry into Zamora had been arranged with partisans inside the town; he must come quickly and secretly to Valladolid. He did, leaving in command in Burgos his half-brother, Alfonso de Aragón, an illegitimate son of Juan's. That expert in siege warfare had recently arrived in Burgos, looked over the work that had been done there, declared that while the double moats and stockades passed muster, the mines were inefficiently laid and the lombards so placed that the shot could not hit the fortress walls, and now had his engineers hard at work.[4]

In Valladolid, Isabel and Fernando conferred for three days, then, Fernando, gathering men—Isabel having instructed authorities in Salamanca, Medina, Segovia, and Avila to send troops at once—left for Zamora, to learn en route that the town had declared for them and the Portuguese had departed for Toro, although leaving a garrison. From early December to March, Fernando lay siege to Zamora's fortress. He was supplied by the people of the town and the surrounding countryside—provisions they had denied to Portugal, including "all the grain in their silos, and they sold it very cheaply."

Isabel traveled north, informed that, Alfonso de Aragón having systematically destroyed the walls of Burgos, the *alcaide* of its castle had on December 2 agreed to surrender within seventy days, the waiting period decreed by chivalric courtesy. Accompanied by the cardinal, she entered the city in a heavy snowstorm but to a warm reception: a great crowd cheering, children dancing and singing. The *alcaide,* young Stúñiga, surrendered to her early, on January 19; she commended his valor before dismissing him from command. In the doing, she also won over his powerful father, who, impressed at her magnanimity and disenchanted with Afonso, announced his own neutrality and opened negotiations with Isabel.

Sermon for a Queen

For Isabel, victory in Burgos marked the end of the first year of her reign, begun with audacity. It had been a year bringing war waged with determination, yet also a year of uncertainty and vulnerability, of the mental and physical toll attendant upon miscarrying a much-desired male heir, and of an awareness imposed of her own lack of experience. She was twenty-five years old. She had functioned as joint ruler and asserted her legal position as sole proprietor of Castile in the face of strong competing claims; and she could not be certain that young Juana was not Enrique's child and rightful heir. War persisted; and if it constituted a trial by combat there was as yet no certain indication from heaven of where the right lay. Moreover, at a time when exemplary models were adjudged all-important guides to conduct, where was a reigning queen to find inspiration? Injunction to demure femininity was no help. Surely she needed exemplars other than Joan of Arc, the peasant virgin of noble spirit who had led a French army; nor were women saints or the ladies of chivalry appropriate models for a reigning queen.

At the end of 1475, in an age when what one did and who one was were assumed synonymous, she sought to fortify her developing sense of what it was to be Castile's queen. She then requested of Hernando de Talavera, her confessor, a copy of a sermon he had delivered to his Hieronymite brothers, a sermon on how all loyal Christians should renew their spirits during Advent (the fourth Sunday before Christmas). Talavera quickly complied, with a version especially adapted for her. What she received was both a devotional tract and a guide for a princess; it was at once spiritual and political, blending piety and power. Whatever its original form, Talavera had turned an exhortation to spiritual renewal into a pep talk for a reigning monarch, a mirror specifically for a queen.

Its point of view, and its author, would have lifelong influence upon her. Talavera, his father unknown, his mother a *conversa*, had shown sufficient ability to gain a chair of moral philosophy at Salamanca and to come to the attention of the cardinal. Talavera had drawn Fernando's will and he had shown financial acumen in suggesting expropriating church silver; now he sat in the Royal Council and was increasingly looked to by Isabel for mundane as well as spiritual advice. As a Hieronymite, he belonged to a religious order inaugurated in Castile by earlier royal ministers who had forsaken the world. Hieronymite rule and name were indebted to the church father and saint, Jerome, who was renowned for being both mystical and practical, a hard worker and a striver for personal perfection, who valued asceticism and direct communication with God, and who preached a modulated apocalypticism. Jerome has been portrayed as both penitent and scholar; often beside him is the lion from whose paw he had removed a thorn. Neither he nor his followers in Spain ever resolved the tension between the pull of a life of apostolic rusticity and one of learned piety; the latter, however, had gained an edge during the fifteenth century. Talavera was also a nephew of another Hieronymite, the learned Alonso de Oropesa, whose advice had been sought by both Juan II of Castile and his son Enrique IV; and he too was a protégé of Cardinal Mendoza.

In January of 1476 Talavera offered Isabel a vision of herself and her role within the divine scheme. In accord with traditions of Spanish kingship and advice to princes, it bound royal power to royal virtue, urged she seek moral perfection, and employed some time-honored exemplars culled from the Bible, the church fathers, Castilian law, and history. It reflected too what has been called 'the moral zoo,' the medieval custom of ascribing laudable qualities to beasts and birds. Isabel, that is, received an updated version of a body of intertwined religious and political principles long associated with and enjoined upon Castile's rulers. Yet, unlike her immediate predecessors, the monarch receiving such advice was young, female, and, judged by her subsequent career, highly receptive. And certainly the tract contained counsel congenial to her own cast of mind as she had revealed it to date: thus Talavera urged she strive for perfection of character and he assumed that "it is a calling to aspire to perfection of your estate. If you are queen, you ought to be an inspiration to your subjects in serving God."[5]

Isabel had shown on more than one occasion that she set for herself very exacting standards and that she subscribed to the principle that the best guide

is one's conscience, that virtuous rulers are guided by the will of God and discern it through heeding their own conscience or heart. Pulgar attributes to her
in those days a prayer to that effect, as well as one indicating the great responsibility she felt, and also a lingering doubt as to the justice of her accession:

You, Lord, who know the secret of every heart, you know of me that not by unjust
means, not with cunning, nor tyranny, but believing truly [I claim] that these kingdoms of the King my father by right belong to me. I have sought to have them in order
that that which the kings my forebears won with so much bloodshed may not pass to
a foreign lineage. And you, Lord, in whose hands is the right of kingdoms, through the
disposition of your Providence have put me in this royal state in which I am today, I
supplicate humbly, Lord, that you hear now the prayer of your servant, and show the
truth, and manifest your will with your marvelous works. If I do not have justice, may
there be no room for me to sin through ignorance, and if I do have justice, may you
give me intelligence and strength so that with the help of your arm, I can pursue and
achieve my charge, and bring peace in these kingdoms, which have suffered so many
evils and such destruction for this reason.[6]

Talavera therefore appears on firm ground in beginning by addressing her
as a wise monarch who was seeking divine guidance in ruling and its analogue,
meting out justice. And he both flattered her and showed his awareness that
she aspired to a clear and discerning conscience in his remarking that,
although ordinarily what is addressed to clergy for their edification is not what
secular people ought to hear, yet "I, who know the excellence of your enlightened intellect and the perfection of your devotion and disciplined will *(orde-
nado desseo)*, find no difficulty in communicating it to your Royal Majesty."
For her request, he went on, was surely inspired by some ray of divine light
which, though it may touch all people, especially touches and illuminates the
royal heart. He recalled those biblical kings—David, and above all the wise
Solomon who sought an educated heart with which to judge his people. And
he addressed to her what Christ had said to his disciples: "that to you is given
to know the mysteries of the kingdom of God."

Although elsewhere Talavera spoke of women disapprovingly, as weak
and too greedy for knowledge they should not have, the queen was clearly a
special case, a woman but, more importantly, a monarch who must be strong
and have knowledge. His attitude toward women was not far from that of
Jerome himself, who, while speaking of women in general as weak and inferior, yet admired certain individuals to whom he dedicated works; on occasion
too Jerome remarked that women had the knowledge and intelligence he
sought in men, and that God valued not gender but heart.[7] Talavera coupled
his admiration of Isabel with an extremely elevated concept of monarchy, akin
to that in the *Partidas* of Alfonso X; Talavera too assumed the ruler to be mod-
eled upon, and in direct contact with, the sovereign of heaven.

He discerned the natural embodiment of laudable royal qualities in that most imposing of birds, the eagle, which he referred to throughout as female. His inspiration, he told Isabel, was a copy of a medieval bestiary she herself had given him. Nor was it a coincidence that the eagle was the symbol of John the Evangelist, whom she had taken as her patron saint. Thus Talavera, addressing Isabel, announced his theme: "how we seek renewal in this holy time in the manner of the eagle, and of the conditions and properties which morally conform to that manner. For as [the eagle] may be queen of the birds, to whom Saint John the Evangelist, because of the height of his elevated evangel and his other lofty revelations, worthily is compared . . . it is worthwhile that Your Highness know these same conditions and properties and the significance and application of them. . . ." He ended that prologue by reminding her that Advent was a holy time of renovation and soul-searching, a time for reading "the holy evangel that mentions the universal justice that we await, in which all the world will be renewed . . ." and we believe that time to be "nearer rather than far off." In effect, Talavera coupled spiritual meditation with eschatological expectation, and he related both to the royal role, which was Isabel's.

The eagle was commonly believed emblematic of Christ and the sun. It was thought to symbolize resurrection, salvation, renewal; and in medieval Europe it stood as an allegory for, among other things, legality of royal descent, rejection of intruders into lawful succession, and even "the undiminished vitality of the [human] race."[8] Moreover Talavera, in noting elsewhere her desire to read spiritual things that would enlighten her and inform her will and her decrees, commended Isabel as the daughter of an excellent father who spent more time in reading than in any other pastime. That reference went beyond compliment to allude to her legitimacy and to rehabilitate, even find exemplary, someone so crucial to her yet generally dismissed as an ineffectual king. Henceforth, she might with good conscience associate the attributes of San Juan and his eagle with her father, Juan II of Castile, that saint's namesake, whose heir she could now more proudly claim to be.

Isabel, in thus rehabilitating the memory and reputation of her father and able to see herself as his direct heir and cut in the same princely mold, could bypass the reign of her half-brother, Enrique, and so lessen the need to be concerned about Enrique's purported daughter. Moreover, the idealization of Juan II of Castile was especially politic in view of the ongoing presence of Fernando's dynamic father of the same name and number who had a claim of his own to succession in Castile. Her growing sense of identification with a father who gave her the legitimacy of succession that Enrique's sometime oath could never do of itself was also reflected in Fernando's having written to her that past June from Burgos that he had made a point of visiting her father's tomb at Miraflores, outside the city, and that he had "kissed his hands" for her.[9]

Talavera developed the relationship between the the eagle and kings through an extended metaphor that elaborated on the fusion of religion with political authority. The eagle nests on the highest cliffs. Christ is a high and firm mountain top and from him all the faithful receive virtue as members of the body receive it from the head. Another very high peak is the Holy Virgin, our lady, Mary, and others are the saints, although less high. Lofty too are the kings and princes, dukes and marqueses. He listed as exemplars the patriarchs—Noah, Abraham, Isaac, Job, Moses—whom he called princes and dukes, and then the kings—Saul, David, and Solomon, who was magnificent in wanting to build a temple to the honor of God. Kings, Talavera mentioned, should love reading and books and they should be surrounded by good counselors, for—and here he made explicit the link between faith and power—"the lord of all will prove to be he who is the true servant of piety." Isabel would concur with that sentiment. She had begun to court, and to gain, a reputation for piety; and she was even then making plans that would demonstrate that she too interpreted temple building as a way of displaying both her power and her religious devotion.

Kings, Talavera continued, clearly placing her within their company, "are viceroys of the King of Kings delegated to rule and govern realms and peoples and to command [their subjects] so that they will know and serve God," and kings should always think more than other men of how to do his will. God commands them to keep the Bible, the book of holy law, at their right hand and each day to study and read it and to consider their great responsibility. And, like the eagle, they should show their young how to fly. "For you, excellent Queen" he explained, "of so many and such great kingdoms by vicarate of God placed as one with the most serene King, your equally worthy husband," there was reason to know those properties of the eagle.

He then discussed the qualities that good princes and kings, prelates and governors must have, through a string of authoritative references—to Old Testament kings, Aristotle, Augustine, and Jerome, and to Spanish legal and political theory as well. Liberality, he said, was the fundamental royal quality, but was to be combined with powerful and sharp sight, for kings must always be watchful; the other essential qualities were charity, constancy, and firmness—because princes must have the love of their subjects, "not as lords to servants through self-interest, but as parents to children for their own good." Rulers had to be consistent and firm in the execution of justice and conservation of the laws. They should be courageous and healthy, never idle nor indulge in frivolity or gaming—a proclivity of Fernando's—and queens, he emphasized, should always be well occupied. Those very qualities he prescribed for good rulers others would come to cite in describing Isabel, with the possible exception of liberality.

Talavera next considered exemplary queens, princesses, and ladies, now adding some ideal feminine qualities to those associated with kingship. Isabel ought to raise her children in good works and noble customs, and be conversant with certain women praised in the Scriptures. Talavera cited the chastity of Sarah, revered by her husband Abraham, "the father of our faith," the modesty and diligence of Rebecca, Leah's hard work, Rachel's devotion and contemplation, the discretion and judgment of Deborah, and so on. Above them all he placed the virtues of "the Queen of Queens and Lady of the Angels, the glorious Virgin, our advocate and lady, Mary," citing her perfect humility and compassion, and admonished Isabel to avoid "the laziness, chatter and frivolous life of our mother Eve." It was one of the few instances where his advice coincided with that which Isabel had received in the *Garden of Noble Maidens*.

Then Talavera returned to the eagle, among whose admirable qualities he discerned love of God and "concern for our salvation and that of those near to us." Teach eaglets to fly, he enjoined Isabel, as our Lord did the Jewish people when he took them from Egypt. Isabel, that is, he charged with developing strong character, behaving and governing in accord with the highest of standards, and having the triple task of emulating patriarch kings, Mary, the queen of heaven, and the good women of the Scriptures. And he ended by exhorting her to

Rise, rise in the air and contemplate the crown of glory . . . for through these works and considerations you will achieve like the eagle the strength and vigor of your youth. . . . Renew through God your noble spirit and gain perfection, for you have the estate . . . of mistress and lady so perfect and so full of all virtue and goodness as has the eagle among birds, in which perfection all kingdoms and domains, and principally all those of yours, have to participate, as do the other birds of her flock. See Your Majesty to what you are obliged, and why you were placed on the peak of honors and sublime dignities.

It was, at a critical juncture in her life, if ostensibly a spiritual tract, nonetheless an exhortation to ascend to the heights of sovereignty and authority on Earth, to exercise absolute rule as divine designate, and it was an exhortation at once impassioned and authoritative enough to demolish any lingering doubts she might have regarding her calling. It was an astute interweaving of religion and statecraft, an injunction to an indisputable queen to soar free, and, through aspiring to it, do heaven's will. Moreover, Isabel, who—as comes through the reconstruction of her tirade on retreat from Toro—had been at pains to bridge the chasm between the demonstrated certainty demanded of a monarch and the conventions of femininity, even noble femininity, here found them reconciled. Subsequently, her reign bore out just how congenial she found this advice; and she kept its profferer close to her through the years, not only as confessor but as one of her two most trusted counselors in affairs of state, relying on him in matters of policy as well as in delicate and detailed financial and diplomatic matters. Talavera presented Isabel with other written advice as well; he drew up a detailed schedule for most efficiently organizing her time in attending to the business of state, which by all accounts she followed closely, to gain a reputation for "prodigious regularity."[10] In accord with his counsel too she was well read. She also continued to rely on him to make clear to her the path to the personal rectitude that both of them considered inseparable from just rule and so, concomitantly, the path to power, fame, and glory for herself and the nation. The consequences for Spain would be many.

In those initial years of her reign, she received advice from other courtiers as well, who also tended to praise her qualities and to look forward to her reign bringing the internal peace and order so desired after years of strife. So Gómez Manrique told her that while prayer was well and good, it was firm rule and stern justice that were now essential.

Peleagonzalo, March 1476

The war, however, had yet to be won and the Portuguese driven out. Indications were promising. With the securing of Burgos, Afonso was fast losing his Spanish allies. Rodrigo Girón sought reconciliation and Pacheco entered into talks with the cardinal. Alvaro de Stúñiga's formidable wife, Leonor Pimentel, sent envoys to begin negotiations, as did most of the late Juan Pacheco's large brood. Only his bastard daughter, Beatriz, countess of Medellín, remained resolutely hostile; she was a force in the war that wore on in Extremadura and Andalusia, fueled by factional strife. But in Castile matters were coming to a head.

Isabel, expecting a new Portuguese offensive in the spring, and perhaps a clash with the French as well, reinforced Burgos immediately after its surrender and sent Alfonso de Aragón to clean out neighboring pockets of resistance—castles held by marauding lords, robber barons. She then took her court to Tordesillas and, on February 9, she sent on the cardinal, Alba, the admiral, and Alba de Liste with their men to Fernando at Zamora. For word had come that Afonso's heir, Prince João —although the Portuguese treasury was exhausted and the gold supply from Africa disrupted now that Castilian ships patrolled the sea-lanes—had raised sufficient funds for twenty-five hundred light cavalry and fifteen thousand foot and had brought those reinforcements to Afonso.[11] The reinvigorated Portuguese first marched on Madrigal, to be surprised by a rain of arrows from the garrison Isabel had reinforced, then proceeded to Medina del Campo, only to encounter Alfonso de Aragón, who came out against them with seven hundred lances, his trained eye leading him "to have more confidence in the troops than in the walls." After a skirmish or two, the Portuguese moved on, to make camp across the Duero River from Zamora. Fernando was encamped on the other side of that river, just outside the walls, thus situated uncomfortably between its hostile fortress garrison and Afonso's army.[12] Yet Afonso, low on funds and with the people of the region withholding provisions, was losing men to desertion and dismissing most of his foot soldiers, while cities and towns from Aragón to New Castile were sending cavalry to Isabel and Fernando. The Portuguese king offered Isabel peace in exchange for Galicia, Toro, Zamora, and money. She replied that, while she would be willing to discuss a cash settlement, she would not part with one bit of Castile's territory.

On March 1 Afonso raised camp, before dawn, and before the day was out the only pitched battle of the war was fought, the last major contest in Castile to be decided by light cavalry and the individual valor of nobles and kings. Late that afternoon, overtaken by Fernando's forces at a place known as Peleagonzalo outside Toro, Afonso drew up his squadrons in battle formation. Although the Portuguese were superior in numbers, and although the Castilians were tired and strung out along the route, their artillery absent and the hour late, Fernando, as he afterward told it, chose to join battle, for he was confident in the right "that I and the most serene Queen, my beloved wife, have to these realms, and in the mercy of Our Lord and of his blessed mother, and in the help of the apostle Saint James—Santiago—patron and *caudillo* of the Spains."[13]

Castilian pride and the habit of centuries did the rest, overcoming the calculated reticence of some of the nobles, but only some. Nonetheless, the cardinal in full armor, stung by Portuguese taunts and mindful of the death on a Portuguese battlefield of the great-uncle whose name he bore, raised the battle cry. The Castilians attacked furiously. Pedro González de Mendoza led his cavalry at a gallop against the foe and fought on undeterred, even after his coat of mail was pierced by a barbed spearhead. Rain and darkness ended the contest three hours later, without a clear-cut victory but leaving Castile in control of the field. Yet, with nightfall, the Castilian soldiers hunted spoils, not the enemy, and the remains of Afonso's army reached Toro over the old Roman bridge. Afonso was thought dead, until the next day, when he was found to have fled to the safety of the nearby castle of Castronuño, having left command of the army to Prince João. Fernando later remarked to Isabel that "if it had not been for the chick, the old cock would have been caught." No matter, Castilians afterward referred to that battle near Toro as divine retribution for defeat suffered in their last contest with the Portuguese, at Aljubarrota in 1385, and as a sign of heaven's favor returned to their land.

Isabel, at Tordesillas, received the news from Fernando, who sent it off even before he regrouped the pillagers. She had had no word since the battle had begun and, as Palencia puts it, "to describe the joy of the Queen would be impossible."[14] She ordered bulls run, celebrations held, and, in the cold and damp of a March day, she went barefoot to give thanks for so marvelous a victory before the altar of the two Saints John in the convent of the Clares. The triumphant Te Deum rose up. Beyond retribution for Aljubarrota, she had received the awaited sign. As she is reported to have exclaimed, "Oh triumph so marvelous where God, who is the true judge, gave his sentence and declared the truth by way of arms!"[15] To Isabel's mind, Heaven had confirmed through trial by combat that hers was the just cause; she the true queen of Castile.

The fortress of Zamora capitulated within weeks; at Toro, although Juan de Ulloa had died, his widow, María de Sarmiento, in control of the town and the fortress, continued to hold it for Afonso, but hers was an isolated case. For the center of the contest then shifted to Extremadura and Andalusia, where support for one side or the other was linked to local struggles among urban factions leagued with one or another great lord, and where the most bitter contests of all were those for the masterships of the military orders.

Cortes at Madrigal

In mid-April of 1476, the monarchs convened the Cortes at last, significantly in the town of Isabel's birth, Madrigal. At the outset, the assembled representatives of the by-then-customary sixteen or seventeen royal towns were instructed "to consider what things comply with the reform of Justice and the good government of our kingdoms," and procedure was stipulated:

They shall give us their petitions so that, providing we see they comply with God's service and our own and the common good of our kingdoms, then we, in accord with Cardinal Mendoza, our very dear and very loved cousin, and with the Duke of Infantado, our uncle, and with the Duke of Alba, our cousin, and with Alfonso Enríquez our uncle and cousin and our Admiral, and with the Count of Benavente and the Bishops of Avila and Segovia, and the other viscounts and knights, *ricos hombres*—men of substance—and the *letrados* of our council, will respond to each petition and will decree as law."[16]

She and Fernando spoke as one at Madrigal, as a single sovereign entity, employing such phrases as "my royal crown" and "my patrimony." The petitions they received even when echoing grievances directed to Enrique in 1465 were a great deal more respectful, and unquestioned there was their right to reign and that of their daughter, Isabel, to succeed them. Conversely, royal statements were couched in terms reminiscent of the most absolutist claims put forth under Juan II. Thus, the invocation stated that as God made kings his vicars on Earth, he gave them greater power than others; and, as the *Siete Partidas* stated, they were obligated to repay in administration of justice, because for this was the power bestowed upon them, for this God made kings and for it they reigned. "For this we were given don Fernando and doña Isabel." In such statements the absolutist *Partidas,* heretofore supplementary law and royal wish, were being taken at face value, as law of the land.

Reiterated from Enrique's reign were complaints of the rising power of nobles and clergy, and of the attendant great diminution of the royal patrimony, particularly the alienation of royal towns and villages. It was asserted that the royal right to make knights was being usurped, that ecclesiastical judges were infringing upon royal justice, and that there was monetary chaos: silversmiths defrauded on weight, precious metals continued to flow out of the kingdom, the currency was unfathomable, and Enrique had left accounts in a mess. To all of those issues, the royal response was an expectation to provide remedy in more peaceful times. The monarchs also promised to examine royal finances, issued regulations for collecting revenues, and acceded to a request that judicial officials for court and chancery be well paid.

A sign of things to come, they agreed to revoke the law that forbade jailing Jews and Muslims for monies they owed to Christians, and they agreed that Jews and Muslims must wear insignia and not have communal officials, *alcaides,* of their own. The delegates further requested that Jews not exercise jurisdiction in their own communities: "well you know, your highness, that following divine law, by the coming of the Holy of Holies [the Messiah] the authority and jurisdictions of the Jews cease."[17] Their grievances delivered, the delegates voted a hefty subsidy.

The most vigorous royal action taken at Madrigal had to do with instituting an overall national *Hermandad* encompassing all existing local militias, the vigilante brotherhoods. It had been a principal reason, together with the oath to Princess Isabel and the need for a subsidy, for having convoked the Cortes. The deputies dutifully suggested that the time-honored remedy "to bring security to travel and trade, most certain and without cost to you, would be to make *hermandades* in all your kingdoms," in each city and village, and that royal ordinances should establish that all the cities league "one with another, and others with others, and all together, some with others." A national organization would help to discourage some *hermandades* themselves from lawlessness or joining rebels. It was a bit after the fact: the minutes of the Burgos city council include a message from the crown of March 30 announcing that a nation-wide council of *hermandades* was even then being set up.[18]

In late 1475, Quintanilla, sent out to pave the way for such a national league, had met with strong resistance. The great nobles objected to what they saw as interference in their jurisdictions and to being joined by *populares* and clergy in their traditional function of providing the monarch with men-at-arms. Unspoken was their dismay that through such an association the crown could directly control a powerful fighting force, expand its influence in municipalities, and open a broad avenue to royal taxation. Towns too resisted, often incited by nobles who dominated them, unhappy at the expense and at royal interference in what they considered their internal affairs. Yet Quintanilla had prepared the ground well enough that at Madrigal deputies made the well-orchestrated request.[19]

And the monarchs graciously complied. The ordinances for an overarching body, a *Santa Hermandad,* were attached to the proceedings of the Cortes at Madrigal. They stipulated that, much as previously, each municipality was to organize a highway patrol within its borders, with jurisdiction over a range of crimes; execution too was to be traditional, by bow and arrow. There is a traveler's description of seeing some *hermandad* archers execute a rebel: they put a target on his left breast, offered a prize of twenty-four *maravedís* for a bull's-eye and a fine of a *castellano* for missing, and only afterward did they hold a trial.[20] In 1476 it was decreed that every municipality was to have in place such a militia within thirty days, and each *hermandad* to keep on hand operating funds raised by taxes—thus Burgos had by June levied a tax on the entry of specific goods to support its brotherhood.

Deputies from the towns met with royal functionaries in May and June to work out *Hermandad* finances and set the numbers of armed men each municipality should send to their majesties. Provincial councils were held and, at the end of July, delegates from those councils arrived at a general assembly held at Dueñas, attended by the queen and king, many nobles, and the court in great state. Awe helped, but not enough. The deputies, hearing the extent of funds and men required, balked. Pulgar has Quintanilla make a day-saving speech, urging defense of the homeland against Portugal, reminding them of the ever-lurking Muslim threat, exhorting them to a campaign against evil, and declaring that the good are also punished when God punishes since they have permitted evils to endure unopposed. And he promised that the *Hermandad* would be temporary.[21]

The deputies came around. Earlier ordinances, envisioning an institution functioning from urban units up, were adjusted to guarantee control from the top down by the national brotherhood's general assembly, and of that body by royal authorities. And locally, *hermandad alcaides* (or *alcaldes*) received much greater jurisdiction, enabling them to override local justices.

Institutional mechanisms were in place; members were enrolled from central Castile and, over time, more municipalities were cajoled or coerced into joining what became a combination of national police force and rudimentary national army, its titular head that siege expert and tactician, Alfonso de Aragón, who was now the duke of Villahermosa. The *alcaides* of the local brotherhoods levied tariffs and fines, collected by taxfarmers overseen by Quintanilla; *Hermandad* receipts also maintained companies of cavalry organized as royal guards. All in all, its establishment proved to be among the foremost of royal measures obviating the calling of Cortes from 1480 to 1498; it

would make possible fielding an army against Granada, and the strategies leading to its introduction would serve as model for imposing other centrally
directed institutions.[22]

Alarums

One other matter of importance was placed before the Cortes of 1476: Isabel
and Fernando requested it ratify an agreement of marriage, of the Princess
Isabel to Ferrante, heir to Naples, whose king, Ferrante's grandfather, was Fernando's cousin. The match was designed to strengthen the coalition against
France, which had invaded Castile in February 1476, been repulsed, and was to
return twice more during the next four months. French hostility had much to
do with *los reyes*' desire to ally with Naples, an aggressively ascending Italian
power not only close to their Sicily but in the very good graces of the papacy,
and thus also crucial to Afonso of Portugal not getting papal dispensation to
marry Juana. At issue too was the trade and strategic control of the Mediterranean. And ever present was the threat of Mehmet, the Grand Turk, who, as
Palencia puts it, was "always interested in promoting discord among Christian
princes and favored by the avarice of the Roman pontiffs."[23] Too, Princess Isabel was six years old, and her parents well aware, especially in view of the
numerous arrangements made for themselves, that this might be only her first
engagement.

As the Cortes ended successfully, little joy was visible; rather, tension was
apparent between Isabel and Fernando. Throughout early May, Isabel seemed
out of sorts and Fernando repeatedly "went off to hunt with falcons."[24] Since
it was to be the only falling out recorded during their lifetimes, it is tempting
to hypothesize that it had to do with extramarital activity on Fernando's part
that would produce two daughters, and Isabel's discovering of it. Both daughters would be named María de Aragón and both would become nuns in Santa
María de Gracia, an Augustinian convent on the outskirts of Madrid, and be
told of their paternity only after Isabel's death.[25] Whatever the reason for that
rift, Fernando, who because of the exigencies of war had repeatedly put off
meeting with his father in the past few years, at the end of the month left to
do so.

He went by way of the northern coast in order to make certain arrangements. By cutting communications, Cantabrian ships had forced the French
to leave Castile and Louis XI to sign a three-month truce at the end of June.
Louis then commissioned a fleet, for France had long relied on Castilian seamen and ships; and Fernando ordered a squadron outfitted at Bilbao in expectation of its arrival. Then, on July 30, he went to Guernica where he took the
traditional royal oath to respect and defend the privileges of the Basque *viz-*

cainos, who had stayed clear of domination by any noble, and where he was then received as lord of Vizcaya under its great oak tree, the symbol of age-old Basque liberties. Those liberties notwithstanding, underlying all his activity in Vizcaya was implantation of royal authority.

It was mid-August before he and Juan met, in Vitoria, their first reunion since Fernando had become king of Castile. Juan insisted, despite his son's protests, on deferring to him as the more powerful king. Juan, who was then seventy-eight, was uneasy, for he feared that his son had come to dissuade him from his passion for one Roxa de Barcelona, who was rumored to have been introduced to him by enemies in order to wear him out. Instead, Juan received criticism on another count, and from Isabel. For at his old ally Carrillo's behest, Juan had ordered the Valencians besieging the town of Villena to change sides and to put themselves under Diego Pacheco, its marqués. Now Fernando gave his father a letter from Isabel conveying her unhappiness at his meddling in Castile's affairs. Juan was certain someone had put her up to it; his implication was that it had been Mendoza.[26]

The meeting at Vitoria, however, centered on larger issues of policy concerning France, Navarre, and relations between Aragón and Castile. Juan was brought around from what had been Aragonese priorities to giving thought to a joint, a Spanish, policy. Although he had vowed to fight France until Rosellón was restored to Aragón, Fernando convinced him to sign a truce with Louis of France and also to agree to a peace in the independent kingdom of Navarre, where a contest for political supremacy was being waged between two factions, one backed by Aragón, the other by Castile. Subsequently, Fernando and Isabel, through astute diplomacy, would make of that principality a Castilian protectorate.

Whatever their personal differences at the moment, Castile's monarchs were jointly realigning its international relations: while not fully abandoning the old policy of friendship with France they were moving closer to the dynasties surrounding it: York in England, Habsburg in Burgundy, and their Trastámara cousins in Italy, and they established connections in Brittany. In 1477 they would hold long secret talks with envoys of England and Burgundy on a combination of political and economic matters. In October 1478 they would arrange a treaty with France and arbitrate the Aragonese claim to Rosellón. International affairs would be of increasing importance, and both monarchs would evince great skill in diplomacy. Yet while Fernando concerned himself with the diplomacy of both Aragón and Castile, Isabel's activity was largely restricted to the interests of Castile where, in late 1476, foreign affairs were less pressing than were some internal considerations.

Within Castile after the battle of Toro, there were many changes of heart and those *grandes* who recanted backing Juana were well received by their queen. So old Alvaro de Stúñiga, as the first, was permitted to keep the bulk of his estates, including Arévalo. And, further evincing a policy of leniency, Isabel confirmed Rodrigo Girón as master of the military order of Calatrava; and when she compensated his hurt and angry rival, Alfonso de Aragón, by giving her blessing to his marriage to Leonor de Soto, a lady of hers of whom he was greatly enamored, it was at bottom a victory for Mendoza, who had advised winning over the powerful Girón and who did not want to see an Aragonese in so elevated a post. The cardinal, for his great service to date, among other *mercedes* then received legitimation of his three sons: the oldest, Rodrigo, was to be marqués de Cenete. As to Carrillo, a royal petition to the Roman curia to remove him from his archepiscopal office availed nothing, although the monarchs did relieve him of his numerous forts. Still, thereafter Isabel would make certain that the papacy paid her more heed.

In August, trouble came from another quarter. Isabel, governing Castile from Tordesillas, sped to Segovia to rescue her daughter. For Cabrera and Bobadilla had joined the queen but left the princess Isabel in Segovia's *alcázar,* in the keeping of its *alcaide,* who was Beatriz's father, and word came that the man he had displaced in that post, seeking revenge, had entered and seized the fortress but that the princess's guards were holding out in the castle keep. Isabel arrived at a gallop, with the Cabreras, the cardinal, Benavente, and a troop of cavalry, to learn that, upon hearing that the queen was on her way, the assailants had retreated. Even so, she found the city in an uproar and entry difficult. Its bishop, Juan Arias de Avila, exiled by Cabrera, had seized the opportunity to return and to exploit widespread grievances against the high-handed administration of the Cabreras and their clique, and the bishop's partisans, among them eminent *segovianos,* were holding a number of Segovia's gates. Arias's adherents appealed to the queen, condemning the Cabreras and requesting she not enter with them nor by the gates they held. Pulgar has her respond: "Say to those knights and citizens of Segovia that I am the Queen of Castile and this city is mine, left me by the King my father. . . . I shall enter by the gate I wish. . . . Say too that all may come to me and may do as I command them, as loyal subjects and that they must stop making riots and scandals in my city, causing harm to persons and property."[27]

Isabel then proceeded without incident into the *alcázar,* but a mob soon gathered outside demanding entry. Against everyone's advice, she had the gates thrown open, had heralds proclaim that the queen wished as many people to enter as the courtyard would hold, and then told the throng that surged in: "Now you, my vassals and subjects, are to say what you want, because what comes from you that is good and to my service it will please me to do for the common good of all the city." The crowd made clear that they wanted Cabrera removed. She assured them that she would consider their petition. and the shout went up, "*¡Viva la reina!*"

Isabel stayed six weeks in Segovia, put Gonzalo de Chácon in charge of the *alcázar*, listened to arguments on all sides and, ultimately faced with either reinstating loyal despots or finding untried replacement for them, she returned a pacified Segovia to the Cabreras. All in all, she demonstrated a response to crisis and a style of adjudicating popular disputes that would persist throughout her reign. And it was arranged that thereafter the princess Isabel would stay close to her mother.

From Segovia, Isabel rode to Toro. She had sent Benavente and the admiral in July to direct the siege of its fortress and, having ordered Quintanilla to bring *hermandad* reinforcements, she herself arrived with supplies on September 28. She observed everything keenly: to get a closer look when Alfonso de Aragón deployed artillery and siege engines for an attack, she made her way through the tunnels up to the moat of the enemy stronghold. When, on October 19, convinced that longer resistance was useless, María de Sarmiento surrendered the garrison of eighty, Isabel assured her she might retain her titles and property; she was after all the sister of Diego Pérez Sarmiento, count of Salinas and chief commander of the valued Basque squadrons.[28]

Of Toro's fall, an admiring chronicler commented, "Not only did the Queen take charge of governing and dispensing justice in the kingdom, but even in affairs of war no man could show such solicitude and diligence."[29] And he added that when women become active in matters of war, men are happier to serve them, for they know that the possibility of being shamed through failing will prod them to greater exertion. Happiness, one gathers, was the result of that process. However that may be, Isabel continued to be active in war, and continued to inspire her knights and men-at-arms in her cause.

Toro had special significance for her. It was the site of the great humiliation of the present war, now avenged; it was also her father's birthplace; and at its shrine of Nuestra Señora de la Vega her mother had, twenty-six years ago, arrived barefoot to fulfill a vow made should she conceive a child; she did, and the child was Isabel. Ironically, this victory at Toro would blot out that association with Mary and her royal suppliant, for out of it came the local memory that, when a Castilian captain left unguarded his position "near that hermitage" to court a young woman of the town, the Portuguese had taken advantage of his absence to attack and Toro would have been lost but for "the intercession of *Cristo de las Batallas*"; consequently that shrine to Santa María became known as the shrine of Christ of the Armies.[30] Most immediately, Isabel wrote to Fernando happily announcing Toro's fall, and he exultantly passed the news on to the councelors of Barcelona. In October he was back in Castile, all strain between him and the queen seemingly gone; he was not to leave again for several years.

Afonso of Portugal had returned to Portugal in June. In September he went to France, where for a year he vainly sought the aid of Louis XI for his Spanish project. At its end, despondent, he withdrew to a French monastery and abdicated in favor of his son, João. Five days after João's formal accession, Afonso reappeared in Portugal; he had changed his mind.

Ubi Sunt?

While Isabel and Fernando had waged war on the *meseta*, in Extremadura that intrepid old knight Rodrigo de Manrique had cut deeply into the vast holdings of the order of Calatrava, controlled by Rodrigo Girón. Manrique had seriously eroded the oppositions' power in taking Almagro, a bulwark of Girón's, and Villena's Ocaña. For such services Isabel confirmed him as master of Santiago; and when, in November of 1476, he died, his son Jorge reviewed his life and death in an elegaic poem that underscored the fleetingness of life and even fame itself. Yet, even while concluding that fame lasts longer than life but that it too ultimately dies, Jorge Manrique gave his father a kind of immortality, achieving through his couplets, as it turned out, what others wrote entire chronicles to accomplish.

As Isabel secured the crown, those couplets cut through Spain's grandiose founding myths and chivalric ethos to reaffirm the rock-ribbed sense of Spanish mission that the old Moor fighter epitomized. Jorge Manrique advised, Forget the Trojans, forget the Romans, we have forgotten even yesterday. And he asked, "What has become of the King Don Juan? The *infantes* of Aragón, what has become of them?" What became of them thereafter was that, in looking back on a fleeting past, Manrique's verses placed both King Juans among the immortals; and those verses achieved fame sufficient to gain to this day an immortality for evanescence. Yet for his own generation, which was Isabel's, he injected new—renaissance—value into old chivalric and patriotic verities in speaking of true honor, fame, and glory and he discerned them residing only in one very Spanish endeavor: "Lasting life is not gained by worldly estates, nor with pleasant living in which lies the sins of hell. But the good monks gain it by prayers and tears, and the famous knights by labors and hardships going against the Moors."[31] Such was the creed of the reconquest, and Isabel herself would soon take that message to heart.

But first, upon hearing of Rodrigo Manrique's death, Isabel rushed from Valladolid to the headquarters of the order of Santiago in the convent-fortress of Uclés, riding the two hundred miles in three days, arriving in a December downpour just as a new master was about to be chosen. She managed to postpone that election until she had ensured a favorable outcome. And so it was that she approved, as new master, Alonso de Cárdenas, *comendador* of León and uncle to Gutierre de Cárdenas, while securing the lucrative administration of the mastership for the crown. From then on, the monarchs supervised the order and controlled its military power, its vast wealth, and its holdings of 83 commendaries or vast estates, 2 cities, 178 towns and villages, 200 parishes, 5 hospitals, 5 convents, and a school in Salamanca.[32]

Fittingly, that January of 1477 while in nearby Ocaña, which held memories for her and which she had just taken from young Pacheco, Isabel received the great crown she had, immediately upon her accession, ordered from Valencia. Made of forty-eight pearls, eight rubies, seven diamonds, and gold from her treasury in Sicily, it was "worked in branches and leaves honeycombed in bright enamel, its eight sections each joined by a small eagle."[33] With only a relatively few pockets of resistance remaining, she could wear it securely, certain she was recognized as queen throughout the realm.

Now too, men once Enrique's critics became Isabel's publicists. Collections of poems and songs, including some hortatory verse written to her father and Enrique, some attacking Enrique, some advising princes, some eulogizing Isabel, all with political and religious components reflecting Isabel's own concept of royal ideology, then circulated among the nobility.[34] "Castile is recovered!" exulted fray Iñigo de Mendoza, who, in one such poem, a guide to princes he dedicated to Isabel, stressed the queen's duty to do justice and generously employed its symbol, the sword, as she herself had done on her accession. That poet, a descendant of both Santillana and Pablo de Santa María, also associated Fernando with the prophesied king of the last days, the Lion King; Talavera had undercut that allusion in connecting Isabel to the queen of the sky, yet also complemented it in endowing the joint reign with explicit heavenly and well as earthly affinity.[35] And Diego de Valera, in a mirror for princes addressing *los reyes* as a promise fulfilled and prophesying a Spain resurgent, now repeated with much more confidence a prediction he had once addressed to Isabel's father: "You shall reform the imperial throne of the noble race of the Goths."[36] He was at last encouraging a ruler who saw herself as charged with doing just that.

Building

At the end of January of 1477 Isabel and Fernando entered Toledo in triumph, displaying royal pomp and captured Portuguese battle standards, riding through the Bisagra gate, associated with El Cid, hand in hand. Toledo's archbishop was not to be seen. The city turned out to greet them, as Isabel had ordered, its notables for the first time donning bright clothing after a generation of strife, gloom, and mourning.[37]

Isabel attended a victory mass in the cathedral, wearing the crown of eagles. "And there [in Toledo] the Queen gave alms to churches and worthy persons, and did other pious works, for the victory that God had given the King and herself. And especially she founded a monastery of the order of San

Figure 4. The joint coat of arms, held in the talons of the eagle of Saint John and flanked by the devices of the yoke and bundle of arrows (1490). Juan Guas. Detail, interior wall of San Juan de los Reyes, Toledo.

Francisco . . . which she had built at great cost, to the exaltation of San Juan, for the memory of king Juan her father, which today is called San Juan de los Reyes."[38] Soaring in aspect, its church was meant as a royal pantheon. The richly emblazoned interior walls still proclaim the legitimacy, the valor, the aspirations of the queen and the king, and their inseparability.[39]

Today, as completed, everywhere are Fs and Ys, everywhere the bundles of arrows, the double yoke, and the motto that came to represent the reign as joint, *tanto monta,* "as much one as the other."[40] And everywhere too, indeed predominating, is the eagle sheltering under its outspread wings both their coats of arms, an image that became the national standard of Spain. It is the eagle of the apostle John. The widespread wings allude to those mentioned in the apocalyptic and messianic vision of the biblical prophet Ezekiel. That ubiquitous eagle also radiates dominance, and it signifies the soaring qualities that Talavera recommended to Isabel. By 1477, Isabel had evidenced that, in taking his injunction to heart, she had but reinforced proclivities of her own.

Through founding and decorating that church, Isabel conveyed that message, one further compounded through dedicating it to Saint John the Evangelist. The Evangelist was known as the herald of the Messiah's second coming. Attributed to him was the Book of Revelation, one of the most familiar parts of the Bible to medieval Europeans. And Revelation had long been a favorite reference for Spanish kings and clergy, who were not unmindful of its popularity. John's apocalyptic prophecies we have seen adapted to royal mission statements and Spanish-centered visions of history, wherein Spanish rulers had a millennial role to play.[41] Isabel, in taking the Evangelist as patron saint and becoming associated with his symbol, the eagle, linked herself publicly and directly to old prophecies of a messianic Spanish ruler. Such prophecies also promised that the Spanish were to be the saved remnant of Revelation, the faithful who would come to universal supremacy at the culmination of all history. The queen, as shall be seen, would soon evoke further comparison with the prophetic visions of Revelation.

Isabel involved herself in planning and raising that church. Initially, she proposed to call it San Juan de la Reina—Saint John of the Queen. But in the end she named it San Juan de los Reyes, attesting to a heightened desire that she and Fernando be identified as ruling inseparably. As its master-builder she chose Juan Guas, who had worked on the cathedral of her Avila. Both churches were built in the late Gothic style originating in northern Europe that, having blended in Spain with *mudéjar* design and construction, is known today as hispano-flemish, or Isabelline.[42] In Toledo (by 1490), Guas achieved a structure visually imparting triumph and expansive thrust in God's service and to God's glory, and to the queen's as well. From 1477 too, Isabel dispensed monies to construct the *cartuja*—the charterhouse of Augustinian friars—of Miraflores, in the same style. At Miraflores, the entire building serves as a long approach to her parents' tombs, which were built a decade later. Everywhere in that church the royal coat of arms bearing the lions of León and the castles of Castile crown the ceiling vaults.

Together, San Juan de los Reyes and the charterhouse of Miraflores represent material evocations not only of Talavera's injunction to her, but of a desire to show herself situated firmly within an unbroken line of Castile's monarchs, and so to put to rest the uneasy memory, held by the public and herself, of Enrique IV and the woman who claimed to be his daughter. Those monuments were thus born of a need to efface the recent years of civil war and the divisions within the realm. They were a bolstering in stone of Isabel's moral position and testaments to her determination, that of a female ruler resolved to assert her preeminence over all rivals, her barons, Fernando's faction, and the absent, but felt, presence of Juan of Aragón. They pointed back, to her proud heritage and her own achievements, and forward, to old prophecies at last being fulfilled and to the defining Spanish mission on the verge of being accomplished.

And it was during that stay in Toledo that opportunity in that direction presented itself: for word arrived that the king of Granada would no longer honor the treaties made with Castile's sovereigns. Yet for the time being, that enterprise had still to be put off, for the land was not yet hers.

Chapter 8
To the Sea: 1477–1478

Andalusia, above all, was a species of new world for the Castilians of the thirteenth century and continued being fundamentally a new and promising land for those that followed, the richest and most open zone of the Castilian crown. . . .
—*Miguel Angel Ladero Quesada*[1]

I have come to this land and I certainly do not intend to leave it to flee danger nor shirk work, nor will I give such glory to my enemies nor such pain to my subjects.
—*Isabel*[2]

In March of 1477, with the *meseta* largely assured and Fernando coping with remaining pockets of resistance, Isabel went southwest and then south, to Extremadura and Andalusia.[3] In those broad expanses great lords and the military orders had long held sway with little royal control, although the endless contests among them had allowed the crown to exert leverage. Civil war, however, had decreased actual royal intrusion and permitted escalation of baronial autonomy and baronial conflict, if in the name of one royal aspirant or another.

In Extremadura, dangerously situated on the Portuguese frontier, opposition to Isabel and Fernando still simmered. It was there that Diego Pacheco, marqués of Villena, had vast holdings and his redoubtable half-sister, Beatriz Pacheco, held Medellín as its countess. In Andalusia, Pacheco sisters were wives of some of the foremost *grandes*, while Pedro Girón's twin sons, the master of Calatrava and the count of Urueña, "had carved out a state" between Seville and Granada.[4] In Andalusia, magnates were yet more freewheeling.

Isabel was determined to restore respect for royal authority in all places and at all levels. But first, en route to Extremadura, she stopped, from late April until mid-May, at Guadalupe, at "the holy and very magnificent house of our lady of Guadalupe," as Talavera put it. There she discovered what was to become for her an oasis. That beautifully situated monastery is constructed of warm *ladrillo,* and within its church stands the small, age-blackened image of the Virgin of Guadalupe. Her chapel is a national shrine; her cult connects nationality and religion. In 1477, Guadalupe had been for 130 years—since the days when Alfonso XI had fulfilled a battlefield vow to Holy Mary by endowing that shrine—a Spanish devotional center, but it was also a bulwark guarding the Portuguese frontier and a royal resource. Kings were wont to consult its Hieronymite friars, many of whom were well born, many *converso,* some both, and who were noted for their piety and their learning.

Guadalupe had multiple attractions for a reigning monarch. It was a haven of peace and renowned as a center of the music Isabel so cherished. The monastery served as a depository for valuables and performed some functions of a bank; it housed a school, a library, and monks trained as lawyers. With perhaps fifteen thousand sheep and twenty-four hundred head of cattle, a center of manufacturing cloth and working leather, possessing mills and timber, and beehives, and feeding more than eight hundred people a day, that establishment was a model of administration and as such greatly admired by Isabel, who is said to have remarked that anyone wanting to fence in Castile should hand it over to the Hieronymites, implying they could transform Castile from wild to tended and manage the confines properly. Moreover, Guadalupe housed a leading medical center, with friars renowned for their knowledge of medicines, anatomy, and surgery, and Isabel, fervently desiring a son, now consulted doctors of Guadalupe. In years to come, she would return there periodically for rest, reflection, and medical attention. Guadalupe was to her, in modern terms, a spa, a spiritual retreat, especially at Eastertime, and a clinic. She would refer to it as "my paradise."[5] In 1477, it was also an ideal place to stop, take stock, and to give thought to how best to secure Extremadura's unruly towns.

Having persuaded the marqués of Villena to put nearby Trujillo under royal jurisdiction, Isabel next resolved to stay in that recent scene of violent warfare despite the objections of her advisors. "Well," she is said to have informed them, "I have come to this land and I certainly do not intend to leave it to flee danger nor shirk work, nor will I give such glory to my enemies nor such pain to my subjects."[6] And so in Trujillo the royal presence was made known and royal jurisdiction imposed. By the end of June she was in the fortress-town of Cáceres, from where she dictated what were becoming usual measures for imposing effective royal control over both urban factions and local lords: she established a *hermandad,* ordered strongholds and towers of local robber barons (usually defined as such by having been on the other side) demolished, and put an *alcaide* over the fort. In Cáceres some three hundred *caballeros* organized in two *bandos* had feuded incessantly, so to restore internal peace she abolished the battleground that was the annual election to the city council, instead ordering that current candidates draw lots, while decreeing lifetime tenancy of council positions and vacancies thereafter to be filled by crown appointment.[7] Those events corroborate that elections of themselves do not necessarily mean freedom, and that, given an alternative, for Castile's people in the 1470s it often seemed a relief, as Pulgar somewhere put it, "to escape into royal liberty."

While almost everywhere her attempts to impose effective royal control in municipal affairs were strongly resisted at first, yet the universal desire for peace and order, some individual hopes of bettering fortunes in a new state of affairs, and Isabel's personal ability to evoke both respect and fear served to achieve an unparalleled imposition of royal authority over cities and towns and their surrounding countrysides. By such measures and in particular by enrolling all Extremadura in the *Hermandad General*, as well as by strength of personality, she also instilled greater central control and new respect for the monarchy.

Even so, boys who grew up in those same Extremaduran towns would recreate the ambience of the preceding years overseas. The *conquistadores* of Peru, the Pizarros, came from Trujillo.[8] That town was taken for Isabel by the powerful Alonso de Monroy, a leader in factional warfare, whose young cousin, Hernán Cortés, from Beatriz Pacheco's Medellín, would carry the militant family tradition across the Atlantic Ocean to Mexico. Hernán's mother was Catalina Pizarro, the daughter of Beatriz Pacheco's *mayordomo*; Hernán's father, Martín Cortés, had fought Isabel for the Giróns; in Mexico, a soldier with Cortés, Bernal Díaz del Castillo, would recall one of his fellows always telling stories about Don Pedro Girón and the count of Urueña. And from wherever they came, most likely those *extremeños* had sailed from Seville.

Seville

On July 24 Isabel made a solemn entry into Seville. With some forty-five thousand people, it was the most populous city of Isabel's realm, and one of the most tumultuous. When Fernando III conquered the Muslim kingdom of Seville, he had gained with that port city a vast hinterland. The city of Seville had continued to dominate those lands, rich in flocks and herds, wheat and olives, vines and fruits, and the timber vital to shipbuilding, a vast area extending along the Gulf of Cádiz to Huelva on the west and southward to Gibraltar. In 1477 Seville was Castile's greatest port and its southern terminus, linking the Mediterranean and the Atlantic, an emporium of both internal and foreign trade. An administrative, mercantile, and financial center, cosmopolitan Seville was home to a diverse populace that included enclaves of Genoese, Florentines, Bretons, English, and Catalans, foreigners visible in the crowds welcoming the queen. The city had been an important source of royal income during the war, and its Italian residents, who were especially forthcoming in lending the crown money, had in turn been wooed with privileges; thus the Genoese were exempted from paying the *almojarifazgo,* the customs duties.[9]

Present at Isabel's entry too, by express request of the city council, were representatives of the large communities of Muslims and Jews, as well as some of the growing numbers of black Africans, who were mostly household slaves or artisans. Many of Seville's blacks spoke Portuguese and were known as *ladinos,* having come by way of Portugal. Others came directly from Guinea: they were Wolof from the banks of the Senegal River near the Portuguese factory of Arguim, or Mandinga from Gambia. People in all walks of life owned slaves, but especially aristocrats and ecclesiastics.[10]

Above the disparate throng, Seville's banner flew from the ramparts, on it a likeness of Fernando III, who had entered the city with his armies as its conqueror, and whose nation-expanding feat and consequent personal renown were not lost that day on a descendant of his. Indicating she was well aware the city was hers by virtue of that conquest, Isabel purposely arrived without her army. Yet army or no, she rode into Seville in state, grandly, having sent ahead her *aposentadores,* whose function it was to make proper arrangements for receiving and housing the monarchs.[11] Having indicated that she assumed Seville was in full obedience, she proposed to stay awhile and to tame Seville's great lords, who since her accession had ruled the city as their own; her self-assigned task was to subdue not the place but the independent-minded traditions of a frontier region never fully incorporated into the crown of Castile.

Chief among Seville's problematic magnates was her viceroy, Enrique de Guzmán, the duke of Medina Sidonia. Married to María de Mendoza, a sister of the cardinal, Medina Sidonia had dominated the city since ousting, after five bloody years of *bando*—factional—warfare, his archrival, young Rodrigo Ponce de León, the marqués of Cádiz, who was married to a Pacheco. Isabel was now resolved to bring that viceroy of hers who was also the strongest and wealthiest of Andalusia's great barons, into line, to reimpose effective royal authority over the proud and cantankerous city, and to set an example for her other noble subjects, particularly those of the region.

No one in all Castile had ridden higher during the years of civil strife than the Guzmán and Ponce de León clans and their powerful neighbors, most prominent among whom were the Aguilar and Fernández de Córdoba of Córdoba. Guarding the southern frontiers, at times raiding, at times cooperating with Muslims or Portuguese, exercising autonomous jurisdiction over rich territory and towns, collecting revenues, and engaging in a host of entrepreneurial activities, they had amassed tremendous fortunes and reached an apogee of near-independent power. Indeed, those border lords of the Muslim and Portuguese frontiers had profited immensely not only from urban revenues, the spoils of war, and royal *mercedes,* but also from the land—its rents and its

products, olives and cereals, wines, fruits and nuts, salt, silk, hides and wool—
and from the sea, through fishing, trading, and piracy—and they had accumu-
lated capital as exporters of artisanry and commercial crops. They carried on
large-scale business and long-distance trade both directly and through agents,
both throughout Castile and abroad. And they owned ships for military reasons, prestige, and profit, for lading, lease, and plunder. The high clergy and
the heads of the military orders belonging to that Andalusian nobility demonstrated similar enterprise.[12]

A prime source of income for them all was coastal fishing, although deep
sea fishing was important as well. The catches were sold locally or shipped
great distances after being salted or preserved in oil; thus the long-standing
rivalry between the Guzmán and the Ponce de León over Gibraltar was linked
to prospects of huge fishing revenues. Isabel herself had, on the eve of the battle of Toro, thought it sufficiently worthwhile to write Seville's council of her
desire to restore the royal tithe on salted fish. And fishing, while profitable of
itself, provided a cover for a number of unsanctioned economic activities, such
as the Guzmán getting around usury laws by selling future catches to Genoese
merchant-bankers; and, above all, fishing gave cover for raiding, trading, and
exploration along African coasts and in the Atlantic.[13]

The best fish were taken on the banks of the Moroccos and off the
Saharan coast and the Canaries. Rights to fishing accompanied the expansion
of Castilian territorial claims, as did expectation of trade with the penetrating
of Africa; so Isabel's father, Juan II, had, in 1449, granted an earlier Guzmán a
monopoly to fish and to explore the African coast to Cape Bojador, in
response to the Portuguese having founded a factory at Arguim the year
before.[14] Such royal grants of fishing rights fishing involved powerful lords and
their private navies in international competition, and served to sanction such
activities as the Andalusian capture of Gibraltar in the 1460s.

Other sorts of royal *mercedes* had further empowered and enriched
Medina Sidonia and the others. For some time the Guzmán had enjoyed a
delegated fifth of such royal revenues as the *almojarifazgo* and the *alcabala*, or
sales tax, in places they controlled, among them Seville, and they had exercised
lucrative influence in Palos, Moguer, and other subsidiary ports. Even so, they
faced competition from other great families who had interests and authority
in Seville, notably the Stúñiga, who played balance of power politics, and the
Enríquez, who enjoyed perquisites in that port city as hereditary admirals of
Castile. Andalusia, it might be said, was an early instance of opening a region
won through war to private enterprise.

Castile's monarchs had long understood that their own political and economic fortunes were bound to those of this southern nobility, and in turn tied
to commerce and finance and the sea. The enduring problem was one of control. So Isabel, within days of taking the crown, had expressed her concern to

Seville's council, which was dominated by Medina Sidonia, regarding the sparse returns to her treasury from the *alcabala*, generally the greatest single source of royal income.[15] Yet the problem was larger, encompassing not only a siphoning off of taxes but revenue lost through smuggling. For as earlier in the north, some Spaniards of Andalusia who fought the Portuguese and the Muslims also traded with them, forming close connections to Granada and Africa, in the main clandestine and so avoiding prohibitions or imposts. Leading culprits were seamen of port towns, employed by nobles or on their own. Such people had fished, raided, and traded along Granadan and African coasts for generations, whatever the political climate or whoever controlled the territory. Although Enrique IV had decreed Portuguese rights be honored, from the 1450s Andalusians, along with broadening Portuguese exploration and commerce, had sailed the Atlantic and made the long and difficult voyages required to raid along Africa's Atlantic coast, voyages taking two or three months outbound, seven or eight on return. But they much preferred to seize Portuguese cargos at sea. So in 1452 a fishing caravel had taken seven men and seven women from a Portuguese ship off the African coast, then sold them in Rota with the consent of Ponce de León (Rodrigo's father). The following year, Dom Henrique of Portugal—Henry the Navigator—requested of Medina Sidonia that his vassals of Palos and Moguer return the sixty-six blacks they had taken from a Portuguese ship. Sanlúcar, Palos, Niebla, and the town of Medina Sidonia became centers of this traffic, principally in Africans coming from Senegambia and the Guinea coast and by way of the Canaries.[16]

Even so, trade in gold was more profitable and less difficult than that in spices or slaves, and also largely surreptitious; and gold was especially scarce in Spain in the 1460s and 1470s and especially valuable. Even so, Seville's mint produced most of Castile's gold coins and it yielded much revenue, theoretically both to the crown and to those enjoying royal *mercedes* in mint fees and customs duties, as well as to those in the business of treating gold coins as a commodity. Nobles, too, minted and did so illegally, although Enrique had on occasion sold or granted them licenses. Temptation was great in all quarters to debase coins, and counterfeiting was profitable. Profit could be made on metal imported and on coins exported, through differential in currency values. In June of 1477, to repay war debts, Fernando himself sought, though unsuccessfully, to have desirable foreign coins minted in Valencia—secretly, at night.[17]

Europeans, despite centuries of effort, had not penetrated Africa to the source of its gold, which was in the West African Sudan and in the lands of the Ashanti. Lying beyond the Sahara, the Bambuhu, Buri, and Lobi goldfields had enriched the Sudanic empires: ancient Ghana, Songhai, and Kamen-Bornu; and in the early fourteenth century Mansa Musa of Mali, regarded as the first African Muslim emperor, was said to have taken forty large camel-loads of gold with him on a combined trading venture and pilgrimage to

Mecca, so much gold that it devalued the currency in Cairo on the way. A Catalan map of 1375 acknowledged the renown of his wealth in portraying Mansa Musa seated on a throne holding a scepter in his left hand and contemplating a large gold nugget in his right, his figure dominating North Africa.

Spaniards, Genoese, and Portuguese had long competed both in the search for those goldfields and for control of terminals of exchange on or near the African coast of the Maghrib (Tunis and Morocco), and recently the Portuguese had coaxed gold caravans to West African coasts as well. Spain's Andalusian ports had especially profited from proximity to North Africa and imports of its gold, and they and all Spain benefited from the exchange of such relatively cheap gold for silver coming in from northern Europe; by all indications both metals gained value in passing through Spain. In that commerce, Genoese and other Italians often acted as middlemen, as carriers and merchants in ports throughout the Mediterranean. For Isabel, control of the trade in gold was important to control of Andalusia and its ports, and to Spanish expansion and its financing.

War at Sea

From the outset of the war with Portugal, Isabel had paid particular attention to promoting Castile's maritime presence in southern waters. In May of 1475 an armed fleet was ordered to patrol sea lanes. By September, on royal orders four Aragonese galleys had arrived at the Guadalquivir, down river from Seville, in a move to discourage Portuguese incursion. And, having appropriated Afonso's titles to Africa, Isabel encouraged Atlantic expeditions from Andalusia but only under strict royal supervision; that same May she had sent to Seville a *letrado* of the Royal Council expressly to assert royal authority over maritime matters. He was, among other duties, to issue letters of marque and to license voyages to Guinea and collect the royal fifth on their return cargos. It was more than coincidental that concomitantly Isabel moved to stabilize and regulate coinage and collection of taxes. And in December of 1475 she ordered each Andalusian caravel that sailed to have on board a royal official to ensure the turnover of the royal fifth. It was a show of authority in the main, for in July she had granted rights to the fifth to the archbishop of Seville, Mendoza, and the bishop of Cádiz in their respective dioceses.[18]

Her rationale went beyond the exigencies of the current war. In a decree of that August, she stated that "the kings of glorious memory, my progenitors, from whom I come, always had [the right to] the conquest of the parts of Africa and of Guinea, and they received a fifth of the merchandise that was recovered [*se rescatavan*], from those places, until our adversary of Portugal, interfered . . . by consent of the king, Don Enrique, my brother, who is in holy glory."[19] She was, in keeping with her stance as her father's direct heir, asserting her lineal right to territories claimed as once held by Spain's Visigoths. The "merchandise" she referred to included captured Africans. She awarded, as a *merced,* the lucrative concession to license such voyages to the faithful Gonzalo Chácon, and subsequently she granted rights to specific sailings to Benavente, Bobadilla, and to a retainer of Cabrera's, all of whom in turn sold them to merchant-adventurers.[20]

Yet those Andalusian magnates, Medina Sidonia and Cádiz, were not to relinquish their freedom at sea readily. Indeed, Rodrigo Ponce de León, the marqués of Cádiz, while maintaining contact with Isabel and Fernando was also in touch with his brother-in-law Pacheco and with Afonso of Portugal. As Palencia puts it, Cádiz and his *gaditanos* wanted to share in the wealth so long denied them. So did other Andalusians, especially since the Portuguese had recently established a West African factory so promising it was known as La Mina de Oro, the gold mine.[21] Relatedly, in 1476 several expeditions from Palos and Puerto de Santa María had gone slaving to Guinea without royal license; one, backed by the *alcaide* of the fort of Palos, Gonzalo de Stúñiga, employed a ruse that would work again later, in America.

Palencia tells the story. The king of the region, who was most likely either Wolof or Mandinga, was accustomed to trading his prisoners of war to the Portuguese and such he assumed those ships to be, especially since on boarding one he was greeted in Portuguese, and so he bartered with them, giving Africans for brass rings, small daggers, and colored cloth. Then, invited to dine aboard and having sent ahead sheep and a calf, he arrived, as arranged, with his brothers, his friends, and his chief people. All of them soon found themselves prisoners. Whose ships were these, he demanded to know, who had so cruelly deceived him? Told they belonged to Spaniards, he asked if they obeyed any king and when answered yes, a most noble one, he expressed confidence that his fellow monarch would soon free him. When put ashore in Palos he refused to walk, instead demanding a horse or mule in accord with his dignity. Gonzalo de Stúñiga, struck by his regal bearing, or thinking of future expeditions, ordered a mount for him; and so the king rode to Seville, majestically, at the head of the column of Africans destined for sale. Isabel, informed of so overt an act of smuggling, ordered Stúñiga to turn over king and people to her commissioner so that they might be returned home. Initially delaying, Stúñiga complied only in sending back the king. Yet once home that monarch managed to capture some old enemies and to exchange them for relatives of his enslaved in Andalusia.[22]

By the spring of 1476 Isabel's policy and Andalusian enterprise together had had effect, for among the reasons Afonso then gave his nobles for his returning to Portugal was that he had to arrange for a fleet to safeguard sailings to Guinea, the source of so much of his wealth. Yet now France was also a factor in war at sea, so that Isabel that spring ordered both more ships to be armed in Guipúzcoa and Vizcaya and a fleet readied in Andalusia for Guinea, its goal to raid Portuguese settlements in the Cape Verde islands, and especially the island of Antonio (now Santiago), named for a Genoese, Antonio da Noli. Noli had resided for a time in Seville, gone to Lisbon, contracted with Dom Henrique to join expeditions to Guinea, and convinced the Portuguese to populate that island and install him as its lord. The settlement had prospered and Noli engaged in the slave trade; trading in gold was reserved to Fernão Gómez, the private concessionaire whose huge annual payments to Afonso had helped finance the campaign in Castile.[23]

Isabel and Fernando, testifying to the royal goals of countering both Portuguese rivalry and Andalusian freebooting, had then sent a watchdog of tried loyalty, Diego de Valera, to oversee the strategically vital royal enclave and customs station at Puerto de Santa María, on the riverine coast up from Cádiz, and they had appointed Valera's son, Charles, *alcaide* of its fort. That same spring of 1476, Charles de Valera received from them command of an expedition to Guinea. Speed was important, for it was known that Fernão Gómez had dispatched twenty ships from Portugal to load African gold.[24]

It was decided, says Palencia, that the royal fleet should consist of thirty light ships, for larger ones were unsuitable for the navigation of those seas, while—and here he attests to the flow of traffic—caravels crossed rapidly from the Cádiz coast to Africa. In addition to the Basques of the fleet and to other Andalusians, Valera recruited from neighboring Palos seamen as well as ships, for, as Palencia explained, "only those of Palos knew from old the Guinea sea, since accustomed from the beginning of the war to combat the Portuguese and take from them the slaves they had acquired."[25] Yet assembling and outfitting the fleet lagged, its overseers, one of whom was Palencia, hampered by inexperience, lack of funds from the crown, and the machinations of certain Andalusian magnates, particularly Medina Sidonia and Cádiz. Medina Sidonia had *sevillanos* withhold all necessaries until the king and queen promised him jurisdiction over the island of Antonio when taken; and the marqués of Cádiz sent two *gaditano* captains to Fernão Gómez to warn him the Castilian fleet was readying, and to request for having done so a share of his profits. Meanwhile, in Palos, Gonzalo de Stúñiga had seized control of the port and was doing his best to stop its caravels from joining the fleet.

Nevertheless, Valera sailed in late May or early June with thirty caravels and three Basque ships for the Cape Verdes, to carry the war to Portugal's lucrative Atlantic fringe and to gain for Castile a base for expansion to the nearby African mainland. He raided thirteen places in those islands, brought back Antonio da Noli, and, having missed the Portuguese treasure fleet, on his way home voyaged to the source of its cargo, the African coast, where he seized two ships belonging to the marqués of Cádiz loaded with five hundred *aza-*

negas, slaves. The men of Palos, however, then sailed off, taking with them Cádiz' ships and cargos. Medina Sidonia, on word of the expedition's success, insisted the island of Antonio and its spoils were his, and both he and Cádiz, who was intent on reclaiming his hijacked property, harried Puerto de Santa María until they obtained the greater part of the booty and slaves taken by Valera. Isabel and Fernando fined the *paleños* for smuggling; and the queen and king prevailed on Medina Sidonia to free the Genoese, Noli, who came to Medina del Campo to thank them, undoubtedly on royal summons because they wished to hear of West Africa and its potential.[26] In years to come, another Genoese familiar with Guinea and the Western Ocean, Cristóbal Colón, or Christopher Columbus, would benefit from an Atlantic interest aroused in Isabel during that war.

Oddly enough, then surfacing was another Colón, one Louis—also referred to as Luis Coulon or Guillermo de Casanove—an erstwhile privateer whom Louis XI, bereft of Spanish ships, had commissioned to assemble and command a French fleet. In 1476, on the French king's orders, Louis Colón escorted Afonso and his fleet from Portugal to France, sailing through the Strait of Gibraltar and up the Mediterranean coast. That fleet stopped to reinforce and provision the Portuguese garrisons at Ceuta, Tangier, Alcázarquivir, and Arzila, for Afonso feared the Moors but even more the Andalusians, and with good reason, for those reinforcements were just in time to repulse an attack on Ceuta ordered by Medina Sidonia.[27]

Medina Sidonia himself, meanwhile, was attending to other business, on strategic Gibraltar. Having received royal funds for its garrisoning, he had instead manned it profitably with *conversos* escaping riots and persecution in Córdoba, indeed charged them for refuge there. But now that they had exhausted their resources in paying for overpriced provisions, his building projects, and his maritime expeditions, he forced them out and was taking charge of Gibraltar personally, hoping such a show of effective possession would buoy his chances to sell the island to the crown.[28]

As for Colón's fleet, upon leaving Ceuta in August it attacked five ships just out of Cádiz, three of them Genoese galleys, with great losses. Diego de Valera writes of five thousand dead, mostly Portuguese, and of six great ships lost: four by Colón and the Portuguese, and a Genoese galley and a Flemish *urca.*[29] Swimming to shore then from one of the vessels involved and so into history was Christopher Columbus, and at the moment his destination was Portugal.

The Canary Islands

Key to the Spanish presence in West Africa were the Canary Islands. A juridical inquiry Isabel had ordered in November of 1476 substantiated claims to Castilian sovereignty over them. Isabel made those claims on a basis given legal standing in her father's reign, that the Canaries were hers by lineal descent, having belonged to the last Visigothic king, Rodrigo. Nor is it surprising that signing that opinion were Hernando de Talavera and the royal jurist, Rodrigo Maldonado de Talavera.[30] Isabel also confirmed, as lords of the four Canary Islands, Inés de Peraza, whose father had bought the rights to them all from Medina Sidonia, and her husband, Diego Herrera, a councilman of Seville. Through bestowing such a grant, Isabel asserted her own overriding sovereignty, and she then bought back from the couple the rights to the Canaries not yet colonized—Tenerife, La Palma, and Gran Canaría. Isabel viewed those places as bases of operation against the Portuguese, and for West Africa—in effect, as Palencia says, as way stations "to the mines of gold of Ethiopia."[31] The name Ethiopia was then redolent of King Solomon's mines and the kingdom of Prester John, thus evoking fabled riches and a land route to the East. Isabel also got from the Peraza-Herrera a devolution of rights to the Torre de Santa Cruz de la Mar Pequeña, a fortified coastal station or factory commanding the valleys of the Draa and Nun Rivers and much frequented by gold caravans from the interior. And she licensed more ships for Guinea, to be organized in annual convoys. All of those measures were directed to economic gain, competing with Portugal, the traditional royal goal of extending reconquest into Africa, and, unifying those purposes and providing overarching religious thrust, was the vision of ultimately retaking Jerusalem.

Isabel would continue to support the conquest of the Canaries and to send men and provisions. Expeditions sailed in the summers of 1478 and 1479; merchants were lured into joining them by permits to ship stipulated amounts of that prohibited export, wheat. While she herself was in Seville in 1478, a fleet of thirty-five caravels sailed for the Canaries, most of the crews from Palos, ostensibly to collect *orchilla,* a precious dye, and the conch shells so valued in the slave trade in La Mina; it was captured by the Portuguese on the return voyage. Nonetheless, conquest of Gran Canaría and dominion over its inhabitants was the true purpose of that expedition; it would be achieved, ruthlessly, by 1483.

From the outset of her reign, Isabel insisted upon royal control of Castilian ventures overseas and at sea. And she wanted not only her sovereignty acknowledged but either a monopoly on trade goods or a percentage of all profits. While in Seville, she forbade any merchandise to be sold before the selling of that belonging to the crown.[32] Yet certain enslaved people were another matter. When Inés de Peraza attempted to sell some natives of Gomera, Isabel opposed it; she also had merchants of Palos and Moguer who trafficked in Canarians sued and the islanders freed. Such captives, was the argument, were the queen's vassals; yet the royal prosecutor made a further point in commenting that, although baptized Christians, they had been treated as though they were Moors.[33] Native peoples in lands Isabel claimed for Castile were declared under royal authority. They were royal vassals, and if legally enslaved, then they constituted royal, not private, merchandise. Moreover, when in 1478 Pope Sixtus IV dedicated certain monies received from sale of indulgences to converting the Canary Islanders, Isabel and Fernando interpreted his bulls as supplying funds not only for conversion but also for conquest by Castile.[34] To the queen, bringing souls to God and vassals to the crown was of a piece, a divine obligation enjoined upon herself. And in practical terms, the religious adhesion of the conquered was crucial to wielding sovereignty effectively. Isabel's experiences with Andalusians and the Canary Islands would strongly influence her policies regarding the lands and people later known as America and Americans.

The Duke and the Marqués

Before coming to Seville, Isabel had had words of her own for the Andalusian lords, and there too the underlying issue was effective dominion. She was unhappy not only at their having delayed Valera's expedition and then appropriating its profits, but even earlier, at their unwillingness to help her during the war with Portugal. Seville under Medina Sidonia had made excuses in response to her urgent letters requesting light cavalry and the guarding of conquered castles and towns, and in Jérez she understood that the marqués of Cádiz had assessed levies of wine and bread for the royal armada and then used them for his own ships. Yet whatever the degree of royal exasperation, she knew too that much royal power resided in arousing a competitive spirit among such magnates for honors and preeminence and accordingly an envoy had gone with stiff letters, first to Medina Sidonia, ordering he move against the Portuguese on the frontier and telling him "that both the King and Queen marvel that Portuguese soldiers have marched from the confines of Sevillian territory to the far provinces of New Castile. . . ."[35] When the duke refused to comply, the envoy informed him that he had instructions in that event to carry royal letters to the marqués of Cadiz requesting that he take command of gathering Andalusian forces against the enemy. Medina Sidonia having remained adamant, and Cádiz having accepted graciously, the duke retaliated by revoking an agreement with the marqués guaranteeing to him the lucrative right to fish freely for tunny off the coast. And, confirming his reputation for arrogance, Medina Sidonia requested that the monarchs uphold that revocation, while Cádiz sought their permission to challenge his long-standing rival to single combat for having broken his oath.

Isabel did not want her *grandes* bashing one another in Andalusia. The war was not over and the frontier with Granada required vigilance. Rather, she wanted her own authority accepted indisputably by those cantankerous border lords. She also wanted to collect the royal rents Medina Sidonia in particular had long usurped, and to be able to tax effectively and have royal authority respected and obeyed in Andalusia, and especially in Seville. Toward achieving those objectives, Palencia had been instructed to sound out *sevillanos* on forming a *hermandad*, which could both rival and confront Medina Sidonia's own forces and loosen his hold on the city. At one stroke, Seville would have a police force dependent ultimately on the crown, not the duke, along with a reserve of manpower, and the populace would know that the duke had bowed to superior royal authority. Medina Sidonia, upon hearing that a friar had come to town who was exhorting *sevillanos* to institute their own armed peace-keeping constabulary, and already smarting at being passed over as master of Santiago, angrily convened the city's authorities and threatened to hang or behead all royal officials, depending on rank. He also terrified the many *converso* notables by telling them that a publicly sponsored *hermandad* might well result in their extermination. Yet, unable to overcome the increasing appeal the *hermandad* had for the populace, he soon did an about-face and began to praise it publicly and highly. Córdoba's principal lord, Alonso de Aguilar, faced with the same situation, behaved similarly. So matters stood when Isabel arrived in Seville.[36]

The queen was received with due ceremony by Medina Sidonia, who exhibited no trace of his recent ill temper in greeting her. He was accompanied by the city's knights, all its municipal and royal officials, and all the clergy. Isabel then made her own show: she rode through the city beneath a canopy of scarlet brocade embroidered with her arrows, its gilded supports borne by eight councilmen. She passed through streets lined with spectators and balconies hung for her entry with householders' most precious tapestries, to Santa María la Mayor, the cathedral, to hear mass, and afterward to the royal palace in the *alcázar*; she would henceforth live for relatively long stretches in that grand warren. For days she was feted with ceremonies, jousts, bullfights, and dances. In return, she admired the city extravagantly, confessing she had never imagined such grandeur.[37]

Accounts differ on her relations with Medina Sidonia from then on. Along with other magnates, he was said to think it a mistake that the queen had come to Andalusia without her husband, that a woman alone could not do what was necessary there, especially given the threat of Muslims and Portuguese and even though she was a woman of great spirit and valor. Be that as it may, he was soon to look forward to the king arriving to soften her impact.

While asserting her prerogative, or negotiating with the powerful to regain control of royal perquisites either alienated by Enrique or simply appropriated in the laxity and disorder of his reign, Isabel was also determined that the entire city should respect and fear the royal presence as never before. This she set about achieving immediately. Her first move was, whether with or without the duke's free bestowal, to have the *alcázar* and the shipyards taken over from Medina Sidonia by her administrators. Yet, more far reaching, she proposed to dispense justice personally—the stern justice announced by the sword she had had carried at her accession. She was as well undoubtedly mindful of the old saw that in effect law was a royal instrument: "there go laws, where kings so command," or "laws go where kings want them to go."[38]

Having informed Medina Sidonia that the principal reason she had come to Seville was to rid the land of tyrants and criminals, that through her understanding and with the help of God she would work until Seville was thus made secure, every Friday she held an *audiencia,* a court of law, in the great hall of the *alcázar.* There she presided from a seat covered in gold cloth, elevated upon a raised dais, flanked on one side by prelates and *caballeros,* who sat a bit lower, and on the other by the learned doctors of her council and the royal secretaries. Judiciary officials, the *alcaides* and *alguaciles,* were seated in front of those dignitaries; a corps of archers stood guard. Isabel heard individual petitions then assigned them to the proper legal experts, instructing them to reach a decision within a few days' time. If they bogged down in technicalities, she often took it upon herself to render a swift verdict. On other days she continued to adjudicate in her apartments. Within two months numerous civil and criminal cases long pending had been settled and those adjudged guilty sentenced, usually severely.[39]

Through rendering justice, writes Pulgar, the queen became loved by the good and feared by the wrongdoers, a great number of whom left the city for Portugal or Muslim lands. He indicates that overall those proceedings had the desired political effect, creating awe of royal majesty, even going so far as to bring eminent Sevillians to be afraid that if justice continued to be dispensed with such rigor no one would be left untouched, for "considering the great dissoluteness of the recent past, there were few in the city without guilt."[40]

The bishop of Cádiz, Alonso de Solís, who also managed the diocese of Seville for its archbishop, Pedro González de Mendoza, came one Friday on behalf of the citizens to plead she proclaim a general pardon. Before a throng of *sevillanos,* among them women whose husbands, sons, and brothers had fled, Solís, tears streaming, argued that, while all mortals are worthy of punishment, if everyone who deserved it received it, "the world would perish in an instant." Justice, he told her, always includes clemency. Isabel, moved, agreed to forgive all civil crimes with the exception of personal injuries, thereby again demonstrating the high value she placed on honor avenged; however, when Solís questioned that exclusion (noting that many such litigants were also frequently defendants in other cases), she withdrew it and issued a general pardon for all crimes except that of heresy, which was both a civil and a religious offense. Whether or not that scene had been staged, more than four thousand of those who fled her wrath, says Pulgar, returned, and thereafter people tended to resolve their differences privately, through shame, or perhaps dreading the verdict of the queen. Whatever the other effects of those public hearings of hers, *sevillanos* had gained respect for the queen, and formed an idea of Isabel's character as formidable.

Her show of strength had reverberations beyond the city. Late one night, after she had retired to her chambers, Rodrigo Ponce de León, the marqués of Cádiz, slipped undetected into the city he had lost to his archrival and appeared at a side gate of the *alcázar*. Isabel, agreeing to receive him, saw before her a red-bearded giant of a man, in his thirties, known to be hot tempered, ambitious, and shrewd, and also more intelligent and decisive than Medina Sidonia. Cádiz proffered her his service, pled innocent to ever having been allied with Portugal, or anyway formally, and offered her his fortresses of Jerez and Alcalá de Guadaira. Isabel was "*muy contenta*" with his proposals and his gallantry. While it was true, she informed him, that she had had no good report of him—her chief informant undoubtedly being Medina Sidonia—his trust in coming and putting himself in her hands obliged her to treat him well, and she assured him that once he had actually turned over to her "those my forts of Jerez and Alcalá, which you hold," she would adjudicate in his quarrel with the duke, guarding his honor.[41] The marqués assigned those strongholds to her; and other holders of Andalusia's forts, who had originally seized them, as had Cádiz and Medina Sidonia, during Enrique's reign, then emulated those two great lords in relinquishing them to her; and in the few instances where they did not, Isabel had those places besieged and their garrisons brought to Seville and hung as rebels. The queen had indeed reconquered the old kingdom of Seville.

Chapter 9
Signs and Revelations: 1478

*Clearly, we see ourselves given a very special gift by God, for at the end of
such a long wait He has desired to give him to us. The Queen has paid to
this kingdom the debt of male succession that she was obligated to give. . . .*

*It seems clear that this Queen was moved to do things by some divine inspira-
tion.*

—Hernando del Pulgar[1]

The king arrived in Seville in September of 1477, to great festivity,
and to the *sevillanos*' vain hope, quickly dashed, that he would soften his wife's
draconian measures. He remained until early October, or as Pulgar puts it: "he
stayed some days in which the Queen became pregnant," an event, the chronicler adds, much desired by all the kingdom. It was known that Isabel, worried,
for her only child was seven years old, had consulted physicians. Whatever
their advice to her, a child was expected in late spring. That fall she and Fernando paid visits to Medina Sidonia in his town of Sanlúcar de Barrameda,
and to its márques in Cádiz, and then wintered in Seville.[2]

They held court grandly in the palace within the *alcázar;* and they lived
there as well, amid the accretion of the Islamic centuries and the assertively
Christian additions of Alfonso X, whose stout Gothic both proclaimed dominance and a defensive stance against the ongoing Muslim threat from Africa.
Isabel's private quarters were in another addition to that royal compound, in
the *mudéjar* palace built by Pedro I, its very presence a visual reminder that
relations between Castile's rulers and Muslims in Spain had long been far from
simple. That palace recalled Pedro's friendship with Granada's Muhammad X,
who had sent to Castile's king workmen from his own Alhambra. The relative
openness of the palace was a reminder too that, Pedro's father Alfonso XI having won the battle of Salado, the threat from Muslim Africa had diminished.
Isabel would later make additions of her own, among them a very *mudéjar*
chapel; by then too she would be acknowledged queen in Granada.[3]

In March, a letter from an agent of Juan of Aragón to Fernando conveyed
a general atmosphere of expectation and the widespread hope that the royal

child would be a boy: "It is good, Your Excellency, for here is the most grave and grand matter of Spain, and nothing is more necessary or desired. . . ."[4] The hope was fulfilled. On the morning of June 30, 1478, Isabel gave birth to a son and heir. Present as the child was born was a midwife and, by royal order, numerous courtiers and city officials, for it was a state occasion and there was to be no question that the child was the queen's. Court and city celebrated for three days and nights. That Isabel's second child was male crowned the successes of those years and was widely interpreted as a sign from God of his approval, and of yet greater victories to come.

Seville resounded with fiesta. On July 9, the baptismal procession made its way from the palace to the cathedral through thronged streets, the prince nestled in brocade cloth in the arms of his well-born nurse, María de Guzmán, the mule she rode flanked by eight councilmen bearing staffs of office and wearing great cloaks of black velvet "provided by the city."[5] Alvaro de Stúñiga, the late great rebel, walked directly behind. Three of the queen's pages strode along at the head of the procession. One held a gold jar, another a gold cup; the third, carrying the customary candle, baby cap, and money offering on a tray, was "so small that he bore the tray on his head, holding on to it with both hands."[6] All the nobles at court accompanied child and nurse, on foot; so did many knights and other people. Silver crosses gleamed above, and trumpets, hornpipes, and sackbutts played ceaselessly.

The prince was baptized Juan in the cathedral, "very triumphantly." That observation was made within the description of those proceedings by a new chronicler of a new sort, Andrés Bernáldez, a militant Andalusian chaplain much less concerned with political relations, much less critical of anyone both orthodox and powerful than Isabel's earlier chroniclers could on occasion be; Bernáldez exuded a crusading patriotism. Officiating at the baptism was Seville's archbishop, Pedro González de Mendoza, chief among courtiers. The godparents were the constable, Benavente, Nicolò Franco, the papal legate, and Leonor de Mendoza, duchess of Medina Sidonia.

A second procession, even grander, took place a month later, on August 9, when the queen went "to present the prince to the temple as was the custom of Holy Mother Church." She had waited until then as was also customary, for a woman was not to enter a church after childbirth until "being purified of her blood."[7] Fernando led the way on a small silver-grey horse. He was opulently regal, wearing heavy brocade lined in gold and trimmed in gold and black velvet, and a broad hat also lined in cloth of gold. (It was sweltering midsummer in Andalusia; little wonder that Fernando reputedly said that all he wished to his enemies were winters in Burgos and summers in Seville.[8]) At the center of that procession rode Isabel, dressed in brocade shimmering with pearls, mounted high upon a white trotter, its saddle of gold encrusted with more gold and with silver. Accompanying her on foot were most of the city's council and many nobles. The constable, Haro, held the right-hand bridle rein of her horse; Benavente held the rein on her left. The infant prince, again swathed in brocade, also rode, carried by his nurse upon a mule with a saddle of velvet. Musicians kept pace, playing trumpets and hornpipes and many other instruments.[9]

The symbolism was patent and glorious. In that solemn, glittering procession Castile's might showed itself subservient to the newly flourishing dynasty. The royal couple demonstrated that it now held Castile through strength and respect, love and fear. In that city until recently so proudly autonomous, where the queen in particular had effected a second reconquest, those monarchs were showing themselves to be worthy successors of their predecessor, Fernando III.

No one spoke much afterward of the total eclipse of the sun that occurred within the month, the reactions to that darkness at noon ranging from fear that the end of the world was at hand to a prescient foreboding concerning the royal infant. Rather, the mood continued joyous. From Barcelona's council came especially hearty felicitations for an heir who, since male, could succeed to Aragon's throne and so become "the unifier of the kingdoms and lord-ships."[10] And Castilians concurred in rejoicing that heaven, so long displeased, was at long last smiling upon them. The Desired One, as one chronicler termed the princeling, was given by the hand of God in response to the prayers of the people; he was "the true promised spouse of these kingdoms, descended from its monarchs and the noble line of the Goths," he who has come to redeem Spain from evil.[11]

Heaven's Smile

Some articulate and well-placed Castilians went further, to see universal significance in the birth. Pulgar, in a letter to a friend whom he assumed to be of like mind, the jurist Rodrigo Maldonado de Talavera, invoked prophecy as was customary upon a royal birth, but he forsook earlier allusions to Merlin and Dante to rely solely upon the weightier authority of the Bible and to convey a more earnest piety. "We here have very great pleasure," Pulgar wrote, concerning the birth of the prince and the good health of the queen:

Clearly we see ourselves given a very special gift by God, for at the end of such a long wait He has desired to give him to us. The Queen has paid to this kingdom the debt of male succession that she was obligated to give. As for me, I have faith that he has to be the most blessed prince in the world, because all those who are born desired are friends of God, as were Isaac, Samuel, and Saint John. . . . And not without cause, for they are conceived and born by virtue of many prayers and sacrifices. Look at the Gospel that is preached on the day of St. John; it is something so fitting that it does not seem but that one birth is the mold of the other; the other Isabel, this Isabel of ours. The other John in those times and this one in these days.[12]

"The birth of the other" was that of Jesus Christ; Pulgar also infers that the Messiah would appear among the Spanish. The other Isabel refers to the mother of John the Baptist, Elizabeth, which is the Latin equivalent of Isabel. That reference further spoke of the tendency to correlate St. Elizabeth with Christ's mother, Mary.

The chronicler Gutierre de Palma, writing in 1479, compared the prince to San Juan, then went on to parallel the mystical union of Prince Juan and Spain to that of Christ and his church.[13] Well attested to by then too was Isabel's predilection for the Evangelist. San Juan el Evangelista was known as Jesus' cousin and sometimes represented as his twin or surrogate; in a poem Gómez Manrique has him say: "I am Juan, that *privado* of my Lord and cousin. . . ."[14] John was also spoken of as "the firstborn of the adopted sons of Mary."[15] In those years, Isabel associated the Evangelist with her reign and dynasty, and with the divine obligation of the monarchy, an association being made patent in those two splendid buildings she had recently commissioned: San Juan de los Reyes in Toledo and the Charterhouse at Miraflores.

Yet, as Pulgar indicates and Palencia states, there was also the allusion made in the name of the prince to Fernando's patron saint, John the Baptist. Palencia says the name Juan alluded to both saints, as well as to both royal grandfathers, Juan II of Castile and Juan II of Aragón.[16] While May 6 was the day of the Evangelist, the prince was born closest to that of San Juan Bautista, June 24. Both saints were closely identified with the Messiah; the Baptist heralded his birth, the Evangelist his second coming. A painting later presented by Isabel and Fernando to the church of San Juan in Granada depicts a *piedad,* or pieta, with San Juan Bautista at one side of the cross and San Juan Evangelista at the other. Fernando appears below the Baptist and, below the Evangelist, Isabel, who holds a tablet inscribed "Make me passionately virtuous in your image and zealous for the faith."[17] In 1478, the two saints sharing one name represented two *reyes* sharing a single crown; they also represented the promise of that crown coming to fruition in a third Juan, who promised a Spain unified politically and religiously.[18]

Yet most immediately, the birth of a prince-son brought high praise to *los reyes* and recognition of her princely qualities to Isabel herself. In the exuberant response to the confluence of peace regained, the promise of a just and strong reign, and an heir come to all Spain, the king and queen were lauded extravagantly, not least by their chroniclers and courtiers. That year Diego de Valera hailed Fernando as another Charlemagne; he was prophesied to be monarch of all Spain, "to reconstitute the imperial seat of the illustrious blood of the Goths, from whom you come."[19] In the same vein, Fernando's old mentor, Joan Margarit, bishop of Gerona, wrote of both monarchs as restoring the lost Spanish unity of the Goths.[20] Pulgar, in sending what he had completed of his chronicle to Isabel, was more specific: "to write of times of such injustice converted by the grace of God into so much justice, of so much disobedience [and] so much corruption into so much order, I confess, *Señora,* requires a better head than mine to produce a lasting memorial of them all."[21]

Valera, after praising Fernando, went on to see in the advent of both monarchs the beginning of a golden age for all Spain; subsequently, however, he indicated he had a clear idea of where power resided. In 1481 he dedicated a concise history of Spain to Isabel, addressing her as "Very Powerful Princess," to whom "Our Lord has given, not without great deserving on your part, little less than the monarchy of all the Spains." Tellingly, he had written it on her command, as a summary centered on the accomplishments of her royal forebears "in these Spains," and so that through their example she might become better informed "of everything it was possible to do to govern and administer these so many and so diverse peoples that our Lord has placed under your royal scepter."[22]

Pulgar's chronicle, highly favorable to Isabel, although not uncritical, was limited to her lifetime. But Valera's history once again situated Spain and its rulers within the universal and providential context favored by Western historians and by Spanish chroniclers from Isidore of Seville on. His history was greatly indebted to those written during the reigns of Fernando III and Alfonso X.[23] Isabel received from Valera, that is, an updated version of the dynastic and national past presented as within God's shaping of time and stressing her royal responsibility within it. It was the sort of history that simultaneously imparted authority and gave advice to rulers. As to its author, he was now seventy-four and still speaking his mind to his sovereign, if much more happily than in the 1460s, for this ruler was listening attentively.

And it was more than a history; Isabel had again sought and received an inspirational treatise. This one, however, went beyond Talavera's injunction to soar, to place her, beyond gender, prominently within a line of illustrious monarchs. It provided a version of the universal past now viewed as leading up to her own reign, and presented history as divine plan. It told her that Spain's monarchy, as signs abundantly indicated, was ever more essential both to its people and the divine scenario encompassing the human past, present, and future.

Queen of Heaven, Queen of Earth

An anonymous chronicler also praised the joint reign as heaven sent: "and so marvelous a happening was not the work of men but a grand divine mystery, that people might see the marvels of God and his power. . . . More than this, God appeared to manifest his very favorable judgment in the King and Queen. . . . For their diligence and virtue, God wished that their works might appear marvelous to men, and extremely different from those of the king don Enrique."[24]

Fernando, the writer continued, had come to Castile to free its peoples, but it was Isabel who was heaven's particular instrument. So, in reflecting on her role in the surrender of Toro, everyone spoke of "how great in excellences was the Queen, the most accomplished person in the world; it was the belief of many that she was born *maravillosamente* for the redemption of kingdoms so lost."[25] All was God's marvel—prudently, he eschewed miracle—accomplished through the queen.

Valera made more explicit, although within a simile, what that statement insinuated: "It can in truth be said," he wrote to Isabel "that just as our Lord wished that our glorious Lady might be born in this world because from her would proceed the Universal Redeemer of the human line, so he determined that you, My Lady, would be born to reform and restore these kingdoms and lead them out from the tyrannical government under which they have been for so long."[26] And it was a poet, Antón de Montoro, who removed the veil, in addressing Isabel as "High sovereign Queen . . . preceding you the daughter of Saint Ann, from you the son of God will receive human flesh."[27] The daughter of Saint Ann, of course, was Mary. Here was religious hyperbole, a blasphemy more usual a generation earlier, when Isabel's mother could hear from another poet, Fernando de la Torre, that "You are my only God in this present life."[28] Indeed, Montoro was an aging *converso*, his verses a relic of that freer expression now frowned upon and soon to be condemned as dangerously heretical.

As to the new *infante*, Juan, tailored to him were prophecies of the Lion King who is to regain Jerusalem and rule in the last days as the final and greatest universal emperor. That popular medieval prediction, in turn based on the dream of four empires in the Book of Daniel, was then given a unique interpretation by the chronicler Gutierre de Palma. In Daniel 2, Nebuchadnezzar has dreamed of a mighty image with a head of gold, breast and arms of silver, stomach and thighs of brass, legs of iron, and feet of iron and clay. A stone, cut by no human hand, smashes that giant statue into pieces. The pieces are blown away by the wind. The stone becomes a mountain and fills the earth. Daniel tells this king of kings that he, Nebuchadnezzar, is the golden head, that his kingdom or empire is to be superceded by three more world empires, of silver, brass, and iron; all of them will fall. Then God will set up a fifth kingdom—the stone—which is his own kingdom and will stand forever. Palma interpreted this prophetic dream as a metaphor for the fortunes of the Trastámaran dynasty; the fourth kingdom ended with Enrique. The statue is shattered, the head of gold remains, and it is Prince Juan.[29] Palma thereby alluded to a medieval accumulation of prophetic imagery conflating Daniel's fourth and fifth kingdoms into a final world empire characterized as a golden age and ruled by a messianic Spanish king. Palma also made much of the Elizabeth-Isabel connection, and so by extension, the analogy to Holy Mary.

Still to be seen on the walls of the Hall of Justice in Seville's *alcázar* are the insignia of the Orden de la Banda, a chivalric order founded by Alfonso XI, purportedly on the battlefield of Salado. The symbols of that prestigious honorary society are a jar (or vase) and lilies, customary symbols both of Mary herself as immaculately conceived and of the annunciation to her of a heaven-sent son. For Alfonso XI and other Spanish kings, Holy Mary was the patron and defender of a Spain chosen to carry out heaven's mission. She was both Mary, La Virgen de las Batallas, bringer of victory and remembered as putting the keys of Seville into the victorious hands of Fernando III, and she was the Virgin Mary, the purest of all women, lily-white, increasingly extolled as without blemish, untainted by original sin.[30] She was, moreover, considered a queen in her own right, descended from King David. Gómez Manrique, in a poetic dialogue for Holy Week, has her say: "I am that Mary / of the line of David."[31] And from that Davidic line was to come the Messiah, royal son of a royal mother.

Now Isabel had given birth to a son, and neither was viewed as ordinary. Valera's statement that Isabel herself was born *maravillosamente* could only have called to mind Mary, born free of the stain of original sin come through Eve, the first woman and mother. Mary, it was said, had come into the world to produce a redeeming son, thus offsetting the damage done by Eve. Isabel had been instructed in that contrast between "the first and second Eve" in her youth in *The Garden of Noble Maidens,* its very title alluding to the Garden of Eden, lost when Eve ate the apple. The not very useful advice Isabel thus received had been supplanted by Talavera's enjoining her to emulate the Eagle. Yet those two tracts had conveyed one message in common.

The metaphor of the Eagle, known as the nemesis of the Serpent, had suggested that Isabel must strive to counteract all that Eve stood for. And around the same time, the audacious Iñigo de Mendoza had explicitly interpreted that as her charge. In an instruction for princes, he addressed her as High Queen, "come by grace of God to remedy our ills, as when our life was lost by the sin of a woman," so that God wants us to restore our health by the means that brought our fall—in other words, again through a woman.[32] God has sent Isabel, he was all but saying, to redress the sin brought on by Eve; she was another Mary. Hers, the poet inferred, was itself a second coming of sorts, enabling the whole Castilian people to advance from past infirmity to present good health. Like the High Queen Mary, this queen had come to the world to restore what was lost.

Isabel had come a long way since being told that as a woman and a crown princess she must endeavor to be the best of the products of Adam's rib. And no matter that neither she nor her mother had conceived mystically, she bore analogy to Holy Mary, even to a Mary with messianic attributes of her own. All those admirers of Isabel's, while adhering to panegyric conventions well established among Europeans, and while also lacing their rhetoric with Spanish historical allusion, yet brought a particularly intense and informed biblical cast of mind to what they said, and, with the probable exception of Gómez Manrique, all of them—Pulgar, Valera, Montoro, Palma, and Iñigo de Mendoza—were of *converso* lineage; they were culturally steeped in assumptions of direct relations between monarch and God of the sort found in the Old Testament, and in prophecies of a messiah to come from the royal line. All of them relayed a scripturally derived expectation of the coming of a messianic age, and all saw that wondrous time heralded by the birth of a heaven-sent son to this Mary-like queen. In the doing, they frequently alluded to the eschatological and apocalyptic prophecies of Daniel and Ezekiel in particular, esteemed among Christians as foreshadowing themes taken up by John the Evangelist in the Book of Revelation. The strong Jewish messianic strain had, like so many Jews, become converted, Castilian, and Christian, and, in 1478, fixed upon Castile's queen and her son.

Thus, with the birth of Prince Juan, Isabel was hailed by contemporaries as Mary's earthly counterpart and a spiritual virginity was claimed for her, a moral purity, a *limpieza* that was the sine qua non of divine election. Moreover, as royal head of the body politic, tradition obligated her to extend that *limpieza,* to cleanse that body, her realm, of the stain—the defilement, infection, and impurity—associated not only with original sin but, and repeatedly in Castile during the recent past, with heaven's displeasure, and with something else. Increasingly, the absence of purity migrated from association with original sin to the defiling presence of peoples of other faiths and at times was extended to their avowedly Christian descendants as well; even then the concept of *limpieza* was showing signs of fanning out from the moral and spiritual to the racial, into calls for *limpieza de sangre,* purity of blood. In 1478, however, it was a Mary-like *limpieza* that was attributed to the queen, as were certain other Marian aspects.

Mary, queen of heaven, was also claimed as the patroness and personification of various cities on Earth. Isabel personified the realm she ruled, the motherland, Spain. It was the blessed Mother Spain of Isidore of Seville; and it was the new Jerusalem to the chroniclers and poets. Her Spanish subjects were the new Israel, liberated by a type of messianic birth, freed to enter a mystical Jerusalem: now, exclaimed one, we are children of the free Jerusalem that is above, which is the mother of us all. That she had borne a son confirmed that Isabel mirrored heaven's queen and she had an analogous and assigned role in the redemption of the earth.

To what extent did Isabel share such views? She certainly approved their being aired and disseminated, often commissioning written and visual media that relayed them. Yet by all indication, her own sense of election had more to do with her inherited role and its responsibilities than with any personal messianic mantle; to her, that mantle was not personal but dynastic, and possibly her son's. Still, to Isabel the divine will revealed itself through history, and Spain's story itself represented a continuation of sacred, biblical, history. Moreover, Isabel also appreciated the stark contrast drawn between Eve and Mary, and certainly she did not object to being seen as a second Eve, like Mary come to right the wrongs of the first—imagery that, after all, paralleled belief in a historical Spain lost and regained. Isabel would commission, or possess, paintings of Adam and Eve expelled from Eden, and others representing the promise inherent in Mary, whether depicting Mary with the Christ child or a Mary with arms outstretched like eagles' wings sheltering Isabel and Fernando and their children beneath them.

Things to Come

For whatever reason, Isabel showed a particular devotion to the cult of Mary of the Immaculate Conception and founded three chaplaincies in her service, in Guadalupe, Toledo, and Seville. At Guadalupe in 1477 she assigned forty thousand *maravedís*—on revenue from Trujillo—to an annual *solemne fiesta* on the day of the Conception of Our Lady. She explained that, to give thanks for the victory over "our adversary of Portugal . . . where Divine Providence was pleased to show me justice," she had chosen to honor la Inmaculada, along with the feast days of San Juan and the Holy Trinity.[33] It was at the same time she had consulted Guadalupe's physicians, wanting a son.

In medieval Europe the Immaculate Conception—Mary as immaculately conceived by her mother Ann—was an event often alluded to in depictions of the Annunciation, in the vase of white lilies present when Mary hears from an angel that she will give birth to Christ. La Inmaculada was, however, taking on an increasing apocalyptic and prophetic dimension. In Isabel's lifetime that symbolic representation would begin to be challenged by another, the Woman of Revelation 12:1–3: "There appeared in the sky as a great sign: a Woman enveloped in the sun, with the moon beneath her feet, and upon her head a crown of twelve stars." The Woman is threatened by the Serpent, but she is borne to safety on an eagle's wings and she gives birth to a messianic son. A popular medieval figure, the Woman was identified with Mary and sometimes with the church itself. Undeniably, it was a particularly apt bundle of symbolism for a reigning queen whose patron saint, the author of Revelation, was

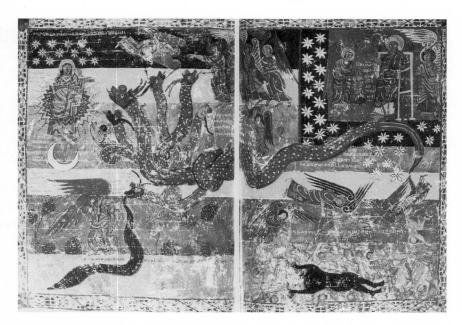

Figure 5. The Woman of the Apocalypse and the Dragon or Serpent. Beatus of Liebana, Commentary on the Book of Revelation. Morgan Library, New York.

represented by an eagle, and who herself had given birth to a much desired son.

La Inmaculada, looking very much the queen of heaven, standing on the moon, surrounded by sun and stars, appeared in miniatures in choir books at Guadalupe and in Isabel's oratorio there.[34] That representation made the connection between Holy Mary and the Woman of the Apocalypse, between queenship, motherhood, purity, triumph over the devil, and the divine promise of freedom from original sin to be fulfilled through the second Eve and in her son. Moreover, that apocalyptic analogy had Spanish precedent of the sort giving it additional significance for Isabel. As her father Juan was born, his mother had cried out "Oh, Sweet Mary!" or so stated a poet, deftly manipulating prophecy. That allusion was meant to affirm the crown prince's august provenance and destiny through relating his birth to the moment in the Book of Revelation when, crying out, the Woman gives birth to a son who will rule the world.[35]

Unquestionably, Isabel sanctioned the vision of her reign and its successes then being put forth so exuberantly, and she welcomed the interpretations of what her son's birth portended. Whatever the timetable of God's universal design, she clearly evidenced that as queen she was determined to further it, that it was incumbent upon her to get Castile ready, which involved purifying the land. In this as in much else, Isabel was a stickler for duty.

Her subsequent activities all fit easily within a providential and apocalyptic view of past and present that dictated a program for the future. Spanish history was the working out of God's design for Spain. God's tendencies regarding reward and punishment, and the sending of an ideal monarch for his purposes, in 1478 permitted seeing recent happy events as sign of and prelude to even greater things to come. And Isabel, however near she believed the last days to be and however she construed her own role in their arrival, surely did not question their imminence, nor did she fault such interpretation; rather, she promoted the insertion of her reign prominently within it. As Spanish ruler she had an assigned role to play, its contours clear, and she would go about it resolutely, her specific policies shaped in interaction with circumstances while conforming to the revealed will of providence.

Pulgar, in chronicling the birth of the royal child, employed cadenced language and allusion reminiscent of the biblical account of the birth of Jesus: "it pleased God that in that city she conceived and gave birth to a son who was named the Prince Don Juan."[36] And here he continued, "in those days that the King and Queen were in Seville, the king of Granada sent his ambassadors. . . ." Again the biblical ring, this time recalling the account of the three kings, yet heightening by contrast and lending discordant significance to what he wrote next. Abū'-l Ḥasan 'Alī, Granada's "king" or, more properly, emir, then demanded an end to Castilian depredations. Gladly, Isabel and Fernando responded to his envoys, tell your king, just as long as he agrees to pay the customary annual sum. The response of that ruler was the stuff of legend; indeed, it was legend: the kings of Granada who were accustomed to pay tribute were dead, he retorted, and the mints that coined it were now forging lances for defense against having to make further payment.

What is thought to have been Isabel's bedchamber in the *alcázar* of Seville, the room now, ironically enough, referred to in guide books as the Harem, has on its walls scenes influenced by *romances de la frontera,* those Castilian ballads exuding respect for Muslims brave and gallant enough to qualify as chivalric adversaries.[37] It was an attitude current in 1478; yet so was an awareness that the years of strife within Castile along with word that Portugal was planning to renew the war against Castile had heartened Granada. Isabel and Fernando did then acquiesce to a truce of three years without tribute, for they had still to negotiate a peace treaty with Portugal and they could not quite count on Andalusian loyalty. And other matters had priority.

Amid jubilation at the birth of the prince that summer of 1478, in Seville's streets and churches crowd-rousing preachers took up the theme of combating "those of the mountains," interpreting that expression as warring against the infidel. But, chiefly and most urgently, they warned of subversive heresy—within the realm and among *conversos* of Jewish lineage.

Chapter 10

Inquisition: 1478–1485

This Queen was she who rooted out and destroyed the heresy that existed in the kingdoms of Castile and Aragón of some Christians of the lineage of the Jews, who returned to Jewish rites, and she made them live like good Christians.

—Hernando del Pulgar[1]

Isabel had imposed her authority on Andalusia, and, not unlike the kings of its first conquest, having done so she entertained ideas of expansion outward, yet reports from her recently introduced officials and clergy there told of an internal threat, heresy, and urged immediate action. From her *alcaide* in Palos came word of secret cells, of "two or three mouths of hell," frequented "by addicts of witchcraft and sorcery," where the devil was worshipped and "our Lord and our Lady, his mother," were not, and of renegades and subversives living openly, with little fear; nor would he speak of matters yet uglier but urged remedy "before this land is alienated."[2] In the telling, he coupled religious deviation with resistance to royal authority, and he blamed on that insidious combination a substantial loss in royal revenues. Another informant also warned that religious laxity was widespread and that "in these kingdoms are many blasphemers, renegades from God and the Saints"; and he proposed as antidote focusing on one outstanding aspect, heresy among converts from Judaism. He was Tomás de Torquemada, prior of the Dominican monastery of Santa Cruz of Segovia and himself a *converso*.[3] Torquemada, reviving proposals made to Enrique in the 1460s, suggested to Isabel and Fernando a statute to stop Jews from influencing *conversos,* then advised an investigation, an inquisition, to uncover and punish judaizing converts.

Sporadic outbursts of violence against Jews had occurred since the later fourteenth century. As Julio Caro Baroja has stated, persecuting Jews served as an escape valve for popular disaffection, a valve sometimes opened by kings and magnates themselves. Mixing metaphors, he adds that at times too those outbreaks spread like a contagion.[4] Especially from 1391 and the time of Vicente Ferrer, such rampages had resulted in numerous baptisms of varying effectiveness. Produced thereby were *conversos,* New Christians—as Christian

converts and their progeny as well were known. Such people, admitted to public office since Christian, had become a factor in urban politics, which were in
turn usually aligned to those of some royal or noble faction. In Toledo in 1449,
New Christians supporting Juan II and Luna became a target of insurgents,
and were collectively condemned as secret Jews, as *conversos*. That charge was
made again in the 1460s, by Espina at Enrique's court. Rulers, their proponents, and the papacy more or less steadily opposed such argument based on
Jewish lineage and favored inquiring into individual persuasion instead. After
all, reflected Fernán Díaz de Toledo, in 1449, some of the best families had
Jewish blood; such had been the number of intermarriages with *conversos* that
who knew who were descended from them?[5]

Living in Seville, Isabel was discovering that *conversos* in Andalusia were
not like those at court or on the *meseta,* that they were more numerous, more
overtly powerful and close-knit, and less indoctrinated in Christianity, and
that they retained more openly at least residual Jewish customs. There were
more than twenty-five hundred of them in Seville, and they lived, as Pulgar
puts it, neither within one law nor the other. That they had tended to favor
Alfonso and then Isabel against Enrique boded not so much continued loyalty
as that they would support the least-pressing authority, which Isabel was even
then striving to ensure would not be her own. Their questionable loyalty to
church and crown was especially worrisome in view of the proximity of Muslim Granada and Africa and of the resurgent danger from Portugal; thus she
ordered, within weeks of Juan's birth, the confiscation of property of some
conversos known to have supported the Portuguese.[6] And had not Medina
Sidonia recently counted upon Seville's leading *conversos* in opposing the
crown-sponsored *hermandad,* known to be a wedge to increase royal control?

In the initial years of her reign, Isabel had honeycombed the major urban
councils, Seville's among them, with appointments of *conversos*. It was a way
of gaining royal control within towns and also of rewarding her *letrados* and
administrators, many of them *converso*.[7] For *conversos* tended to function as
tight-knit families, satellites orbiting their star, who was usually a court figure,
and dependent upon royal service. So in Seville she had recently ordered public offices restored to *conversos* dispossessed by application of local statutes of
purity of blood. But now in Andalusia those people who had appeared to be
part of the solution seemed to have become a part of the problem and the
solution appeared to lay elsewhere.

Relatedly, by the later 1470s municipal councilors, their seats inheritable
and their salaries minute, customarily made money through accreting land,
selling influence, and both setting tax rates and farming taxes. That is, municipal councils, no longer representative, were becoming closed enclaves of privilege and within them factions frequently formed around Old and New
Christians. Isabel, desiring to keep peace between them while dominating

both, faced the challenge of maintaining control of her early *converso* supporters, while not alienating Old Christians. For those purposes an inquisition
seemed just the thing, useful to sort out the spurious from the faithful, keep
powerful *conversos* in line, and foster religious and political solidarity. She was
presented with the strong argument that an inquisition would not only
uncover religious deviance and mete out punishment, but also head off recur-
rences of the populace taking that royal attribute, justice, into its own hands.
Such a tribunal would literally instill the fear of God and of the monarchy as
well, indeed reinforce the inseparability of the two in the popular mind. By
1478, she was sponsoring measures to investigate and separate true from false
converts in Seville. Preachers had appeared to alert the public to an ascending
threat of heresy, of Antichrist abroad; the parallel to the royal sponsoring of
fear-inspiring street-corner sermons advocating the *hermandad* is unavoid-
able.

Alonso de Ojeda, a Dominican of Seville, was chief among those warning
Isabel that heresy was rampant in the city. He was though only the most active
and ardent proponent of an inquisition. During her stay, he thundered against
conversos as such, much as had Espina and other Franciscans over a decade
earlier at Enrique's court. Ojeda, however, did so to the public at large and
quickly earned the reputation of being a *"Fray Vicente el segundo,"*[8] even
though Vicente Ferrer had sought to have Jews convert to Christianity while
Ojeda and the others lumped and excoriated those who had, and who, in good
part due to Ferrer, are estimated to have numbered at least 250,000 throughout Spain, many of whom, due to such coercive means, were shaky Christians.
In 1478, Seville itself had relatively few Jews and many wealthy and well-placed
conversos who retained some Jewish customs and constituted a powerful faction in the city.[9] Ferrer had alluded to prophecies that Jews must vanish before
the second coming; Ojeda extended that stipulation to New Christians. Moreover, it was exactly Espina's earlier wholesale condemnation of all *conversos*
as crypto-Jews that some of the most vociferous advocates of an inquisition
disseminated, along with the old hate-arousing myths of atrocities committed
by Jews and now laid to *conversos*.[10] It was the same stance the first proponents
of a statute of *limpieza de sangre,* of purity of blood, had taken at mid-century
in Toledo and soon in Seville as well, and it had gained adherents. A recent
escalation of mob violence in Andalusia revealed a widespread conviction, patently false, that all *conversos* were secret Jews, members of a race, as Bernáldez—
himself an Andalusian priest—stated, whose survival was an offense to God,
polluting the land.

In Córdoba, *conversos* were numerous, wealthy, ensconced in city government, and protected by its lord, Alfonso de Aguilar. There a brotherhood had
formed of Old Christians, mostly artisans, who termed themselves "pure" or
"clean Christians." During Lent of 1473, as the members of that Cofradía de la

Caridad, or Confraternity of Love, or Charity, marched in procession through the streets, a young girl emptied some water from a window, as often happened, but the house belonged to *conversos* and the water splattered an image of Holy Mary. From the marchers came shouts that it was urine and thrown on purpose, that it was an insult to the faith that must be avenged, that all *conversos* were traitors and heretics. The cry went up of "Death to the *conversos*!" The populace and a majority of the knights and squires and many foreign merchants responded "quickly and violently," inspired, wrote a witness, "with more greed to rob than zeal for the service of God." Within days, all Córdoba's *conversos* had been thoroughly fleeced, their houses demolished, and many of them killed. Girls and women had been raped. "And from the uprising a fiery spark leaped out from the city to all the neighboring places."[11]

Aguilar, beholden to *conversos* for their past support, protected them at first but subsequently came to agree that everyone of Jewish lineage must leave the city and forever be forbidden public office. Some Córdoban *conversos* fled to Seville, and it was during anti-*converso* rumblings there as well that Medina Sidonia recruited a number of them to garrison Gibraltar, then ousted them.[12] Now, four years later in Seville, on street corners and in plazas, preachers, particularly Dominicans, once again provoked public outrage against *conversos* by depicting them all as secret Jews who had insulted images of Christ and crucified Christian children.

Isabel, it is worth noting, became a tertiary sister of the Dominican order in 1477.[13] Still, she must be counted with those, among them many *conversos,* who hoped by an inquisition to put suspicion of true converts to rest, to protect the sincere Christians by separating out those who were not. New Christians were after all numerous among the nobility and among her most valued advisors and administrators, and they predominated among her chroniclers. Indeed, she and Fernando both were of Jewish ancestry, if remote. Fernando had Jewish forebears through his mother, Juana Enríquez, and Isabel's paternal grandmother Catalina, Catherine of Lancaster, was the granddaughter of a *conversa,* María de Padilla. Also of Jewish lineage was Leonor de Guzmán, mother of the first Trastámara, Enrique II, and a common ancestor of both Isabel and Fernando.[14] Even so, the term *converso* usually referred only to those Jews who had converted during the mass baptisms of 1391 or thereafter and their descendents.

Step by Step

Nicolò Franco, the papal legate who was Prince Juan's godfather, had been charged by the pope in 1475 with looking into the *converso* problem in Castile and supported instituting the Inquisition there.[15] That same year Isabel and

Fernando had named a Dominican, Filippo de Barbieri, as inquisitor general for Sicily, signaling their joint interest in invigorating the tribunal already existing in that kingdom of theirs. Sicily and its parent kingdom, Aragón, had long had an official but none too active Inquisition, under the authority of bishops and the papacy. Castile had none. And in 1477 first Isabel and then Fernando confirmed a privilege (a forged one, supposedly originally granted in 1233 by the emperor, Frederick II) allowing Sicily's new inquisitor general to retain a third of all confiscated property. They referred to Barbieri in that confirmation as a confessor to them both, and the grant sounds most like a *merced*. It indicated, that is, that at the outset they recognized that profit might be had from instituting the Inquisition and that they considered inquisitorial procedure in their realms to be under royal, rather than the usual episcopal, aegis. Barbieri, in turn, vigorously advocated to them that the Inquisition be introduced in Castile as well, telling them that the terror it would arouse and its exemplary punishments would be greatly beneficial to the faith.[16]

Toward the end of 1478 *los reyes* received a papal bull, of November 1, conceding them the faculty to appoint two or three priests as inquisitors in Castile. Most probably Isabel had requested it; her name must have of necessity been attached to its solicitation.[17] There is every reason to believe that the decision to institute the Spanish Inquisition and to do it as a royal endeavor was a joint one of *los reyes,* and that it paralleled royal purpose and strategy in instituting the *hermandad.* Everything indicates that the tribunal was expected, besides encouraging religious conformity, to heighten popular adhesion and internal control and stability, and to bring in funds. Moreover, its introduction flowed so naturally from the reforming climate pertaining since Isabel had arrived in Seville that imposing it could well have been accepted as the queen's royal and sacred duty.

The enabling bull, nonetheless, had been solicited with great secrecy, for no mention of royal interest in bringing in the Inquisition appeared in the proceedings of the Castile-wide ecclesiastical assembly held in Seville during the summer of 1478. And, once obtained, that bull was not implemented for two years. While Isabel left Seville that October cognizant of *converso* strength and worrisome connections to the great nobles and the Portuguese, most immediately she faced a contest with the papacy over control of Castile's clergy, and possibly another with those nobles and ecclesiastics from whom she was determined to regain Enrique's and Alfonso's grants of royal property and income. Moreover, it was the papacy that customarily directed the Inquisition through bishops. All in all, the time was not opportune to install a tribunal as a crown enterprise; and an Inquisition under the bishops was not to her purpose, especially since its principal proponent was Carrillo. Certainly, from the time she had agreed to the slower but more certain route to the crown as Enrique's successor, she preferred when possible to innovate by degree, to impose her programs gradually, building consensus; and thus did she proceed in this quest for religious conformity.

Accordingly, in 1478 she appointed not inquisitors but a commission to look into the religious condition of Seville's *conversos* and to try to persuade questionable converts to embrace Christianity wholeheartedly. Her nominees indicate the scope of her thinking: Cardinal Mendoza, represented by the bishop of Cádiz, he whose tears had gained *sevillanos* a general pardon in civil matters, but also Diego de Merlo, on the rise as the royal deputy through facing down Andalusian nobles, and Fray Ojeda, a prime proponent of initiating a Holy Tribunal or Holy Office, as the Inquisition was more formally known. In addition, Hernando de Talavera, whether or not a member proper, was highly influential in the workings of that commission.

Mendoza, as archbishop of the vast province of Seville, began by circulating to all churches and having posted in all parishes a pastoral letter detailing the proper forms of the sacraments and observances of Christian life and insisting they be followed. It stated, among other necessities, that Christian houses were to have "a painted replica of the cross on which our Lord Jesus Christ suffered, and some painted images of our Lady and some *santos o santas* which will arouse devotion in their inhabitants." Charged by him, clergy preached in public and instructed in private in an effort to drive home to deviating *conversos* "how much perpetual damnation of their souls and perdition of their bodies and possessions" they were bringing upon themselves by practicing Jewish rites.[18]

In Isabel's world, the criteria of orthodoxy was heavily weighted to conformity in outward observance and habits of everyday life; they were considered sure indicators of interior disposition. Eight months later, that commission not surprisingly reported the measures taken insufficient. The predisposition of the commissioners aside and no matter what the religious preference of individual *conversos,* in view of the generations of custom those instructions sought to eradicate so quickly and completely the result was a foregone conclusion. As Pulgar observed to Mendoza:

I believe that there are some there [in Seville] who are bad [Christians], and others, the largest number, are so because they follow those bad ones, and would also follow good ones if there were any. But since the Old Christians there are such bad Christians, the New Christians are such good Jews. I believe without a doubt, My Lord, that there must be ten thousand maidens in Andalusia from eighteen to twenty years of age who since they were born have never left their house, nor have heard or know any other doctrine than what they have seen their parents do.[19]

Yet had the criteria of orthodoxy applied been Jewish, the great majority of Seville's *conversos* would have also been found wanting. Even so, Jewish custom and Jewish law were so intertwined with, and had for so long so permeated, every aspect of daily family and communal life that many converts lacking solid indoctrination in Christianity, whatever their sincerity, tended to remain at least culturally connected to their age-old faith, and the practices so retained and embedded in everyday life were the very ones now being flamboyantly denounced and equated with apostasy.

Bernáldez, who was chaplain to an inquisitor, indicates this rule of thumb, and in language and tone similar to that of street-corner preachers. To him, judaizing was discernible in the customs "of the stinking Jews themselves."[20] Secret Jews he declared recognizable as gluttons who had never lost the Jewish habit of eating foods containing onions and garlic, refried with oil, and meat stewed in oil in order to avoid bacon, so that their breath reeked, and their houses stank, and they themselves smelled like Jews because of those dishes and because they were not baptized. Baptismal water, it was held, removed that stench instantly. Yet now it was admitted that baptism had not sufficed. Talavera, in a tract more to the point but only slightly less vitriolic, listed among customs identifying secret Jews the keeping of Saturday sabbath, circumcision, and washing the dead and burying them outside Christian cemeteries, and very deeply, which he was certain gave heretics a good start on their journey to hell. Moreover, *conversos,* and especially the women, had Jews come to instruct them at home. As predictable, *conversos* did not mend their ways sufficiently; rather, they then fled Seville in droves, particularly to places within seignorial jurisdiction.[21]

So matters stood when, in September of 1480, Isabel and Fernando, with a treaty with Portugal in hand and the nobles and clergy having shown themselves more tractable, named two inquisitors, Dominicans, for Castile; they were probably at work in Seville by mid-October. Isabel, when the immediate response was riots and a greater exodus of *conversos* (some of whom went to Rome to appeal to the pope), ordered both the provocateurs of such outbreaks and subjects who neglected to denounce fugitives punished and their goods confiscated. Named one of the two royal receivers of such property was the trusted Diego de Merlo, his appointment another indication of Isabel's awareness that financial value attached to insisting on orthodoxy. In January of 1481 the inquisitors banished all Jews from Seville and its hinterlands, and, armed with the queen's edicts and in a bravura show of royal might, they summarily ordered the marqués de Cádiz and all nobles to seize and turn over to them within fifteen days the Jewish fugitives they harbored.[22]

On February 6, 1481, six *converso* men and women of Seville who had been sentenced by the inquisitors for judaizing, after secret denunciations and without public trial, were burned at the stake. Such was the inaugural *auto de fe.* (That day, too, Ojeda preached a celebratory sermon that was to be his last, for he died of plague a few days later.) Shortly after, in a second *auto,* three *conversos* who had plotted to kill the inquisitors were similarly executed; such had been their prominence that Isabel had in April of 1478 confirmed to the ringleader, Diego de Susán, a seat on the city council.[23] That *conversos* had formed a sizable militia in Seville during the troubles of 1473 and subsequently been alerted by Medina Sidonia to resist the *hermandad* by force were good reasons why Susán's coterie was prepared with weapons and thinking in terms of resisting by arms another threatening royal institution. That by hindsight their plot appears to have been suicidal attests to the relatively sudden upending of power relations wrought by royal determination.

On March 26, seventeen more people from all walks of life went to the stake and yet many more did so in April. Outside Seville's walls a great field was designated as the *quemadero*, literally "the burning place," and there, it is said, statues of prophets were erected to which the condemned were tied when executed.[24] Those figures silently spoke of the Messiah having come and been denied by Jews, and reminded the crowds of onlookers that the second coming would occur only after the world was rid of heretics and Jews. The *auto de fe*, quickly becoming a popular spectacle, itself served as metaphor for purifying the land through fire, and offered the assembled a graphic representation of both judgment day and hellfire, palpably reinforcing an atmosphere of combined expectation and dread.

More *conversos* fled Seville that year of 1481; and, as plague reached epidemic proportions, the inquisitors also escalated their activities, and pursued them for several months. In the city of Seville by November 4, 298 people had died at the stake, and 79 been sentenced to perpetual imprisonment; in that year in the archbishoprics of Seville and Cádiz as many as 2,000 were burned to death and 1,700 penitents—wearing *sanbenitos*, yellow tunics inscribed with their names and crimes, and *corozas*, high conical caps—had been paraded through the streets at a time, with calculated effect on both participants and onlookers, offering entertainment and warning, enhancing fear and awe of royal majesty.[25] The Holy Office was soon extended to Jerez, Puerto de Santa María, and Córdoba, all jurisdictions of nobles who, through the 1480s and 1490s, nonetheless tended to protect *conversos*, including those penanced and "reconciled" to Christianity.

At the heart of inquisitorial procedure was what has been described as "a rapid, severe, and inflexible justice," appealing in its simplicity.[26] The inquisitors and their staff, working from reports of informers, secretly investigated, tried, and sentenced converts for heresy. Those who repented received lesser sentences and had to wear *sanbenitos* and *corozas*, those highly visible reminders to everyone of the awesome reach of church and state, for a designated period. The progeny of both those executed as heretics and those reconciled to the church were excluded from public office and much else for at least two generations. Were the condemned in fact heretics? It is instructive that in Spain today the expression "to wear a *sanbenito*" connotes unjust condemna-

Figure 6. Inquisition (1495). Pedro Berruguete. *Auto de fe*, detail. Prado, Madrid.

tion.[27] And while the Holy Office was licensed to function only against heretics, in practice it exercised jurisdiction over proselytizing Jews as well.

The *auto de fe* was a joint venture of the Inquisition and the crown, popularly recognized as such, enhancing belief in the power and sacred attributes of monarchy. Ostensibly the church sentenced the prisoners, then turned the condemned over to the state for execution. That was the operative fiction, a specious distinction. For church and state cooperated in every aspect of the Spanish Inquisition. Thus, against strong pressure, Isabel and Fernando supported inquisitors' keeping secret the identity of those making denunciations. Isabel is said to have believed that otherwise *conversos* would wreak vengeance against such witnesses.[28] It was a stand consistent with her often expressed conviction that seeking vengeance was a natural and pervasive human trait, indeed on one's own part imperative to survival.

Opinions

How did Isabel regard the Inquisition in those early years of its operation? Information is sparse, yet the opinions of some men close to her survive; their outlooks provide a good deal of insight into her own. One of the few who did not welcome the institution and its procedures was Pulgar, who, clearly not in complete conformity with her point of view, early on wrote in an open letter to Mendoza that "the Queen Our Lady does what she ought to do as a most Christian queen is obliged to do, and her duty to God requires no less." Still, he asked, might she not be misguided in executing essentially ignorant people instead of having them penanced and instructed in Christianity? For, while he himself has seen "the great extent of the blind stupidity and stupid blindness of those people"—the *conversos* who judaized—that did not mean they should be burned alive.[29]

Pulgar's demur stands almost alone among surviving statements in its spirit of Christian charity. It recalls the principle of jurisprudence he cited as having been expressed to Isabel by the bishop of Cádiz in urging that she make an example of Seville's foremost culprits, but not punish everyone in the city. Her response then had been forward looking: she was persuaded to grant a general pardon to all except heretics. Now it was to her that Pulgar attributed the introduction of the Inquisition, an institution practicing retributive justice if justifying itself as soul saving and nation cleansing, and clearly not one based upon the premise that the example of punishment of a few outstanding culprits would suffice. As was common knowledge, that tribunal and the queen who introduced and sustained it were determined to show themselves dedicated to extirpating heresy root and branch, and at the same time, as other commentators explained, to saving souls through drastic means.

Accordingly, Pulgar's outlook evoked a heated response from an anonymous *familiar,* or functionary, of the Holy Tribunal, addressed to the queen. While, he insisted, the Inquisition might punish some innocent people, "the harm from ignoring sin and withholding punishment is greater than the harm that would follow from administering it, for from that error would ensue the breaking of the faith, the corruption of true doctrine, and the destruction of virtuous life; and even though the punishment [of the innocent] create a scandal, it is the doctrine of Christ to punish, and not to open the door of pardon either to the few or to the many; for it is better to enter Paradise with one eye than to suffer in Hell with two. . . ."[30] That reference to getting to heaven with one eye became a staple among proponents of wholesale punishment by the Inquisition, as did the remarkable notion that "it was the doctrine of Christ to punish." The Christ of the Inquisition, and surely of Isabel at its inception, was not the Christ of the Sermon on the Mount.

Presenting himself as public minded, that functionary continued: "In this punishment, we are dealing with the common good, the preservation of which lies in punishing obstinate sinners, and disregarding their distress, for that must be subordinated to the common good, which is considered divine; just as for the survival of the body it is advisable to cut off the rotten limb." He concluded that the Bible was full of acts of God's vengeance and that "God, once the evil men are eradicated, will bring His mercy." Now, was his hawkish message and that of the Inquisition, must be a time of purging, of cleansing the body politic of every bit of infection. Underlying it was an apocalyptical vision of a stark world where good and evil eternally clashed, of a world at war as Castile had been for so long, if no longer at overt civil war; yet still the good, directed by heaven, were battling the devil's stealthy adjutants, those judaizing *conversos* who had outstayed their welcome on Earth. "And if you do not know their name," he instructed, "read the last part of the first letter to the Corinthians, where the Apostle calls them *marrantha,* which in our language means, plainly and simply, *marranos*"—that is, pigs.

Pulgar, responding, refuted any charge that he himself had impugned the Inquisitors; but arguing from Christian compassion, he defended minorly erring *conversos* and forgave his attacker, for "I believe that he who seeks vengeance rather tortures himself than avenges, and becomes so greatly changed that he tortures his body and does not save his soul," and him, Pulgar says, he will leave to heaven.[31] Yet Pulgar's opponent had inferred that in attacking the Inquisition the chronicler was attacking the queen, and to that charge Pulgar referred indirectly, in saying that her highness the queen had thought that she was doing right when she entrusted the fortress of Nodar to Martín de Sepúlveda, but he rebelled and turned it over to the king of Portugal; similarly, he implied, it was no great wonder that she may have been wrong in setting up the Inquisition, thinking that she was doing right.

His nuanced views in that exchange may have gotten Pulgar exiled from court, but not permanently, for he was again in Isabel's good graces by 1484. Still, that letter was quite possibly his final blast at the Inquisition. No one criticized the Holy Tribunal. Among the last to do so publicly was also the outspoken *converso* poet, Anton de Montoro, who, in concluding a poem of uncertain date addressed to Isabel, both indicated the increased social tenuousness of New Christians and displayed great confidence in the queen's protection, even in her appreciating his mordant sense of humor, by requesting that he not be burned at the stake at the moment, that it wait "at least until Christmas-time when fire is welcome."[32] Such levity was to be no longer tolerated as the 1480s wore on.

Christians of Jewish lineage, nonetheless, generally retained their posts at court; undoubtedly, such people did not display any distinguishing Jewish characteristics. They remained prominent among Isabel's most trusted and valued lawyers, administrators, and advisors. While the Inquisition did condemn some highly placed *conversos,* in those years none close to her were publicly prosecuted by the Inquisition, although some royal administrators and other prominent people were secretly reconciled. And clearly, Isabel herself held the view that baptism and belief made a Christian; she did not then endorse the essentially racial concept of *limpieza de sangre.*

Yet, as time went on, court figures were not exempt from public punishment and the attendant humiliation and loss of reputation. Shortly to be called before the Inquisition was Juan Ramírez de Lucena. A diplomat and Isabel's sometime chief notary, he had written that lapsed *conversos* were not heretics, for their baptism was not valid since forced, and like Pulgar he had denounced inquisitorial violence and urged clemency rather than burning. Yet that does not seem to have done him in. Rather, condemning Lucena's statement that "the monarchs our lords do not imitate God," another courtier countered with the official stance as projected by royal publicists, the Spanish church, and *los reyes* themselves: "Heaven must be praised," he countered, for wishing "to give us monarchs who follow the heart of God."[33] The Spanish Inquisition rested on that assumption.

On Behalf of the Queen

In 1481, as the inquisitors went to work, Hernando de Talavera once again wrote a tract at Isabel's request, and once again she would give every indication of endorsing his sentiments. Indeed, from all indications they represented the official and predominant ideology at the moment, justifying religiously both imposing the Inquisition and harsh treatment of Jews for refusing to accept Christianity. Talavera, like Pulgar, ardently defended sincere *conversos* as true Christians and was himself one. A seventeenth-century historian caught his spirit: "he detested the evil custom prevalent in Spain of treating members of the sects worse after their conversion than before it . . . so that many refused to accept a faith in whose believers they saw so little *caridad* and so much arrogance."[34] He also supported death for backsliding judaizers, equating judaizing with practicing Jewish customs, which he loathed, and he claimed a good deal of credit for bringing the Inquisition to Seville.

The queen had come to him, he explained, with a tract by an anonymous *converso,* "a malicious heretic," who defended the old within the new, who straddled Judaism and Christianity, and whose assertions had upset her. They infuriated him, as the refutation he quickly wrote entitled "Catholicism Impugned," fulsomely attests.[35] The unknown writer, Talavera declared at the outset, although claiming to be moved by prophecies and authorities and God's inspiration, was but a schismatic and sower of discord who divided Old and New Christians. He had the temerity to assume all New Christians to be of his own cast of mind—of his *patria,* nature, disbelief, infidelity, heresy and apostasy—not seeing that the day was coming of anger, vengeance, calamity, and misery for sinners, the day when he and his fellow-thinkers would descend into hell. He was, Talavera declared, nothing but an obstinate and malicious Jew, a heretic of the sort warned of by Daniel and Saint John, akin to the apostate friars and priests recently burned in Seville.

Contemporaries described Talavera as Christlike in his appearance, way of life, and attitude. It is a comparison most enlightening as to notions of Christ at the time. For that confessor of Isabel's viewed God as mostly vengeful, stern, and terrible, his judgment *cruel.* Talavera and his God sought from human beings a constant striving toward perfection and redemption; and the friar saw the good life as ascetic, a life of the soul and not the body. Now the time was fast approaching in which all the world would be renewed, "the universal justice which we await" coming soon. That being so, heretics such as "that madman" were intolerable. He had been influenced by Satan, "the old enemy of the human race who spoke through the serpent that deceived our mother, Eve and, through her, our first father, Adam." He was a subject of the devil who, as Job said, was the king of the arrogant and the father of liars, and who was also the destroyer-king of the Apocalypse of San Juan. Still, Talavera took care to defend sincere converts, writing that the saints stated and the civil laws desired that New Christians be honored and treated well. All of them should not be classified as *marranos,* but only those who, although baptized and showing some signs of Christianity, yet kept the ceremonies and rites of Muslims or Jews. Such people in truth ought to die.

Jesus Christ, according to "that lunatic," was a Jew. Talavera demurred, arguing that lineage commonly came from the father, that Christ was of no human lineage but was the Son of God. He then went on to provide explanation for his own attitude, and for inquisitorial prosecution seemingly based upon a person's residual habits. God, he said, had detailed in the Law given Moses that conduct was one with religious observance and faith, so that behavior signified belief. Indeed, he Talavera had preached in Seville that the law of Moses was without force since the fulfilling of the prophecies through the coming of Christ, the Messiah; since then, the Mosaic law was old and black and dying, not bad in its time but that time was past.[36] Any Christian holding to the old law sinned gravely and was an apostate or heretic; even Jews sinned more in holding to it than in breaking it. The new law in force was the Holy Evangel and all the New Testament; it was God's will concerning how human beings must live. For a new covenant had been made with a new Israel. Now "the people of Israel" signified those Christians whom the holy apostle had called Israel-in-spirit.

The Jewish people were no longer the people of Israel, nor were they true Jews; rather, they were the synogogue and *ayuntamiento,* council or court, of Satan, as the Lord said to Saint John in his Apocalypse (3:9); for although of the blood of Abraham, Isaac, and Jacob, they were not their children, nor of their line, for they had not their faith nor had they performed their works; they were but dry branches without yield. He despised, he said, those who insisted on being Jews. They were anomalies of history, which revealed God's plan, and hindrances to the Second Coming, and they insisted on claiming exclusivity as Israel, the chosen of God, when the chosen, the true Israel was, rather, the people of the Christian church militant.

Talavera also indicated something of how the religious climate contributed to royal stature. Ten years ago the law of the land had not been obeyed. That was due to the malice of the people or the defect of the ruler, as became clear in the improvement after "our most serene Lord and Lady" came to rule. There was now so much justice and good government in those kingdoms it was as if they were monasteries. The Lord had enhanced the monarchs' virtue and lives; they were his very excellent and fitting vicars, and had done the Lord's work in bringing about reform—the Inquisition clearly within it.

"Catholicism Impugned" closed on Talavera's old theme of self-perfection: people desire perfection; they seek the true good that is discernible only to those with a healthy, clean, and enlightened heart. The true good of human beings and their true and principal perfection is the glory of heaven that is to see God, to know him clearly and love him with all one's heart, and to do so a very clean heart is necessary as well as the very clear light of the holy Catholic faith. Those miscreants who abhor the light and who, like bats, love the darkness of night reach their desired end, the everlasting and consuming fire of hell. Seen from Talavera's vantage point, which undoubtedly greatly influenced Isabel, the *auto de fe* efficiently and relatively humanely dispatched those allies of darkness who insisted upon awaiting Antichrist as their messiah. It would continue to do so for some three hundred years.

Whose Inquisition?

The pope, Sixtus IV, in authorizing the introduction of the Inquisition in Castile, expected the usual procedure, that it function under episcopal jurisdiction with appeal to Rome. Isabel's instructions to the first inquisitors, however, while supposedly based on the papal bull of 1478, declared the Holy Tribunal a royal institution. With its imposition, his holiness was soon hearing from fugitive *conversos* and irate clergy of such uncanonical procedures as secret denunciation, false accusation, unjust imprisonment, unusually severe torture, and inquisitors appropriating for themselves the goods of the condemned. Accordingly, the pope made a stab at exerting papal and episcopal oversight. Yet while in January of 1482 he recommended less inquisitorial severity, in February Sixtus conceded to the monarchs the faculty to name the eight additional inquisitors they had proposed for Castile; preeminent among them was Tómas de Torquemada, who became Spain's inquisitor general.[37]

Fernando and Isabel had by then named inquisitors for Aragón, in December of 1481. And while in January of 1482 Sixtus denied their request to extend their version of the Holy Tribunal there, in April he changed his mind, although at the same time he complained of inquisitors there and in the Aragonese provinces of Valencia, Majorca, and Catalonia, who were moved to torture and condemn Christians by a lust for wealth. Sixtus, it appears, was fighting a weak rearguard action.

In 1478 Aragón already had an Inquisition run by its bishops. But Fernando, on becoming king of Aragón in 1479, had taken charge of the decrepit medieval institution in his lands; he reinvigorated it and extended its jurisdiction despite protest from clergy, town councils, and *conversos*. To all such Aragonese opposition to royal incursion and a Castilian inquisitor, the king always responded that the Inquisition had nothing to do with infringement of customary provincial rights, that it was a creation of the papacy.[38] Be that as it may, in October of 1482, the pope having suspended inquisitorial procedures in Aragón, it was Isabel he heard from. She well knew that the papal act posed a challenge to royal control of the Inquisition, one not restricted to Aragón. Sixtus soon received from Spain's queen a long handwritten letter. She was aware, Isabel wrote, that His Holiness had received complaints of the Inquisition and been told that she and Fernando wanted *conversos'* wealth, but such charges were untrue; rather, she explained at length, theirs was a deeply religious impulse.

In late February of 1483, the pope responded, reassuring the queen that he had not heard any such criticism and that no one could persuade him of anything against her religious devotion and that of her royal spouse. "We rejoice in our heart, beloved daughter," he told her, "at the determination and diligence you put into things so desired by us. We should always put diligence in applying the necessary remedies to such pestilential harm."[39] Accordingly, he approved and thanked God for her so holy endeavor and he exhorted "that you take upon yourself this cause of God, because in nothing else can you serve Him better than in this." She was to carry on the work underway and he would deny her nothing he could honestly concede.

Patently, Sixtus had backed down—he needed the monarchs' aid against France in Italy—and the Inquisition was theirs. It was a major victory for Isabel and Fernando. It gave them the first institution cutting across the heretofore separate administrations of Castile and Aragón, and greater leverage regionally, within towns, and in places under nobles' jurisdiction. In August of 1482 Sixtus had sanctioned secret reconciliation. At some point in the 1480s, Tomás de Torquemada emerged as chief inquisitor for all Spain.[40]

Within Castile, more tribunals were established, one in Córdoba in 1482 and, in 1483, others in Jaén and Ciudad Real. With Carrillo's death, the latter in 1485 moved to Toledo despite the protest of Toledo's *corregidor*, Gómez Manrique, who, undoubtedly mindful of the religious warfare in Toledo in the past, also publicly spoke out against any measure based on the concept of *limpieza de sangre*.[41] Inquisitors also went to work as well in Segovia, Àvila, Sigüenza, and Valladolid. Torquemada headed a growing bureaucracy, which he staffed in collaboration with the monarchs, and, when a realm-wide council of *la Santa Inquisición* was established (by 1488), he cooperated increasingly closely with royal *letrados*, until his death in 1498. Untiring and remorseless, Tomás de Torquemada extended the Inquisition throughout Spain. Although surrounded by pomp, he himself lived, as did Talavera, as a friar-ascetic.

Isabel and Fernando were present in Seville when, in November of 1484, Torquemada and the assembled Spanish inquisitors drew up a regulatory code. The royal pair then organized and attended another such assembly in Valladolid in 1488 that produced additional ordinances that extended inquisitorial power and autonomy, condoned great secrecy, and brooked no criticism. Moreover, Isabel sought economic security for the inquisitors and got them ecclesiastical benefices and some of the most secure revenues of the kingdom; even so, for such benefices some of them paid the crown large sums that they had accreted from confiscated goods.[42]

The monarchs saw to it that the Inquisition expanded, authorizing tribunals particularly for places with concentrations of *conversos*. Such tribunals tended to prosecute heresy vigorously and often on dubious evidence. Torture was normal procedure. Cases commonly began with secret denunciations. Denunciation was mandatory as the duty of all good Christians, and denouncers and witnesses remained secret. Two of the early tribunals, in Avila and Guadalupe, were both unusually active before they migrated elsewhere. In small Guadalupe in 1485 seven *autos de fe* were held in which fifty-two Judaizers, forty-six disinterred dead bodies, and two effigies of fugitives were burned at the stake; sixteen people were imprisoned for life, and yet others were sent to the galleys or sentenced to wear the *sanbenito* perpetually. Hieronymite friars figured among them.

When the Inquisition arrived in Toledo in 1485, a group of *conversos* plotted, as some had earlier in Seville and as Henry Charles Lea put it, "to raise a tumult and dispatch Inquisitors, and seize the city." They were betrayed and six of them hung. There too, as in Aragón and Seville, Jewish rabbis were ordered to have their people, although legally forbidden to testify against Christians, report to the Inquisition on backsliding *conversos*.[43] In Toledo, on Sunday, February 12, 1486, 750 men and women were reconciled after having been made to march in procession from the church of San Pedro Mártir to the cathedral, in freezing cold weather, the men without hats and shoes, the women naked, all carrying unlit candles and taunted by a great crowd, for people had come from miles around to see the spectacle. The reconciled wept and wailed; "it was believed more for their dishonor than for their offense to God."[44] Their prescribed penance was to repeat that procession, flagellating themselves as they went, on the five Fridays of Easter and on Holy Thursday. Again on Sunday, April 2, another 900 men and women were reconciled in similar fashion (if warmer weather). They were, however, forgiven one Friday's repetition and instead fined a fifth of their wealth for the war then underway against the Moors. Another 750 were similarly reconciled a month later. And on August 16, 25 men and women were burned at the stake, among them a member of the city council and other notables, all in conical hats and yellow *sanbenitos* bearing their names followed by the words "condemned heretic."[45] On December 10, 900 more people were reconciled; thereafter *autos de fe* were held periodically. In 1486–87, an estimated 5,200 people out of Toledo's population of 18,000 to 20,000 were punished for judaizing. There is no record but strong evidence of many additional secret and undoubtedly purchased reconciliations. Throughout Spain, it is estimated, 2,000 people were condemned and 15,000 penanced in the decade after 1481.[46]

In Zaragoza in 1485 some *conversos* stabbed to death an inquisitor, Pedro de Arbués, while he prayed in the cathedral. Retaliation was swift. One, apprehended and imprisoned by the civil authorities, had his hands cut off, then was dragged alive to the market and hung. His body was afterward cut down, decapitated, and quartered, his hands affixed to the wall above the door of the regional deputation, and one quarter of his body hung along each of the four highways out of town. Several others were executed similarly. Two committed suicide. But a brother of Gabriel Sánchez, the royal treasurer, somehow got away, and Sánchez himself, although implicated, was not charged, but did leave court for a while. On hearing of the assassination, the monarchs ordered to be burned summarily every *converso* throughout Aragón found to perform Jewish rites, "and all their property applied to the *cámara* of the king and queen, of which," says Pulgar, "there was a great quantity," for there were many *conversos* in Aragón and they abounded in wealth.[47] In Aragón, moreover, and despite his disclaimer, Fernando demonstrably used the Inquisition to cut through regional jurisdictions and as a listening post, as in instructing an inquisitor in Valencia to report on its civil officials. In Aragón too, the crown obtained papal permission to appropriate over half the incomes of condemned heretics.[48]

Did such wealth motivate Isabel to sponsor and support and expand the Holy Tribunal? Early on, the queen supported the Inquisition, Pulgar wrote, even though aware that *conversos* had fled Andalusia to the point that its great commerce had diminished, and thus her rents been very greatly reduced. Seville's revenues are estimated to have dropped by a third with the flight of thousands of *converso* families, including those of numerous merchants and tax farmers. Isabel, Pulgar averred, then gave little consideration to the diminution of her rents, for, putting "all interest aside, she wished to cleanse her kingdom of the sin of heresy, for she knew it was to the service of God and herself. And the supplications that were made to her in this affair did not make her change her mind about it."[49] Palencia concurred, making what were becoming the standard vituperative comments on judaizers: "The establishment of the Inquisition, indispensable recourse to punish the depraved heresy, had also augmented penury"; yet the royal course held steady: "It is certain," said Palencia, "that this was considered trivial in respect to eternal happiness, since true riches are the possession of the true Catholic. Thus don Fernando and doña Isabel put before any inconvenience whatsoever the ripping out of the multitude of judaizers from among the Andalusian people, so that those infected by error would return to the road of eternal health by means of a true reconciliation or would perish among the flames if they remained pertinacious." Accordingly, he went on, many had been burned, "for among *conversos* most women practiced Jewish rites. And most men fled, carrying their wealth or hiding it," so that "Andalusia remains exhausted of gold and silver."[50] That may be so, but Andalusia nonetheless appears to have recovered and found sufficient resources to serve as principal supplier of men, ships, and material in the war against Muslim Granada then beginning and lasting for a decade. Further, over the years funds from confiscations, fines, and reconciliations supported the Inquisition itself and flowed in to royal coffers, or should have: in 1487, the first receiver of confiscated goods to be called to account was accused of siphoning off a million and a half *maravedís,* and he was not the last.[51]

Debated still is whether or not the Inquisition was a source of profit to the crown. Miguel Ángel Ladero Quesada, the leading historian today of Isabelline Spain, estimates that in Andalusia between 1488 and 1497, confiscations reached 50 million *maravedís*. And Pulgar mentions that in Andalusia the queen directed that property confiscated from the condemned, including of the many who fled and were tried in absentia, was to go to the war against the Moor.[52] Records indicate it also went to finance the construction of San Juan de los Reyes, the Dominican convent of Santo Tómas in Avila, the royal residence—the *hospedaría*—in Guadalupe, built in 1485, and to make *mercedes*. It would appear that the inquisitors and the monarchs profited handsomely from inquisitorial activity; and that to the question of direct royal benefits must be added the assignments of confiscated wealth applied to numerous royal projects. That does not mean that royal motivation was solely material, for plainly there was political and spiritual profit to be had as well.[53]

Initially, Isabel had sought the imposition of an investigatory institution, then from its introduction in Castile employed it as a royal vehicle, and ever after, despite knowledge of its ruthlessness and abuses, she endorsed it and profited from recurrent, secret, paid reconciliations as well as confiscation of property. As to the dread it engendered, she believed firmly that a monarch needed to inspire fear in gaining respect. That the Inquisition promoted a secretive, distrustful, vengeful view of the world she could not have foreseen clearly; still, a part of her had always viewed the world in those terms. Another part, however, could temporize, as in mediating between Torquemada's zeal and the remarkably lenient inquisitors at work in Medina del Campo, that mercantile hub and source of substantial royal revenues.[54] Pulgar tells yet another sort of story, of the moral maze resulting from inquisitorial activity and of one way Isabel threaded through it. He tells of Jews in Toledo who, since forced to testify, through envy or malice or fear bore false witness leading to death sentences. The truth becoming known, Isabel ordered the liars be treated as perjurers; accordingly, eight of them were tortured with pincers and stoned to death.[55] That series of events can only be adjudged a spiraling of injustice.

There remains too an account of the inquisitorial impact on everyday lives otherwise not directly effected by the workings of the Holy Tribunal, if in this case within the royal household. One day in the 1480s, Prince Juan and his pages were playing at Inquisition, drawing lots for who would be the judges and who the accused. The boy judges then proceeded to read out the sentences, strip bare those condemned, and were tying them to the stake when an older page, realizing the game had gone too far, sped to the queen's apartments. Isabel herself, interrupting her siesta, hiked her skirts and came running, to find the boys at the point of actually garroting their victims. Zeroing in on the prince, Isabel gave her son a resounding thwack, then untied the prisoners and bore them off, wrapped in hastily found capes. It is further instructive that at least one of their parents, her secretary Fernán Alvarez de Toledo Zapata, was a *converso,* and revealing of her attitude regarding such matters that he was compensated with royal *mercedes.*[56]

There is no question that for Isabel the Inquisition was a means to achieve a bundle of political, religious, and economic ends: among them, extending, heightening, and maintaining monarchical authority, nurturing a broadly Spanish consensus based upon religious orthodoxy, keeping sweet those ordinary people who claimed social superiority as Old Christians, and removing a proven destabilizing tactic in local factional warfare. The Inquisition, in vigorously and highly visibly pursuing the goal of cleansing Spain of heresy, intensified not only certain nasty aspects of Spanish religious tradition but also boosted Spanish patriotism, public order, and political conformity.

As time went on, and as in other projects once embarked upon, the queen became ever more obdurate in support of the Holy Tribunal and ever more convinced of its efficacy, brooking no argument. So she moved steadily toward a closed mind on the matter and a closed society for Spain. Isabel did on occasion attempt to curb those abuses that could be construed as disrespectful of royal authority, and after a decade she sought to call inquisitors to fiscal accountability, but she certainly did not put full energy into either. Over time, she came to view as a logical extension of that institution's findings the expulsion of Spain's Jews; and in the end she condoned policies of *limpieza de sangre.* The Inquisition endured into the nineteenth century, having reached a peak in activity and executions in the later sixteenth century under her great-grandson and great fan, Philip II.

*   *   *

In his bull of August 2, 1483 in effect authorizing a crown-directed Inquisition for all Spain, Sixtus IV looked forward to two things: converting the Jews and the fall of the infidel kingdom of Granada. That bull accorded with Spain's historical mission; still, in Spain the papal hope of converting the Jews was passé. The Inquisition as it swiftly evolved there was not so much about encouraging conversion as containing it. The bull dovetailed with growing royal conviction in stating that *conversos* as such were known to backslide, constituting the sin of heresy, and that they raised their children in heresy, infecting Christians. The pope and *los reyes,* then, stood somewhere between recognizing the existence of sincere converts and condemning them as a group. In the circumstances it was perhaps inevitable that within the Holy Tribunal and throughout the land ostracism for those lacking "*limpieza de sangre*"—racially uncontaminated blood—would gain adherents. To Isabel, overriding all other considerations was the welcome convergence of religion, royal program, and popular opinion. And the pope's sentiments concerning Granada appeared extremely timely.

Chapter 11
Readying: 1478–1481

When Isabel joined Fernando for Christmas at Guadalupe in 1478, peace had been made with Portugal's ally France and with Carrillo. Soon after, the defeat of a last incursion by the Portuguese and of their supporters in Extremadura, along with the unpopularity of the war in Portugal itself, signaled its end. France remained at war with Aragón; and that contest was soon Fernando's responsibility, for his father died, on January 19, 1479, in his eighty-first year.

At the last, Juan II of Aragón could claim vindication for his reliance on prudence (as he understood that virtue) and for his foresight in engineering the marriage of Fernando to Isabel. Juan, born in Castile, was indisputably *the* architect of a unified Spain. His son was king of Castile; his grandson was heir to both Castile and Aragón. To the end of his long life he had governed his kingdom strongly and personally. His example, followed selectively, would earn Fernando a reputation as Europe's most astute statesman-king.

That year, from June through October, Fernando was in Aragón. Isabel, in Castile, personally took charge of peace negotiations with Portugal. On invitation of her aunt, Beatriz of Braganza, the powerful dowager duchess of Viseu, who was King Afonso's sister-in-law and mother-in-law to his son João as well, aunt and niece met in Alcántara in March. Agreement foundered on the very first clause the Portuguese proposed: that Isabel's son Juan marry Juana, sometime known as *La Beltraneja* and referred to by the Portuguese as the Excellent Lady; she was now seventeen years old and her diminished prospects had dampened the ardor of Afonso of Portugal but not his desire to save

Figure 7. Fernando II of Aragón. Staatliche Museen Preussischer Kulturbesitz, Berlin.

face. Isabel remained adamant that the potentially troublesome girl must go to a convent, declaring she would sooner break off all conversation than listen to anything further on the subject. She also refused to promise her own daughter Isabel to Afonso's son and heir, João, a widower with children. She had firm support; there is an annotation in her hand in the margin of her dictated report on the talks: "The King conferred with the Cardinal on all this and sent to say they agreed entirely."[3] Isabel departed at impasse.

Matters went better in June. Isabel then sent to Portugal the jurist Rodrigo Maldonado de Talavera with full powers to negotiate a treaty, but not to do it without getting Juana to a nunnery and arranging that the *infanta* Isabel marry not João but his son and heir, Afonso. Isabel did not like or trust João, whose intervention in Castile's civil wars had nearly brought her cause to grief. His son was more personable and closer in age to her daughter, and a child of theirs might well one day wear Portugal's crown. The god of irony was surely smiling at her determination in that matter.

Maldonado wrote to the queen daily, as instructed, and Isabel, foreshadowing the diligence of her great-grandson, Philip II, personally read and annotated the copious memoranda he sent, including the reports she had ordered on Portugal's military strength. On September 4, 1479, came a treaty of peace that essentially reestablished the status quo ante bellum. Castile renounced all claims to Guinea, the Mina de Oro, Madeira, the Cape Verdes, and the Azores, and to any lands undiscovered between the Canaries and Guinea. But Isabel retained the Canaries.[4] And on July 26, 1480, a complementary accord guaranteed that Castilians might trade in Barbary and the Portuguese in Granada. The way was cleared thereby for Castile to extend its influence along the North African coast and to expand westward into the Atlantic from the Canaries; and thereafter Isabel pursued a policy of maritime expansion. During Cortes in Toledo, the tame deputies suggested that the monarchs order galleys and *naos* to be constructed in Vizcaya or Seville, "so that they might be as powerful at sea as on land and surpass all other kingdoms in seapower."[5]

In September of 1479, Isabel confirmed the peace treaty, betrothed young Isabel to João's son, and signed a second agreement, stipulating that Juana was to enter a nunnery or be otherwise confined. So concerned was she that that stipulation be honored that she agreed to send that daughter of hers—of whom all accounts state she was inordinately fond—to Portugal as earnest of her own intention.[6] Juana entered the elegant convent of Santa Clara in Coimbra as a novice, and although Isabel strove to see that no loophole should enable her to leave, she came and went as did many highborn ladies; and João, becoming king when Afonso died of plague in August of 1481, had Juana to stay at the palace despite Isabel's admonitions. Isabel pressed on, sending Hernando de Talavera to Portugal to make certain that Juana took the veil. And an accord was reached with João guaranteeing that Juana would not marry or leave religious life or Portugal. (She did none of those things, and she lived until 1530.)

Toledo, 1479–1480

With peace with Portugal confirmed, Isabel immediately went to Toledo, where the Cortes, postponed from June of 1479, at last met, from October 1479 through May of 1480.[7] Toledo, hallowed as the old Visigothic capital and as a principal staging area of the reconquest, was also perennially a major seat of unrest and revolt. Its population fluid and cantankerous, Toledo was plainly overdue for a royal stay entailing a mighty display of royal power. Moreover, by imposing her commanding presence at that center of his archdiocese, Isabel—to whom revenge was always sweet—could further serve notice on Carrillo, whom she had only officially forgiven for his defection. Nor was it happenstance that the convocation coalesced with the raising there of the great monastery of San Juan de los Reyes.[8]

On October 14, 1479, Isabel made a brilliant entry into the city with her infant son, Prince Juan; the swearing of the oath to him as her heir had been the ostensible reason for calling Cortes. It also spoke well for dynastic continuation that the queen was obviously again well advanced in pregnancy, and in Toledo in November she gave birth to an *infanta*, Juana. Fernando arrived nine days after Isabel, his entry equally splendid but far more exotic. For in his entourage was an elephant, the gift of an embassy from Cyprus, its presence evoking the imperial grandeur of Alexander the Great, remembered as a world conqueror. It alluded as well to Hannibal's crossing of the Alps, and it pointed up a comparison being made by panegyrists—of Fernando to Charlemagne, who had received a gift elephant and supposedly obeisance from Harun al Rashid, the sultan holding Jerusalem. Medieval legend also foretold the coming of a second Charlemagne who was often conflated with the last great world emperor. This new Charlemagne, Christ's champion, would come forth like a lion, lead Christians against the infidel, and finally inaugurate from Jerusalem a universal period of peace and plenty.[9] For what *los reyes* were about to propose, that elephant so ringed with allusion was an appropriate symbol.

Yet other significant spectacles were in store in Toledo. The royal governor, or *corregidor,* who was Gómez Manrique, staged a very different event. Alarcón, Carrillo's alchemist and influential advisor, having confessed to "having caused many scandals in the kingdom and disturbing the peace," Manrique had the old fraud publicly beheaded and his severed head dropped into a garbage basket, in order (says Pulgar) to engender the fear that leads to peace.[10] Public theater continued in Toledo's cathedral, with Castile's mightiest—lords, prelates, knights, and *ricos homes*—attending. While the queen, the king, and the prince stood before the high altar, one by one, on a missal held by a priest, those worthies solemnly swore "to have for king of those kingdoms of Castile and León the prince Don Juan, the first-born son of the King and Queen, after the days of the Queen, who was the proprietress of those kingdoms."[11] Those ceremonies but raised the curtain on the show of royal power that was to follow. Isabel and Fernando had convoked that Cortes to confirm the order of succession and to raise money: it voted them a *servicio* of 104 million *maravedís,* a huge amount even taking inflation into account. Moreover, they treated it as a forum in which to unveil a fuller program of reforms designed to cement royal authority and centralize administration. That the representatives would comply was a foregone conclusion. The delegates came from the usual sixteen or seventeen royal towns, their selection more strongly influenced than ever by the crown.[12] And while they were customarily elected by each municipal council and restricted "to honorable persons who were not manual laborers or town officers," they did include several *corregidores,* those royal watchdogs who tended to exercise a balance of power between urban councils and the lords or abbots often bent on dominating them. The ubiquitous Gómez Manrique presided over those *procuradores.*[13]

A tangle of networks threw up those representatives. As one commentator explains, most urban council members were interrelated; "and being delegates to Cortes remained an exclusive privilege of a few families." That situation was not only understood by *los reyes,* but promoted by them within a conscious policy of control of that assembly. During their reign what had been a social concentration of the delegates became further consolidated and frequently benefited specific families who rose socially and politically through adherence and service to the monarchs. Linked thusly were Cortes delegates, royal counselors, and administrators of basic governmental institutions.[14]

The Cortes neither represented the entire realm (except as a corporate body) or its estates nor enjoyed the legislative powers associated with modern parliaments. It was called when rulers so desired. Its discussions were limited to subjects proposed by the crown. It did not hold the purse strings; rather, expected of its cities was the concession of a *servicio,* a sum proposed by the crown. Carefully controlled, both sounding board and rubber stamp, it was nonetheless a legitimating and affirming device, its oath customary to establishing royal succession, and its sessions good places to announce and advertise royal policies. And, softening royal authoritarian demeanor, keeping the crown in touch with local concerns, and holding out hope of what is today known as pork-barrel perquisites, delegates were permitted to present petitions regarding local matters, and they were compensated personally, by salaries and gifts, or assigned percentages of the *servicio.* At Madrigal the Cortes had chiefly cleared the way for introduction of a general *hermandad* requiring the participation of the towns; at Toledo it mediated many more royal initiatives. There *los reyes* would "utilize the opinion of the *procuradores* about certain laws to assure a greater unanimity and efficacy between king and realm."[15]

The proposals put forth and the promises made in Cortes at Toledo in 1480, while on all points carefully citing precedent and frequently emanating from measures conceived or even introduced in the previous two reigns, nonetheless would at last be implemented in Isabel's time and so bring about a revolution in the scope and efficacy of royal government; her enactments would go far to convert medieval realm to modern state. The legislation introduced at Toledo built upon the vision of strong personal monarchy propounded in her father's time, and on the orthodoxy and reforms suggested or demanded by royal critics during Enrique's reign, as well as on promises made at Madrigal in 1476. Those measures enacted at Toledo reflected the same vigorous spirit of straightening up morally, spiritually, and administratively then also propelling the setting up of the Inquisition and the royal scheme of ecclesiastical reform (of which more later), and the same spirit spurring the rapid hardening of attitudes toward Jews and Muslims.

There is no conclusive evidence that Isabel and Fernando had mapped out what looks by hindsight like an overall program, but certainly by then they had given much indication of proceeding in determinedly orderly and systematic fashion. At Toledo, they set forth governing principles from which, as the measures they took from then on attest, they did not swerve. In broadest terms, those principles accorded with historical and traditional, time-honored, royal goals as the reigning couple understood and represented them.

From the outset, the monarchs persuaded the delegates to sanction a great increase in royal authority and power by convincingly presenting their measures as long desired by everyone present and as highly beneficial to the realm as a whole. In the doing, they made reality of some old ideals, such as were expressed in the *Partidas* or in legend, and particularly they took an absolutist view of monarchy, and they claimed territory purportedly held by the Visigoths as theirs by right of descent. The very ordinances approved in 1480 helped to ensure that for the remainder of Isabel's reign, Cortes was seldom called, only when thought necessary to recognize changes in the order of royal succession.[16]

The Larger Picture

For Isabel and Fernando, reinforcing royal control of the Cortes fit within a program of centralizing power and administration in themselves. And, as Pulgar indicated by what he chose to write, the functioning of a conciliar system was of more moment than was the workings of the Cortes. "In that Cortes of Toledo, in the royal palace where the King and Queen stayed, five councils sat in five apartments," states Pulgar, describing the Royal Council and its sub-divisions, several of which would become separate councils by the end of the reign. One group handled affairs of state including relations with other rulers and the papacy, its decisions binding. It included *grandes,* favored royal coun-selors, the royal secretaries, and the king and queen when matters warranted. A second, devoted to justice, heard petitions and cases and passed sentence; it was composed of prelates and *letrados.* Both of those subdivisions were to remain within the Royal Council, although justice would be shared with the royal chancery.[17] Two others, however, would become separate councils. One of them was made up of knights and *letrados* native to Aragón, Catalonia, Sic-ily, and Valencia, and handled the business of those kingdoms; it would become the council of Aragón. In the other sat the representatives of the *her-mandades* of all the kingdom and their royal overseers. In the fifth and last chamber, there gathered "the *contadores mayores* and officials of the books of the treasury and royal patrimony," who estimated revenues and assessed taxes, arranged for their farming, and received and recorded payments. In Toledo in 1480, "all these councils had recourse to the King and Queen with anything doubtful come before them. And their letters and provisions were of great importance, signed on the back by members of those councils, and signed inside by the King and Queen." Isabel's loyal minions controlled each of those divisions; Cardinal Mendoza presided over the council of state.[18]

For decades, the control of the Royal Council had been the focus of con-tests among the great nobles, but that was changing. While monarchy and nobility in tandem continued to dominate the realm and while the council included nobles, spheres of authority and power as delineated at Toledo kept the nobility as a whole at a remove from affairs of state. The days of Isabel's avowed insistence on consulting the great lords of the realm on all matters of moment had passed; now the queen relied most heavily on a smaller, private *cámara,* a cabinet, made up of chosen members of the Royal Council. And expanding in importance was the post of royal secretary, held by several *letrados,* who among other functions oversaw the process of choosing delegates to Cortes.[19]

Within the evolving governmental institutions, *letrados,* lawyers, were of increasing importance. Lawyers comprised not only a majority on the council of state, but staffed the expanding administrative bureaucracy, which also included some lesser nobles. *Letrados* who were royal secretaries were particu-larly influential through direct and continual contact with the king and queen and through enjoying royal favor and confidence. And *letrado* families, indeed clans, formed an influential network linking localities and central administra-tion so that the royal presence was felt throughout the realm. A later Mendoza would comment that the sovereigns "put the administration of justice and public affairs in the hands of *letrados,* whose profession was legal matters, middling people between the great and the small without offense to one or the other." Such people, he said, lived quiet, simple, honest lives. They did not visit or take gifts or form close friendships. They neither dressed nor spent extravagantly. They were moderate and humane.[20] He did not mention the web of relationships they wove.

While hindsight had idealized that description, its substance was corroborated by Isabel's chroniclers. One of them, Lorenzo Galíndez del Carvajal, himself a *letrado* and a later member of her council, recalled that she kept in a book the names of meritorious men of middling social background who possessed talent and moral rectitude, as a pool of worthies for all vacant positions, civil and ecclesiastic.[21] Such people proved invaluable to her, as they did to other European monarchs, in establishing a modern state. Moreover, in seeking trained administrators, Isabel supported the *colegios mayores,* the schools within the universities that were for her the prime sources of well-educated bureaucrats and where education was strongly centered on civil and canon law. The revival of Aristotelian Thomism within the schools was supportive of royal authority, particularly at Salamanca, under the Dominicans. (The outstanding Thomist there then was Diego de Deza, who would become Prince Juan's tutor and then succeed Torquemada as chief inquisitor.) Later that year, Isabel and Fernando visited Salamanca. The favor they showed the university remains commemorated on its facade where a medallion bears their portraits; surrounding them is a Greek inscription, which, playing on their motto, *tanto monta,* translates as: "the Monarchs for the University; the University for the Monarchs."

Laws and Profits

For Castile, the ordinances endorsed by the Cortes of Toledo cleared the way for constituting a nation-state that was in form close to an absolute monarchy, and they were the work of jurists experienced in promoting royal interests. Thus Alfonso Díaz de Montalvo, one of two royal secretaries, who three decades earlier at the behest of Isabel's father had found law to support absolute royal authority and had drawn up the crown's indictment of Alvaro de Luna, in 1480 was charged with preparing a single compendium of Castilian law. The result, completed in 1484 and printed in eight large volumes in 1485, proved less a collection of existing laws than a regalist code with imperial Roman provenance. For as Montalvo himself explained it, he had gathered royal ordinances and pragmatics, but omitted "laws superfluous, useless, revoked, derogated, and those which are not or should not be in use, conforming with the use of the court and royal chancery."[22] Each municipality was ordered to have a copy. That code, put in force as supplementary law by Isabel, became a basis of juridical decision for more than fifty years. Such a body of otensible precedent served to obviate having the Cortes promulgate laws and to elevate reliance upon royal decrees. Similarly, administration of royal justice was subsequently expanded by introducing regional tribunals—*audiencias* (one sat first in Ciudad Real, in 1494, and later in Granada; another sat in Jaén)—and through reinvigorating the original royal chancery at Valladolid, which, from 1480 on, sat permanently in the mansion where Isabel and Fernando were married, for its owner, Juan de Vivero, had been charged with the death of his wife and the crown had commandeered his residence.

The greatest coup of 1480, however, was reclaiming the royal patrimony, the numerous territories and revenues so generously dispensed as *mercedes* by Enrique and Alfonso, a move valuable to the monarchs both for the revenues regained and the principle imposed. The majority of such grants existed in the form of *situados,* liens on specific income-yielding royal imposts, or as *juros,* bonds, transferrable rights presented to individuals or institutions for term, life, or in perpetuity. Both *situados* and *juros* were royal permits to receive annual sums on revenues produced by a stipulated *renta pública* such as specified *alcabalas,* sales taxes. Since most ordinary royal income derived from *alcabalas,* those outstanding obligations cut deeply into the funds at the disposal of *los reyes.* Moreover, by 1480 some *rentas* were mortgaged so far beyond what they produced that Isabel had ordered payments to bondholders confined to a proportional distribution.

At Toledo, all such grants made by her brother Alfonso were rescinded, and those adjudged bestowed from 1464 through force or deceit exercised upon Enrique were ordered separated from those awarded properly by him, following a formula proposed by the cardinal. Among other things, its adoption says something about Isabel's attitude to the recent past, for the plan assumed that the civil war had been an assault of nobles on monarchy. This *mercedes* reform was just the reverse, and it proclaimed no high opinion of the validity of either Enrique's or Alfonso's reigns, and represented Isabel as returning Castile to proper governance.

In 1478, indicating the direction of the wind, Fernando de Mexía, a poet and member of the city council of Jaén, had written a *nobiliario* that stated nobles were made by either God or the crown and in no other way; his further point, like Isabel's in 1480, was that position in secular society was not held independently of royal fiat. Diego de Valera had said much the same thing earlier.[23] Even so, at bottom the arrangements of 1480 were viewed as an exchange. The monarchs pardoned all nobles and high clergy who had been on the wrong side in the late war and assured to them their property and positions; in 1486 Isabel would guarantee their holdings in perpetuity through confirming the institution of *mayorazgo,* the right to entail estates. Nobles were to return only part of the royal rents acquired from 1464 on, the crown would recognize and legitimate all the rest. In accepting those arrangements, the nobility acknowledged the authority and jurisdiction of the crown as superior to its own and conceded the royal right to create law and to administer justice everywhere throughout the realm. In turn, the crown affirmed the economic and social standing of the nobles, and they retained much de facto local and regional power as well as strong, if lessened, political influence. At Toledo, that is, Isabel both constrained and reassured the nobility.

In implementing the retrieval of *mercedes,* she left to the many-faceted Talavera the sorting out of legitimate claims from illegitimate ones. He sent out royal *pesquisidores,* investigators, who traveled for three years ascertaining just who held royal lands or enjoyed usufruct of royal rents and in what amounts. He then scrupulously applied the criteria decided upon and his report became the basis of final settlement. In the end, roughly half of the grants were allowed to stand. Notable among those losing least was the cardinal. Cabrera and Bobadilla, however, gave up an amount in *juros* only exceeded by the loss sustained by Beltrán de la Cueva, but the Cabreras were granted the prestigious and income-producing *marquesado* of Moya, and Beltrán soon did well as a leading lieutenant in the Granada campaigns. Isabel also generally opposed reclaiming grants made to monasteries, hospitals, and the poor. Although nobles, treasury officials, and tax farmers would continue to siphon off royal income beyond that granted them, nonetheless the monarchs recouped quite a bit; they had also made their point.[24]

At Toledo too, Isabel and Fernando, indicating that they well understood the three-pronged basis of secular power in Castile—monarchy, nobility, and towns—further extended royal control over municipalities as well. With peace, Castile's cities were experiencing greater well-being and a surge in growth, and they were seeing in the crown their best assurance of continuing protection against encroaching nobles. So when given the choice of relinquishing their *juros,* often uncollectible, or of facing new exactions, they gave up most of their *juros.* Concomitantly, royal *pesquisidores*—investigators—were sent out to restore old municipal boundaries encroached upon by nobles and to hear complaints against *corregidores.* In 1480 too the monarchs ordered *corregidores* situated in all cities of the realm, "so that nothing may be done to our prejudice and that of our jurisdiction without it then being remedied or reported to us."[25] Isabel charged Talavera with implementing that directive as well, and ordered him also to have his agents recompense individuals for losses of horses and other goods, and provide for the women and children of men killed in the late war.

Currency reform also received attention at Toledo. The monarchs imposed a gold standard, justifying it as holding down prices after years of currency clipping, devaluation, inflation, and loss of confidence in Castilian coinage. They confirmed in Cortes prohibition of exports of both gold and silver, setting a death penalty for taking out of Castile more than five hundred *doblas*. In 1481 they ordered *excelentes,* equivalents of the Venetian ducat, coined in Valencia, both to promote international exchange and as a way to strengthen the money of account, the *maravedí*. Minting, it is worth remembering, was a regalia of the crown and itself a producer of income, including a fee for coinage. They also had currency devalued. One effect was to raise the value of gold and so benefit the royal treasury since it had, foresightedly, put in reserves of that precious metal. Finances, it should be noted, had remained in the hands of those three time-tested stalwarts, the *contadores mayores*— Cárdenas, Chacón, and Rodrigo de Ulloa; Chacón, moreover, held the post of *mayordomo mayor,* chief steward or head of the royal household, which included oversight of the royal *hacienda,* or estate, which was indistinguishable from the treasury of Castile.

The reorganization of Castilian finances, as ordered at Toledo, resulted in a great rise in royal revenue, already mounting, and which more than doubled between 1477 and 1482. Ordinary royal income increasingly came from commerce and additional monies from the *tercias reales,* two-ninths of the ecclesiastical tithe, as well as from customary levies on Jewish and Muslim communities; and two-thirds of all royal income derived from central Castile and Seville. Still, there were leaks: there remained the thorny problem of the many nobles who considered the *alcabala* in their jurisdictions their own, and a third of Castile's population resided in noble jurisdictions. Moreover, and among the consequences of the steps taken at Toledo, the Mesta, the association of owners of great flocks, became extremely powerful, especially from 1485 when a royal councilor was made *juez pesquisidor* of the sheepwalks, succeeding the count of Buendía, Carrillo's brother.[26]

The Queen and the Church

Repeated at Toledo was the familiar assertion that the monarchs had the place of God on Earth and were to function as his viceroys. Coupled with that assumption of a divine mandate was a belief in the queen's right, indeed responsibility, to intervene in religious matters. Not only had the decision to hold Cortes in Toledo advertised the containing of its archbishop, it had also accorded with Isabel's dual interpretation of ecclesiastical reform, to cleanse the church in Spain and to tighten royal control of it. The consequent measures taken involved redrawing the boundaries of bishoprics, notably Toledo but others as well, and, since she could not seize ecclesiastical property as she had that of great nobles, it meant battling with the papacy for the right to name bishops.[27]

Through the centuries, Spanish clergy and crown had functioned in close working relationship and mutual reliance. Isabel's father had let the pope know that by custom the king had the right to name masters of the military orders, and that church *cabildos* could propose bishops but customarily bowed to royal preferences. Her father-in-law, Juan II of Aragón, had simply and arbitrarily named bishops at his pleasure, among them both a son and a grandson born out of wedlock. The agreement between Isabel and Fernando immediately after she took the crown had stated that archbishoprics, bishoprics, masterships, and so on be requested in both their names but "at the will of the Queen" and that the men put forth be *letrados*. Six months later *los reyes* jointly instructed their ambassador to Rome to make certain the pope bestowed no Spanish benefices save at their request, as in accord with ancient custom. They would take much the same line in negotiations concerning the naming of a new bishop for Toledo on Carrillo's death in 1482. Isabel, having stated that questionable assertion as hallowed tradition, would then seek juridical basis for it, charging a *letrado* of her council to find canonical titles. She would also make the additional argument that Spanish sees held castles that could not be put in the hands of untrustworthy persons, especially foreigners.

Hernando de Talavera had in 1475 drawn up for her criteria for provision of bishoprics. They were to go to honest, lettered, native Castilians of middle-class background, that is, no longer to foreigners or powerful nobles. He then presented that view as the royal one in July of 1478 to the Castilian clergy meeting in Seville. Its being accepted there without demur provided a valuable endorsement and a basis for future precedent; some ancient custom began at that point. Yet even before the issue of ecclesiastical patronage was raised at Toledo, tension with the papal curia had broken into open conflict.

Without consulting Isabel and Fernando, however, Sixtus IV bestowed the bishopric of Cuenca on a cardinal-nephew of his in 1479. On hearing, Isabel sent an embassy insisting that bishoprics and benefices given to foreigners be revoked and that no episcopal appointment be made in the future without having been proposed by *los reyes*. "And this," she directed her envoys, "you must procure with all insistence because we do not intend to accept anything else."[28] The following year in Cortes her argument was made with equal firmness; there it was baldly stated by the crown that left to his own devices the pope would not make appointments in Castile's interest and that absentee foreigners kept worthy Spaniards out of sees; and Isabel added that the monarchs knew better than the popes who was worthy. An ordinance of that obedient Cortes forbade foreigners to hold benefices in Castile.

Two years later a concordat with the papacy signaled a partial victory. Isabel's long-time royal confidante and sometime confessor, fray Alonso de Burgos, then became bishop of Cuenca; the papal nephew received Salamanca as consolation, and the papal son, Rodrigo Borja, who was after all of Valencian descent, was to be bishop of Cartagena. The pope, while conceding he would receive the royal preferences for episcopal appointments, retained the right to provide them. Yet Isabel did then get from him the *cruzada,* the royal license to sell bulls of crusade, indulgences, in Spain, the proceeds to go to the war against the Moor, and she got a tithe on the rents of the clergy as well; she agreed, however, to cede back to Rome a third of each for the war against the Turks. That accord was signed in Córdoba on July 3, 1482. Within days of it Carrillo died, evoking from Isabel little show of grief but a determination that Pedro González de Mendoza become archbishop of Toledo. The pope concurred; both the monarchs and the papacy were beholden to the cardinal for mediating the dispute over Cuenca and most other matters between them.

Defense, control of great revenues, and residence in the diocese were arguments Isabel made for choosing as bishops Spaniards by birth. Conversely, bishops, including Mendoza, were told to reside in their sees. The queen also wanted bishops celibate, although here tradition was strongly against her; and she had already recognized the three sons of the new archbishop of Toledo. Undaunted and looking ahead, Isabel, enlisting his aid and that of Talavera, encouraged establishing Spanish seminaries to train Spanish clergy, who were in turn expected to exemplify and instruct the populace in morality, and she chose for ecclesiastical offices earnest and obscure but gifted friars who lent tone and swelled the ranks of the upright and the loyal.

Yet, despite her hewing to the principle that bishops reside in their dioceses, they were expected to appear at court and some were employed there. Also at court were some not trusted by *los reyes,* notable among them the bishop of burgos, Luis de Acuña, Carrillo's brother. Acuña, who had been on the other side in the civil wars, was kept running royal errands for years, and so away from making mischief in his base of power, until his death in 1495. The queen also had assemblies of Castile's clergy meet periodically, the first at Seville in 1478. That council not only supported the royal prerogative, but also expressed great concern at the dismal moral state of the Roman curia.[29]

Throughout her lifetime, Isabel worked to strengthen a national church, one dependent on the crown at the expense of regional, episcopal, and papal power. She would increasingly promote clerical reform, and she and her administrators were to continue to come into conflict with clergy in matters of jurisdiction, including in disputes between clergy and royal *corregidores* and *audiencias,* in attempts to make royal justice superior in civil cases, and in determining competence in cases mixing civil and religious elements. Royal representatives would clash with clergy over a host of jurisdictional boundaries. At dispute were temporal cases tried in ecclesiastical tribunals, ecclesiastical authorities imprisoning laymen, cases of commercial debt, the excommunicating and interdict of royal officials and municipalities for defending the royal prerogative, and cases involving the finances of churchmen. For, although sincere in desiring a morally upright clergy, Isabel was in fact moving the crown into what had been ecclesiastical and papal territory, and the most efficacious manner of doing it was in the name of reform. While there is no doubt that Isabel was devout, her thrust for church reform went beyond piety. From the next pope, Innocent VIII, she and Fernando extracted high appointments for native sons, favorite ones: the archbishopric of Seville for Diego Hurtado de Mendoza, a nephew of the cardinal; a move from Cuenca to Palencia for Alonso de Burgos; and the bishopric of Avila for Talavera.

First, the Turks

In Spain in the 1460s and again in the 1470s, the papacy had promoted the sale of indulgences—bulls of crusade—to raise money for war against the advancing Ottoman Turks. And as Isabel came to the throne, Rodrigo Borja had been enforcing a subsidy on the clergy equal to a third of their tithes for that crusade. The preaching of crusade against the Turks at that time, and again in 1479, when preachers advocated an inquisition as well, contributed to intensifying the hostility of Christians against Muslims, Jews, and suspect *conversos*. Augmenting that hostility too were the restrictive measures, particularly against Jews, emanating from the Cortes of 1476 and 1480. At Toledo, Isabel ordered old laws of segregation, of *mudéjares* into *morerias* and Jews into *alhamas*, be strictly enforced, and they subsequently were.[30]

The royal thrust for religious reform and conformity within Spain converged with the call for renewed holy war. For Isabel, it was above all time to reconstitute Spain, to regain lands lost to Muslims. The royal intention to go to war against Granada was announced during Cortes at Toledo, the occasion presenting itself in the investiture of new master of the military order of Santiago. He was Alonso de Cárdenas, a valiant captain in Isabel's cause during the late war and the uncle of Gutierre, he "who had reached great *privanza* with the Queen." At some time after *los reyes* arrived, the cathedral of Toledo was the scene of another dramatic entry, recounted by Pulgar and Palencia. Those attending solemn mass saw the new master stride down the central aisle, accompanied by four hundred commanders and knights of Santiago. A veritable army clothed in white habits emblazoned with red crosses advanced to the high altar. Then Cárdenas alone entered the choir, where the king and queen awaited him, and fell to his knees before them. With great solemnity, they gave into his keeping the banners of Saint James—"in that bestowal he was given to understand that they made him captain and standard-bearer of the apostle Santiago, patron of the Spains"—and they enjoined him "to go with God against the Moors, enemies of our holy Catholic faith."[31] Cárdenas kissed their hands and promised that indeed he and all his knights would enter the land of the Moors and war on them, thereby to serve God and themselves and to fulfill the statutes of his order. The monarchs then assured him that they were planning to declare war against the Muslim kingdom of Granada soon, but that first they must send an armada against the Turks.

*   *   *

Mehmet II, emperor of Constantinople, "a great prince of the Muslims, lord of a great part of Asia," was then poised to invade Italy. Since taking Constantinople in 1453, he and his Ottoman Turks had spread over the Crimea and the Black Sea, moved into the northern Aegean and the Balkans, and advanced westward in the Mediterranean. When, in May of 1480, Mehmet, as Bernáldez construed it, "died and descended to hell," his successor, Bayazet II, called Ilderim, meaning lightning, was as good as his name and immediately launched a double offensive, by land into Trieste, and by sea laying siege to the island of Rhodes. But, says Bernáldez, it did not please God that Rhodes should fall, "and some Turks confessed that in that battle a very frightening knight, dressed in white, had vanquished them, and they said it was San Juan, the glorious apostle, whose order held that city, come to defend it."[32] Be that as it may, in August came dire news: the Turks had taken Otranto, in Naples, establishing a base in western Europe and putting to the sword all its priests and most of its Christians, although taking into captivity the young people, male and female. They had sacked the city, left a garrison of five thousand, and were thought to be preparing a fleet for an invasion of Sicily.[33]

A great terror gripped Europe. Sicily's sovereigns, Fernando and Isabel, says Pulgar, "ordered daily prayer to God in the churches of their kingdoms, because it should help to lift his anger and free the Christians from the forces and power of that enemy." And they immediately requisitioned from merchants of Burgos arms and ammunition—lances, shields, armor, helmets, artillery, and military stores. Isabel, having receiving from the *junta* of the *Hermandad* a petition, surely solicited, to form an "armada for the [Mediterranean] sea for the service of God and the exaltation of the faith and the royal service," ordered allocated to that purpose all the *Hermandad* contributions of Galicia, Cantabria, the lands of Medina Sidonia and Cádiz, and the towns of Moguer, Palos, and Santa María del Puerto, as well as confiscations made by the Inquisition. And she immediately sent Quintanilla, the *Hermandad's contador mayor,* and its governors north to Vizcaya, Guipúzcoa, and the mountains of Asturias to commandeer ships and gather men, supplies, arms, and artillery, that is, to ready an armada to protect Sicily and support the Neapolitans in retaking Otranto.

The inhabitants of those northern places, although suspicious of that royal delegation and zealous for their traditional liberties, were once again brought around by Quintanilla, his rhetoric as reported by Pulgar an indication of royal tactics to come. "He changed suspicion into pride and their excuses into extreme diligence," convincingly arguing that he and the others had in fact come to protect their liberties. He expiated on how holy was the enterprise, how ungodly the Turk who was shedding Christian blood, how great the honor of serving king, country, and religion. He praised the northerners: how wise they were in navigation, how valiant in battle at sea. And he appealed to their honor: surely they were better than the Portuguese, so why would they remain sulking at home and allow the Portuguese to reap honor in combatting the Turk? Seventy Spanish ships sailed for Naples on June 22, 1481. But glory eluded them. They arrived with their crews decimated by plague to find Otranto already retaken and its duke selling the vanquished garrison into slavery—many of them into the galleys—and also selling back to the Turks their artillery. And it was known that for the moment Bayazet's energies were deflected by court intrigue, halting further Turkish advance. Nonetheless, there remained the pervasive sense of threat to Christendom, a great fear, which Isabel and Fernando directed masterfully against Granada.

Claiming and Reclaiming

The king and queen, explained Pulgar, "knowing that no war should be started except for the faith or for security, always had in mind the great thought of conquering the kingdom of Granada and of casting out from all the Spains the rule *(señorío)* of the Moor and the name of Muhammad."[34] War against Granada had been promised in their marriage agreement and civil war had been justified as prelude to that highest of aspirations. It had been argued, in proposing that the *Hermandad* become a national militia, that such a marshaling of men and resources, even a general mobilization, was necessary to prepare the country for war against the Moor. Readying for that enterprise had been claimed too as cause for the measures proposed at Toledo against heretic and infidel, and argued in negotiations with the papacy for retaining crusading funds in Spain.

Palencia, in the preface to his account of the war of Granada, echoed royal cognizance of the general satisfaction felt that so lofty an aspiration so long advocated by Castile's monarchy had become the immediate project: "The pleasure with which I begin the narrative of the campaigns against the Granadan Moors, long interrupted and today at last industriously resumed, is only comparable to the repugnance with which in other times I saw myself obliged to write the annals of happenings sufficiently shameful." Castile, that is, had progressed from ignominious civil strife, a sure sign of the frown of divine providence, to glorious endeavor: "Nevertheless this same misfortune awakened the beneficent energies of the illustrious couple," Fernando V of Aragón and Isabel of León and Castile. "On them Providence appears to have bestowed the gifts necessary to dispel the inveterate habits of anarchy of the natives and to vanquish the tenacious enemies of Christianity in Spain."[35] Palencia, his prose ponderous as ever, had at last come to respect, even to appreciate, the queen. Yet it was a sign of the times too that during Cortes in Toledo, Isabel dropped him as official chronicler because he would not present his writing for official review.

Toledo had been a triumph for the king and especially for Castile's proprietress, the queeń. Leaving that city in August of 1480, it was time to carry out three projects necessary to completing royal ascendency in Spain, as Isabel conceived of Spain: to implement the ordinances of that Cortes throughout Castile, to firmly attach Aragón, and to regain the emirate—called kingdom—of Granada. Relations with Portugal boded well through the engagement of the *infanta* Isabel to João's son, Afonso. They stopped at Arévalo to visit Isabel's mother and to carry out the pleasant task of reclaiming that town of her youth. Alvaro de Stúñiga having died, it was held by his widow, the redoubtable Leonor de Pimentel, who relinquished it to the queen in exchange for Plasencia and the mastership of Alcántara for her son, although he was under age, and with the proviso that the crown was to retain legal authority over the order.

They moved on to Medina del Campo and Fernando left for Aragón. From September through January Isabel stayed in Medina del Campo, the hub of Castilian trade and banking. Attributed to her is the conceit that she would be glad if God were to give her three sons so that one could inherit her kingdom, another be archbishop of Toledo, and the third become an *escribano*, a notary, of Medina del Campo, for such people validated all business contracts and Isabel well knew a great amount of lucrative business was transacted in Medina del Campo.[36] The town was a headquarters ideal for a queen desirous of preparing financing and provisioning for campaigning against Granada. As the year ended she also fulfilled, far less enthusiastically, the wrenching obligation of sending off her first-born daughter to Portugal as hostage to the peace.

On April 9, 1481, she joined her husband, who was now Fernando II of Aragón, in Calatayud to open the Corts of that kingdom. Although no woman could succeed to Aragón's crown, Fernando had ensured that Isabel be recognized as co-regent, governor, and general administrator there. She was designated by its new king as an *"otro yo"*—"another I"—whether he was present or absent.[37] He had, after all, parental precedent. And on May 19 Isabel saw her son sworn heir to Aragón's crown. That same month, presaging events and policies to come, there arrived at court some leading and ostensibly converted Canary islanders, *guanches,* captured and converted to Christianity in the current Castilian campaign spoken of as pacifying those islands. Isabel declared them to be under royal protection, free from enslavement, and parallel in privilege to her Castilian subjects.

In June, the royal family solemnly entered Zaragoza, the venerable capital of Aragón; then, while Fernando progressed through his new realm, Isabel remained in Zaragoza's splendid *mudéjar palacio de la Aljafería,* which was of special importance to her. It was the birthplace of her ancestor, Santa Isabel, the *infanta* of Aragón and queen of Portugal who was first in the long line of royal Isabels. Isabel and Fernando would attend to restoring that palace so evocative of their ancient, honorable, and intertwined heritage. She rejoined him in Barcelona on June 28, her presence during the next three months helping to finally bring that most recalcitrant of cities to obedience and even affection.[38] From there they proceeded through Tarragona to Valencia where, at year's end, they received word that the Granadans had stolen a march; they had taken by surprise the frontier fortress-town of Zahara.

Palencia tells of Zahara's *alcaide* having gone to Seville, "where he was giving himself up to a licentious life," so that "the sagacious Moors, advised of this negligence," on the dark and stormy night of December 27, 1481, scaled the wall in a section thought inaccessible, overpowered the fortress without the least resistance," and before dawn became masters of the village. Those Granadans had carried off all of Zahara's inhabitants and left a strong garrison "for the grave harm and ruin of the Christians in those regions."[39] The news was received in Castile—thus Bernáldez begins what is the most complete chronicle on the war—as a spark to kindling heaped high in a basket of dried straw.

Retaliation was swift: "knowing the desire of the monarchs to seize some place or fortress of the Granadans before declaring war on them openly," and resolved to satisfy them, continues Palencia, on February 28, 1482, Diego de Merlo and the marqués of Cádiz, along with some other Andalusians and some members of the queen's guard, surprised and occupied the treasure town of Alhama, thirty miles from the city of Granada itself.[40] By then, Isabel and Fernando were again in Medina del Campo, where they turned the surrounding fields into barracks and exercise grounds for foot soldiers and light cavalry, chiefly men mustered by the *hermandades* of the towns; the king and queen also dispatched orders for gunpowder, provisions, and siege weapons. And now they had war against the Moor proclaimed along the entire Andalusian frontier from Lorca to Tarifa.

To Granada, they sent a formal demand for the customary tribute owed by its kings to those of Castile, although the treaty they had renewed with Granada for a year in March 1481, without tribute, had some weeks to run, and although such tribute had in fact been paid only sporadically from the time of Fernando III and never to Isabel. There had been three treaties with Granada's emir since her accession; none had mentioned tribute. It is hardly surprising that Abū'-l Ḥasan 'Alī now refused to pay up. Bernáldez attributes to him yet another memorable response of doubtful veracity but enduring legend: the Granadan ruler replied that those who had paid tribute were now dead, and so were those whom they had paid.[41] He was right, but it did not matter.

During Cortes at Toledo the monarchs had, while retrieving *mercedes* and announcing effective extension of royal authority, also promised to Castile's nobles, cities, and people the imminent probability of material and spiritual enrichment, individual and collective, in taking up the conquest of Granada. Now the climate was propitious, and the enterprise pronounced divinely favored, indeed dictated by heaven.

Chapter 12

The Queen's War I: 1482–1485

*By the solicitude of this Queen was begun, and by her diligence was contin-
ued, the war against the Moors, until all the kingdom of Granada was won.*
—*Anonymous*[1]

*The towns suffered great fatigues, both because they favored the war against
the Moors and because the Queen was very feared and no one dared to contradict her orders.*
—*Hernando del Pulgar*[2]

In February of 1482, Isabel called to war all knights holding royal
lands and subsidies. Foot soldiers and light cavalry from the *meseta* towns and
the north arrived at Medina, as did Aragonese and Swiss mercenaries. Some
of the queen's jewels then went to Valencia, to be held in the sacristy of its
cathedral under triple lock as surety for loans; she would send yet others over
the years of war.[3] Fernando left for Andalusia in mid-March. Isabel tarried,
not feeling well. She was expecting twins in June. Should one be a son, he was
to have the title of king of Granada.

In early April, having sent *corregidores* into key towns and cities and left
the admiral with royal powers in Castile, she too went south. Stopping in
Toledo at Easter, she presided over the ingathering of magnates and their *mesnadas* customary to royal campaigns, welcoming Gutierre de Cárdenas, Chacón, Cabrera, the Mendozas, and everyone important who was ever on any
side of a Castilian embroilment (Pulgar fills a page with their names). Jubilation was general at the news of Alhama's capture; Pulgar wrote of everyone
seeing in the destruction of its populace God's wrath and justice done, a warning to sinners.[4]

It was, from the outset, Isabel's war. The king, aware of her great suffi-
ciencies, wrote Pulgar, "gave over and entrusted to her all things," relying on
her proven ability and good natural intelligence. Palencia said of Fernando
that since Zahara had been conquered from the Moors by Fernando de Antequera, his grandfather, "the King took it as a personal affront and was irresist-
ibly impelled to break openly with them"; yet the usually crusty chronicler also

acknowledged that at bottom the king resolved to war on the Granadans "to second *los vivos deseos* of his most beloved wife."⁵ For now, he explained, with Otranto free of the Turks and France and Portugal allied to Castile, their majesties could proceed against "the ferocious enemy of Catholicism" who for centuries had dominated so much territory properly claimed by Castile. Too, as Isabel herself observed, it would keep her nobles busy.

The city of Granada and its surrounding *vega*, its countryside, comprised "one of the richest irrigated places in Europe."⁶ A town under the Romans, then attached to al-Andalus, Granada came into its own, as an emirate or kingdom, only in the thirteenth century, when Muslim power in Spain splintered and the Christians streamed into Andalusia. With the fall of the kingdoms of Córdoba and Valencia, Muhammad I al-Ghālib, the prince who was to found the Nasrid dynasty, Granada's greatest, negotiated a treaty with the Castilian conqueror, Fernando III, promising tribute and military aid, and he provided it during the conquest of Seville. His successor, backed by the sultan at Fez, reversed course by attacking the Christians. Thereafter, relations seesawed. They were at their friendliest in the later fourteenth century, when Muhammad V sent workmen from the Alhambra to Pedro *el Cruel* for his palace in Seville's *alcázar*. He also sent Pedro three galleys to use against Aragón and fifteen hundred *jinetes* to employ against his half-brother, Enrique de Trastámara. Granadan relations with the Trastámara were understandably less cordial, coming closest to friendly under Enrique IV, which did nothing for that king's popularity among his own people.

The emirate of Granada embraced today's provinces of Granada, Málaga, and Almería, the southernmost area of Spain. Two hundred miles long and sixty-five miles wide, the size of Switzerland, Granada was protected by mountains on three sides and the Mediterranean Sea on the fourth. It was comprised of fourteen cities, one hundred fortified towns, and in 1481 perhaps three hundred thousand people, many of them refugees from places taken by the Christians. The fifty thousand inhabitants of the city of Granada were so crowded in, it was said, that "three men had to share the ownership of one fig tree." The city housed not only Iberian Muslims, many of them refugees, but Africans, Christian renegades, many Jews, and some Genoese merchants (there was a larger community of Genoese in the principal Granadan port, Málaga).⁷

Towering above this last Islamic stronghold in Iberia, emblematic of "the distilled splendor of al-Andalus," rose what a contemporary described as the stupendous towers and marvelous walls, harmoniously constructed, of the fortified administrative complex of the Alhambra, Dominating the city, the Alhambra contained not only the royal palace but also the mansions of courtiers and high functionaries, as well as mosques and schools, workshops, markets, grain warehouses, barracks, stables, and an armory.

Granada was part of an intricate network of trade and communications uniting east and west. An Egyptian cotton merchant, 'Abd-al Bāsit, coming to the city from Alexandria aboard a Genoese ship in 1465, wrote of his delight in this western emporium, which conserved the heritage of seven centuries of al-Andalus. It reminded him of Damascus, so rich in splendid buildings and monuments, in religious congregations, literary culture, and technical skill; Granada had running water, he observed, and an impressive garrison of (an improbable) eighty thousand archers, as well as poets, scientists, and artists that were "among them the best men of our time."[8]

On the hill opposite the Alhambra, the Egyptian ascended the steep and winding streets and admired the wares of the Albaicín, an autonomous urban area with its own governors and justices. There he found weavers producing brocades and taffetas, woolens and linens, and artisans making leather, ceramics, jewelry, and weapons—all of those products to be shipped out from Málaga or carried overland into Castile, destined for other European lands of the eastern Mediterranean or to be traded with the African Maghrib in exchange for Sudanese gold. From the heights of the Alhambra, 'Abd al Bāsit admired the rich *vega* irrigated by the Genil River, abounding in fruit, vines and fig trees, and the soft and agreeable odors rising from vegetable and flower gardens along the river Darro. Yet he sensed an uneasiness among Granada's inhabitants, for the infidel held the greater part of the land of al-Andalus and many of the fortified cities renowned throughout Islam. Border raids, ambushes, and skirmishes were part of everyday life. In both Muslim and Christian towns along the extensive frontier, there were justices especially charged with negotiating with their counterparts concerning stolen people or cattle or other grievances. It was a de facto and edgy coexistence punctuated by spurts of hostility, which at times took on the aspect of sporting contests between members of two societies geared for war. Muslims and Christians alike saw in military prowess a height of achievement; and those possessing horses and arms subscribed to the ideal of a chivalric code of conduct and participated in games honing military skills. Both societies celebrated special occasions with bullfights and *juego de cañas,* a tourney of two teams on horseback fighting with strong reeds and leather shields. Popular frontier ballads conveyed a mutual respect for one another's chivalric qualities, affirming the adage that a worthwhile enemy was one equal in valor.[9]

Yet Granada was far weaker than its neighbors. It had endured chiefly by playing off Morocco against Castile, and it was beset internally by factional struggle. Since the days of Fernando III, Castile had viewed Granada as by rights a tribute-paying vassal kingdom and it is never clear whether royal sallies against it, including the campaigns of Isabel's predecessors, Juan II and Enrique IV, were designed as steps to its conquest or to keep friendly dynasts on its throne and extract tribute from them. Tribute or no, Granada profited

Castile's crown by contributing to the royally taxed flow of trade; and it sent Castile not only silk, sugar, and leatherwork, but also African gold. Yet the recently defiant emir, Abū'-l Ḥasan 'Alī, had stepped up attacks on bordering Castilian settlements, raiding, burning, and carrying off Christians, undeterred by treaties he made with Isabel and Fernando in 1475, 1478, and 1481. Those treaties, after all, did not cover such minor incursions; customarily, sieges of three days or less and forces not publicly called up did not count, and such indeed was the taking of Zahara and Alhama.[10] By 1482, however, Isabel was determined to complete the Christian reconquest of Iberia and considered that the best defense against the threatening advance of the archfoe, Islam, including the Turks, was ridding the peninsula of the Muslim presence and then moving into Africa. And now the situation within Granada was propitious, and the pretext given.

Although esteemed as a brave warrior, Abū'-l Ḥasan also delighted in sensual living, imposed burdensome taxes, and neglected government, or so said his critics. On becoming king in 1463 he had renounced his wife, Fatima, the daughter of a previous ruler and the widow of another, and married a young Christian captive, Isabel de Solís, known as Zoroya. Fatima, who had borne him two sons, became the soul of the opposition. The depth of distress within Granada at the loss of Alhama—a grief immediately echoed in the popular ballad, "Ay, de mi Alhama"—allowed Fatima and her supporters to seize the moment, evict Abū'-l Ḥasan and replace him with her elder son and his, Muhammad XII, known as Boabdil. As a result, Granada was torn by civil strife through the 1480s, to the advantage of Castile. (It is worth mentioning that remarkably similar, and at least equally useful to Castilians, would be the political situations later encountered among both Aztecs and Incas in America.)

Mustering: 1482

In the Christian camp, there was worry whether Alhama, being so deep within Granadan territory, could be held. Isabel refused to listen to any suggestion that it could not. She well knew, Pulgar explains, that since she and Fernando had decided to proceed with conquering the kingdom, "and since that city was the first that was won, that it would be imputed to cowardice if it were abandoned."Accordingly, from Córdoba in mid-May of 1482 Fernando reinforced and provisioned Alhama's garrison formed, according to Pulgar, of four hundred *hermandad* lances and captains and one thousand foot; forty thousand[!] mules then carried in enough supplies for three months.[11]

In Córdoba, where Isabel arrived in late April, a council of war convened. Overriding a suggestion by the marqués of Cádiz to invest Málaga, the assembled magnates preferred to besiege the smaller town of Loja. Isabel made ready. Immediately, she assessed all Castilian cities, villages, and religious orders a stipulated number of knights and foot and instructed them to bring lombards, cannon, and much gunpowder. She also ordered them to send specific quantities of bread, wine, cattle, salt, and pigs, commanding that half be delivered to the encampment before Loja by the end of June and the other half in July, adding the inducement that she would not fix prices, "each might sell at the best price he could get." The Granadans, on their part, had sent messengers throughout Africa seeking aid. To discourage African response, Isabel and Fernando sent an armada, including some Genoese carracks, to patrol the Strait of Gibraltar. Very quickly, Isabel found that the armies of the nobles were costly to the crown, heavily weighted to cavalry, and theirs to command. Accordingly, short of money yet desiring the greatest control possible, the queen relied on the *hermandades* and the municipal councils to provide soldiers and supply them. Soon, however, she found the cities and towns disappointingly reluctant to comply with royal quotas, and the army assembled in Córdoba smaller than planned.

On June 28, as Fernando prepared to depart from Córdoba to invest Loja, Isabel went into labor, at the council table. She gave birth to a third daughter and a stillborn female twin. The surviving child, in a marked departure from giving family names, was baptized María, surely a demonstration of devotion to the cult of Holy Mary, and most likely, given the circumstances, in her guise as Protectress of the Armies. However that may be, María was as it turned out the most fortunate of Isabel's children. More immediately, according to Palencia, many people saw in the death of one twin a bad omen. And hindsight once again did not fail him, for from the time Fernando left two days later, Isabel received nothing but bad news. Cádiz had warned that his force was too small to invest Loja, and, on making camp, he informed Fernando that the site chosen was too low and too narrow. Another seasoned warrior, Alfonso de Aragón, commanding the *hermandad* recruits, informed the king that the men were undisciplined, that no provision had been made for a counterattack, and that food was in short supply. While, as Fernando ordered, the camp was being moved, Lojans streamed out to do battle and the Castilians, panicking, ignored Fernando's insistence that they hold their ground. He, refusing to retreat, fought furiously and nearly alone, until Cádiz rode in and pulled him to safety. Many Christians, says Palencia, died, and some one thousand were taken prisoner. Fernando returned to Córdoba, sadder but as he subsequently demonstrated wiser.

Isabel was immensely distressed, Pulgar recounts, "because with great diligence she had worked to provide all necessary things, and for the pride the Moors took in seeing themselves so soon free." Nonetheless, she hid her feelings so that "no one could tell from her words or actions."[12] She now knew much more of war than she had six years ago when she berated all concerned for retreating from Toro. And from Loja on, says Bernáldez, rancor mounted against the Moor. Immediately, great engines of war were ordered, including many large cannon and catapults. The timing was propitious. Skilled Spanish artisans, profiting from the European-wide technological improvements in mining and increase in metal production, had already begun to shift from the casting of bells to bronze guns and from the forging of iron utensils to wrought-iron ordnance.[13]

If there was bitterness at court at the rout inflicted at Loja by the infidel, there was also satisfaction at the extirpation of heresy in nearby Seville. During August and September, says Palencia, the Inquisition burned in Seville or submitted to diverse tortures many *conversos,* "for from day to day their perverse errors became more patent and the punishments were repeated."[14] In 1483, the monarchs and the Inquisition ordered all Jews expelled from Andalusia. It is hard not to see the two simultaneous campaigns, both strongly motivated by fused religion and politics, as of a piece.

Late that summer, Fernando again reinforced and provisioned Alhama and he laid waste to swaths of Granada's countryside, already suffering, as was all Andalusia that year, from poor crops. In October, he and Isabel went north, stopping at Guadalupe, and then Madrid. That winter of 1482–83 they gave attention to international matters, organizing a league—with Milan, Florence, Ferrera, Naples, and the papacy—against France. Negotiations to have England join, while unsuccessful, did serve to confirm Isabel's tenacious memory for slights. Her envoy then informed Richard III that she "was turned in her heart from England in time past" for the unkindness shown her by the late king, Edward IV, "whom God pardon, for his refusing her and taking to wife a widow of England."[15] *Los reyes* also explored closer ties to Flanders in order to offset France and establish an Atlantic connection desired by Burgos merchants and Basque seamen. At the same time, they opened discussion with an envoy of Maximilian of Habsburg about the possibility of marriage between one of their daughters and Maximilian's son Philip, the heir to Flanders.

Looking toward the next spring's campaign, Isabel was cheered by a subsidy voted by the clergy, and by promise of funds to come from what was to prove the greatest source of royal wartime revenue, returns from the sale of the bulls of crusade. Did those returns attest to the popularity of the war? Or simply to the effectiveness of the clergy selling them? In Castile, Talavera, the new bishop of Avila, managed the business of those indulgences. A Valencian, Luis de Santángel, received the same charge in Aragón. Then named too as collector of the tithe and the share of the *cruzada* for the papacy was a Geneoese, Francisco Pinelo, who resided in Castile and was associated with the papal envoy, Dominico Centurione, and with the bank of Centurione, which handled papal finances. Bulls of crusade were being printed and distributed by the spring of 1483; an example of that date survives from the press of a Dominican convent in Mendoza's new see of Toledo.[16] Certainly the hawking of bulls of crusade by salesmen-preachers deepened the public sense that this was a holy war against unbelievers—Turks and Moors—and waging it a religious duty. And so it was meant to do. As has been said, "the conquest of Granada by *los Reyes Católicos* was *a crusade against the Moors, enemies of our holy Catholic faith,* besides being an enterprise of recovery or *territorial reconquest.*"[17]

A Rout and a Prize: 1483

In 1483 Isabel, accompanied by Cardinal Mendoza, spent most of the spring in Madrid and the summer in Santo Domingo de la Calzada, an old town comfortably near Aragón—where Fernando then was—and redolent with dynastic significance. There Enrique II, the founder of the Trastámara dynasty, had died in 1379, and there his heart was buried. And Isabel, even while raising troops for that year's campaign against Granada, then paid great attention to dynastic affairs. Talavera was again sent to Lisbon, where he convinced King João to accept the *infanta* Juana as hostage in exchange for her sister, Isabel, whom he brought back to her mother. The queen also sought to tighten the Spanish hold on Navarre by arranging the engagement of Prince Juan to its child-queen, Catalina. Isabel was now faced with the possibility that she might not bear another son, that Juan was not strong, and that it was her namesake, the *infanta* Isabel, who might inherit the crown. Nor, the marriage alliance notwithstanding, did she overlook the fact of ongoing rivalry with Portugal in the Atlantic, a contest centered on territory, strategic advantage, the wealth of Africa, and, ultimately, a route to the East. Accordingly, she now sought people and provisions to support the conquest and settlement of Gran Canaría.[18]

Certainly her own star was rising, her reputation growing for intrepid diplomacy and her passionate waging of a latter-day crusade. Amid her formal reception by the Basques as their queen, one Basque diplomat then eulogized her as greater than those stock biblical heroines, Queen Esther or Judith, who killed Holofernes to liberate her people; she was, he indicated, another Mary. *La reina* Isabel, he stated, "like Our Lady the mother of God has protected the human line, for by her virtue she has saved all Spain, and even all Europe, especially since the militant enemy of humankind"—that is, Satan—"was striving to sow discord in order to be able to throw off their highnesses from the very holy project on which they are embarked."[19]

A heightened respect was obvious too when, that March of 1483, many more of Castile's magnates responded to the renewed call to war against the Moor. Most of Andalusia's young knights then sought to join one or another border lord, hoping to repeat the *hazañas*—the noble deeds—of Alhama and gain rich booty. And now the captains and men of the *hermandad* came in in greater force. With the monarchs absent—Isabel was in Madrid arranging the Portuguese marriage and Fernando was attending to factional strife in Galicia—Alonso de Cárdenas and the marqués of Cádiz exercised joint command. Once again Cádiz proposed a swift attack on the strategic port of Málaga, having had word that its *alcázar* was then poorly garrisoned and counting on Castile's ships to prevent its provisioning by sea, and once again he was overridden. Instead, Cárdenas's proposal to lay waste the lush countryside around Málaga was approved, despite Cádiz's warning of the savage, broken terrain of the only landward approach, through a region known as the Ajarquía.

The armies departed the forward base at Antequera, three thousand light cavalry and relatively few, perhaps one thousand, foot; bringing up the rear were the usual merchants ready to buy the spoils of war. Castilians advanced, pillaging and burning Muslim towns and villages as they went, until, on March 21, in the narrow defiles of the gorges of Ajarquía, as the sudden mountain darkness fell, that inexperienced force was ambushed and massacred. Ringed round by "ten thousand candles of fire," and with arrows and rocks hurtling down upon them, the horses stampeded and many fell, entangling, pinioning, and killing riders. Cárdenas spurred ahead, giving no command. Cádiz and his men, in the rear and cut off from the main squadron, relying on his *adalides*—scouts who knew the terrain—fell back to Antequera. Most of the other Castilians, weighed down by armor and spoils and terrorized by Muslim war cries, were killed or captured as they attempted flight.[20]

The monarchs soon heard that nearly eight hundred Christians, the flower of Andalusian knighthood, had died, and fifteen hundred been taken captive, including four hundred nobles. "Our Lord consented to it," concluded Bernáldez, "because it is certain that most of those people went with intent to rob and to do business, rather than serve God"; and he noted that many knights had carried money from friends to buy slaves and silks.[21] Bernáldez has Cárdenas, rather than mention his own lapse of judgment, lay the debacle to the usual suspect, heaven's wrath, which was turned "against us for our sins so that it has pleased Him to punish us at the hands of the infidel." The official reason when given was bad guidance by the *adalides*. However they construed the cause, from then on Castilians displayed a heightened animosity to the Moors, a more intense dedication to holy war, and a strong desire to avenge that rout and regain honor.[22] Immediately, the monarchs resolved on a new expedition. Isabel ordered security tightened along Castile's borders and resolved that thereafter Fernando would command the armies and Cádiz be his first lieutenant and principal counselor.

Rodrigo Ponce de León, the marqués of Cádiz, was "a man of great heart." In his late thirties, that redheaded giant was determined to live up to if not exceed the deeds of El Cid, for whom he was named, and to whom his checkered history of relations with his sovereign and with Muslims bore a certain similarity; Cádiz's allegiances advantageously shifted before submitting to Isabel, but thereafter he remained steadfast. Fighting his first battle at the age of seventeen, he had been given up for dead after a lance traversed his arm, yet within weeks had sufficiently recovered to join his father, the count of Arcos, in taking Gibraltar. Like El Cid, too, the marqués was an outsider, if in his case since born out of wedlock. Yet his father, who had no legitimate sons, had at length married his mother, Leonor Núñez, and in 1469 Rodrigo had inherited the title and his most valuable single jurisdiction, the port of Cádiz. In 1471, driven out of Seville by Medina Sidonia, he had fortified Jerez and through the good offices of his father-in-law to be, Juan Pacheco, been elevated to marqués of Cádiz. Although his past relations with Muslims, Pacheco, and Portugal did not bear scrutiny, Cádiz was to demonstrate amply that he considered his personal honor to be bound up with the royal recovery of the kingdom of Granada.

Exactly a month after the rout at Ajarquía, everyone's sense of honor was partially assuaged when Diego Fernández de Córdoba, the count of Cabra, and his nephew of the same name fortuitously captured the sometime ruler of Granada, Boabdil. Surprising a large Muslim raiding party at Lucena, uncle and nephew resorted to a ruse. On their orders, trumpets blared on either side of the Granadans, "who thought all Castile was there" and who, certain they were outnumbered, fought fiercely but only briefly.[23] Among the seven hundred captured Granadans was one who at first claimed to be a certain captain's son, then admitted, after having nearly died because that captain had killed his captor's brother, that he was Boabdil. Fernando, on hearing, advanced the royal captive funds for appropriate raiment and retinue, had all Córdoba's streets cleaned, and welcomed that prize prisoner there in May. It was agreed Boabdil was to receive fourteen thousand ducats and turn over a brother and son as hostages, and that fall he was freed, as a Castilian vassal committed to warring against his father, Abū'-l Ḥasan. The combination of war and diplomacy, of frontal attack and fomenting internal division was to serve Castile as it once had worked for Juan II of Aragón within Castile itself.[24]

Isabel, rejoined by Fernando at Vitoria in late September, thanked Boabdil's captors, the Fernández de Cordoba. She had them join the royal family at table and honored them with "a stately and cadenced dance" to the music of trumpets and flutes. She also granted Cabra the right to place on his coat of arms the nine Muslim battle flags he had taken, as well as the head of a king on a chain.[25] A month or so later she heard from Cádiz. Not to be outdone, he and his companions, wild at recognizing the armor, horses, and trappings of relatives or friends killed or captured in the Ajarquía, had fallen upon a larger force of Muslim *jinetes*. Then, having exacted vengeance of a satisfactory sort through killing most of them, they had gone on to regain Zahara. Fernando's response was a high compliment, the promise to Cádiz of an annual gift of his own clothing. Isabel wrote congratulating the marqués and urging him on. She would make it a habit to write him hortatory notes, and he to inform his queen of his estimable deeds in her service.[26]

That winter, spent in Vitoria and Tarazona, was again a time of attending to international relations, to some matters of joint importance to Castile and Aragón. Isabel's plans for Prince Juan's marriage were dashed by Catalina of Navarre's engagement to a French lord, and although Louis XI had recently died and the new king, Charles VIII, was a child, the French would not yield the provinces of Cerdaña and Rosellón; accordingly, Spanish troops were stationed along frontiers bordering both France and Navarre. At the same time, the monarchs decided to reestablish relations with Egypt in order to restore Barcelona's trade, in decline for a century, and to reassert former Aragonese hegemony in the Mediterranean, which was impossible without the concurrence of Alexandria. Those decisions fit within the larger policy, thought imperative after Otranto, of establishing cooperative relations with the Muslim rulers of Africa against the common enemy, the Turk. Within that overall plan, Sicily was viewed as a bulwark and Italian equilibrium was vital.[27]

Most pressing, as ever, was the need for funds. It was now that, as Pulgar put it, the flight from the Inquisition so augmented royal penury that Andalusia remained exhausted of gold and silver. However that might be, the four arms of the Corts of Aragón—ecclesiastic, noble, military, and popular—were summoned to Tarazona to vote subsidies. And a head tax was imposed in Castile, for Isabel was determined to pursue the war.[28]

Gaining the Vega: 1484

The queen vented that determination in no uncertain terms in Tarazona that April. Although the Corts was still in session, "that war against the Moors was much on her mind." She had, she told Fernando, resolved to go to Andalusia, "because," or so Pulgar reports her saying, "it was so just and holy an enterprise, that among all the Christian princes nothing was more honored, nor could be; because pursuing it truly had the help of God and the love of the people." Fernando argued that they must suspend the war with the Moors, for it was voluntary "while war with France was necessary, to recover what was theirs," the provinces of Rosellón and Cerdaña. But to Isabel, what was theirs to be recovered was Granada. Still, she graciously heard him out before reminding him that they had fought the Moors for two years on sea and land at immense cost. He should remain in Aragón with some men-at-arms and do as he wished. She was going south to carry on the war against Granada.[29]

Taking with her the cardinal and her children, Isabel returned to Córdoba. Yet she forsook her customary route, instead choosing to make a highly symbolic entrance into Andalusia, through the pass of Despeñaperros, the imposing defile where victory by her royal predecessor, Alfonso VIII, had opened the way to the conquest of al-Andalus.[30] She also stopped in Ubeda and Jaén "to introduce royal justice" much as she had done previously in Seville, so that in those towns too, as Pulgar puts it, "the ministers of justice had great fear of the Queen." In making that point, he singled out one decree of hers, a sentence of death for anyone found gambling with dice, and he comments that so great was the fear of the queen and so thoroughly was the decree carried out that no one with dice could be found anywhere in the kingdom, and that no one dared sell them. Yet in noting that the decree was repeated a year later, Pulgar appears to undercut his own assessment of royal efficacy, for such repetition tends to indicate that prohibition fell short of complete compliance.[31] Yet does he? For complete compliance was undoubtedly less the purpose of that prohibition than was instilling fear and respect for royal authority and reaffirming the fusion of monarchy and morality. It was that same year of 1484 that a traveler from Burgundy, Nicolás de Popielovo, attested to the effectiveness of Isabel's self-representation, for having been at court he observed that the queen was more feared than the king by nobles who hurried to carry out her orders.[32]

She was in Córdoba by May 15, organizing that year's campaign. Nobles and knights, especially from Seville, and many foot soldiers answered her call to arms. French and German engineers arrived to make guns, cannon, and siege weapons. Hundreds of carts brought wood and iron for weapons and stones for catapults; and some thirteen thousand *bestias*—donkeys, mules, and oxen—were hired to pull them and to transport provisions. "Following the Queen's opinion," says Palencia, a small armada was fitted out to intercept the Genoese and Venetians, who were being well paid to ferry Muslim troops from Morocco to the Granada coast. That fleet of *naos,* galleys, and carracks was also to guard the Strait of Gibraltar and blockade Granada's ports. And warnings went out to the senates of Genoa and Venice and to leaders of Italian enclaves in Seville and Cádiz that if they did not desist from aiding the enemies of Christianity they would be made to suffer a more terrible vengeance than any that might be inflicted by the Moors.[33]

With Isabel's dedication and perseverance, her very presence setting an example, writes Pulgar, her ministers and servants worked extremely diligently. She had the army readied within two weeks and, with Fernando absent, she gave command to the cardinal. Moreover, the council with Isabel present now unanimously favored the proposal of the marqués of Cádiz, "that noble and powerful *caudillo,* as practiced in affairs of war as fecund in plans to wage it," that they besiege Alora, midway between Antequera and Málaga. His opinion was also approved by Fernando, who arrived unexpectedly on May 29, ready to resume command in the field; the Corts of Aragón had refused to fund a campaign against the French.[34]

On June 9 Fernando departed, this time with an army that was well provisioned and marched in good order, and one that carted more and better artillery, siege weapons, and firearms than ever before. Isabel sent along six great tents for the wounded, as well as bedclothes, physicians, surgeons, medicines, and male nurses.[35] Chronicles and subsequent histories never fail to mention that field hospital when celebrating her womanly compassion. Much less frequently do later histories mention that Isabel had shown herself to be the guiding force behind waging war and had overseen all arrangements for the armies. Compassionate she was, but only to a point. For to Isabel, while in that war lives were to be saved and suffering allayed to the extent possible, loss of life and limb were to be borne, for the cause was the highest and most imperative.

Alora surrendered within nine days. Shot from the new lombards had demolished two gate towers and pierced a great wall heretofore considered impregnable. Then fire power like nothing ever seen before leveled the town and terrified Alora's people into submission. Those who fled to Málaga were vilified there as cowards, for the *malagueños* would not believe such destruction possible. On May 20 the banners of the king and queen and the pennon of the *cruzada*, the holy cross, flew over the highest tower still standing in Alora. Neighboring towns surrendered rather than face similar demolition. Fernando, satisfied with what was achieved and ever low on funds, prepared to return to Córdoba.[36]

Isabel had daily dispatched money and provisions, relentlessly dunning everyone for more men, more mules, more food. In letters to Murcia's council she marveled at its notables' tepid response to the royal call to war and she warned them that rumors had reached her of their trading with Granada. Now, upon hearing that Fernando was planning to return, she wrote to him that, if it pleased him, he ought first to lay waste the Granadan *vega*, or besiege some other town, for enough of summer remained. It appears to have pleased him.[37] Following her orders, Medina Sidonia and Cabra headed expeditions with the same purpose. She also sent Fernando five thousand *bestias* laden with provisions for Alhama. That August, she conceded to Rodrigo Ponce de León the titles of duke of Cádiz and marqués of Zahara. In September Fernando, on Cádiz's advice, besieged and retook the fortress town of Setenil not far from that bastion of western Granada, the town of Ronda.[38]

The monarchs, in Seville from October into February, refused the belated offer of Abū-l Ḥasan to pay them tribute, and they encouraged Boabdil to work at keeping Granada embroiled in civil war. That they then received an embassy from the king of Fez, a traditional ally of Granada, bringing gifts of horses and harness for the king and silks and perfumes for the queen, indicated a growing awareness abroad of their new strength, as well as the efficacy of their naval blockade. The upbeat mood that winter was reflected in a new *romance,* recited to musical accompaniment in the royal chapel and indulging in grandiose prophecy. It spoke of the royal desire to reconquer Granada and then annihilate from end to end all the sect of Muhammad. "And to regain the Holy House [Christ's tomb in Jerusalem], as is prophesied, and place on the Holy Sepulcher your royal crusading banner."[39]

Readying for a major strike against Granada, Isabel and Fernando then took steps to tighten their grip on Castile's towns—crucial to providing them with wherewithal. *Los reyes* then put into effect the ordinance of 1480 ordering the investigation of all *corregidores,* their conduct in office to be reviewed within the year through *residencias,* the taking of evidence within their jurisdictions. *Pesquisidores,* those most onomatopoeic of royal functionaries, were dispatched to investigate complaints of municipal lands having been usurped by nobles. Moreover, the monarchs could count on a staff of several hundred *continos,* retainers who served them as personal envoys, and spies. Often of noble blood, the *continos* were always available to travel on crown business, particularly to notify municipalities of amounts of money, men, and provisions they must deliver; and they were empowered to confront local and private authorities in securing compliance. Some *continos,* too, traveled with the armies, gathering provisions and keeping an eye on their distribution and on monies paid out or collected.

Through such men, a royal order of November 23 was conveyed to the realm stipulating that, in addition to the royal guards, the *Hermandad,* the prelates, and first-rank nobles, all *caballeros* with their arms and horses, and all *hidalgos,* lesser nobles, also with arms and mounts, or at least bows and lances, were obliged to present themselves in Córdoba in March of 1485, or to send a deputy. In that society organized for war, military service was intrinsic not only to nobility but also to position on municipal councils.[40] Excepted were the clergy, Jews, and Muslims, all of whom were assessed special war taxes. Those men who served militarily were promised a salary and certificate of service. Those who did not, without just cause and without sending a deputy, would lose all exemptions of *hidalguía.* It was the first general call-up of Castile. Individual *hermandades* now came closer to meeting assigned quotas of men and provisions, and the *Hermandad*'s national council, overseen by Quintanilla, Alfonso de Aragón, and Alonso de Burgos, conceded for the war the great sum of two million *maravedís.*

Now too the Andalusian town of Ecija became a foundry; artisans were attracted to it by tax exemptions and in some cases by grants of property confiscated by the inquisitors, who were themselves proving very industrious. That January of 1485, while the monarchs were in residence in Seville, nineteen men and women were burned at the stake. It is not known whether or not *los reyes* attended that *auto de fe;* it is known that three men, a captain of artillery, an expert in gunpowder, and a trumpet player—the monarchs made certain that musicians, so important to morale and to discomfiting the enemy with blaring trumpets and rolling kettledrums, were always with the armies— received houses and corrals confiscated from *conversos* condemned for heresy.

Ronda: 1485

The court remained in Andalusia that winter. That same January, against Isabel's advice, Fernando attempted to take Loja, and failed. Still, there was diversion: hawking and hunting; Medina Sidonia set up suitable accommodations in a pleasant area of the forest then surrounding Seville for the king, the queen, the *infanta* Isabel, and all their retainers. And Seville's *alcázar* received attention: an order survives from Isabel and Fernando to have gardeners sent from Valencia to tend its grounds; they were to bring trees with them.[41] (They were probably Muslim, for Valencia had a large Muslim population, and *mudéjares* were known as the best gardeners in the Spains.) Yet respite was brief, for late in January some people in the palace fell ill of plague, and the royal family, Cardinal Mendoza, and those knights and functionaries permanently attached to the court left immediately for healthier towns. Nonetheless, by late March the monarchs were again in Córdoba for the general muster.

That spring Isabel was more determined than ever to impose upon the expanding army a higher morality, consonant with holy endeavor and conducive to better behavior and tighter control. The great lords, or their sons or nephews whom they sent with their *mesnadas* to Córdoba, arrived to a literal dressing down from the queen and the king; they were upbraided for spending too extravagantly on their clothing, their persons, their showy retinues of people useless in war, their overflowing tables, and their paraphernalia, especially torches and torchbearers, on everything, that is, that seemed necessary to them to demonstrate high estate. They were, they were told, setting a bad example to other knights. The monarchs, it was clear, also had in mind a new sort of army, wherein what counted most were numbers, efficiency, discipline, and economy.[42]

Leaving Córdoba in April were perhaps eleven thousand horse and twenty-five thousand foot. Heading the large Sevillian contingent were veterans of Ajarquía, many of them rescued or ransomed from Muslim prisons.[43] Engineers and *maestros,* masters in military technologies, some of them Frenchmen and Bretons, went along to tend the lombards, catapults, and other siege engines, and with them came specialists in making shot of rubble and the new iron balls. There were experts in gunpowder, carpenters with their tools, and blacksmiths with their anvils. A thousand wagons carted the artillery and siege machines. Corps of foot soldiers with pickaxes and hoes accompanied them to clear the way. There were oxen conscripted from Avila and Segovia, mules that had been requisitioned and others that had been hired, and there was cattle for food—for scavenging in Christian-held countryside was punishable by death. There were the six commodious tents and all the necessities of the queen's hospital. Isabel sent along Gutierre de Cárdenas to dispense funds for provisions and pay, and to keep an eye on the tremendous amount of money on hand. The lombards just founded at Ecija and a conscript army were patently making obsolescent heavily armored knights and private armies.[44] Within decades, this new-model Spanish army would evolve into the most powerful in Europe and from it would come the close-to-indomitable captains fighting in Europe and America.

The objective for 1485 was to isolate Málaga through conquering its satellite towns. In early May, Fernando having taken Coin after a week's siege and hard fighting and Cartama having fallen to him within another week, Isabel sent off one of her congratulatory notes, mentioning that should he wish to pursue conquest elsewhere, there was sufficient summer remaining and she would send the necessary provisions. Now it happened that Cádiz, who was with Fernando, had had a letter too, from an old acquaintance, Yuze el Xarife, the *alguacil,* or bailiff, of Ronda, informing him that the town's populace was depleted, disheartened, and an easy target, that civil strife in the city of Granada meant no relief would come from there, and that he himself was ready to serve their majesties if they would show him their gratitude. Accordingly, as Pulgar tells it, Fernando, employing a feint, had a Muslim prisoner first tricked into believing he had overheard plans to attack Málaga, then allowed to escape and spread word that the Castilian army was headed for that port. While Fernando ostentatiously marched off in the direction of Málaga, Cádiz left camp in the dark of night. On May 9, as day broke, *rondeños* awakened to find their town encircled by his army while much of its garrison had gone to meet the threat at Málaga. And soon they saw that Fernando had doubled back and joined forces with Cádiz before Ronda's high walls.[45]

Ronda, Granada's western bastion, enjoyed a situation magnificent but daunting: it was defended by escarpments and strong fortifications on three sides, and, on the fourth, a gorge cut by a swift mountain stream, the river Guadalevín. As an Arab visitor, Abū al-Fiḍa, saw it, Ronda had clouds for a turban and torrential rivers for its swordbelt. The Guadalevín was Ronda's chief water supply and so steep was the descent to the gorge that to fetch water from it required traversing 130 steps down a narrow zig-zagging passageway cut into the cliff inside the walls; fetching water was generally left to Christian prisoners. Control of that water supply was crucial to victory, and more than once Cádiz and his men, waist-deep in the swift current, battled contingents of Ronda's small but fierce garrison. In command of that garrison was a doughty old warrior, Aḥmād al-Tagrī, whose men were mostly African mercenaries, Gomeres, "whose whole business," as has been said, "was to fight."[46] It was Tagrī who had been chiefly responsible for harrying the Christian forces at Ajarquía, and, it was thought, for that disaster itself.

On hearing, Isabel immediately ordered relay stations established, and she sent massive supplies—thirty-four hundred mules and six hundred pairs of oxen are recorded, and there were more—and much light artillery and projectiles. To pay for it all, she pressed everyone for funds with a high degree of success; when they lagged, her royal order was followed by her royal ire: "I marvel greatly," she wrote Seville's council, "that in so needy a time, the King my lord being where he is, that you should delay sending the aforesaid *maravedís.*" And she insisted all *aljamas* of Muslims and Jews in Spain immediately pay all war taxes in arrears.[47]

Ronda surrendered after two weeks of siege, on May 22. Its capitulation was due to a number of factors. The new siege engines, those giant cannons, the lombards, their thunder terrifying, had battered the town, and fireballs were employed for the first time. There was too the essentially traditional, chivalric derring-do of the marqués of Cádiz, the king's generalship, and the queen's unrelenting support; and there were some *rondeños* who had no interest in heroism. Ronda's inhabitants were expelled with what they could carry; *continos* arrived to see to apportioning houses and property to Christians wanting to settle there or in the other captured places; and meticulous ordinances were drawn up for each town. The exiled townspeople went to Granada and Africa, Isabel ordering that they be protected en route and that anyone who robbed them be punished, with—says Pulgar—some degree of success. Excepted were perhaps one hundred leading families, the group who had preferred surrender to loss of life and property; they removed comfortably to Carmona or to Alcalá de Guadaira, outside Seville, receiving property the Inquisition had confiscated. Fernando went on to take the port of Marbella and forty neigboring places; in those surrendering promptly, he permitted the populace to stay as *mudéjares,* tribute-paying royal subjects, "promising them on his royal word to conserve the law of Muhammad."[48]

In conquered towns, however, mosques were ritually purified and rededicated as churches, to Santa María de la Encarnación, to the Espíritu Santo, Santiago, San Juan el Evangelista, and San Sebastián, the last quite possibly a barbed response to the Muslims increasing use of poisoned arrows. The mystery of the Incarnation, that from Mary Christ took human form, was the theological principle on which Muslims and Christians diverged most sharply, to the extent that Muslims considered Christians polytheists, and so the Incarnation was a doctrine worth imposing to signify victory. To all those churches Isabel sent crosses, chalices, silver censers, silk and brocade vestments, and altarpieces, images, books, and bells. (The Muslims hated bells.) And she graciously received the four hundred Christian captives discovered in the dungeons of Ronda: emaciated men, women, and children wearing rusted leg irons, hair and beards waist-length, in rags or naked. Many of the men had been taken at Ajarquía. Now they were "redeemed," a term alluding to their delivery from captivity as analogous to a wider redemption of Castile from evil through so just a war. Isabel had them fed and each given eight *reales* with which to get home. Their broken fetters she had sent to Toledo, to be hung on the facade of San Juan de los Reyes.[49]

On June 28, Isabel welcomed Fernando at the entrance of the palace in Córdoba ceremoniously; with her were their daughters Isabel and María and many women attendants, all of them wearing brocades and silks "and other rich fabrics." He had returned in triumph; and throughout all Spain, indeed throughout Christian Europe, the fall of Ronda was publicly acclaimed. In Seville, a procession of thanksgiving was immediately organized by the councils of the church and city. Rome too celebrated; on June 3 Fernando had written of Ronda's capitulation to the pope, "so that Your Holiness should see and know on what Spain spends its time and money."[50] But heaven did not smile on a second campaign mounted that year. In September, Fernando failed to take Moclín; losses were high. Boabdil's formidable uncle, Muhammad ibn Sa 'd, known as al-Zagal, who had gained supremacy in Granada, enhanced his standing there when a war party of *jinetes* returned from Moclín with eleven Christian captives, eighty trophy heads, and ninety warhorses.

Back in Córdoba, Fernando came down with fever and Isabel, who was pregnant, suffered a spell of uncharacteristic despondency. Pulgar reports it equally uncharacteristically, for he has heretofore accentuated her steadiness and resolve, and now he describes her as appearing perturbed, indecisive about resuming the campaign, and, although greatly concerned with how to provision Alhama, refusing the cardinal's offer to go himself to do so, "for since his company was a great consolation and his council a great relief and remedy for things as they occurred, she would not permit him to leave her."[51] Thus too does Pulgar, perhaps as a nod to the patron he esteemed so highly, offer a glimpse of the *privanza* enjoyed by Mendoza, affirming that he was Isabel's constant and chief counselor and that she relied on him greatly, although he did not dominate the royal will or the government as had the *privados* of the kings who preceded her. That fall the cardinal remained at her side while captains provisioned Alhama, and Fernando, having recovered, took the Muslim castles of Cambril and Alhabar threatening Jaén, in terrain so rugged that the chronicler reported seeing more than six thousand men leveling a mountainside to permit passage of the artillery.

In late October, the court went north to Alcalá de Henares, a place Isabel had known well under vastly different circumstances. At Alcalá, once Carrillo's

Figure 8. Pedro González de Mendoza, cardinal and archbishop of Toledo, with Prince Juan and the *infantas* Juana and Isabel (1485). Diego de la Cruz and workshop. *Virgen de la Misericordia,* detail. Monastery of Las Huelgas, Burgos.

favored residence, her host was Toledo's current archbishop, Mendoza. Again there was plague in Seville, and, rather than strain Andalusia's resources further—the court now numbered in the hundreds and the royal children each had a court in miniature—the monarchs chose to spend the winter accepting the hospitality of the archbishop. Her bout of weakness past, Isabel was a demanding guest, insisting that royal justices and jurisdiction must pertain in Alcalá during her stay. Mendoza argued that his own archepiscopal jurisdiction should prevail as customary. She, obdurate, declared her jurisdiction superior to all others everywhere in her kingdoms, even in church lands. Neither would budge; each appointed five *letrados* to meet and settle the dispute. They could not. Argument over that principle persisted throughout the winter while in practice sometimes royal and sometimes ecclesiastical officials adjudicated, and the queen and the cardinal conferred on state business as usual.

And there were family matters. A document of December 20, 1485 attests to Prince Juan having acquired a tutor. He was Diego de Deza, a Dominican friar and doctor of theology of the University of Salamanca, who would succeed his fellow Dominican, Tomás de Torquemada, as inquisitor general of Spain.[52] And in Alcalá, on December 15, 1485 was born the *infanta* Catalina, the last of Isabel's children. "The birth of a son," says Palencia, "would have caused *los reyes* greater happiness, for a succession depending on an only son inspired no small fear, and the fecundity of their daughters boded difficulties for future relationships."[53] That is, the birth of another daughter increased the dreaded possibility of disputed succession. Even so, of all the children, Catalina would most resemble her mother. She too would be a queen, but her circumstances would be far different.

*   *   *

Castile having gained with Ronda the countryside all the way to Gibraltar, and with seamen of Jerez and Puerto de Santa María industriously raiding African coasts, grandiose visions of Castilian expansion then proliferated. Fernando wrote to Iñigo López de Mendoza, the count of Tendilla, a nephew of the cardinal's, of "making Spain a microcosm of Christianity." And in seeking recruits for the next season, Cádiz reminded Castile's nobles of old prophecies attached to Spain's kings and about to be fulfilled, and the messianic *El Encubierto*—the Hidden One—to be truly revealed. For, he explained, the king and queen having been jointly chosen and sent by the hand of God, and as was well known, "the heart of the King [being] in the hand of God," the time had arrived for a king from Spain, born "in the cave of Hercules," to escape it like a lion. That hidden one, now revealed, would destroy the Moors of Spain and all renegades, conquer Granada, subjugate Africa, destroy Egypt, raise his banner in Jerusalem, and become emperor of Rome and monarch of the world, destined to rule it until its foretold end.[54] Certainly that expansive vision was in accord with *romances* then recited at court and with the operative royal ideology of the Granada war. It fit with royal aspirations to influence powerfully affairs in Africa and the eastern Mediterranean and to be viewed as protectors of Jerusalem's Christian holy places. And it represented the coalescence of Castilian and Aragonese spheres of interest in allusive prophecy. It was in 1485, too, that Gil de Siloe designed the flamboyant Gothic tombs of Isabel's parents in the Cartuja de Miraflores, conveying a similar message.

It was not unrelated that in 1485 appeared Pulgar's gloss on *Mingo Revulgo,* those scurrilous verses of a generation ago attacking the court of Henry IV. His commentary strove to soften their condemnation of nobles and crown while leaving intact the great emphasis their anonymous author had placed on divine retribution for human sin. His point was that when the people had been bad they got a bad shepherd, but that God had now relented and sent another, and that one was Isabel. And within a year there was published in Toledo, bound together and among the earliest works printed in Spain, Pulgar's circulated letters and his *Claros varones,* short biographies of illustrious Castilians, written in humanist mold emphasizing the positive and offering a rehabilitation of the royalty and nobility of the last generation. Those exculpating portraits were dedicated to Isabel, "the very excellent and very powerful Queen, our lady."[55] Taken together, they publicized, and provided with a substantiating history, the vaunted and continuing harmony among Spain's brightest and best, its monarchs, great nobles, high clergy, and its most distinguished *letrados*. Common cause was proving a powerful unifier, even after the fact.

At the same time, late in 1485 or early in 1486, occurred the first event in a chain that would bring Isabel and her descendants much advantage and lasting renown. She and Fernando then gave a brief audience of little moment to them at the time: "Thus," says Bernáldez, "Christopher Columbus brought himself to the court of king Fernando and queen Isabel and made them relation of his imagination, to which . . . they did not give much credit, and he talked with them and said he was certain of what he told them, and showed them a map of the world, so that he aroused in them the desire to know those lands."[56] Given the expansive mood reflected in the play of imagination then being indulged in by Cádiz and courtiers, it was an ideal time to lay before them a map of the world.

Chapter 13
The Queen's War II: 1486–1492

In the spring of 1486, having stopped at Madrigal and Arévalo, the monarchs again came south by way of Guadalupe. There Cardinal Mendoza had prepared festivities, but Isabel opposed them, for it was Lent.[3] She was no longer the young queen who would reign over a tourney in Lenten-time. Now she had an oratorio built above the choir at Guadalupe where she prayed the canonical hours; and tradition has it that when the choir sang she sang along. There too she commissioned a royal hostelry, described as a true palace.[4] It was paid for by funds acquired by the Inquisition.

And since her last visit the Inquisition had intensely affected life in that center of the Hieronymite order. In Guadalupe, three friars had been burned at the stake. The others, declaring themselves shamed and dishonored, in chapter meeting had ordered all houses investigated and decreed that no New Christian could take the habit or their order until the kingdom was cleansed of heresy. That convocation also sanctioned a statute of purity of blood in proposing that Hieronymites who were *conversos* be excluded from the offices of prior and vicar. That proposal elicited from the monarchs a message warning of carrying matters too far. Still, Cardinal Mendoza's own advice to its proponents was telling: have patience. Mendoza, although often seen as a moderating influence on Isabel, put such statutes into his own dioceses of Toledo, Seville, Sigüenza, and Calahorra, and in the Colegio de Santa Cruz he founded in Valladolid.

That spring the armies at last took Loja—defended by Boabdil who had reconciled with al-Zagal—and also Illora and Moclín, towns west and north-west of Granada commanding those approaches to the city. Isabel had called up a larger force than ever, perhaps twelve thousand light cavalry and forty thousand archers, lancers, and musketeers. She had requisitioned seventy thousand *bestias* with provisions and artillery, and she sent along some six thousand foot to clear the way and build bridges. She was ill when, on May 13, Fernando left Córdoba with the armies, but five days later wrote him one of the very few personal letters of hers that survives. She begins by thanking him profusely for the great concern he had expressed about her health. She is completely well, rid of the fever and feeling fine. Let her know where the siege will be. The children are all well. That note of hers reflects cognizance of their shared royal station, a touch of wifely demeanor, and her adherence to convention—so she addresses Fernando as your lordship—and yet it is warm and loving.[5]

She wrote again on May 30, providing rare insight into her state of mind; rare too, she becomes reflective. She could not know that Boabdil had just surrendered Loja, so she cheered Fernando on. She prayed to the Lord, she said, to continue granting victory "until he gives you the city and all the kingdom. This [the war] has been a marvelous thing and the most honorable in the world. . . . The dead weigh on me heavily, but they could not have gone better employed"; and she mentioned in particular one Velasquillo, who, because "he was afraid of dying even so honorable a death, had to show he was no coward, that he knew how to live and to die." She was dispatching reinforcements and although it would take more time to send them well provisioned still she would do it, for she did not know the state of supplies in camp. He was to tell her what he needed and on what day and she would see to it, "because we do not want to err in anything." She marveled that the Muslim kings put themselves at such great disadvantage; "they would do better to concert with us." And she suggested promising Baza and Guadix and their lands to Boabdil as his own, then caught herself. "Pardon, Your Lordship, because I speak about what I do not know"—the iron fist in the velvet glove. More advice nonetheless followed. She closed by telling him that they were all well. May the Lord guard him and bring victory, as she desired. In that letter, too, she observed of the Moors that "they are fickle and they rise and fall quickly."[6] It was strong criticism, given the high value she put on constancy, and it was a transference to the enemy of qualities associated with the workings of fortune, to her a heretical alternative to divine providence.

Isabel's verbal mingling of authority and subservience is reconcilable as within the canons of chivalry; above all, she and Fernando continued to write to one another and demonstrably treat each other as lady and knight. Yet ironically, the chivalric code was, along with heavy cavalry and private armies, making a last, grand stand in this war of theirs (a straight line would run from there to Don Quixote). For by hindsight, in the course of that conflict the age of modern warfare clearly dawned. Still, old usages persisted. In one notable instance of the tenacity of the old order and although most Castilian magnates were tiring of the war, the cardinal's nephew, the duke of Infantado, did arrive, with some six hundred lances and two thousand foot and obviously little disposed to heed their majesties' condemnation of extravagant attire. Infantado came to war draped in cloth of gold, man and mount, with fifty of his *caballeros* and their horses nearly equally resplendent; all the rest, from head to hoof, were clad in silks. Yet Infantado fought bravely, and when his men flagged he rallied them with "Hear, *caballeros,* if you show yourselves in rich trappings, you must distinguish yourselves even more in great deeds!"[7] Isabel was undoubtedly torn. She immensely enjoyed chivalric display, but now knew it unproductive to waging this war. Still, much as Infantado, she valued attracting brave men inspired by that code to do their utmost.

The possibility of doing great deeds, and in a crusade within Europe, also brought to Spain some of that disappearing breed, knights-errant. They came from France, and Ireland, and most memorable was an English noblemen, Anthony Woodville, Lord Scales, who was related to Isabel through her forebears of the house of Lancaster: her paternal grandmother Catalina of Castile, and her maternal great-grandmother, Philippa, queen of Portugal. Scales had fought for Henry VI against Richard III on Bosworth Field, says Palencia, who then goes into one of his tirades: a century before Shakespeare and far from his spirit, Palencia recounted the horrible deeds of Richard III, termed the contest between Lancaster and York bloody and seditious, censured both sides, and lambasted all the English. "This nation is so inclined to cruelty," he concluded, "that it appears never satiated with seeing bloodshed; this fever takes so many devious forms, especially among the nobility, that among the English he is reputed happiest who is at the point of exposure to the most atrocious death."[8] So much for chivalry, never Palencia's strong point.

Scales, was Palencia's point, had had enough of civil conflict; he now wanted to engage in a just and holy war. He had, therefore, come to gain pardon for his sins and to serve God by making war on the Moors, "those tenacious enemies of the Christian religion." He had brought with him some three hundred English knights, and musketeers, cross-bowmen, and foot soldiers with lances and battleaxes. The Englishman insisted on being in the thick of skirmishes, and, in leading a scaling operation he lost, along with some men, two of his teeth. Fernando, offering what was meant as consolation, told Scales he should rejoice, for his virtue had knocked them out and consequently remained highly visible. Scales obviously took the point. Isabel, in commiserating with him later, according to Palencia, received the gallant reply, "I have opened a window so that through it Christ—who built this structure—may more easily see what is hidden inside."[9]

Yet after a bloody battle had secured the outskirts of Loja, it was not chivalry nor scaling operations but a single day's heavy pounding—by the lombards and other siege machines, their very names rolling thunder: *tiros e cortaos e pasabolantes e cebretañas e ribadoquines e pasabanías*—that secured the fortress-town.[10] On a Sunday, May 28, "the rigor of the gunpowder having vanquished the fury of the Muslims," Boabdil, although wounded, rode out, dismounted, and in token of surrender kissed Fernando's feet. Fernando insisted he remount and that sometime vassal rode away, to do further mischief within Granada itself. Loja's inhabitants were expelled, but permitted to resettle as *mudéjares* in Castile, Aragón, and Valencia. On word of the town's surrender, the queen, with her daughter Isabel and her ladies, went on foot from Córdoba's cathedral to its church of Santiago. She also gave alms to churches and monasteries and had constant prayers of thanksgiving for victory said; and she prepared to depart for the front.[11]

On June 11, having visited Loja, Isabel reached the camp before Illora, some twenty miles from Granada and "called by Granadans their right eye," to find that Fernando had taken the city. Arriving five days earlier, he fired the artillery on June 7, and on June 9 its populace had departed en masse for Granada. What fighting there was had taken place within the Christian camp, between the Asturians and the *sevillanos*. On June 10, severe punishments had been meted out; the next day the entire chastened camp turned out to greet Isabel. She rode in with great show, regally attired. The queen wore a scarlet cloak of Moorish design, a velvet outer skirt, velvet and brocade underskirts, and, under a broad-brimmed black hat, thickly embroidered, her hair was caught in a silk net. She sat on a brown mule, its blanket made of gold-embroidered satin and its silver saddle richly gilded. She was accompanied by ten ladies and some thirty male retainers; and she was met with an unprecedented display blending respect and enthusiasm. Fernando, equally on display and astride a fine horse, greeted her with warmth and ceremony. The king wore for the occasion a loose brocade robe over short yellow satin skirts, a crimson vest, a plumed hat, and a scimitar. *Los reyes* once again demonstrated that other sorts of acceptance do not necessarily accompany taking up the material aspects of another culture.

Immediately behind Fernando was Lord Scales, and while to the Castilian eye Fernando's skirts, hat, and scimitar were not novel, Scales "looked very pompous and strange." For the English lord was in full armor and over it had put on a short French cape of black brocade; sweeping plumes adorned his white French hat, and he carried on his left arm a small round shield banded in gold. Odder still, his stirrups were long and his horse covered from head to hoof in azure silk edged in mulberry and ablaze with gold stars. Scales' five pages were thought equally exotically fitted out, in silk hose and suits of brocade. What is more, as the monarchs progressed into camp, the Englishman rode back and forth, drawing up alongside them to offer gallantries then moving away to show off the gaits of his steed, his antic behavior even more astounding to the Castilians than his outlandish attire.[12] Even so, before he left, Isabel presented him with expensive gifts: two beds with linens and bed coverings, one embroidered in gold thread, and twelve horses and some field tents. The memory of her grandmother, Catherine of Lancaster, Palencia explains, had sufficed. And she grieved when Scales died soon after, fighting in Brittany against France.

It did not hurt the queen's image as divinely favored when on June 16, having come with the army to besiege Moclín, another Muslim fortress town, perched high and extraordinarily difficult of access, on the night of her arrival *una bomba* fired by a mortar directly hit the town's stores of powder, sulpher, niter, and provisions. That fireball appeared to the besiegers to have been carried by divine providence, and the town capitulated three days later. Seemingly equally providential, Castilians, upon entering Moclín singing the Te Deum, heard themselves joined by other voices. The voices seemed to come from beneath their feet and guided them to subterranean dungeons holding Christian prisoners of war.[13]

Upon Moclín's surrender, Isabel visited some wounded knights and *continos* of her household. While solicitous, she told them that they should be happy to have faced such danger as would strengthen their faith and aggrandize their country, and that if they were not repaid in this life God would not forget them in the next. She also had her treasurer give expense money to each of them, according to his estate. By the end of June, after Fernando had raided the Granadan *vega* and taken several more towns, the monarchs returned to Córdoba. What before had taken a year had been done in a month.

Isabel's pursuit of internal order continued, of a piece with the war against Granada, and each made the other more imperative to her and more popularly acceptable as well. Isabel had made clear her determination to keep Castile on a war footing, administrators efficient and as honest as possible, nobles obedient, clergy compliant, the realm strong and united in high purpose, and everyone fearing and respecting the rulers and acknowledging their unchallenged supremacy. Accordingly, that summer she and Fernando brought under royal sway the last regional cluster of recalcitrant nobles. She had, the year before, on receiving word of insurrection in Galicia—where the count of Lemos had seized Ponferrada, a royal town—become so exasperated that she had spoken of going personally and instantly to put it down. But the war had priority and she had sent Quintanilla with a *hermandad* force and, when he failed, Benavente with his men, who did no better. Now, a year later, the audacious young count of Lemos in defying royal authority had inspired other Galicians, so that the situation was not only infuriating to the queen but dangerous to the internal peace of a realm at war.

Both monarchs went north. Leaving Prince Juan, María, and Catalina in Jaén, they took with them the queen's near constant companion, the *infanta* Isabel. The royal presence proved sufficient. Since the rebels insisted that Lemos had told them he was defending Ponferrada for the crown against the attempt upon it by Benavente, Lemos had no recourse but to surrender that town, and he was made to give up his own castles as well. He was called to account, fined, and exiled.

Isabel and Fernando entered Santiago de Compostela on September 15; Galicia's nobles flocked to court to proffer service. Graciously accepting apologies for past behavior, the monarchs took away with them the major troublemakers, then toured Galicia, where they ordered more than twenty castles demolished, and, on departing, left a royal governor with instructions to reclaim all towns, monasteries, abbeys, and lands appropriated over the years by the aristocracy, and to ensure that the *gallegos* contributed liberally to the war against Granada. Isabel, while there for the first and last time, visited the shrine and tomb of the apostle Saint James—Santiago, for five centuries the patron saint of the reconquest.[14] After that journey he loomed larger in the pantheon of saints to whom she dedicated religious establishments, but still well below San Juan and Holy Mary.

On their return, Isabel and Fernando stopped in Salamanca, its university a prime source of their valued *letrados,* then went on to Avila, where Talavera was bishop, and where, assisted by Luis de Santángel as *contador,* and associated with a papal commissioner sent to ensure Rome's portion, he oversaw the hundreds of people who printed the bulls of crusade, sent them to each treasury, sold them, and kept an eye on one another. The monarchs, while keenly encouraging that operation, showed far less zeal regarding the one-third interest due to the papacy. Rome would repeatedly protest abuses in receiving its share from the sale of bulls of crusade and from a tithe that now the crown rather than the church was collecting from the clergy. Cardinal Mendoza, having established strong financial bonds with the pope's Genoese bankers and initially negotiated the arrangements concerning the *cruzada,* also saw to farming that tithe. The monarchs again wintered in his Alcalá.

Isabel, with the campaigns against infidel and heretic going well and the papacy valuing Spanish support in Italian affairs, then took further advantage of the moment. She secretly ordered her ambassador in Rome to obtain a bull enabling her alone, if need be, to administrate the military orders. It was, her envoy reported, the most difficult business he had ever done in Rome, "because the pope and all the cardinals held it as contrary to law and as a monstrous thing that a woman would be able to have administration of [military] orders." She was granted only co-administration with Fernando, and only of the masterships as they fell vacant.[15] To Isabel it signified one of those first steps she tended to count on, an opening wedge, and it did provoke admiration at home. Thus that court wit, fray Iñigo de Mendoza, is credited with saying that if Saint Helena was to be esteemed for finding a cross, the holy cross on which Christ was crucified, our queen should be all the more so for finding three: the crosses emblematic of the three military orders of Alcántara, Calatrava, and Santiago.

When word came that year of the Turks, possibly in alliance with Egypt, preparing for another attack on the West, Fernando and Isabel were certain it was directed in support of fellow Muslims in Granada and against themselves. It was, they decided, imperative they take Málaga.

Málaga: 1487

Municipalities and nobles were notified to have specified quantities of cavalry and infantry at Córdoba by March 27, a general call went out to all knights, and amnesty was offered to all fugitives from justice who presented themselves for service. And breaking with custom, Isabel now decreed that no camp followers and prostitutes go with that army. The *hermanded* agreed to a mammoth levy of ten thousand foot with salary for eighty days, and a host similar in size to the previous year was assembled. The plan was to take advantage of the renewed strife within Granada between al-Zagal and Boabdil, their partisans incessantly fighting through its narrow streets.[16] Money came in from the bulls of crusade, and through huge individual loans: 11.3 million *maravedís* from Medina Sidonia, 8.3 million from the Mesta, 5 million from Benavente, and a million and a half from Cádiz.[17]

Isabel was in Córdoba with her children by March 2. Arrangements having been made with supporters of Boabdil within Málaga, only a brief campaign was expected, and in early April she saw the army off to the base camp at Antequera. It was to invest first the outlying town of Vélez Málaga, thereby cutting Málaga off from Granada. The campaign began inauspiciously: there was an earthquake the following day. She heard from Fernando of his having spent an anxious, sleepless night concerned for her safety and of his wish that "Our Lord guard you above all others."[18] Then came torrential rains, and floods washing out roads and swamping pasture lands, slowing the host to five leagues a day.

Vélez Málaga sits behind a daunting barrier of mountains a half league from the sea. Into that rugged mountainous terrain moved an advance unit of two thousand foot soldiers and along with it carpenters who built bridges over *arroyos* and filled in deep pools of water, while another four thousand *peones* wielding iron pikes and poles leveled and paved the ground. The army that followed is estimated at twelve thousand cavalry and forty thousand infantry.[19] Once Fernando was encamped before the town, on April 16, trouble persisted.

Only a part of the artillery had arrived, the lombards remained mired down in Antequera, and twelve hundred sick and wounded lay in the field hospitals. The *gallegos,* Asturians, Basques, and other mercenaries were proving unruly. And rain had ruined a great deal of food. Still, ships brought provisions to the coast, and people from Málaga brought some out—until Málaga's *alcázar* was taken from Boabdil's *alcaide* by partisans of al-Zagal.

Isabel, hearing through her swift couriers that al-Zagal himself was coming to relieve Vélez Málaga with one thousand horse and twenty thousand foot, urgently called upon knights from all Andalusia—the cardinal offered to pay personally all cavalry volunteering—and she ordered all Andalusian men from twenty to sixty "to take arms and go to the King and serve him." Al-Zagal indeed arrived, by April 25, but almost immediately heard that some of his men in fleeing from a skirmish with Boabdil's partisans had induced a general panic in Granada. He hurried back, only to find himself locked out and in disgrace and Boabdil proclaimed king.

Boabdil had had help. At his urgent request, Fernando and Isabel had sent him Spanish cavalry and foot and also arms, money, and provisions. Granadans, the monarchs had assured him, might leave the city to sow their crops and travel to Christian lands to secure necessaries, anything but arms.[20] In response, Isabel had a welcome letter from Boabdil of April 29, announcing his triumph and reaffirming the obeisance he had sworn at Loja. And an agreement was reached between them in which, much as Isabel had suggested, he would turn over Granada when he could, in exchange for places in the eastern part of the kingdom, which was, however, as yet loyal to al-Zagal.

Vélez Málaga surrendered on April 27, followed by all the places between it and Málaga, their people permitted to remain and retain their religion and customs, a leniency calculated for effect.[21] On May 6, Fernando made camp before Málaga itself, Granada's great Mediterranean port, renowned, as Palencia says, for the opulence of its inhabitants and "its decided commercial inclination," and known to be harboring numerous Christian renegades and many fugitive *conversos* and expelled Jews. Yet initial hope for its speedy surrender was soon dashed; negotiations quickly foundered.

Two weeks later Isabel arrived with her oldest daughter and a large entourage,[22] to an impressive panorama. The Castilian camp sprawled over beaches and countryside on three sides of the city. Her fleet stood off the fourth, blockading the port, firing upon it, and ferrying provisions to her armies. Málaga itself, beautiful and apparently impregnable, its fortifications designed to protect its sizeable populace (then more than eleven thousand) and tremendous wealth, stood "nearly at the end of the eastern sea and at the entrance of the western sea"—between Mediterranean and Atlantic—"near the Strait of Gibraltar which separates Spain from Africa."[23] Málaga had three strong fortresses, two of them had just been seized by Aḥmad al-Tagrī, that fierce lieutenant of al-Zagal, and his Gomeres; Palencia estimates his garrison at five thousand men. Isabel had come at Fernando's urgent request, to allay the rumor rife within Málaga that the queen so feared the pestilence afflicting nearby villages that she had ordered the Christians to decamp. Beyond the firm intent her coming conveyed, her presence attracted more volunteer knights and foot, for everyone "thought that with the arrival of the Queen the Moors had to surrender."[24] Such was the conviction her very presence exuded that a treasurer of hers, one Ruy López de Toledo, was transformed into an ardent soldier and captain and at Málaga was seen to fight so boldly and valiantly and to so inspire others that the cardinal told the queen that in him she had another Judas Maccabeus. That comment reflected both an easy familiarity with the Old Testament and alluded to the fact that the treasurer was, like so many of Isabel's staff, a *converso*.[25]

She and Fernando then demanded that Málaga surrender immediately or all its inhabitants would suffer captivity—a euphemism for slavery—when it did fall. Al-Tagrī refused, expecting torrential rains that would make Málaga's unprotected harbor so dangerous an anchorage that ships could no longer provision the Christians daily, and he awaited help from Africa. In the interim, his Gomeres killed or terrorized all dissenters while a holy man buoyed Málaga's increasingly hungry populace, prophesying that one day they would feast on the mountains of food in the Christian camp.[26]

Within a month of Isabel's arrival, another Muslim holy man came into the Christian camp and, brought before Cádiz, convinced him that he had information that he could give only to the king on how to take the city. Fernando, however, was asleep and Isabel would not then see him, so the man was taken to a nearby tent, where, seeing among others a Portuguese nobleman and Beatriz de Bobadilla, he mistook them for the king and queen. As Bobadilla, frightened by his expression, hurried to the entry, he lunged at her companion with a dagger. Ruy López de Toledo, who was also there, seized the assailant from behind and guards, running in, hacked him to pieces. Those pieces were then catapulted into Málaga, where, says Pulgar, they were gathered up, sewn together with silk thread, washed and perfumed with oils, and buried with great ceremony. Al-Tagrī retaliated in kind, killing a principal Christian captive, disemboweling the corpse, tying it to an ass, and driving the animal into the Christian camp. God, was the interpretation, had wished to protect the sovereigns. Still, thereafter Isabel had a personal guard, of two hundred men-at-arms.[27] Or so say the chronicles.

Summer wore on. Fernando and Isabel, hoping not to destroy the town, had initially subjected it only to the fire of the middling artillery, if several hundred pieces of it. But when, a month into the siege the seven great lombards arrived, they were brought into play. And in a move both practical and emblematic, Fernando ordered to be carried from Algeciras, "now depopulated, all the lombard stones that the king don Alfonso [XI] his great-great [-great] grandfather had fired against [Algeciras and Gibraltar] when he laid siege to them."[28]

Still the starving *malagueños* held out, and within the Castilian camp tempers frayed; many of the men were sick, desertion was endemic, and rumor rampant. Thus the monarchs banished all *mudéjares* from the camp, for it was being said, in a time-honored accusation made against outlanders, witches, and infidel, that they were poisoning the wells; and severe and summary punishment was meted out for all offenses.

The sea proved of crucial advantage. Fernando and Isabel, low on gunpowder, quickly procured some by sending a galley to Valencia and a caravel to the king of Portugal. And when they called on Medina Sidonia for aid, he came in person with all his knights, and a loan of twenty thousand *doblas de oro* and one hundred ships as well. Proving their blockade and privateers effective, ambassadors arrived from the king of Tlemcen (Oran), opposite Granada, offering service and requesting that the sea be opened to his subjects. They graciously complied, for Africa's Mediterranean coast figured in royal plans—economic, political, and religious.

Isabel and Fernando had solicited and received papal permission to keep open both African trade and that of Málaga. Málaga had formerly traded heavily with Barcelona and more recently with Valencia, in Granadan and re-exported African products—saffron, wax, hides, sugar, fruits and nuts, silks, and gold—and in spices and other Eastern wares brought by caravan or ship to the Barbary coast. The ships involved were often Genoese, and they traded with Italy, England, and Flanders as well.[29] It is tempting to tie such Genoese activity to the fact that Christopher Columbus was requested to come to the royal camp before Málaga, and to speculate that he may have served as a contact with resident fellow Genoese within that city, in arranging continuation of its trade, or even its surrender. However that may be, it was not to be his last appearance at court.

In the third month of the siege, in August, when Fernando offered a reward for information on conditions in the town, a group of *gallegos* hid among the tombs in a Jewish cemetery outside the walls, waylaid five men who came out to find grass for their goats, and managed to bring one of the fellows alive to the king. Fernando at length induced him to reveal that the inhabitants were subsisting on dogs, rats, and weasels; that few horses or burros survived; yet that the holy man was inciting the populace to resist, and that the Berbers, and renegades, *conversos,* and apostates, who could expect no mercy from the Castilians, would hold out to the death.

Even so, a leading *malagueño* merchant, 'Alī Durdūsh, who was partial to Boabdil, sounded out the monarchs, who insisted now on unconditional surrender; the siege had proven unexpectedly long, hard, and costly. In reply to that demand, the city fathers threatened to kill the six hundred Christian prisoners, and Fernando in turn responded that, should one die, he would kill every Muslim in Spain. Durdūsh continued to negotiate, with Gutierre de Cárdenas. On August 18, overcome by starvation, Málaga capitulated. Al-Tagrī and his garrison surrendered two days later.[30] As the royal standards and holy cross appeared on Málaga's ramparts, the queen, the *infanta* Isabel, and the entire camp knelt and prayed to "*nuestro Señor e la Virgen Santa María gloriosísima,*" and to *el Apóstol Santiago,* while the Te Deum rose up. Isabel and Fernando were in command of the chief port of Granada. Málaga was the second city of the emirate and had been Muslim for 770 years.

When the corpses had been cleared away, the stench abated, and the mosques been made churches—Talavera headed the clergy reconsecrating the principal mosque, to Santa María de la Encarnación—Isabel and Fernando entered the city gates. Even earlier, there came to their tent outside the walls the Christians released from the city's dungeons, more than six hundred men and women, emaciated and yellowed from hunger and disease. Reportedly, they fell to the ground, attempted to kiss their monarchs' feet, but received their hands instead, as well as the customary funds with which to return home. Looting was forbidden and Málaga placed under heavy guard. The monarchs stayed at Málaga until September 11. They oversaw an incoming Christian population receiving houses and lands. They arranged that the city would be the seat of a bishop and capital of a region including the Ajarquía and the *serranía* of Ronda, and they drew up ordinances for its governance in consultation with the cardinal and the Royal Council.

As to the *malagueños,* Durdūsh had not revealed to his fellow citizens the full terms of surrender. Isabel and Fernando had resolved, and Durdūsh knew, that renegades would die by sharp pointed reeds, *conversos* and judaizers come from Spain would be burned alive, Gomeres would be enslaved, and most other inhabitants would be held for ransom, a near impossible thirty *doblas* for each man, woman, and child, to be paid within sixteen months, and enslaved if not ransomed.

Street by street, the inhabitants were registered individually, under the direction of Gutierre de Cárdenas. They were divided into three lots. One was to be exchanged for Christians held by Muslims. Another was to be parceled out to all knights, council members, captains and other *hidalgos,* officers and soldiers, whether Castilian, Aragonese, Valencian, or Portuguese, who had come to the war, in accord with their rank and services. (It is unclear if until ransomed, or permanently.) A third, "to help meet the expense of the siege," was reserved to the crown until ransomed. The monarchs requisitioned all valuables as an initial ransom installment. As for Málaga's Jews, they were allowed their moveable property and transported en masse to Carmona where they were to be locked in its castle until the ransom set for them was completely paid; in Carmona too were incarcerated al-Tagrī and the demagogic holy man. Some of the *malagueños* to be ransomed were sent to Seville, to serve householders there and in Córdoba, Jerez, and Ecija, as hostages until the entire sum set for them all should be paid in full. It never was.

*   *   *

Most *malagueños* became and remained slaves. They were, states Bernáldez, "corralled and counted and enslaved and sold."[31] From 2500 to 3000 men and women were distributed immediately among Christian nobles and prelates: the cardinal received at least seventy. Fifty young women went to Fernando's sister Juana, queen of Naples, and 30 more to the queen of Portugal. Isabel bestowed a great many *malagueñas* on ladies of Castile and took others to serve in her palace. And royal account books list nearly two million *maravedís* received from the sale of 192 "heads of Moors." The pope received a gift of 100 of the surviving Gomeres, who arrived in Rome in February 1488 during a celebration of a consistory during which he doled them out: one, two, or three apiece to the assembled clergy.[32] Many unredeemed Muslim captives remained in Andalusian cities and over 3000 in Málaga, serving its new Christian inhabitants. Sales of 4,363 such people are documented, sold with their goods for over 56 million *maravedís;* moreover, the crown customarily collected sales tax on the transfer of such "slaves of war."

'Alī Durdūsh had arranged exception for himself and some relatives, somewhere between eight and forty households, who were permitted to stay in the city as Castilian subjects. Málaga's Jews—450 "souls," mostly women speaking Arabic and dressing in Moorish style—were at length ransomed for the huge lump sum of ten thousand *castellanos de oro.* It was raised by Abraham Señor, the high judge of Castile's *aljamas.*[33]

Returning to Córdoba, the king and queen were met at its gates by Prince Juan, now ten, accompanied by the knights of his guard and other dignitaries. Everyone proceeded solemnly to the cathedral, where Isabel and Fernando prayed before the high altar and received the episcopal blessing.

New Faces: 1487–1489

That fall of 1487 Aragón required attention. The monarchs left their younger daughters in Montoro, safe from the plague raging in Córdoba, took with them the *infanta* Isabel and Prince Juan, and stopped en route to be royally entertained by Infantado in Guadalajara. In Zaragoza from mid-November through mid-February, they held Corts. In that capital city, and elsewhere in Aragón, they introduced the *hermandad,* that proven remedy for factional disturbances, enhancer of royal authority, and harbinger of a national army. They also diverted some Aragonese revenues to the war, and they made certain the Inquisition was doing its job.

The following May, of 1488, with Andalusia beset by plague and near famine, they went instead to Murcia, where Juan Chacón held sway, to set up headquarters for the campaign in eastern Granada. The example of Málaga had had effect. With little or no fighting, on June 5 Lorca surrendered and soon after the port of Vera; numerous other places sent *alfaquies,* elders, empowered to surrender on condition their people might remain as *mudéjares.*

At campaign's end, Isabel went north to Valladolid and summoned leading inquisitors to organize the Holy Tribunal realm-wide. Either the queen alone or both monarchs—Fernando joined her in December—oversaw the issuance of ordinances reinforcing inquisitorial power and autonomy, condoning great secrecy, and brooking no criticism. Isabel then reconfirmed inquisitorial scope and procedures, and paid attention to regulating abuses to do with major peculation; so one receiver of confiscated goods was called to account for siphoning off a million and a half *maravedís.* She also attended to the royal chancery, making a string of new appointments, all doctors of law, having dismissed several members for sending a case on appeal to the papacy.[34]

With *los reyes'* rising reputation abroad came offers of marriage alliances. Ambassadors from Burgundy sought a pact against France and the hand of the *infanta* Isabel for the widower and holy Roman emperor, Maximilian of Habsburg, whose sizable realm included present-day Austria and Flanders. They also requested Juana be engaged to his son, Philip, heir through his mother to Burgundy. Yet it remained to be seen whether or not the Habsburgs could come to wield effective power in their far-flung domains. The queen, temporizing, replied that the *infanta* Isabel was promised to another and Juana not yet of age, but promised to reopen the conversation when she was. She and Fernando also begged off joining Burgundy against France because of the war with Granada, but sent to its aid a manned fleet.

The Spanish monarchs received an embassy too from England's new king, Henry VII. He had earlier proposed that his infant son and heir, Arthur, marry the infanta Catalina and so well had preliminary discussions in London gone, their resident ambassador reported, that at their conclusion Henry— who as a Welsh upstart saw the match as a step to solidify the dynastic Tudor hold on the crown—had joyfully broken into a Te Deum. Isabel "made [the English ambassadors] very particular honor," for she prized her Lancastrian kinship with this Henry, saw a connection with England important to Spanish preeminence in Europe, and was resolved to impress the envoys. According to English accounts, she succeeded. Summoned on March 14, at dusk, they were brought by torch-light before "the kings" (as the English referred to them). Isabel and Fernando sat side by side in a great hall, framed against a tapestry woven of cloth of gold emblazoned with the quartered arms of Castile and Aragón. They were also robed in cloth of gold, trimmed with sable. Isabel had not stopped there. In addition, she wore a riding-hood of black velvet, slashed to reveal the gold cloth beneath and trimmed in solid gold and jewels—"so rich," reported the awed emissaries, "that no one has ever seen the like." Over one shoulder she had thrown a short cloak of crimson satin fringed with ermine. An enormous balas ruby "the size of a tennis ball" decorated her girdle (the belt or sash around her waist). She wore a necklace of white and red roses of enameled gold, at the center of each a large jewel, the roses undoubtedly meant as a complimentary allusion to the reconciliation of the houses of Tudor and York. And "suspended on each side of her breast" was a ribbon studded with large diamonds, rubies, and pearls The visitors estimated the value of her attire at two hundred thousand crowns of gold. "Seated next to the Queen on the same high-backed bench" they reported, was the cardinal; and many great lords and ladies were in attendance. The ambassadors duly presented their letters and made the expected speeches, in Latin. The bishop of Ciudad Rodrigo made reply. "But the good bishop was so old, and so toothless, that what he said could be made out only with great difficulty."[35] No matter, it was only the beginning.

The next evening the Englishmen stated their business to the monarchs, whom they encountered once again extravagantly attired. Isabel wore a ruby necklace, one of several she appeared in during their stay. At the envoys' request, they now saw Prince Juan (in rich crimson velvet) and the *infanta* Isabel (dressed in cloth of gold under a green velvet robe with long train). Four days later at royal invitation the Englishmen joined the monarchs at the hour of compline in the chapel and afterward sat with them to watch young courtiers dance, observing the *infanta* Isabel among them and that, as protocol dictated, she danced with one of her ladies, the one she liked best, who was Portuguese.

Several days later, the envoys attended a tilting match, followed by minstrels, dancing, and dinner, where they encountered the queen more richly bejeweled than ever and escorted by the cardinal. They met the *infantas* María and Catalina, also opulently dressed and well attended. Finally, a bullfight was held in their honor, and afterward one hundred knights "skirmished and ran with dogs in the way they fought with the Saracens." They sat watching with the royal family in the scaffolding—the bleachers—"and it was beautiful to see how the Queen held up her youngest daughter, the infanta donna Catherine, [who was to be] princess of Wales; and at that time she was three years of age." Again dancing followed, mother and daughters again resplendent in rich attire and jewelry. Culminating those festivities was the signing of the treaty of Medina del Campo, promising mutual aid and defense and the marriage of Catalina and Arthur; it would guide relations between Castile and England until their deterioration in 1525 when Carlos I of Spain, who was also Charles V, Holy Roman Emperor, jilted England's princess, his cousin Mary, Catalina's daughter.

Baza: 1489

Threading through that fall and winter were preparations for the upcoming campaign against Baza, the key to hemming in al-Zagal, who was in Almería; it would prove to be the costliest siege to date. In November the junta of the *Hermandad* again agreed to provide ten thousand infantry and eighty days pay. Again the city councils were assessed and, in February, a forced loan was levied on them, with amounts specified for each place, payable in a year, and *continos* instructed to see to their collection. Nor were Jews and Muslims, although they paid other levies annually, exempt from new extraordinary imposts. The Mesta too was charged a special tax on each head of cattle, to be paid to Talavera. Individual nobles and bishops once more "loaned" large sums. The clergy voted a subsidy as well as paying a tithe, each amounting to over 13 million *maravedís*. And the bulls of crusade brought in tremendous sums. A royal pardon was again promised to criminals in Galicia and Asturias who would volunteer for a year. In February, purchase orders went out for grain, wheat, and barley, with prices stipulated.

Isabel, early in the spring of 1489, visited her mother in Arévalo and then went to Guadalupe. By mid-April she and Fernando were in Córdoba and, in May, in Jaén. There she set up headquarters and remained until late fall, along with her children, Mendoza, Talavera, and most of her council, while the siege of Baza began. Lasting from mid-June through December, it would be among the longest, the hardest, and the final campaigns of the war.

Baza was surrounded by jagged mountains on three sides; in a river basin on the fourth lay its *huerta* of irrigated farmland, protected by a low wall. Fernando reportedly lay siege accompanied by thirteen thousand horse and forty thousand foot, but encountered prodigious rains and faced a well-garrisoned and fortified city. After an initial and fierce twelve-hour battle ending in a draw promised a long siege, Fernando considered raising camp and attacking some other place. In the council, opinions varied. Cádiz wanted to stay, Gutierre de Cárdenas to go. "And about all this," says the anonymous chronicler, the king "decided that he ought to consult the Queen, who had charge of arranging all provisioning, to get her opinion about the things needed if the siege was to continue." Isabel had his account of how matters stood, carried by relays of couriers, within ten hours. Nor is the tenor of her reply unanticipated. She responded equally quickly that her council did not know enough to give an opinion, that he should decide, but if he did resolve to continue the siege, which at the beginning all had agreed to, then with the help of God she would arrange that the armies should be well provided with men and money and provisions and all the other things necessary until the city was taken. The king chose to continue the siege, because, Pulgar observed, "those things the Queen offered are the principal ones that sustain wars."[36] And he added that, her resolve known, the rank and file now wanted to see it through, that men who were originally reluctant or simply bent on booty had adopted the royal cause as their own.

Isabel pressed everyone for more funds. Luis Santángel, who had arranged international loans, made advances against them. Cádiz and other magnates accepted seignorial jurisdictions in exchange for loans. The Genoese merchants of Seville contributed handsomely; and one of them, Francisco Pinelo, who was associated with Talavera and Santángel in the *cruzada* enterprise and other financial activities, came up with three times as much as did the others together. And it is now that, the ransom period having expired and the need for funds pressing, Málaga's people were being sold into slavery; handling that business too were Santángel and Pinelo.[37]

Even though hard-pressed, Isabel punctiliously sent Boabdil money monthly and saw Granada remain satisfactorily torn by factional strife. Appealed to by Granadans, Qā'it Bay, the sultan of Egypt, now requested of the pope that he inform the king and queen of Spain that they must end the war against Granada and, if not, Christians in his domain, which included Jerusalem, would be treated as they treated Muslims. The sultan's unlikely envoys were two Franciscan friars attached to Christ's tomb in Jerusalem; the pope sent them on to Fernando and Isabel, whose response was that their progenitors had held those lands the Muslims now unjustly ruled, that those Muslims had warred on Christians, and that they would treat the many Muslims in their realms as the sultan treated the Christians in his. Yet they wrote directly to Qā'it Bay as well, in more conciliatory terms: it was not a religious war, they explained; rather one to reclaim vassal states of theirs that had tried to break away. (They were consistent; several years later Isabel's envoy to Egypt, Pedro Mártir, would make much the same argument.) They themselves, the monarchs stated, had always respected the religion of the vanquished, as their agreements upon surrender attested. And to show the sultan their good faith they suspended for the moment the preaching of holy war that accompanied the sale of bulls of crusade. They were not greatly concerned, for the sultan also requested the help of an Aragonese fleet against the Turks. His friar-emissaries had found Isabel in Jaén. She talked extensively with them, pledged them one thousand ducats annually from her revenues on Sicily for maintenance of Christ's tomb, "and she gave them a veil that she, moved by devotion, had made with her own hands, to cover the holy sepulcher."[38]

As she had promised, Isabel kept the camp at Baza well supplied. For five months she continually sent money and provisions, bread and wine and meat, as well as armorers, saddle makers, harness makers, and all other necessities. Merchants from Castile, Aragón, Valencia, Catalonia, and Sicily flocked to the Spanish encampment, bringing brocades and silks, cloths and linens, hangings, and other things then welcomed by men at war with pay and booty to spend. But no merchant would carry provisions on his own account. So she ordered wheat and barley to be purchased in Andalusia and the lands of the military orders, and with dearth and doubled prices in Andalusia that year, she permitted shipment of more from the Barbary Coast. She arranged the transfer of those purchases to the mule trains that went daily to the camp, and had the grains sold at a fixed price. She also made arrangements for milling flour and transporting it there.

In July, Isabel decreed severe punishment for desertion and absence without leave, and, with a long siege likely, in August she coaxed infantry reinforcements and their pay out of the cities, and also additional loans. She dunned towns in arrears, levied further forced loans upon them and on prelates, knights, and ladies as well, and she insistently urged merchants to lend all they could. The response was good, indicating a firm patriotism and confidence in the queen's credit. She drew relatively heavily on Talavera's see of Avila and on the *cruzada,* Talavera as its *comisario general* having recourse to its huge revenues. She also sold bonds payable on the rents of municipalities directly under the crown. And she sent jewels into pawn; her most splendid ruby necklace was again in Valencia in August, surety for a loan of twenty thousand florins. In December, a crown of gold and diamonds followed it to ensure a loan of thirty-five thousand florins arranged by Santángel. Meanwhile, within Muslim Baza, the women gave their jewels to pay the soldiers of the garrison.

Although the fall was extraordinarily mild, Fernando prepared for the winter snows and winds habitual to the region. He and the great lords had houses built, with mud walls covered by tile and wood; within four days, over one thousand went up, situated along newly laid out streets. The foot soldiers built sheds of branches or huts for themselves. No sooner was this tour de force completed than a great storm hit, ruining houses and rendering all roads impassable. The dwellings were promptly rebuilt, and only one day's supply trains failed to arrive. For the queen had immediately sent artisans and six thousand *peones* to repair roads and build causeways and bridges, so that one route was kept open for supply trains going to the camp and another for those returning. Other provisions came by sea, through the port of Vera, transported principally by Andalusian ships. Overseeing the obtaining of those supplies and their distribution within the camp was a formidable team, testimony to the importance of that task: two royal secretaries, Hernando de Zafra and Fernán Alvarez de Toledo Zapata, and the *letrado* Rodrigo Maldonado, now a member of the Royal Council.

Letters from the duke of Cádiz kept Isabel informed of the campaign.[39] Fernando, nobles, and knights repeatedly requested that she come to camp, for, they told her, should the Moors but see her they would surrender. She hesitated, until she heard that within the war council one faction, which now included Fernando, was ready to raise camp. She arrived at Baza on November 7, with her daughter Isabel—from whom, Pulgar observes, she was now never parted—and her cardinal and ladies; the entire encampment turned out to greet her, except the posted guards. The chronicler, who was there, indicates that to men bored after a siege of six months, the queen's coming at the very least brought welcome novelty. And, among the besieged, it certainly appeared to have immediate impact; all artillery fire and skirmishing then ceased and shortly thereafter Sīdī Yaḥyā-al-Najjār, the military governor of Baza, was ready to negotiate. So was Isabel.[40]

Gutierre de Cárdenas having assured the governor that should he not come to terms the Spanish were prepared to stay all winter, Baza surrendered. The royal forces entered the city in blinding snow on December 4. The terms given were among the most lenient of the war: the garrison might leave; the inhabitants might stay but they must move outside the walls, pay tribute, and become royal subjects, *mudéjares*. Fernando and Isabel swore they might keep their faith, their laws, and their *fueros* or customary rights. Surrender of other settled places from Baza to Almería followed rapidly under the same terms; Castilian *alcaides* were sent to take charge of their forts. Then came word from al-Zagal in Almería; he also would surrender for, he explained, "it appears that the will of heaven is to take this land from me and give it to you." The Christians saw it all as a marvel attributable to the divine will that such strong cities had fallen to them with no further exertion on their part. On December 10 al-Zagal signed a capitulation, and he turned over Almería on December 22. Although Isabel, held up by heavy snow until December 23, missed that ceremony, she was in time for the reconsecration of Almería's mosque. When al-Zagal surrendered Guadix on December 30, the monarchs wrote to Seville that the war was over. They were too optimistic.

Perhaps twenty thousand Spanish had died in that campaign, the great majority of them from sickness and cold. Isabel decreed the families of the dead and wounded exempt from future war exactions and granted them funds from fines levied on deserters and no-shows.[41] And, seeing the end of the war at least near, Mendoza instructed that there be carved on the choir stalls of Toledo's cathedral the fifty-four scenes still to be seen there commemorating the surrender of each of fifty-four Muslim towns and cities.[42]

Royal Wedding: 1490

Isabel had tried in vain to have the Portuguese accept another of her daughters for Prince Afonso. But Afonso, it was said, wanted only the *infanta* Isabel;

and, being the oldest, with her too might one day come all Spain. In February, Portuguese ambassadors arrived, urging that the marriage take place; Afonso, five years younger than his intended, was now of age. The *infanta* Isabel was twenty and had become her mother's inseparable companion. As a child she had been placed in the care of Teresa Enríquez, the wife of Gutierre de Cárdenas, a woman renowned for her devotion and piety. Intelligent and dutiful, she had been hostage to the Cabreras and then to the peace between Castile and Portugal. She knew Afonso well, for both had lived for over three years in the care of her great-aunt, Beatriz. She was, in effect, still a hostage; she must marry, and her choice of husband was limited, either to Afonso, a boy she knew and liked, or Maximilian, a stranger and a middle-aged widower in a far land. Of the two, her mother preferred the prince of Portugal because he was closer to her daughter in age and customs as well as geographically, because he shared a lineage, and because it was also a way to keep Portugal sweet in matters of Africa and the Atlantic.

Isabel's relations with Portugal's king, João (who had taken the title lord of Guinea and was reaping from Portugal's African enclaves the gold that had once gone to Algiers, Tunis, and, hence, often to Spain), while never good, had worsened since 1483, when he had executed that most powerful noble, the duke of Braganza, on suspicion of plotting with herself and Fernando, which Braganza well may have done. Yet, since she must send her daughter off once more, she would show the world how valued was her firstborn, and how powerful Spain's royal family had become.

Arrangements were made with the Portuguese by Talavera and Cárdenas. Isabel, accustomed to supplying an army of tens of thousands, in providing a handsome dowry and in everything else having to do with the wedding manifested a war-reinforced habit of thinking on grand scale. According to the royal household accounts, her daughter's silver and gold plate alone cost over three million *maravedís*. She paid for splendid public festivals in May lasting fifteen days, spending over 500,000 *maravedís* for the trappings of the mounts of the court ladies attending the jousts, over 100,000 *maravedís* for the harness of Prince Juan's horse. She paid 26,554 *maravedís* for the stage sets for the customary *momos*, which were ostensibly commissioned by twelve-year-old Juan in honor of his sister, much as his mother had once done for her brother.[43] The wedding arrangements and celebrations demonstrated, as they were meant to do, both the prosperity of the court and its capacity to mobilize funds.

On Easter Sunday of 1490 Cardinal Mendoza officiated at a proxy ceremony in Seville; the actual wedding would take place in Portugal. Attending were knights come from Castile, Aragón, Valencia, Catalonia, and Sicily. The one hundred *caballeros* of the royal household appeared everywhere in silks and cloth of gold. *Grandes* too shone in such raiment and in gold chains studded with gems and insignia. Isabel herself wore cloth of gold and she and the soon-to-be princess of Portugal were accompanied constantly by seventy women in brocade and jewels; at night eight or nine torchbearers escorted each one of those ladies. A great jousting field was set up between the shipyards and the Guadalquivir River, just outside the city walls (assumedly a sufficient distance from the *quemadero*). In short, it was November before the *infanta* Isabel left, her parents and her brother riding with her as far as Constantina, where everyone shed many tears at parting. Then the cardinal and a large escort accompanied the *infanta* as far as the border. In Portugal the marriage was celebrated with another month of extravagant festivities. Pulgar will not have Castile outshone: although in their own subsequent festivities the Portuguese strove to outdo in grandeur the king and queen of Castile, he sniffs, they showed themselves of a greater mind to spend than of a sufficient faculty to do it in good taste.[44]

Six months later, on July of 1491, Afonso was galloping on uneven ground along a river bank when his horse slipped and, in falling, crushed the prince to death. Queen Isabel, upon receiving word of the tragedy and that her daughter, overcome by grief, was neither eating nor sleeping, determined that the *infanta* must return to Castile. And so young Isabel came back, in deepest mourning, to rejoin her parents, her grief inconsolable, her tragic figure a portent of greater woe to come.

Murmurings

Isabel, preparing to move against Granada itself, sought yet more funds. The years at war had forged in the people of Castile a sense of high Christian mission. Success had enhanced the prestige of the monarchy to the point where towns, cities, individuals, and religious bodies paid on demand the monies requested of them. But approval was not unalloyed. Indicative of opposition was criticism by one Hernando de Vera, a councilman who was angered by tremendous subsidies demanded of Jerez, where he sat on the town council. Vera's vehicle was a reprise of the corrosive couplets of *Mingo Revulgo*, popular in the 1460s, berating a shepherd for poorly tending his flock. The shepherd meant had once been Enrique, but now it was Isabel. Vera scored too a poor friar who had become tremendously rich, possibly Talavera or Alonso de Burgos, and "the old dog who runs always at your side," undoubtedly Mendoza. "The seven rapacious serpents," with a dragon at their head and another behind, signified the closest royal cohorts and linked them to the evil monster of the Apocalypse. Influenced perhaps by a comet appearing in 1490 and considered an ominous sign, he foresaw an eclipse of the moon, "an eclipse like *Luna*." Having badly misjudged what was then permissible, Vera was sentenced to death for those verses, but managed to stay alive until 1497, when they were no longer topical and he was pardoned.[45] In 1491 however, having persevered for a decade, Isabel would brook no dissent; she was determined to achieve her goal.

The End of the War

It was time to lay siege to Granada. Boabdil, although he had promised to turn over the city when the eastern provinces fell, did not, for he was leery of the strong Granadan war party made up of the military and the refugees, nor would Isabel and Fernando agree to grant him the lands he considered guaranteed to him in exchange. When he subsequently attacked some Christian forts, the Castilian monarchs termed it rebellion. It was, most opportunely, the spring of 1491, time for another annual campaign, meant as a culminating one. Isabel, in what proved a prelude to national conscription, called up all nobles and knights and ordered all men of Castile between eighteen and sixty to enlist in companies under captains. In April and May, Fernando raided the *vega* from the camp at Los Ojos de Hachure on the outskirts of the city; he had been joined by his former foes, the *caudillo* of Baza, who came with 150 horse "and took the most dangerous place," and al-Zagal, with 200 *jinetes*.

Isabel arrived in early June, with Prince Juan, the *infanta* Juana, and a large entourage; her daughter Isabel rejoined her at the end of July. In the interim, Prince Juan had a birthday. The past February, Fernando had ordered him turtles from Valencia, gifts to delight a boy. But Juan was thirteen years old that June; he had come of age. And so, encamped before Granada, Fernando knighted his son. Juan's *padrinos,* godfather-sponsors, were Medina Sidonia and Cádiz. Juan received a helmet and a coat of mail, campaign breeches and a dagger. Isabel handed him the coins for the liturgical ceremony, twelve Castilian doublons. The prince was now a *caballero* with horse and armor who could accompany his father on expeditions and in turn knight the young sons of the high nobility.

During June of 1492, too, Castile's queen fulfilled a long-harbored desire; from a high window in a house in the hamlet of Zubia she could at last see Granada's walls and towers, a view undoubtedly signifying to her that she was on the verge of achieving the centuries-long goal of Spain's kings. It was to Isabel an occasion of sufficient moment to commemorate later by constructing a Franciscan monastery where that house had stood. She had come to that vantage point accompanied by Fernando, their children, and a number of courtiers, and escorted by Cádiz at the head of a detachment of cavalry. She had instructed the marqués that should the Granadans come out, there be no skirmishing, no responding to taunts; she wanted no one to die because of her caprice. Yet the regal procession passing before Granada's walls went beyond caprice; it was a defiant show, flaunting its strength and embodying determination, made even more provocative by Cadiz's men galloping back and forth in high spirits. When hundreds of *jinetes* streamed out of the city, those knights, resisting goading only so long, engaged, with losses on both sides.[46] Ballads would tell of it, and of the Muslim noblewomen watching the fray from the Alhambra's towers.

Such encounters were indeed the stuff of ballads, and chivalric doings were frequently indulged in during that final siege, for spirits were high, and there was not much else to do; capitulation seemed only a matter of time. Redolent of chivalry too was the conduct of Cádiz, who faithfully escorted his queen whenever she was in "the lands of the Moors, because he was so feared by them."[47] Large in stature and reputation, he cut a truly heroic figure, made more so by pursuing that campaign despite suffering from a painful wound received in a skirmish, a lance thrust that traversed his right arm, from which he was never to fully recover.

Looking back with nostalgia on it all as a simpler time before the more deadly and less idealistic Italian wars, the Venetian ambassador, Andrea Navagiero, who was there, recalled the conquest of Granada as the last war waged as giant tournament, with challenges to single combat on both sides and chivalric rules respected:

It was a beautiful war, with little artillery as yet, and brave men were readily seen to be brave. There were daily encounters, and every day there was some fine feat of arms. All the nobility of Spain was there, and all were competing in the conquest of fame. The Queen and her court urged each one on. There was not a lord present who was not enamored of some one of the ladies of the Queen, and these ladies were not only witnesses to what was done upon the field, but often handed the sallying warriors their weapons, granting them at the same time some favor, together with a request that they show by their deeds how great was the power of their love. What man is so vile, so lacking in spirit, that he would not have defeated every powerful foe and redoubtable adversary, risking a thousand lives rather than return to his lady in shame? For which reason one can say that this war was won by love.[48]

He was wrong in that Granada was won over the long haul and by unified effort, superior technology, manipulation of internal factions, money, and tenacity. As one scholar, taking the larger and longer view, concludes, Muslim al-Andalus, "despite its greater evolution with respect to Christian society in Spain," was chronically weakened by ethnic differences and divisions; and so it fell before a "dynamic Christian society, whose strong national sentiment served it as a motivating force of great vigor."[49]

Nonetheless, and especially during the siege cf Granada, resurgent chivalry, injected with a righteous sense of Christian purpose, had a field day. Crucial to the chivalric code was service to a lady, and in that war the lady served universally was the queen, who approached becoming the very embodiment of national sentiment. Religion and chivalry intertwined, mutually reinforcing her prestige. Isabel contributed to that conjunction by behaving as Joan of Arc might have had she been a married queen, and by ceaselessly demonstrating her own dedication to both chivalric usages and holy war.

Chivalry and an act of God appeared associated too in her greatest brush with danger during the final siege. In the early hours of July 14, Isabel, who had left a candle burning beside her bed, awakened to a tent in flames. Shepherding Juana and her servants outside, she encountered Fernando running out of his tent in his nightshirt, dagger and sword in hand, cuirass on his arm, thinking it a surprise Muslim attack. Then, while Isabel and her daughter, escorted by a page also in nightshirt, went to Cabra's nearby tent, Cádiz, gathering (it is said) three thousand men, rode out to make certain that Muslims did not take advantage of their plight. His marquesa sent the queen clothes and all necessaries, and on return he himself relinquished to her his own tent. Yet that night, despite the efforts of the entire army, the fire, fanned by wind, consumed much of the camp.[50]

The Christians rebuilt. The men of the *hermandades* and the military orders raised tiled houses, the experience at Baza standing them in good stead, so that "it appeared a well-ordered city." Isabel sent a painting on cloth of the new encampment to the Portuguese court. Replete with walls, moats, battlements, and towers, its orderly streets conforming to the shape of a cross (visible as such from Granada's battlements), it was called Santa Fe, the Holy Faith. Everything was in abundance, says Pulgar, silks, cloths, brocades, and all the rest, "as though it were a goodly fair," the queen having seen to its provisioning. In Granada, eight miles distant, there was great unhappiness at such strong indication that the Castilians had come to stay.

Within Granada, although a holy man incited a popular outcry against surrender, Boabdil convinced his council that with no hope of rescue from abroad, the city could not hold out. Accordingly, the formal documents of surrender, the *capitulaciones,* were signed on November 25, and Boabdil was given a customary chivalric period of grace, sixty-five days, to ready for the event. The terms were relatively lenient. Granadans might remain. Isabel and Fernando guaranteed their lives and property, promised to respect the existing laws and religious institutions, and acknowledged their right to practice their religion freely. Education was to remain under Muslim *doctos* and *alfaquíes.* Inhabitants would receive three years' exemption from taxes. Boabdil and his family were to have ample domain, in the Alpujarras, and he was to receive thirty thousand *castellanos de oro.* Granada was to be subject to Castile and to have a Castilian governor.[51] Henceforth its peoples would be *mudéjares.*

Events surrounding the surrender itself further attest to chivalry at work, and to planning awry. Formal surrender was set for January 2, 1492. But on the first of January, along with the six hundred noble Muslims that Boabdil sent as hostages to the camp at Santa Fe, he sent a message: a force must come into the Alhambra, secretly that night, to secure it against any trouble during the next day's formalities. The monarchs accordingly dispatched Gutierre de Cárdenas with a contingent of armed men; and that night, in the Torre de Comares, Boabdil turned over to him the Alhambra's keys, although not without getting a written receipt for them. Cárdenas stationed guards at all towers and doors, then alerted Iñigo López de Mendoza, count of Tendilla, the experienced warrior and diplomat named Granada's new governor, who immediately joined him. It is unclear if it was then or the next day that the banners of Castile and León as well as that of Santiago were hoisted on the Tower of Comares, while the great silver cross of the cardinal, who was Tendilla's uncle, was raised on the Tower of the Winds, which was also the highest tower. Whenever it was, Isabel was watching and waiting, and when she saw the holy cross gleaming and her banners flying atop the Alhambra and heard the cry go up all around her of "¡*Castilla*! ¡*Castilla*! For *don* Fernando and *doña* Isabel!" she fell to her knees and gave thanks to God. Her chapel resounded with the triumphant Te Deum. "Everyone shouted and cried with joy."

The official surrender took place the next day as planned. The king, the queen, Prince Juan, an unspecified *infanta*—either Isabel or Juana—the cardinal, the court, everyone splendidly dressed, proceeded to within a half-league of the city, then reined up by the bank of the Genil River. Fernando continued on, fording the river to meet Boabdil, who rode out of Granada's gates on a mule, accompanied by fifty knights on horseback. Beforehand, in negotiations on protocol, Boabdil and his indomitable mother had been adamant against his kissing any hands, while Isabel and Mendoza were equally so in refusing to cede on any bit of due ceremony. At length it had been agreed that Boabdil had only to take one foot from the stirrup and to doff his hat, then Fernando would signal he need do no more. And so it went. The two kings then rode back together to Isabel, who also refused Boabdil's kissing of hands in submission, but she did admonish him henceforward to behave himself.

In due form, Boabdil gave the keys of the city to Fernando. He passed them to Isabel. The keys then went farther, but there is no agreement as to just where: either from her to Prince Juan, and finally to Granada's governor, Tendilla, or from the queen to Tendilla and then to her factotum, Gutierre de Cárdenas. Whatever the progression, the city was hers.[52] Tendilla and the new archbishop of Granada, Hernando de Talavera, then led a contingent of one thousand horse and five thousand foot up to the Alhambra. En route they met, coming the other way, a straggling procession, a band of Christian captives just released from the dungeons carved in the rock below the Alhambra. Rag-

Figure 9. Cardinal Mendoza, Isabel, and Fernando entering Granada, 1492 (c. 1521). Felipe Bigarny. Royal Chapel, Granada.

ged and malnourished, dragging their chains, they advanced in single file behind a cross and an image of the Virgin Mary, singing to the God of Israel—the God of war and the deliverer from captivity.[53] He seemed the most appropriate deity.

There is the enduring story of Boabdil returning to the Alhambra in tears, to meet his mother's reproof that he should not cry like a woman for what he could not defend like a man. And there is another, often told and equally suspect: just beyond the Alhambra is an eminence where Boabdil is said to have turned to look back sadly as he left Granada; it has become known as the Moor's Sigh. However that may be, Boabdil went with his family to Val de Purchena in the Alpujarras, where he had been granted three towns, and where he was not to stay long.

Isabel and Fernando made solemn entry into the city on January 6, Epiphany, the Day of Kings, an event commemorated in yet another unreliable but telling anecdote. Against the monarchs specific prohibition, a knight rode into the Alhambra ahead of them. They ordered him beheaded, then they reconsidered, for he had fought in all their campaigns ever since Toro, and so "they forgave him and made him *mercedes* in that city and kingdom."[54] Here the transition from war to peace began.

Afterward

The monarchs stayed for three months more in Santa Fe, going into Granada only during the day, until advised that the city was safe.[55] After some rapid repairs in the Alhambra they spent the night there in early April. Thereafter, they occupied the palace and, while leaving most mosques in the city intact, they had the royal mosque converted into a Christian church. Despite having ordered all arms in the city collected, uprisings were attempted and a large cache of weapons found, "about which they made much justice." *Los reyes* also had Granada's Jewish quarter demolished; it is estimated that twenty thousand Jews were cast out within what soon became a realm-wide expulsion. Throughout the predominantly Muslim region, they had fortifications erected or strengthened and garrisoned. They ordered new construction techniques employed to counter new artillery technology. In the Alhambra itself, walls were reinforced and gates reconstructed. The *puerta de hierro* remains emblazoned with the royal coat of arms then prominently placed upon it; and their Fs and Ys, yoke and arrows, are still visible on the palace ceilings.[56]

Although Tendilla showed himself acutely sensitive to the disposition of Granada's inhabitants, he was essentially a military governor of occupied territory whose difficult assignment it was to incorporate the still-Muslim city within the crown of Castile. To achieve it, he worked in tandem with Granada's first archbishop, that mainstay of royal government and the royal conscience, Talavera, in making and reviewing decisions of every kind. While there Isabel, who stayed through May, assumed major responsibility for transforming the Muslim kingdom into a province of Castile. In that process, she counted on both men and also upon Hernando de Zafra, an experienced royal secretary and administrator who continued to work closely with them both after she left, and to keep her well informed.

Throughout the decade, the monarchs had placed large, important subjugated Muslim areas and their towns and cities in *realengo,* that is, directly under royal jurisdiction. Others, usually of great size but very rural, they ceded to powerful nobles in return for wartime services. Thus, Cenete became the head town of the *mayorazgo* of its new marqués, Rodrigo de Mendoza, a bold captain and one of the cardinal's sons. Muslims of Guadix, Baza, Almería, and Almuñécar were allowed to settle in his domains, for to Cenete and other noble proprietors much of the value of such concessions was precisely the presence of Muslim farmers, so hardworking and so experienced in cultivating lands in mountainous regions. Veterans or simply immigrants, incoming Castilians settled mainly on royal domain, where they received small holdings. Coming principally from Andalusia, New Castile, and Murcia, they also settled along what had been nearly deserted frontier. The crown parceled out to them lands and goods through *mercedes,* through purchase, or in *repartimiento* (in the redivision of lands in places where Muslims had been expelled), as in Málaga, Ronda, and Baza. Royal officials having inventoried moveable property and real estate in those towns, grants were made from their lists, and an initial freedom from taxes and a chance to live better attracted settlers. It was anticipated at court that through this system royal revenues would soar. Castilians also gravitated to the city of Granada. Although no reapportioning of land occurred there, they enjoyed the advantage of belonging to the dominant faith and culture, an advantage that would increase with time.[57] In 1495, when the three-year moratorium ended, heavy taxes were levied on all *mudéjares* and the heaviest on those of the former kingdom of Granada. The Muslims of Granada were indeed a subject people by then, and worse was to come.

From Granada in 1492, the monarchs instructed anyone holding Muslims as captives or slaves to turn them over to royal officials, disclosing their cost under oath, and the crown would see that they were reimbursed. Yet such slavery endured. A traveler several year later wrote of seeing numerous Muslim slaves on the estates of the duke of Cádiz. Isabel herself retained female Muslim slaves in her domestic service. The suspicion arises that, especially with peace, exceptions were made to general regulations.

The tithes of benefices in Granadan churches had been stipulated beforehand: a third to go to the parishes and two-thirds to the crown. To endow such new churches, the goods and rents of mosques, hospitals, and religious groups were simply taken over, serving a double function in strapping Muslim institutions. Her account books reveal Isabel's own ongoing donations to those establishments, a long list of bells, organs, benches, images, missals, candelabra, monstrances, chalices, ornaments, altar cloths, vestments, and other necessaries.[58] In many churches dotting the former kingdom of Granada, a piece of velvet altar cloth or an embroidered vestment is revered today as having been embroidered by Queen Isabel herself; the tradition is an old one, the fabric usually of more recent date. Crown and archbishop constructed monasteries for the principal religious orders. Above all, religious dominance was yet again made manifest through dedicating new establishments to those Christian doctrines most repugnant to Muslims: the divinity of Christ and the virginity of Mary. One royal directive, to an artillery engineer, instructed he recast the alarum bells of fortresses into church bells. The victors continued to ring out the old and ring in the new with an incessant pealing of church bells, so much a symbol of Christian triumph and so despised by the Moors. "How come you don't have the cows," the besieged *malagueños* were supposed to have scoffed, "but you ring their bells?"[59]

Bent upon convincing leading Muslims to become Christian, Isabel repeatedly made them gifts including sums of money. Her archbishop, Talavera, true to his principles, was both determined to convert all Muslims and to do it without force, through the weight of reason, example, and persuasion. Opposed to mass baptism, seeking sincere Christians, and well knowing the terrible effects of forcing Jews to convert, he studied and analyzed Muslim customs in order to battle old ways and to introduce Christianity more compellingly. He and men he trained learned to speak Arabic and, among those Granadans won over, he strove to eradicate customs associated with Muslim ceremonies: the traditional ways of celebrating birth, marriage, and death. Bathing, ringed with ritual, was discouraged. He expected heads of families to learn Christian rudiments, make the sign of the cross, kneel in church, revere the images, and recite the Paternoster, the Ave Maria, and the Credo. Infants were to be baptized within eight days of birth. Marriage bans and wedding ceremonies had to be the province of priests. The dying had to receive last rites, and the dead be buried in consecrated ground. Families had to attend mass and vespers and family heads go daily to church to pray and receive holy water; the church was to replace the mosque as the site of daily gathering. New converts were to form Christian *cofradías* (confraternities or mutual aid societies) and send their children to church schools, ideally to learn to read, write, and sing, but at least to learn prayers; and they were to sustain one or two hospitals for their poor and sick. With Isabel's sponsorship and at his own cost, Talavera founded in Granada a seminary for priests, the Colegio de San Cecilio, teaching his approach. He also put up *segundones,* younger sons, of the old high nobility in his own house, teaching them *ciencia y virtud.*[60] Tendilla gave him wholehearted support. An accretion of the military, administrative, and proselytizing experience gained during the Granada wars would be carried to the New World, and there it would be most firmly implanted by missionaries and royal officials, a number of them both trained by Talavera and Tendilla in Granada.

III

Toward Empire

Chapter 14
The View from Granada: The Grand Design, 1492

As God did his deeds
defense was unavailing
for where He put his hand
the impossible was nearly nothing.
—Juan del Encina, on the fall of Granada[1]

"We write of the great mercy that Our Lord has shown us in giving us this city. . . . We assure you that this city of Granada is greater in population than you can imagine; the royal palace is majestic and the richest of Spain."[2] So read the bailiff of Valencia in a letter of January 1492 from their majesties. They wrote much the same thing to their bishops and to the pope, and they instructed all their subjects to say prayers and to hold processions of thanksgiving for a Spain restored after 780 years. God had given them victory, to His own glory and that of the faithful, to their honor and the increase of the realm, and to the honor of their loyal subjects.[3]

Isabel and Fernando informed Europe's other kings as well. As Francis Bacon recalled, very detailed letters were received in London from Spain's king and queen, "signifying the final conquest of Granada from the Moors; which action, in itself so worthy, king Ferdinando, whose manner was never to lose any virtue for the shewing, had expressed and displayed in his letters at large, with all the particularities and religious punctos and ceremonies, that were observed in the reception of that city and kingdom."[4] Henry VII, Bacon continued, "naturally affecting much the King of Spain, as far as one king can affect another, partly for his virtues, and partly for a counterpoise to France," sent all the nobles and prelates at court and the mayor and aldermen of London to St. Paul's Church, where the lord chancellor told them that they were assembled "to sing unto God a new song"; that for now, through "the prowess and devotion of Ferdinando and Isabella, Kings of Spain, and to their immortal honor," was recovered the great and rich kingdom of Granada, for which all Christians must thank God; and that this conquest was obtained "without

Figure 10. Isabel and Fernando praying before the Virgin and Child, with Prince Juan and the *infanta* Isabel, or perhaps Juana (c. 1490). Dominican in conception, behind them stand Saints Dominic and Thomas Aquinas. From the Convento de Santo Tomás, Ávila, built by Tomás de Torquemada. Prado, Madrid.

much effusion of blood. Whereby it is to be hoped, that there shall be gained not only new territory, but infinite souls to the church of Christ, whom the Almighty, as it seems, would have alive that they may be converted." And throughout Europe the victory was seen as well as a step toward redressing the loss of Constantinople.

The prestige of Isabel and Fernando soared, and that welcome state of affairs was reflected back to them in lofty prose by ambassadors: from Henry of England, from Venice, and from the pope.[5] Hieronymus Münzer came "on behalf of Maximilian and other Germans" and to see with his own eyes the marvels of which he had heard. He told the king and queen that their noble deeds were known throughout the universe and that they filled the princes and lords of Germany with admiration, especially for having turned discord and civil war into peace and prosperity. "We see," he recalled saying to them, "the rulers through whose arm God has caused regeneration of their vassals and the submission of kingdoms and men of other races." Now were the chains of the captive broken, the peasant secure, the traveler confident, and Spain in tranquility.[6]

In such accolades the monarchs were jointly spoken of, as Isabel had long insisted they be, as dual sovereign heads, *los reyes,* or, as Bacon put it, "the kings of Spain." Even Münzer, with no high idea of woman's place, came to concede that Isabel had proven herself impossible to overlook: "Such is her counsel in the arts of war and peace, that nearly all hold it above what it is possible the female sex can do . . . I believe that the Omnipotent on high, on seeing Spain languishing, sent this most admirable woman, so that, in union with the King, it might be restored to sound state."[7] Pedro Mártir, stating what "*los reyes*" implied, called them "two bodies animated by a single spirit, for they rule with one mind."[8] Their motto, *tanto monta,* now above all signified joint sovereignty: "as much one as the other."

The Next Step

True to her usual mode of operation, with one grand-scale enterprise completed, Isabel contemplated a project of yet broader scope viewed as its continuation: she and Fernando planned advance into Africa and the Atlantic. The Spanish claim to the domain of the Visigoths in Africa and the Canary Islands, that claim that had in her father's reign passed from hortatory rhetoric to legal argument, was transformed once again, into current program. Recovering *lo suyo,* her own, that which Christian Spaniards once held, had, with her prompting, in the late 1470s provided justification for the seaborne ventures whose goals were territory and gold, security against the Muslims, and besting Portugal. The treaty with Portugal in 1479, distinguishing between eastern and western Barbary as divided by the Strait of Gibraltar, had recognized Spanish economic interests across the strait from Andalusia in eastern Barbary, a region nearly coterminus with the kingdom of Fez. Since then, Castile's African commerce had surged. Isabel had asserted royal oversight, and, although instructing her subjects planning to trade along the western coast as far as Cape Bojador to seek license from Portugal, she insisted that the seas off that coast were free. Yet she also claimed a monopoly of her own, and collected fees, for fishing in those waters.[9]

The Canaries continued to offer a base to Africa and beyond, and gold to remain a magnet. With Gran Canaría under Castile's jurisdiction, on July 13, 1492 she and Fernando signed an agreement with Alonso Fernández de Lugo; he was to take La Palma and Tenerife for Castile, a conquest "to be gained at his own cost and expense." Lugo's expedition, underwritten by some Genoese and Florentines and by Medina Sidonia, sailed in 1493 with twelve hundred people and twenty thousand goats and sheep. The monarchs also garrisoned a small enclave on the Guinea coast itself, Torre de Santa Cruz de Mar Pequena (Mar Pequena was the name given the waters between Africa and the Canaries), which did a brisk business with Melilla, a Saharan gold terminal. And they profited from a royal monopoly on Canarian products, principally the dyestuff, *orchilla* (red and of mediocre quality), and cowrie shells, which sold well to the Portuguese since they were used as a medium of exchange on the Guinea coast.[10]

Although rulers of North Africa had proffered friendship, still there was good reason to be concerned about Granada's extensive coastline, so exposed to attacks from the opposite shore, especially those of Barbary pirates. For these and other reasons, Isabel made it her business to bring all major ports held by nobles under the crown. Through a combination of firmness, diplomacy, cash, and exchange she took over Cartagena from Juan Chacón, Gibraltar from Medina Sidonia, and, most important, Cádiz—ports viewed as crucial to defense, as naval bases, and as points of enforcing royal customs collection.

In August of 1492 that mainstay of the war, Rodrigo Ponce de León, died, not yet fifty but having achieved the victory and glory he sought. Isabel and Fernando put on mourning for him; they also extracted from his widow the port of Cádiz. Situated at the intersection of two trade routes—one from the Mediterranean to Flanders and England, the other from the Barbary coast to Atlantic Andalusia—Cádiz from then on superceded Puerto de Santa María as the royal port of entry for cargo from North Africa and the Atlantic. Thereafter, any merchant might go to Africa but had to stop at Cádiz on return and pay to the crown a fifth of the value of goods brought back. That merchandise was usually slaves and gold. The gold coming from Africa through Spain was estimated as worth over two hundred thousand *ducados* annually; it constituted the principal shipments of the metal received by Europe.[11]

By that year of 1492, the Portuguese Bartolemeu Dias had rounded Africa's Cape of Good Hope. But there remained other routes to Asia—through Africa, where Prester John was possibly to be contacted, or through the Mediterranean, then dominated by Muslims; and there was the scheme of the Genoese seaman, Columbus, to outflank both Portuguese and Muslims to reach Asia by sailing westward into the Atlantic. For Asia promised wealth, national enhancement, and, although roundabout, an approach to the Holy Land. Yet other plans were afoot. Isabel and Fernando then sent spies to North Africa, among them the future chronicler Lorenzo de Padilla, who explained that "as the souls of the King and Queen were great, not contenting themselves with having conquered Granada, they then planned to conquer Africa."[12] Münzer, visiting in 1494, noted the readying of ships, men, and provisions, that the king was to go with the armies, that no doubt Africa would soon belong to the crown of Castile, and that with Africa conquered, it would be easy for *los reyes* to reach and take Jerusalem.[13]

In 1492 an envoy was dispatched from court to Jerusalem, holiest of cities and often depicted on Christian maps as at the center of the world. Just as the analogy of "the destruction of Spain" in 711 at its conquest by Muslims to that of the Muslim conquest of Jerusalem was an old commonplace, so too was the pairing of the restoration of the two. In turn, to Spain's rulers and people Jerusalem was not simply a spiritual center but heaven's analogue and the ultimate goal of Christians, as it had been viewed by crusaders for centuries, and surely as not impossible to retake for monarchs—or their dynasty—who had seemingly reversed singlehandedly the Muslim onslaught on the West.

During the war, prophecies and popular *romances* had celebrated the royal desire to reconquer Granada, annihilate "the sect of Mahomet," and regain Christ's tomb. During a royal audience, Münzer ventured that "nothing remains to Your Majesties except to add to your victories the reconquest of the Holy Sepulcher of Jerusalem, this triumph is reserved for you, to crown your triumphs. . . . Now we see the saviors of all Spain."[14] His rhetoric, if overblown as customary in such circumstances, yet attested to a widening cognizance that Granada's conquest might be but a piece of a far grander design. What had heretofore served as a militating and legitimating mission statement for more limited objectives could become actual agenda. Even earlier, in verses directed to *la Reina Doña Isabel,* Pedro de Cartagena, a *contino* of the court who had died at Loja, had foreseen: "You will not be well content until the royal standard is raised in Jerusalem." The rulers of Aragón had long included Jerusalem among their titles, but now it was associated with Castile's queen as well. The I in Isabel, Cartagena told her, stood for *Imperio,* empire.[15] Talavera too had addressed Isabel as queen of Jerusalem. And, as we know, Isabel herself was of a literal cast of mind.

Certainly during the war years, a broadening, collectively Spanish sense of purpose had come to transcend the conquering of Granada. Early on, Diego de Valera had looked forward to ongoing Christian conquest, Spanish led; and by 1486 Cádiz assumed himself speaking for widespread sentiment in viewing ongoing military success as a sure sign of the advent of the warrior-emperor of the last days, the Lion King, who was to redeem Jerusalem. By 1492, that prophesied final world emperor had application to *los reyes* jointly. Pope Innocent VIII, in writing to Isabel in 1489, had spoken of the eleventh hour as near; in 1492 it seemed eminently possible that Isabel and Fernando together were inaugurating that eleventh hour, the approach of the Last Days, the time, as one old prophecy had it, of "the Age of Triumph, when peace and material goods would abound, Jew and infidel be converted, and Jerusalem would be glorified."[16] This was panegyric, but went beyond panegyric, for it was inspired much as was Isabel herself by the thrust of Spanish history as Spaniards understood it.

A treatise published in 1493, congratulating both monarchs for restoring lands lost for eight hundred years and retrieving infinite souls captured by the Moors, referred to another sign of the final times, triumph over evil, in stating to them that "Heaven must be praised for giving us monarchs who follow the heart of God" and who have done everything to the glory of Jesus Christ "and so against Satan, who in the form of a dragon and through snares had sown in your lands . . . *tanta zizania*," *zizania* meaning, roughly, confusion or chaos.[17] Victory over Granada unleashed expectation of Satan's imminent defeat, that necessary prelude to Christ's second coming and the final judgment. Now prophecy was widely spoken of as being fulfilled: as the Eagle having ascended and the Lion having roared forth to combat the Serpent. Granada's fall was interpreted as a major victory within the war against Antichrist, Muslims, and Jews, a war that Christendom seemed likely soon to win, led by a Spanish king. Hymns sung in Spanish churches after the conquest of Granada delved into Spanish history to speak of divine retribution and now not only as gained for the Spanish defeat by the Portuguese a century ago but for the Muslim conquest nearly a millennium ago! Where social harmony had been elicited in the 1470s by seeing civil war as foreign aggression, now it was again solicited in bundling the late victory as at once avenging attack from abroad, Muslim pretensions, and heresy in general.[18] Given Isabel's own propensity to value revenge, she surely did not take exception to this political theology.

Whatever the intensity of Isabel's own apocalyptic or millennial convictions, by all indications conquest of Granada confirmed to her the elect nature of the Spanish and their rulers, and the great responsibility she and they bore as Christendom's divinely designated champions. Throughout her reign, she amply evidenced that she believed herself directed by the Lord; assuredly the conquest of Granada had shown that she and Fernando were on the right course and must forge ahead, that their hearts were truly in the hand of the Lord. Moreover, they were both quite aware of the political value of saying so.

With 1492, in sum, among Spaniards the vision of Jerusalem as ultimate goal endowed recent victory with transcendental religious meaning; it gave impetus to ongoing militancy and enfolded all the various royal initiatives embarked upon shortly thereafter: expansion into Africa, the Atlantic, and the Mediterranean; the expulsion of the Spanish Jews, the sponsoring of Columbus, and even involvement in Italy and some further Portuguese marriages;

and it provided explanation for a Spanish alliance with Egypt (which, handily, Merlin was said to have prophesied was to precede the world's end).

For Spain's queen, such enterprises were to be the stuff of what would be the last decade of her life, integral parts of a grand, indeed grandiose, dynastic and imperial scheme to extend Spain into an overseas empire and to further hegemony over all Christendom. To Isabel, residing with Fernando in the Alhambra, that splendid symbol of the vanquished might of Muslim Iberia, it would not have seemed impossible that they, or at least their progeny, were to defeat Islam abroad and liberate Christendom's heart, Jerusalem.

That year of 1492, the humanist Elio Antonio de Nebrija recalled that, during a visit of the queen to Salamanca, he had told her of his plan to write a Castilian grammar, the first in any European vernacular. She had asked why so, and Hernando de Talavera had answered before Nebrija himself could "that after Your Highness subdues beneath your yoke many barbarous peoples and nations speaking foreign tongues, with defeat they will have to receive the laws conquerors give the conquered and, with them, our language." It was a sentiment that Nebrija himself, in dedicating to Isabel a Spanish grammar, expressed more succinctly as "language is the companion of empire."[19]

To Talavera and Nebrija, and to Isabel and many of her subjects in 1492, Christian conquest had become synonymous with lofty purpose and forging an empire beyond Iberia. They subscribed to a grand design that involved dominating and converting other peoples; an enterprise of national and religious expansion, its composite goals were the gaining of subjects and territories that would in turn yield material and spiritual profit, and glory.

The Fruits of War: Economy and Monarchy

War had undeniably proved a stimulus to implementing the royal program unveiled at Toledo in 1480. During it, the monarchs and great noble families had forged a more mutually satisfactory relationship. The nobility had gained wealth and aggregated titles. The monarchs had granted to the fifteen great lines a third of all royal *mercedes*. Those *grandes* had enjoyed an expansion of their holdings, and (from 1489) they had invested heavily in royal *juros*. At the same time, nobles by birth who held court posts had markedly declined, superceded by *letrado* administrators and men more recently ennobled by Isabel; preeminent among them were Chacón, Cárdenas, and Cabrera, all of whom were tremendously wealthy by the end of the war. Spain's aristocrats now bridged two worlds, those of medieval baronies and modern court. And if baronial autonomy and military function had diminished, older militant aspirations had not. Rather, reinforced by war and taken up by the new men, aristocratic chivalric values had altered but survived; they had become permeated with patriotic ideals in turn suffused with religion and had spread throughout society.

War too, had been kind to lesser nobles, the urban *caballeros*. They had gained power locally, on town councils, in *hermandades,* and were generally prospering within the growth attendant upon a wartime economy. Greater cooperation and more direct relations with the crown had brought them a good deal of independence from the high nobility and a greater preeminence over *el común,* the 80 per cent of the populace who alone paid taxes. And population had mounted. Initially wartime requirements had elicited a census, taken by Quintanilla in 1482, who came up with 1.8 million householders, translating into perhaps as much as 5 million people in Castilian lands (not counting Granada) and another million or so under Aragón. With more people than ever before, towns and surrounding rural areas grew, as did the domination by both towns and the nobility of hinterlands and their villagers. Still, these alterations occurred under the watchful eye of *corregidores,* who had become generally accepted in towns, fixtures, overseeing everything, symbols of the royal presence.[20]

The war had also furthered royal goals in some ways most likely not anticipated. During it, heightened demand and the use of money had expanded the production of goods and services, stimulated transportation and communication, and advanced the economic integration of Spain's regions. War had bolstered the navy and merchant shipping, the production of cotton and wool and the working of them into cloth, and the output of foodstuffs. The bulk of royal income had until 1480 derived from sales taxes (the *alcabala*) and customs duties (the *almojarifazgo*). But during the war revenue had vastly increased through some extraordinary imposts that the monarchs sought to retain thereafter. Prominent among them were the *cruzada,* church tithes, subsidies voted by ecclesiastical assemblies, and the levies on prelates, the *hermandad,* and municipalities, as well as solicited gifts and loans, and forced loans (some repaid, many others covered by *juros*). They also continued to count on the mortgaging of future income, and funds coming through the Inquisition. Isabel and Fernando, that is, succeeded in having exactions initially imposed as emergency measures continue to generate most royal income after the war; it was to double by the century's end. Along with greater and more direct control of society, war had brought Isabel and Fernando invaluable experience in financial management. Even so, royal expenses outran receipts, and after 1492 the crown continued to sell *juros* and mortgage future returns, amassing considerable public debt.

It was not yet the time of comprehensive economic programs; to the extent *los reyes* had an overall policy it has been termed empirical mercantilism. Many of their specific decrees, before and after 1492, had to do with economic matters and their diplomatic and political measures had large economic components; vying for African gold as metal, merchandise, and money remained a large factor in the rivalry with Portugal, and access to the port of Alexandria, a hub of trade with the East, persisted as a primary reason why good relations with Egypt's sultan were deemed vital.

Just what Isabel's economic interests and priorities were can only be pieced together. Overall, the economy was to benefit the royal treasury to the greatest extent possible. Seen as crucial to that end was effective collection of taxes; and taxes were in turn based upon duties and sales, preponderantly of raw materials, so that much depended upon a thriving commerce. Nor can the suspicion be dismissed that Isabel and Fernando knew that royal income was not necessarily contingent upon prohibiting bullion from leaving the country. Decrees against exporting gold were issued seemingly to discourage its export per se, but other reasons readily present themselves: to curb smuggling, to encourage payments abroad in products of the land, to have as much gold as possible go through royal mints, and to make money through sale of exemptions to that ruling. It was also most desirable that any gold and silver leaving Spain be in coins and yield royal customs returns and sales taxes, and that the exchange of gold and silver for one another profit the treasury. They attempted to make Castilian gold coinage uniform with Europe's best, promoted better flow of silver, and demanded sounder silver coinage. And while amassing bullion was a prime royal desiderata, the most advantageous way of procuring it had proved to be not necessarily the most direct.

The monarchs adopted some specific means to stimulate the economy as they understood that process. In 1491, among other steps toward more efficient customs collection, they had a list drawn of *almojarifazgo* charges. They also limited export of cereals, arms, and iron, thus keeping them more affordable internally and making a good business of selling royal licenses for their export. Isabel herself invested in ships dedicated to the Flanders trade; both king and queen sent olive oil there on their own accounts, and Fernando took a personal interest in large-scale trade in wheat. They licensed corsairs, and royal squadrons guarding Castilian shipping also dabbled in piracy; thus in 1484 royal ships seized two Venetian galleys off the Maghreb that were laden with gold. The Venetians were, after all, known to be in league with the Turks and suspected of supplying the Granadans; then too, the crown was to receive a royal fifth on confiscated cargos.[21]

Chiefly interested in profit from distribution of Spanish goods and only secondarily in their production, Isabel and Fernando protected their merchants abroad and foreign merchants in Spain, and they encouraged both sorts of traders and such production as was ultimately most lucrative to commerce and so to the royal treasury. Accordingly, they promoted manufacture of iron, so vital to war and so profitable an export. They encouraged shipbuilding, especially of the large vessels preferred for war. In Granada, they protected the silk industry and its much sought after, high quality satins, damascenes, and velvets. And while their ordinances outlined the economic functions of municipalities, they left agricultural production and localized distribution to the town councils and the nobles. They frowned on internal customs barriers, for such revenue redounded chiefly to localities or local lords. And, a spur to seeking royal control of the military orders—they took charge of Calatrava in 1487, Alcántara in 1494, and Santiago in 1499— were the great revenues of those august bodies, for all three owned huge flocks of sheep and together they dominated a tenth of Castile's land and its population.

Los reyes, bent on promoting those elements of the domestic economy that they perceived as advantageous to the royal treasury and integral to profitable foreign trade, assisted nobles involved in producing for, and distributing to, expanding overseas markets. And especially did the crown increasingly favor the owners of large flocks, who were generally the nobility and the military orders, and they smiled upon the distributers of wool as well. Thus in 1492 the monarchs confirmed the exclusive privileges of the Mesta, which had supplied funds to them during the war, and whose wool was a staple of trade with Flanders, Brittany, and England. Thereafter, the crown continued to collect revenues on the sale of Mesta wool and on the seasonal migrations of its vast flocks, which had doubled in numbers within the century, to somewhere close to three million sheep. By 1492, moeover, great nobles were consolidating control within the Mesta and owners of smaller flocks dwindling.

In 1494, Isabel licensed an exclusive *consulado* or guild for Burgos merchants, who sent wool to England and the continent in Basque ships and had their own enclaves in key ports abroad. During her reign wool became *the* export of Castile; at length, its production was to prove disastrously inhibiting to both agriculture and industry.[22] So those satirical wartime verses accusing her of extracting *tanta lana,* so much wool that a mantle made from it could cover the country, indicated that "wool" was thought of as synonymous with wealth, yet may well have also alluded to her favoring of wool interests in making the poet's point—that she was squeezing her subjects unmercifully.

During the war, the use of currency had surged, while the vast wartime operations and their funding had brought experience in the uses of credit. Royal ordinances had accordingly made credit easier and, in doing so, stimulated the economy. By 1492 a complex monetary and banking system was evolving, with sophisticated mechanisms, including various sorts of bonds, to get around canonical condemnation of usury. Barcelona, once a center of banking and commerce, was recovering. Valencia was at its height and prospering from relations with thriving Castile. Within Castile, greater economic integration among its diverse regions paralleled the expansion of exterior trade. More merchants than ever before and greater numbers of ox carts and mule trains plied an expanding network of roads. Isabel and Fernando personally kept an eye on the royal fairs of Medina del Campo, among Europe's largest, which they continued to enjoy attending, and which, despite devastating fires in 1491 and 1492, were more popular than ever as centers for internal exchange and long-distance trade and banking; the monarchs had made certain that all nobles who held competing fairs had ceased doing so. From 1492 until Isabel's death in 1504, although with fluctuations, Castile flourished. That was particularly true of the south. Seville was Spain's leading commercial and banking center and Castilians increasingly profited from Granada's wealth and commerce.[23] In the euphoria of 1492, it was simply assumed at court that all subjects must in some way or other benefit from the realm's prosperity.

The monarchs relied in economic and financial matters on Quintanilla and Cárdenas, and ultimately on Talavera (until 1492) and Mendoza, who in turn made use of Genoese, Florentine, and Venetian merchants and bankers. Venice had been a traditional ally of Aragón, but the Genoese were increasingly favored by both Isabel and Fernando as merchants and bankers, as they were by the pope. At the end of Isabel's reign there would be three hundred Genoese merchant companies in Spain. Where formerly the court had relied strongly on Jewish and *converso* funding and services, it was more frequently the Genoese, among whom there were also *conversos,* who provided them. Although Spanish *conversos* and other Spaniards continued to engage in commerce and finance, the Italians especially enjoyed the advantage of established international networks on which depended large transactions and long-distance trade.[24]

In accord with her devotion to order, Isabel's economic instinct was toward thrifty and efficient management of resources; and thus the remark attributed to her, that anyone wanting to put a fence around Castile should hand it over to the Hieronymite friars, whom she knew at firsthand to be hard-working, productive, and skilled in administration.[25] In 1492, it was to her a moral imperative that all her subjects should become more industrious, and more devout as well.

Cleansing the Realm

With peace at hand, Isabel shifted some wartime (and warlike) energies to eradicating "corruption" throughout society, beginning by endeavoring to reform the institution responsible for propagating, upholding, and policing morality, the Spanish church. Such reform she thought her duty and she expected would improve the learning and morals of the clergy, filter outward to most Castilians, and strengthen respect for royal authority. Thus, as Granada capitulated, royal decrees signaled an escalating severity toward erring priests and friars, whose prevalence was soon to be commented upon in a "tragi-comedy," *La Celestina,* wherein the procuress, Celestina, remarks: "The clergy were so numerous that there were some of all kinds: some very chaste, and others whose duty it was to support me in my profession. There are still some of these, I think."[26] Indeed, *La Celestina* depicts the postwar society Isabel sought to reform. Royal orders went out that concubines of clergy, until then commonly accepted as a fact of life, were to be publicly scourged, and heavy penalties to be levied as well upon laymen who kept concubines.[27]

Other sorts of behavior deemed highly immoral were punished brutally. Münzer wrote of seeing, on leaving Almería in 1494, the bodies of six men dangling from a tall post. He learned that they were Italians who had been convicted of sodomy—that is, homosexuality; the men had been hung first by their necks, then by their feet, but only after "their genitals had been cut off and hung around their necks, because in Spain they hate this sin greatly."[28] Three years later, Fernando and Isabel, concluding the existing penalties were "insufficient to eradicate such an abominable crime," decreed conviction for sodomy carried with it guilt of heresy and high treason. They did not explain the connection. In Isabel's final decade, royal authority reached ever more persistently into private life to impose an orthodox morality. Interestingly, some offenses punished severely were ones at one time or another linked to royal behavior, to Fernando's often commented upon fondness for gambling, and to Enrique IV's purported homosexuality. That homosexuality was associated with Antichrist was not lost on Enrique's opponents or on publicists who in the 1490s bundled orthodoxy with prophecy, royal mission, and the imminence of the Last Days.

Nor was the papacy exempt from Isabel's penchant for propriety. Her opinion of the new pope, Alexander VI, who succeeded Innocent VIII in July of 1492, had never been high. Even though as a Valencian he might favor Spain, to her he remained Rodrigo Borja and she did not think much of him. The doctrine of papal infallibility lay in the future. She confided to the papal nuncio that should His Beatitude hear of her censuring him he should know she did so not through animosity but through love. Then she dropped the other shoe: it distressed her to hear it said that the wedding festivities of his daughter Lucrecia were scandalous, and she wished he would show less heat in the affairs of his son the duke Caesare and his brothers.[29] A chronicler, the newcomer Alonso de Santa Cruz, echoed her sentiments in summing up Borja's reputation: the pope was ambitious and greedy and his sons were thought not very good Christians.[30] Santa Cruz's inference was that his monarchs were much better ones. They thought so too.

The Spanish Inquisition affirmed the royal championing of orthodoxy, the ongoing power struggle with the papacy, and the constant need to do battle against Satan. That tribunal, spoken of ever more respectfully and attracting crowds to its public events, ensured perpetuation of a sense of national unity

born of wartime commitment and that such social cohesion rested on an apocalyptic faith. In 1491 the monarchs confirmed the ascending power of the Holy
Office in sanctioning an accusation of heresy made against the powerful and
esteemed bishops of Segovia and Calahorra, their parents and relatives, and
against other ecclesiastics as well. And since trials of bishops were reserved to
the papacy, another contest with Rome ensued, which the monarchs would
win, to emerge as the most assiduous of Christians.

Patently, in the cleansing and consolidating of the body politic and the
campaign for moral regeneration there was no room for cultural or religious
plurality. The Inquisition both continued to impress that point and to inten-
sify belief in its validity, in the process making appear ever more anomalous
Spain's housing of diverse faiths and peoples. The Muslims were seen as a
problem on its way to eventual solution through baptism or emigration. As
for the Jews, their value to the crown had diminished as had their numbers
and wealth and, ever more unpopular, they were viewed as a threat to the
orthodoxy of New Christians and to the internal peace of the realm. To Isabel
by 1492, Spain's Jews were a stubborn remnant of a people whose time had
come and gone. Her decision to expel them that year (of which more pres-
ently) attested to the continuation of a war-reinforced crusading spirit and to
a recognition that the presence of Jews made Spain look old-fashioned and
heterodox internationally, and so was a hindrance to its assuming what had
clearly become important to her, a rightful position of primacy in Europe and
all Christendom.

Primacy in Europe appeared very possible in 1492. Her son Juan would
inherit a united and expanded Spain, indeed an empire. The marriages
arranged for her children were expected to cement alliances with Atlantic
Europe, but they also looked beyond immediate European concerns. She had
had the *infanta* Isabel marry in Portugal not only because of a shared border
and lineage and for strategic and economic reasons, but also to merge dynasties, so that one day a grandchild of hers would come to the other Iberian
throne. Equally, the marriages planned with England and the Habsburgs confirmed, and might well augment, dynastic power and stature. Those marriage
alliances were also expected to hem in France, Spain's chief competitor in
Europe. The ambitions of the new young French king, Charles VIII, in Italy
were of particular concern in 1492; they would soon derail Spanish plans to
move into Africa.

By 1492, Isabel herself had achieved a standing unheard of for a monarch
who was female, one no other European queen had as yet attained. She had
made her mark in foreign courts and with the papacy as well. The war had
proved to be one of those situations of crisis, change, and innovation in which
the impact of individuals is greatest, and none had been greater than that of
the Spanish queen, Isabel.

The Queen at Forty

In 1492 Isabel was forty, and at a height of power and prestige. Pedro Mártir was not alone in thinking that she surpassed all women and all of the ancients in rectitude, constancy, and "the valor to undertake great enterprises," nor in acknowledging that she was dowered with many more and more powerful kingdoms than possessed by the king, nor that "in everything, whatever she orders is done." As he confided to an Italian friend," she commands in such a way that she always appears to do it in accord with her husband, so that edicts and other documents are published with the signature of both. . . . These virtues, unheard of in a woman, together with the magnanimity of her strong heart, have won her merited fame." As for Fernando, Mártir observed, "The King does not disagree with this [verdict], for with her counsel she alleviates for him many preoccupations and cares."[31] Lucio Marineo Sículo, like Mártir an Italian humanist, and at court in 1497 on Isabel's invitation and soon to be Fernando's secretary, would concur, in stating that although both rulers showed a true majesty, "in the judgment of many, the Queen was of greater beauty, more lively intelligence, a heart more grand, and greater gravity."[32]

Isabel was not small, by forty she was not slim, and she was reckoned a force. Münzer in 1494 thought her most imposing, and remarked that she looked no more than thirty-six. With Fernando, Isabel had established a highly effective modus vivendi, sharing a history, indeed a universe, as well as a highly developed mutual understanding and appreciation, a working partnership in the exercise of authority, and a mutual love and reliance, each fully confident of their conjoined power, of together personifying sovereignty and dynasty. At bottom, as Pulgar had seen, love held their wills joined. Their closeness and trust, there from the beginning, had since become widely recognized and admired, indeed was being written of as a marvel of the world. Even so, Isabel was jealous. She loved the king her husband so much, says Marineo Sículo, that she continually watched for signs he might love another. And if she felt he was looking at some woman of the court with any sign of love, she prudently found a way to remove that lady. She had cause, in that Fernando had had children by other women.[33] Loving him intensely, respecting him greatly, she was at once a jealous wife and a queen regnant, and in both roles she always stood her ground tenaciously. Her husband and her faith were for her monopolies, to be preserved from poachers.

Her will, always strong, iron, forged by inculcated moral principles and religious beliefs, had been converted into steel in the crucible of war; now well tempered, it even proved slightly flexible when necessary. She was not known to smile readily. Reserved, she nonetheless showed a maternal warmth transformable as the occasion might demand into a matriarchal concern, and she demonstrated a compassion for individual suffering, although it was allayable in the aggregate, or in consideration of ends she viewed as highly principled and desirable, or if the individuals in question were not Christians.

And to Isabel, vengeance remained a fact of life, although after 1492 she appears to have lost some of her former enthusiasm for exacting it. Yet she remained a stickler for retributive rather than exemplary justice, as well as for being loved and feared, fashioning herself a stern judge in the manner she most admired, that of Old Testament and old Spanish kings. She thought of herself as highly reasonable; she delighted in being proven right and, as Pulgar admitted, although she listened to advice, she altered her opinion only with great difficulty. There is the story that when Fernando wanted to dispatch a certain knight on important business, although she suggested the man not be sent because he had poor judgment, Fernando sent him, and he did well. But it was only when the same man went on another royal errand and botched it that she had her secretary award him a *juro* of thirty thousand *maravedis*. The mystified secretary asked why she gave that fellow *mercedes* now, when she had not done so when he had acquitted himself well. Isabel replied: Because now he had done what was reasonable to expect of him in going wrong, as he had not before in getting it right.[34] Isabel displayed a tendency to equate what she expected with what was reasonable, but she also demonstrated a gift for surrounding herself with very loyal and very capable people; and repeatedly she revealed a great propensity for irony.

Münzer spoke of her as extremely devout, pious, and sweet, qualities he obviously admired highly in women; and Marineo Sículo, himself a court chaplain, noted that she had many chaplains and collected about her the wisest priests.[35] He did not say that they were the most observant or the holiest. He also recalled that from his arrival in the later 1490s every Thursday of Holy Week both monarchs imitated the apostles: they had twelve paupers brought in and they washed their feet, fed them and served them at table, and gave them new clothes and a gold ducat apiece. Yet it was Fernando whom Marineo singled out as punctilious in personal devotions. As to Isabel, she "was desirous of great praise and illustrious reputation." She had always desired them; and within the tenets of the Christian humanism recently introduced at court, she could in good conscience view those pursuits as eminently virtuous. And certainly she had, as she would acknowledge to Talavera in 1493, achieved greatness and prosperity.

Pulgar had earlier admitted that, although she was naturally inclined to be truthful, "wars and changes" made Isabel sometimes deviate, and he confirmed her reliance on inspiring a combination of love and fear in stating that, while she made many bountiful grants, she said that queens should conserve lands, because in alienating them they lose the rents with which to make *mercedes* in order to be loved, and so diminish their power to be feared. She also valued ceremony and wished to be served by the highest of nobles, with great reverence and great show of humility. Pulgar made excuses: it was said to be a vice that she displayed so much pomp, but *el rey* is superior and ought to shine above all the estates, for he has divine authority in the land.[36] *El rey* was she, a woman of great heart.

She possessed remarkable stamina and a strong constitution and had suffered but few illnesses. Yet sometime in 1491 she had written to Torquemada saying that she had not responded to his letters, hoping each day to write by hand, for she had been indisposed with eye trouble and tertiary fevers and was unable to write, but that "now, thank God, I am better."[37] While encamped at Santa Fe, she had also suffered with swollen legs, then attributed to too much riding. Eye trouble, fevers, and swelling would all recur.

While there is a story that she took an oath not to bathe until Granada fell, and another that she did not bathe at all, it would be very odd behavior in someone so fastidious in all else, who so intensely associated some other sorts of cleanliness with holiness. Yet bathing was linked to Muslim and Jewish rites and customs, and the Inquisition, having made burning religious issues of cultural habits, considered frequent washing of the body among the most blatant indications of heretical behavior. Too, from the twelfth century on the church had held that bathing aroused erotic notions. Years earlier, when Sánchez de Arévalo had praised Enrique IV in saying he bathed little, it was understood not as a compliment to his orthodoxy but as refuting charges of his "Roman effeminism." In 1492 Isabel did restore the Alhambra's baths but, with public baths in full disrepute and anything resembling ritual bathing a matter for the Inquisition, whatever the queen did privately, she did not publicly indicate she often bathed.[38]

Isabel, as she so often demonstrated, loved music and valued it tremendously in devotions, public display, war, and court life. Musicians had always accompanied her processions and her armies. A chapel traveled everywhere with her, composed of twenty singers, two organists, and a choir of fifteen to twenty-five boys; it was among the best in European courts, as were her composers and musicians. Notable still are Juan de Anchieta, who among other pieces composed a mass for the queen on the surrender of Granada, and Juan del Encina, who not only wrote music but collected in his *Cancionero del Palacio* of 1496 more than three hundred songs of the court, among them many ballads sung to lute and viol.[39] And Isabel enjoyed theater, as was observable from the time she commissioned and played in Gómez Manrique's *momo* and, ever after, in her calculated, sustained, superb performance as queen of Castile.

Dynasty

In everything she did there was a sense of dynasty. When visiting her mother in Arévalo she waited on her personally and thought it instructive to her children to see her do so.[40] To them she showed strong maternal love and in them she found a promise of continuity. She centered much affection and her dynastic hopes on her son and heir, Juan. She paid great attention to his education and did not stint on his court, his activities, his clothing, and his retinues, nor on his participation in court pageantry and festivities. He was given his own household and there waited upon as befitted a great prince, with exact protocol maintained from rising to retiring. A hierarchy of servants made a ritual of dressing and undressing him; *grandes* attended him. She attached to his household her own mentors: Gonzalo Chácon, now known as *el viejo*—the old one—and whose grandson of the same name was one of Juan's companions, and Gutierre de Cárdenas as Juan's *mayordomo mayor* and *contador.* Juan's tutor, Diego de Deza, who had taught theology at Salamanca, was a nephew of yet another of her longtime comptrollers, Rodrigo de Ulloa. She arranged her son's daily routine. Each morning there were prayers with Deza, then mass, then lessons. Since Juan particularly enjoyed music, she would often send to him during his daily two-hour rest period her music master and four or five choirboys, and he would sing with them, tenor. He was given his own musicians as well and he owned and played a number of instruments, among them the first Spanish *claviorgano,* a combination of organ and plucked string instrument, made by one Mofévrez, a Muslim grandmaster from Zaragoza; it was a present from his half-brother, young Alfonso de Aragón, archbishop of Zaragoza, Fernando's son.[41]

Yet Juan's health was always delicate. Isabel had his diet and regimen carefully monitored. Each morning doctors visited and he reported to them on how he had slept, and on his digestion and bodily functions. Münzer, indicating physical disability, wrote of having saluted the prince in Latin and of Juan's understanding it but ordering Deza to reply for him since, said Münzer, he suffered from a weakness of the lower lip and tongue that impeded his answering plainly. Isabel spoke of her son as "my angel," and had him sent treats considered good for digestion: strawberry conserves, lemon blossom candies, other sugared sweets, and jars of quincemeat from what she referred to as "Valencia del Cid."[42]

Juan's upbringing tells a good deal about Isabel. One of his pages later recalled that in his education the queen had cared as much for letters as for other abilities and, above all, for virtue.[43] Manly virtue included proficiency in arms. Juan was given a master of arms, and the prince slept with a sword at the head of his bed and was instructed in its use. His father had knighted him before Granada. His mother had even earlier provided as companions for him ten knights, five mature, five young, "a species of *colegio.*" One, who had fought at Granada, dedicated to the boy a translation into Castilian of Caesar's commentaries, avowedly to convey that arms would not benefit him without good counsel.[44] Juan corresponded with the humanist Marineo Sículo and with the poet Juan del Encina, who adjudged him as learned in *sciencia* as in empire. Juan was, that is, raised in the atmosphere then permeating the royal court and compounded of a fervent and militant piety, a resurgent chivalry, and a rising vogue for humanistic classicism.

Isabel gave much thought to Juan's education, designing what she conceived to be the ideal upbringing for a Christian prince. She followed principles akin to those of the *Siete Partidas* and the mirrors of princes as though glossed by current usages and humanist studies, but their essential base and hers was orthodox religion. That unusual attention to his education and her ideas about what constituted it were reflected in a treatise written by a courtier close to her, Alonso Ortiz. Ortiz composed the work as a dialogue between the queen and Cardinal Mendoza. Surely echoing her own concerns, the principal question the treatise raised was how to achieve the spiritual health of the prince; the answer it gave was through learning good habits in childhood. In that treatise, Mendoza presents a highly traditional Christian rationale with some humanistic overlay. Thus he cites a Christian Platonist and somewhat Pythagorean understanding of purification in stating that the stars incline us and the wiles of the demons push us toward vices, that original sin infected everyone, corrupting the flesh and weighing on the soul; that the flesh submitted to the influence of the stars but the will remained free, subject only to God, yet needed instruction in order to gain wisdom. Training in will power, he explained, would develop natural abilities and correct bad inclinations; it could purify. Accordingly, he advised an education consonant with the stages advocated by Plato and Aristotle, an education leading to virtue, both moral and intellectual, and so to the happy mean. Virtue and vice he declared within human power, life a pilgrimage toward blessedness and bliss, toward the eternal life of which Saint John speaks. That dialogue was itself a guide for a prince's education, as it simply assumed much of what such guides had heretofore customarily stated, that the monarch's spiritual health was the same as the common good. Taking for granted the importance of the prince, it concentrated on this specific prince's personal development in wisdom, justice, moral qualities, and high character. In passing it revealed a good deal about humanistic education as understood at the Spanish court in the 1490s.

That treatise states that fables have the purpose of teaching children good customs easily and pleasurably. Although by all indications mirroring Isabel's outlook, the examples given seem not to have much to do with good customs as now understood. Rather, they have to do with the behavior of Hercules and the pagan gods and they stem from "all the theology of the ancients [that] brings with it the lightning, the shield, the trident, the battle-axe, the dragon, and the staff of Thyrsus [carried by Dionysius and his attendants]—all the arms of the gods."[45] There is good indication that Isabel subscribed to such views and found in them a rationale for her own enjoyment in reading fables, fabulous history, and chivalric tales. Yet she also increasingly recognized the value of the new humanistic studies and established a school at court for the sons of nobles. She wanted them educated as loyal future leaders and suitable companions for the prince, and she appointed a humanist, Pedro Mártir, as their schoolmaster. For as Ortiz indicates and Isabel and Mártir well understood, religion and learning could reinforce one another; Christianity and humanistic studies were at the time not mutually exclusive. And in late fifteenth-century Spain, where the queen took so lively an interest, they came together in ways amenable to royal interests.

Isabel approved of her son being instructed in a very Christian humanism, in a combination of Greek and Latin classics and Christian philosophy. She also placed closest to him as his tutor Deza, the Dominican theologian whom she would later appoint inquisitor general. It was said that Deza "neither in words nor deeds ever indicated he knew nor even suspected anything lewd or indecent," and that unlike most of his peers, he was a virgin.[46] Her choice of Deza promised an education firmly grounded in both a severe Christian morality and the scholastic method of Thomas Aquinas. Monies went out for Aquinas's *Summa Theologica* and for a book by St. Bonaventure, a breviary, a Bible, "and a book on ethics." And in 1493 Isabel commissioned the bishop of Coria to write a manual of Christian edification for the young nobles at court. In Isabel's world, where the ruler was held to personify the realm, and religion and politics intertwined, every bit of this education constituted training in statecraft. Nor was experience in governing forgotten: designedly "in order to learn to dispense justice," at eighteen Juan received his own court and council, and, from the age of ten on, his parents had him sit with them from time to time in deliberation on affairs of the realm. Mártir in praising Juan effusively relayed his mother's hopes for him: "for us you are a *vice-dios* on earth."[47] Isabel also carefully saved some of her son's Latin copybooks. Nor did she, mindful of her own inadequate preparation, neglect readying her daughters to become queens, if in their cases most likely queens consort, although she was well aware that Juan's health was delicate. When later the humanist Luis Vives, in counseling that young women be educated in spinning and handwork and in letters as well, observed that "they are honest exercises that remain to us from that golden century of our predecessors," he was referring to the upbringing Isabel had given her four daughters.[48] All of them had letters, that is, Latin, instructed by friar-tutors and from 1493 also by the humanist Alejandro Geraldini, who had been invited to court by the queen.[49]

All were accomplished. The *infanta* Isabel was in 1492 a widow devoting herself to good works, but she was also welcomed to participate in her parents' discussions of state matters. The *infanta* Juana, according to Münzer, recited and composed verses and was highly learned "for her age and sex." Later, in Flanders, she would speak fluently the French of her new court as well as some

Latin. Juana enjoyed dancing and her passion was music; she played several instruments, among them the clavichord. Catalina was proficient on clavichord and harp; moreover, she was learned in philosophy, literature, and religion, and had Latin, Castilian, French, English, and German. During her years as England's queen, between 1509 and 1527, Catherine of Aragón attracted to court the learned and the wise, among them Luis Vives and Erasmus, scholars who praised her piety and erudition. María, who would become queen of Portugal, if apparently the least gifted of Isabel's offspring, would be known for providing her seven children with an excellent education, so like her own.[50]

The Queen Studies, the Queen Prays

In the 1480s, Isabel herself began studying Latin. Within a year she thought that she understood enough to take note should any preacher or choirboy err in pronunciation and afterward she would correct him. It had bothered her that she had not the learning prescribed in mirrors for princes and possessed by her closest advisors, the letters thought to complete an aristocratic education and burnish a royal image, the Latin necessary to read what were considered the best and most useful writings on law and government and war, the Latin her father had. Nebrija had not as yet ventured that Castilian Spanish was highly estimable. And here as in much else she was determined to set an example, and so she did. Asked the humanist Juan de Lucena, rhetorically, "Do you not see how many have begun to learn, admiring your highness? What kings do, good or bad, we all try to do. . . . When the king gambles, we are all gamblers. When the queen studies, we become students."[51]

That penchant of hers for study went beyond Latin. Isabel was an avid reader by all accounts and she encouraged the new art of printing; Valera, in praising to her a German who with several of his compatriots had introduced printing into Spain in 1472, referred to him as "a familiar of Your Highness."[52] The printing press arrived in 1478 in Seville, the same year as the Inquisition and, like it, proved a boon to the royal reach. In the early 1480s Talavera had presses set up to print bulls of crusade; and printing ensured that the royal laws Montalvo compiled were, as ordered in 1480, available to every town and city; the press also enabled wide dissemination of his edition of the *Siete Partidas*, printed in 1491. And, much as Isabel set the tone for study, it is obvious that even where she did not commission a book herself, her policies and her taste in reading influenced what was printed.

Isabel owned, in manuscript and in print, in Castilian and in Latin, nearly four hundred volumes; many of them were additions made during her reign to the royal library she had first encountered in Segovia. As she knew from its various guides for princes, and as Talavera had reminded her, good rulers should love reading and books. Most of the royal library was as expected. There were the traditional treatises on the education of the prince, some in manuscript possibly inherited, others recently printed. There were also numerous religious works, including Bibles, books of hours, psalters, commentaries, and the philosophy adjudged Christian of Aristotle, Seneca, and Boethius.[53] Even so, the books she reportedly most enjoyed were chivalric *romances*. Those she owned were among the earliest of published works and included *The Prison of Love*, a courtly *romance* appearing in 1492 (and quickly going through twenty Spanish editions) and *Tirant lo Blanc* (1490), the adventures in Africa and Asia Minor of a knight steeped in fortitude and the sexual forbearance of courtly love. Isabel possessed as well several compilations of the prophecies of Merlin. Her serious opinion may have coincided with the informed one of the day, that "it is said the Devil was Merlin's father and I would not advise anyone to waste time in such reading."[54] Still, by classifying his prophecies as fables, she could read collections like the *Baladro de Merlín* with clear conscience; and certainly she did not dismiss one prophecy found there, that of a lion-like ruler who would be a Christian champion. Far places and distant times interested her; she owned Sir John Mandeville's book of his travels, generally recognized as mixing fact and fable. Her library reflects something else. Isabel, if determinedly decorous, was earthy, not of delicate sensibility. Two of her favored courtiers, both priests, Alonso de Burgos and Iñigo de Mendoza, were renowned for being ribald. And some of her books were erotic and reflected the late medieval delight in playful obscenity; such were Boccaccio's *Decameron*, the tales of the archpriest of Hita, and a purported biography of Aesop illustrated with "scabrous engravings."[55]

* * *

That Isabel found the past highly instructive, as well evidenced in her self-representation and commissioning of chronicles, is corroborated in her large and wide-ranging collection of histories. She owned Livy's *Decades*—morally reinforcing and instructive in military strategy and in acquiring an empire. She owned chronicles supposedly of Troy, which was considered from Isidore of Seville on as cradle of Spain's own classical antiquity. She had as well several copies of works on Alexander the Great and Hercules, figures believed historically linked to Spain's glory and its rulers. Among her three hundred-odd tapestries as well, there were five bed-hangings depicting the conquests of Alexander, and six wall hangings of the Labors of Hercules; some teemed with knights and ladies and all made visual chivalric ideals. In much the same vein, she had three tapestries illustrating Arthurian legends and others taken from chivalric romances.

Isabel also possessed many Spanish histories, the old royal chronicles blending the mythical and the factual, seeing Spain as a nation bringing together and culminating all previous history, and certifying to its queen's august genealogy. It was said she particularly enjoyed the chronicles of her father's reign; certainly she saw herself as fulfilling the program of reconquest and moral regeneration they told of having been urged upon him. And there were of course the chronicles of her own reign. How they differed from earlier histories and how they themselves varied over time provides insight both into her own views concerning her royal calling and her changing vision and representation of the significance of her reign.

Her initial chroniclers, notably Pulgar, Palencia, and Valera, concentrating on Castile's queen, king, and nobles, and on the character, personality, and morality of such notables, chiefly wrote of current events, if within an implicit framework of universal providentialist history. Bernáldez then brought a righteous post-Inquisition spirit to his account, more sharply explicating the present reign as the working out of providential design. Yet Isabel herself, early in her reign, had Valera write a history of Spain set centrally within universal context; and after the conquest of Granada, the scope of Spanish chronicles was again that of medieval universal histories, notably those written in Spain from the reign of Fernando III.

Again like those chronicles, accounts written in the 1490s tended to integrate Christian and classical backgrounds. But there was a significant difference. Now written by humanists, they did so within an altered mindcast, diverging even from the outlook of Isabel's earlier years. That shift becomes very apparent, as Robert Brian Tate has shown, in comparing Pulgar's chronicle with Nebrija's *Decades* of 1495, dedicated to Isabel. Regarding speeches, Tate observes, "Pulgar argues either from Biblical example or immediate political exigencies whereas Nebrija debates against a background of ethical humanism. . . . Where [in Pulgar the duke of Medina Sidonia] calms a quarrel over the distribution of booty by warning his men against the power of the devil, Nebrija puts in the Duke's mouth a Ciceronian proverb and a condemnation of '*auri sacra fames.*'"[56] What had changed was that classical allusions and values had come to substitute for religious dictum, but far from completely. Yet one aspect remained constant; whether the rhetoric was biblical or classical, the histories written in Isabel's reign continued to stress the divinely assigned, even messianic, role in human history of Spain and its rulers. Moreover, their writers, steeped in both biblical and classical learning, drew from both sources in focusing more intensely on the universal historical significance of those rulers. So in the prologue to his *Decades*, Nebrija stated that just as movement of the heavens and stars is from east to west, the monarchy of world had migrated westward, from the Assyrians, through the Medes, Persians, and Macedonians, to the Romans, Germans, and Gauls, and that "now, who cannot see that, although the title of Empire is in Germany, its reality lies in the power of the Spanish monarchs who, masters of a large part of Italy and the isles of the Mediterranean Sea, carry the war to Africa and send out their fleet, following the course of the stars, to the isles of the Indies and the New World." This is to allude both to Danielic prophecy and classical imperial rhetoric in stating that Spain is, as destined, the last, the greatest, and a messianic empire. Elsewhere, Tate mentions that Nebrija's history celebrated the triumph over the Muslims—Spain's recovery of itself, purified of external, alien presence.[57]

Isabel the young queen and her aspirations can be found in Pulgar; yet by 1492 she had come to envision a Spain set within a much larger, imperial, context coated with the enhancing veneer of classical humanism. Paralleling the evolution of the chronicles she commissioned, and in all the histories undertaken from 1492 in Castile, she and Fernando were portrayed as promising to return Spain to the more virtuous time of the Visigoths but also as restoring and extending what was now termed an empire in the combined Danielic and Roman sense. In the 1490s, both Juan de Lucena and Pedro Mártir wrote of Spain as having entered a golden age. When, similarly, Juan del Encina proclaimed to *los reyes* that "with you begin the golden centuries,"[58] it was well understood that he alluded to the future as foreseen both by biblical prophets and Virgil, as a worldwide empire brought about by an elect people slated for greatness under a divinely designated ruler.

Mártir and Marineo Sículo and Geraldini brought a new wave of Renaissance humanism to Castile—Renaissance but far from secular. Those Italians were priests and devout, although Mártir admitted to becoming a priest in Spain because it was the only way for a man of letters to gain respect. As similar people in other European courts were then doing, they put their learning to reinforcing the ruler they served through a combining of national history, chivalric and humanistic ideals, Christian piety, patriotic rhetoric, and messianic monarchy;[59] and they were also mindful of the particularly strong religious thrust of Spain's rulers. Marineo Sículo attested to that blend in speaking of "our Christian sovereigns, who in the beauty of their lives and the glory of their deeds surpass ancient and modern alike."[60] Those émigré Italians, stung by the consensus in Italy that Spain was uncivilized, came to the conclusion that there was something corrupt about Italy and its Romans, and that their adopted country was purer, *más limpia*. Theirs was a political theology welcomed as royal ideology. As medieval gave way to early modern times, that age of gold they saw dawning was one both classical and having much in common with what Talavera had spoken of as the final age of justice predicted by Saint John.

Isabel was given prominent place in that glorious dawn. She was now hailed as another Minerva or "the very resplendent Diana." The classical goddesses of wisdom, the hunt, and the moon supplanted earlier biblical paragons in eulogizing her. And now the queen was in one instance addressed as "*Diana, primera leona.*"[61] That allusion not only breached old categories of gender, but rolled into one classical deities and Christian prophecy, that of the Lion King and the primordial earth goddess of folklore who had become associated with Diana. Isabel was also compared, not unfavorably, to the queen of the Amazons, as well as to Astraea, come down from the sky—the virgin Astraea, standing for justice, and whose descent Virgil, Ovid, and Dante saw as heralding the return of the golden age, and the beginning of an imperial era.[62]

Praise for the queen, however, also took a more complex cast. While Talavera later affirmed that the restoration of Granada to Spain was to a great extent "the work of the counsel, strength, and labor of the Queen,"[63] at the fall of Ronda Valera had introduced another note in writing to Fernando that Isabel "fought no less with her many alms and prayers and by giving order to the things of war than you, My Lord, with your lance in your hand." But the efficacy of Isabel's piety alone was echoed in Juan del Encina's *romance* on Granada's surrender. Encina stated that the Visigoth king Rodrigo had lost the city and don Fernando and "*la reyna doña Isabel,* the most feared and loved, had regained it: she with her prayers, and he with many armed men." Yet he did indicate those prayers were not ordinary in exclaiming "*Viva* the very grand lioness! High Queen prospering!"[64] "High Queen" was usually an epithet reserved to Holy Mary.

Still, from 1492 Isabel became celebrated for her piety more frequently. She also took on the role of civic patroness in the tradition of pagan goddesses, the figure of Roma, and Holy Mary. After 1492 her image, the very concept of queenship, underwent alteration. Talavera's soaring eagle and Gómez Manrique's injunction to leave off prayer and rule was giving way to a more quiescent concept of piety. Isabel's image was being reshaped to conform to more modern, peaceful times, and to strengthen the bonds between religion and peacetime patriotism. Isabel, triumphal panegyrics aside, tended henceforth to exemplify the repository of the gentler virtues responsible for the humane, cultured, and civilized ordering of society. So Marineo Sículo, in a royally commissioned work, newly emphasized the queen's piety in order to see in it a source of Spain's civility and ongoing strength: because of her prayers, merits, and holy works, he observed, God looked benignly on her people and kingdom and aggrandized, defended, and exalted Spain.[65]

With peace, it was not thought civilized for the queen to be hailed as dunning towns for funds and soldiers or riding off to war. She should, rather, be an exemplar of civic virtue and the power of turning to prayer, and so she soon was. In the chapel of San Juan in Granada, in the *Pieta* that portrays Isabel directly below John the Evangelist, the tablet she holds reads, "Make me passionately virtuous in your image and zealous for the faith." And that image of Isabel on her knees, hands steepled in prayer, endured. It does not reflect the piety of the good monarch obligated to be energetic, moral, and devout as conveyed in the old histories, the mirrors for princes, the *Partidas,* and by Talavera, the monarch she had striven to be. Rather, it relays a more spiritual, more humble sort of supplication bringing to mind the piety idealized in female saints. It is closer to the piety advised to a princess long ago in the *Garden of Noble Maidens*; and indeed that treatise was published in 1500. In time that interpretation of the nature of her religiosity would take over almost completely; she would be buried beneath it for five hundred years. Clearly, before 1492 it was off the mark. Yet, how true to life was it afterward?

Certainly, gone were the days of her calling Fernando to a tourney on Passion Sunday. After 1492 she would in fact become more contemplative. During the war years, even while apocalyptic expectation of the Messiah's Second Coming heightened and was regarded as a highly militant affair, devotion spread to Christ come to the cross to suffer for the sins of humanity. A living, suffering Christ was to be emulated by the devout in simple living and spiritual contemplation in order to achieve personal salvation. Isabel treasured a Flemish book of hours originally belonging to Juana Enríquez, beautifully illustrated with the life of Jesus. In the 1490s, she commissioned paintings of Christ's life and death and a manual on Christian life, and she encouraged translating and publishing an *Imitation of Christ,* a handbook of spiritual exercises and private contemplation.[66] And, as the decade wore on, amid newer currents of pietism and mysticism and under the press of events, her religious sensibility assimilated the new while retaining aspects of the old. That said, whatever her private devotions, unmitigated humility was impossible to a reigning queen.[67]

Writ in Stone: Virtue Restored

Skilled *mudéjar* artisans were summoned from Zaragoza to repair the Alhambra immediately after Granada's fall, and Isabel refused to let the great mosque in Córdoba be altered or razed. A Granadan *morisco*—a Christian of Muslim culture—reminded her great-grandson, Philip II, of that patronage and its reason: *Los reyes* "sustained the rich *alcázares* of the Alhambra . . . as they were in the time of the Muslim kings, in order always to manifest their power, to recall the triumph of the conquerors."[68] At the same time, Isabel and Fernando, too, as customary among European royalty, had religious institutions constructed, their number and grandeur expected to reflect their own stature and their vision of their reign as well. Among those structures were not only the royal hospice at Guadalupe but the monasteries of St. Thomas in Avila and Santa Cruz in Segovia, a hospice for pilgrims in Santiago, and a church of St.

Figure 11. Tomb of Juan II of Castile and Isabel of Portugal (completed 1493). Gil de Siloe. Charterhouse of Miraflores, Burgos.

Francis in Rome. Isabel founded two convents of St. Isabel, one in Toledo and one in Granada. Even so, most striking and telling were the two monuments she commissioned earliest, San Juan de los Reyes and the tombs of her parents housed in the charterhouse at Miraflores. Both were dedicated to dynastic splendor; both were completed in the years around 1492; and both sought to allay mortality. Grandiose and full-blown, they spoke of her illustrious heritage and her commitment to uphold and cap it.[69]

The tombs at Miraflores and the surrounding sculpture, designed in 1480 and built between 1489 and 1493, reveal a good deal about Isabel that did not change.[70] There, sculpted in alabaster in a wall niche, her brother Alfonso kneels in prayer, his face young and fresh and remarkably like portraits of her, his hat a mass of spring flowers; those flowers are signs of a new beginning and the hat sidesteps the problem of a crown. Above the figure of Alfonso and to one side is carved a pulled-back curtain, the whole conveying not death but promise and anticipation. Nearby, Isabel's parents, Juan II of Castile and Isabel of Portugal, lie below the high altar within a great, raised, star-shaped white marble confection, their effigies ringed by the cardinal virtues personified, outstanding among them the figure of Justice, who has been given two swords, undoubtedly temporal and spiritual. Saints surround them, and Old Testament prophets, angels, and a great array of flora and fauna. Birds and beasts abound, and most frequent are eagles. The four evangelists guard the four corners of the tombs and, among them, most carefully carved is San Juan with his eagle. High above are other eagles, ending the ceiling vaults, sheltering under their wings the royal coat of arms.[71] The whole bespeaks a powerful dynasty chosen to forward God's design.

The choice of a star shape to encompass the tombs has been described persuasively as an allusion to heaven and divinity, and as conventionally standing for another astral body, the sun, symbol of Christ, so that Isabel's parents are ringed round by divinity. The equivalent of a halo is implicit in the circle formed by the design around King Juan's head.[72] Yet the allusions are more multiple: they call to mind the phrase of St. Jerome taken up by Sánchez de Arévalo: "In the West the sun of righteousness has risen"; and Jerome's own implicit East-West contrast in seeing the East as contaminated by the devil and his demons whom Spaniards then tended to identify with Muhammad and the Muslims. By extension, the star commemorated as well the crusade of Juan and his daughter against the influence of magic and ways of thought in Spain associated with the non-Christian or heretical East. The star also recalls other stars such as those surrounding the Woman of the Apocalypse, who represented at once the church, the queen of Heaven, Mary, and her temporal counterpart, Isabel. Conveying allusion to Isabel too is the star's evocation of Astraea, equated with the constellation Virgo, and whose return is to announce the arrival of a golden age of justice. The star recalls Alfonso X's astronomy (translated from the Arabic) where in the constellation Aquila, now known as Altair, the brightest star is called "the flying eagle."[73] And hovering on the edge of astronomy and astrology, Vicente Ferrer had preached of twelve ages of the church, likened them to the twelve signs of the zodiac, and predicted that with the death of Antichrist "the sun of justice" would appear in the penultimate sign, Aquarius, when all unbelievers would be baptized. Miraflores reflects all this messianic and millennial expectation and centers it on Isabel's dynasty.[74]

The star at Miraflores has eight points. To Francisco Imperial, the poet who had offered prophecy to Juan II, the number eight had special symbolic value in regard to that king's birth.[75] Eight was, moreover, the symbol of new life, surely that of Juan's daughter. Imperial also spoke of "the Star Diana" in undoubted conflation of Diana, the goddess of the moon, who was thought to help women in childbirth, with both the Virgin Mary, whom Imperial saw as having a similar responsibility, and the Woman of the Apocalypse, standing upon the moon and surrounded by stars. Nor can it be happenstance that all of them had become referred to in conjunction with Juan's daughter Isabel, Castile's queen.

On his tomb at Miraflores, King Juan holds a scepter, echoing a verse of Mena's: "Justice is a scepter that the sky created."[76] And the scepter is in the shape of an orb, symbol of the globe and its universal dominion, and, more precisely, of its center, Jerusalem. Above the royal tombs, in the glittering altarpiece, the splendid, powerful, and devout patrons, Isabel and Fernando, kneel in prayer. Miraflores is a visual reclamation: in this dynastic statement Isabel has aggrandized her parents—and so herself. Miraflores speaks of her own dedication to shouldering her father's responsibilities, and to fulfilling the blighted promise of another Isabel, her mother. Miraflores as completed was also meant to surpass all other funerary structures in Spain, and its iconography to affirm royal supremacy in the face of the self-aggrandizing imagery and architecture favored by the nobility.

Palaces, religious institutions, and public buildings reflecting the royal aesthetic, their patrons often employing the same people to build, sculpt, and paint them, were being commissioned by obviously prospering nobles, bishops, and chief courtiers, particularly by Cardinal Mendoza, who was all of those things. He had earlier had a hand in the splendid Hispano-Gothic Mendoza palace in Guadalajara with its facade and great hall embellished with *salvajes;* he was responsible for the expansion of the cathedrals of Seville and Toledo and for their altarpieces, the most spectacular in Spain. He was also careful to tie his power, as slightly lesser, to that of the monarchs. He commissioned the choir stalls of Toledo's cathedral depicting the taking of fifty-four Granadan towns, his choice of location confirming that conquest and its perpetrators, himself included but principally *los reyes,* had fulfilled a holy mission. In Valladolid the progress of his Colegio de Santa Cruz, the College of the Holy Cross, paralleled the changing outlook at court, but was at the same time forward looking. Begun in 1487 in Gothic style, it was completed by 1492 as the first major Renaissance structure in Castile.[77] Mendoza himself, bald-pated, looking more banker than great lord, appears on its tympanum. He is on his knees before St. Helena, the emperor Constantine's mother, held to have rediscovered the true cross—the *Santa Cruz*—while visiting Jerusalem. The analogy is patent to another mother, of a son whom it was hoped would be another Constantine—to Isabel. The cardinal, through his dedication to Christ's cross, rendered homage not only to his title proper, *cardenal de Santa Cruz,* but to his close connection to Spain's monarchs and to their royal goals.

In Valladolid, too, another powerful longtime associate of Isabel's, Alonso de Burgos, then bishop of Palencia and president of the *Hermandad,* between 1487 and 1496 sponsored two buildings, the church of San Pablo, and, adjacent, the Colegio of San Gregorio, their facades a flamboyant prophetic vision consonant with official ideology. The two Saints John grace the church of San Pablo, while over the central portal of San Gregorio the royal escutcheon rests in the topmost branches of a huge pomegranate tree; the pomegranate, symbol of both Granada and resurrection, was added in 1492 to the royal coat of arms. Here it is held not by an eagle but by two lions, possibly a reference to *los reyes* as dual Lion Kings. The tree takes the form of a Tree of Jesse, traditionally imparting a messianic genealogy, but here amid its branches sprout a chivalric array of pages, heralds, and knights. A row of naked hairy wildmen stand at its base, four abreast on each side of the portal, armed with knightly maces and shields. They fill a space "which, since the beginning of Gothic architecture, had been reserved for the prophets and the saints."[78] Those *salvajes,* prophets of a sort, are symbols and ensurers of Spanish destiny and more than mortal.

That iconography, depicting among other things the emergence of the chivalric from the barbaric, was no anomaly; in Isabel's Spain it conveyed a sense of Spanishness at once religious, political, cultural, and patriotic. As employed on noble and royal monuments, those stalwart *salvajes* recalled Spain's legendary founders, the Visigoths and Hercules, and reflected the proud descent claimed from them by nobles and monarchs alike. In visual response to the noble challenge to royal absolutism, that Tree of Jesse commissioned by a royal booster also displayed the ultimate superiority of royal power as divinely dictated. San Gregorio—the pope Gregory I the Great—had himself viewed human society as a divinely ordained hierarchy, mirroring heavenly arrangements; communal leaders as such were morally superior and at its top, whatever their path to power.[79] The tree spoke at once of heaven and earth, and of past, present, and future, of history, social structure, and prophecy.

The *salvajes* symbolized all that. As Isabel's chronicles fulsomely attest, the Visigoths, or West Goths, were seen as Christianity-bearing forefathers, by the 1400s depicted as noble barbarians. So Gómez Manrique, whose family proudly claimed descent from the Goths, in his masque for Alfonso's birthday and in the subsequent prose and poetry he addressed to Isabel presented the Visigoths as royal and noble ancestors, savages arrived in Spain who had rapidly become humane, magnanimous, liberal, and devoted to the arts and sciences. So Livy and Tacitus had praised the rustic simplicity of Germanic tribesmen, and so Sánchez de Arévalo had similarly lauded the early inhabitants of Spain: they were robust and avoided "the effeminate pleasure" of hot baths.[80] The emblematic *salvajes* were often satyr-like or figures of fun elsewhere in Europe.[81] But they could also signify to the Spanish, and to humanists in Spain, rejection of the Italian view of Spain as barbarous. They proudly celebrated the barbarity of the Visigoths, who according to Spanish histories out-ancestored, outfought, and outshone Rome.

Salvajes, untamed and uncorrupted, noble and pure, bore resemblance to Hercules, another of Spain's mythical founding figures. So in the *General History* of Alfonso X, the first age of six is a golden age; then men knew no evil, no laws were necessary; it was the time of Hercules. In the centuries intervening between Alfonso *el Sabio* and Isabel, Hercules had taken on combined patriotic and religious significance. Those emblematic wildmen recalled both Hercules and the Goths, common ancestors, and like them stood for primitive and Christian virtues, and for Spain's antiquity, integrity, moral and physical strength, and proud destiny. Depicted as quintessential guardians, they joined chivalric motifs on noble tombs—as in Avila and Luna's chapel—and residences—such as the castles of Cádiz and the Mendozas, as well as on San Gregorio's facade, and in the royal palace of Segovia, now Isabel's. At Miraflores, wildmen stand guard with staffs and shields at the tombs of her parents. Exemplars of virtue, proud defenders of nationality, and figures of chivalric romance, they sometimes appeared with female counterparts, Amazons, with whom some accounts say the Goths intermarried. Dilating on the excellences of Isabel, Pulgar's anonymous continuator compares her to the queen Semiramis and her Amazons, but states that while they "have some stain," Isabel, no less strong, is *castísima.*[82] Even so, in her Spain *salvajes* could connote a form of purity in that Visigothic descent was equated with pure blood, *limpieza de sangre.*

The sumptuous Isabelline buildings themselves, conceived from the late 1470s on to commemorate idealized origins and announce the dawn of a new age, reflect a great surge of assurance and prosperity in the 1480s. The years of their construction paralleling the Granada war and intense activity by the Inquisition, they underscored court-driven cultural assumptions of pursuing a religious and national mission under the monarchy. Isabel herself commissioned some of those structures and inspired others of them; she had come to personify their common message.

The Court

In 1492 the court was swelling in size, its offices proliferating, its habitués alert to positions coming open as chief ministers aged and some stalwarts died. Still peripatetic, now numbering over one thousand people and including the royal guards, the royal chapel, and the many servants, it was a traveling city. More than ever the center of social and political power, attracting great lords as the place to be, the court was as well the hub of a growing administrative apparatus. And within its bureaucracy, the ascending value to the monarchs of the *letrados* was ever more apparent. Mendoza's Colegio de Santa Cruz, had been founded for their education. The University of Salamanca, which in 1494 had five thousand students, no rival in Spain, and was principally dedicated to legal studies, had been expanded at royal expense. While competition for position intensified after the war, a haphazard system of rewarding secretaries and jurists endured, so that in 1493 Isabel could hear from Talavera that some especially worthy, loyal, and hardworking men were grossly underpaid, and his comments leave the impression that rivalry within court circles was fierce and intensifying.

Nobles, although no longer dominating the Royal Council, did retain power and influence at court, as well as enjoying resurgent strength in the towns and the economy. Through the 1490s titles escalated and dukes in particular proliferated; there had been few at Isabel's birth. The nobility was closing ranks, procreating apace, intermarrying, and entailing estates. Sons succeeded fathers, and younger sons more often received titles of their own. Isabel favored families who had rendered great service during the war, and she tended to back them in their numerous disputes with town councils over municipal lands. Those councils themselves—their offices proliferating, more often sold, and becoming hereditary—were increasingly the sinecures of a few families who were little responsive to public interest. And royal *corregidores,* with longer terms and less oversight by the crown, were accreting local property and power. Yet if nobles throve in a decade of economic expansion, so did propertied townspeople. A postwar society, more mobile, less idealistic, greedier and more urban, was clearly reflected in *La Celestina.* Within it behavior was very much at odds with royal injunctions, very non-Isabelline. Münzer, touring Spain, described a conjunction of prosperity, ostentation, and moral laxity. People dressed very showily, he observed, in gold, brocades, and silks, even though the monarchs prohibited such excesses.

The court set no example of austerity in that expansive postwar atmosphere. Expenses soared for the royal household as the monarchs displayed an ascending opulence they considered appropriate only to themselves and their children. Castilians had long expected their rulers to dress and live splendidly, befitting their station, and Isabel, although avowedly opposed to superfluity and extravagance, when the occasion merited was happy to oblige her subjects. Yet for Spain as a whole, her goal remained a highly moral and wholly Christian society and, as a next step in that direction, she addressed the matter of the presence of Jews.

Chapter 15

The Expulsion of the Jews: 1492

And the kingdom and the dominion, and the greatness of the kingdoms under the whole heaven, shall be given to the people of the saints of the Most High; their kingdom is an everlasting kingdom, and all dominions shall serve and obey them.

—Daniel 7:27

For behold, I create new heavens
And a new earth,

. . . .

And I will rejoice in Jerusalem.
—Isaiah 65:17, 19

The royal decree of expulsion of all Spain's Jews was, appropriately, given in Granada. Dated March 31, 1492, but not made public until the end of April, it gave them until the end of July, three months, to leave the country. They were not to take out of Spain gold, silver, money, arms, or horses. The decree explained the expulsion as evolutionary: that since there were bad Christians in the realm, and a great cause of their condition was communication with Jews, segregation of Jews from everyone else had been ordered in the Cortes of 1480 and the Inquisition been established. Nevertheless, contact with the Jews occasioned great harm to Christians, because it subverted "our holy Catholic faith." Jews held meetings where they read and taught. They managed to circumsize *conversos* and their sons and to give them books of prayer. They informed *conversos* of the history of their law, and notified them of holy days and instructed them in their observance, even carrying to their houses unleavened bread and ritually slaughtered meat. Partial, exemplary expulsion in a spirit of royal clemency had been tried: "We, knowing that the true remedy of all these harms and inconveniences is separating the Jews from all communication with the Christians and expelling them from our kingdoms, had wished it to be enough to order them to leave all . . . Andalusia where it seemed they had done the most harm." It was thought that it would suffice to warn all Jews to leave off proselytizing. It had not sufficed: "Each

Figure 12. Spanish Jews (later thirteenth century). Alfonso X, Cantigas de Santa María.

day it is found that the Jews increasingly continue their evil and harm. . . ."[1] It was an explanation according with the process usual to Isabel, the incremental imposition of dire measures, one of reassuring herself and convincing everyone else that at every step she had proceeded judiciously. That being the case, it is difficult to ascertain just when expulsion was decided upon, and for how long premeditated.

Whatever the date a nationwide expulsion was first conceived, to Isabel in 1492 emptying Spain of Jews was a necessary next step, taken much like a logistical decision to cut off the enemy from allies and provisions; in that sense it was an extension of a war-nurtured ruthlessness. War had accustomed her to uprooting great numbers of people; war and the Inquisition contributed to her thinking dispassionately of people en masse. And by 1492 the Inquisition had found some thirteen thousand converts guilty of Jewish practices. Even so, a more neutral analogy was made in the decree:

for, when some grave and detestable crime is committed by some members of some college or university, it is reason enough to dissolve and annihilate the entire body . . .

and those who pervert the good and honest life of the cities and towns and by contagion can harm the others may be expelled from the towns and even for other less serious causes that may harm the Republic, then how much more [should Jews be expelled] for this greatest and most dangerous and contagious of crimes, as is this.

Invoked, that is, was the old organic metaphor of cleansing the body politic of disease. In effect, all Jews by their very existence were assumed guilty of causing such contamination.

A sense is conveyed of royal patience at an end, and something more: "Because of the weakness of our humanity, the diabolic tricks and enticements that continually war against us could quickly triumph if the principal cause of this danger is not removed"; that "principal cause" being the Jews. Inquisition language spilled over into the royal decree, and carried with it an assumption of incessant warfare necessary against the devil and those prime instruments of his, the Jews. It is hard to conclude anything but that Isabel herself believed in the this-world venue of the contest between heaven and hell. Although on occasion she expressed disdain for the *opinión del vulgo* concerning the devil's power, she denied only its potency in relation to God's might. Concerning the Jews too she was acutely attuned to the public temper, and, once again, she had had much to do with molding it.

Relatively early in her reign she had employed the traditional royal formula in insisting: ". . . all the Jews of my kingdoms are mine and they are under my protection and power, and they belong to me, to defend and protect and maintain in justice. . . ." That claim was as much an assertion of royal authority as anything else. In 1476 in Cortes at Madrigal, she had signaled the direction of her thinking in statutes that catered to urban constituencies and popular prejudices and were proclaimed throughout the realm. Those statutes resurrected discriminatory ordinances fallen into disuse: Jews and Muslims were to wear special badges or signs, Jews to wear on their right arm a six-pointed star. Neither were to dress in luxurious fashion. Debts to Jews were excused if usurious.[2] And at Madrigal and thereafter, in policies toward the Jews Isabel spoke as one with Fernando.

Prophecy and Precedent

The expulsion decree reflected adhesion to a centuries-long animosity toward Jews as a clannish people of wrong-minded belief and different culture, as foreigners among Us, and with antipathy to Them known to be immensely valuable in defining Us. That hostility—displayed in civil and church law, sermons, drama and literature, art and architecture, and acted upon sporadically—had long and ably been played upon by Spanish kings, who had kept it both alive and tamped down. Alfonso X's *Partidas,* drawing on Visigothic and Roman precedent, had formulated its precise terms: "Jews are a manner of men who do not believe in the faith of Our Lord Jesus Christ, but the great lords of the Christians have always suffered them to live among them. . . . And the reason why the Church and the Emperors and the kings and the other princes suffer the Jews to live among the Christians is this: because they shall live as in captivity forever and shall remind men that they come from the line of those who crucified Our Lord, Jesus Christ."[3]

Elsewhere the *Partidas* spoke of Jews as helpmates of the devil, alluding to the belief that in the last days, Antichrist, archdevil and tyrant, was expected to arise. Antichrist needed no explanation in medieval Spain; he was, as Daniel had dreamed of him and the Book of Revelation portrayed him, a horned monster, a serpent, the principle of destructive power on earth, indistinguishable from Satan. The edict of 1492 assumed Jews to be doing Satan's work: "the tricks and enticements of the devil could quickly triumph if the cause of this danger is not removed. . . ." Such doomsday assumptions, enshrined in royal law and at times preached under royal auspices, stoked animosity to a large and distinct group whose chief protection lay in the same people who spoke of them thusly, the monarchs.[4]

On becoming queen, Isabel had claimed the customary guardianship of Jews and exhibited the customary disdain. She knew that in Spain had lived and worked since Roman times one of the largest, if not the largest, populations of Jews in Europe. The Jews had lived throughout the realm, within largely self-governing enclaves in towns and cities, directly under royal authority, their presence a fact of everyday life. Yet with her Trastámara predecessors had come more restrictive legislation, more anti-Jewish riots, greater pressure on Jews to convert, and many more *conversos.*

She was certainly aware that most *conversos* dated from 1391, when, after mob violence against Jews had broken out in conditions of weak royal control, thousands of Jews had converted, perhaps more than had not. And she was surely cognizant that in 1412 such violence had flared again, during her father's minority when, fanned by the incendiary warning of Vicente Ferrer that the Last Judgment was not far distant and that Jews must disappear as soon as possible, popular "wrath had burned . . . as a sea aflame."[5] Nor had it done so without royal compliance, for Ferrer had been favored by the regents, Fernando's grandfather, Fernando de Antequera, and her paternal grandmother, the dowager queen Catalina. Again coerced mightily, many Jews accepted baptism, but received little or no instruction in Christianity.

A statute of purity of blood, promulgated in Toledo in 1449, classified Jews and *conversos* as a single group, with identical lineage. Some eminent *conversos,* put on the defensive, had then argued that all Jews should convert for such was God's plan. While proud of their highborn Jewish ancestry, several bishops and royal secretaries then declared that the Jewish people had been chosen to announce and produce the Messiah, but that with his coming they had, in remaining Jewish, outstayed their place in the divine scheme; those Jews who refused to accept this truth were obstinate and perverse, and possibly malicious, for their God wished them to become Christian. From 1449, Jews were said to pose a particular threat to sincere converts.

Isabel had been with Enrique's court in the 1460s when, after a quiescent period allowing partial recuperation for *aljamas,* partisans of an inquisition had clashed on whether or not *conversos* remained Jews but agreed that Jews were despicable and a threat to Christianity. One position was aired in a tract of 1464 by the Franciscan friar Alonso de Espina, that all New Christians continued to be Jews by blood and so belonged to a depraved race. As evidence Espina repeated old slanders: Jews sacrificed innocents on Good Friday, they profaned the host, and they poisoned wells. Even more ominous, since the fall of Constantinople they were making astrological computations calculating just when their Messiah—commonly thought to be Antichrist—would appear. Opposing Espina's racism and condemnation of all *conversos* was Alonso de Oropesa, who was of *converso* stock and who declared Christians to be the new Israel. Oropesa defended Christian *caridad* and the right of *conversos* to Christ's faith, and he declared it estimable to belong to the race of Abraham, for Christ was born into it. Israel, imperfect beforehand, had by Christ's coming been offered perfection. Those Jews who had not accepted the Messiah as having come were an anomaly, the source of all the difficulties confronting New Christians and the greatest danger to Christianity, a contamination. It was, the Hieronymite concluded, necessary to afflict them so that vexation and pain might open their eyes to understanding for, as Isaiah had prophesied, Jews were to suffer before their own redemption. Although sharply divided in their opinions of converts, Espina and Oropesa agreed about Jews.

By Isabel's accession a number of *conversos*—including new converts and those whose forebears had converted from 1391—had joined those Old Christians who viewed contemporary Jews both as a bad influence on converts and as stiff-necked and dangerous in resisting conversion themselves. Royal decrees indicate the queen coincided in sentiment. Some among the people she trusted, and particularly Gómez Manrique, loathed and insulted Jews. Quite possibly he and other knights claiming Goth ancestry subscribed to the Visigothic detestation of Jews found preserved in Visigothic law codes and histories.[6] By 1481 Talavera, in the tract written at Isabel's request applauding the coming of the Inquisition, had demonstrated how much the court attitude toward Jews had hardened. As we have seen, he declared Jews to be despicable, vestigial, anomalies of history; the true Israel was now the Christian church militant and the law of Moses was a dead letter. So blind were those people that they even awaited a messiah of their own, who was in reality Antichrist.

Jews, he had then concluded, either too thickheaded to see the truth or too malicious, were damning their own souls and putting others in jeopardy.[7] Certainly the Inquisition, while ostensibly focused on insincere Christians, had much to do with exacerbating antipathy to Jews, as will be seen its actions in the case of the infant of La Guardia. Even so, initially Isabel temporized; yet she gradually imposed greater royal authority at local level through measures restricting Jews.[8]

Talavera, royal ideologue, was also a powerful administrator who influenced policy. Thus he had dispatched instructions to Burgos when drought had left that city without bread in which he linked heaven's wrath to the presence of Jews. God, he informed the town fathers, was punishing sin; in order to regain His favor no bread or meat or wine or fruit were to be sold on Sundays—Sunday was holy to Christians but not to Jews. Jews and Muslims, he said, had to wear distinctive symbols and no silk "or any other noble fabric."[9] He was informing Isabel's Christian subjects that royal protection for the Jews was evaporating. The message conveyed was that sufferance, notably that of the queen, for such people was wearing thin.[10] By Isabel's time, to the extent that the crown had relied on Jews to provide administrators and handle finances, it now looked largely to New Christians. Having during the Cortes at Madrigal indicated a desire to restrict Jewish activity, Isabel did so a few years later, within the eschatological atmosphere thickened by the birth of her son and the preaching of friars sent out by the court. She had in 1478 supported the cardinal in pressuring Seville's Jews to convert as prelude to introducing the Inquisition. That institution in ferreting out secret judaizers harped on the anomalous presence of Jews per se. Yet at the time, Isabel's more immediate interest was in insincere converts.

Quarantine

That message was corroborated in the severe restrictions imposed within the royal program set out in the Cortes of 1480. Jews were to live segregated in *aljamas* and subject no longer to their own justices but to municipal and royal officials. Magistrates were to be named in each urban unit, whether it was dependent on a noble or the crown, to establish the places in which Jews must live, and to see to it they were resettled in them within two years. Jews were forbidden to sell goods during Christian holidays, to spend the night outside their *aljamas,* to have shops in plazas or Christian streets, or to build synagogues larger than those now existing. From 1481, those measures were applied with rigor and they were sanctioned by a bull of May 31, 1484 that the monarchs had obtained from Sixtus IV.[11] It also authorized their expelling Jews from Seville, Córdoba, and Cádiz, that is, from most of Andalusia; it was issued after the fact, for under royal directive that expulsion had been decreed by the inquisitors on January 1, 1483. Probably many Jews then paid and stayed, for numerous Jews left Andalusia only in 1492.

In the process of implementing segregation, Isabel and Fernando jointly, conscientiously, and conspicuously, showed themselves as graciously performing the royal function of supreme mediator. And mediation was very necessary, for their stance—and their Inquisition—had by then encouraged a spate of local anti-Jewish measures resulting in appeals to the crown. Thus, Jews of Avila complained of being robbed as a result of ordinances at Madrigal in 1476. And those mandates had put Jews who lent money in a particularly difficult situation, for war, inflation, and fluctuation in currency had brought increasing recourse to borrowing yet made lending risky and so subject to high interest rates. In that volatile economic climate, the laws against usury emanating from Madrigal were wilfully misinterpreted by some Christian borrowers. Again in Avila, both sides appealed to the crown. The initial reaction of Jews of that city to those laws had been simply to refuse to make loans. When, upon the urging of the municipal council, they had relented, they soon found that their debtors would not repay the sums borrowed, claiming them usurious, and would not heed the *corregidor*'s orders to do so. Isabel sent mediators, who in turn evoked new Jewish protests. It was a state of affairs highly inflammatory, yet advantageous to demonstration of royal authority within municipalities and conducive to bolstering the royal treasury. So it proved when, in June of 1485, the monarchs accepted an offer from all Castile's *aljamas* of four thousand *castellanos de oro* in return for a decree freeing their residents from any suit to reclaim usurious interest.[12]

By the later 1480s, all pressures on Jews intensified in tandem with demands of war and the spread of the Inquisition and its mentality. Very little is known about the role of the nobles in relations with Jews in these years, only that some, such as Medina Sidonia and Medinaceli, allowed *juderías* to remain relatively undisturbed within their jurisdictions. Municipalities, however, taking their cue from the hardening royal attitude, were enforcing proscriptive laws with such vigor as to overstep royal ordinances.[13] To Isabel and Fernando, following their lead was one thing, abusing their laws and thus subverting their authority another. They repeatedly intervened, affirming royal power and appearing more or less evenhanded. In 1486 they annulled a new ordinance in Burgos that limited the number of Jews who might live there and that directed any who had married in the past three years to leave. Yet at the same time, they left undisturbed the prohibition, consonant with their decrees and Talavera's injunction, against Jews selling food in the *alhama* on Sundays and Christian holidays. And when Segovia in 1488 forbade Jews to sell salted or dried fish in the plaza, or to buy fish on Fridays or meat or poultry on Thursdays until afternoon, and its Jews appealed, the monarchs again demonstrated a talent for exquisite fine-tuning in having that decree modified to the extent that Jews might buy meat on Thursday mornings beginning at eleven. They did, however, completely revoke an ordinance of Medina del Campo that in 1489 prohibited sale of firewood, charcoal, and bread in the Jewish quarter. Even so, the next year they approved of Medina's prohibiting Jews having shops in the plaza, thereby cutting them off from both local trade and the fair; yet after hearing an envoy from Medina's *aljama* (and in such appeals, a gift to their majesties was not unusual) they again changed their minds. So it went, the crown exerting its authority in such cases and often being rewarded monetarily for doing so. When Plasencia's council complained that Jews would not stay in the new *judería,* then admitted that it was not fit to live in, a royal appointee supposedly sent to better their situation made it worse. Although he was replaced and an official edict of May 18, 1491 promised security to that *aljama,* it was not to last long.[14]

That the royal tone had altered a great deal since 1476, from conveying the assertion of royal authority that was implicit in jurisdiction over Jews to sending a message of bare sufferance, was evidenced in the language of a decree of 1490 prohibiting inhabitants of Bilbao from harassing the Jews of the village of Medina de Pomar. That order ran: "By canon law and in accord with the laws of our kingdoms, the Jews are tolerated and suffered, and we command you to tolerate and suffer them, that they may live in our kingdoms as our native-born subjects."[15] Imparted was an impatience to have done with the Jewish presence, although not quite yet. In 1490 too the *aljamas* paid a special levy of ten thousand *castellanos de oro,* as well as the high ransom set for Jewish *malagueños.* They had met extraordinary tributes repeatedly during the war; and in October 1491 a last-minute extraordinary war assessment was levied on Jewish communities, half due at the end of November and the rest in mid-January 1492.

As the war ended, mounting hostility to Jews, the spreading activities and influential attitude of the Inquisition, and the professed royal stance of segregating Jews as a contagion to be contained set the stage for perhaps the most notorious of Inquisition cases, resulting in an *auto de fe* that preceded the decree of expulsion by only four months. In 1490, the Inquisition had charged a *converso* of La Guardia, near Toledo, with having gotten hold of a consecrated wafer and plotting with five other New Christians and six Jews to use it, along with a human heart, to cast a spell that would bring insanity and death to all Christians. A year later, additional arrests and torture brought confessions that the heart was that of a Christian child crucified by the plotters. Although no child was anywhere missed and the confessions impossibly inconsistent, at Avila in November of 1491 three Jews, by then dead, were burned in effigy, two others were torn apart alive with red-hot pincers, and the six *conversos* were reconciled to Christianity (and so first mercifully strangled) before being burned at the stake.

Testimony extracted by the inquisitors stated that it was the spectacle of the initial *auto de fe* at Toledo that had frightened those people into a novel recourse to black magic; yet at the same time, the sentence passed on them contradicted that evidence, in identifying the alleged crime as a usual one, as a ritual murder customary among Jews and among *conversos* who judaized. That sentence was widely disseminated, even translated into Catalan; a cult of the martyr, the holy child of La Guardia, sprang up and still endures, although not sanctioned by the Catholic Church.[16] Apart from malicious fables, there is no proof such a crime was ever committed anywhere. It was yet one more of the many recurrent and widespread false accusations often accompanying other sorts of attacks on Jews in Europe—a groundless allegation that has continued to be repeated down to the present.

Immediately after that *auto de fe,* the monarchs received from the Jews of Avila a request for guarantees that they would not be slaughtered. The publicity attending that case had been so intense and so successful in raising anti-Jewish sentiment to a boil that it is hard to escape the conclusion that such outrage was purposely fanned as prelude to expulsion. Conversely, an inquisitor and others declared that that ritual murder had great influence on the monarchs' decision to expel the Jews. Such was indicated within a month of that public execution, in December of 1491, when legislation reserved to the crown the right to supervise the tax farming system and cancel contracts "inconsistent with reorganization plans of the state."[17] Since there were still some Jews among principal tax farmers, it may well be that the expulsion was even then contemplated. Still, given Isabel's modus operandi, the suspicion lingers that it had been planned even earlier.

Whose Decision?

Historians have tended to see the decree of 1492 as principally the work of Fernando, basing their opinion on his correspondence endorsing it, influenced by the Machiavellian reputation he acquired later, and noting that in 1486 when an inquisitor in Zaragoza was murdered by *conversos* and riots ensued he had ordered Zaragoza's Jews expelled.[18] Yet ringing true is an account that lays that edict at least equally to Isabel. Its author was Isaac Abravanel, who in 1492 shared with Abraham Señor the leadership of Spanish Jewry, and who was both a writer of philosophy and Cardinal Mendoza's chief tax farmer. Abravanel had been called to court in 1484 and had subsequently, together with Señor, loaned Isabel millions of *maravedís* for the war and become a trusted financial advisor of hers. In March of 1492 he was proud of having gained royal favor, appreciation, and esteem and later recalled his complete surprise at the edict of expulsion. As soon as he learned of it, Abravanel said, he quickly went with the octagenarian Señor and Señor's son-in-law and successor as chief tax farmer, the rabbi Mair Melamed, to urge the king to cancel the decree. Fernando agreed only to delay it. Upon Abravanel and Señor offering him a great sum, possibly three hundred thousand ducats, the king reconsidered but finally refused, telling them that it had been a joint decision of *los reyes* and was irrevocable. And so Abravanel went to the queen. Clearly he knew Isabel, and he chose to meet her on her own ground, moral certitude. If (and here Abravanel's biographer paraphrases his reminiscence) "she thought that, by measures like expulsion, the Jews could be brought to surrender and to extinction, she was greatly mistaken. He pointed out to her that . . . the Jewish people had outlived all those who had attempted to destroy them, that it was beyond human capacity to destroy [them], and that those who tried to do so only invited upon themselves divine punishment and disaster."[19]

Her response, as he gave it, was consistent with what we know of her and is fundamental to understanding her reasons for expelling Spain's Jews: "'Do you believe,' she asked him, 'that this comes upon you from us? [Rather], the Lord hath put this thing into the heart of the King.'" Abravanel, plunging ahead, asked her to influence Fernando to withdraw it. "No, she could not . . . , even if she desired it. 'The King's heart,' she said, 'is in the hands of the Lord, as the rivers of water. He turns it whithersoever He will.'" It was an instance of the value to *los reyes* of their subjects having to deal with two crowned heads rather than one; and as Isabel did not choose to say to Abravanel but had so often demonstrated, she believed the queen's heart too was that of a king and directly in God's keeping.

Abravanal and Señor came to the conclusion that in fact Isabel, rather than Fernando, was chiefly responsible for the edict and the refusal to rescind it, and they were convinced that they had no recourse. She insisted, moreover, that the two of them convert and stay. Señor accepted baptism, at Guadalupe, his sponsors the sovereigns and the cardinal. But Abravanel, despite cajoling, threats, even a plot to kidnap and baptize his grandson, would not consent and in early August took ship at Valencia for Italy. Isabel's exchange with Abravanel was at bottom a confrontation of competing claims to being God's elect, a contest of wills concerning God's will. Her implication was plain: it was the Lord who viewed the Jews as anachronistic and that, as Talavera and others had put it, her own Christian people were the New Israel, the spiritual heirs of the initial chosen ones, and that, the Messiah having once arrived, it was past time for Jews to disappear. Moreover, and to the extent possible, it was the Spanish monarchs who were implementing the divine timetable for the Second Coming. At the very least they had been designated to set an example to the world by cleansing Spain.

Consequences

Abravanel had made his stand by affirming that it was the Jews who were and would remain God's elect. Later, in exile, in the first of three messianic works, he took pains to establish that Jewish triumph was soon to come, arguing that Jews were the fifth kingdom of Daniel, the select people of the saints of the Most High. During Isabel's reign, as their numbers shrank and pressures upon them mounted, Jews expressed a growing sense of impending disaster and a rising messianic expectation, for suffering was prophesied to precede the coming of the Messiah. Upon learning they must leave Spain, many reacted with panic, hysteria, and despair; then, once past the initial shock, some came to see exile as an ordeal set by God. It was the assigned suffering preliminary to total triumph and boundless prosperity. The prophesied Day of Wrath had arrived; it would be followed by entry into the Promised Land or by the coming of the fifth kingdom. However construed, when faced with conversion or expulsion, most chose to leave.

The chronicler Bernáldez described the observable impact of the decree on Spain's Jews and something of the Spanish reaction to it. Wholly sympathetic to the Inquisition, indeed a functionary of it, he yet wrote compassionately; much like Isabel, he sympathized with individual suffering even when believing it necessary to attain a higher good. Bernáldez reiterated the old saw: it is better to enter heaven with one eye than not at all. Certainly the Jews had to suffer before the Last Judgment; and with his sovereigns he shared the equally essentially eschatological assumption that it was past time for Jews to go. The spirit of his chronicle is much like that of the 1492 decree, and it tells of its immediate consequences, the events Isabel set in motion.

"Having seen the very great harm proceeding from the obdurate opinion and perpetual blindness of the Jews, and how they nourished the depraved Mosaic heresy," his account begins, "and being at the siege of Granada in 1492, [the king and queen] commanded and decreed that the Holy Evangel and Catholic faith and Christian doctrine be preached to all the Jews of Spain and all its kingdoms." The monarchs, that is, sent out yet another of those friar-vanguards such as they had dispatched preliminary to imposing the *Hermandad* and the Inquisition, this time seeking to convert all of Spain's Jews. Although it was preached to the Jews that the Messiah whom they awaited was Jesus Christ, Bernáldez says, yet they ignored it, fearing the truth and "having been deceived by the false book of the Talmud, . . . where there are very obscure lies and abominable mad things against the law of God and against the law of nature and against the law of the Scriptures." Indeed, "the wise men among them were intoxicated as much as the simple, . . . although they saw before their eyes their own exile and perdition, and although they were importuned and threatened," yet "they remained pertinacious and unbelieving although forced to hear; never have they willingly received in their hearts a thing that benefitted them."[20]

Apologists for the expulsion until today adhere to that same argument, that it was after all by choice that the Jews left, for they had only to convert in order to stay. Bernáldez blamed the rabbis for misleading the others: "Even before they left off hearing the evangelical preaching, their rabbis preached to them the contrary, and strengthened them and gave them vain hope, and said to them that they were to know for certain that [impulse for their expulsion] came through God, who wished to take them from captivity and carry them to the promised land and that in this exodus they would see Israel." Neither Bernáldez nor other Spaniards viewed the Jewish return to Jerusalem as an eschatological necessity, as would evangelical Protestants from the next century on; rather, they tended to speak in terms of cleansing Spain and of themselves as the new elect. In 1492 it was Jews who, in reaction to expulsion, expected end-time events to occur—to return to Jerusalem and to greet the Messiah.[21]

Bernáldez gave historical explanation for there being Jews in the world. They would not recognize or receive Jesus Christ, or give ear "to the great miracles and marvels he worked, before maliciously persecuting and killing him; and the error made, never did they repent of it." The chronicler compacted time and bent Scripture to find the origin of the dispersion of the Jews by Rome in that refusal, as his contemporaries tended to do. So the emperor Vespasian, who was responsible for the Jewish diaspora, had been an instrument of divine vengeance sent because the Jews did not repent the crucifixion. As for Isabel, who read Josephus on Vespasian's destruction of the temple in Jerusalem, there was no reason to think otherwise.[22]

After that dispersion, said Bernáldez, "many [Jews] came to Spain at many times" and "from them come those who live now, in lineage as in contumacy," of which there were over 30,000 households. Scholars tend to accept his figures but disagree on the proper multiplier, seeing it as between three and five. At the most, then, it indicates that some 175,000 Jews were in Spain in 1492. Most lived in the lands held by lords, Bernáldez went on, and were "merchants and vendors and farmers of the *alcabalas* and stewards of nobles"; others were "cloth-shearers, tailors, shoemakers, tanners, weavers, spice merchants, peddlers, silk dealers, silversmiths, and of other similar occupations." All were "people who never broke the earth nor were farmers nor carpenters nor masons, but all sought easy jobs with little work." Still, they prospered, for "they were very subtle people and people who lived communally" and, profiting through usuries in dealings with Christians, "in a short time many of the poor became rich." His account omitted some occupations, particularly physicians and proprietors of landed estates; yet it corroborates that many Jews were skilled artisans. Then, as from time to time occurred, the observer momentarily overcame the polemicist: "Among themselves they were very charitable. Although they paid tribute to lords and kings . . . they never became very needy because their councils, called *aljamas,* supplied their necessities."

Returning to reaction to the decree of 1492, Bernáldez relayed a pervasive sense among Jews of the time having arrived for their being led by God in another exodus to the Promised Land and told of how that exodus was then organized:

The rich Jews paid the cost of departure of the poor Jews, and they treated each other with much care and generosity; so that none wished to convert, except for very few of the most needy. The Jews, simple and lettered, in that time commonly held the opinion, wherever they lived, that just as God, with strong hand and arm extended and much honor and riches, had through Moses led the people of Israel from Egypt miraculously; that thus He would return to them and lead them from these parts of Spain with much honor and riches and without any loss of belongings to possess the holy promised land, which they confessed to having lost through their great and abominable sins, which their ancestors had committed against God.

Yet, he went on, they were sadly mistaken, for the Jews who left Egypt had been good and humble, and the Egyptians bad and gentile and idolators. "And now, on the contrary, the Jews are bad and unbelieving and idolatrous, and not sons of Israel, but sons of Canaan, and of perdition, and the Christians are good and sons of God, of law, of benediction, and of obedience, and people of God." The Christians, to Bernáldez as to his queen, were the true successors to the Old Testament Jews.

And so the Jews prepared to depart Spain:

In the time of six months [effectively three] allowed by the edict, they sold and sold cheaply what they could of their estates. . . . The Christians got their very rich houses and heirlooms for little money, for they encountered no one who would buy them and so gave a house for an ass, and a vineyard for a little cloth or linen, because they could not take out gold or silver; although it is true that they took infinite gold and silver secretly, and especially many *cruzados* and *ducados* embedded in their teeth. They [also] swallowed them and carried them out in their stomachs, . . . and the women swallowed most, for it so happened that some would swallow thirty *ducados* at once.

The chronicler's pride in accurate observation, and belief that it was necessary that Jews suffer as preliminary to the redemption of humanity, produced some sympathetic counterpoint. "And, before leaving, they married all the young men and women who were over twelve to one another, so that all the women would be accompanied by a husband; and they began to leave Castile in the first week of July." All of them, he continued,

confiding in their vain blind hopes left the lands of their birth, children and adults, old and young, on foot and in wagons, and the *caballeros* on asses and other beasts, and each journeyed to a port of embarkation. They went through roads and fields with many travails and [mixed] fortunes, some falling, others rising, others dying, others being born, others falling sick, so that there was no Christian who did not feel sorry for them and always invite them to be baptized. And some sorrowfully converted and stayed, but very few. And on the way the rabbis heartened them, and had the women and youths sing and play tambourines to cheer the people, and so they went through Castile and arrived at the ports. . . . When those who went to embark arrived at Cádiz or Puerto de Santa María and saw the sea, they shouted loudly and cried out, men and women, great and small, in their prayers demanding mercy of God, and they expected to see some marvel of God and that he would open a path through the sea for them. . . .

Instead of a reprise of the Red Sea dividing, they encountered hardship and suffering. Many were robbed and murdered at sea and in the lands through which they passed by both Christians and Muslims. Many others sailed from Cartagena and other Aragonese ports; some went to Navarre, France, and Germany. Those on the Andalusian coast waited many days on the shore, then had to crowd into twenty-five ships. Seven sailed to present-day Morocco, to Oran, where, encountering a pirate fleet in port, they were allowed to depart only on promise to pay ten thousand *ducados,* and went on to the Spanish port of Arcilla, their destination Fez. Some changed their minds: one hundred fifty Jews disembarked in Cartagena and four hundred in Málaga and were baptized. Those who went to Portugal—Bernáldez says seven hundred households, but most scholars think more, indeed the great majority of those expelled—were told they could stay only six months and were charged an entry fee of a *cruzada* apiece. From Portugal, some went on to Italy, others to Fez or Turkey, and many converted and returned to Castile. In March of 1493, all were expelled from Portugal, but six hundred of the richest households were permitted to remain for a time on payment to the king of one hundred *cruzadas* for each member, another one hundred houses paid eight *cruzadas* per person, and more than one thousand other Spanish Jews were enslaved by the king because they had not paid the entry fee. João's successor, Manoel, freed them on coming to the throne in 1495; but two years later, fulfilling a stipulation made by his Spanish wife-to-be, the *infanta* Isabel, he insisted all Jews in Portugal convert or leave.

Those who went to North Africa fared worst. Jews who had left Gibraltar, although they had hired a guard of Muslim soldiers in Arcilla to escort them to Fez, "were, by order of its king, robbed along the way and the girls and women and their bundled belongings carried off, and women were raped in the sight of their fathers and husbands" and otherwise molested, so that, hearing of it, many who had remained encamped outside Arcilla went into that town and were baptized. Many others subsequently returned from Fez. For those who had gone inland to Fez there had been even worse treatment in returning to Arcilla, for Muslims seized them and "made them open their mouths to get gold and they put their hands [into their private parts] below for it, . . . or stripped them and raped the women and killed the men and cut them in half looking for gold in their stomachs."

People from both groups continued to return to Spain from 1493 to 1496. Bernáldez said he himself had baptized more than one hundred, among them some rabbis, whose citing of Isaiah 10, which speaks of extermination from which only a remnant shall be saved, he saw as their accepting the prophecy of the coming of Christ. For Bernáldez, a remnant saved was good reason for the Inquisition and for expelling the Jews, just as it was said it was for Isabel. Bernáldez did not mention that Isaiah 10 begins "Woe unto them that decree unrighteous decrees."

Many of those who returned to Spain from North Africa, he noted, "came naked, barefoot, and full of lice, dying of hunger and having been very badly treated, so that it was a sorrow to see them. . . ." On he went, chronicling the suffering he had seen as resulting from unbelief and inherently necessary to the prophesied apocalyptic scheme. Informed estimates place the number of Jews returning to Spain at between thirty thousand and fifty thousand, most of whom were baptized preemptorily, swelling the *converso* population and providing raw material for the Inquisition.[23] In 1499, a royal edict declared death for any Jews reentering Spain, unless advance word was sent that they were coming to be baptized and it was done and notarized at the point of entry. Records show that the edict was enforced stringently in 1500 and 1501, and also that Jewish slaves were then ordered deported or converted. With the Jews gone, calumny of them escalated, justifying having cast them out and serving individuals as an assertion of orthodoxy to ward off inquisitors. And as the century ended, it was Muslims and *moriscos,* the new forced converts, who would receive royal attention.

Cleaning Up

While income was probably not among the most compelling reasons for the expulsion, still, as has been seen, the crown profited in the event.[24] In Aragón, where Fernando most blatantly used the Inquisition for political ends, the expulsion itself was carried out by inquisitors and Jewish property was categorized as that of heretics, and so subject to confiscation. Inquisition and expulsion, that is, were fused, to inquisitorial and royal profit. Zaragoza—a case in point—ever since the royal command of 1486 to expel its Jews, had received "a confusion of orders and counterorders, edicts and threats, along with secret instructions and exceptions for individuals"; there all Jewish property was first ordered inventoried, then sequestered, and, while frequently given out by authorities to their cohorts, still much came to the crown.[25] In Castile, the expulsion of 1492 was supervised by secular, civil officials, and there royal measures indicate that the intention was to continue to protect Jews while getting them out, and in the process to take in as much profit as possible. Thus, royal escorts went with some of those departing, following upon reports of others having been robbed, or subjected to extortionate duties, or having paid for protection never supplied. Yet, once arrived at ports, Jews were charged a royal embarkation tax of two ducats apiece, and the crown confiscated any gold, silver, coins, horses, and arms they sought to take with them. At issue was only who was to fleece them.

A royal edict of May 14 allowed Jews to sell their lands, although in Aragón not until royal taxes were paid and courts had decided any questions of debts. Everything owed Jews was ordered paid them so that they could pay their own debts, which they were to do promptly or forfeit their property. A subsequent decree of May 30 ordered claimants to come forward immediately and courts to adjudicate by mid-July. Unable to collect monies owing before leaving, Jews sold rights to them cheaply to Christians, who soon found them encumbered, for on September 10 a royal order suspended payments on all such debts until it was decided if interest charges on them were usurious. That suspension, however, was not to affect the rights held by Cardinal Mendoza, the Toledo church, and the creditors of Abravanel. From October 6 on, a series of orders went out for tallying Jewish debts, and directing all debts, goods, and letters of exchange in Spain still belonging to Jews be confiscated.

Letters of exchange remained the only means for Jews to retain the money they received for debts and property; Italian, particularly Genoese, bankers, did well in their drawing up. After the expulsion, the crown "invited" Genoese creditors to declare those letters, promising their holders a fifth of their value, while exposing such funds to confiscation. In July of 1494, arguing the Jews had taken prohibited goods with them, the monarchs ordered all debts still owed them be collected and deposited in the treasury. In Burgos alone, the government collected an estimated seven million *maravedís* in assets left behind by Jews.[26] Abravanel estimated that Jewish property was worth 30 million *ducados*. The figure is probably too high, but whatever it was, the crown did its best to get the lion's share.

The royal treasury confiscated *aljamas*, synagogues, and cemeteries, all the communal property Jews left, often redistributing it as *mercedes*. Thus, Fernando and Isabel in March of 1494 granted Torquemada the old Jewish cemetery in Avila on which to build the convent of Santo Tomás. Cardinal Mendoza received the Jewish goods of his *señorío* to compensate, said the grant, for vassals and rents he had lost, and other nobles received similar gifts. Indicative of a more general practice, at the end of 1492 Isabel conceded to Toledo's cathedral the gravestones from its Jewish cemetery, and she gave the land on which they stood to the city.[27]

The Heart Has Reasons

The queen had moved, slowly but inexorably, from the traditional view that, although Jews were an anomaly, they were the monarch's own subjects and a royal resource, to believing it imperative that Spain have no Jewish inhabitants. They had been valuable as a source of regular income, been considered a reserve much like gold and jewelry, and served as a resevoir of financial expertise, but their wealth and usefulness to the crown had diminished, and Isabel increasingly had available other sources of funding and professional expertise. By 1492, she had also come to rely less and less on Jews as tax gatherers—they were no longer the only people who could get together enough capital to farm taxes—and on monies from *aljamas*. Funds were more available elsewhere and expanding royal bureaucracies, with *conversos* prominent within them, handled much of the assessing and collecting of royal revenues. Over time, baptism had brought many of the more skilled, talented, and educated Jews into the social mainstream. Nor did Isabel rely any longer on Jewish physicians but on *conversos*. And in financial matters, there were also the Italians.

Isabel's intentions were of the highest, as usual and as she saw them. And also as usual, in casting out the Jews she saw herself doing God's will, which was synonymous with what was best for Spain, the faith, and the crown. She was cleansing the realm. And she was helping to clarify, amid rising and contending messianic expectation on the part of both Jews and Christians, just who were now the Chosen People. Moreover, in tolerating the Jewish presence Spain had appeared benighted. She was mindful that those other powerful states of western Europe, France and England, had long ago expelled the Jews. As to Italy, Isabel's court humanists knew the opinion of its men of letters.

Her humanists bridled at their Italian counterparts' sneers at Spain as a nation of *marranos,* of secret Jews. In this sense, the Jews had to go for the old reasons, those of Revelation, so the golden age might arrive, and for newer reasons, those of progress, so the golden age might arrive. Yet for an up-to-date monarch, eschatological or millennial reasons alone would not do publicly or even, perhaps, personally, but social contamination by untrustworthy and disruptive elements within the body politic was an eminently acceptable explanation. After they had left, with no flesh-and-blood individuals to deflate heated imaginations, in Spanish depictions of them Jews became mysterious and monstrous beings, scary bogeymen. Their expulsion was increasingly justified at court in religious and racial terms and with increasing emotion—as Pedro Mártir's remarks made on royal behalf to the sultan in Egypt in 1502 demonstrated.

For several years after 1492, Isabel continued to consider *conversos* of proven persuasion as fellow Christians, indicating a belief that baptism made a Christian and that Jewish ancestry was no blight, only Judaism. Yet, and

although she and Fernando had in 1486 stopped the Hieronymites from passing a statute of purity of blood, they also had in effect elicited the shame pre-
cipitating it. The members of that religious order had then proposed that
exclusionary measure, they said, because, a friar of Guadalupe having been
burned at the stake, their fear of further dishonor was great, a fear aroused
"because they saw the warmth the King and Queen bestowed upon the business of the Holy Office of the Inquisition."[28] We have seen that Cardinal Mendoza indicated where he stood on the issue by placing a statute of *limpieza de
sangre* in the founding constitutions of his Colegio de Santa Cruz and in his
past and present sees, of Sigüenza, Osma, Seville, and Toledo.[29] At the century's end, Isabel herself was to sanction such exclusionary measures, and the
assumption that Jews were a race would take firmer hold on queen and country. The *Partidas,* after all, had stated as much in commanding that "other
Jews must not molest converts."[30]

Welcome praise for expelling the Jews came from abroad, and principally
from Italy. Rodrigo de Borja, Pope Alexander VI, termed it a fine service to
the faith. The humanist Gian Pico della Mirandola praised the sovereigns,
recounted the sufferings of the exiled, and made the point that the expulsion
had given the lie to Jewish astrological calculations connected to the arrival of
their Messiah.[31] Similarly, Machiavelli termed it a a "pious cruelty."[32] Guicciardini later wrote of Castile as anarchic under Enrique IV when it was full of
Jews and Muslims but now freed of Jewish heretics; he declared Spain had
been on the verge of forsaking Catholicism before the expulsion, and he
applauded the burning of 120 *conversos* in one day at Córdoba.[33] Far less
enthusiastic were Jews who chronicled the events of 1492; some of whom spoke
of the anguish caused by the malevolent and perverse Isabel, that she-bear.[34]

As her prestige abroad ascended with success against the Muslims, and as
she sought good marriages for her children, Isabel, courting world opinion as
well as that of her Christian subjects, had expelled the Jews. It would no longer
do to have those sad, benighted, stubborn, and outmoded people in the land,
insufferably claiming to be God's elect, nor did she need them any longer. It
was what powerful kings did; and *los reyes* of Spain had a historic obligation to
God to make Spain catholic, and so to impose order and harmony and ready it
for greater things. So the expulsion would announce to all Europe. Moreover,
in 1492 their reputation among their Christian peers, so glowing at present that
it was not to be dimmed by small failures, permitted taking an occasional risk,
such as sponsoring the voyage of Christopher Columbus.

Chapter 16
Christopher Columbus and the Queen:
To 1492

I saw the royal banners of Your Highnesses placed by force of arms on the towers of the Alhambra, which is the citadel of the city; and I saw the Muslim king come out of the gates of the city and kiss the royal hands of Your Highnesses and of the Prince, My Lord. . . . After having driven out all the Jews from your realms . . . Your Highnesses commanded me that, with a sufficient fleet, I should go to the said parts of India.
—Journal of Christopher Columbus[1]

Cardinal Mendoza, a man equally worthy for his qualities and his wisdom, was of the opinion that Nicholas of Lyra was a very able theologian and Saint Augustine a doctor of the Church, renowned for his doctrine and holiness, but that neither of them was a good geographer.
—Alejandro [Alessandro] Geraldini[2]

Three months after entering Granada, between the drafting of the decree expelling the Jews and its issuance, Isabel and Fernando agreed to sponsor Christopher Columbus on an expedition of exploration westward into the Atlantic. The Genoese seaman and sometime merchants' agent had come to them in late 1485 or early 1486 with a plan to reach the East by sailing west, after having been turned down by João II in Portugal. Just when and where they first gave him audience, most of the facts of his life before then, and exactly what he proposed, are conjectural. The combination of his learning, information on Portugal, experience at sea, including in Guinea, and connections with fellow Genoese and some court figures was sufficiently rare and potentially valuable to gain him a hearing and consequent attention by rulers now bent on overseas expansion.

In 1493, on returning from his first voyage, Columbus himself gave some indication in the dedication of his journal of that voyage, of what he had proposed initially to the Spanish *reyes*:

. . . information which I had given to Your Highnesses concerning the lands of India, and concerning a prince who is called Grand Khan, which is to say . . . King of Kings.

How many times he and his ancestors had sent to Rome to beg for men learned in our holy faith, in order that they might instruct him therein, and how the Holy Father had never made provision in this matter, and how so many nations had been lost, falling into idolatries and taking to themselves doctrines of perdition; and Your Highnesses, as Catholic Christians and as princes devoted to the holy Christian faith and propagators thereof, and enemies of the sect of Mahomet and of all idolatries and heresies, took thought to send me, Christopher Columbus, to said parts of India, to see those princes and peoples and lands and the character of them and of all else, and the manner which should be used to bring about their conversion to our holy faith, and ordained that I should go . . . by way of the west, by which down to this day we do not know certainly that any one has passed.[3]

The grand khan of India was generally believed allied with (the legendary) Prester John. And Columbus, in alluding to the Spanish monarchs' extending the holy work they were accomplishing within Spain worldwide, and to their taking up a labor the papacy had let drop, implied that they were greater champions of Christendom than was the pope. It was an appealing formulation, one not foreign to their own.

Indicative of their piqued curiosity, Fernando ordered from a Valencian bookseller a copy of a prime source of Columbus's notion of the globe, Ptolemy's *Geography,* probably for Isabel, since he read little.[4] Talavera, who had had a hand in arranging that interview, received instructions to form an investigatory commission, "to call together people who seemed to him most versed in that matter of cosmography, of whom there were few in Castile." The commission met a number of times in Salamanca, frequently with Columbus, who was at court often for several years. It concluded that not only were his promises and offers weakly founded and uncertain, even impossible, but that should the queen and king sponsor him they would gain nothing, lose money, and derogate royal authority. Still, his proposal coalesced remarkably with their own grand design. It was another of those projects that Isabel did not forget but postponed to a more appropriate time; and the decision of the commission not withstanding, Columbus had the support of some of her most trusted people.

Experienced in the ways of the Portuguese court, somehow he had met and convinced the right people in Castile to plead his cause, especially to Isabel. He had secured an introduction to Talavera, perhaps dating to Talavera's days in Portugal negotiating the peace treaties, and he had met Mendoza. At some point, the cardinal had arranged an audience for him with Isabel and Fernando, whom he had assured that he found Columbus astute, intelligent, able, and versed in cosmography. He had also suggested that their majesties should help the Genoese seaman with some ships, for they would venture little and might gain much. Concurring with him was the humanist and courtier Alessandro Geraldini, who criticized the attitude of the investigatory commission. Here Geraldini observed that while some prelates saw manifest heresy in denying Nicholas of Lyra's views concerning the terrestrial globe and St. Augustine's conclusion that there were no antipodes it was the cardinal's opinion that neither of them was a good geographer. (Nor, as it turned out, was Columbus.)

Columbus was kept on retainer. Talavera signed authorizations for stipends to him, the first known in May of 1487 for three thousand *maravedís*, another on July 3; and in August while in Córdoba, Columbus received four thousand *maravedís* to get himself to the camp at Málaga, "for some things pertaining to the service of their highnesses," and three thousand more in mid-October.[5] To Isabel and Fernando, that the most active and influential merchants in Granadan Málaga were Genoese, that among them were Columbus's old associates the Centurione, that contacts within that city were considered all important to its conquest, and that it was thought imperative that Málaga, once taken, should be fitted into the Castilian port system to the benefit of the crown may well have had as much to do with that summons as the far less immediate interest in Atlantic exploration.

The emirate of Granada has been described as virtually a Genoese colony, and the Centurione, sometime papal bankers, were also powerful within a Genoese network extending to Seville and Córdoba, and they were affiliated with the Negrón and Spínola who traded with Barbary, mostly in gold and slaves, principally out of Jerez and Cádiz. As the Spanish historian Rumeu de Armas has said, "the Genoese used Cádiz like an African trampoline."[6] Columbus also had connections with Florentines, whose commerce linked the North African coast with the Canaries, the Azores, and the Madeiras, those bases for West Africa and the Atlantic.

Yet the purpose of calling Columbus to Málaga may have been even more complex, having to do with his Portuguese connections. Information was scarce on the Portuguese search for the source of African gold, but it was known that Diego Cão had recently contacted peoples up the Congo River, purportedly inhabitants of the lands of Prester John. Worrisome was João II of Portugal having sent agents eastward by land, and now in 1487 commissioning Bartolomeu Dias to find a sea route to Asia and sending two seamen to seek land to the west of the Azores. That same year, when Columbus brought to the attention of Spain's rulers a request from João that he return to Portugal, another subsidy of three thousand *maravedís* was forthcoming. Later, Columbus claimed to have been present when Dias returned to Lisbon in December of 1488; if so, quite possibly it was at the behest of Isabel and Fernando.

The Andalusian Connection

For Isabel, Columbus's proposal was a logical extension to her policy of exerting Castilian control over Atlantic exploration and the Canary Islands. When in 1488 Pedro Mártir wrote to a friend that Queen Isabel "has brought under submission to her empire the mysterious Fortunate Islands—if such are the Canaries," the inference was that although he was skeptical of their worth, Isabel was not. However that may be, when not at court Columbus gravitated to Seville, Puerto de Santa María, Palos, and Moguer, all principal ports of African and Atlantic endeavor. In Andalusia, too, he sought out Luis de la Cerda, duke of Medinaceli, one of the region's powerful lords keenly interested in maritime enterprise. Indeed the La Cerda, who were of royal blood, retained the title of "Princes of the Fortunate Isles," referring to their century-old claim to the Canaries. Is it coincidence that Medinaceli was the cardinal's first cousin, and that his daughter was married to one of Mendoza's sons? According to Medinaceli, by 1489 Columbus had spent two years as his guest.[7] Medinaceli's seat was at Rota and he shared jurisdiction over Puerto de Santa María with those royal officials Diego Valera and his son Charles.

Since the time of Alfonso X, Puerto de Santa María had been a strategically vital royal enclave on a maritime frontier that was otherwise dominated by great lords. It was, we have seen, a port crucial to Castile's defense, to contact with Africa and the Atlantic, and to royal collection of customs duties along coasts long notorious for smuggling. Situated between Jerez and Cádiz, the Puerto could monitor the traffic of the estuary formed by the Tinto and Odiel Rivers, including that of Palos and Moguer, places largely dedicated to seaborne expeditions and to piracy. It was at once a naval yard for layovers and repairs, a fishing port, and a commercial town. In 1485 Isabel and Fernando ordered that all African ventures must go through that royal enclave. It was that year too that seamen from the Puerto and Jerez raided African coasts and returned with more than four hundred women and children to sell as slaves. Situated just beyond the Strait of Gibraltar, it had prominent Genoese residents, most of them *converso,* and was a favorite stopping place for Italian merchant ships. Little wonder that Columbus came initially to that region, and undoubtedly with purpose beyond that of leaving his son, Diego, with Diego's aunt or with the Franciscans of Santa María de la Rábida, just outside Palos. And that monastery, too, had close ties with Atlantic exploration; it had led in sending out missions to the Canaries.

Isabel's trusted *corregidor* in Puerto de Santa María—that astute and outspoken old knight, Diego de Valera, courtier, royal chronicler, advisor, and *converso*—was valued by Medinaceli as well; in 1486, Medinaceli, stating his appreciation for their many services, granted to Diego Valera and his son Charles some houses whose former owners had come afoul of the Inquisition. The Valeras were also well acquainted with Genoese in the area; indeed, Charles de Valera's fourth (and final) wife was a Spinola.[8] During his stay with Medinaceli, Columbus and the Valeras surely met, drawn by mutual interests. And Diego de Valera, who had assured Isabel that he would always keep her informed, would have apprised her of any worthwhile information about Columbus.

The Valeras and Columbus had much to talk about. Columbus had sailed to Guinea from Portugal at a time when many Andalusians, especially those of Puerto de Santa María and Palos, had much contact with the Portuguese, either through cooperating with them or through poaching on their shipments of gold and slaves. Those seamen knew the Canaries—some had sailed there with Charles de Valera—and they knew that from those islands it is possible to find winds favorable to sail westward. The geographer Carl Sauer has suggested the speculation then occurring: "What if . . . one followed downwind from the Canaries? Were the Canaries to remain the end of Spanish venture or to become a starting point for parts unknown and promising? . . . Land, current, and genial skies invited exploration."[9] Abounding too were rumors of ships out of Andalusia blown off course, to Guinea and even to other lands in the Western Ocean. Surviving still is conjecture that an unidentified sailor had reached the Caribbean before 1492 and that Columbus knew of it. If Columbus had heard of any such voyages, it is likely that so had the Valeras, and so had Isabel.

According to Fernando Columbus, his son and biographer, his father had conversed at length with a mysterious one-eyed sailor of Puerto de Santa María. And men of Palos recalled Columbus staying at La Rábida during 1488–89 and frequently coming into town to talk to one Pero Vásquez, or Pedro Velasco, who was skilled in ocean sailing. Forty years earlier, Vásquez had gone exploring as pilot with a certain Diogo de Teive, a former page to Dom Henrique of Portugal. The two had vainly sought the legendary island of Antilla, appearing on some maps to the west of the Canaries and Azores. Antilla was said to have seven cities populated by Visigoths who had escaped the invading Muslims in the eighth century, and to have been rediscovered by a Portuguese ship blown off course. Whatever Columbus knew when he arrived and whatever his purpose in coming to Andalusia, he surely gathered—along with the usual yarns of lost isles and the voyaging of St. Brendan and of St. Ursula and her eleven thousand seagoing virgins—further information on Atlantic navigation from its seagoing residents; and he undoubtedly met the Valeras.

Indeed, coinciding remarkably with Columbus's later cast of mind were the words that in 1485 Diego de Valera had addressed to Fernando on taking Ronda: "It is clear that our Lord intends to carry out what has been prophesied for centuries . . . to wit, that you shall not merely put these Spains under your royal scepter, but that you will also subjugate regions beyond the sea."[10] Coinciding too was the allusion made the following year, by the marqués who held Cádiz and had long sponsored Andalusian seafaring, to the old prophecy that "he who will restore the ark of Zion will come from Spain."[11] Columbus would subsequently say much the same things. In addition, his years in Portugal had surely exposed him to Dom Henrique's goals and to King Afonso's claim to be *El Encubierto,* that same prophesied restorer of Jerusalem; indeed it was in Portugal in 1481 that Columbus first expressed an apocalyptic sense of his own.[12] He would also later speak of a ruler who was destined to subjugate far places and finally Jerusalem; and like some friar-preachers and humanists of Isabel's court, he would equate Christian unity and Jerusalem regained with the coming of a final millennial age.

A Meeting of Minds

By early 1489 Isabel had received from Medinaceli a request to permit him to back Columbus. She denied it. After Columbus's triumphant return from his initial voyage, Medinaceli presented to the cardinal a face-saving account of that interchange, one incidentally reflecting the great esteem in which the queen was then held: "And as I saw that this enterprise was [properly addressed to] the Queen Our Lady, I wrote about it to Her Highness from Rota and she answered that I was to send it to her. I sent it to her then . . . Her Highness received it and passed it on to Alonso de Quintanilla."[13] Isabel had long ago decided all such ventures must be under royal patronage. In responding to Medinaceli, she graciously expressed pleasure in having in her realm a person, himself, of such generous spirit and such inclination to heroic endeavors, but, she told him, such an enterprise was only for monarchs.

Within two months of refusing Medinaceli, Isabel, urged by the cardinal and Diego de Deza, recalled Columbus to court. A letter patent corroborating that summons, drawn in both royal names, survives, given in Córdoba, May 12, 1489:

The King and Queen to the members of the councils, justices, *regidores* (members of town councils), knights, squires, officials, and honest men in all cities and villages of our kingdoms and *señorios:* Christopher Columbus must come to this court and to other places of our realm, to concern himself with some matters to be carried out in our service; whereby we command you that when he should pass through said cities and villages, or stay in them, he be put up and be given good lodgings for himself and those with him, without charge if not at inns; and provided with maintenance at fair prices. And you must not quarrel with him or with those he may bring with him. And you must do nothing to hinder him in any way, under pain of our justice and a fine of ten thousand *maravedís* apiece.[14]

That June, while Fernando was camped before Baza, Isabel received Columbus at Jaén and gave him "certain hope, once the matter of Granada was resolved," which was then expected to occur shortly, once Baza fell. At the time, she conversed with him at length. Columbus was self-avowedly unlettered, but he was also singularly cultured, courteous, and entertaining. His bearing and appearance were to his credit; "He looked like a Roman senator: tall and stately, gray-haired, with dignified face."[15] He was a remarkable combination of mariner and gentleman—adventurer, of the sort her Portuguese grandmother would have recalled her own noble husband retaining; indeed, Columbus's father-in-law, Bartolomé Perestrello, a Genoese who in 1449 became hereditary captain of Porto Santo near Madeira, had been in the household of that grandfather of Isabel's. Perestrello had also had an interest in Atlantic exploration and been somehow associated with Dom Henrique, Henry the Navigator. Columbus had Perestrello's papers.[16] Surely he had both familial and entrepreneurial matters to discuss with the queen.

Isabel had given some thought to encircling and defeating the Muslims and regaining Jerusalem, the same scheme that great-uncle of hers, Dom Henrique, had considered. And now she had before her a seaman of experience and imagination who proposed to carry it out; he might one day prove useful to Spain. Too, his moral universe aligned with hers; indeed, it became no less congruent as time passed and he came to understand hers better. Isabel remained intrigued and all accounts indicate that Columbus was intriguing, in both senses of the word. Moreover, his enterprise offered her a means for Castile to challenge what Dom Henrique had begun and João of Portugal had assiduously taken up, the search for a sea route eastward; and that Bartolomeu Dias had just returned to Portugal, having rounded the Cape of Good Hope and found such a route, lent urgency. Columbus had Portuguese contacts; he had recently written to João, perhaps visited him; he could and surely did expiate on the significance of Dias's voyage to her.

Isabel undoubtedly heard from him something of his own voyages as well—of his claim to have sailed everywhere; of his trading in gold and jewels, spices, sugar, and slaves; of what he had learned in Portugal and Andalusia regarding exploration and discovery, navigation and geography; of his reading of Ptolemy, Marco Polo, John Mandeville, and others considered authorities on cosmography; and of what he had gathered from his father-in-law's papers and from other sailors about the Western Ocean. Isabel we know had copies of her own of Mandeville's *Book of the Marvels of the World and Voyage through Jerusalem, Asia, and Africa*, itself a compendium of earlier compendiums, and their combination of fact and myth.[17] Columbus later attributed to Mandeville his idea of circling the globe, of going west and returning by way of Jerusalem and Rome to Seville. He also frequently cited Mandeville as an authority on such entities as the Antipodes, and the kingdom of the Christian king-priest Prester John in India (more accurate writers put it in Ethiopia), and the existence of the earthly paradise—the Garden of Eden—which Mandeville placed in eastern Asia; there too, as legend, prophecy, and Mandeville had it, Amazons, Gog and Magog, and the twelve lost tribes of Israel survived, hidden until the Last Days.[18] Diego de Valera, too, in the historical summary he wrote at Isabel's behest, had borrowed freely from Mandeville in describing the regions of the world, and also in recounting the popular story of the world-conqueror Alexander the Great, who, Valera said, encountered noble savages on an eastern island then, finding them completely devoid of material desire, had admired them and 50 left them undisturbed.[19] Isabel's own understanding of geography could not have been uninfluenced by such legends or by Mandeville, or by St. John the Evangelist's apocalyptic cosmography, for, although questioned by scholars, they all remained standard authorities; they also substantiated the tall tales still current of her great-uncle Dom Pedro's encounters in his far-flung travels.[20]

Columbus would have learned of Isabel's policies regarding the Canaries, her desire to compete with Portugal in Guinea and beyond, and the components and the moral intensity of her commitment to reconquest, for they were assuredly no secret, either at court or beyond it. Nor could Columbus have been unaware that ascending in Spain and radiating throughout Europe was an appreciation of the Spanish monarchs as religious and military bastions of Christendom. He was at court when the queen had displayed her great interest in Jerusalem, when, in Jaén, Isabel conversed intently with the friars from the Holy Sepulcher, promising them one thousand ducats annually and proposing to work a covering for Christ's tomb with her own hands.

By 1492, Columbus had assuredly encountered another recent Italian arrival at Isabel's court, the humanist Pedro Mártir, who readily admitted himself captivated by the dedication, the moral rectitude, the effectiveness, and the sheer power exuded by *los reyes*. The two compatriots displayed an affinity of outlook regarding Spain's rulers; Mártir would also be the first to chronicle Columbus's exploits, the first historian of what became known as the Spanish Indies.[21]

Expectations

Columbus's writings reflect the far reaches of royal ideology remarkably faithfully; yet they also attest to how both Isabel's world view and his own fit within a system of belief widely held not only in Spain but among Western Christians, so that Columbus shared an overarching, European, religious frame of reference with the queen. They also both drew on a Western Christian store of belief of proven adaptability to royal ideologies and to visionary missions in general. This confluence goes far to explain, to whatever extent it occurred, the meeting of minds between Isabel and Columbus. They would have something else in common as well: both came to believe too literally in their own roles in an all-important divinely assigned task.

In this sense, Isabel surely had some strong but heretofore unnoticed influence on Columbus. He, probably from the outset, astutely evoked what one commentator has aptly termed "the intermingled destinies of himself and their majesties."[22] He also did his utmost to insert himself indispensably within the royal construction of that destiny. Much of the vision he subsequently imparted to Isabel was in apocalyptic and messianic terms quite familiar to her. Columbus drew on potent rhetorical elements long current in Europe and long since specifically adapted to Iberian traditions, and particularly to those associated with the crown-centered Spanish version of universal history. He would later affirm to Isabel and Fernando their right to Africa based upon the Visigothic heritage, then go on to strengthen it through supposing a land bridge had once existed between Iberia and Africa. So too his recollection that in 1492, "I saw the royal banners placed by force of arms on the towers of the Alhambra," and that their highnesses, "having driven out all the Jews," had commanded him to go to India. This deliberate inversion served to align those events in proper sequential order with the well-known circumstances prophesied for the arrival of the Last Days.

Familiar with the royal vision, Columbus would later present his own enterprise in much the same terms. He would not only allude to prophecies of being rid of Jews and freeing the holy places associated with Christ as necessary preliminaries to a final golden age, but also state that his own ultimate goal was to bring light to the holy city and free the rest of the world from pagan darkness. Cognizant of the royal stance of being poised for empire, he inserted his own mission prominently within Isabel's aspirations as he perceived them. But that is to get ahead of the story.

Isabel's Jewels

When, Baza and Almería having capitulated, Boabdil did not surrender Granada as he had promised, hope for immediate victory evaporated and Isabel once again dismissed Columbus from court. Then, in the fall of 1491, just as Granada's surrender was assured, she had word of him. Columbus, back at La Rábida, had encountered a sometime chaplain and *contador* of hers, the Franciscan Juan Pérez, now its guardian. Pérez then wrote to her on Columbus's behalf and she responded within two weeks: Pérez was to come to the encampment at Santa Fe, Columbus to stay at La Rábida and await her good reply. Having sounded out Pérez, she sent back with him a summons to Columbus to come to court, and twenty thousand *maravedís* in florins for suitable clothing and a mule. He arrived at Santa Fe in December 1491, in time for the triumphant royal entry into Granada, which he later wrote of in terms of prefiguring his own enterprise.[23]

Shortly thereafter, Isabel called that conclave of nobles, prelates, and *letrados* to consider the enterprise of Columbus. His project "was discussed by a Council made up of the men most eminent in rank" and opinions were divided. But the wait had been too long; other projects were afoot, and Africa now of most moment. Mendoza and Talavera were no longer enthusiastic; everyone thought Columbus asked too much, and competition with Portugal had receded with João's failing health and young Isabel's marriage to his son and heir. Once again, Isabel dismissed Columbus.[24]

Then the stuff of high drama: Columbus left for Córdoba, with thoughts (he later said) of going to France or even Genoa. He was overtaken outside Granada, at the bridge at Piños, by a royal messenger: he must return to court. The queen had changed her mind. Fernando later claimed he had had a hand in it. Las Casas attributes that recall to Luis de Santángel, the Valencian who "managed the accounts of the royal household." Santángel, together with Pinelo, both *conversos,* had superceded Señor and Melamed in their positions: as treasurers of the *Hermandad,* administrators of tax farming, and general receivers of taxes for the Royal Council. Immediately after Columbus had departed, Santángel (according to Columbus's son, Fernando) had gone to the queen on his behalf. Santángel had chided Isabel for not taking so small a risk for so large a possibility of glory to God and church, and for the glory and aggrandizement of her kingdoms and estates. He had told her that, should some other prince sponsor Columbus, she would be criticized by friends and retainers, and enemies as well, and that she and her successors would regret it. But should she and Fernando back him, whatever the outcome, they would be judged as magnanimous and generous princes for having intended to know the greatness and secrets of the universe, which had brought other kings and lords great praise.[25] He appealed most strongly, that is, to Isabel's desire to appear preeminent among rulers and in royal qualities, particularly in liberality, never her strong point, as well as in one quality traditionally viewed as a sign of God's special favor, the ability to uncover what yet lay hidden of the universe. And, he concluded, the cost was small.

It was an effective argument. She thanked Santángel for his good advice, accepted it with pleasure, but suggested its execution wait until some reparations from the war allowed funding the project; however, if he thought it pressing, the quantity could be had quickly through pawning some jewels of hers. She need not pawn the jewels, Santángel answered, because he would be pleased to perform so small a service as to lend Her Majesty from his own funds the twenty-five hundred ducats necessary to outfit a fleet of three ships. Small it was. In 1491 he had personally advanced the crown over ten million *maravedís.*[26]

Did Isabel indeed offer to pawn her jewels? Probably, for their value as surety for loans was one reason rulers owned jewels, and the sum was little and reimbursement anticipated. Her gesture need not be viewed as a tremendous commitment to Columbus's project, for in any case she was not offering prized possessions so much as customary collateral. Many of her jewels, among them the ruby necklace that was her wedding gift, were already in pawn in Santángel's Valencia, and not for the first time, serving as guarantee for three loans totaling sixty thousand florins borrowed for the protracted campaign against Baza. And four years later, on the eve of her childrens' weddings, she would borrow back her crown of eagles, which had been in pawn in Valencia since 1489 as collateral for thirty-five thousand florins. In her suggestion to Santángel, therefore, she may have been indulging in some of her habitual irony, for the amount was scarcely worth her jewels. The florin was worth roughly two-thirds of a ducat; by comparison to other transactions, the twenty-five hundred ducats for Columbus was a minor outlay. Nor did Santángel actually open his own purse. Rather, he advanced funds from crown monies to which he had access. Threading through the labyrinth that was royal financing, the monies for Columbus appear ultimately to have came from *cruzada* receipts and to have been actually dispensed by order of yet another person skilled in royal finances, the archbishop of Granada, Talavera.[27]

Wherewithal assured, on April 17 Isabel and Fernando signed the *capitulaciones,* the articles of agreement, drawn by the friar Juan Pérez, who represented Columbus, and affirmed by the royal secretary, Juan de Coloma. They did not mention a religious mission or purpose, but dealt with territory and trade. Columbus was to be royal admiral, viceroy, and governor-general over all he might find, with rights to a tenth of any treasure and with permission to trade duty-free. A safe conduct of the same date, though, did mention religion, if rather cryptically, in stating purpose: "We send Cristobal Colon with three caravels through the Ocean Sea to the Indies, on some business that touches the service of God and the expansion of the Catholic Faith and our own benefit and utility."[28] Columbus would sail for Isabel's Castile, which, unlike Aragón, had a well-documented claim on Atlantic exploration, a reminder that Spain was as yet united only in the persons of its sovereigns.

The king and queen initially found those concessions exorbitant. By them Columbus would, if successful, become effective lord of eastern Asia or even of an unknown continent en route. Yet they were agreed to, for Isabel was experienced in modifying such grants, over time and in ways favorable to the crown, as she had shown in acquiring royal control of the Canary Islands. And neither those, nor any other documents known, specifically delineated Columbus's salary and rights.

On April 30, she and Fernando sent out directives ordering ships fitted out, confirmed Columbus's titles and offices, and provided him with a blanket letter of recommendation—meant, according to Bartolomé de Las Casas, for the grand khan and all the kings and lords of India and anywhere else he might discover. That letter stated only that the object of the voyage was islands and mainland in the Ocean Sea—in the Atlantic—although secret documents at the same time referred to Eastern trade and to sailing to the Indies, and to contacting an unnamed Asiatic prince, probably one of those denizens of legend: Prester John, or perhaps the grand khan.

To the Indies

Isabel, to whom vengeance was sweet, in May 1492 wreaked it on her disobedient subjects of Palos, who were so prone to smuggling, ignoring royal duties and monopolies on trade, and fishing in forbidden waters. So, in Palos on May 23, her new admiral had a royal order read out before the church of St. George: "Know you that whereas, for certain things done and committed by you to our disservice you were condemned and obligated by our council to provide us for a year with two equipped caravels at your own charge and expense."[29] The Pinzóns of Palos provided the *Pinta;* from nearby Moguer, whose seamen were accustomed to joint ventures with those of Palos, the Niño family supplied the *Niña.* Columbus chartered his third, largest, and least seaworthy ship, the *Santa María,* from its Vizcayan owner, Juan de la Cosa, who had been sailing out of Puerto de Santa María. The admiral of the Ocean Sea, that is, requisitioned ships, crews, and master mariners from Castilian ports whose men were accustomed to voyaging the Atlantic southwestward, the one thousand miles and more to Guinea and the Canaries. He sailed with ninety men on August 3, 1492. He had, he stated in his journal of that voyage, contracted with the queen and the king to sail a westward route to Asia, ally with its grand khan, open its lands and people to the faith, and find there in King Solomon's mines enough treasure both to regain Jerusalem and enrich Spain.[30]

In March of 1493, Isabel and Fernando, in Barcelona, had word from him: Columbus had discovered the Indies, lost one ship, and left a settlement, La Navidad, on the island of La Española (or Hispaniola), where there was gold and docile people; he had also sighted the mainland of Asia, for so he thought Cuba. On March 30, they sent a congratulatory letter to "Don Cristóbal Colón, our Admiral of the Ocean Sea and Viceroy and Governor of the isles that he has discovered in the Indies." They took, they said, great pleasure in what he had written, "and that God has given you such a good end in the work you undertook, whereof He will be greatly served and ourselves and our realms receive so much benefit."[31] And they requested he hurry to the court at Barcelona, for he must also return within the year to the lands he had discovered.

In response, they received from him suggestions on governing the Indies.

Found three or four towns, he advised, each having an *alcalde* and clergy who would minister to the townspeople and also see to conversion of the Indians, yet his main concern at the outset was regulating gold mining and ensuring that the crown received half of all gold found. He advised too that their majesties regulate all trade between Spain and the Indies.

That letter of highly practical content he signed *Christo-ferens*, Christ-bearing. His sense of election, his high mission, he now felt had been confirmed. On reaching the Caribbean and encountering native Taínos, he concluded they were Indians, people of lands off Asia, unknown to Europeans.[32] Having come upon unknown lands and peoples, he was certain he had been chosen as divine agent. He was to bear the Messiah, Christ, in a double sense. He was to carry Christianity to those people, and he was instrumental in the revelation of hidden things prophesied to precede the Second Coming.

Royal Mission Reflected

In an entry dated December 1492, Columbus further elucidated in his journal:

I hope to God that when I come back here from Castile, which I intend to do, that I will find a barrel of gold, for which these people I am leaving will have traded, and that they will have found the gold mine, and the spices, and in such quantities that within three years the sovereigns will prepare for and undertake the conquest of the Holy Land. I have already petitioned Your Highnesses to see that all the profits of this, my enterprise, should be spent on the conquest of Jerusalem, and Your Highnesses smiled and said that the idea pleased you, and that even without this expedition you had the inclination to do it.

Merlin, he went on, had prophesied great treasure would be revealed in the ends of the earth.[33]

The quest for gold, after all, fit within rationales for exploration traditional to both Columbus and Isabel; it was justifiable as abetting Christian spiritual advance, and it comfortably aligned with the ongoing Spanish goal, articulated centuries ago by El Cid, of "winning our bread," which assumed an earned right to treasure as booty. Certainly Isabel was at home with the many mixed political and religious references made by Columbus and assuredly she was not at all unhappy about his dedication to searching for King Solomon's lost mines.

Columbus returned to Spain in 1493, to a triumphal audience at court, bearing evidence of his discoveries. Whatever their limitations might prove to be, he had launched Isabel's Castile, and all Spain, into empire.

Chapter 17
Isabel and the Indies: 1492–1504

My confidence in God and her Highness, Isabel, enabled me to persevere. . . .
I undertook a new voyage to the new heaven and earth, which land, until
then, remained concealed.
—Columbus, letter to Juana de Torres (1500)[1]

What power of mine has the Admiral to give anyone my vassals?
—Isabel[2]

On or about April 21, 1493, in the great hall of the old palace of
Barcelona's counts, the queen, the king, and Prince Juan greeted Christopher
Columbus, who encountered them seated "in all majesty and grandeur on a
rich throne under a gold-brocaded canopy," with a host of notables in attendance.[3] Pedro Mártir reported it all to Tendilla and Talavera: "Raise your spirits, my two wise old men! Hear about the new discovery! Remember, because
you should, that he has come back from the western antipodes." Columbus
had encountered seven islands, more land than Spain, and brought back
remarkable things: gold, and cotton, cinnamon, pepper, and dyewoods, and
nude people.[4]

Isabel was presented with *hutías* like small grey rabbits, though with the
ears and tail of a rat; chili peppers, burning the tongue, sweet potatoes, and
monkeys, and parrots, and some gold. "Most admired," reported Pedro
Mártir, were the six men wearing gold circles in their ears and nostrils, who
were not white, nor black, nor dark brown, "but the color of cooked quinces."
Those Taínos were called Indians, and subsequently baptized, the king, the
queen, and the prince standing as godparents. One, named Juan de Castilla
after the prince, remained at court as a page, but briefly, "for God soon called
him to Himself."[5]

Bartolomé de Las Casas tells of streets crammed with people along
Columbus's route, of "a solemn and beautiful reception," of the monarchs on
hearing his account sinking to their knees in gratitude to God, of a Te Deum
sung out by the royal chapel choir, and of faces streaked with tears of joy.

Mártir relates how Isabel and Fernando insisted Columbus sit down in their presence, which "is among our kings the greatest sign of benevolence and honor that they concede for great deeds." And they urged him to sail again immediately. It was imperative he explore further and claim for them the land he had assured them must be the mainland of Asia.[6]

The information he brought was too scant to enable assessing the geographical position or economic or religious potential of those lands. Still, as to Spain's admiral having reached India or any part of Asia, Mártir, keenly attuned to royal sentiments, was among the first to express doubt, in a letter of October of 1493: "I do not deny it completely, although the magnitude of the globe appears to indicate the contrary." Yet, a year later, he hedged, in writing that Columbus had found a new archipelago; much as Columbus himself referred to an *otro mundo,* an other world, Mártir spoke of "the new world" and placed it off the Golden Chersonese, the Malay peninsula of Asia.[7] Tellingly, he prefaced that statement with "they say." Certainly, it was the politic opinion most conducive to reaffirm the international reputation of *los reyes* and to establish their territorial claims.

Reactions

Pleased with her admiral, Isabel's deepest reaction to Columbus's success was concern about instituting a Castilian monopoly over the newfound lands in anticipation of a counterclaim by Portugal. Talavera, shortly after Columbus's return, expressed a similar disquiet in writing to her: "O that [the matter] of the Indies may come out certain!" And he added, chiding, "of which Your Highness has not written me one word."[8] "We are now," Isabel replied archly, "[negotiating] with the king of Portugal concerning those islands Colón found, those same ones about which you say I never wrote you."[9] She was coupling that business with arrangements underway for her widowed daughter, Isabel, to marry again in Portugal, with Dom Manoel, the nephew João had designated his heir. Even so, on word from Medina Sidonia that the Portuguese were preparing a fleet to follow Columbus's route, on May 2 she wrote back that he was to have his caravels ready to intercept it should it sail.[10] While she wanted her daughter to marry Portugal's heir, she did not want to share the Indies with her in-laws.

Whatever the reason she did not mention Columbus's discovery to Talavera, it was not because it did not cause excitement at court and among the populace. Most remarkable was the speed with which its details were known, and not only within Spain; the news spread all over Europe through a letter purportedly written by Columbus to Luis de Santángel. In Barcelona, that letter was circulating by the time Columbus arrived there. It was printed in Rome and elsewhere soon after, and by 1497 had gone through seventeen European editions. It emphasized those aspects of his voyage most conducive to Isabel and Fernando securing a papal bull confirming their possession of the new-found lands; the letter spoke of God's gift of the Indies to Castile, their proximity to the Canaries, and how very apt the Indians were to receive the faith. Whether it was written by Columbus or, as some scholars assert, was a fabrication by the royal chancery, it still fits within what is known of Columbus's own outlook, and provides no reason to lessen belief in the affinity of Columbus's interpretation to that of the monarchs concerning the meaning of his landfall.[11]

Cardinal Mendoza himself went with the ambassador, Diego López de Haro, to Rome in May. Sent officially to congratulate Rodrigo Borja on becoming Pope Alexander VI, López de Haro while there lectured the new pontiff before the papal consistory for having promoted war in Italy, corruption and venality in the curia, and the sale of benefices. He was but relaying the opinion of Isabel and Fernando, who, having waged holy war and espoused religious reform at home, felt free to announce their assumed position of moral superiority to that pope. A week later, their resident ambassador in Rome, the cardinal Bernardino de Carvajal (who was Mendoza's nephew), in a speech before the college of cardinals proclaimed that by the will of Christ *los reyes* had subjugated to their dominion the Fortunate Islands—the Canaries—"and now He has given them many others toward India, until now unknown . . . and it is expected they will be converted to Christ in a short time by persons the sovereigns send there."[12] Accordingly, his monarchs requested bulls confirming the Indies to them. They also sought papal permission to apply receipts of bulls of crusade, which had gone to fund the war against Granada, to "the conversion of new found peoples"; and upon receiving the solicited document, their chancery added to it the words "and conquest."

Las Casas reported Alexander VI having received the news as of "a hidden world, full of nations centuries behind, infinite, to be led to the Church in what is, following the parabola of Christ, the eleventh hour."[13] Certainly the pope quickly issued a bull, which went to Spain on May 17 confirming to Isabel and Fernando dominion of the islands Columbus had discovered, as well as any others found by men they had sent out, provided that such lands had never been held by any Christian prince. Two years earlier, João of Portugal had obtained bulls confirming Portugal's right to the African coast and lands south of the Canaries and west of Guinea, and the Portuguese continued to insist that grant included any lands southward and no matter how far west. The pope limited that Portuguese claim in issuing two more bulls; they drew a line of demarcation in the Atlantic from north to south, just nicking the tip of Brazil; everything to the west was to belong to Spain. A fourth bull canceled all previous grants to those areas, which (although it did not say so) were claimed by Portugal. The Portuguese, unhappy, sought direct negotiation with Spain and, at Tordesillas in 1494, with Isabel and Fernando in residence, Gutierre de Cárdenas, Rodrigo Maldonado de Talavera, and a battery of *letrados* thrashed out with their Portuguese counterparts a treaty, indeed several, in accord with the papal bulls but compromising in moving the demarcation line a little further west, thereby allotting to Portugal the bulge of as-yet-undiscovered Brazil.

It was now that Isabel and Fernando sent scouts to Africa; they received as well a bull for African crusade and the sale of indulgences for that enterprise. Although in 1479 Isabel had agreed that Fez was within Portugal's sphere, at Tordesillas that area was left open—thus in effect reopened—to arbitration. The result was that Tremecen, Argel, Bugia, Tunis, and Tripoli were henceforth considered fields for Castilian expansion. In 1494, Isabel and Fernando planned, once the conquest of the Canary island of Tenerife was completed, to occupy the port of Melilla, principally because it was near Tafersit, a west African hub of gold exchange between the coast and the Sahara Desert. With that aim in mind they recognized Portuguese claims to western Barbary in exchange for acknowledgment of their own right to Melilla, which fell to them in 1497. The several treaties of Tordesillas allowed them not only Atlantic and Mediterranean expansion. Their terms attested to a conceptual linking by Castile's monarchs of Africa, the Indies, and Asia. Columbus was indeed a piece in a global project.[14]

The Second Voyage

Isabel and Fernando kept Columbus at court for five or six weeks, while arrangements concerning his second voyage were worked out. Warmth prevailed. They granted him not only *mercedes,* including a coat of arms, ten thousand *maravedís* annually for life, and his titles "for now and for always," to pass on to his children, but also the right to propose officials and name lieutenants in the Indies. Even so, during those same weeks, rapidly, in "document after document, directive after directive, it was the sovereigns who were establishing the fundamentals of colonial government: naming public functionaries, provisioning the fleet, recruiting peasants and laborers . . . ," setting up their own monopoly on the Indies, all culminating in their instructions to Columbus of May 29.[15] The first colony in the Indies, they stipulated there, was to be made up of male employees, mostly laborers, salaried and provisioned by the crown, and overseen by Columbus as their viceroy with the help of a few royal officials. As a return for their expenditure and for the impulse that at God's behest they gave to evangelizing the Indians, they and their successors were to be overlords to any potentate encountered. They were, as Las Casas interpreted it, to be "as sovereign emperors over all the kings and princes and kingdoms of all these Indies, islands and mainland, discovered and to be discovered."[16] It was a traditional way of extending sovereignty over peoples and places.

This second voyage was expected to do three things: strengthen the Spanish claim through a strong presence in the islands, extract gold, and encounter the Asian mainland; and it was a major enterprise, of seventeen ships and twelve hundred men. It was readied speedily, within five months, by a protégé of Talavera's, Juan Rodríguez de Fonseca, archdeacon of Seville and sometime chaplain to the queen. As directed, Fonseca laded a cargo of arms and tools, biscuit, wine, wheat and flour, oil and vinegar, cheeses, rice, chickens, mares, and a few stallions, as well as other necessaries for the journey over and to sustain settlement. Columbus, stopping in the Canaries, took on more hens, and cattle, goats, sheep, and also eight pigs—at seventy *maravedís* apiece, from whence, says Las Casas, had come all the *puercos* then in the Indies, which were infinite.[17] Columbus added also the seeds and pips of oranges, lemons, apples, melons, and everything grown in gardens, their yield also infinite.

As ordered, Fonseca also loaded trading goods belonging to the monarchs; there was to be no private commerce. Most of the recruits were peasants, meant to labor, till the soil, and mine gold. Las Casas says that "if they had known what the work would be I do not believe that one of them would have come." There were too some artisans, some *caballeros* from Seville, twenty mounted troopers from Granada's new *hermandad,* a few men of the royal household, and a physician. There were no women. Among the *caballeros* was one Alonso de Hojeda who, in order to get the attention of the queen during a visit she made to the tower of Seville's cathedral, had climbed out on a ledge and dangled by one leg. Her reaction is not recorded, but Hojeda's audacity was to lead him, in 1499, to brave further dangers to prove that Venezuela was part of a mainland. On Española, Hojeda demonstrated he was ruthless as well; he would be instrumental in annihilating many, if not most, of its indigenous inhabitants.

The monarchs sent with that fleet a royal comptroller, a bailiff of the court, an inspector, and a treasurer, all of them crown officials, their appointment indicating that the greatest royal interest lay in revenues and in establishing royal jurisdiction. And upon departing, all members of Columbus's second expedition took an oath to be loyal and obedient to the king and queen and to the admiral and the justices, and to respect the royal treasury. Disloyalty to the sovereigns in the New World would be very rare; relations to resident royal authorities were another matter.

Two unofficial royal watchdogs went as well: an Aragonese noble and soldier, Pere Margarit, and a Catalan friar, Bernardo Boyl (or Buyl, or Boil, or even Buil), a humanist turned Benedictine monk, who had been Fernando's secretary. Boyl went under both royal and papal auspices. Stated the monarchs: "We send our devoted *padre Fray Buyl,* together with other religious . . . to procure that the Indians may be well informed about our faith and understand our language."[18] The natives were looked upon as ready to be converted, as without law or sect of their own. Columbus, as admiral, viceroy, and governor was to see that they were well treated, given gifts from the royal store of merchandise, and brought to the faith. Boyl had been empowered by the pope to choose missionaries to accompany him. Known to have gone in that fleet was a Hieronymite friar, Ramón Pané, a Catalan, who would write on Taíno life and customs and learn something of one Indian tongue; and, it seems likely, there were also several Mercedarians and three to five Franciscans.[19] But the absence of interpreters guaranteed little proselytizing. While on Española, Boyl destroyed what Spaniards considered idols and, in the new Spanish town of La Isabela, in what was to be called America he dedicated the first church, to the Word Incarnate and the Most Holy Mother Mary (heretofore the customary dedication in Muslim places). Isabel herself provided its ornaments, including a velvet cloth for its chapel, preserved for years almost as a holy relic "for being the first and for the Queen having given it."

Boyl did not stay long. He was soon at odds with Columbus; Las Casas says over the admiral's severity in whipping and hanging Spanish miscrants, but those punished were mostly men under Margarit, and more likely the quarrel signified a power struggle in which Boyl joined a fellow Catalan. The friar placed the admiral under interdict; Columbus retaliated by withholding Boyl's ration of food. In late 1494 Boyl returned to Spain to present his grievances; their majesties listened and considered their viceroy less indispensable.

Isabel had written Columbus a long letter on September 5, 1493, revealing her concern about Portuguese claims and requesting that he always let her know everything about what he had found and what he was doing.[20] She received a response only the following March, by way of Antonio Torres, the captain general of the Indies fleet, who had returned to Cádiz for supplies. Columbus had come upon more islands, which he named Guadalupe, Montserrat, and Antigua; he had returned to Española to find the original settlement, La Navidad, destroyed and he was building La Isabela—public buildings of stone, houses of thatch—in proximity to gold mines he believed located in Cibao. He sent the king and queen twenty-six of what he described as cannibals, "men and women, boys and girls, which your highnesses can order placed in charge of persons from whom they may be able better to learn the language while being employed, gradually ordering that greater care be given them than to other slaves." It would be good for them, he was certain, to speak Spanish, to break old habits, to be baptized, and so "secure the welfare of their souls."[21] Clearly, Columbus had sent those people as a sample. That he did so indicated he was finding little gold and a lot of people—estimated are 800,000 to 1.5 million Taínos at contact on Española—and that he was adjusting his notion of the source of wealth in the Indies. He knew too that within Castilian and canon law, cannibalism was just cause for enslavement. Pedro Mártir wrote of seeing eight of the Caribs sent by Columbus, among them the queen of the cannibals and her son, and he assumed their slavery justified in that Spaniards had reportedly found in Carib huts on Guadalupe human joints ready for cooking.[22] Isabel and Fernando, temporizing, replied to their admiral only that they were not ready to make a decision on slaving.

Although Torres brought them relatively little gold, only thirty thousand ducats worth, and inferior or bogus spices, and along with them an urgent request for additional provisions, still Isabel and Fernando wrote encouragingly to Columbus on April 13, 1494. They sent out his brother Bartolomé and three caravels of provisions, and they welcomed his sons, Diego and Fernando, to court as pages to Prince Juan. That summer they heard that their admiral had come upon Jamaica and had coasted Cuba, but insufficiently to determine it a mainland. Isabel wrote to him again on August 16, beginning with reassuring cordiality: "It seems to us that all that you told us at the beginning you have been able to achieve for the most part, that all has come true as though you could have seen it before you told us about it; we hope in God that all that remains to be known will continue in the same way, for which we will remain very much obliged to give you our favor."[23] There is equivocation in her "for the most part." While clearly curious, what she most desired was more information from him in order to evaluate the situation. She wanted, she told him, to hear more about what he had discovered: what names he had given each place and what he had found in each one, about planting and seasons; he should send birds and all else, "for we wish to see everything." Each month she would dispatch a caravel to Española and one should also leave there monthly for Spain. Let her know what she should send, she wrote him, much as she had once written Fernando in prodding him on. In dealing with everyone there, he should "give them as much contentment" as possible, but not allow them to overstep in anything that they were ordered to do for her; as to problems with Europeans—she had undoubtedly heard they roved the island, looting and raping women—he must do as he thought best.

A month later, royal expectations were lowered considerably by reports from Boyl and Margarit. They stated that the enterprise was a farce: there was no gold, expenses would never be repaid, famine and syphilis were rife at La Isabela; Columbus had jailed their comptroller, and the tribute system he had introduced, based on having chiefs collect a set amount of gold from every Indian, was unworkable, for there were no mines and little gold. (Española, Cuba, and Puerto Rico had only placer mines and gold-bearing quartz veins.) Neither of them mentioned that there was great starvation among the Indians, nor that terrible penalties were inflicted on Taínos who could not produce enough gold to pay the tribute. They reported only that the natives were fighting the gold hunters.

At the end of 1494 Torres returned to Española with an invitation for Columbus from the monarchs to come "advise them on negotiations with Portugal"; he did not accept. Mártir, who so often reflects the royal mood, was still sanguine about the presence of gold, writing around then that large chunks, "*pepitas de oro en bruto*," were to be plucked from streams, but in January of 1495, while still praising the climate and productivity of those lands, he for the first time failed to mention gold at all. And within weeks his emphasis shifted significantly, onto the value of converting many thousands to Christianity.[24] Although royal hope was ebbing for treasure, there was still the wealth of souls to be gained, especially important because it was the basis of the papal confirmation of Castile's claim to dominion over the land and people. The trade in live bodies was another matter, neither publicized nor resolved.

By 1495, Columbus, disappointed in the attempt to obtain enough gold to support the colony, repay the crown, and ensure his own wealth and fame, not to mention fund an expedition to retake Jerusalem, had turned to the slave trade. That February he had fifteen hundred Taínos brought to La Isabela and sent the five hundred he thought best to Fonseca to dispose of for the crown. Columbus declared them legally enslaved since they had warred on the Europeans. By then, two hundred had died at sea, and most of the others would not live long. That April, the monarchs wrote Fonseca that Andalusia seemed the best place to sell those Indians, but four days later they informed him that they wanted a commission of *letrados,* theologians, and canonists to look into if, in good conscience, they could sell them for slaves at all, and certainly that could not be done without having on hand the letters Torres had brought from the admiral detailing the cause of their captivity. Meanwhile, then, Fonseca was to sell them provisionally.[25] That August Pedro Mártir's tone changed markedly: while "Admiral Colón supposes [Española] to be Ophir, Solomon's gold mine," had he found the Indies at all and was Cuba anything more than an island?[26]

Columbus returned to Spain in the spring of 1496. Despite reports from Española of "infinite cattle, especially pigs," and many chickens but little gold and much trouble, on July 12 Isabel and Fernando wrote him a gracious note, if understandably less warm than formerly, extending permission to join them whenever he wished. He came to court that fall, to Burgos. His son, Fernando, there as a page to Prince Juan, later described the scene. His father arrived with more things of the Indies—birds, animals, trees, and plants, masks and belts adorned with gold, and gold dust and nuggets. The monarchs greeted him with affection and due ceremony. They heard a rosy account of the progress of mining and a proposal for a third voyage, requiring eight ships, two with provisions for Española and six to seek a mainland Indians had said was to the south. Yet this time they were in no hurry to accommodate him. His venture was after all proving unprofitable, unspectacular, and relatively unimportant. Nor did it help Columbus's cause when, after they had heard from a pilot-captain, who arrived from Española in October of 1496, that he had brought them three ships full of badly needed gold, they discovered that the gold referred to was the estimated worth of Indians he had shipped to be sold. Isabel, since the commission had not yet decided whether or not such people could be legally enslaved, ordered Fonseca to sell fifty of them who were between twenty and forty years old as rowers for the royal galleys, but to get receipts in case they had to be freed, so that if need be he could ship back to Española the ones still living.[27] Moreover, from January of 1496, a royal decree ordered all vessels arriving from the Indies to make port only in Cádiz and there to turn over whatever gold they carried only to Fonseca.

The Third Voyage

Whatever the monarchs' disillusionment with Columbus and his Indies, Portugal was then sending out Vasco da Gama and this was not the time to relinquish their advantage in the Atlantic. On April 23, 1497, the orders they issued to prepare another voyage clearly sought to rectify what were thought of as previous errors. They granted Columbus the eight ships he had requested and permission to recruit three hundred settlers, but those conscripts were to be salaried and to include sailors, artisans, squires, gold miners, a physician, an apothecary, a herbalist, and peasants who would double as foot-soldiers, and, in addition, thirty women, unsalaried, their status not specified. They may have been the first European women in the Indies, although some might have gone out earlier with Torres. The monarchs advanced funds for food, specifying they be repaid after those people had made money. They set salary scales and prices for provisions, and loaned wheat to farmers to sow, directing that from their crops they must tithe to God; and they decreed that mares, asses, and twenty yokes of oxen be shipped to work the soil. The goal was to establish settlement.

Subsequently, the monarchs authorized Columbus to take another 170 people, unsalaried; and, at his request, criminals were permitted to go "to serve us through our Admiral." They were to work—for two years if serving a death penalty, otherwise for a year—before being pardoned; not eligible, however, were heretics, traitors, murderers, counterfeiters, arsonists, sodomists, or anyone who had exported money from Castile. Each settler was to receive lands with wood and water and to build a house. They were to plant gardens, vineyards, cotton, olive trees, and sugar cane, and they might construct mills and sugar mills. The crown reserved for itself all deposits of gold and silver, and the valuable dyestuff, brazilwood. Financing was found for that expedition with great difficulty, most of it advanced through the Genoese Centurione clan in Seville. Almost as a postscript, on June 15, Columbus was directed to take priests to administer the sacraments and convert Indians.[28]

On this third voyage, of January 1498, Columbus devoted himself to seeking Cathay and its grand khan, knowing that Mandeville described it as the richest province in the world and close to the lands of Prester John. Late that year, he notified the monarchs he had reached the Asian mainland. He had in fact coasted Trinidad, come upon present-day Venezuela, sailed into the Gulf of Paría and discovered the mouth of the Orinoco. He wrote, however, of having encountered "an other world" in the East Indies, south or southeast of the Chinese province of Mangi (so he thought Cuba). He had, he reported, reached the continent where lay the earthly paradise, "because all men say it is at the end of the Orient," and that it lay on a promontory he compared to "the nipple on a woman's breast" atop a pear-shaped land.[29]

His mysticism had become more pronounced with ill health—painful arthritis and sore eyes—and diminishing esteem. That discovery, he explained, was yet another sign that all things were being revealed through him; even so, the malice of Satan was stopping him from finding enough gold to get to Jerusalem. And there was urgency. For that year of 1498 da Gama reached the Malabar coast of India, and the monarchs heard from an envoy in London that for the past seven years Bristol had been sending ships out "following the fantasy of that Genoese Cabot," who sought the fabled isles of the Seven Cities and Brazil, and who in 1497 had reached Newfoundland and Nova Scotia. They were misinformed in that ships of Bristol had explored the Western Sea since 1480. Fonseca, now paying no attention to Columbus's monopoly, quickly licensed Hojeda to explore where the admiral had left off, and furnished him with Columbus's charts. It was Hojeda who named Venezuela, although greater renown would accrue to his shipmate, Amerigo Vespucci.

Isabel had applied to the Indies the model of settlement established by Spaniards and Portuguese in the Canaries and other Atlantic islands. There they had founded fortified enclaves where paid laborers or sharecropper peasants worked under a few merchant proprietors (some of them Genoese), and where urban European social strata were not reproduced. But the first Spaniards in America were either intent on making a fortune quickly and returning home or they had in mind another model, that of Christian settlement in places taken from Granada's Muslims, with themselves as overlords. Columbus himself aspired to both the stature of the new lords of Granada and the merchant princes of the islands.

In 1498, Isabel received from him steady complaints regarding settler pretensions. It was easy to discern that he was not succeeding as either lord or merchant prince. Upon return to Española, he found Europeans in revolt, 160 of them ill with syphilis, and that either God or Satan continued to conceal the gold. He requested more men and ships. He would send to Spain brazil-wood and slaves; and he wanted priests sent, to evangelize the natives and also to reform the Spaniards, and a royal magistrate to dispense justice, "since without royal justice the religious will profit little." The chief justice had been Francisco Roldán, who had become chief rebel, and in trying to appease him, as Isabel learned only later, Columbus had instituted a system of *repartimiento*, literally a parceling out of Indians who must work for those Europeans receiv-ing them, and it was understood that with such human consignments went the benefit of their lands. It was an arrangement not only detrimental to Indi-ans, but reminiscent of the sort of autonomous lordships the queen had so recently abolished in Spain.

When that year Columbus again requested a magistrate, one had already been chosen. Francisco de Bobadilla was sent with the double-edged title of judge investigator and chief magistrate, instructed to look into the entire situa-tion, including the activities of Columbus. Bobadilla, a *comendador* of the mili-tary order of Calatrava, was renowned for bravery in war against the Moors and a former captain of the Alhambra guards.

Indian Policy

A story Las Casas tells rings true: when in May of 1499, the queen heard that three hundred settlers had returned, each with a slave presented by Columbus, she loosed her wrath: "What power of mine has the Admiral to give anyone my vassals?"[30] She had it proclaimed throughout Granada and Seville, where the court was, that all Indians given by Columbus to individuals must be returned home on pain of death; some went back with Bobadilla in June of 1500.[31] Isabel's confessor, Francisco Jiménez de Cisneros, also sent with Bobad-illa four Observant Franciscans and a Benedictine as missionaries; once there, those friars simply baptized Indians en masse.[32] Isabel had concluded that Indians were royal vassals in whom Christianity must be instilled, and, on that count alone, that enslaving them was unjust. Yet in Spain that order of hers was confined to Indians Columbus had presented, and did not affect the oth-ers held there, nor those in the New World.

Once in Española, Bobadilla liberally granted Indians in *repartimiento* to Europeans; and to encourage mining he lowered royal imposts on gold, so that under his jurisdiction placer mining began in earnest and with Indian labor.[33] And, a veteran of infighting within a military order on the Castilian frontier and familiar with the hazards of divided command, Bobadilla had Columbus and his brother siezed and, in October of 1500, he shipped them to Spain for trial, in chains.

Isabel and Fernando, on hearing, sent orders by rapid post to free them, or so says Pedro Mártir; a more recent and perhaps less subjective account, that of Samuel Eliot Morison, says the order came only after the two Genoese had spent six weeks in a Cádiz prison.[34] Whatever the timing, and although Columbus's son, Diego, recalled that the queen then declared that Columbus had done all he had promised, of undoubted weight were requests from the friars on Española that Columbus not come back. He wanted no priests there, they said; he was turning the island over to the Genoese, and he would soon destroy everything, this pharoah-king. Columbus's other son, Fernando, who was with the court in the Alhambra that summer, recalled fifty or more idlers returned from the Indies who "having bought a great quantity of grapes, sat in the patio of the Alhambra spitting seeds and shouting at Their Highnesses and the Admiral that they had made them live that way by paying them badly"; and they taunted him and his brother: "Look at the sons of the Admiral of the Mosquitos, of the one who has discovered lands of nonsense and deceit for the misery and burial of Castile's hidalgos!"[35]

Still, just before Christmas of 1500 the monarchs summoned Columbus and granted him two thousand ducats for a fourth voyage. They wanted him to explore further, and his earlier voyages, although disappointing, had enhanced their standing as singled out to forward heaven's purposes. Thus verses written to Isabel in 1499 by an old retainer, Juan Alvarez Gato, offered a vision of peoples of all lands flocking to bow to her. Then too another poet, Diego Guillén de Avila, felt the time ripe to reiterate the prediction that she and Fernando would conquer Africa and go on to rescue the Holy Sepulcher from the infidel.[36] Yet immediately some more pragmatic action was called for; on Española Isabel replaced Bobadilla with Nicolás de Ovando, a member of the more austere military order of Alcántara, a *caballero*-friar of Cistercian vows—of poverty, chastity, obedience, and fighting infidels—who had proven himself both loyal to the crown and adept at administration within his order, and who had lately been one of the knights making up Prince Juan's entourage.[37]

Ovando and the *letrados* and secretaries he took with him were salaried, where before officials' income had come from a percentage of colony revenues. With him went twenty-five hundred colonists in the thirty ships of his fleet, some for a specified term and some with families and assigned lands; such people were expected to reside in towns and to help extract gold. The monarchs directed Ovando to inform them completely of all his decisions. He arrived at La Isabela in April of 1502, to find only some three hundred Europeans surviving. With Ovando too went the first full contingent of clergy: twelve or thirteen Franciscans and four or five priests, all recruited by Cisneros. At Barcelona in 1493, everyone had been cheered by the Tainos' "multitude and simplicity, gentleness and nudity . . . , by their most apt disposition and ability to be lead to our holy and Catholic faith," as Las Casas put it. "Their royal highnesses, especially the holy queen doña Isabel" felt that with divine favor and with royal expenditure—although, he noted, little outlay was required—a great many infidel nations would be discovered and led to the universal church in a land more extensive than Granada.[38]

The monarchs had evidently pledged to send missionaries to the Indies; the papal bull of May of 1493, confirming to them the Indies, alluded to that promise. Yet it was not until four years later, when it was realized that gold was scarce and Indians the greatest natural resource of the islands, that, in instructions for Columbus's third voyage, the monarchs ordered him to take clergy to minister first and foremost to the Indians. The sending of the friar missionaries with Ovando coincided with *los reyes* receiving from the pope in 1501 the direct use of tithes in newly found lands, but on condition that they not only introduce and maintain Roman Catholicism in them but also see to the instruction and baptism of their inhabitants. Even so, once on Española those friars too attended chiefly to Spaniards, although they also took on a few highborn Indian boys to instruct. Subsequently, other friars did arrive who sought to save indigenous souls by example and instruction—and to find themselves allied with the crown in mounting competition with Europeans for jurisdiction over ever fewer Taínos.

Isabel's Subjects

Earlier experience with Canarian conquest, administration, and religion set precedent for royal handling in America of conquerors, settlers, and indigenous inhabitants. It established precedent for *capitulaciones* with conquistadores, for adaption of *repartimiento,* for regulating slavery, for cultivating sugar cane, and for the blending of mercantile and conquistador mentalities and activities. And much of the precedent thus set was attributable to the queen.

Isabel had earlier opposed Inés de Peraza selling Canarians as slaves, and had had merchants of Palos and Moguer who trafficked in them fined, ordering that those islanders, and Africans as well, be freed and returned to their homelands.[39] The queen's interest, while humane, lay in collecting import duties, prohibiting illicit slaving, and imposing the principle that peoples of newly conquered lands were royal vassals, or, in certain circumstances, royal merchandise. Isabel did not question the legality or morality of the institution of slavery itself, indeed she employed in her court Muslims enslaved at Málaga. The norm endured of slavery as it had existed in Murcia at her birth.

In 1481, she and Fernando had treated some high-ranking baptized Canary Islanders when brought to court more or less as subject potentates. They and their people were privileged to enjoy royal protection, "like the

Christians they are," and were free to travel and trade in Castilian dominions, and not to be enslaved. Yet while the earlier success of Franciscan missionaries and such treatment by the monarchs did gain them adherents in the Canaries and had made Vera's conquest there easier, in effect by dividing the natives, within two years the resistence Vera met was such that he chose to turn to fire, sword, and the profitable business of enslavement. In the Canary Islands, natives were enslaved and provided most labor, supplemented by black Africans. Canarians were also valuable to Madeira's sugar industry, until 1490, when the Portuguese king prohibited their use, asserting that they were royal vassals and thereby building precedent.[40]

From the outset, Isabel did not want the Indians enslaved—instructions of 1493 to Columbus had been to treat them lovingly; yet she did want to make use of Indian labor to mine gold and to maintain the Spanish presence in newly conquered lands. Her solution was to have the natives become Christian and to impose the principle that they were royal subjects, to be treated as such by resident Europeans, who might have access to their labor only with the approval of the crown. Accordingly, she rejected the essentially Aristotelian notion, presented to her early on in the prologue to the *Garden of Noble Maidens,* that "barbarous people are those who live without law; the Latins, those who have law; for it is the law of nations that men who live and are ruled by law shall be lords of those who have no law, because they are by nature the slaves of the wise who are ruled by law." Yet while Isabel viewed the Indians as royal vassals rather than as rightful slaves of the resident Europeans, she did think that "they have neither law nor sect," as instructions for Columbus's second voyage stated. Still, she did think they could become civilized if brought to Spanish ways and faith, which, as she contrued them, were inseparable. Together they were the aim of a civilizing mission that served as justification for Spanish dominion in the Indies, as in accord with the papal confirmation. Through Ovando, Isabel resolved to battle Spaniards in the Caribbean for the labor and revenues of "her vassals." There she lost, for the vassals she claimed were within a decade decimated by ill treatment, overwork, starvation, and the disruption of their societies; disease soon followed. Yet she made her point; the legal principles and the royal authority she then imposed in the Spanish Indies endured for more than three hundred years.

Ovando had been instructed: "We want the Indians well treated as our good subjects." The instruction added that, as vassals, the Indians "should pay tribute to us through their chiefs who will collect from each; and since their work is needed for gold and other labors, they must be made to serve us through work, and be paid a just salary, nor should they live outside of villages." Ovando was responsible for instilling in the Europeans a healthy respect for royal authority. He was to "make anyone who treats them [the natives] badly understand that you will punish them in such a way that from then on no one will dare to do them harm." The Franciscans whom Cisneros sent with him were counted on to underscore that point of view.[41]

In March of 1503 Ovando received additional instructions: "we are informed that, for what complies to the salvation of the souls of the Indians, they must live in villages, each in a house with a wife, family, and possessions, as do the people of our kingdoms, and dress and behave like reasonable beings." In those villages, there must be a church and a chaplain charged with teaching them the Catholic faith as well as "a person who in the royal name is in charge of the place as though he holds it as an *encomienda*. And it would be well if the Indians mined gold for us, retaining a certain part for themselves. . . ."[42]

By 1505, Ovando had introduced the system of *encomienda*, which entailed the commending of the services of Indian communities to individual Europeans. In Castile *encomienda* had been a concession, commonly made in places taken from Muslims to members of military orders, of extensive lands and their castles and peoples, who nonetheless remained in principle royal vassals; the *encomendero* was obliged to serve the crown militarily, yet he was also given legal authority and exempted from the jurisdiction of regional authorities and thus highly autonomous, in effect a petty king. In the castle-less Indies, where Isabel wanted no lords, *encomienda* quickly became a seignorial system having more to do with holding people and enjoying their labor and tribute rather than holding plentiful land, and it largely replaced *repartimiento* and slavery. Under Ovando, royal government was effectively imposed. The Europeans' access to Indian labor was mediated by the royal government. Spain's was not a policy of genocide; yet the population would continue to decline. Soon, extended to the mainland, *encomienda* would become the initial central institution maintaining Spanish domination of indigenous peoples in America.

In October of 1503, Isabel did sanction certain types of slavery in a decree affirming that cannibals might be justly warred against and enslaved "as punishment for crimes committed against my subjects." For, she said, since the Indians should become Christians and live like reasonable men, she had ordered some captains to accompany clergy who were to preach and indoctrinate the natives in the faith and in what was required of those in her service. Only the cannibals had resisted. They had also killed some Christians and warred on Indians in her service and eaten them, so they might be punished for both crimes against her better-behaved subjects. Moreover, she said, although enjoined repeatedly to convert and live peacefully, they remained obdurate in their idolatry and "in continuing to eat the said Indians." While Isabel did not accept the hypothesis, put forth by Bernáldez among others, that the Indians were, like the Muslims and Jews, subjects and instruments of the devil, neither did she entirely preclude its applicability to those who practiced

idolatry. She decreed that anyone under her orders might try to bring the cannibals to her service and the faith; if failing, they could capture them and take
them to other places and sell them, "paying the portion that belongs to us."
For in serving Christians they might more easily be converted to Christianity
and its ways.[43] Cannibalism and idolatry, was the inference, could be construed
as of a piece, one or both opening a door to legally enslaving their prac-
titioners. Some cannibals there were; but the number revealed to the Spanish
approached the miraculous.

That December she further conceded that the Indians of Española might
serve the Christians—for the natives must work, but they were to be paid for
day labor, because they were free people.[44] That is, she now sanctioned another
form of *repartimiento* having to do with conceding to resident Europeans the
forced labor of the Indians, but this version, unlike the first, upheld the principle that those natives were royal vassals. Ovando's instructions had also raised
the possibility of employing blacks as slaves, and some were sent from Spain,
until he reported that they could not be stopped from escaping and joining
Indians and asked that no more come. The trade stopped, then began again
after Isabel's death. (Those instructions of 1503 also set policy regarding mixed
marriages; they were permitted only of Spaniards with indigenous noblewomen, daughters of *caciques*.)

The codicil to Isabel's last will of 1504 indicates a lasting uneasiness with
Indian policy. A clause of that codicil that stipulated that "if the Indians have
received some offense, it must be remedied and resolved" was very much after
the fact. Those instructions of hers came too late, because, by then, contact
with her Spanish subjects had decimated the inhabitants of the New World.[45]

The Last Voyage

In 1500, the Portuguese Pedro Alvarez Cabral, en route to India, bumped into
Brazil while on a *volta*, the wide arc required to sail southward with the winds
in navigating the West African coast. Within the year, the Spanish monarchs
acceded to Columbus's request to make yet a fourth voyage of exploration and
in September of 1501 they decreed that with him should go a gold founder and
marker, a treasurer, a ranking royal official, and a commercial agent (who was
one Francisco de Monroy, of the Extremaduran clan from whence would soon
come another adventurer, Hernán Cortés). Columbus sailed in May of 1502
with four ships and with specific instructions to stay away from Española.

He coasted Central America, seeking a strait across what he wrote of as
the Malay peninsula, and he obsessively sought gold. He wrote to the pope
embellishing his finds—Cuba was still to him the Asian mainland—and recall-

ing his promise to the monarchs to provide enough wherewithal for an army to reconquer Jerusalem; he reiterated that he would have done it before had he not been prevented by the malice of Satan. He also wrote to Isabel and Fernando in the same vein; "the hands of the Christians are destined to rebuild Jerusalem and Mount Zion, as God has declared by the mouth of his prophet [Isaiah]," he told them; moreover, "he who should do this was to come from Spain" and Saint Jerome had shown the Holy Woman the way to accomplish it.[46] In that letter, and in similar statements he addressed to the king and queen in his *Book of Prophecies,* he was still evoking what he believed were views they all shared. He made flattering allusions to Fernando and Isabel as the Lion King and the earthly emanation of the Holy Woman, and he put his own activities in a light of highest importance: "I was aided not by intelligence, by mathematics or by maps. It was simply the fulfillment of what Isaiah had prophesied."[47]

Columbus was shipwrecked for nearly a year on Jamaica. By then, his monopoly on exploration like his position in Española had evaporated. The monarchs licensed other venturers: Isabel, although ill, sent off one of her handwritten hortatory notes to the *conquistador* Pedro Arías de Avila (known as Pedrárias Dávila).[48] Vicente Yáñez Pinzón reached Brazil. In 1503, Isabel also instituted the Casa de Contratación, the Board of Trade, in Seville, under the direction of Fonseca.[49] On behalf of the crown the Casa oversaw every aspect of the enterprise of the Indies: all commerce, justice, technology, and cartography. The government and trade of the Indies were to remain a royal Castilian monopoly. Isabel also insisted that the property Bobadilla had taken from Columbus be returned, but not his titles or authority. On November 7, 1504, he returned to Spain from his final voyage, bitter and worn out. At the last, Columbus addressed the queen as his principal supporter and his inspiration, yet he was not to see her again. She died less than three weeks later.

For the Indies as elsewhere, Isabel sought a symbiotic balance between God's work and royal benefit. Following the news of Columbus's landfall, Mártir had observed that "the thoughts [of the king and queen], even when they sleep, are only about the augment of our religion." Nor did he have to add that they now had basis for absolute correlation between the extension of the faith and the extension of Spain overseas, possibly to world empire.[50] Isabel sought to gain souls in the Indies, and also sovereignty, monopoly, revenues, and firm royal control over both Spanish and indigenous subjects, which entailed royal jurisdiction prevailing over both, and, lacking gold, required profiting from indigenous labor. Royal benefit also involved parceling out the business of consolidating conquest among delegated administrators, financial experts, and justices, as well as supporting those clergy who carried on the missionary work equated with the civilizing process. The civilization sought was European and Spanish, and required communities organized as social and political hierarchies, at their heads the monarch. The concept of civilization settled on America was Isabelline. It was not to go unchallenged.

Isabel died well before Magellan's expedition, in circumnavigating the globe, proved the West Indies were not the East Indies, and America not Asia. Even so, it had become obvious to her that the Indies had not the proverbial wealth of Asia, and so she treated them as a waystation to the East, as she did the Canaries in relation to Africa. Yet to the last it was politic to speak of the Indies as part of eastern Asia. And, whether or not a new continent had been discovered, it was a new world to Europeans. An implication of the term "new world," as employed by Columbus, Las Casas, and Pedro Mártir, was that its inhabitants, uncivilized though they were said to be, like other *salvajes* had something to teach Europeans about morality. Columbus spoke of coming upon a happy world of people who lived simply and innocently without being forced to by laws, and without quarrels, judges, and libels, "content only to satisfy nature." That interpretation reflected those golden age conditions, once obtaining in Eden, that were to be found in noble savages and to return everywhere in the Last Days. That belief, implying contrast to a corrupt Europe, was consonant with Isabel's deep sense of the need to reform Spain itself. The moral virtue she sought personally and for her subjects, and which those observers ascribed to the Indians of the New World, she strove to impose at home through starting with the clergy, those supposed exemplars and disseminators of the will of God, and that of the monarchs, among the Spanish populace.

Chapter 18

The Catholic Kings: 1492–1499

And now, who cannot see that, although the title of Empire is in Germany, its reality lies in the power of the Spanish monarchs who, masters of a large part of Italy and the isles of the Mediterranean Sea, carry the war to Africa and send out their fleet, following the course of the stars, to the isles of the Indies and the New World, linking the Orient to the western boundary of Spain and Africa.
—Antonio de Nebrija[1]

The Pope, our Lord, for the great merits of Your Highnesses in the Catholic faith and Christian religion, has deliberated jointly with the holy college to entitle Your Highnesses with the title of Católicos, *as your progenitor is Alfonso [I] el Católico, and most meritoriously he has done it, and I know the French are very pained.*
—Bernardino de Carvajal[2]

On October of 1492 Isabel and Fernando had entered Barcelona in state. There Isabel saw her son received as heir apparent by the often truculent Catalans. There too, on December 7, Fernando presided over a regular Friday dispensing of public justice. Then afterward, as he descended a staircase, he was savagely attacked. He was felled by a knife thrust in the back of the neck. Only the heavy gold chain he wore, in deflecting the blade, prevented the amputation of the royal head.

So wrote Pedro Mártir to Talavera and Tendilla the next day, and Mártir continued to keep them informed. The king's life was despaired of. The assailant, a Catalan peasant, one Joan de Canyamás, was taken alive and readily confessed: he had been told by a demon to kill the king so that he himself might claim the kingdom that was rightfully his. Upon hearing of the assault, the queen "flew in search of her husband," but fearing a plot, she first commanded that war galleys be rowed to the embankment before the royal residence in order to protect Prince Juan, who was heir to Aragón should his father die. "An entire battalion of doctors and surgeons has been called," said Mártir; "we lurch between fear and hope."[3] Nine days later, Mártir wrote again to Talavera. While the king seemed out of danger, his tongue was terribly swollen and his cheeks burned with fever; still, he was taking food from the queen's own hands. On December 23 Mártir reported that Fernando was still housebound, and that people were undertaking pilgrimages to pray for his life, "through mountains, valleys, coasts and wherever there is a sanctuary. The entire royal family has gone on foot to [the shrine of Our Lady of] Montserrat."[4]

On December 13 Isabel had her secretary, Alvarez, inform her deputy in Castile that she had ordered an investigation by members of the Royal Council and the dignitaries of Barcelona, and that they had learned from the prisoner himself, through torture and otherwise, and through reputable witnesses, that he was subject to fits of temporary and violent insanity. He had further confessed that a diabolic spirit had moved him. It was decided that he must do penance in all his erring members. On December 12, upon a high platform visible to everyone, punishment was meted out: the right hand that had wielded the knife was removed, as were the feet by which he had come to do it, the eyes by which he saw the way, and the heart that had prompted him. Pincers tore the flesh from all his body and then it was turned over to the people to be stoned and burned, for everyone wished to have vengeance on it. "And so that traitor met the end he merited." In truth it was a marvel, Mártir commented, that the prisoner had not been torn to pieces on coming out of the jail. The king was much better and sitting up in bed; the queen was reading him letters and keeping him informed of affairs. Another account stated that she had ordered the assailant garroted before execution. Whether or no, a public display of retributive justice was the object. Isabel's secretary's explanation for it all was that "it is believed that the Devil had sought through the hand of that man to do that on the person of the king, Our Lord, to see if in that way he could stop all the good that His Highness has continually done."[5]

Isabel wrote to Talavera personally on December 30, ruefully and revealingly beginning "For since we see that kings can die of some disaster like other people, there is reason to prepare to die well."[6] While she had thought of death often before, "greatness and prosperity has made me think of it and fear it more." Still, there was a vast difference, she continued, between thinking of death and coming face to face with it. She hoped never to die in such a way, and especially not with her debts unpaid. And so the purpose of that letter: she wanted from Talavera a list of her debts. Isabel wanted to know, that is, her literal debts, the sums she owed on loans received as *servicios,* how much on wartime indemnities, how much on old *juros* incurred when she was princess, "and all the things that seem to you must be repaid and satisfied in some way. . . . It will be the greatest relief in the world to have it." Tantalizingly, she mentioned that she had incurred other sorts of debts, but she did not say what they were. Sensibly, she appealed to the man who had been both her confessor and chief accountant, who could tally obligations both financial and otherwise.

Yet nowhere does her no-nonsense literal-mindedness come clearer; to her, debts were primarily monetary. And ever certain of the omnipresence of divine purpose, she had, as usual, extracted from near catastrophe some practical lessons.

Unburdening herself to her old confessor and counselor, she spoke of her own anguish, Fernando's dire condition and great popularity, and God's activity: "the wound was so great, according to the physician of Guadalupe, that I had not the heart to see it, so large and so deep, of a depth of four fingers, of such size that my heart trembles in saying it. . . . But God made it with such compassion that it seems he directed it so as not to prove fatal." God had then sent a life-threatening fever, like an infernal night. "But believe, Father, that never was such [popular concern] seen before anywhere." Everyone spontaneously prayed or went on pilgrimage for the king's recovery. Now Fernando was up and about. "The pleasure of seeing him get up was as great as had been the sadness. We are all restored. I do not know why God shows to us this great mercy and not to others of much virtue. . . . What shall I do, who have none? And this is one of the sorrows I felt: to see the King suffer what I deserved, not meriting it, but paying for me"; it was this that "killed me most of all." She has prayed to God, she said, that she will serve him henceforth as she ought. Had she a guilty secret? Or was this the sort of expression of pious humility the situation seemed to require? Or was it, as has been said, that in Catholic cultures suffering tends to be seen as a sign of God's attention and love?[7] If so, then about her greater deserving of suffering may there have hovered not only love but competition.

She ended the letter on a note of relief; she has been reassured that the assailant was out of his mind and acted alone. At the end he had seemed to awaken from a dream, and she had insisted that a confessor be called when everyone else wanted him to lose both body and soul. There was a postscript: her secretary had found a list of her debts after all; perhaps Talavera had some additions. She hoped that she had not tired him but felt compelled to write at length and that he would suffer her daring to do so. She showed him affection and great deference, addressing him as *reverendo y devoto padre mi confesor;* and yet, as a subsequent exchange between them indicates, within the changes of the 1490s, certain actions of hers that she justified as promptings of her conscience, on which she relied so heavily, were diverging from his views.

On January 19, 1493, the monarchs signed a treaty with France returning the long-contested provinces of Rosellón and Cerdaña to Aragón, but at a price. Fernando and Isabel then agreed that the French king, Charles VIII, might traverse Italy to fight Ferrante, king of Naples, in order to determine whose claim to Naples was better; they agreed, that is, to a trial by combat, a medieval arrangement that, as it turned out, was to bring Spain's army into modern times. Isabel, in writing to Talavera, mentioned that the attendant festivities held for the French ambassadors had wearied her. Talavera's reply began opaquely; he enjoined her to strive for her own moral perfection, reminding her that what God wills must be constantly guarded in return for His gifts. Then he became more specific: "since your very excellent prudence will not be content with this generality," he would say what she might not want to hear and what he had become tired of saying, that while he was not censuring such festivities, nonetheless certain things required prudence: among them, having the French dining with her at table, her lavish bestowals of gifts and *mercedes,* her taking pleasure in showy military exercises, and her profligate spending on new clothing; and "what I see most offending to God . . . was the dancing, especially of one who ought not dance." Isabel, he knew, loved to dance. Irony unsheathed, he wielded it unstintingly: he marveled that she could dance without sinning and he lamented the mingling of French knights and Castilian ladies at supper, reminding her (as she herself had once reminded her half-brother) how far the French departed from Castilian decorum and gravity. It was to provide a bad example to her country; how much his queen and sovereign lady had lost through it! He cited biblical queens who had behaved far better in similar circumstances. He alluded to her daughter's widowhood of two years as though it had just occurred. "And what can I say of the bulls, that without dispute are a condemned spectacle?" Conscious of how important to Isabel was her own prestige, he warned her that international embarrassment would follow upon such cruelty and crudity as a bullfight entailed. And then he delivered the *golpe de gracia,* worthy of a master matador: "Pardon all, Lord; do not inflict the merited punishment. Amen. Amen." His parting stiletto thrust indicated her sense of duty and purpose had gone seriously astray. She would do better, the archbishop of Granada told the queen, to turn her attention to commemorating the battle of Salado, where her ancestor Alfonso XI had triumphed over the last Muslim invaders from Africa. He did not mention that during recent feast-days he had praised her profusely, as another Deborah and another Judith.[8] It may have been just as well, for at court now the preferred analogy was to Diana or Athena.

Her response, coming only at the end of 1493 and quietly self-exonerating, indicated a distancing from his way of thinking. In entertaining the French, she explained, she had not danced nor had she worn new clothes, only a silk dress with some gold trim, the simplest possible. Men and women had dined together; it was a French and Burgundian custom. She too was opposed to bullfights. She then closed the discussion in royal fashion by changing the subject, in both alluding to their old intimacy and affirming she was engrossed in more pressing matters than dress and dancing. Isabel wrote that she had been in bed all day. She was not sick. Rather, she had had too much work to do to take the time to get up. Certainly the tenor of her response and the months she had allowed to elapse before giving it suggest that she now found him out of touch with her court and with a changing world, and that his influence upon her was diminishing.

Francisco Jiménez de Cisneros

Isabel had a new confessor. Mártir wrote to a friend of her satisfaction with him: "The Queen, because she fears and respects God, appears to have encountered what she has so ardently desired, the man to whom she can disclose with tranquility her innermost secrets . . . and this is the cause of her extraordinary content. They say he is called Francisco Jiménez."[9] In the spring of 1492, when she was about to leave Talavera in Granada as its archbishop, she had, recounted a chronicler, sought a person of honest and holy life as a confessor, and God had provided him. Once again, heaven's instrument was Cardinal Mendoza, who had known just the man, Francisco Jiménez de Cisneros, once his vicar in the diocese of Sigüenza and since become a Franciscan of strict observance and contemplative life.

Cisneros, born in 1436, his father a receiver of tithes for the crown and undoubtedly a *converso,* had early displayed several sorts of strength. He had stood up to Carrillo, showing himself equally contentious in an argument over a benefice; he had ridden into Sigüenza with Mendoza, who had had to take up his appointment there by force of arms. Cisneros had then proved a brilliant administrator of that diocese. Then in 1484, rather suddenly, he retired into a remote monastery and took up the most austere Franciscan regimen. "Fearing the inconstancy of the world," as Mártir explained the decision, "and the snares of the Devil, he abandoned everything in order not to become caught up in pernicious gratifications and delights."[10] Cisneros, was the suggestion, was bent on mastering temptations that strongly attracted him. Mártir described the Franciscan as pale and emaciated, like the desert saints, displaying the acuity of Saint Augustine, the abstinence of Jerome, and the severity of Ambrose. Certainly, Cisneros had acquired a reputation for holiness. He reputedly wore a hairshirt under his robe, scourged himself frequently, experienced ecstacies, spoke with heavenly beings, and could be spiritually carried away in contemplation of the divine mysteries. Isabel, eager to sound out this paragon of everything, interviewed him on some pretext and, a few days later, invited him to become her confessor. He accepted, on condition he continue to reside in his cell except when summoned by her. She soon found him indispensable.

Taken together, Isabel's reaction to the attempt on Fernando, her letters to Talavera, her reliance on Cisneros, and the policies of the years following the war indicate that now imposed on her consciousness was a sense of finite time and of much still to be done. Moreover, after the attempt on Fernando, a wariness in the face of general well-being never left her. Ever after, she was protectively watchful of family and faith, nor did she cease preparing to die well. There is a thought-provoking mention in a letter of Mártir's at the end of 1494. He recalls the comment of a former student of his, that no one was content at court, that "even the Queen herself, whom the entire world in part respects, in part fears and admires, when permitted free access to her, you find her to have become closed off in sadness."[11] Mártir's own response was that the only true happiness lay in good use of intelligence. Implicit in it was a disapproval of nonrational pursuits and the implication that her new confessor, much more singlemindedly than her old, was given to them.

Indications are that her sadness may have stemmed from a new quest, for spiritual closeness to God, a closeness she had heretofore simply assumed natural to a queen who behaved and felt as she ought. Just when, that is, she had succeeded in an enterprise expected to achieve entry to God's good graces, he had seemed to recede, to become less knowable than ever. Marineo Sículo reported that in the 1490s Isabel heard mass daily and prayed the canonical hours like a nun. Certainly, at a time when within religious thinking and observance greater attention was being paid to Jesus Christ, to his death and resurrection and the promise of the Second Coming, and when his life and sufferings were being widely construed by lay people as individually exemplary, Isabel herself showed an awakened interest in meditating on Christ's life and cross as a way to approach God. She was undoubtedly swayed by Cisneros, himself devoted to contemplation and belonging to a branch of the Franciscans holding as models for emulation the life of Christ and his apostles. Printing played its part in this trend. In writing to Talavera in 1493 Isabel mentioned her impatience to see printed the *Vita Christi,* the *Life of Christ,* written by the Carthusian Ludolf of Saxony, and then being translated into Spanish by a friar of San Juan de los Reyes; and she referred to it as a book of secret consolation. She herself commissioned Pedro Jiménez de Prejano, who was bishop of Coria, an inquisitor, and a protégé of Talavera's, to write an inspirational manual especially for young nobles at court. He called it *Lucero de la vida cristiana,* the *Guiding Star of Christian Life,* and its dedication to *los reyes* combined an assumption of royal holiness with a heightened spirituality. To "Your Sacred Majesties" he said, "It is not you who speak, but the Holy Spirit who speaks through you."[12]

Still, there were other, more mundane reasons for Isabel's sadness. She was losing her old stalwarts one after another. Gómez Manrique and Rodrigo de Ulloa had recently died. The cardinal, mortally ill, had retired to Guadalajara. Her son's health was worrying. Her daughters must soon marry and so depart. Although she had striven so hard to unite her realms in peace and godliness, everything was becoming more divisively complex, including Spanish society, and in her eyes more immoral. Her plans were often disrupted now. The contest with the French in Italy and Fernando's rising involvement in Aragón meant that, although *los reyes* were more powerful than ever, she could no longer singlemindedly act in accord with her own priorities. Too, she was approaching the age at which her father, the longest lived of the Trastámaras, had died. Perhaps the sadness observed by Mártir stemmed from all of those things: from getting older, from a new spiritual insecurity based on a revised view of God's will just when she had thought to have fulfilled much of her religious obligation, from a sensation of a world growing in complexity and ever more difficult to control, from the disappearance or inefficacy of many old and more simple ways, and from the sidetracking of the all-important mission symbolized by Jerusalem.

Jerusalem Recedes

For the first time since the early days of their marriage, she and Fernando were seldom apart. They spent all of 1493 in Barcelona, and there greeted Columbus on return from his initial voyage. Until then Fernando, long embroiled in Castilian affairs and the war with Granada, had given but cursory attention to Aragón. Since succeeding to its crown in 1479, he had but reaffirmed the limited monarchy traditional there and governed through viceroys. Still, he had shown himself adept at resolving some of its long-standing problems. In Barcelona, he had gained respect through promoting commerce and mediating among powerful rival cliques; and in 1486 he had, by the Sentencia de Guadalupe, freed those Aragonese peasants who had been, much like serfs, tied to the land, and he had made them proprietors in all but name. Now he brought Aragón's old Royal Council within the larger system of Spanish advisory councils, signaling the monarchs' decision to rule over their realms as separate entities confederated only under a common composite sovereign, *los reyes.* That arrangement was proving eminently suitable too for expansion into dynastic empire, allowing, in Aragón, in America, and anywhere else imaginable, the leaving in place of a facade of existing institutions, legal, political, and social, the crown maintaining old hierarchies of authority and taking control at the top of each and every one of them and so gathering all those disparate entities into a de facto empire.

That system, dependent on all power converging in *los reyes,* could not tolerate any threat posed by former heads of once independent states. Thus when, upon hearing of the attempt on Fernando, Boabdil had sent from his dominion in the Alpujarras an emissary with his good wishes, Gutierre de Cárdenas took advantage of the opportunity presented. He paid the envoy well to agree to his lord being recompensed for his Spanish holdings and transported to Africa. Although Boabdil was furious when he heard and informed their majesties such were not his wishes, they nonetheless had Tendilla send three ships to Almería and, in May of 1493, Granada's last Muslim ruler "passed over into Africa where he lived miserably and was deprived of the sight of his eyes," and where, soon after, that tragic figure died.[13] "Of the going of the Moor king," Isabel wrote to Talavera, "we have had much pleasure; and of the going of the *infántico,* his son, much pain."[14] When Boabdil had been freed after his capture at Lucena, he had given the child as a hostage and Isabel had become attached to him. She had, however, greater success with Boabdil's younger and more compliant half-brothers. A contemporary described them as tall and courtly, good Christians who had been baptized as "don Fernando and don Juan." Isabel treated them like *infantes;* she married Fernando to a grand-daughter of the duke of Infantado and Juan to a daughter of the count of Castro. Their mother, Zoroya, whom she had convinced to return to Christianity, was, on baptism, herself named Isabel.

*   *   *

Returning to Castile, Isabel and Fernando spent 1494 on the *meseta,* in Valladolid, Medina del Campo, Segovia, and Madrid. And it was in Tordesillas that May and June—and resulting from a combination of Columbus's success, the campaign for the Canaries, Portuguese rivalry, and a Valencian pope—that a satisfactory agreement was reached with Portugal on spheres of influence and power in global areas long of great concern to Isabel and with ramifications beyond dividing up what would be America. Soon after, the conquest of the Canary Islands was completed.

Having overcome fierce resistance, Alfonso Fernández de Lugo had at last subjugated Gran Canaría and La Palma, and led expeditions to Tenerife; all were private enterprises contracted with the monarchs; one was backed by some Genoese, another by the duke of Medina Sidonia. Tenerife offered the most resistance. Lugo, who needed war to acquire booty and to enslave its inhabitants legally, purposely stirred them up to armed resistance, then formed a mercantile company and sold those captured as slaves. When in 1498 the monarchs sent an official to retrieve those enslaved guanches from their masters and resettle them on their own lands, for many of those islanders as for their American counterparts it was too late. All of the Canary Islands were occupied by 1496; and in 1495 and 1496, Diego Cabrera headed a royal expedition from Gran Canaría to the opposite coast of Africa, where he got Saharians transporting gold to that region to agree to a protectorate by Castile, and he brought back great quantities of gold. It was also arranged that a watchtower be built, as the monarchs wished, on the African coast at Santa Cruz del Mar Pequeña, as an outpost and a point of contact between Africa and Castile. In 1494 bulls of crusade were printed and sold throughout Spain for carrying the war against the Moor to Africa; those indulgences were expected to raise funds, advertise holy war as advancing overseas, and help to keep alive among the populace the crusading spirit of the Granada wars.

Yet Africa soon had to wait. That same year Charles VIII, invading Italy, informed the pope and the world that not only was Naples his by right, but that it was a necessary base for a crusade against the Turks and that he himself was the emperor destined to conquer Jerusalem. Relying on French prophetic tradition, this brash young king represented himself as a second Charlemagne prophesied to rescue Christ's tomb. Charles VIII, that is, entered the competition for the role of awaited warrior king of the Last Days. Nor did international rivalry stop with prophecy. When Ferrante of Naples, who was married to Fernando's sister, Juana, died and was succeeded by a bastard son, Alfonso, both Charles and Fernando claimed a superior right to that kingdom, Fernando through his paternal uncle, its king Alfonso V, known as the Magnanimous.

Isabel and Fernando had sent emissaries to Rome in 1493 not only to secure bulls confirming to Spain the lands Columbus found, but also to form an alliance with Alexander VI against French pretensions in Italy. To assure the Borja pope's goodwill, they catered to his desire for Spanish estates for his children—they then permitted his son, Juan, duke of Gandia, to wed María Enríquez, Fernando's niece. Isabel soon had cause to complain of the duke's behavior. For once in Spain, Gandia, chafing under the moral sobriety of the Spanish court and finding his wife a model of the discretion he hated, quickly gained a reputation as a gambler and a womanizer, and a coward as well. The queen spoke her mind to the papal nuncio. Gandia returned to Rome, and there one night in 1497 he was murdered, rumor had it on order of his brother Caesare, the cardinal of Valencia. The aphorism that God works in strange ways was in this case particularly apt, for "this bad example," as Isabel referred to him, and María Enríquez were the grandparents of Francisco de Borja, knight and saint, and renowned general of the Company of Jesus—the Jesuits.

As to Alexander VI, although he called Charles VIII in against young Alfonso, Ferrante's heir in Naples, he changed his mind when the French entered Rome, then changed it yet again after Charles threatened to reveal papal dealings with the Turks and to back a council on church reform. In this situation, Fernando and Isabel drew closer to Portugal and England, and they formed a Holy League—holy since, despite the questionable behavior of the pope, designed to defend the papacy. It was composed of Spain, Venice, Milan, Maximilian, and at length the nimble Alexander VI. The league's diplomats having reached every major Italian city-state, the French king feared for his line of communications and left for home with half his army, perhaps nine thousand men, sacking Rome on the way.

Consequently, war against France was proclaimed throughout Spain. Fernando and Isabel dispatched to Italy an expeditionary force of veterans of the Granada wars commanded by Gonzalo Fernández de Córdoba, an Aguilar second son who had distinguished himself in the Granada wars. It was an inspired appointment. At the beginning, Fernández de Córdoba lost several battles to the French, but he soon realized that his skilled allies, the Italian *condottieri,* had much to teach him. Within the year he was relying upon light infantry with great firepower and mobility and demonstrating a genius for strategy, timing, and leading men; Naples was all but his and he was celebrated internationally as *El Gran Capitán,* the Great Captain. "From that campaign," runs the verdict of posterity, "came the Spanish army that would dictate to Europe until the seventeenth century."[15] More immediately, Spain became a power in Italy; the Spanish defeated a French fleet at sea, regaining from it the treasures of Naples accreted by that renowned patron of the arts, Alfonso the Magnanimous; and European relations became uppermost in Spanish policy.

The monarchs planned a standing army; at home they instituted a militia wherein royal captains within set geographical zones recruited men, promising to pay them monthly. Thus was established a direct chain of command from crown to recruit, a substitute for the *hermandad,* which was disbanded in 1498. And to offset burgeoning expenses. they levied a head tax on their taxable subjects, those neither noble nor clergy.

Pedro González de Mendoza

In September of 1494, Isabel and Fernando visited Cardinal Mendoza in Guadalajara, for he was gravely ill and confined to bed, the diagnosis an abscess on a kidney. Thereafter Isabel sent physicians to him and kept informed of his health, for, reported Mártir, she and Fernando were then "convinced that they will lose a goodly part of their own selves" if they were deprived of so great a man and his frequent counsel.[16] Pedro González de Mendoza, archbishop of Toledo and cardinal of Spain, died on January 17, 1495. He was seventy-five years old, a prince of the church, primate of Spain, and *grande* of Castile, and, as Mártir had so often reminded him, also "the third king of Spain," without whom *los reyes* made no difficult decisions.[17]

Mendoza, instrumental in Isabel's gaining the crown, was for twenty years her principal minister and her closest advisor; he was more constantly at her side during the decades of war than was Fernando. Pragmatic, learned in law, valuing rationality, skilled in shaping opinion, he was also a militant, indeed fighting cleric. Yet his urbanity balanced the passionate religious zeal of that other intimate of Isabel's, Talavera, whom Mendoza had introduced at court and with whom he worked closely. Between them, they had not only supported and advised the queen, but had constructed and administered her apparatus of state. She could not have done it without them. Was Mendoza as moderating a force as he seems? Or is it that he too preferred to innovate gradually, as in his backing of the piecemeal introduction of the Inquisition, or in suggesting to supporters of statutes of purity of blood that they bide their time, even while including such a statute in the constitutions of his own Colegio de Santa Cruz? The cardinal understood power, indeed enjoyed it doubly, in wielding it for the monarchs and being trusted by the papacy. A prime exponent of absolute royal authority, he was ever mindful of the best interests of his Spain, and protective of his own power, as when he so tirelessly disputed with Isabel jurisdiction within his see of Toledo.

The marqués de Santillana, Mendoza's father, had been a great lord, and a famous warrior and poet. Pedro González was a lawyer and priest, statesman, patron of arts and architecture, Renaissance collector, and operative head of Spain's most powerful clan. To his sons he left numerous titles and estates; and he left Isabel bereft. Their esteem had been mutual; in his will he named her his executrix, granted her full powers to emend it if she thought best, and in his own hand stated his complete trust in her judgment. That show of confidence in the queen surely serves to allay any lingering suspicion that he might have been a puppet-master. He also gave her three final pieces of advice: she should make peace with France; she should not concede the archbishopric of Toledo to a nobleman; and, surely most disquieting to her, she should marry prince Juan to Juana, "Queen Juana's daughter."[18] She would follow only one of those recommendations.

The omnipresent Münzer, in attending the cardinal's funeral, was most impressed by the immense wealth he had accrued, estimating money, jewels, and moveable property as worth more than two hundred thousand ducats, and declaring the Mendoza palace in Guadalajara as among the most beautiful in Spain and most lavish in its use of gold. The cardinal was, said Münzer, known to have spent sparingly on his own person but exuberantly on everything else. Isabel has been credited with commissioning his imposing tomb in the Capilla Mayor of the cathedral of Toledo, but it would be surprising if Mendoza had not arranged for it himself. Münzer described the royal couple and their court a week after his death, everyone dressed in black, deep in mourning.

Yet such were the exigencies of monarchy that even while Mendoza lingered Isabel fought the curia for jurisdiction over the see of Toledo. And at his death, despite the opposition of the cathedral *cabildo*, she quickly and for the first time imposed nominees into such offices within the vacant see that she construed as secular, observing that "we much marvel" at questioning of the royal right to do so. Equally indignant, that *cabildo* retaliated by attempting to seize all Mendoza's funeral paraphernalia and to prohibit erecting the funeral bier ordered by the rulers. But little by little it gave way before the threats and pressure exerted by a royal attorney. Isabel had expanded royal control over church administration in general, as was evidenced in her decrees on such administrative matters having moved from the justificatory preamble, "*e porque . . .*" ("and because . . .") of 1480, to the forthright command, "*Ya sabedes . . .*" "Now know you . . ." in 1495. She also personally oversaw the inventorying of Mendoza's vast estate.[19]

Isabel followed his advice regarding the social category of his successor. It had become her practice to prefer men of middling background and proven ability, and she was fully cognizant of the opportunity now presented to extend royal control over what was at once the leading archdiocese and the greatest barony in Spain. So in naming Mendoza's successor, having resisted Fernando's desire to appoint to Toledo his son, Alfonso de Aragón, then bishop of Zaragoza, she sent off an envoy to the pope with the name of a worthy Franciscan friar, and then she sent another, to say that she had changed her mind and was naming Francisco Jiménez de Cisneros as archbishop of Toledo. Alexander VI confirmed her choice; at the moment he preferred Spanish backing in Italy to asserting papal power in Spain; it was then that Isabel and Fernando, knowing his priorities—Italy and his children—understandingly yielded the see of Valencia to his son, Caesare Borgia.

Isabel did not tell Cisneros of her decision regarding him beforehand, knowing that he would oppose it, and when, without comment, she simply showed him the papal bull, he turned his back on her and strode out of the palace. He held out for six months. Isabel waited; she had become very good at it. In October he consented, although he refused to put away his friar's robe and put on the customary archepiscopal silks and ermines. He only recanted when ordered to do so by the pope, and even then with the proviso it be only in public.

At court Cisneros was feared and respected but not much liked. "The archbishop," as a later chronicler of Aragón explained, "had a mind that soared with great thoughts more usual to a king than a friar."[20] He and Fernando had their differences. "He was a man of warlike and even disquiet condition,"[21] wrote a later Mendoza, implying Cisneros was not mentally well balanced. Whether he was a mystic or epileptic or both, unquestionably he experienced flights of ecstatic transport; still, the meditation and solitude he valued proved no barrier to his bringing great vigor to public affairs. In the troubled years following Isabel's death, he would become inquisitor general and twice regent of all Spain, and he would set in motion trends in political and religious life reverberating to this day. While she lived, and despite his earlier demurs, Cisneros was frequently at court, the most influential of counselors, temporal and spiritual, throughout the last decade of her reign. Cisneros was to take the place with the queen of both Talavera and Mendoza for the rest of her life.

VĒ ĐZA. ‖ F.FRĀCISC?XIMENEZ.DEC
N.1495. ‖ ROS. ĊRIĐNAIIS.OB. ꝫ.NOV

Figure 13. Francisco Jiménez de Cisneros as archbishop of Toledo (1509–11). Juan de Borgoña. Sala Capitular, Toledo Cathedral.

While his personal influence was enormous, Isabel, in conceding the archbishopric of Toledo, traditionally the most powerful position below the monarch's, to a non-noble friar, ended the possibility of nobles like Carrillo employing it as a personal fief. She also seized the opportunity to diminish the size of the archdiocese to royal benefit and to assert the royal right of patronage. She could rely so heavily on Cisneros because he owed his position to her; he had no other power base.

Cleansing the Country

To whatever extent Isabel saw ridding society of corruption, immorality, and heresy as a necessary preliminary to the advent of the Second Coming, she assuredly hoped that a clergy morally uplifted would in turn uplift the populace. Mendoza and Talavera, expecting it would set precedent among Spaniards, had sought reform of the way clergy lived, established seminaries in their own residences, and favored obscure but gifted friars who swelled the ranks of the educated and upright. Even so, as matters stood, among the perhaps forty thousand secular and regular clergy in Spain, many had no formal training but had simply been appointed by bishops; many too were married, of bad reputation, and did not wear habits. The first church assembly of Isabel's reign, held at Seville in 1478 and dominated by Mendoza and Talavera, had ordered every bishop to make certain that each priest have a shaven crown, the size of an old *blanca*—a large silver coin—and wore a habit falling four fingers below the knee. Isabel, in soliciting a papal bull to that effect, added her own more precise specifications: the tonsure should be "the size of the seal on the bull of His Holiness, the hair short enough to see the ears, the habit of decorous color, black or dark blue or dull tawny or drab, closed in back and pinned at the chest, and long enough to reach the instep, and it must be worn for four months before committing a crime"—that is, before the cleric could come under ecclesiastical rather than royal jurisdiction. She informed her ambassador in Rome that men who took clerical habit often did so to escape punishment for crimes they had committed rather than to serve the Lord and thereby compounded their guilt; that huge numbers of clergy had no religious vocation, lived with women, and went about armed; and that monastic life was particularly scandalous and she wanted to appoint a prelate or a religious to oversee monastic reform.[22]

From 1485 on, she and Fernando had tried without success to secure from the papacy the necessary faculties for a general reform of the clergy. Once again, the royal strategy became to introduce reform piecemeal, for Alexander VI would only authorize reformation within certain religious orders. The process began in women's convents. Moreover, with Isabel's staunch support, Cisneros became provincial of his own Franciscan order in Castile; he toured the monasteries in his charge in 1495, traveling on foot, eating by begging alms, and assiduously imposing reorganization.

Pedro Mártir recorded one result. Mártir had been asked to secure a pardon for one Lorenzo Vaca, a *comendador* of the Holy Spirit and a fugitive from justice, who was charged with having given the habit of his own religious order to Franciscans fleeing Cisneros's rigor. "*Mis reyes,*" as Mártir put it, "plan to check, restrain, and return to the primitive spirit of their order the lascivious friars of the order of Saint Francis." What punishment then did Vaca not merit—asked Mártir archly—for having thwarted that plan? Even so, he had personally asked mercy for Vaca of Cisneros, who was "a man of holy probity—as they say; a man of highest integrity—as is the rumor; the Queen's confessor—as is commonly said; and the promoter of such a great enterprise." The interview, as reported by Mártir, was a disaster:

Turning to me with furrowed brow he said: "Pedro Mártir, do you defend this man, who has dared to profane such holy decrees of the monarchs?" And he threatened me with the hatred of the Queen if I dared to say one more word in [Vaca's] favor. This man [Cisneros] . . . is he who through his counsel makes everything happen now in

Spain. He, through the dynamism of his talent, through his gravity and wisdom, through outdoing in holiness all the cenobites, hermits, and anchorites, has so much prestige with the monarchs as no one ever achieved before. They judge it a sin to contradict his counsel, for what he says they do not believe comes from the mouth of man.[23]

It was useless in that business, he concluded, newly critical of *los reyes,* to speak to them on the subject without first placating Cisneros. Mártir, annoyed at that so recent ascendency and at receiving such dismissive treatment, and highly partisan to the supplanted Talavera, was far from objective and prone to exaggerate for effect. For when Franciscan houses resisted radical reform, Isabel did admonish Cisneros for going too far too fast. And, however much she learned from him, she showed to him the efficacy of patience and incremental advance—until, in 1499, papal license arrived to reform all mendicant orders.

There is no mistaking, however, that after 1492 and with Cisneros's ascendency, royal decrees tended to approach ever more closely to holy writ and Spain to be portrayed in them as a prime battleground of good and evil, so that the wartime crusading language and spirit was shunted into fighting evil within Spanish society. And intrinsic to that process was Isabel's ongoing and wholehearted support of the Inquisition, which ever more blatantly confirmed a symbiosis operative between crusade, personal salvation, apocalyptic hopes and fears, social control, royal power, and benefit to the royal treasury. In 1498 Torquemada, the inquisitor general, died. Appointed to that office was Prince Juan's old tutor, Diego de Deza, signaling no distancing of the Holy Office from the court. The Inquisition was now firmly entrenched and the monarchs wanted it accountable, at least financially, and its activities profitable to themselves. Between 1495 and 1497, the royal treasury finally managed to extract some accounting of finances from the inquisitors, although royal investigators continued to find it difficult, for somehow many tribunals could not locate their records.

Still, indications mounted that the Inquisition benefited the royal treasury. In particular, the crown then levied on all reconciled converts a direct fine, explained as a one-time buying of rehabilitation. Huge numbers of purchases of rehabilitations into public life by the penanced resulted. The implicit rationale for that levy was that, with Jewish influence removed, it was among final steps required before Spanish society was unifiedly Christian and the Inquisition could wither away. The papal nuncio had another explanation: Isabel and Fernando wanted the money and were expecting so many millions that it was his opinion that the faculty to impose such a fine be granted them only in return for some extraordinary service to the curia. By 1497, it has been estimated, the crown had received through the Inquisition somewhere near 15 million *maravedís.*[24]

The Inquisition did not, however, disappear. Isabel continuously defended the Holy Office to Rome. Cisneros would later tell her grandson, Charles V, with only slight exaggeration, that the peace of his kingdoms and even his own authority depended upon that institution. Nor was there Christian unity. Rather, increasing emphasis was put on *limpieza de sangre*, carrying the message that all *conversos* and their offspring were a race apart, that they bore continual watching, and that they were continually being watched. When in 1497 the Queen dismissed the president and all the magistrates of the royal chancery it was said to be because 'they were all new Christians and little clean of hand.' Too, the story was told that in 1498 Isabel, on hearing that a *converso* was resisting expulsion from the prestigious Colegio de San Bartolomé in Salamanca, which had instituted a statute of purity of blood, did not hesitate to respond that "if he will not leave by the door, throw him out the window."[25] However that may be, by 1500 the monarchs opposed *conversos* entering the church and sanctioned a norm of excluding them and their near relatives from public position. The following year the concept of purity of blood was introduced within their government by an edict barring any relapsed *converso* to the second generation from a seat on the Royal Council. To what extent those statutes were implemented is unknown, especially in view of the fact that some of that edict's principal proponents were themselves of Jewish lineage. Jewish blood, however, increasingly became a taint, a legal barrier to advance in church and state; yet certificates of pure blood could be bought, removing that stigma.

*   *   *

On December 2, 1496, as the French withdrew from Italy, Alexander VI and his curia showed their appreciation of the merits of Fernando and Isabel. A papal bull commended those monarchs for having unified and pacified their kingdoms, conquered Granada, and expelled the Jews, for having promised now to carry the crusade against the Turk, and of course for ridding the papal states and Naples of the French. Fernando and Isabel were, in consequence, henceforth to be known as *Los Reyes Católicos*. That specific honorific was decided upon in the curia only after much discussion of possible alternatives, among them *religiosos, defensores,* and *protectores.* Certainly *católicos* was the broadest designation and the most likely to offend Charles VIII. The Spanish ambassador in Rome, Carvajal, reported to the monarchs that their new title had indeed upset the French.[26]

Royal Weddings

In 1495 Prince Juan was seventeen; at the end of January Isabel sent him as royal representative to the French frontier with a guard of 135 knights and all

Figure 14. Fernando and Isabel, *Los Reyes Católicos* (sixteenth century). Facade, University of Salamanca.

the nobles of the military orders. That month too, Maximilian of Habsburg signed a double wedding contract: Prince Juan was to marry his daughter, Margaret of Austria; and the *infanta* Juana to wed his son, the archduke Philip. The monarchs now considered Maximilian a satisfactory connection; he had beaten back the Turks at Villach in 1492 and had regained and unified the Habsburg lands of Austria and Hungary. For his part, Maximilian was well disposed to linking his dynasty with this ascendingly powerful one. It had been through his own marriage to Mary of Burgundy that he himself had risen from a minor princeling to control much of central Europe. The Habsburg luck was to hold; for in several generations that dynasty would rule yet more of Europe and many lands beyond.

In 1495, Isabel could feel, with reason, satisfaction at the powerful unions she had arranged for her children. Catalina was to marry England's crown prince, Arthur. And when João died that year, she redoubled previous patient efforts to coax young Isabel to remarry in Portugal, to its new king, Manoel, who had lived for several years in Castile's court and who had refused to accept María instead. Yet her oldest daughter firmly resisted. Mártir wrote in 1494: "She does not want to know any other man and renounces a second marriage."[27] Two years later, Pedro Mártir lamented that the princess was "thinner than a dry trunk," that since becoming a widow five years earlier, she had continued to say she would not marry anyone. She had not returned to eat at table, but mortified herself with fasting and vigils, devoted herself to working church ornaments, and blushed and became very agitated when it was suggested she remarry. Yet he felt that some day her parents would persuade "this daughter that they love so extraordinarily to wed a good king."[28] In point of fact, they had already signed her marriage contract, negotiated by Cisneros, on November 30, five days before that comment of his. And, unbeknowst to her mother, the bride-to-be had made the stipulation that, before her arrival, Portugal must be rid of Jews and must begin to prosecute heretics.

Even though the suspicion arises that Mártir's many prescient remarks, such as that concerning young Isabel someday marrying a good king, may well be the result of his post facto editing, his letters are among the richest of sources for the events of those years at court. Certainly he best evokes the royal weddings and what came after. One letter of his, dated August of 1496, tells of the queen, saddened by separation from the king (who was readying an army against the French in Perpignan), going with all her children to Laredo, a port on the Cantabrian sea, to send off Juana to Flanders and her prospective spouse. "A powerful fleet had been readied, of two Genoese carracks and 108 caravels, carrying, it was said, 10,000 armed men come from between the mountains of Cantabria and the Basque country, because it was to sail along French coasts." The admiral of Castile, Fadrique Enríquez, was in command; many nobles, knights, and ladies were to accompany the *infanta*. Isabel spent two nights on board with Juana; then the fleet set sail on August 22. "The Queen, after crying for her daughter, whom she thought she might never see again, left for Burgos . . . where we are now, awaiting the King with great anxiety."[29] In Burgos, Isabel received reassuring news of Fernando every eight or nine days by relay riders, but, Mártir confided, still she "suffers greatly because of her daughter, for she does not know how the furious winds, immense reefs, and high seas will treat the delicate maiden and she is tormented with uncertainty as to her having escaped the Charybdis-like whirlpools of the British sea. . . ." Day and night, he said, the queen kept at her side expert mariners whom she constantly queried about winds and possible causes of delay, and she lamented having felt herself obliged to send Juana to remote Flanders when the sea was nearly impassable with winter near and with communications cut by land due to the enmity of the French.[30]

"While those preoccupations were torturing her mind," the queen received word that her mother had died in Arévalo. Mártir says that although Isabel of Portugal died "consumed by age"—she was in her sixties—that did not stop her daughter from crying. (The dowager queen was first interred in the Franciscan convent outside Arévalo, until, in accord with her daughter's orders, in 1505 her body was laid beside her husband's in Miraflores.) Then, on October 21, Fernando returned from Aragón, and Isabel received welcome word at the end of November that Juana had arrived safely. Yet Isabel worried still, for Margaret was to set sail for Spain in the same fleet as soon as the weather broke. She had other cause as well, for before its return, most of the men-at-arms of the bridal fleet froze or starved to death at sea or in the ice and snow of Flanders.

After a stormy voyage and a near shipwreck, Margaret arrived—at Santander, on March 8, 1497 with a large entourage and the first carriages seen in Spain. Isabel received her in Burgos, in the palace courtyard with numerous ladies, formally. Everyone wore gold and precious jewels, says Mártir, according to their station, and everyone shone and glittered during the days of festivity that followed. Isabel had again borrowed back from Valencia her pawned crown. The wedding took place on April 2, although it was Lententime. "Our prince," Mártir explains, "burning with love, got his parents to dispense with protocol in order to get to the desired embraces." There was one somber note, a knight died jousting. Mártir, at his most prescient, worried that it was a portent of unhappiness to come.[31]

In a letter of June 13 he described Margaret: "if you saw her, you would think you were contemplating Venus herself." Yet he trembled to think that some day that beauty might lead to unhappiness and the loss of Spain. For the prince, carried away with love of her, was pale and thin and "bore himself sadly." The doctors and the king were counseling the queen that some of the time the two should be separated, "for too frequent copulation constitutes a danger to the Prince." Sexual overindulgence, they told Isabel, was softening his bone marrow and weakening his stomach. They got nowhere. It was not fitting, she insisted, that men separate those whom God had joined in matrimony. The prince from infancy had been weak by nature, they rejoined, raised on chicken and other digestible foods like an invalid; she must not confide in the example of her own husband, who from his mother's womb was naturally gifted with an admirable robustness of body.[32]

Isabel would listen to no one. She showed herself obdurate, a quality that in her mature years she had been at pains to hide. Mártir professed astonishment: "She has been transformed into another whom never until now have we suspected in her. I always have proclaimed that she was a constant woman; I would not have called her contumacious; I was too confident." Yet God willing, all would go well. The monarchs were then in Medina del Campo, but leaving soon to take the *infanta* Isabel, now consenting to marry Manoel, to meet him at the Portuguese border.[33] Clues to Isabel's obstinacy lie in her strong desire for dynastic continuity, her chivalric notions of the primacy of love, and her belief in the holiness of marriage and that on no account should a man and wife be kept apart. Did she have in mind Luna's treatment of her mother and father? She insisted that marriage was so holy that the devil could not affect it, overlooking that the pope had declared the union of her half-brother Enrique and his first wife Blanca bewitched. To Isabel, wedlock was so sacrosanct that only God could have power in it. Isabel was a remarkably happily married woman.

In mid-July, Mártir relayed news of Juana to Talavera. She had been well received and was esteemed by the Flemings, for they believed her very suitable for motherhood. It was said that Philip, her husband, lacked nothing of what a woman could desire in a man: he was of admirable age, physique, beauty, and habits, possessing a steady character and all natural attributes. "Our monarchs," he reported, "are content with him and with their daughter-in-law, unless her beauty harms the Prince their son." From both marriages they awaited exemplary grandchildren, "the greatest and most insatiable desire of parents."[34]

Knives of Sorrow

Two months later, Mártir announced a tragedy. On September 13 with ominous portents—"*con hados adversos y aves infaustas*"—the court left Medina del Campo. The king and the queen, who was not well, were accompanying their oldest daughter as far as Alcántara, and Juan and Margaret were going to Salamanca, its jurisdiction assigned to the prince when he married, where they were to live. They arrived to a jubilant reception; that city dedicated to letters went wild for its future king, who from his youth had loved and cultivated learning. Three days later, Juan lay desperately ill of a high fever. Relay riders sped the news to his parents. While Isabel remained to see the Portuguese wedding arrangements through, Fernando rushed to Salamanca, where, according to Mártir, he found their son pale but lucid, and implored him not to give up hope. Juan replied he was resigned to death. Mártir, ever the humanist, praised the prince for being so philosophical, and attributed to him a marvelous exaltation of spirit owing to his having read many volumes of Aristotle.[35] Still, there is something to be said for Fernando's insistence on exerting a will to live. Less than two weeks later, on October 4, Juan died.

Fernando wrote Isabel only that some days Juan was worse, some better, and he ordered that no word of their son's death reach her until he rejoined her and they could console one another. When told, she was only heard to say, "God gave me him, and He has taken him away." Juan's body was interred in the Convento de Santo Tomás in Avila. Mártir echoed the general sentiment: "There was buried the hope of all Spain." Yet one hope remained. Margaret was pregnant.

Ten days later Mártir informed Talavera that *los reyes,* "orphans of so grand a son," were trying to dissimulate their profound grief, "but we divine it inside them, crushing their spirits. When they are seated in public, they continually look at one another, not knowing what to do on discovering what lies hidden within," their eyes full of a grief too deep for words. He worried that they would cease being human beings of flesh and blood and become harder than diamonds if they did not give vent to their enormous loss.[36] Spoken of henceforth were Isabel's knives of sorrow, in implicit reference to Mary's suffering and Christ's passion. The king and queen went into relative seclusion, to Alcalá de Henares with Cisneros, and remained there through April of 1498.

More tragedy lay in store. Margaret miscarried: "Instead of the desired offspring, she has aborted; instead of the longed for heir, we have been given an unformed mass of flesh worthy of pity."[37] From Portugal, Manoel and Isabel were immediately called to take up the succession. They came, after Manoel had been guaranteed the continued separateness of Portugal and young Isabel been assured all hereditary rights as proprietary queen of Castile. They received the oath from the Cortes, called to Toledo on March 16, and within the month were in Zaragoza, where problems arose. For by Aragón's ancient constitution no queen could bear the scepter, yet since young Isabel was pregnant, it was conceded that the oath could be taken to her child, if male. The queen, it is said, was so thoroughly exasperated at that disrespect shown by the Corts that she declared that a more honest remedy would be to conquer Aragón.

Some five months later, on August 24, 1498, young Isabel, queen of Portugal, died in childbirth. She, lamented Mártir, had the gifts of soul of her mother, her great virtue and magnanimity, but was so different physically. The mother was stout, the daughter thin, so thin she could not support the anguish of giving birth. She had frequently predicted her own death and had had the *viaticum* and friars on hand to confess her. To her mother, she had left one compensation, a grandson who could become the sovereign of the Iberian kingdoms.[38] The child, named Miguel, was not strong, but a month later the signs that he would survive were sufficient that his father Manoel, leaving the infant with his grandparents, returned to Portugal. Isabel lay abed, ill beforehand and now stricken with grief at the death of her favorite daughter. Yet she rallied to attend the Corts, which now recognized this male heir, although with the proviso that should Fernando ever have a legitimate son, the oath was null.

Marineo Sículo, admiring the fortitude of the king and queen, gave an explanation for the degree of resilience they did show, that "they had from youth been accustomed to dangers and work and great changes in matters of their estates."[39] He did not exaggerate that resilience. In Zaragoza in early July, Isabel had been so sick with "tertiary fevers" that there was fear for her life. Cisneros, who was with her, informed his cabildo on July 6 that she had been bled twice and was feeling much better, yet also that processions were being held for her health, and masses and prayers said. Young Isabel died a few weeks later; her mother never fully recovered. Yet life went on within the ever expanding court. With the French quiescent, attention to Africa seemed more urgent than ever with the return from Calcutta of Vasco de Gama. Then, on April 8, 1498, Charles VIII died, to be succeeded by his uncle, Louis XII, who renewed the Italian imbroglio.

Winter in Alcalá

During that long stay at Alcalá after Juan's death, Isabel worked with Cisneros on projects dear to her heart. Artists designing an altarpiece for the *capilla mayor* of Toledo each brought his maquette to Alcalá so the queen might see them all and give her opinion. She and Cisneros furthered arrangements for clerical reform. And, related, Cisneros was then planning a university that would rival Salamanca and reverse its priorities; theology rather than law would be its fundamental field of study. For there remained, in a Spain so assiduously championing religious orthodoxy, much confusion as to just what constituted it.

For Isabel, Cisneros had become a mainstay; and from then on he was increasingly influential, including in making key appointments at court. He had proven energetic, authoritative, arrogant, ruthless, and politically astute, even flexible, demonstrating in everything tremendous force of will and high intelligence. He had found a way both to practice contemplative spirituality and exercise rigorous administration. Cisneros was also less concerned than was Talavera with how he achieved a desired goal; he lacked Talavera's insistence on principle applied at every step of the way, and was, more like Mendoza, sometimes empirical in the relation of means to ends, although more grating in manner; Cisneros had neither Mendoza's more genial worldliness nor his sense of noblesse oblige. And while Cisneros did take care to express himself with great moderation, the effort showed. He has been described as chaste and modest, and having much self-control, quite possibly implying he found it necessary to curb his passions. His warnings of the emotional snares set by the devil probably convey firsthand experience. Nor would he stay over-night in any dwelling where women were, although he treated women with extreme courtesy. He was to show himself "a harsh prophet of Spain's messi-anic destiny"; neither was he unsympathetic, as P. E. Russell has put it, "to the prophetic dreams which enjoyed wide sympathy among some churchmen at this time and which foretold an imminent *Renovatio mundi* which would both transform the Church and . . . introduce the Christian millennium."[40]

In that holy pursuit mundane affairs mattered to him; the readying was lofty purpose enough for engaging in government vigorously and for carrying a crusading mentality into civil and ecclesiastical administration, to say noth-ing of engaging in crusading itself. Cisneros was to personally lead an expedi-tion against Oran in 1509. Before that, he was part of, and played upon, an expectant messianic atmosphere compounded of the presence of the Inquisi-tion, royal success against Muslims and expulsion of Jews, the advance toward Jerusalem, and the advent of the year 1500, which was ringed with millennial speculation. Says one scholar, "I think that people met in the streets and dis-cussed prophecies as long as Cisneros lived."[41]

Was meditation and a greater spirituality the form of consolation Isabel turned to under the influence of Cisneros? Indications are that Talavera's met-aphor of reigning queen as soaring eagle was not so much displaced as joined by an inner vision of soaring soul. That is, to Talavera's pointing the way to perfection of the soul through self-confidence, self-control, and diligent work, to his valuing most highly Christian practice, and to the assumption that the monarch was in direct contact with the divine will, were added Cisneros's con-cerns with reform of temporal life and a personal obligation to strive to know God more intimately, with meditation and prayer as avenues toward such spir-itual ascent. It was only then that Isabel's religiosity seems to have assumed many of the characteristics today associated with the term piety. Moreover, while, like her father in his last years, she was drawn to attempts to reconcile classical philosophy and Christianity, she went further than he did, to favor especially those authors who saw in philosophy a preparation for the imitation of Christ. More than ever, the books and art she acquired reflected those new, more transcendent concerns of hers, as did the books whose printing she encouraged. However she felt about prophecy, Isabel demonstrated a continu-ing interest in the dual religious and geophysical reaches of the grand design: in 1501 she ordered arrears be paid and her commitment honored thereafter on the one thousand ducats she had promised annually to the Franciscans of

Mount Zion in Jerusalem. She then also arranged Pedro Mártir's embassy to Egypt.[42]

In addition, the sense of her own mortality, with her ever since the attempt on Fernando, may well have intensified both her devotions and her already exacting moral code. To ensure morality, in 1502 she and Fernando decreed means of controlling the printing and circulation of books. Royal magistrates were to examine them before being printed and authors were to pay a fee. *Los reyes* also forbade blasphemy and gambling—"inspired by God," said a courtier, for gambling led to robbery, murder, insanity, and gamblers would go to hell, while blasphemers "say things against the honor of God." They also decreed that homosexuals were to be burned alive. Similar directives were being issued in England and elsewhere, so that such decrees also signified that Spain's rulers were abreast of European trends.[43] Too, in 1499, the monarchs enacted more stringent measures against Jews who might return and seek baptism, and others against Gypsies, as well as sumptuary laws against excessive luxury in dress beyond one's social rank.

Those people meant to be Christian exemplars, the clergy, proved recalcitrant. Isabel persevered. In 1500 she notified the bishop of Calahorra that priests in his diocese still lived publicly with concubines or kept mistresses and went armed to prevent detention. In Bilbao, after the royal *alcaide* did disarm a priest, six or seven men had entered his bedroom and beaten him; and in Seville, when an assembly ordered priests living with women to separate from them, it was a signal for gangs to eject such women and to loot their houses, and those of innocent priests as well. Isabel wrote to those places prohibiting entering such houses by force, though to little avail, and she chastised officials who had joined in the looting. Assaulting people seen to be in royal disfavor was a habit well established, in Seville and elsewhere, but until then directed principally against Jews.

Yet if Isabel appeared less well and more devout, she did not abandon directing the affairs of this world. And if, increasingly, she left international relations to Fernando, it was also the case that they were increasingly bound up with Aragón's traditional interests in Italy. In November of 1500 both Isabel and Fernando signed a treaty dividing Naples with Louis XII; they retained possession of the port. Isabel remained especially concerned and involved with those foreign affairs that had to do with her daughters, Juana and Catalina. Matters of foreign trade and Castilian shipping continued to be important to her, and figured prominently in negotiations with England and France. She paid attention, too, to ongoing relations with Portugal. María was to marry Manoel; on October 12, 1499 the Cortes voted the tremendous subsidies needed for the dowries of María and Catalina. And Isabel did not neglect the affairs of the Indies.

As the century turned, she also insisted that Medina Sidonia relinquish

Gibraltar to her, "because it complied to her service."[44] There was every indication as well that the monarchs' Italian and European policies continued to be part of a broader plan, imperial in scope and encompassing Africa, the Mediterranean, the Spanish Indies, and ultimately Asia and Jerusalem. Between 1497 and 1500, an interval in the Italian wars, she and Fernando turned again to Africa. It was then that they occupied Melilla, tightened their protectorate over Tunis, and sponsored an expedition that tried but failed to reach sub-Saharan gold sources. At the same time, they ringed the Tyrrhenian Sea with *consulados,* reinforced Malta, and acquired Otranto and Tarentum as bases on the Mediterranean. And they formed a league with Portugal, England, and Scotland against their strongest Islamic adversaries, the Turks, who had taken Venetian colonies in Greece and again threatened Sicily, Naples, and the whole western Mediterranean and who continued to stand between them and Jerusalem. Royal directives once more went out for prayer and sacrifice for Christian well-being and the triumph of Christian arms against the infidel; for in July of 1499 Isabel and Fernando had returned to Granada, and once again it was war against the Moor.[45]

Chapter 19
The Queen and Her Daughter: 1499–1504

The first knife of grief that stabbed the spirit of la Reyna Doña Isabel *was the death of the Prince, the second was the death of Isabel, her firstborn child, queen of Portugal; the third stab of grief was the death of Miguel, her grandson, with whom she had consoled herself. From these times on [she] . . . lived without pleasure, her life and health foreshortened.*
—Andrés Bernáldez[1]

The court returned to Granada in July of 1499, for the first time since 1492. Although Talavera and Tendilla proudly pointed out to the monarchs the city's tranquility and progress toward Christianity—Talavera had instituted and Tendilla supported a policy of converting through persuasion and indoctrination—the monarchs were surprised at how Muslim it still was. The Turks were again threatening the Mediterranean; Barbary pirates in league with Granadan Muslims were marauding along coasts; and while Granada remained Muslim any Spanish advance into Africa was threatened. By November Cisneros had come, most likely in response to a royal summons, and, by the time Isabel and Fernando left for Seville at the month's end, he had launched an intensive campaign of forced religious conversion.

Cisneros sought to convert Muslims through sermons, bribes, and threats, especially pressuring notables to be baptized as examples to everyone else. The recalcitrant were locked in and preached to daily; he who held out for twenty days, as has been said, was considered a man of iron. Cisneros and the clergy he brought in began by preaching only to Muslims baptized as Christians but found backsliding, *elches*; Cisneros received and wielded inquisitorial powers against such renegades. Some Muslims found themselves faced with the choice of baptism or the Inquisition; one recalled being told with no basis that "your grandfather was a Christian who embraced Islam."[2] The children of ascribed *elches* and some others were also baptized, without parental permission.

Muslims saw those innovations as violations of the *capitulaciones* of 1491. On December 18, 1499, when a bailiff entered the Albaicín to arrest a purported apostate, the inhabitants of that quarter, fearing a general forced con-

Figure 15. Isabel (1500). Attributed to Juan de Flandes. Pardo Palace, Madrid.

Figure 16. Baptizing Muslims. Felipe Bigarny (c. 1521). Royal Chapel, Granada.

version, arose, killed him, and organized an armed resistance. For three days the city's Christians, relatively few, feared for their lives, until, acting in concert, the two *ancianos,* Tendilla and Talavera, personally stopped the uprising from spreading, and through their immense prestige managed to restore order. Tendilla then cordoned off the Albaicín; Talavera went in to calm the *barrio* and win over its leaders with a combination of promises and threats.[3] Nonetheless, they also called upon Andalusian towns to send troops. Cisneros found positive value in that uprising. He reported to his cathedral *cabildo* on December 23 that he having on the eighteenth converted three hundred Muslims before midday meal, the Moors had risen because "Satan always procures to overturn all good things. . . ." Yet it had been for the best, for "with the fear [the insurgents] had of what they had done, it has pleased Our Lord that where they had thought to upset conversions," that trouble had instead "been the cause that today 3000 souls are converted and baptized. . . ."[4]

Isabel and Fernando, in Seville, heard rumors of all Granada having revolted before an accurate account arrived and, enraged by Cisneros's provoking of near disaster, Fernando at once wrote to Tendilla of "the archbishop of Toledo, who never saw Moors nor knew them," and instructed that only those who killed the bailiff be punished. Then, with report of damage contained, he and Isabel changed their minds. They wrote to Cisneros and Tendilla that while they marveled at not having been informed immediately, yet they were pleased with how the uprising had been handled, and had decided that, "as to what touches the service of Our Lord and the augment of our Holy Catholic Faith, our desire is that in conversion you make all the fruit you can make."[5] By mid-January of 1500 Cisneros was of the opinion that all the city was Christian; and that now the entire kingdom of more than two hundred thousand souls awaited conversion by the Lord. Be that as it may, more than nineteen thousand *mudéjares* living throughout Castile suffered backlash; Isabel wrote to Arévalo and other places that Muslims were under royal protection and must not be harmed.

Although the monarchs proclaimed mass conversion throughout the kingdom of Granada to be against their instructions—Isabel in January 1500 personally assured envoys from Ronda that the treaties made at the time of surrender remained in force—they also interpreted the insurrection in the city as a Muslim breaking of the *capitulaciones,* so that Fernando, back in Granada at the end of January, "made known it was his will and the Queen's" that everyone must convert, that "there is no salvation for the soul in any other law, only in that of Jesus Christ."[6] Tendilla had pardoned all the insurgents who agreed to be baptized; Fernando offered amnesty to everyone converting by February 25. Mass conversion ensued, of perhaps fifty thousand people. The archbishop of Toledo had counseled *los reyes,* says Mártir, to offer baptism or death "in order that they [the infidel] not be lost";[7] while it is unclear whether

Cisneros meant infidel souls or infidel obeisance, most probably he coupled them. Talavera, less sanguine, warned that such converts lacked true understanding of Christianity, and that there would be trouble.[8]

Cisneros, undeterred, forcibly carried the campaign to the surrounding region, where he met resistance. Güejar rose. Gonzalo Fernández de Córdoba crushed it with troops that had been about to embark for Naples; Güejar's people were enslaved. When, consequently, various places in the Alpujarras, fearing forced conversion, revolted and sought aid from Muslims abroad, Fernando, going with an armed force during the first week in March, resolved to make an example: in some rebellious villages he had all the inhabitants slain; in Lanjerón, "the occupants were baptized before perishing."[9]

In January the monarchs had noted that the archbishops of Toledo and Granada had had some differences, and that it was "to God's service and our own" that they reconcile. Talavera, resigned to the sovereigns' having abandoned his own patient policy based on persuasion and individual indoctrination, wrote ruefully to the royal secretary, Miguel Pérez de Almazán, making a parable on that abandonment and his own present powerlessness: "Although one swallow does not make a summer or, better said, a winter, Our Lord has broken the wings that can, and our own wings and strength to fly to heaven." And he closed with a bitter pun: "From Granada, in truth very *desgranada,* picked over, and turned to nothing."[10] A general accord was reached by Granadans and royal government on July 30, 1500; between August and October, most of the kingdom's Muslims were perfunctorily baptized en masse. Isabel, suffering as well from broken wings, had returned to the Alhambra in July; she was to remain there for over a year, until October 20, 1501. By July 1500, Cisneros had left. The monarchs took charge in the city and requested more clergy to minister to the baptized, especially priests who spoke Arabic. To great effect, they assured converts they might keep their lands; and, levying an overall fine of fifty thousand ducats on rebels throughout the kingdom of Granada, they exempted converts, so that the entire weight of payment fell on those who remained Muslim. By September all Baza had asked for baptism; by 1501 calm had returned to the entire eastern region.[11]

Then, early in that year, Ronda and the surrounding Sierra Bermeja rose, repelling all pacifying expeditions. One terrible rout left among the dead Alonso de Aguilar, a seasoned veteran and Gonzalo de Córdoba's older brother. That lord's body was so hacked up, reports Mártir, that it was scarcely distinguishable in the immense pile of corpses of servants, familiars, and loyal friends who perished with him.[12] Still, Fernando, while determined to subdue the rising, is said to have replied forebearingly to a suggestion that in retaliation to the mass rebellion he put all remaining Muslims there to the sword, observing that "when your horse does something wrong you do not reach for your sword to kill him before you give him a slap on the rump and throw a cloak over his eyes; so my opinion and that of the Queen is that those Moors be baptized, and if they should not be Christian, their children or grandchildren will be."[13] Even so, in the field he took no captives and gave no pardons. By April 11, he had attained a treaty with the rebels and sent it on for Isabel's approval and signature; many of the defeated were granted the permission they requested to go to Africa and were given passage there.

Isabel recalled Cisneros to Granda; the royal position had crystallized. She had resolved that all Muslims in her realms be baptized, but stipulated it be accomplished without recourse to force or reward, for that would be scandalous. Rather, "they must either convert or leave our kingdoms, for we can not harbor infidels."[14] In her view, to be given a choice was not to force compliance—as Pedro Mártir would soon explain to the sultan of Egypt. In July of 1501, *los reyes* forbade Muslims to reside in the kingdom of Granada, since, was the rationale—reminiscent of that for the expulsion of the Jews—they disturbed the indoctrination of converts. On February 12, 1502, a decree to that effect was issued for all Castile; by April 20 all adult Muslims of Castile had to choose between baptism or exile. Overwhelmingly, they accepted mass baptism; but as *moriscos* they assimilated neither socially nor culturally, and they too would at length be expelled. In Castile, Muslims were a small minority. The large and productive Muslim enclaves of Aragón, valued by both crown and aristocracy, were left for later. Subsequently, the sale of Granadan rebel captives and spoils brought in over five times more than royal expenses in putting down the uprisings; and anticipated were two-thirds of tithes to be paid by New Christians, conceded to the crown by the pope in March of 1500.[15]

In short, most Castilian *mudéjares,* deeply attached to their lands, converted. In Isabel's lifetime all Castile became Christian, if nominally. As guarantor against backsliding, there was the Inquisition.[16] Nonetheless, such *moriscos,* to employ an anachronism, slipped beneath its radar; they appear to have remained solidly Muslim. As has been said, "the policy of Isabel I was the last intended to regulate a [Christian] coexistence with Muslims of Castile and Granada, and the first manifestation of its definite collapse."[17]

As for Isabel herself, while farsightedly looking to ensure the religious condition of the great-grandchildren of her subjects, she was more aware than ever of her own mortality, and greatly uncertain of the future of the dynasty. The deaths in her family had taken their toll, and they were not at an end.

An End to Dynasty

In Granada, on July 20, 1501, the infant Miguel, the heir to Castile, Aragón, and Portugal, not yet two and never strong, died, in his grandmother's arms. "Such great grief," wrote Marineo Sículo, who was there, "has swept over our most Christian princes and the whole court that no one has been able to approach the Queen, for the King and the Queen are bowed down in deep distress."[18] A month later Mártir told a friend, "The death of the little *infante* Miguel has disheartened his grandparents profoundly. They declare themselves powerless any longer to support with serenity of mind so many blows of fortune. . . . Nevertheless, they conceal those dark feelings all they can, and show themselves in public with smiling and serene countenance. It is not difficult, however, to divine what goes on inside them."[19] Bernáldez again found comparison for Isabel's misery in Mary's sufferings: ". . . the third stab of grief was the death of Miguel, her grandson, with whom she had consoled herself." And he added, "From those times she lived without pleasure, her life and health foreshortened."[20]

Fast couriers went off to Ghent immediately, to Juana, who was next in line of succession. Reports about her had been disturbing: that she was excessively enamored of her husband, Philip of Burgundy, archduke of Austria and count of Flanders, that he was neglecting her, and that he was evidencing a clear predilection for France. Even so, it was unthinkable to change the order of succession. Yet that Philip would, upon Juana's accession, become king consort in Castile was, to Isabel, not a happy prospect. Philip was no Fernando; on the contrary, he was said to be extremely dependent upon a *privado,* his old tutor the archbishop of Besançon. And Juana was no Isabel. In the circumstances, it seemed prudent to speed arrangements for the marriages of Catalina to Arthur, prince of Wales, and María to the widower, Manoel of Portugal, and so to establish through those other powerful sons-in-law counterweights to Philip and so to France.

In May marriage had been contracted between Manoel and María, who was then seventeen and whom Isabel had wanted him to marry in the first place. The monarchs also extracted from Manoel a promise to prohibit Muslim worship in Portugal. Alexander VI rushed a dispensation in exchange for Luis Borja, yet another son of his, now receiving the archbishopric of Valencia.

María went to Portugal on September 30, that haste dictated too by Manoel's need for an heir. For the death of Miguel having left no direct heir to the Portuguese crown, Portuguese factions were forming behind perspective claimants that could prove dangerous to internal peace and to Castilian interests. And ever worrisome to Isabel was the presence in Portugal of "the Excellent Lady," Juana. Isabel soon heard that María's marriage was a happy one, Manoel solicitous and giving his bride magnificent presents, María beaming and, reassuringly, spending much time with her sagacious great-aunt, Beatriz of Braganza.[21] María, least promising of Isabel's children, proved the happiest, the longest lived, and assuredly the most fertile, raising seven children of her own. Plans for Catalina's marriage to England's crown prince went less smoothly, although it was obvious Henry VII wanted both the promised

Figure 17. Juana. Juan de Flandes (1496–1500). Kunsthistorisches Museum, Vienna.

dowry of two hundred thousand *escudos* and Spanish trade. The wedding had been celebrated by proxy in 1499, nonetheless there was news that Philip had initiated negotiations to have his sister Margaret, Prince Juan's widow, marry Arthur instead. Even so, Isabel delayed sending Catalina until Arthur was fourteen, that is, considered of an age to consummate marriage.

Juana and Philip were plainly in no hurry to come to Spain. On word of Miguel's death, envoys had flocked to them from all Christendom, among them many Spanish nobles, and Alexander VI had sent them the papal Rose of Love and Friendship.[22] It was a heady experience for Philip and his advisors and a difficult one for the Spanish monarchs. Juana and Philip had had a daughter, Leonor, in 1498 and in February of 1500 Juana had given birth to a son. Yet even that welcome news was not unmitigated, for it was known that Margaret, just arrived, had asked her brother that the child be named Juan, but that Philip had preferred he be baptized Charles, after his Burgundian grandfather, Charles the Bold. More distressing was word that Juana had held herself aloof from the attendant celebrations and that her state of mind troubled her retainers. Still, Isabel and Fernando had instructed their ambassador, Gutierre Gómez de Fuensalida, to relay the pleasure they took in the son the Lord had given to Juana and Philip; may it please God to protect him "and that they might have of him much delight, and might see children of the children of his children, and of them more children who would give them much pleasure."[23] In that child now resided their hopes for Spain. Nor would they have been disappointed in Charles I, king of all Spain, who was also Charles V, Holy Roman Emperor.

At the moment, however, disquieting reports continued, of Juana confiding only in her husband, who relayed everything she told him to the archbishop of Besançon; of Philip wanting 'the usual princely freedom from his wife'; of a policy in force among Philip's counselors to isolate Juana, especially from affairs of state; and of Philip determined to assert his authority over her. In that situation, the quick-tempered Juana was lashing out, not directly at Philip and his people, but at those about her. From Flanders one exasperated Spaniard wrote in August of 1501 to the royal secretary, Almazán, "of one thing I am certain, it is attributable to her alone that she has not a living soul who will help her."[24] This daughter was in straits foreign to Isabel; Juana was far from home, mired in powerlessness, ringed by unfriendly courtiers, and passionately enmeshed in unrequited love for a husband whose political interests ran counter to much of what she represented. And she was showing little aptitude or even inclination for statecraft.

As early as 1498, her parents had instructed their ambassador to inform Philip that he had no claim on the Spanish inheritance and to advise him to be friendlier to his in-laws; in other words, he was to be less friendly to France. By late 1500 his ministers had, instead, arranged the marriage of the infant

Charles to Louis XII's only daughter, Claudia. Shortly thereafter, in January of 1501, there arrived in Spain not the eagerly awaited young couple but Flemish envoys, one of them the archbishop of Besançon, their stated business to get an agreement to the French marriage before Philip and Juana would set foot in Spain. Isabel and Fernando accepted the match, which could have its dynastic advantages, and they entertained the Flemings lavishly for three months. Isabel patiently and repeatedly pointed out to them that Juana and Philip should live in those kingdoms that they would one day rule.[25] It was Juana whom she particularly wanted, together with her son Charles, who would inherit both Castile and Aragón, so that the child would be raised in Spain.

The Flemings were persuaded only that both Philip and Juana had to be there in order to receive the indispensable oath in Cortes. Pedro Mártir once again interpreted matters astutely: "there is no doubt Juana will come if her husband does, for she is lost in love of him, although she would not be moved by ambition for so many kingdoms and love of her parents and of all those others with whom she was raised. Only her attachment will drag her here, to the man they say she loves with such ardor."[26] Yet, as Fuensalida reported from Flanders, Juana had recently shown herself torn; she had refused Philip her power of attorney for negotiations with France and Spain with the explanation that she first had to consult her parents. He had, in response, spoken to her so abusively, stated Fuensalida, that he himself, unable to hold his tongue any longer, had complained to Philip on behalf of his sovereigns. Bleakness was not unalloyed: Fuensalida also reported that the children, Charles—"*Musyor de Lucenburc*"—and "*madama Leonor*," were very well, that Charles maneuvered a go-cart with the strength of a three-year-old, and that Leonor was very pretty.[27]

News from envoys in England brought more cause for concern. Recent French advance in Italy and word reaching London from some Genoese in Cádiz who exaggerated the difficulties in Granada had made Philip's proposals more appealing to Henry VII; Catalina must come as quickly as possible. Isabel could delay no longer and in May of 1501 sent off her youngest child, from Granada, with a fittingly regal escort headed by steadfast Gutierre de Cárdenas. She could not take Catalina herself, as she had planned to do, as far as La Coruña on the northwest coast. For both she and Catalina had been very ill with tertiary fever that spring and Isabel was still not well enough to make the trip. Instead she worried, particularly on hearing that the fleet had sailed on August 17 only to be blown back to Laredo by a storm. It set sail again only in October.[28] Then came good news: Catalina had arrived and, as Henry VII wrote, been "welcomed by the whole people."

A surviving anecdote corroborates a truly popular reception: along the way to London Catalina was offered a glass of English beer. She gamely tasted it, made the appropriate courteous remark, but then turning to a retainer, she

Figure 18. Catalina. Michel Sittow. Kunsthistorisches Museum, Vienna.

pronounced her true verdict: "This is the sponge of ice and vinegar given Our Lord." Catalina and Arthur wed in November. Isabel would not live to see tragedy overtake this daughter most like herself and whose keen intelligence and good judgment were so markedly in contrast with those of her sister Juana, the daughter who was known in England as Catherine of Aragón.

The Habsburgs Arrive

In Flanders there was yet further delay, the explanation given that Juana was again pregnant. After the birth of a second daughter, assuagingly named Isabel, Juana and Philip departed for Spain on July 15, 1501. His insistence on taking the land route, through France, did not allay concern and unhappiness in Spain with his behavior to date, for boundaries between the French and Spanish areas of Naples were being disputed and war again likely. Nor did Philip and Juana hurry. Instead, they spent months at the French court, staying through Christmas, when Philip, it was heard, offered Louis the customary coins given in token of vassalage, and it was some small satisfaction that Juana would not do so.[29] In late January of 1502, a year and a half after being urgently summoned, the archduke and archduchess arrived at Fuenterrabía, where Gutierre de Cárdenas met them. Fernando joined them en route and, at last, on May 7, Isabel received them in Toledo at the gates of the palace, and in state, although after the customary formalities she took Juana by the hand and led her off into her own apartments.

A state banquet followed, and tourneys in which Philip showed his mettle, even learning quickly to ride *a la jineta.* No one, observed Mártir, was more affable, more valiant, more handsome; but his insatiable hunger for the scepter had clouded his intelligence. Isabel and Fernando were extremely cordial to everyone, even when the Flemings intruded themselves in negotiations between France and Spain, and even when word came that Catalina's husband, Arthur, had died of the plague, and that Philip was now secretly and assiduously negotiating to have his sister Margaret marry Arthur's younger brother, Henry, England's new crown prince.

Isabel and Fernando, resolved to outspeed their untrustworthy son-in-law, within the month sent an ambassador whom they instructed first to talk to Henry VII about sending back Catalina along with half her dowry, then to broach as possible alternative her marrying young Henry and she and her dowry staying in England. By June, Henry VII was speaking of the match as probable. He was, however, less interested in aiding the Spanish monarchs in Italy against France, which, Isabel had written him, "has the lack of shame to make war on us."

On May 22, the Cortes and most of Castile's luminaries dutifully took the oath to Philip and Juana as *los príncipes* of Asturias, heirs apparent to the crown of Castile, although some among its members made known to the monarchs reservations stemming from Philip's not speaking the language or knowing the customs and being unwilling to remain in Spain any longer than absolutely necessary. Concomitantly, when word came from Portugal that María had given birth to a son and named him Juan, it was an irony lost on

no one. The *archduques* traveled on to the Corts at Zaragoza, after assurances
from the Aragonese that there would be no problems with the oath of succession this time. Fernando accompanied them. Isabel was not well and remained
in Toledo.

She heard from Fernando, from Calatayud, his letter of July 30 providing
a rare glimpse of how little they differentiated between public and private matters in their ordinary exchanges, as well as corroborating their intimacy. He
worried, he wrote, for he had not heard from her since she had been given a
purge. He had heard from her secretary, Lope Conchillos, and congratulated
her on something she had said to Besançon. Yesterday letters had come from
England. Its king was well and whatever Besançon had told her was a lie; however, he could not read them more closely, for his secretary Almazán had not
brought the cipher with him; have Lope send it. Authorities at Perpignan
reported that the French were moving to the frontier and with artillery, "a lot
of it, even against us a lot." He should reach Zaragoza Tuesday or Wednesday
morning. He expected her to follow, but she should avoid the bad road from
Sigüenza to Monreal. He awaited an envoy from the king of France. "I close
kissing the hands of Your Ladyship whom may Our Lord guard more than all
others, as I desire."[30] Whatever the references to Besançon signified, that thorn
in Isabel's side was removed soon after, for he sickened and died in Toledo.[31]

Fernando wrote to her again, from Zaragoza on August 15. He had heard
from her and was delighted she was better, though undoubtedly still in much
pain. He asked her not to work too hard. Since she was organizing financing
for the defense of Perpignan against the French, he suggested that in order not
to rely further on Genoese loans—the Genoese were then handling the funding of the war in Italy—they levy *sisas,* taxes on foodstuffs, sell public property,
and farm out the taxes on Seville and other places too large to handle. There
would, he thought, be no peace with France until there was war. He was awaiting "my children," for he very much wanted to talk to Philip of the great harm
he was doing to foreign relations and to affairs within their kingdoms, and to
tell him that she and he could see they had no assurance that he, Philip, would
act in their interests. He was pleased she had sent the duchess of Alburquerque
with Juana; it seemed good to him that the women of those kingdoms should
love the princess. Although Isabel, having heard rumor of French ships in the
Mediterranean, had expressed fear of traveling, she should not worry; even if
the French had many more ships, they themselves would still be all right. They
had next to go to Barcelona to receive the oath there. He wanted her to come.[32]

It was that September that Pedro Mártir returned from Egypt, writing to
Talavera and Tendilla of having arrived at the most secure port of all, *la Reina
Católica,* and that she had received him four times, "with composed and
serene countenance," and asked him many questions.[33] Yet, a month later, on

October 27 as, breaking tradition, the Corts at Zaragoza accepted Juana, a woman, as *"primogenita sucesora,"* Fernando heard that Isabel was gravely ill. He was at her side in Madrid within three days. Philip, whom he had left to preside, followed on November 3, leaving the Corts to Juana, who stayed twenty days more then came as well. Isabel's dire condition made succession seem an imminent possibility; the court boiled with intrigue. Yet by November 21 she had recovered sufficiently to send a letter to Manoel: such had been her health, she told him, that she could not answer his letters; she had improved and then had two setbacks but she was now much better, although she still could not write by hand.[34]

Several weeks later she had so clearly rallied that Philip was impatient to leave, to return to Flanders and by the route he had come, through France; after all, a five-month truce had been arranged in November. Isabel insisted that he ought not think of such a thing with Spain's relations with France still so bad, that he must stay and spend time with his subjects if he wanted to be obeyed later, and that certainly Juana, who was pregnant, should not travel. Philip agreed only to Juana's staying, despite her entreaties that he take her with him. If his obduracy was hard on the queen, observed Mártir, "it was much harder on his ardent spouse, who is a simple woman, although daughter of so great a woman; she did nothing but cry. Nor did it soften Philip. He is harder than a diamond."[35] He did not mention that, Besançon and some others of his entourage having died in Spain, Philip feared for his life.

Fernando went in February to Zaragoza to conclude the Corts, then to face problems Philip had left in his wake: revolt in Rosellón and French resurgence in Naples. And, exasperated that talks between Philip and Louis of France had ended in agreement that Naples would go to Charles and Claudia when they wed but in the interim be governed for them by the French and the Flemings, Fernando sent more troops to Gonzalo de Córdoba in Italy.

Fernando spent most of 1503 in his kingdoms of Aragón securing his position, for the French were pressing and should Isabel die he would, according to the terms of their marriage, lose all authority within Castile. In October he rushed to Perpignan in order to reinforce nearby Salsas against a French siege. In France, Philip sickened and lay deathly ill for two months; poison was rumored. Another event that month appeared relatively unimportant, but was not: on October 25 María had a daughter, Isabel, who would one day wed her cousin, Charles, become queen of Spain, and give birth to its next king, Philip II.

The queen effectively functioned as head of state, although she had not fully regained her health, and although anguished by war with France, by Juana's unceasing pining for her husband, and by the loss of longtime counselors and friends. Gutierre de Cárdenas and Juan Chacón died, within a few days of one another. Cárdenas, heavy and hearty, had accrued position, high trust, and tremendous wealth since the days when he had escorted Fernando into Castile to wed its princess. *Comendador* of León, *contador mayor* of the royal treasury, her *maestresala,* and a force in the Royal Council, she had entrusted him with the most delicate of missions and negotiations and with overseeing her son's household. Cárdenas, as was said, had "always lived in the palace." Juan Chacón had long ago ensured that Isabel was proclaimed queen in the crucial town of Avila, and in reward she had arranged he marry the daughter and heir of Pedro de Fajardo, Murcia's powerful *adelantado,* or governor, whom he succeeded in 1482; and he had proved a force in the campaign against Granada. Remarkably, his father, Gonzalo de Chacón, who had attended Isabel since her birth, yet lived; past seventy and a widower, he had recently taken a second, very young wife, in order, he explained, to warm his bed.[36] (Upon yet another death Isabel did not grieve, that of Alexander VI, rumored poisoned at a banquet by a drink his son, Caesare, had meant for a rich cardinal.) Mártir could only compare the queen to a gigantic rock in the sea, pounded by waves on all sides.[37] Early in January of 1503 she went with her daughter Juana to Alcalá, the residence of Cisneros, the principal statesman left to her.

There the gloom lifted. On March 10 Juana gave birth to a second son and his grandmother happily celebrated what would be her last state occasion. On the following Sunday, Isabel attended a mass of thanksgiving. She was elegantly attired "in a French skirt of fur, colored scarlet, with a large jewel at her breast, a gleaming medallion on her coat, and on her right arm an emerald and ruby bracelet that reached from wrist to elbow." Her ladies wore marten and ermine, gold and precious stones. One of the great lords present carried a gold sword; others wore gold chains and velvets, and several nobles dressed in the new style, completely in black. In the sermon that day the bishop of Málaga praised Juana and he spoke of the great armada that had carried her safely and magnificently to Flanders, the husband who contented her, and the children she bore with no pain. The last was an obvious allusion to Mary's having painlessly given birth to Jesus, and the enumerating of God's blessings upon her in a dexterous attempt to present the princess as divinely chosen to rule. Afterward Isabel and Juana dined, then they and their ladies watched from a window as the nobles and their retainers jousted in celebration.[38]

The following week it rained incessantly. Isabel ordered the baptism set for that weekend put off, until she heard the bishop of Burgos preach that postponing the ceremony placed the infant in danger of mortal sin. A solemn, and soggy, procession wended through the downpour, the child so completely wrapped in brocade that only the top of his head was visible. In Alcalá's main church, with six bishops in attendance and his grandmother looking on, the primate of Spain, Cisneros, baptized him Fernando. Cisneros was experienced; he had given thousands of Muslim converts the same name. Afterward, Isabel and Juana received well-wishers, and, the steady downpour notwithstanding, bulls were run and jousts held. That grandson of Isabel's would grow up in Spain, but then leave to rule the vast Habsburg domains in eastern Europe.

Isabel remained in Alcalá into July. She had a daughter she needed to try to train in statecraft, and a healthy grandson who proved a greater comfort than did Juana's small appreciation of queenly priorities. Isabel referred to Juana as "my mother-in-law" not only because she looked like Juana Enríquez, but because she too was inordinately headstrong. What Isabel did not mention was that Juana showed many more, and more disturbing, signs of resembling her own mother, Isabel of Portugal, in her mental distress. Juana now lived, wrote Mártir, "with furrowed brow, not speaking except to reply rudely when spoken to," and interminably insisting on returning to Philip. Her behavior, he commented, employing a graphic phrase of which he was particularly fond, was tearing at her mother's entrails; it was, he said, reviving the grief brought on by Juan's death and deepening Isabel's preoccupation with what would become of the realm.[39] Even so, Isabel continued to be active. By the time she closed the Cortes convoked the previous year, the queen had secured the needed subsidies for the renewed war in Italy; that May the Great Captain took the city of Naples.

Isabel's pleasure in that victory, however, proved short-lived, for in retaliation Louis XII sent a large force to besiege Salsas and Fernando went to relieve it. She was upset, she informed him, not so much by his being there, for she received three or four letters from him each day, but because that war was between Christians and Christian lives would be lost. She entreated him to avoid battle if possible; she prayed and she had prayers said in churches and monasteries. Seemingly in answer, the French decamped. As to exacting vengeance for the bother they had caused the Spanish, wrote Mártir, she would leave them to God.[40] Isabel had had enough of warfare among Christians, from which she seemed to exclude war in Italy.

While, in what was to be the last year of her life, she came to eschew revenge, at least in one instance, yet it might well be that she had come to prefer achieving it through statecraft. Louis XII had worked against Spanish interests in the independent kingdom of Navarre, and she sought to offset his influence there through the betrothing of her Habsburg granddaughter, Isabel, to the Navarrese prince and heir, Enrique. And, in mid-April, to bring matters to a head with Henry VII, she ordered the Flanders fleet to go to England to bring home the widowed Catalina. On June 23, the king of England, apprized on Isabel's instructions and cognizant that the Spaniards were destroying the French army in Italy, signed the contract for Catalina's marriage to the son who was to succeed him as Henry VIII.[41]

Impasse

In June Isabel was again very ill, and again seemed to be recovering, until on the twentieth her doctors had cause to write to Fernando. They had bled her, they wrote, and she had had only a low fever and little pain; but yesterday, having left her apartments to see Juana, she had returned terribly altered, her face drawn and drained of color. She had spoken of feeling cold and of great internal pain, then for four hours she ran so high a fever that they had despaired of her life. Today, praise God, although still in much pain she had sweat copiously and at midnight the fever had abated, the pain had subsided, and she had eaten a little and was better. "Your highness must believe," they concluded, "that it is a great danger to the health of the Queen to have the life she has with the Princess."[42]

Isabel had good cause for being upset. Such was "the disposition of the Princess" as the physicians described it, "that not only should it pain those who see her often and love her greatly, but also anyone at all, even strangers, because she sleeps badly, eats little and at times nothing, and she is very sad and thin. Sometimes she does not wish to talk and appears as though in a trance; her infirmity progresses greatly." It was customary, they explained, to treat Juana's infirmity through love, entreaty, or fear; but the princess had proven unreceptive to entreaty, and even "a little force" affected her so adversely that it was a great pity to attempt it and no one wanted to try, so that, beyond the queen's customary immense labors and concerns, this weight of caring for her daughter fell upon her. It has been conjectured that Isabel's illness could have been cancer, endocarditis—infection of the heart valve— chronic dropsy, or several of them combined. By the following June she had a visible tumor, although it is not known where or of what sort.[43]

In August she took Juana to Segovia, which she had seemingly avoided for years, telling her it was a step toward the north coast and her departure for Flanders. There Isabel continued to try with little success to get her to turn her mind to affairs of state.

Juana showed little interest in government and in her child, and a good deal of disregard for religious matters of any sort, and for public opinion as well. The princess appeared to disdain much of what Isabel valued, and even to represent the antithesis of the very qualities her mother valued most highly. Even so, Juana was her designated successor, and Isabel was determined to keep her in Spain and do her best to train her to be its queen. So the arguments against Juana's departure were patiently repeated: the season, the sea, the French, that Philip should be safe in Ghent before she traveled, and did she not want to see her father before she left? The hope remained that Juana would stay and Charles join her, so that Isabel might have him educated in Spain's customs and come to prefer its people. And with Juana and Charles there and

Philip not, should Isabel die, Fernando, still king of Aragón, could surely manage to guide their daughter in governing Castile.

It was November. A treaty with France—arranged by the queen of France, Anne of Brittany, and Margaret of Austria—had been signed, and an envoy arrived from Philip requesting that Juana return to Flanders. Isabel, playing for time, responded that the princess, although better, was not well, that relations with France were still such that it was not safe for her to travel by land or, now that it was winter, by sea, that she had better wait until spring, and that "following her frame of mind and *la pasión* she has" that Juana should not be where there was no one who could quiet and restrain her for it might be dangerous for her.[44] The implication was that Juana was emotionally out of control. Exactly what was meant by "restrain" we do not know.

Isabel, hoping to cheer her daughter up and keep her from leaving, sent her to Medina del Campo at fair time, holding it out as a further step toward taking ship on the northern coast. Once there Juana, receiving letters from Philip urging her to come immediately by land or by sea, for the French had assured safe conduct, insisted on departing, although, as Isabel herself later recounted the episode to Fuensalida, "against our will." Nonetheless, Juana ordered her bags packed and her household readied. Isabel, advised, said she then sent Juan Rodríguez de Fonseca, who was then bishop of Córdoba and who had been Juana's tutor, to talk her out of it, "for it would appear to everyone to be a very bad thing, of such shame for her and of so much disrespect for us."[45]

Fonseca arrived to encounter Juana standing outside the inner door of the castle of La Mota where she was staying, just about to leave, and pleaded with her to return to her apartments and await her mother's permission to depart. Juana held her ground. Fonseca, caught between duty to his queen and ruining his future by alienating her successor, temporized, ordering, in the queen's name, that no horses be brought. Juana countered; she would walk to the stables through the city streets. He, "in order to see that, in view of her authority and the estimation of her person, she did not do so unreasonable a thing in sight of the natives and strangers who were there for the fair," had the outer doors of the fortress closed. She threatened him with death and refused to go back into the castle. Fonseca went for Isabel.

Despite everyone's pleas, Juana remained between La Mota's inner and outer gates, during one of the coldest nights of that winter—burning with the fury, said Mártir, of an African lioness—and the next day she retreated into an adjacent fruit-storage shed. Isabel sent notes to her by courier, to no avail, and then dispatched Cisneros and the admiral of Castile, who could not budge her either. After four or five days of stalemate, the queen came herself, traveling the sixty miles from Segovia within two days, in a litter, as she informed Fuensalida, "with more effort and speed and making longer daily journeys than good for my health." Upon arrival, Isabel entered the shed to find Juana crouched under a table. Isabel suggested she return to her apartments, and met rebuff: "She spoke to me very resentfully words of such disrespect and so far from what a daughter ought to say to a mother, that if it were not for the state in which she was, I would not have suffered it in any manner." Patiently, the queen who had swayed thousands managed to coax her daughter back into the castle and on various pretexts to continue to delay her departure. If she would wait, Isabel promised, a fleet large enough to protect her would be readied to sail as soon as the weather broke—that is, in the spring. Juana stayed, and so did her mother.

Isabel had managed to keep her daughter in Spain for over a year. In January of 1504 Philip seemed willing to send Charles to Spain in exchange for the governance of Naples. In March, Isabel at length agreed Juana might go to the coast, and the distraught woman who would one day wear Castile's crown departed, only to be forced to wait for two more months in Laredo for clement weather.

Medina del Campo: 1504

Isabel remained in Medina del Campo, in the royal great-house or palace on the plaza. She had come full circle; this was the closest place to home, to Arévalo and Madrigal, that could accommodate her court. It was the town that her brother, Alfonso, had given her long ago. Time and again she had come with him and then Fernando to its fairs. From Medina, she had had war proclaimed against Granada. From there she now sent off her grandson, the infant Fernando, whom Juana had left behind and whom Isabel pampered, to be raised as she had been, in Arévalo by trusted retainers. But it was his older brother, Charles, whom more than ever she wanted to have in Spain.

Juana arrived in Flanders in May. Isabel received dismal reports: her daughter did not want Charles to come to Spain and, finding the so-desired Philip cool to her, in a fit of jealous rage Juana had attacked one of her ladies whom she suspected of being a rival for his affections. Philip had upbraided her, perhaps even hit her, and declared that he would no longer "spend time" with her. Isabel, highly indignant and hugely frustrated, could only instruct Fuensalida to do his best and to chide Philip for not treating his wife kindly, for she was so obviously of unsound mind.[46] That fall Isabel's health again worsened. Fernando arrived in Medina del Campo in time for Christmas, and he stayed.

A letter from her secretary, Conchillos, to Fernando's, Almazán, written early that December of 1503, revealed Isabel hard at work, getting off dispatches at midnight and permitting him little sleep. She signed ordinary documents until May of 1504, then until September only those of great importance. Sometime during that period, Prospero Colonna, ally and *condottierre*, arrived from Italy, declaring that "he had come to see she who ruled the world from her bed."[47]

Bedridden, she had her room hung with certain tapestries: some depicted themes from the Apocalypse of St. John, some represented God the Father, and a series of them graphically illustrated a popular legend wrongly attributing to Pope Gregory I the Great a heaven-sent vision of the literal presence of Christ's blood in the host. She chose too a tapestry of death personified and several of greenery and one of Cupid and the triumph of love. On her bed hangings were three scenes from the life of that legendary forebear of hers, Hercules, the preeminent royal exemplar of power.[48] Exemplary too was the woman lying amid that visual potpourri so emblematic of her diverse sources of inspiration. As spring approached, she had a door and eight windows cut into the walls of the room to admit air, light, and the smell of flowers.[49]

On April 5 there was a great earthquake. It signified to the credulous, of which there were many, a new time of woe for the kingdom, and indeed pestilence and hunger followed. The tremor was especially devastating in Andalusia; nonetheless the queen and king felt the shock while at the Hieronymite Monastery of La Mejorada, not far from Medina, where they had gone for their customary Eastertime retreat. Mejorada had the feel of the royal houses in which Isabel had been born and raised. It offered familiarity and a sense of continuity with the atmosphere of Guadalupe, which was too far for her to travel now. It offered too the religious approach of Talavera's Hieronymites, and so in effect a comforting alternative to Cisneros's less accessible God.[50] They stayed at Mejorada for over two months, then, within days of returning to Medina on July 26, both Isabel and Fernando developed a high fever. His illness and consequent absence deeply upset her; she once again feared for his life. He recovered fully; she did not. Even so, in August she could write Fuensalida, unhappily, that "the discontent and lack of love" between Juana and Philip "weighs on us greatly"; that he must do what he could. With all her strength of will and her remarkable lucidity, Isabel saw herself reduced to impotence precisely in what was most important to her.

After September 14 she signed no state papers and she developed an insatiable thirst, diagnosed as a sign of worsening dropsy.[51] On September 26 Fernando sent word secretly to Philip and Juana: Isabel was dying. She had had fever since July, and serious seizures recently; they should be prepared to come. "Fever consumes her," wrote Mártir on October 7.[52]

Legacies

On October 12, Isabel did sign one more document, a will; it was customary to do so only in one's final days. It reveals much of her state of mind at the end of her life, of how far she had or had not traveled mentally and spiritually. While her body was infirm, it began, "of an infirmity that God wished to give me," her mind was "healthy and free." Then, as customary, she invoked God and the Virgin Mary and certain other heavenly protectors, her choice of saints highly personal and unusually meticulously explained. She called upon "the powerful, Father and Son and Holy Spirit, three persons and one divine essence," the Trinity that was the "universal Creator and Governor of Heaven and Earth and of all things, visible and invisible," and on the Virgin Mary, "Queen of the Heavens and Lady of the Angels, our Lady and advocate"; and she went on to single out certain other members of "the court of Heaven."[53] The kingdom of heaven, she clearly assumed, was structured much like her own; she had always seen hers as its earthly counterpart.

Next she invoked the help of "that very excellent Prince of the Church and the *Cavallería angelical,* the archangel Saint Michael, and of the glorious celestial messenger, the archangel Saint Gabriel," observing that the two were of first rank. She then singled out, above the other *sanctos y sanctas* of the court of Heaven "especially that very holy precursor and herald of our Redeemer Jesus Christ, Saint John the Baptist," and those princes among the apostles, Saints Peter and Paul, and "all the other apostles, particularly the very blessed saint *Juan Evangelista,* beloved disciple of our Lord Jesus Christ and great and shining eagle, to whom He reveals his very high mysteries and secrets. . . . This holy Apostle and Evangelist I have for my special advocate in this present life."

It not surprising that one of the first words of that testament of hers is *poderoso,* full of power, and that in her regard for heaven's court the queen manifested the punctilious sense of hierarchy and protocol she had shown all her life. In calling upon both Saints John and a dual devotion, Isabel voiced her closeness to Fernando and reaffirmed that the two saints, in being identified with the Juans of her life, linked Spain's kingdoms as well. The two saints served also to entwine biblical revelation with millennial expectation and with the belief that she herself and her people were chosen to carry out God's plan. Isabel had not abandoned certainty of her own direct relationship with God; quite the contrary. She still assumed that He had singled her out to suffer, unquestionably with purpose. Now she was bearing it well through her last display of self-mastery on earth; she was making a good death. And making a good death was very much on her mind: "For while it is certain," she had dictated, "that we have to die, it is uncertain when or where we will die, so that we ought to live as though each hour we might have to die."

It was the Evangelist especially whom she expected to be her advocate in the hour of her death, and "in that very terrible judgment and stringent examination, most terrible against the powerful, when my soul will be presented before the seat and royal throne of the Sovereign Judge, [who is] very just and very evenhanded, by whom, according to our merits, all of us have to be judged." Moreover, the Evangelist would then unite with his brother, Saint James, whom the Lord had given to her kingdoms as patron, and also with Saint Francis and "those glorious confessors and great friends of our Lord, Saint Jerome and Saint Dominic, who as evening stars shine resplendently in the western parts of these my kingdoms, to the eve of the end of the world."

It will be recalled that when Constantinople fell shortly after Isabel's birth, some Spaniards had discerned, even laid claim to Spain being, a new sun, or a new star, rising in the west to counterbalance that loss and redress it. That symbolism had found reflection in her parents' tomb, and, for Isabel, at the end of her life, it was those two saints, the twin evocations of the western star, who were to guide that westering progression of empire to her realms and so to its final, golden conclusion. Isabel then invoked one more special advocate, a surprising one—St. Mary Magdalene, with no explanation. A generation later, a humanist would provide enlightenment in noting "Look how we divide among our saints the functions of the gentile gods. Mars has been succeeded by Santiago and Saint George . . . and, in place of Venus, *la Magdalena.*"[54]

Isabel had formed a very clear idea of how she ought to die and how best to arrange for reaching and entering heaven. She sought, she said, to imitate "good king Hezekiah," in disposing of her *casa,* her earthly goods, as if she had to leave this world immediately.[55] She commended her spirit to Jesus Christ, then voiced a concern of the sort she had expressed to Talavera a decade ago: "And if none can justify themselves before Him, how much less can we of great kingdoms and estates who have to give account?" She requested that Mary, queen of heaven, and her chosen saints be her advocates when she should stand before him. And she made a further request: "I wish the blessed prince of angelic chivalry, the archangel Saint Michael, to receive my soul and to shelter and defend it from that cruel beast and ancient serpent who will then wish to swallow me, and not to leave [my soul] until through the mercy of our Lord it may be placed in that glory for which it was created." Her concept of Michael reflects her often observed fusion of the chivalric and the holy.

The beast and the serpent—apocalyptic creatures from the Book of Revelation of Saint John the Evangelist—were usually construed as Antichrist and Satan.[56] She had attacked and thrust out of her realms those whom she had come to see as their minions—the Muslims, the heretics, the Jews—and now she feared their vengeance. This queen who had spent so much of her life at war dreaded being at the mercy of old enemies and, while certain her soul was destined for glory, yet looked to a sword-wielding saint to guard her way to it. Her view of death was an extension of her view of life; both were perilous passages between good and evil and along the way constant war must be waged by everyone, and especially by monarchs such as she, against the forces of darkness. Belief in that incessant battle between good and evil had been central to the religion of her childhood and then to her developing sense of what she as a queen must do and be. It had been reinforced in the years of fighting the Moor. It had if anything intensified after 1492, justifying her policies regarding infidel and heretic, escalating her animosity toward Jews and Muslims, and intensifying her striving to be seen as behaving morally, as God wished.

In what has since been termed a messianic outbreak as the century turned, and within messianic expectation earlier, Saint Michael was often substituted for Christ militant in saving worthy souls and in crushing Satan permanently at the Second Coming.[57] In earlier illuminations of the Beatus of Liebana's commentary on the Book of Revelation, it is Michael who binds the dragon in the abyss; on a Catalan altarpiece Michael disputes the fate of a soul with the devil. Michael was also often depicted with a balance for judging souls in his left hand and a sword in his right; and Michael slew the dragon on the seal used by Rodrigo Borja as papal legate in Spain in 1472.[58] The grandson whom Isabel had expected to inherit the realm had been baptized Miguel, although no forebear of hers had held that name. Thirty years previously in Segovia, it was before the church of San Miguel that Isabel had been proclaimed queen of Castile. The powerful Saint Michael was also an easy substitute for Saint George, whose specialty was dragon slaying and on whose day she was in fact born. And Michael as patron saint was much favored by European monarchs.

Her last will abundantly corroborates that, whatever changes of heart or mind she may have experienced in conformity with new religious trends, several early traits of hers persisted. Isabel had not relinquished Talavera's righteous, personal, punishing, and essentially rational deity, nor her sense of her own direct relationship with God the Father, nor her lifelong vision of heaven as organized much like the kingdoms she knew, with a monarch and court. There were jousts and balls in paradise. And there remained much chivalry in her theology. Like a proper knight she had quested to find herself and striven to serve her Lord; she had fought to recover a kingdom, even to establish an empire, and she prized honor highly. Her concept of heaven remained essentially that of the kings who had preceded her, notably Alfonso X, whose *Partidas* spoke of God having organized his court in hierarchical order—of archangels and angels, saints and pious souls—within a hierarchic universe. And in her will she frequently referred to her own "absolute royal power."[59]

Still, she displayed one aspect of the humility then in fashion among Europe's mighty. She instructed that her body be interred in the Franciscan monastery of Santa Isabel in Granada and be clothed in the habit of the order of Saint Francis, "that blessed poor man of Christ," and that her tomb be low and unadorned, but then added: if the king chose to lie elsewhere, her body was to be buried with his, "because I hope that the *ayuntamiento*, the physical intimacy, and [the intimacy] of our souls we had while living, we may in the mercy of God have in heaven, and that our bodies laying in the ground may have and represent it."

She requested no extravagant funeral honors, and she stipulated that what was customarily spent on mourning instead go to pay for clothing for the poor. All her debts must be paid. She charged the consciences of her executors with carrying out everything she considered most conducive to achieving the welfare of her soul. To that end, they were to do several things: have masses said, twenty thousand of them, in the most devout churches and monasteries;[60] have *maravedís* given to dower poor girls for marriage and convent; see to clothing two hundred poor "so that they may be special supplicants to God for me," and redeem two hundred captives from the infidel, "so that the Lord grant me jubilee [on judgment day] and remission of all sins and blame." They were to have alms given, in the cathedral of Toledo and to Our Lady of Guadalupe and to other pious foundations, as was customary.[61] They were also to comply with her father's last will, and to honor and care for the tombs of her parents and brother in Miraflores. At the last, she could surely rest secure in having established, to her own satisfaction, her position within the direct line of Castile's ruling monarchs. What she could not do, however, was be sure of its survival on the throne.

To discharge her conscience, for as a monarch she must render account to God for the well-being of the realm, she declared she now regretted some recent decisions she had countenanced that confirmed practices she felt detrimental to the crown and the public good. She asked God's pardon for the proliferation of offices in the realm, wanting their number restored to what it had been "in accord with the good and old custom of the kingdoms." She wanted annulled certain *mercedes* of questionable legality, revoking one such grant in no uncertain terms: "by my own will and certain knowledge and absolute royal power which in this situation I want to employ and do employ. . . ." Further, her heirs must never alienate either the *marquesado* of Villena or Gibraltar; undoubtedly she remembered the mischief done by Pacheco as the powerful marqués de Villena, and she wanted to ensure dynastic control of the strategic Strait of Gibraltar in the interests of trade, defense against Islam, and advance into Africa. Moreover, when Gibraltar had been won from Muslims in her youth, she had seen its conquest viewed as emblematic of Spain as the final imperial world power and as fulfilling prophecy, that "in the West the sun of righteousness had risen." Gibraltar's domination had gained and retained symbolic as well as real value; it was corroborative of royal purpose and of God's.

Isabel had, she confessed, allowed some nobles to collect taxes that were rightfully hers; they must not be permitted to claim that permission as custom and so continue collecting them. She had heard that some great nobles and others impeded recourse to royal justice; that situation should be remedied.

Certain revenues of Seville that she had conceded to her daugher, María, queen of Portugal, were María's for her lifetime only. Isabel also warned against making the *juros* given in exchange for funds for the war against Granada perpetual; her successors should redeem them, with the revenues of Granada if possible, so that the crown would not face ongoing debt. And she directed that the dowries of María and Catalina promised to Portugal and England be paid.

While designating Juana her heir, she made her lack of enthusiasm for the prospect plain: "conforming with what I ought to do and am obliged to by law, I order and establish and institute her as my universal heir . . . to be received as true queen and natural proprietress." All fidelity should be given to Philip, as her husband; Isabel meant as king consort, not as king. And, immediately following Juana's accession, all the *alcaides* of *alcázares* and forts and the lieutenants of cities, towns, and places should take an oath to her, and the fortified places be held for her alone. Isabel returned to a favorite theme in requesting that, fulfilling her obligation as queen and in accord with laws made by her progenitors, no royal post or ecclesiastical dignity be given to a foreigner, for those not native-born did not know Spain's laws or customs and the people would not be content. She stated it twice, and commanded "the Prince and Princess, my children," to guard and comply with that request and do nothing contrary to it. Isabel, who had never left Spain, did not trust foreigners and especially those surrounding Philip. And she specified that "the isles and mainland of the Ocean Sea" and the Canary Islands belonged under the crown of Castile. As for America, she showed no continental sense of it; for her it remained principally a way station to the East.

To the last, Isabel was a crusader. She commanded "the Princess and Her Husband" to honor God and the faith and to take up the obligation to protect and defend the Holy Mother Church, as they were obliged to do, and in that connection she coupled overseas conquest and internal orthodoxy, insisting "that they not cease the conquest of Africa and the fight for the Faith against the infidel, and that they always favor highly the things of the holy Inquisition against the depraved heretic [now the common term for secret Jew]."

She did as much as she could legally to see that Fernando retained power. At the behest of the deputies of the Cortes of 1502 and after having consulted some nobles and prelates, she instructed that, should Juana come to the realm and then leave it or cease governing for any reason, then "the King, My Lord, in such cases ought to rule and govern and administer these kingdoms for the Princess," or, "if she does not wish to govern them or can not take charge of governing them, the King is to do it until the *infante don Carlos* is of age, that is, at least twenty years old." Thereby having tried to give Fernando many years of rule in setting Charles's majority so high, she went on to ask him expressly to accept that responsibility. She relied, she explained, on what he had always done to increase the royal patrimony, and she requested he take an oath to continue to do so. She ordered her people to obey him. And, revealing her own doubts, she asked "the Princess, my daughter, and her husband always to be very obedient and subject to the King, and honor him as obedient children ought to honor a good father and, for the good of the realm, follow his orders and counsel." She asked them all to live in love and unity and harmony. In short, she did not want Juana to rule Spain, thinking her not competent to do it, and she particularly did not want Philip ruling it for her. Isabel now did her best to give to Fernando all the power that she herself had insisted, years before, in limiting in the interests of assuring her inheritance as a woman and the primacy of her own authority. It was another in the long string of ironies threading through her life. Yet the most dreadful irony was that, of her remaining children, the least competent was to inherit the crown.

In her will, she eulogized Fernando. He should, she said, be honored and respected for being so excellent and renowned a king, gifted with such virtues and so many of them. He had worked mightily "in recovering my kingdoms, so alienated at the time I succeeded," and in combating the great ills and wars and turbulent movements of the time, and no less had he risked his royal person in gaining the kingdom of Granada and thrusting from it the enemies of the faith, "and in bringing those kingdoms to the good government and justice in which they are today by grace of God." She and he, she declared, had always lived in much love and concord, and she charged her children, Juana and Philip, to have for one another that love and union and conformity she expected of them. Yet again, she returned to what she owed Fernando for having taken great care in administering her realm. And, since Granada, the Canaries, and the isles and mainland of the Ocean Sea must, in accord with the papal bull, remain within the kingdom of Castile, there was reason that he be "in some way served by me and those of my kingdoms, although it can not do as much as Your Lordship merits and I desire." Accordingly, beyond the masterships of the military orders he held for life, she instructed he be paid annually half the revenues of the islands and mainland of the Ocean Sea and other stipulated rents.

Mercedes were to be given her servants, *continos,* and familiars, among them the marqués and marquesa of Moya and Gonzalo de Chacón, for having served her loyally. And she established the order of succession: after Juana, Charles, his descendants, males to be preferred over females, conforming to the *Partidas,* down through Catalina, princess of Wales, and her progeny. As for her possessions: the jewels given her by Juana and Philip were to be returned. "The relic that I have of the breechcloth of Our Lord" should be given to the monastery of San Antonio in Segovia; all the rest of her relics were to go to the cathedral of Granada. All the things she had in the *alcázar* of Segovia must be sold to pay her debts and bequests, and everything else given to churches and monasteries, except that the king was to take any jewels and things he wished, "because seeing them he can have more continuous reminder of the singular love I always have had for him, and because since he knows he must die and I hope it is in another century, that with this memory he can live more holy and justly."

As executors she named Fernando and four of her counselors—Cisneros, "*mi confesor;*"; Antonio de Fonseca, her *contador mayor;* Juan Velázquez, Juana's *contador mayor;* and Diego de Deza, Fernando's confessor—and also a secretary and *contador* of hers, Juan López de Lecarraga. Once her body was interred in the monastery in the Alhambra, the body of her daughter Isabel should be carried there as well, and a tomb of alabaster be made for the burial of her son Juan in the monastery of Saint Thomas in Avila. A royal chapel should be constructed in the cathedral in Granada. (It was, and her tomb is there next to that of Fernando.) The original copy of her will was to be deposited in the monastery of Guadalupe. She signed it before a notary and seven witnesses, among them three bishops.

A month later, on November 23, she added a codicil. It principally had to do with some specific matters she said she had on her conscience, and so sheds light into some dark corners. The Holy See had conceded bulls of crusade specifically for campaigns against Granada, the Muslims of Africa, and the Turks, all "enemies of our holy Catholic faith"; if those funds had been spent on other things, she directed, they should be paid back. She had wanted to put order in the laws, and now charged Juana and Philip with it, although nothing should be enacted against ecclesiastical immunity and liberty. She acknowledged that measures taken to reform monasteries had sometimes exceeded the powers vested in the reformers; and she worried about how just was the pricing of the *alcabalas,* "because they are the greatest and most principal of royal rents," and of other taxes. Well she might, for administrative corruption and financial fraud had soared in the last decade, and the obvious need to reform the mechanisms of royal income had recently led to an official investigation that was still underway.

She instructed further that twenty thousand masses be said for the souls of her dead retainers, and that her mother's servants be provided for. And she asked that, since the papacy had conceded the isles and mainland of the Ocean Sea in order to convert those peoples, Fernando and Juana do no harm to those Indians or their goods, but treat them justly and well, and "if they were receiving any harm, to remedy it, so that it did not exceed the apostolic letter of concession." That injunction, while part of her great concern to die with a clear conscience and so a requisite for salvation, was also an admission, in circuitous and least self-incriminating fashion possible, of having transgressed moral and legal bounds in regard to the people of the Indies. Interpreted within context, of prime consideration to her was not so much the welfare of the natives as that she might have jeopardized her soul in overstepping the papal concession, and endangered Castile's holding of the Indies as well.

A dispatch sent from Flanders on November 1 had arrived at Medina on November 21, with no good news. Philip was avoiding Juana, and Juana was behaving very oddly, constantly washing her hair and bathing and allowing only her Moorish slave women near her. Philip, irritated, had sent orders that she must dismiss them. Juana refused. He came personally to insist. When Juana asked why he had ordered the slaves sent away, Philip replied it was because she wished to do nothing he wished, that she must be attended by decorous older women, and that he would not sleep with her until she complied. Within a week he had sent home those women of hers and locked Juana in, fearing she too would leave for Spain. He was, in fact, considering coming to Spain without her.[62] Heaven did not seem to be smiling on the queen of Castile's lifelong work. Given that situation, Isabel, by her codicil, sought to make doubly sure that she was seen to have done her best in God's sight. As for her kingdoms and her family, she could but leave them to heaven, and, as far as morally and legally permissible, to Fernando.

For fifty days public processions and prayers had been made for her recovery; now, "seeing it the will of God to carry her to her rest," she ordered her people to cease importuning God to restore her health.[63] She avowedly put aside things of this world, and command, and royal dignities. In her illness she could not sleep, said a contemporary; but in those vigils God gave her consolation, compunction, and understanding of his secrets, so that she said never had she had so much of all of them in her life. She thought about many passages of the Holy Scriptures and she said never until then had she understood the readings from Job that are said in the office of the dead. She had, that is, prayed and meditated on biblical texts, as advocated by Cisneros and in accord with the new spirituality, but the texts she chose, her interpretation of them, and her concept of making a good death were nonetheless highly traditional. As her will attests, a central aspect of the new spirituality, the imitation of a humble and pacific Christ, was not a foremost concern of hers at the last. Undoubtedly that way of approaching God was too removed—from being a queen as she construed it, from the militant faith she knew, and from those religious principles that traditionally sanctified reigns on Earth, including her own.

Isabel died on November 26, a Tuesday, between eleven and twelve in the morning, having received all the sacraments, although her modesty was such that in receiving extreme unction from the prior of La Mejorada she would not allow her clothing to be raised above her feet.[64] So runs the usual interpretation. Yet extreme unction was widely feared and put off until the last minute, for it was commonly believed that once received one could have no further sexual relations, a belief responding to the custom of anointing not only the loci of the five senses but the kidneys as seat of sexual desire. However that may be, Isabel the literalist expected life eternal and she had assuredly precluded the anointing of her kidneys. Fernando recounted her last minutes: "she received the sacraments of the Church very much awake and with contrition, which certainly in part alleviates our work."[65] He was, that is, certain of her going to heaven and of having an advocate there. As the friar intoned the last rites, at the phrase "*in manus tuas*," it is said she sighed and made the sign of the cross, and when he said "*Consummatum est*," she died. ". . . And thus the most excellent Queen *doña* Isabel ended her days."[66]

Requiem

Reminiscent of her device, the bundle of arrows, hers were a bundle of qualities, shaped in interaction with her world and circumstances, within what was possible. Her sense of morality, perceived by her as promptings of the royal conscience, bound them firmly together. Hers was a moral sentiment of time and place, culturally derived. She saw herself as an absolute monarch within Spanish tradition and strove conscientiously to fulfill her obligations and moral responsibilities to God and to her realm.

To Isabel, morality and piety were of a piece, as were position and self. All were inseparable and mutually supportive. We know that she believed in heaven and hell, and in God's revelation through John the Evangelist of Christ's apocalyptic Second Coming and the divine schema for the end of the world. Whether or not she herself believed that the last days were imminent, she knew many of her subjects did, and she did believe that during that final time certain conditions had to prevail, notably the absence of infidel, heretics, and Jews, and that the devout alone were then to inhabit the Earth, most likely under a single world emperor. She repeatedly endorsed that conviction and she did everything in her power to bring about those conditions. That mindcast enabled her to construe as inevitable the death and destruction she inflicted, to see the campaigns against Muslims and Jews and the workings of the Inquisition as ultimately to good purpose and the salvation of souls. Within the general climate of practices and convictions of her time, Isabel could believe that her intentions were essentially good, her cause the highest. That said, the suffering she caused was monstrous.

Yet if God as she conceived of him, the stern and militant God of the Old Testament, had designed a punishment for her, it could not have been greater: to lift and then dash her hopes of dynasty so indistinguishable from children well raised and well married and grandchildren in the same mold; to inflict a string of family deaths, killing her slowly, excruciatingly, and, at the end, leaving the one child who could undo her life's work, because of the precedent she herself set, as her successor. Still, she never lost her sense of her own direct and personal two-way relationship with God. Explanation for her torment she found in the tribulations of Job.[67] And there we must leave her, entrusting her soul to Saint Michael to shepherd past the apocalyptic beast and the old dragon.

Epilogue
"A Queen Has Disappeared . . ."

A Queen has disappeared who has no equal on earth for her greatness of spirit, purity of heart, Christian piety, equal justice to all, [or for] her spirit of conserving the old laws and putting order in the new, or for the creation of a rich patrimony and a strong economy, which is most important for the realm and the people.

—Francisco Jiménez de Cisneros[1]

She, besides being such a person and so very close to us, deserved so much for being in herself gifted with so many and such singular excellences, she who was in her lifetime exemplary in all acts of virtue and the fear of God; and she so loved and saw to our life, health, and honor that we were obliged to love her above all the things of this world.

—Fernando[2]

The Queen is in hell, for she oppressed people. . . . Those kingdoms had been very badly governed; and the king of Aragón and she did nothing but rob those kingdoms and were very tyrannical.

—a denunciation made to the Royal Council, 1506[3]

Isabel's funeral cortege traversed the realm, from Medina del Campo to Granada, at its head a silver cross was carried, lent by the Franciscan monastery in Arévalo and draped in black cloth. Prelates and priests and Pedro Mártir, Beatriz de Bobadilla, and many of Isabel's household escorted the plain coffin, trussed with cords and protectively covered with calf hide. Through Arévalo, Toro, Cardeñosa, Toledo, and Jaén they went, as though marking off Isabel's milestones. They proceeded, for weeks, through unceasing rain, over roads and rivers so flooded that Mártir declared he had not encountered such perils in the whole of his hazardous journey to Egypt. It is said the sun only broke through on the day they reached Granada, December 18. Isabel was interred, as she had stipulated, in the Franciscan monastery in the Alhambra, "with such sorrow and sentiment of all the city that I never saw nor heard so marvelous a thing,"—Tendilla wrote Fernando—"and now this treasure lies in this monastery."[4] To that faithful lieutenant and many others the queen's

Figure 19. Coffins of Isabel and Fernando, Juana and Felipe, in crypt below tombs. Royal Chapel, Granada.

body was close to being a holy relic. Nor had the deluge been unexpected: well-known was a prophecy of Merlin's that foretold an iron monarch and heretics burned, and predicted that "a great rain will fall so that the earth will be as wet as when it lies under water."[5]

On the day she died, Fernando had written to Philip that "she was the best and most excellent wife that ever a king had, the sorrow of the absence of her is ripping my entrails . . . but otherwise seeing that she died as holy and Catholicly as she lived, is to believe that our Lord has her in her glory, which for her is a better and more lasting kingdom than that she had here. . . ." He had no doubt she would soon have status in heaven commensurate to that she had enjoyed on Earth.[6] Two days before her death, he had instructed Fuensalida to "say clearly to the Prince our son, and to his people, if they talk about it, that, if the Queen dies, may God protect her, the Princess has to come to take possession and governance of these kingdoms as proprietary *señora,* that they then will be hers, and that without her the Prince has no part, nor will he be received in any manner."[7]

Isabel might truthfully have said on more counts than one, "after me, the deluge." Fernando had lost not only his wife but Castile. The very afternoon of her death he gave indication of what he would do about it. He had the customary banners raised for Juana as *reina propietaria* of Castile, and he also had himself proclaimed governor and administrator for her. Messengers carried word to the realm's dignitaries and municipalities that all Castile was to follow that formula and to obey his commands and decisions and to show him obedience and loyalty, as conforming with the desires expressed in the Cortes of 1502.[8] Now he quickly convoked Cortes in Toro, where he had triumphed in battle nearly thirty years before; undoubtedly he meant to remind Castilians of his exertion on their behalf ever since. On January 11, the delegates heard Isabel's last will, declared it the law of the land, and, in accord with it, took an oath to Fernando as governor and administrator. And, in secret session, they unanimously agreed that if Juana was ill, Fernando should be permanent regent and that Philip was to be informed of that decision.[9] The week before Isabel died, Mártir reported nobles scurrying to Philip; gain, he commented, was always to be had when there was discord about succession. Thus, notably absent at Toro were most of Castile's great lords. Still, Fernando counted on Alba and a few others, on Cisneros, on the towns (once again beset by nobles), and on Tendilla, who made certain Granada and all Andalusia stayed calm.[10]

In May of 1505, Juana wrote de Vere, the Flemish ambassador in Spain, that it was maliciously being said she had lost her wits and that the king her father was pleased for he wanted to govern; and she instructed, "speak to him for me, for I do not believe it." If she had shown temper, she went on, it was because of jealousy, which was not unique to her. "My lady, the Queen, who is in God's glory, who was so excellent and renowed a person was also jealous, just as it pleased God to make me"; and she added (with pathos and hope) that in Isabel's case, time had amended it.[11] Unfortunately for the succession, it was one of the few of Isabel's traits her daughter Juana could claim.

Not until the spring of 1506 did Juana and Philip return to Spain, and then with an armed host. Even then, Philip was in no hurry to leave Galicia until seeing who would come to join him. In the interim, Fernando had stunned everyone by allying with Louis XII of France and, on October 12, 1505, he contracted to wed Louis's niece, Germaine de Foix, claimant to the crown of Navarre. (Even earlier, he had tried unsuccessfully to marry Juana, the Excellent Lady.) He married Germaine less than a month before the arrival of Juana and Philip. Now Fernando was in León from where, conscious of having attracted far fewer of the nobility than had Philip, he sent emissaries of welcome to his daughter and son-in-law. He also sent Cisneros, who arranged for Fernando and Philip to meet. They did so in June at Remesal, with great formality. Philip arrived with an army, Fernando with his best resources, patience and a plan. He got Philip to recognize his, Fernando's, position in accord with the terms of Isabel's will; then both agreed that Juana was incompetent to rule and that Philip was to exercise exclusive power. They had, thereby, gone against the will, as Fernando knew and stated in a secret document in which he repudiated those agreements as having been signed under duress and in order to avoid civil war. He further swore that he would gainsay neither Isabel's will nor Juana's rights.

Fernando retired to Aragón and in September he sailed for Italy. In Castile, the Cortes confirmed Philip and Juana as king and queen, and Philip took power. He turned over to his current *privado*, the Castilian noble, Juan Man-uel, a number of forts, including the *alcázar* of Segovia, and lavished upon him other *mercedes*, making him Castile's most powerful lord. Others of his retinue grabbed towns. Then, having ruled for less than three months, Philip fell ill and, within days, he died, on September 25, 1506. There was rumor that Fer-nando had him poisoned, but his doctors insisted it was plague and anyway Fernando was in Italy and in no hurry to come home.

Throughout Castile, factions were once again feuding violently, backed by nobles now unrestrained. Mártir beseeched Almazán, Fernando's secretary, to "come save us from the wolves." Medina Sidonia was stopped from retak-ing Gibraltar, indeed Andalusia held, by the redoubtable Tendilla. Muslims raided the coasts; Isabel had been prescient. As for Juana, she provided raw material for legend. Lucidly, she revoked all of Philip's *mercedes* in one day, but she did not govern. Juana traveled Castile's roads with a cart carrying Phil-ip's body, although lacking the heart, which had been sent to Flanders, and the entrails, which had been interred in Miraflores. She may well have feared the Flemings would otherwise steal it away to Flanders, and so decided to take it to be entombed in Granada. On the road, she gave birth to her fourth child, Catalina.

It was Cisneros who at seventy, having emerged as the most astute and respected statesman in Castile, managed Fernando's recall. Even then, Fer-nando delayed another seven months, letting events play themselves out in Castile while he reintegrated Naples into the crown of Aragón, so that what-ever happened, he would have a base for influence in Italy, control of the Med-iterranean, and forays into Africa and even Asia. In the process he dislodged the viceroy of Naples, the Great Captain. Fernando was suspicious of Gonzalo de Córdoba's ambitions and loyalties, uncomfortable with his splendor and magnanimity, uneasy at his popularity, and cognizant that had it not been for the feats of that hero, his own military exploits against Granada might well stand as the greatest of the age. Nor was it a good idea to have a powerful Castilian viceroy in a kingdom he was reclaiming for Aragón. He made the Andalusian great promises, of lordships in Italy and Spain, of the mastership of Santiago, and got him back to Spain.

Fernando himself then returned to see Juana and to receive her power of attorney in August of 1508. She had been torn between father and husband; now the decision was not difficult. Juana retired to Tordesillas, where she lived on, well into the reign of her son, Charles. Castile was now Fernando's to gov-ern as regent. There ensued echoes of the 1470s, many nobles having come to realize they were better off under Fernando's firm and experienced hand, yet powerful exceptions remained troublesome. In Córdoba, for example, Aguil-ar's son the duke of Priego jailed and expelled his envoy. Immediately, Fer-nando himself went south by forced marches and reimposed royal authority.

And, when Fernando proposed that the fourteen-year-old duke of Medina Sidonia marry his grandaughter—the daughter of his son Alonso de Aragón, archbishop of Zaragoza—and the duke's guardian, Pedro Girón, count of Urueña, instead engaged him to his own daughter, Fernando swooped down, placing the entire dukedom under the crown.

Since 1500, in an Andalusia suffering famine and plague, an inquisitor, one Lucero, supported by the inquisitor general, Deza, had plundered, tortured, and burned *conversos,* many of whom were known to be good Christians. He and his confederates, ran one report to Almazán, were "discrediting all these kingdoms and destroying a great part of them without God and without justice, killing and robbing and raping virgins and married women, to the great revilement and ridicule of the Catholic religion."[12] By January of 1506, so unsettled was Andalusia and so powerful was Lucero that he had jailed and tortured Talavera's sister, his nephew, and three nieces, and only awaited the necessary papal permission to charge with judaizing the archbishop of Granada himself. Talavera wrote to Fernando. He lamented the great offense to God that the Inquisition had become, that it was separating Christians on the basis of lineage, that Isabel would never have allowed matters to come to such a pass, and declaring Fernando himself negligent. Even at that Talavera was being diplomatic, for it was well known that Deza and the Inquisition were in Fernando's camp.[13] Nor was it forgotten that when Isabel lay dying many *conversos* had fled to Flanders, knowing Philip to be unsympathetic to the Spanish Inquisition.

Talavera was more successful with an appeal to the pope, who sent a nuncio who secured absolution for him and his family. It was at length Cisneros who saw to it that Lucero and Deza were deposed, and that he himself became inquisitor general, but not before Talavera, near eighty, died, on May 14, 1507, his family still in prison. Granada mourned its archbishop as a saint; the friar's robe that was his shroud was torn to shreds by relic seekers. Whatever else he was, Talavera was a mainstay of Isabel's reign, who along with Mendoza was instrumental in organizing the realm into a modern state, and it was he who had confirmed its queen in a dual reliance on revelation and on the promptings of her own conscience.

For the next two years, Fernando attained a new height of power and reputation as the arbiter of Europe. His former daughter-in-law, Margaret, was instrumental in allaying tensions between the Spanish king, her father Maximilian, and Louis XII; and now once again a widow, she also took charge of raising her nephew, Charles, in Flanders. Fernando was at last free to turn to Africa. Yet recruits were a problem, for men were now more interested in venturing to the Indies. Even so, conforming with Isabel's injunction in her will, his armies conquered Oran in 1509, led and paid by Cisneros, took Tripoli in 1510, and came to dominate all of the African coast facing Andalusia except

Tunis, which his grandson Charles would take. Fernando jubilantly spoke of going on to regain the eastern Mediterranean and making effective his hereditary title of king of Jerusalem; and with his African campaign reverberating throughout the Christian West, Pope Julius II addressed him as "the strongest athlete of Christ." Fernando, as has been said, knew how to join earth and sky.[14]

Henry VII of England had died in April of 1509. His strapping heir, another Henry, eighteen years of age, wanted to marry Catalina, to Fernando's great satisfaction, and on June 11 they wed. Two weeks later, London celebrated the coronation of Henry VIII and Catherine of Aragón. Fernando corresponded a good deal with his intelligent, energetic, and still malleable new son-in-law; and Catalina wrote to her father: "Our English kingdoms enjoy peace and the people love us, as my husband and I love one another."[15]

That May, Germaine de Foix gave birth to Fernando's son, who was named Juan and who did not live out the day. There were no more children. Four years later Fernando, at sixty, became gravely ill; he nonetheless insisted on continuing the custom he had shared with Isabel of retreating to a monastery at Eastertime. At Mejorada his fever soared and for a day he was delirious. He never recovered completely. Pedro Mártir explained that illness as the effect of a potion taken to enhance his sexual potency, or perhaps inclination. Mártir said that so he might make his wife pregnant, Fernando had for over a month taken a concoction of bull testicles prepared either by her French cook or by two of her ladies. In November he was still unwell, and he was deeply depressed. From 1513 on, irascible and withdrawn, he showed little interest in politics. He refused, however, to be confined to a sickbed. A holy woman had told him he would not die before conquering Jerusalem and he wanted to believe it.[16] In late 1515, seemingly determined to outspeed his own mortality, he started for Andalusia, but having reached the hamlet of Madrigalejo, near Guadalupe, he could go no farther. There he signed a last will with the old customary flourish, an F intertwined with a Y. It instructed he lie beside Isabel in the cathedral of Granada, as they both had always desired. He died in Madrigalejo, in a house of the Hieronymites of Guadalupe, on January 23, 1516.

Fernando, wise in the importance of the judgments of history, had helped on those concerning himself and Isabel. He undoubtedly commissioned the monumental tombs of Isabel and himself for the Royal Chapel in Granada, begun in 1514 by Domenico di Alessandro Fancelli in Carrera marble.[17] He had the chronicles of the reign of her father, Juan II of Castile, and of her half-brother, Enrique IV "corrected and coordinated" by Lorenzo Galíndez de Carvajal. Of at least equal consequence, Galíndez, who had entered the council of Castile in 1503, kept that body functioning on Isabelline lines until the coming of her grandson Charles, then ensured continuity within it in the initial years of the young king. And, in advising Charles on governing, he frequently cited

Figure 20. Tombs of Isabel and Fernando (1514–17). Domenico Fancelli. Royal Chapel, Granada.

the example of "the Catholic Queen, doña Isabel, and the Catholic King her husband, Your Majesty's grandparents."

Fernando had designated Cisneros regent, and it was Cisneros, then in his eighties, who governed Spain for nearly a year before Charles arrived from Flanders. Cisneros or a cohort of his then wrote an *instrucción* for Charles, urging he return the kingdom to the condition in which Isabel had placed it. The worldwide empire constructed by Charles V, Holy Roman Emperor, would come to be viewed as far different than Isabel's Castile. Yet Charles himself and his son Philip II as well would justify much of what they did and thought regarding governing as within the tradition of Isabel. They would take her achievements and those of *Los Reyes Católicos* together as the measure for their own. In that sort of emulation too Isabel had set them precedent. She took up her own version of old customs and institutions, and she so reinvigorated and extended what she claimed as traditional usages through forceful exercise of royal power and authority as to transform them and Spain. Arguably, she left a legacy of personal, absolute monarchy so strong that Spain had to wait centuries for representative government.

Isabel and Fernando transformed the old crusading spirit of Spanish reconquest into a vision of universal monarchy and Spanish empire, a vision their descendants would make reality in ruling Mexico, Peru, and the Philippines, forging a Christian empire girdling the world and inaugurating a golden age in Spain. The imperial heritage of *los reyes* was Spain's grand design and they passed it on. Especially made for Charles's baptism had been four figures from the Old Testament and three from the New, exemplifying the fulfillment of the former in the latter and of all prophecy in Charles.[18] And while regent, Cisneros disseminated the idea that in the person of Charles was fulfilled the prophecies of world emperor and second Charlemagne.

From high in the courtyard of Philip's palace in the Escorial, a gallery of Old Testament kings look down, appropriated by that grandson of Isabel's as spiritual ancestors of Spain's kings. Among Philip's inherited titles was that of king of Jerusalem, and he most closely identified himself with the most august of them, Solomon. And it is not beside the point that his mother was yet another Isabel, the daughter of María and Manoel of Portugal.

That grandaughter of Isabel of Castile, the empress Isabel, her cousin and husband, Charles, and their son, Philip, were all zealous for the faith. Philip II celebrated attaining the throne with an extravagant *auto de fe,* and he saw the defeat of his Glorious Armada as an act of God, and possibly even as God's favor confirmed through tribulation. Perhaps nowhere in western Europe did the power of revealed prophecy and the expectation of apocalypse so long and so pervasively affect statecraft as in Spain. The Inquisition nurtured such beliefs, and the monarchs and nobles shared the conviction that Spain and its people were God's elect and that God himself directed Spanish destinies. One concomitant that endured for several centuries was expressed by Philip's viceroy in the Netherlands, the duke of Alba, who is said on his deathbed to have told his confessor that "his conscience was not burdened with having in all his life shed a single drop of blood against it," for, was the point, all the blood he had shed was that of heretics and traitors.[19] His remark recalls Isabel's unhappiness in her last years with war, when waged against Christians.

In his history, Francis Bacon declared Isabel's reign "the corner-stone of the greatness of Spain that hath followed."[20] During the reign of Charles, one chronicler wrote of her as "honored throughout the Spains and mirror of women."[21] Another, Baldassare Castiglione, papal nuncio to Charles's court in the 1520s, reported that while Spanish opinion recognized Fernando as magnificent, yet Charles and everyone else would do well to see in Isabel "a mirror for princes."[22] A principal aspiration of hers had been achieved. Remembered as an ideal monarch, she had become for posterity what she had striven to be. Nor was it any longer her own guides to rule, the *Partidas* or the mirrors for princes or the moralistic monarchists of her father's court and their followers, that inspired Spain's kings so much as it was this progenitrix of theirs who had taken the advice of all those mentors in turning herself into the reigning queen of Castile.

Yet the image of herself that she projected so efficaciously, so closely approximating that of an ideal ruler, set an impossible standard for Spain's monarchs and for Spain itself, from our vantage point misdirecting them as it had misdirected her. And the hold some of the lofty ideals she fostered continued to exert evoked a world-renowned reaction: the ironic questioning that Miguel Cervantes submitted those old beliefs to through his high-minded and hapless knight, Don Quixote. The world of Don Quixote's imagination was that of Isabel's aspirations and her vision of Christian chivalry, a lost Isabelline golden age.

If Isabel's princely qualities inspired acclaim and emulation by her immediate Habsburg successors and other Europeans, yet as time went on that image faded and gave way to another, that of the devout and pious queen, on her knees humbly praying, a view of her culminating in the current attempt to have her canonized as a saint. Viewed in the round, however, her faith embraced qualities today adjudged unholy. Certainly she aspired to an ideal of monarchy now no longer generally associated with saintliness, and her piety was integral to that aspiration. Within the world as she knew it, Isabel strove mightily to be just and pious. She would not have understood today's condemnation of so much that she did and for which she stood, for mainstream Christianity has left behind her militant God and her intolerance of other faiths and cultures. And a morality considered universal has long condemned the Spanish Inquisition.

Conjugal love, family ties, and ambition to excel as a monarch are the keys to Isabel's story. But that history is also a cautionary tale concerning extraordinary reserves of will, resolution, and courage, and the purposes to which they are dedicated. That complex combination of qualities in one monarch five hundred years ago has left an indelible imprint—on Spain, on Europe, on America, on the world.

Notes

Preface

1. Nieto Soria, "Los fundamentos ideológicos del poder regio," in Julio Valdeon Baruque, ed., *Isabel la Católica y la Política* (Vallodolid, 2001) 213.

Prologue

1. Pedro Mártir de Anglería, *Epistolario*, ed. José López de Toro (2 v., Madrid, 1955) 1: epís. 6.

2. He is Pietro Martire d'Anghiera in his native Italian and becomes Peter Martyr in English. That, however, is a given name; Anglería is considered his surname. Still, he is usually referred to by his given name. Here he will be cited as "Mártir."

3. Mártir's account of this meeting: Petri Martyrus Anglerii, *Opera: Legatio babilonica* (Seville, 1511; repr. Graz, 1966); there is a Spanish translation by Luis García y García, *Una embajada de los Reyes Católicos a Egipto* (Valladolid, 1947). See also Luis Suárez Fernández, "Las relaciones de los Reyes Católicos con Egipto," in *En la España Medieval* 1 (1980) 507–19; and Antonio de la Torre, "La embajada de Pedro Mártir de Anglería," in *Homenaje a Antonio Rubió y Lluch* (Barcelona, 1936).

4. The *Chronicle of Alfonso III* (ca. 880), as translated in Kenneth Baxter Wolf, ed., *Conquerors and Chroniclers of Medieval Spain* (Liverpool, 1990) 168.

5. The instructions received by Mártir of August 8, 1501, in Antonio de la Torre, ed., *Documentos sobre relacionales internacionales de los Reyes Católicos* (6 v., Barcelona, 1949–66) 6:268. See also David A. Boruchoff, "Instructions for Sainthood and Other Feminine Wiles in the Historiography of Isabel I," in Boruchoff, ed., *Isabel la Católica, Queen of Castile: Critical Essays* (New York, 2003) 1–24, for royal acuity regarding the potency of rhetoric.

6. Bernard McGinn, *Visions of the End* (New York, 1979) 328n43: Egypt as Babylon and temporary ally of the prophesied last emperor is found in Merlin's cry. Popular in Spain was "Demanda de sancto grial" ("Quest of the Holy Grail"), a subsection of an anonymous work known as *The Cry of the Wise Merlin, with His Prophecies,* a title derived from Merlin's outcry when he is locked away by the nymph Nimue, or in some accounts by the Lady of the Lake. See Pedro Bohígas, ed., *El baladro del sabio Merlín según el texto de la edición de Burgos de 1498* (3 v., Barcelona, 1957, 1961, 1962).

7. See Chapter 5.

Chapter 1. Walls and Gates

1. Anon., *Cronicón de Valladolid* (Madrid, 1848) 20–21, in Martin Fernández de Navarrete, Miguel Salvá, and Pedro Sáinz de Baranda, eds., *Colección de documentos inéditos para la historia de España* (112 v., Madrid, 1842–95) (hereinafter Codoin) 13:20.

2. Hernando del Pulgar, *Letras,* ed. J. Domínguez Bordona (Madrid, 1929) letra 6, p. 35.

3. Juan Torres Fontes, *Estampas de la vida murciana en el reinado de los Reyes Católicos* (Murcia, 1960, 1984) 321–24.

4. Leopoldo Torres Balbas, "El ambiente mudéjar en torno a la Reina Católica y el arte hispanomusulmán en España y Berbería durante su reinado," in Consejo Superior de Investigaciones Científicas, Instituto de Estudios Africanos, *Curso de conferencias sobre la política africana de los Reyes Católicos* (2 v., Madrid, 1951) 2:95–97.

5. Jorge Manrique, "Coplas a una beuda que tenía empeñado un brial en la taberna," in his *Obra completa,* ed. Miguel de Santiago (Barcelona, 1978) 188. Lucio Marineo Sículo, *De los cosas memorables de España* (Alcalá de Henares, 1539) lib. 2, fol. 11: "*Madrigal muy nombrado lugar por su vino blanco de buen olor y mejor sabor.*" See also Alonso de Encinas, *Madrigal de las Altas Torres: Cuna de Isabel la Católica* (Madrid, n.d.); and Miguel Angel Ladero Quesada, *España en 1492* (Madrid, 1978) 74, 77. Some of the forests remained into the nineteenth century. Encinas, 10–42, has drawings of the town done by Miguel Ourvantzoff in the 1950s, when some of the walls still stood.

6. Pulgar, *Letras,* letra 35.

7. Alonso Fernández de Palencia, *Crónica de Enrique IV,* ed. Antonio Paz y Meliá (3 v., Madrid, 1973–75) dec. 1, lib. 3, cap. 2. See also below, chapter 2, note 18.

8. Diego de Valera, *Memorial de diversas hazañas,* ed. Juan de Mata Carriazo (Madrid, 1941) cap. 33, p. 110. See also Lorenzo Galíndez de Carvajal, "Crónica de Enrique IV," in Juan Torres Fontes, *Estudio sobre la "Crónica de Enrique IV" del Dr. Galíndez de Carvajal* (Murcia, 1946) 253; and *Colección Diplomática 2: Memorias de Don Enrique IV de Castilla* (Madrid, 1835–1913) (hereinafter CD), doc. 109, p. 364.

9. Gonzalo Chacón, *Crónica de Alvaro de Luna,* ed. Juan de Mata Carriazo (Madrid, 1940) xiii. This chronicle was published only in 1546. It is not certain Chacón wrote it; Carriazo and Menéndez y Pelayo think he did, particularly since, after Luna, it presents him in the best light. Chacón's patron may have been Alfonso Carrillo, archbishop of Toledo and Luna's nephew, which would explain a lot. Carrillo later sought to play a Luna-like role with Isabel, to no avail. See also Robert Brian Tate, "El cronista real castellano durante el siglo quince," in Horacio Santiago Otero, ed., *Homenaje a Pedro Sáinz Rodríguez III: Estudios históricos* (Madrid, 1986) 665n20.

10. Juan José de Montalvo, *De la historia de Arévalo y sus sexmos* (2d ed., 2 v. in one, Avila, 1983; facsimile of Valladolid, 1928) 10; M. Serrano Castello, *Isabel la Católica: Arévalo, pasajes históricos, sus honores* (Madrid, 1951) 26–27.

11. Luis Suárez Fernández, "Las rentas castellanas del infante don Juan, rey de Navarra y de Aragón," *Hispania* 19 (1959) 192–204; Gerónimo Zurita y Castro, *Anales de la corona de Aragón,* ed. Angel Canellas López (8 v., Zaragoza, 1977) 4:39; Palencia, *Crónica,* dec. 1, lib. 4, cap. 4.

12. Palencia, *Crónica,* dec. 1, lib. 2, cap. 8.

13. Fernán Pérez de Guzmán to Santillana, in *Cancionero castellano del siglo XV,* ed. R. Foulché-Delbosc (2 v., Madrid, 1915) (hereinafter CC) 1:680.

14. Valera, *Memorial,* cap. 3, pp. 8–9; Palencia, *Crónica,* dec. 1, lib. 2, cap. 3.

15. While the term "the reconquest" was coined later, it is useful to describe the activity—a crusade in the first instance within Spain to regain lost Christian territory and drive Muslims holding it from Iberia—that provided the Spanish with common cause.

16. CD, doc. 46.

17. Gómez de la Torre, *Corografía de la provincia de Toro* (Madrid, 1802) 1:84–85.

The church later became dedicated to *Cristo de las batallas* and memory of it being a shrine to Mary disappeared. See Chapter 7, n. 30.

18. Anon., *Carro de las Donas* (Valladolid, 1542) lib. 2, 43rb; Juan Meseguer Fernández, "Isabel la Católica y los Franciscanos (1451–1476)," *Archivo Ibero-Americano* (hereinafter *AIA*) 30 (1970) 266–310; Meseguer, "Franciscanismo de Isabel la Católica," *AIA* 19 (1959) 155–57. Whatever her attachment to the Franciscans, Isabel later also relied on and patronized Dominicans and Hieronymites.

19. See Gil González Dávila, *Teatro eclesiástico de las iglesias de España* (Madrid, 1959) 2:262ff.; Vicente Beltrán de Heredia, *Cartulario de la Universidad de Salamanca (1280–1600)* (6 v., Salamanca, 1970–73) 1:474–99.

20. *Carro de las Donas*, 44vb.

21. Hernando del Pulgar, *Claros varones de Castilla,* ed. J. Domínguez Bordona (Madrid, 1969) 150; Pulgar, *Crónica de los Reyes Católicos,* ed. Juan de Mata Carriazo (2 v., Madrid, 1943) cap. 24.

22. See Chacón, *Crónica de Luna,* tit. 46; V. Campo and V. Infantes, eds., *La Poncella de Francia: La historia castellana de Juana de Arco* (Madrid, 1997); Adeline Rucquoi, "De Jeanne d'Arc a Isabelle la Catholique: L'image de la France en Castille au XVe Siècle," *Le Journal des Savants* (January–June 1990) 155–74: Rucquoi questions Chacón's entire account, yet whether or not Juan II and Luna made much of the Maid, the chronicler certainly did.

23. Gutierre Díaz de Games, *El Victorial,* ed. Juan de Mata Carriazo (Madrid, 1940), caps. 8, 19, 21. For Diego de Valera and tenets of chivalry in Spain: Jesús D. Rodríguez Velasco, *El debate sobre la caballería en el siglo XV* (Salamanca, 1996) especially pp. 380–82. See also Diego de Valera, *Espejo de verdadera nobleza,* in *Biblioteca de Autores Españoles* (hereinafter BAE (Madrid, 1959) 116: 89–116.

24. Montalvo, *Arévalo.* See Thomas F. Glick, "Convivencia: An Introductory Note," in Vivian B. Mann, Thomas F. Glick, and Jerrilynn D. Dodds, eds., *Convivencia: Jews, Muslims, and Christians in Medieval Spain* (New York, 1992) 1–9.

25. Hernando de Baeza, *Relación de algunos sucesos de los últimos tiempos del reino de Granada,* ed. Emilio Lafuente Alcántara (Madrid, 1868) 4; Miguel Angel Ladero Quesada, *Granada* (Madrid, 1979) 147; Rachel Arié, *L'Espagne musulmane au temps des nasrides (1232–1492)* (Paris, 1973) 141; Pedro de Escavías, *Repertorio de principes de España,* ed. Michel García (Jaén, 1973) 210. Elena Lourie, "A Society Organized for War: Medieval Spain," *Past and Present* 35 (1966) 69: *a la jineta* entailed "a fairly low saddle and a plate-bit which [forced] the horse to turn far more quickly than by pulling at the sides of its mouth."

26. Alfonso [Alonso Fernández] de Palencia, *Epistolas latinas,* eds. R. B. Tate and Rafael Alemany Ferrer (Barcelona, 1982) lln8, cites a letter signed and dated December 4, 1458 by Palencia, "*cronista y secretario de Latín.*"

27. Pedro Carrillo de Huete, *Crónica del halconero de Juan II,* ed. Juan de Mata Carriazo (Madrid, 1946) 540; *CD,* doc. 87; Miguel Angel Ladero Quesada, *Andalucía en el siglo XV* (Madrid, 1973) 16–17. His aunt had married Luna; he himself was the second son of Juan Pacheco, an intimate of Enrique's.

28. See P. E. Russell, *Prince Henry the Navigator: The Rise and Fall of a Culture Hero* (New York, 1984; New Haven, Conn., 2000) 120–27: Europeans knew, however, that a real Prester John existed in Ethiopia. See also Charles Julian Bishko, "The Spanish and Portuguese Reconquest, 1095–1492," in *Studies in Medieval Spanish Frontier History* (London, 1980) 435–38, 448: "The Portuguese, [while] stimulated by the expanding trade of their western and southern coastal cities with Andalusia and the

Maghrib, obliged to protect their merchant shipping against attack by Barbary pirates or war navies, and determined to secure a sphere of interest in western Morocco . . . never lost sight of reconquest goals."

29. Oliveira Martins, *Los hijos de don Juan I* (Buenos Aires, 1946) 60–109; Francis M. Rogers, *The Travels of the Infante Dom Pedro of Portugal* (Cambridge, Mass., 1961).

30. See Tarsicio de Azcona, *Isabel la Católica: Estudio crítico de su vida y su reinado* (Madrid, 1964) 112.

31. Diego Enríquez del Castillo, *Crónica de Enrique IV*, ed. J. M. Flores, cap. 37, BAE 70.

32. Luna in his chronicle repeatedly overcomes adversity through perseverance and fortitude. R. B. Tate, "A Humanistic Biography of Juan II of Aragon," *Bulletin of Hispanic Studies* 34 (1962) 10: Juan II of Aragón's life is presented in his chronicle as a perfect illustration of the moral advantages of adversity; it mirrors Seneca's *De Providentia*. Tate, however, errs in claiming it not providentialist. Overcoming tribulation is also Pauline, especially Heb. 12:4. See also Chapter 18, note 7.

33. See Galíndez de Carvajal, "Crónica," 90–92; Chacón, *Cronica de Luna*, xiii, xxxiii–xlvii; and Juan de Mata Carriazo, "Tres cortesanos de los Reyes Catolicos: Gonzalo Chacón, Gutierre de Cárdenas, y don Diego Hurtado de Mendoza; Semblanzas ejemplares de Gonzalo Fernández de Oviedo," *Clavileño* 2 (1951) 14, citing Gonzalo Fernández de Oviedo on Chacon's *privanza*.

34. Chacón *Crónica de Luna*, 437; José María de Azcárate, "Sentido y significación de la arquitectura hispano-flamenca en la corte de Isabel la Católica," *Boletín del seminario de Estudios de Arte y Arqueológia* (1971) 205; José María de Azcárate, "El Tema iconográfico del salvaje," *Archivo Español de Arte* no.82 (1948) 91; and González Palencia, "La capilla de Don Álvaro de Luna en la Catedral de Toledo," ibid. (1929) 109–22.

35. See Chapter 14.

Chapter 2. The Wrong King

1. *Agrio-dulce es reinar.* Juan de Contreras y López de Ayala, Marqués de Lozoya, "El monasterio de San Antonio el Real en Segovia," *Boletín de la Academia de Historia* (hereinafter BAH) (1919).

2. Miguel Angel Ladero Quesada, "Fernando II de Aragón, el Rey Católico: El Estado," in Esteban Sarasa, Presentación, *Fernando II de Aragón: El Rey Católico* (Zaragoza, 1995) 14: Aragón had 850,00 people, under 14 percent of the peninsular population, and some 18 percent of Iberian territory. The crown of Aragón also had Mediterranean interests and incorporated Sardinia and Sicily.

3. Palencia, *Crónica*, dec. 1, lib. 3, cap. 2. The anonymous *Crónica incompleta de los Reyes Católicos*, ed. Julio Puyol (Madrid 1934) begins *"quiero dezir en suma las felicidades de su buena fortuna en los primeros años de su reynar, y las grandes desaventuras de los postrimeros . . ."* (p. 48). Its author is generally assumed to be Juan de Flores: see Joseph J. Gwara, "The Identity of Juan de Flores: The Evidence of the *Crónica incompleta de los Reyes Católicos*," (1989); Carmen Parrilla, "Un cronista olvidado: Juan de Flores, autor de *La crónica incompleta de los Reyes Católicos*," in *Literary Studies in Memory of Keith Whinnom*, a special issue of the *Bulletin of Hispanic Studies* (1989). See also William D. Phillips Jr., *Enrique IV and the Crisis of Fifteenth-Century Castile, 1425–1480* (Cambridge, Mass., 1978); and José Luis Martín, *Enrique IV de Castilla* (Hondarribia, 2003).

4. See Angus Mackay, *Money, Prices, and Politics in Fifteenth-Century Spain* (London, 1981) 59–97; and Miguel Angel Ladero Quesada, "Para una imagen de Castilla, 1429–1504," in *Homenaje al Dr. Don Juan Reglá Campistol* (Valladolid, 1975) 1:201–15.

5. Charles T. Wood, "Review article: The Return of Medieval Politics," *American Historical Review* (hereinafter *AHR*) 94 (1989) 391–404, states that medieval European government was about limited resources and their allocation and controlling and managing society. Effectiveness depended on the personal ability of the monarch: "on the interest he took in practical administration of his realm, and on the extent to which he was able to translate his own desires into politically useful action, something which required constant interchange between the king, his officials, and the notables of the realm" (p. 401). By this measure Enrique comes off very poorly.

6. Palencia is vituperative regarding Enrique; certainly he got a bad press from the chroniclers of the next reign, but even his friendliest chroniclers, such as Sánchez de Arévalo and Galíndez de Carvajal remain critical, just not as critical: so Gálindez de Carvajal states that Enrique campaigned against Granada more seriously and vigorously than does Pulgar. See Phillips, *Enrique IV,* especially pp. 1–16; he has taken issue with my reading of Enrique as being plagued by physical problems, personal demons, and lack of political acuity. See also Luis Suárez Fernández, *Enrique IV de Castilla: La defamación como arma política* (Barcelona, 2001) for a detailed political explanation of Enrique's troubles.

7. Letter of July 20, 1462, "Tratado de los Epistolas enviadas por Mosen Diego de Valera," in Mario Penna, ed., *Prosistas españolas,* in BAE 116:3, epís. 4, pp. 8–9, urges Enrique to take steps to counteract the present danger to himself and the common good posed by the deplorable state of the kingdom, and says he will not mention "the thirteen Goth kings who died in Spain by the hands of their vassals for their bad governance."

8. See Palencia, *Crónica,* dec. 1, lib. 1, cap. 2; Enríquez del Castillo, cap. 1, pp. 100–101, says Pacheco kept Enrique subject with philters.

9. Palencia, *Crónica,* dec. 1, lib. 1, cap. 2.

10. See Enríquez del Castillo, 112.

11. CD, doc. 35.

12. Palencia, *Crónica,* dec. 1, lib. 3, cap. 6–8,10; Valera, *Memorial,* cap. 7, p. 19; Enríquez del Castillo, caps. 13–14.

13. Pulgar, *Reyes,* caps. 1,3.

14. "Itinerarium Hispanicum Hieronymi Monetarii, 1494–1495" (hereinafter Münzer), ed. R. Foulché-Delbosc, *Revue Hispanique* 48 (1920) 125–26. See also Angus MacKay with W. J. Irvine, "Medical Diagnosis and Henry IV of Castile," in Angus MacKay, *Society, Economy, and Religion in Late Medieval Castile* (London, 1987) xv.

15. On both sides, Muslim and Christian, crusading as waging holy war had to do with a combination of militant faith and political domination. Moreover, for a king, such a war (unless or until unsuccessful) was a proven stimulant to popular cohesion and political approval. See the remarks on crusading by Bernard Hamilton in the *American Historical Review* 108 (2003) 1204: "the crusade movement was part of an ongoing war between Christian and Muslim powers dating back to . . . the seventh century."

16. Palencia, *Crónica,* dec. 1, lib. 3, cap. 4; lib. 4, cap. 8; Valera, *Memorial,* cap. 3, p. 7; Phillips, *Enrique IV,* 55–56; Azcona, *Isabel,* 58–62; José Goñí Gaztambide, *Historia de la Bula de la Cruzada en España* (Vitoria, 1958).

17. Valera, *Memorial,* cap. 5, p. 17.

18. See ibid., caps. 6, 8, 10. See Alfonso de Palencia, *Gesta Hispaniensia ex annali-bus suorum dierum collecta,* ed. Brian Tate and Jeremy Lawrance (2 v., Madrid, 1998) dec. 1, lib. 4.5 (1:145); and see that edition for bibliography and for helpful annotation on matters covered by Palencia to 1468.

19. Palencia, *Crónica,* dec. 1, lib. 3, cap. 8.

20. Rodrigo Sánchez de Arévalo, *El Vergel de Principes,* ed. Mario Penna, pro-logue, in BAE 116 (Madrid, 1959) 312–13; Robert B. Tate, *Ensayos sobre historiografia peninsular del siglo XV* (Madrid, 1970) 98–100: Sánchez de Arévalo also justified Castil-ian preeminence historically and morally through a supernatural favor; the nation was chosen by God to carry out the divine scenario.

21. Ibid., 21.

22. Palencia, *Crónica,* dec. 1, lib. 5, cap. 5. My appreciation to Bill Knight for bow-sorting.

23. For Arías, see María del Pilar Rábade Obradó, *Una elite de poder en la corte de los Reyes Católicos* (Madrid, n.d.) 101–69.

24. Fernán Pérez de Guzmán, *Generaciones y semblanzas,* ed. R. B. Tate (London, 1950) 47.

25. Palencia, *Crónica,* dec. 1, lib. 4, cap. 3.

26. Fernando del Pulgar, *Claros varones de Castilla,* ed. R. B. Tate (Oxford, 1971) 62.

27. Palencia, *Crónica,* dec. 1, lib. 5, cap. 2.

28. Galíndez de Carvajal, "Crónica," 154–64; Enríquez del Castillo, ch. 31, p. 118: Zurita, *Anales* 7:lib. 17, cap. 3; Palencia, *Crónica,* dec. 1, lib. 4, cap. 9.

29. Enríquez del Castillo, cap. 37.

30. Ibid., cap. 38, p. 120.

31. "Relacion de Schaschek: Viaje del noble bohemio León de Rosmithal de Blatna . . . . 1465 a 1467," in José García Mercadal, ed., *Viajes de extranjeros por España y Portugal* (Madrid, 1952) 267, reports thirty-four kings, "made of pure gold." Valera, *Memorial,* cap. 100, p. 294. Elias Torno y Monzó, *Las viejas series icónicas de los Reyes de España* (Madrid, 1917) indicates that all were destroyed by fire in 1862, but drawings done in the 1830s by Hernando de Avila survive, in *Album cronolitográfico de la decora-ción de las salas regias del alcázar de Segovia* (Madrid, 1915). See also F. Collar de Cá-ceres, "En torno al Libro de los Retratos de los Reyes de Hernando de Avila," *Boletín del Museo del Prado* 4:10 (1983) 5ff.; Joaquín Yarza Luaces, "Imagen del rey y la imagen del noble en el siglo XV castellano," in Adeline Rucquoi, coord., *Realidad e imágenes del poder: España a fines de la Edad Media* (Valladolid, n.d.) 273. Philip II added ten more kings, including Isabel and Fernando, removing some of the queens to make room.

32. Alfonso de Oropesa, *Lumen ad revelationem gentium et gloria plebis tuae Israel, de unitate fidei et de concordi e pacifica aequalitate fidelium;* only fragments survive. There is a résumé in José de Sigüenza, *Historia de la orden de San Jerónimo* (2 v., Madrid, 1909) 1: cap. 19, pp. 367–73. The title is from Mark 2:32. Cf. Albert A. Sicroff, *Los Estatutos de limpieza de sangre: Controversias entre los siglos XV y XVI* (rev. ed., Madrid, 1985) 92–100; and see Enríquez del Castillo, 130; and Luis Alfredo Díaz y Díaz, "Alonso de Oropesa y su Obra," *Studia Hieronymiana* (Madrid, 1973) 1:253–313. Cf. B. Netanyahu, *The Origins of the Inquisition in Fifteenth-Century Spain* (2nd ed., New York, 2001) passim.

33. Azcona, *Isabel,* 66, says the papal nuncio, Antonio Giacomo Venier, brought to Spain in March of 1462 a bull granting the faculty to repress heresy, but also thinks that it was due to Venier personally that no broader Inquisition was then introduced.

34. Palencia, *Crónica,* dec. 1, lib. 6, cap. 10; lib. 5, cap. 7.

35. CD, doc. 92. The term *grandes* appears in this transcription.

36. Galíndez de Carvajal, "Crónica," 212.

37. Enríquez del Castillo, 137.

38. Valera, letter of July 20, 1462, in "Epístolas," pp. 8–9; see also Valera, *Memorial,* cap. 20, pp. 72–75; Palencia, *Crónica,* dec. 1, lib. 5, cap. 4; Pérez de Guzmán, *Coplas de vicios e virtudes,* appended to his *Semblanzas.*

39. See R. B. Tate, "An Apology for Monarchy: A Study of an Unpublished Fifteenth-Century Castilian Historical Document," *Romance Philology* 15 (1961) 113.

40. Circular letter, September 28, 1464: CD, doc. 98, pp. 334–35; Antonio Paz y Meliá, *El cronista Alonso de Palencia* (Madrid, 1914) doc. 11, pp. 60–69. On homosexuality, see Philippe Aries and A. Bejin, eds., *Western Sexuality* (New York, 1985) 40–76. McGinn, *Visions,* 302n30: homosexuality was an apocalyptic sign in the *Pseudo-methodius,* the popular medieval text on Alexander the Great.

41. Palencia, *Crónica,* dec. 1, lib. 3, cap. 1.

42. CD, doc. 96, 102, 103, 106; Enríquez de Castillo, 138.

43. CD, doc. 109.

44. Palencia, *Crónica,* dec. 1, lib. 4, cap. 2; see also Enríquez del Castillo, 139.

45. Julio Rodríguez Puértolas, ed., *Fray Iñigo de Mendoza y sus coplas de Vita Christi* (Madrid, 1968) estr. 186.

46. Codoin 14:369–95, 136–44. See José Manuel Nieto Soria, *Iglesia y génesis del Estado Moderno en Castilla, 1369–1480* (Madrid, 1994) 272–86, regarding clergy taking sides in this conflict and as politically radical.

47. *Cronicón de Valladolid,* 67; Valera, *Memorial,* caps. 29, 30; Galíndez del Carvajal, "Crónica," 16, 206, 238–39; Palencia, *Crónica,* dec. 1, lib. 7, cap. 8. *Cf.* Angus MacKay, "Ritual and Propaganda in Fifteenth-Century Castile," *Past and Present* 107 (1985) 3–43; the criticism by K. Sorensen Zapalac and MacKay's masterly rejoinder, in ibid. no. 113 (1986) 185–208.

48. Antonio Serrano de Haro, *Personalidad y destino de Jorge Manrique* (Madrid, 1966) 17; see also José Antonio Maravall, "La tradición de la herencia goda como mito político," in *El concepto de España en la Edad Media* (3d ed., Madrid, 1981) 299–340. With the Trastámara, royal chroniclers had gotten out of the habit of celebrating the Goth ancestry of kings, while nobles had taken it up as exclusively theirs (i.e., Pero Niño in *El Victorial*). But Barrientos, Sánchez de Arévalo, Valera, and other fifteenth-century chroniclers went about reclaiming it as belonging chiefly to their royal patrons.

49. Versions of Mendoza's speech in CD, 489–90; Pulgar, *Crónica,* lib. 1, cap. 1. See MacKay, "Ritual," 40. In Palencia, *Crónica,* dec. 1, lib. 8, cap. 8, cf. the religious basis of the pro-Enrique arguments of the learned and influential *converso,* Francisco de Toledo.

50. CD, doc. 119.

51. Ibid., doc. 119, pp. 490–92.

52. Severino Rodríguez Salcedo, "El reinado del primer Alfonso XII en Palencia," *Publicaciones de la Institución "Tello Téllez de Meneses"* no. 5 (1950) app. 1, pp. 71–73; Luciano Serrano, *Los Reyes Católicos y la ciudad de Burgos* (Madrid, 1943) 80, 87.

53. Angus MacKay, "The Hispanic-*Converso* Predicament," in MacKay, *Society,* XIII; cf. *CD,* doc. 119.

54. Gabriel Tetzel, *un patricio* of Nuremberg, who was traveling in Spain with Leo of Rozmital, brother-in-law of the king of Bohemia: "Relacion de Tetzel," in García Mercadal, *Viajes,* 298; see also Escavias, *Repertorio,* 220. Both sides encouraged partisan preachers and consulted theologians: Valera, *Memorial,* ch. 34; and see above, note 46.

55. Anon., "Coplas de Mingo Revulgo," in Julio Rodríguez Puértolas, ed., *Poesía crítica y satírica del siglo XV,* (Madrid, 1981) 221–32. Rodríguez Puértolas attributes those verses to fray Iñigo de Mendoza. The metaphor of the good shepherd was time honored; Valera in his *Doctrinal de principes* (BAE 116, cap. 1, p. 174) of the 1470s cited Ezekiel's reference. That figure stands too as a sign of redemption—for Christ the Redeemer and the idea of one shepherd, one flock to come in the last days; conversely, the bad shepherd stands for Antichrist: see André Grabar, *Las vías de la creación de la iconografía christiana* (Madrid 1985) 28.

56. Anon., "Coplas del Provincial," in Rodríguez Puértolas, *Poesía,* 237–63; and see his introduction to both satires.

57. CC 1: no. 149, p. 269.

58. Gómez Manrique, "Pregunta a Pedro de Mendoza," in CC 2: no. 352.

59. Gómez Manrique, "Esclamación e querella de la governación," in CC 2: no. 415 (s. 2); "Coplas . . . Diego Arías," in CC 2: no. 377 (s. 47).

60. Enríquez del Castillo, cap. 87.

61. CD, doc. 125.

62. July 6, 1465, Zamora, Enrique to Afonso of Portugal: CD, pp. 504–5. That letter is repeated within a *cédula* of Afonso of Portugal of September 15, 1465, from La Guardia, enclosing agreements made with his sister, Juana, empowered by Enrique.

63. Valera *Memorial,* cap. 36.

64. Ibid.

65. Alfonso to the city of Murcia on September 16, 1467: he has taken Segovia. Juan Torres Fontes, *El principe don Alfonso* (2d. ed., Murcía, 1985), 152.

66. CC 2: no. 391; Charles F. Fraker, *Studies on the Cancionero de Baena* (Chapel Hill, N.C., 1966) 100.

67. Cristóbal Espejo y Julián Paz, *Las antiguas ferias de Medina* (Valladolid, 1908) 49; see also Miguel Angel Ladero Quesada,"Las ferias de Castilla: Siglos XII a XV," *Cuadernos de Historia de España* no. 67–68 (1982) 269–347.

Chapter 3. The Right Marriage

1. Paz y Meliá, *Cronista,* doc. 14, p. 72.

2. Galíndez de Carvajal, "Crónica," 316.

3. Ibid., 313.

4. Palencia, *Crónica,* dec. 1, lib. 7, cap. 1.

5. CD, docs. 146 and 147.

6. Palencia, *Crónica,* dec. 1, lib. 9, cap. 9; Galíndez de Carvajal, "Crónica," 330–34; Valera, *Memorial,* cap. 40, Enríquez del Castillo, 112, 118; Isabel del Val Valdivieso, *Isabel la Católica, princesa (1468–1474)* (Madrid, 1989) 56–61.

7. Juan Torres Fontes, "Itinerario," in *Principe,* 165–66; Gálindéz de Carvajal, "Crónica," 331; Phillips, *Enrique IV,* 106.

8. CD, doc. 87.

9. Torres Fontes., *Principe,* app. docs. 1–2, pp. 203–7; Galíndez de Carvajal, "Crónica," app. 505–6.

10. Jorge Manrique, "Coplas por la muerte de su padre," in J. M. Cohen, ed. and trans., *Penguin Book of Spanish Verse* (London and New York, 1988) verse 20.

11. CC 2: no. 417, pp. 149–50. Thus Manrique made implicit messianic reference: see below, ch. 5.

12. Palencia, *Crónica*, dec. 1, lib. 10, cap. 10.

13. Valera, *Memorial*, cap. 41.

14. Galíndez de Carvajal, "Crónica," xxx, 331; Palencia, *Crónica*, dec. 2, lib. 1, cap. 1; Valera, *Memorial*, cap. 40; Phillips, *Enrique IV*, 106.

15. Azcona, *Isabel*, 119.

16. Paz y Meliá, *Cronista*, app.(b), pp. 321–26.

17. *CD*, doc. 152.

18. Valera, *Memorial*, cap. 42; Palencia, *Crónica*, dec. 2, lib. 1, cap. 4.

19. Valera, *Memorial*, cap. 50.

20. Martín de Córdoba, *Jardín de nobles donzellas: A critical edition and study*, ed. Harriet Goldberg (Chapel Hill, N.C., 1974).

21. *CC* 2: no. 390.

22. Paz y Meliá, *Cronista*, doc. 16, pp. 77–90; Miguel Gual Camarena, "El matrimonio de Fernando e Isabel (1469), documentación valenciana," in *Homenaje al Professor Carriazo* (3 v., Seville, 1971–73) 3:67; Zurita, *Anales* 4: fol. 157v.; Jaime Vicens Vives, *Historia crítica de la vida y reinado de Fernando II de Aragón* (Zaragoza, 1962) 99–100.

23. Palencia, *Crónica*, dec. 2, lib. 1, cap. 7.

24. Paz y Meliá, *Cronista*, doc. 14, pp. 72–73.

25. *CD*, doc. 156; Pulgar, *Reyes*, cap. 5.

26. Diego Clemencín, *Elógio de la reina doña Isabel* (Madrid, 1821) app. doc. 8, pp. 585–90; see Azcona, *Isabel*, 154–55; Gual Camarena, "Matrimonio," doc. 1.

27. Paz y Meliá, *Cronista*, doc. 18, pp. 80–81.

28. Andrés Bernáldez, *Historia de los Reyes Católicos*, in BAE 70:574; Palencia, *Crónica*, dec. 2, lib. 1, cap. 7.

29. Pulgar, *Reyes*, cap. 8.

30. Palencia, *Crónica*, dec. 2, lib. 1, cap. 9; Valera, *Memorial*, cap. 47.

31. Palencia, *Crónica*, dec. 2, lib. 1, cap. 10.

32. Pulgar, *Reyes*, cap. 2; Biblioteca del Archivo Histórico, Madrid, *Colección Salazar*, A-8, 123, transcribed in Félix de Llanos y Torriglia, *Así llegó a reinar Isabel la Católica* (Madrid, 1927) 163.

33. *CD*, doc. 168, pp. 605–9. Cf. Paz y Meliá, *Cronista*, doc. 21, p. 85.

34. Amalia Prieto Cantero, "¿Dónde están el collar de balajes y la corona rica de la reina católica?" in *Estudios genealógicos, heráldicos, y nobiliarios en honor de Vicente de Cadenas y Vicent* (Madrid, 1978) 197–222; Vicens Vives, *Historia crítica*, 204–5.

35. Pulgar, *Reyes*, cap. 23. Marineo Sículo, in *Cosas memorables*, later described Fernando as of medium stature, well-proportioned members, very fair, with a happy, indeed glowing aspect, chestnut hair, wide-set eyebrows, his eyes clear and nearly smiling, a small nose, rosy cheeks, and small white teeth in a small mouth.

36. Report of Miralles, notary of the diet of Valencia, in Vicens Vives, *Historia crítica*, 190–91, 196.

37. Pulgar, *Reyes*, cap. 3; Vicens Vives, *Historia crítica*, 533–34.

38. Marineo Sículo, *Cosas memorables*, f. 188; Vicens Vives, *Historia crítica*, 207–8; Félix de Llanos y Torriglia, *En el hogar de los Reyes Católicos y cosas de sus tiempos* (Madrid, 1943) 28.

39. *CD*, doc. 170.

40. *Crónica incompleta*, 88–89.

41. Palencia, *Crónica*, dec. 2, lib. 2, cap. 4.

42. Tarsicio de Azcona, "Isabel la Católica bajo el signo de la revolución y de la

guerra (1464–1479)," in Julio Valdeón Baruque, ed., *Isabel la Católica y la política* (Valladolid, 2001) 69.

43. Valera, *Memorial,* cap. 52; Palencia, *Crónica,* dec. 2, lib. 2, cap. 5; Galíndez de Carvajal, "Crónica," 366; Clemencín, 585–92; Gual Camarena, "Matrimonio," 74–75; Azcona, *Isabel,* 148–55; Phillips, *Enrique IV,* 113–14; Val, *Isabel,* 191–97.

44. Clemencín, app. 1.

Chapter 4. To the Crown

1. M. Grau Sanz, "Así fue coronado Isabel la Católica," *Estudios Segovianos* 1 (1949) 24–36.

2. Vicens Vives, *Historia crítica,* 265. Isabel's council then consisted of Cárdenas, Chacón, the treasurer Alfonso de Quintanilla, the *letrado* Rodríguez de Lillo, the secretaries Fernando Núñez and Palencia, and the friar Alonso de Burgos. See also Azcona, *Isabel,* 133; and for a more detailed narrative: Luis Suárez Fernández, *La Conquista del Trono* (Madrid, 1989).

3. Palencia, *Crónica,* dec. 2, lib. 9, cap. 1 (2:118).

4. *Cartas autógrafas de los Reyes Católicos (1475–1502),* transcription and study by Amalia Prieto Cantero (Simancas, 1971) carta 2.

5. See Otis Green, "Courtly Love in the Spanish *Cancioneros,*" *Publications of the Modern Language Association of America* 64 (1949) 283–86, regarding the particular warmth of conjugal tenderness and respect expressed by Spanish nobles, from El Cid on. In chronicles of the time, Juan of Castile dotes on Isabel of Portugal, Juan of Aragón on Juana Enríquez, the count of Plasencia is devoted to his strong-minded wife, Leonor Pimentel, and Isabel and Fernando's children would tend to adore their spouses. Santillana assumed ineluctable passion is inherent to the human condition, as did a treatise attributed to Tostado and the diagnoses of love sickness in medical treatises: see Arnaldi de Villanova, *Opera medica omnia,* v. 3: *De amore heroico,* ed. Michael R. McVaugh (Barcelona, 1985). The idea of love as a sickness also appeared in Arabic medical works.

6. Enríquez del Castillo, cap. 144, p. 199; Palencia, *Crónica,* dec. 1, lib. 12, cap. 7 (1:302).

7. Val, *Isabel,* 101.

8. Paz y Meliá, *Cronista,* doc. 30, p. 101; Val, *Isabel,* 206.

9. Paz y Meliá, *Cronista,* doc. 31, p. 102; Enríquez del Castillo, cap. 145, p. 201. With Enrique's French accord in November of 1469, French influence on the curia bore heavily against the couple.

10. Isabel to Diego de Cabra, October 2, 1470 (in Archivo de Albuquerque); appended to Alonso Andrés, "Documentos originales de los Reyes Católicos en archivos particulares," *Revista de Archivos, Bibliotecas, y Museos* (hereinafter RABM) 57 (1951) 639.

11. Paz y Meliá, *Crónista,* doc. 34, p. 108; Vicens Vives, *Historia crítica,* 280.

12. CD doc. 179, pp. 619–21; Enríquez del Castillo, cap. 147, pp. 203–4; Suárez Fernández, *Conquista,* 42.

13. Torres Fontes, *Príncipe.* 207–31, a better transcription than CD, doc. 187. Santa Susana was a popular figure in miracle or mystery plays. A reference to Santa Susana appears too in an instruction of Juan II to Isabel of September 29, 1469: Paz y Meliá, *Cronista,* doc. 24, p. 91.

14. CD, doc. 187, p. 335. See also Val, *Isabel,* 233. Cf. Vicens Vives, *Historia crítica,* 282–87.

15. Paz y Meliá, *Cronista,* doc. 33, p. 106; Enríquez del Castillo, cap. 27, p. 115; cap. 145, p. 201; Pulgar, *Libro,* 11–15.

16. To the bishop of Coría, 1473, in Pulgar, *Letras,* letra.25, p. 131; Enríquez del Castillo, cap. 148, pp. 204–5; Phillips, *Enrique IV,* 115. Real Academia de la Historia, *Cortes de León y Castilla* (7 v., Madrid, 1861–1903) 3:75: the nobles rise higher; the people suffer.

17. Galíndez de Carvajal, "Crónica," 18, 241–42, 261–62, 267; *CD,* docs. 191, 192; Phillips, *Enrique IV,* 98–99; Isabel del Val, "Resistencia al dominio señórial durante los últimos años de reinado de Enrique IV," *Hispania* 34 (1974) 53–104; Modesto Sarasola, *Vizcaya y los Reyes Católicos* (Madrid, 1950) 48–57; Juan Torres Fontes, *Don Pedro Fajardo, adelantado mayor del reino de Murcia* (Murcia, 1953) 232.

18. Paz y Meliá, *Cronista,* doc. 41, pp. 121–22, of June 12, 1471: Isabel and Fernando dispatched Juan Ramírez de Lucena to Flanders to negotiate with Charles the Bold. Thomas Rymer, *Foedora, conventiones, literae . . .* (20 v., London, 1726–35) 11:70; Suárez Fernández, *Conquista,* 53–54.

19. Palencia, *Crónica,* dec. 2, lib. 6, cap. 4 (2:59).

20. CC 2: no. 402.

21. Vicens Vives, *Historia crítica,* 314–15.

22. Paz y Meliá, *Cronista,* doc. 27, pp. 93–94. See also Vicens Vives, *Historia crítica,* 296–97; documents in Gual Camarena, "Matrimonio," 76–80, for other jurisdictions she extracted from Juan.

23. Clemencín, 325–30, who argues convincingly this account dates from 1473.

24. See Eloy Benito Ruano, "'Los Hechos del arzobispo de Toledo D. Alonso Carrillo,' por Pero Guillén de Segovia," *Anuario de Estudios Medievales* 5 (1968) 517–30.

25. See Rucquoi, "Jeanne d'Arc," 155–74.

26. Vicens Vives, *Historia crítica,* 301–2, 345. Both Fernando and Juan signed the treaty of Abbéville with England and Burgundy.

27. Palencia, *Crónica,* dec. 2, lib. 7, cap. 6 (2:79–81).

28. Bull of December 1, 1471: Clemencín, app. 6, pp. 592–93; Vicens Vives, *Historia crítica,* 308–10; Suárez Fernández, *Conquista,* 56.

29. José Sánchis y Sivera, "El Cardenal Rodrigo de Borja en Valencia," *Boletín del Real Academia de Historia* (hereinafter BRAH) 84 (1924) 149.

30. Vicens Vives, *Historia crítica,* 319–21.

31. Paz y Meliá, *Cronista,* doc. 44.

32. Vicens Vives, *Historia crítica,* 323–25.

33. CD, doc. 197; Palencia, *Crónica,* dec. 2, lib. 7, cap. 6, 7 (2:79–82).

34. Isabel to Juan II, Talamanca, April 29, 1473, in Paz y Meliá, *Cronista,* doc. 49, pp. 129–30.

35. See Alain Milhou, "La Chauve-souris, le Nouveau David et le Roi Cache (trois images de l'empereur des derniers temps dans le monde ibérique des XIIIe–XVIIe siècles)," *Mélanges de la Casa de Velázquez* 18 (1982) 61–78, 67.

36. *Cartas autógrafas,* no. 1, p. 16.

37. Andrés Alfonsello, *Los reys d'Aragó y la seu de Girona desde l'any 1462 fins al 1482,* ed. Fidel Fita (2d ed., Barcelona, 1873) 1:51–52; Vicens Vives, *Historia crítica,* 339–44.

38. Palencia, *Crónica,* dec. 2, lib. 8, cap. 1–2 (2:93–96); Hernando del Pulgar, *Crónica de . . . Fernando e Isabel,* ed. Cayetano Rosell, BAE 70 (Madrid, 1953) lib. 1, cap.

6, 246–48 (hereinafter Pulgar, *Crónica*); Enríquez del Castillo, cap. 88, p. 159; Suárez Fernández, *Conquista*, 63–64; Francisco Márquez Villanueva, "Conversos y cargos concejiles en el siglo XV," RABM no. 63 (1957) 518–19.

39. Pedro de Bobadilla, Beatriz's father, had tended Alfonso and Isabel in childhood, and surely Isabel and Beatriz had then known one another. Beatriz too was a strong personality. See Rábade Obradó, *elite* 186 and passim.

40. CD, doc. 199: pact between Cabrera and Isabel, Segovia, June 15, 1473. Enríquez del Castillo, cap. 104, p. 170; cap. 144, pp. 199–200. Francisco Pinel y Monroy, *Retrato del buen vasallo . . . Andrés de Cabrera* (Madrid, 1677) 158–60. *Crónica incompleta*, tít. 8: Cabrera was in poor health; it was Bobadilla who mediated successfully among the parties.

41. See Suárez Fernández, *Conquista*, 66, and Val, *Isabel*, 322. Palencia, *Crónica*, lib. 5, cap. 8 (2:112–14), insists it all a conspiracy of those nobles and Enrique IV to do in *los principes;* most sources see it as a valid attempt by all concerned (except Pacheco, and perhaps Carrillo) to reach agreement.

42. See Galíndez de Carvajal, "Crónica," 442–43; Enríquez del Castillo, cap. 154, pp. 217–18; Suárez Fernández, *Conquista*, 63–67; and Val, *Isabel*, 322.

43. Palencia, *Crónica*, dec. 2, lib. 8, cap. 10 (2:113–14); see also Pulgar, *Letras*, letra 6, pp.32–33.

44. Palencia, *Crónica*, dec. 2, lib. 8, cap. 10 (2:114); cf. Pulgar, *Crónica*, lib. 1, cap. 7, pp.248–49.

45. Palencia, *Crónica*, dec. 2, lib. 9, cap. 1 (2:118–19).

46. Pulgar, *Crónica*, pt. 2, cap. 6 (p. 259), cap. 12 (pp. 262–63); Pulgar, *Claros varones*, 63–64.

47. Cárdenas to Fernando: Paz y Meliá, *Cronista*, doc. 69, p. 168. Pedro Fajardo to his brother, November 7, 1474, in ibid., doc. 71, p. 172. and Juan to Pero Vaca, doc. 11, app. to Vicens Vives, *Historia crítica*, 562–64.

48. Palencia, *Crónica*, dec. 2, lib. 10, cap. 9 (2:152–54).

49. Ibid., dec. 2, lib. 7, cap. 3 (2:152–53); Pulgar, *Crónica*, pt. 1, cap. 11 (p. 251); Paz y Meliá, *Cronista*, doc. 67, pp. 160–64; Azcona, *Isabel*, 203–4. Pedro Salazar de Mendoza, *Crónica de el gran cardenal de España, Don Pedro Gonçález de Mendoça* (Toledo, 1625), f. 142: Mendoza had convinced Enrique to call Cortes to recognize Isabel, but Enrique died beforehand. Galíndez de Carvajal, *Anales breves*, in BAE 70, 254: A secret will left the kingdom to Juana; Fernando and Isabel got hold of it much later, but Isabel lay dying, too ill to read it, and Fernando had it burned. Tarsicio de Azcona, *Juana de Castilla mal llamada La Beltraneja (1462–1530)* (Madrid, 1998) 141, concludes that the documentation points to Juana's legitimacy. There is no knowing.

50. CD, doc. 206. See also Pulgar, *Crónica*, pt. 1, cap. 11; Palencia, *Crónica*, dec. 2, lib. 10, cap. 9 (2:152–54); Paz y Meliá, *Cronista*, doc. 67, pp. 160–64; Enríquez del Castillo, 217–18; Salazar de Mendoza, f.142; Azcona, *Isabel*, 203–4. Phillips, *Enrique IV*, 118, thinks he was poisoned. It is quite possible, and may be what the innuendos in the letters above infer.

51. Palencia, *Crónica*, dec. 2, lib. 10, cap. 10 (2:154); her letter to Murcia of December 12 in Torres Fontes, *Pedro Fajardo*, 237–38, doc. 23.

52. Palencia, *Crónica*, dec. 2, lib. 10, cap. 10. See Isabel, letter from Segovia, December 20, 1474, imparting Enrique's death, in Juan de Mata Carriazo and Ramón Carande, comps., (5 v., Seville, 1929–68) 1; the series contains documents of the Archivo Histórico Municipal de Sevilla preserved in its *cartulario*.

53. The ceremony is described in Grau (see above, note 1), transcribing the rela-

tion of the *cabildo* notary García de la Torre, who wrote an account of her accession on her orders.

54. See above, note 1.

55. The notary's account ends here. MacKay, "Ritual," 19, 23–25, notes no coronation ceremony was usual in Castile, and thinks the popular acclamation *the* key element; see also Valera, *Memorial,* 5; José Manuel Nieto Soria, *Fundamentos ideológicos del poder real en Castilla (siglos XIII–XVI)* (Madrid, 1988) 60–67; Nieto Soria, *Ceremonias de la realeza* (Madrid, 1993) 33–34, 106–11.

56. Palencia, *Crónica,* dec. 2, lib. 10, cap. 10 (p.155). Palencia adds *grandes* to her procession.

57. Ibid.

58. For sword imagery, see *Siete Partidas,* bk. 3; *Poema de Alfonso XI* (stanzas 127–29); Pinel y Monroy, 198; the preface to Fernán Pérez de Ayala, *Rimado de Palacio,* ed. German Orduna (Madrid, 1987); Nieto Soria, *Ceremonías,* 188–90, and his *Iglesia,* 234–35.

59. Nicholás Popielovo, in García Mercadal, 319.

60. See Frances A. Yates, *Astraea: The Imperial Theme in the Sixteenth Century* (London, 1985) 3–4, 9.

61. M. de Foronda y Aguilera, "Honras por Enrique IV y proclamación de Isabel la Católica en la ciudad de Avila," *BRAH* 63 (1913) 427–34.

Chapter 5. A Royal Heritage

1. See Thomas F. Glick, *Islamic and Christian Spain in the Early Middle Ages* (Princeton, N.J., 1979); Ladero Quesada, "Imagen," 205–15; MacKay, *Money,* 20–21, 31–32, 105; J. N. Hillgarth, *The Spanish Kingdoms, 1250–1516* (2 v., Oxford, 1976) 2; Olivia Remie Constable, *Trade and Traders in Muslim Spain* (Cambridge, 1994) 242–58; and Wendy R. Childs, *Anglo-Castilian Trade in the Later Middle Ages* (Manchester, 1978).

2. See "Crónica del Rey Don Enrique, Tercero de Castilla y León," BAE 68: 161–257; Luis Suárez Fernández, *Estudios sobre el regimen de Enrique III* (Madrid, 1954); Luis Suárez Fernández, *Relaciones entre Castilla y Portugal en la época del infante don Enrique, 1393–1460* (Madrid 1960).

3. See Ron Barkai, *Cristianos y musulmanes en la España medieval* (Madrid, 1984) for the medieval entrenchment of both Muslim and Christian self-images, in which each saw the other as the enemy.

4. Isidore of Seville, "History of the Kings of the Goths," in Wolf, *Chronicles,* 81–110. See also J. N. Hillgarth,, "Studies in Historiography and Iberian Reality," *History and Theory* 24 (1985) 23–43; Hillgarth, "Historiography in Visigothic Spain," in Hillgarth, *Visigothic Spain, Byzantium, and the Irish* (London, 1985) III; Marc Reydellet, "Les Intentions Idéologiques et politiques dans la Chronique d'Isidore de Seville," *Mélanges d'Archéologie et d'Histoire* 82 (1970) 363–400.

5. Glick, *Islamic and Christian Spain,* 32.

6. Angus MacKay, *Spain in the Middle Ages* (London, 1977); J. A. García de Cortazar, et al., *Organización social del espacio en la España medieval: La Corona de Castilla en los siglos VIII a XV* (Barcelona, 1985).

7. See now Joseph O'Callaghan, *Reconquest and Crusade in Medieval Spain* (Philadelphia, 2003). See also Chapter 2, note 15.

8. Maravall, "Tradición," 309–12.

9. Kenneth Wolf, "Christian Views of Islam in Early Medieval Spain," in *Medieval Christian Perceptions of Islam*, ed. John Victor Tolan (New York, 1996); Wolf, "Earliest Spanish Christian Views of Islam," *Church History* 55 (1986) 281–93.

10. Jeffrey Burton Russell, *Lucifer* (Ithaca, N.Y., 1984) 69n13.

11. Leopoldo Torres Balbas, *Algunas aspectos del mudéjarismo urbano medieval* (Madrid, 1954) 21.

12. Miguel Angel Ladero Quesada, "Isabel y los musulmanes de Castilla y Granada," in Valdeón Baruque, *Isabel*, 91–94. An English version, "Isabel and the Moors," appears in Boruchoff, *Isabel*, 171–93.

13. See "Relacion de Tetzel," in García Mercadal, 298, who states that the inhabitants of Olmedo are largely infidel, "the king has many [infidel] in his court," and also many Moors and Jews.

14. *Anales Toledanos* in *España Sagrada*, Enrique Flórez, ed. (2d ed., 16 v., Madrid, 1754–87) 10:23; Maravall, "Tradición," 299–331; Américo Castro, *The Structure of Spanish History* (Princeton, N.J., 1954) 323.

15. Ladero Quesada, "Isabel y los musulmanes," 93.

16. *Siete Partidas*, Partida 2, tit. 2, ley 3 (referring to Prov. 21:1); tit. 1, ley 5; also see ley 7; tit. 13, ley 26; tit. 5, ley 4; also, on expectations of kings: Partida 1, tit. 2, leyes 1, 4.

17. Francisco Sánchez Canton, *Libros, tapices, y cuadros que coleccionó Isabel la Católica* (Madrid, 1950) 32. She also owned a copy of the the harsh Visigothic law code, the *fuero juzgo*.

18. Sánchez Canton, 33–34.

19. See Carlos Alonso de Real, "Amazonas y Godos," *Hispania* 23 (1963) 324–41.

20. Alfonso X, *General estoria*, Part 1, ed. A. G. Solalinde (Madrid, 1930); Part 2, ed. Antonio G. Solalinde, Lloyd A. Kasten, and Victor R. B. Oelschlager (2 v., Madrid, 1957, 1961); Alfonso X, *Primera crónica general de España*, ed. Ramón Menéndez Pidal (2 v., Madrid, 1955). See also Charles F. Fraker, *The Scope of History: Studies in the Historiography of Alfonso el Sabio* (Ann Arbor, Mich., 1996) 114–77.

21. See Alan Deyermond, "The Death and Rebirth of Visigothic Spain in the *Estoria de España*," *Revista Canadiense de Estudios Hispánicos* 9 (1985) 345–67.

22. Sánchez Canton, 29.

23. See McGinn, *Visions*, 255.

24. Rodrigo Yáñez, *Poema de Alfonso XI*, mentions Merlin in coplas 405, 242–45, and 1808–41; *Poema de Fernand González*, ed. Zamora Vicente (Madrid, 1946); and see María Rosa Lida de Malkiel, *La Idea de la Fama en la Edad media Castellana* (Mexico, 1952) 197–207; Maravall, "Tradición," 323, 342; Joaquín Gimeno Casalduero, *Estructura y diseño en la literatura castellana medieval* (Madrid, 1975) 131–35. The poet also sees in Fernán González another Alexander the Great: vv. 351, 357, 437. Chroniclers declared Alfonso XI an Alexander and a Fernán González.

25. The literature is vast: see Adolf Bonilla y San Martín, ed., *Libros de caballerías*, (Madrid, 1907) 1:155–62; and above, Prologue, note 6. William J. Entwistle, *Arthurian Legend in the Literatures of the Spanish Peninsula* (London, 1925), 226–27, thinks the *Baladro* was translated into Spanish and dedicated to Alfonso X's son, Sancho IV, about 1291. See also Paul J. Alexander, "The Legend of the Last Roman Emperor and Its Messianic Origin," *Journal of Warburg and Courtould Institutes* 41 (1978) 1–15.

26. Lion King: Pere Bohigas, "Profecies catalenes dels segles XIV y XV," *Boletín de la Biblioteca de Catalunya* (1925) 24ff.; and see notes 24–25.

27. Nieto Soria, *Fundamentos*, 52–53; and his *Iglesia*, 191–93: "the divine dimen-

sion of monarchy" surged with the Trastámara, and "was much popularized during the fifteenth century as a literary recourse."

28. Pablo de Santa María, *Siete edades del mundo,* ed. Jean Sconza (Madison, Wis., 1991). He wrote in poetry, he explained in his prologue, to avoid boring the prince. He earlier dedicated that same poem to the queen and regent, Catalina (d. 1418).

29. *Siete edades,*54; Judith Gale Krieger, "Pablo de Santa María: His Epoch, Life, and Hebrew and Spanish Literary Production" (Ph.D. diss., UCLA, 1988) 317.

30. *Siete Edades,* s. 332. See also Alan Deyermond, "Historia universal e ideología nacional en Pablo de Santa María," in *Homenaje a Alvaro Galmes de Fuentes* (3 v., Oviedo, 1985–[1987]) 2:313–24.

31. Pedro M. Cátedra, *Sermon, sociedad, y literatura en la Edad Media: San Vicente Ferrer en Castilla (1411–1412)* (Salamanca, 1994) 244; McGinn, *Visions,* 258.

32. Cited in Angus MacKay and Dorothy S. Severin, *Crónica del sereníssimo rey don Juan II* (Exeter, 1981) 6.

33. Aurelio González, "Romances de la época de los Reyes Católicos," in Valdeón Baruque, 387–406, indicates how prominent figures became widely known and lodged in collective memory. See Alan Deyermond, "La ideología del estado moderno en la literature española del siglo XV," in Rucquoi, *Realidad* 71–93; Nieto Soria, *Fundamentos,* for a comprehensive thematic approach to concepts of royal power in Castile. See also José Manuel Nieto Soria, *Orígenes de la monarquía hispánica: Propaganda y legitimación (ca. 1400–1520)* (Madrid, 1999); and his "Propaganda and Legitimation in Castile: Religion and Church, 1250–1500," in Allan Ellenius, ed., *Iconography, Propaganda, and Legitimations* (New York and Oxford, 1998) 105–20, for paths of diffusion.

34. CD doc. 25, p. 44. See also Nicholas G. Round, *The Greatest Man Uncrowned: A Study of the Fall of Don Alvaro de Luna* (London, 1986) particularly pp. 87–129.

35. Palencia, *Crónica,* dec. 1, lib. 2, caps. 9, 10 (1:52–55); Pérez de Gúzman, *Semblanzas,* 44, 47.

36. Iñigo López de Mendoza, marqués de Santillana, *Obras completas,* ed. Angel Gómez Moreno, et al. (Barcelona, 1988) 410–13. Cf. Anon."El *Libro de la consolación de España,* una meditación sobre la Castilla del siglo xv [c. 1434–49]," in Julio Rodríguez Puértolas, ed., *Miscelánea de Textos Medievales* (Barcelona, 1972) 1:189–212.

37. Valera to Juan II, 1441, 1447, in "Epistolas," epís. 1, 2, pp. 3–7.

38. Juan de Mena, "Laberinto de Fortuna," in CC I: coplas 255, 271.

Chapter 6. Contests

1. *Crónica incompleta,* 144–45.

2. Palencia, *Crónica,* dec. 3, lib. 1, cap. 1.

3. *CD,* doc. 206.

4. Palencia, *Crónica,* dec. 3, lib. 1, cap. 4.

5. Grau, 37–39; Bernáldez, cap. 10. Fernando sent out letters describing his splendid entry: Vicens Vives, *Historia crítica,* 394.

6. Pulgar, *Crónica,* pt. 2, cap. 2.

7. Palencia, *Crónica,* dec. 3, lib. 1, cap. 4.

8. Ibid.

9. Alfonso de Madrigal (?), "Tratado que hizo el Tostado de cómo al ome es nec-

esario amar," in Antonio Paz y Meliá, ed., *Opúsculos Literarios de los siglos XIV y XV* (Madrid, 1892) 221–46.

10. *Crónica incompleta*, 144–45.

11. Pulgar, *Crónica*, pt. 2, cap. 2.

12. Palencia, *Crónica*, dec. 3, lib. 1, cap. 5.

13. Zurita, *Anales*, lib. 19, ch. 16. A copy of the agreement annotated by Zurita was published in José Diego Dörmer, *Discursos varios de historia* (Zaragoza, 1683) 295–302.

14. Palencia, *Crónica*, dec. 3, lib. 1, cap. 5.

15. See Antonio Beltrán, "Temas de las monedas a nombre de los Reyes Católicos," in *V Congreso de Historia de la Corona de Aragón* (5 v., Zaragoza, 1955–62) 224; Claudio Sanz Arizmendi, "Las primeras acunaciones de los Reyes Católicos," RABM, (3a. época; 1920) 68–80; Carlos Castán Ramírez, *Las monedas de los Reyes Católicos* (Madrid, 1972) 2ff.; A. Navarro Guglieri, *Catálogo de sellos de la sección de sigilografía del Archivo Histórico Nacional: I. Sellos Reales* (Madrid, 1974) 425, 431–33; José A. Vicenti, *Catálogo general de la moneda español, 1475: Reyes Católicos* (Madrid, 1974); Antonio Vives y Escudero, *Reforma monetaria de los Reyes Católicos* (Madrid, 1898); Remedios Morón Martín and Eduardo Fuentes Ganzo, "Ordenamiento, legitimación, y potestad normativa: Justicia y moneda," in Nieto Soria, ed., *Orígenes*, 229–38.

16. Suárez Fernández, *Conquista*, 87–88, 110.

17. *Crónica incompleta*, 208.

18. Ibid., 157; cf. Vicens Vives, *Historia crítica*, 402–4.

19. Tarsicio de Azcona, "Isabel," in Valdeón Baruque, 76, states that the marriage did take place, by proxy, in Trujillo, that it was indispensable to the Portuguese decision to enter Castile.

20. See Palencia *Crónica*, déc. 3, lib. 2, cap. 1 (2:184); Bernáldez, cap. 16.

21. Peralta to Juan II. Alcalá, May 16, 1475; Paz y Melia, *Cronista*, doc. 82, p. 182. Vicens Vives, *Historia crítica*, 389, 411.

22. Paz y Melia, *Cronista*, doc. 76, p. 176.

23. Pulgar, *Crónica*, pt. 2, cap. 1: on February 7, 1475. For Pulgar's instructions: A. P. V. Morel-Fatio, *Etudes sur l'Espagne* 1:1ère série (Paris, 1895) 187–88. Palencia, *Crónica*, déc. 3, lib. 24, cap. 6 (2:239), praises Pulgar as skillful and sagacious, ingenious in conversation and trustworthy. His respect for the other great chronicler of the reign, a man of very different temperament whose interpretations often differed from his own, makes relying on both of them a good deal easier.

24. Paz y Meliá, *Cronista*, doc. 78, p. 178. The implication is that Juan may have suggested that Fernando instruct her in international matters.

25. Pulgar, *Crónica*, pt. 2, cap. 10; Palencia, *Crónica*, déc 3, lib. 1, cap. 9 (2:174–76).

26. *Cronicón de Valladolid*, 92–94.

27. *Crónica incompleta*, 166–68, for the following description.

28. Palencia, *Crónica*, déc. 3; lib. 2, cap. 3 (2:186–87).

29. *Crónica incompleta*, 168.

30. See Palencia, *Crónica*, déc 3, lib. 2, cap. 3 2:186–87; *Cronicón de Valladolid*, 92–94; Miguel Angel Ladero Quesada, *Los Reyes Católicos: La corona y la unidad de España* (Valencia, 1989) 94–95.

31. Dörmer, 302–5. In that agreement, conceded by Isabel, she reaffirmed the power "that I have and to me belongs as heir and legitimate successor of these kingdoms and lordships."

32. *Cartas autógrafas*, carta 2.

33. CD, doc. 209, p. 708.

34. Palencia, *Crónica*, déc. 3, lib. 2, cap. 1. (2:184).

35. J. N. Lincoln, "Aljamiado Prophecies," *Publication of the Modern Literary Association of America* 52 (1937) 640; Milhou, "Chauve-souris"; Nieto Soria, *Fundamentos*, 230.

36. December 4, 1475: ASCT, doc. 455, capa 30/16; printed in Margarita González Cristóbal, comp., *Inventorios documentales monasterio de Santa Clara de Tordesillas* (Madrid, n.d.).

37. See Torres Balbas, "Ambiente mudéjar," 99; Juan Agapito y Revilla, "Restos del arte árabe o mudéjar en Santa Clara de Tordesillas," *Boletín de Sociedad Castillana de Excursiones* 3 (1905) 21–26. Isabel was in Tordesillas in April and July of 1475, from February 19 to March 28, 1476, and again at the end of June through July of 1476: Antonio Rumeu de Armas, *Itinerario de los Reyes Católicos (1475–1516)* (Madrid, 1974) 50–54.

38. Galíndez de Carvajal, *Anales*, 353: Palencia, *Crónica*, déc. 3, lib. 1, cap. 6 (2:169–70); CD, doc. 209, p. 708; *Cronicón de Valladolid*, 98; *Crónica incompleta*, tit. 22.

39. *Cartas autógrafas*, carta 3.

40. Paz y Meliá, *Cronista*, doc. 85, pp. 187–88; Palencia, *Crónica*, dec. 3, lib. 27, cap. 2 (2:303–5); and Pulgar, *Crónica*, pt. 2, caps. 22, 23.

41. Azcona, *Isabel*, 299–304.

42. Vicens Vives, *Historia crítica*, 415–16, cites A. Paz y Meliá, ed., *Noticias históricas y genealógicas de los estados de Montijo y Teba* (Madrid, 1915) doc. 105, pp. 232–37.

43. Pedro de Alcántara Suárez, *Vida del venerable don Fray Hernando de Talavera* (Madrid, 1866) 59–63.

44. *Cartas autógrafas*, carta 4.

45. *Crónica incompleta*, 210–18, whose wealth of detail implies the writer was there; and Fernando to his father: Paz y Meliá, *Crónista*, doc. 87, pp. 195–96.

46. *Crónica incompleta*, 225–26.

47. Ibid., 239ff.

48. Palencia, *Crónica*, dec. 3, lib. 3, cap. 6.

49. *Crónica incompleta*, 244–46.

50. Ladero Quesada, *Reyes Católicos*, 181: the amount garnered was more than thirty million *maravedís*.

51. Beltrán, "Temas"; and see above, note 15.

Chapter 7. Resolutions

1. *Colación de cómo se deven renovar en las ánimas todos los fieles cristianos en tiempo de adviento.* This manuscript dating from the early sixteenth century is in the Fundación Lázaro Galdiano (Madrid) ms. 336 (M 2/18). It is transcribed in José Amador de los Ríos, *Historia crítica de la literatura española* (Madrid, 1865) 7:541–61.

2. The advice of William Marshal to Matilda of England, as recounted in Georges Duby, *William Marshal: The Flower of Chivalry* (New York, 1986) 61.

3. Fernando to Juan II, November 14, 1475, Paz y Meliá, *Cronista*, doc. 94, pp. 204–5. Juan had made a six-month truce with France, and so could and did send to Fernando and Isabel Valencian troops against the marquesado of Villena, four galleys to the Guadalquivir, and war supplies, especially siege engines: Zurita, *Anales*, 4:246v.

4. Palencia, *Crónica*, dec. 3, lib. 2, cap. 8.

5. All quotations are from the *Colación*. Soon after, Isabel asked Talavera about the attributes of Saint John the Evangelist, and he replied in a *Tractado de loores de San*

Juan Evangelista, bound with *Colación* in the Lázaro Galdiano manuscript, in which he associated the properties of the saint and the eagle, as borrowed from the popular medieval book given him by Isabel: Bartholomaeus Anglicus, *De Proprietatibus Rerum*; see John Trevisa, trans., *On the Properties of Things* (Oxford, 1975) 1:602–6: The eagle is strong, bold, hardy, and virtuous, surpassing all other birds.

Isabel later sponsored that book's printing in Castilian: Sánchez Canton, 28.

6. Pulgar, *Crónica,* lib. 2, cap. 11.

7. See Eugene Rice Jr., *Saint Jerome in the Renaissance,* (Baltimore, 1985) 69–75, 96.

8. See Rudolf Wittkower, "Eagle and Serpent: A Study in the Migration of Symbols," *Journal of the Warburg Institute* 2 (1938–1939) 293–325: the Word of the apostle John is symbolized by the eagle; it is the weapon by which the sin of the world, often symbolized by the snake, is conquered. (Thus in effect the eagle sets to rights mischief done by Eve; Isabel too was to wreak vengeance on the serpent.) Marjorie Reeves and Beatrice Hirsch-Reich, "The Seven Seals in the Writings of Joachim of Fiore," *Recherches de Théologie ancienne et medievale* 21 (1954) 211–47: Joachim of Fiore had prophesied of the Lion King that "he will take to himself the wings of the Eagle." The eagle appears too in Mena, "Laberinto," stanzas 13–14. In an illustrated commentary on Revelation by Beatus de Liebana, an illumination of the angel of the fourth trumpet shows a flying eagle, traditionally the church. See Leslie G. Freeman, "Commentaries on the Apocalypse of the Blessed Apostle John," in Umberto Eco, et al., *Estudio de manuscrito del Apocalypsis de San Jan de Beato de Liebana de Escalada* (Valencia, 2000) 477, 479. Mary in turn stood for the church, and Isabel would soon be alluded to as another Mary. The eagle is also associated in Christian symbolism with the light, which is Christ (John 1:1).

9. *Cartas autógrafas,* 29.

10. Talavera, "De como se ha de ordenar el tiempo para que sea bien expendido," in Amador de los Ríos, *Historia crítica,* 7:94ff. See also Talavera, "Memorial para la Reyna cerca la orden que debía tener en el despacho de los negocios," (undated), in Vicente Rodríguez Valencia, ed., *Isabel la Católica en la opinión de españoles y extranjeros* (3 v., Valladolid, 1970) 1:367–69, who transcribes Archivo General de Simancas, *Estado Castilla* leg. 1 (2), fol. 81; also in Codoin 36. Cf. Alcántara Suárez, 59–63: Talavera to Fernando on becoming king.

11. Palencia, *Crónica,* déc. 3, lib. 25, cap. 6; Vicens Vives, *Historia crítica,* 431: Fernando to the councilors of Barcelona, February 5, 1476; Fernando to Juan, February 6 and another of February 7, 1476; Pulgar, *Crónica,* lib. 2, gives a running account of the war.

12. Palencia, *Crónica,* déc. 3, lib. 25, cap. 8.

13. CD, doc. 212; Codoin 23:396.

14. Palencia, *Crónica,* déc. 3, lib. 25, cap. 9.

15. Bachiller [Gutierre de] Palma, *Divina retribución sobre la caida de España en tiempo del noble rey Don Juan el Primero,* ed. José María Escudero de la Peña (Madrid, 1879) 58–59. The title refers to Isabel and Fernando achieving divine retribution for the Spanish defeat at the battle of Aljubarrota of 1385.

16. "Cortes of Madrigal, April 27, 1476," *Cortes de los antiguos reinos de León y de Castilla* 4 (1882) pp. 1–109. See Chapter 11, regarding Cortes representation and procedure.

17. Ibid., 4:94.

18. Luis Suárez Fernández, "Evolución histórico de las hermandades castellanos,"

Cuadernos de Historia de España (1952) *separata;* Miguel Angel Ladero Quesada, *Hacienda castellana entre 1480 y 1492* (Valladolid, 1967) 201–18; and Martin Lunenfeld, *The Council of the Santa Hermandad* (Coral Gables, Fla., 1970) 31–38.

19. See Palencia, *Crónica,* déc. 3, lib. 24, cap. 6; Pulgar, *Crónica,* pt. 2, cap. 51; cf. Pulgar, Gloss on Mingo Revulgo, bound with Pulgar, *Letras,* 215; *Crónica incompleta,* tít. 51, p. 305; Galíndez de Carvajal, *Anales,* 261–62.

20. Rozmital, in Codoin 127:107. "All I know is that the Holy Brotherhood has something to say about those who go around fighting on the highway, and I want nothing of it," says Sancho Panza in Miguel Cervantes, *Don Quixote,* 1:ch.10.

21. Pulgar, *Crónica,* pt. 2, cap. 51.

22. See Miguel Angel Ladero Quesada, *Castilla y la conquista del reino de Granada* (Granada n.d.) 106; Ladero Quesada, *Hacienda,* 19–20, 40, 214–18; Azcona, *Isabel,* 337; Vicens Vives, *Historia crítica,* 457; and J. Lasuén, "Alfonso de Quintanilla, Contador mayor de los Reyes Católicos," *Boletín de la Instituto Fernán González* 30 (1951) 713–24.

23. The Turk was restrained from dominating Europe only by the Venetians and by Hungary, which was also torn by factions.

24. Paz y Meliá, *Cronista,* doc. 107, p. 229.

25. See Chapter 3, note 38; Vicens Vives, *Historia crítica,* 452–53, 457; Prieto Cantero, commentary to *Cartas autógrafas.* Llanos y Torriglia, *Hogar,* 28: their mothers are unknown; one was a *vizcaina* and the other a Portuguese or Valencian noblewoman; he gives no source. Münzer, "Viaje por España y Portugal," trans. Julio Puyol, in BRAH 84 (1924), 68, mentions a daughter, María, in the Convento de la Trinidad, Valencia. In 1509 Fernando wrote his ambassador in Rome seeking to legitimize them so they might hold positions in the convent; he requested a papal *breve,* "the briefest possible," and apparently received it. One became prioress, the other vicaress, either in Madrid or Madrigal.

26. Paz y Meliá, *Cronista,* doc. 109, p. 230. See Juan Torres Fontes, "La conquista del marquesado de Villena en el reinado de los Reyes Católicos," *Hispania* 50 (1953).

27. Pulgar, *Crónica,* lib. 2, cap. 65.

28. Palencia, *Crónica,* déc. 3, lib. 27, cap. 8.

29. *Crónica incompleta,* 310.

30. William Christian Jr. has written to me of a response received to a questionnaire about the shrine, dated October 12, 1969, that contains the story of the young captain. However, that cult was not immediate, for in 1481 it is recorded that Rodrigo de Ulloa and his wife, Aldonza de Castilla, gave to the shrine of Nuestra Señora de la Vega a magnificent altarpiece: José Augusto Sánchez Pérez, *El Culto Mariana en España* (Madrid, 1943) 429. See also above, Chapter 1, note 17.

31. Jorge Manrique, "Coplas por la muerte de su padre," in Cohen, *Spanish Verse,* v. 36, p. 54. "Don Juan" was Juan II of Castile; "the *infantes* of Aragón" were the future Juan II of Aragón and his siblings, who were notorious for meddling in Castile.

32. Phillips, *Enrique IV,* 22–23, estimates the military orders had about one million vassals, revenues of more than forty thousand ducats a year, and fifteen hundred titles to bestow in patronage. See Paz y Melia, *Cronista,* doc. 135, p. 267; Zurita, *Anales* 8:lib. 20, ch. 1–2

33. Prieto Cantero, "Collar de balajes," 207–8.

34. See Dorothy Severin, *Del manuscrito a la imprenta en la época de Isabel* (Kesel, Belgium, 2004).

35. Fray Iñigo de Mendoza, "Dechado del Regimiento de Principes," in R. Foulché-Delbosc, ed., *Cancionero castellano del siglo XV* (2 v., Madrid 1912) (hereinafter CC)

1:72–78; Rodríguez Puértolas, *Fray Iñigo de Mendoza,* 237–44. Mendoza, "Coplas a [los Reyes Católicos] en que declara como por el advenimiento destos muy alto señores es reparada nuestra Castilla," in CC 1:72; see also 1:67. And he addresses Fernando: "Y el propheta, en conclusión, / dize: 'Rey, según venís, / como brumará el león / y castigará el blason / la contraria flor de lis!' "

36. Valera, *Doctrinal de principes,* in BAE 116:173.

37. Palma, 60–66.

38. Pulgar, *Crónica,* pt. 2, cap. 84.

39. San Juan de los Reyes was also meant to commemorate victory, particularly over Portugal, to erase Castilian defeat at Aljubarrota; see also Azcona, "Isabel," 78.

40. "Tanto monta" had compound meaning, including favoring a pragmatic solution, as did Alexander the Great when faced with whether to cut or untie the Gordian knot; that knot often appears with the device of the yoke and was probably originally a device of Fernando's. Ladero Quesada, *Reyes Católicos,* 94–95: *tanto monta* was suggested by Nebrija. Tate and Lawrance, xliii: *tanto monta* was suggested by Mendoza. See also Azcona, *Isabel,* 219; Suárez Fernández, *Fundamentos,* 19. Some see it as exclusively Fernando's device: Pedro Aguado Bleye, "Tanto monta: La empresa de Fernando el Católico," *Santa Cruz,* no. 8 (1949) 7–12; and Vicens Vives, *Historia crítica,* 400–401. Yet clearly that limited interpretation changed to earn it a prominent place among other symbols in Castile advertising royal togetherness and conjoined high purpose.

41. See Chapter 5.

42. See Azcárate, "Sentido," 201–7; and documents in José María de Azcárate, "Datos histórico-artísticos de fines del siglo XV y principios de XVI," in *Colección de documentos para la historia de arte en España* (Madrid and Zaragoza, 1982) 2:242–43.

Chapter 8. To the Sea

1. Ladero Quesada, *España en 1492,* 15–16.

2. Cited in A. de la Torre, *Homenaje a Isabel la Católica en Madrigal de las Altas Torres* (Madrid, 1953) 14.

3. Pulgar, *Crónica,* pt. 2, cap. 65: some nobles opposed Isabel's venture south, but Fernando backed her going "because he knew her to be a woman of great spirit."

4. Ladero Quesada, *Andalucía,* 33.

5. Münzer, 112; Albert A. Sicroff, "The Jeronymite Monastery of Guadalupe in Fourteenth and Fifteenth Century Spain," in M. P. Hornik, ed., *Collected Studies in Honour of Américo Castro's Eightieth Year* (Oxford, 1965) 397–422; Guy Beaujouan, *La science en Espagne aux XIV et XV siècles* (Madrid, 1973); J. R. L. Highfield, "The Jeronymites in Spain, Their Patrons and Successes, 1373–1516," *Journal of European History* 34 (1983); B. L. Díaz, "Centro de amplicación de estudios médicos en Guadalupe," *Revista del Centro de Estudios Extremeños* 1 (1927) 237–42. Talavera, Isabel's intimate, in his *Católica impugnación,* written about 1480, singled out "the holy and very magnificent house of our lady of Guadalupe" as chosen by Jesus Christ for serving and praising him.

6. See note 2; Palencia, *Crónica,* déc. 3, lib. 29, caps. 2, 3 (3:35–37).

7. Pulgar, *Crónica,* pt. 2, cap. 69.

8. Isabel while in Trujillo learned that one Diego Pizarro, who had recently been given the new post of *alcaide* among Jews and Muslims, was accused of maltreating his charges. In May of 1476, Jews protested that Pizarro had forced them to clean stables,

haul manure, and wash chamber pots. Isabel informed them she was suspending his appointment until the Council reviewed the matter. Reflecting ongoing maltreatment from Caceres in July of 1477 came Isabel's letter of security to the Trujillo *aljama* stating that Jews were no longer to be abused by other inhabitants: see Luis Suárez Fernández, *Documentos acerca de la expulsión de los júdios* (Valladolid, 1964) docs. 9 (p. 93), 10 (pp. 94–95), doc. 14 (p. 116); and 18 (p. 116).

9. Escavias, *Repertorio*, 25–32: in this 1474–75 chronicle, Hercules brings in Seville's original population. See also Miguel Angel Ladero Quesada, *Historia de Sevilla, 2: La ciudad medieval* (2d ed., rev., Seville, 1980) ch. 3, 4.

10. Alfonso Franco Silva, *La esclavitud en Sevilla y su tierra a fines de la Edad Media* (Seville, 1979). See appended documents to José Gestoso y Pérez, *Los Reyes Católicos en Sevilla (1477–78)* (Seville, 1891); Enrique Otte, *Sevilla y sus mercaderes a fines de la Edad Media* (Seville, 1996); and Diego de Valera, *Crónica de los Reyes Católicos,* ed. Juan de Mata Carriazo (Madrid, 1927) 74–75, regarding a Sevillian merchant who comes from Barbary and describes the slave trade and merchants. See also William D. Phillips Jr., *Slavery from Roman Times to the Early Transatlantic Trade* (Minneapolis, 1985) 107–13.

11. Isabel's entry: Zurita, *Anales,* lib. 29, cap. 12 (8: 292). Palencia, *Crónica,* déc. 3, lib. 29, caps. 7–8 (3: 47–49); Palencia, who was there, has come at last to indicate respect for the queen's judgment.

12. Miguel Angel Ladero Quesada, "Aristocratie et régime seigneurial dans l'Andalousie du XVème siecle," *Annales* 6 (1983) 1346–68; Ladero Quesada, *Andalucía;* Ladero Quesada, *Historia de Sevilla* 2:119–22; Ladero Quesada, *Hacienda,* 127–42; see also Wendy R. Childs, *Anglo-Castilian Trade in the Later Middle Ages* (Manchester, 1978).

13. Archivo Historia Municipal de Sevilla, Cartulario; Juan de Mata Carriazo and Ramón Carande Thobar, eds., *Tumbo de los Reyes Católicos* (5 v., Seville, 1929–68) 1: doc. 87; Ladero Quesada, *Andalucía,* 6–7. Antonio Rumeu de Armas, "Las pesquerías españolas en la costa de Africa (siglos XV–XVI)," *Hispania* 35 (1975) 295–300.

14. Florentino Pérez-Embid, *Los descubrimientos en el Atlántico y la rivalidad castellano-portuguesa hasta el tratado de Tordesillas* (Seville, 1948) 196–210; Antonio Rumeu de Armas, *España en el Africa atlántica* (2 v., Madrid, 1955); and Pierre Chaunu, *European Expansion in the Later Middle Ages* (Amsterdam, 1979) ch. 3.

15. Isabel, December 20, 1474: *Tumbo* 1:1–3.

16. Alfonso Franco Silva, "La intervención de Portugal en el comercio de esclavos de Andalucía a fines del medievo," in *Actas de III coloquio de historia medieval andaluza* (Jaén, 1984) 346–47. Palencia, *Crónica,* déc. 3, lib. 25, cap. 4 (2:261–62), views such activity as defensive against Portuguese insolence and mentions that three or four fishing boats of Palos had seized many Portuguese ships returning from Africa, killing the crews and claiming their cargos, including enslaved blacks.

17. Vicens Vives, *Historia crítica,* 466–67; Pulgar, *Crónica,* pt. 2, caps. 62, 70; see also Angus Mackay, *Money.*

18. Antonio de la Torre and Luis Suárez Fernandez, eds., *Documentos referentes a las relaciones con Portugal durante el reinado de los Reyes Católicos,* (3 v., Valladolid, 1958–1963) 1:87–89, 97–99.

19. Torre and Suárez, *Documentos* 1:92–93; *Tumbo* 1:31.

20. See Torre and Suárez, *Documentos* 1:97–99, 117–19; and Roger Highfield, "The De La Cerda, the Pimentel, and the so-called Price Revolution," *English Historical Review* 87 (1972) 499.

21. Pulgar, *Crónica,* pt. 2, cap. 70; P. E. Russell, "Fontes documentais castelhanas

para a historia da expansão portuguesa na Guiné nos últimos años de D. Afonso V," *Do tempo e da Historia* 4 (1971) 5–33; Juan de Mata Carriazo, introduction to Diego de Valera, *Crónica* . . . *Reyes;* Vicenta Cortés, "Algunos viajes de las gentes de Huelva al Atlántico (1470–88)," *Anuario de Estudios Americanos* 25 (1968) 565–74; J. Vogt, *Portuguese Rule on the Guinea Coast, 1469–1482* (Athens, Ga., 1979). See also Cesareo Fernández Duro, "Viaje por España, Portugal, y costa de Africa en el siglo XV," BAH 32 (1898) 17–21: an account by a Belgian trader, Eustaquio [Eustatius?] de la Fosse, in 1479, who went to La Mina de Oro from Seville with merchandise from Flanders. A fort was built at San Jorge da Mina in 1481. See also Chapter 16, note 6.

22. Palencia, *Crónica,* dec. 3, lib. 25, cap. 4 (2:260–62). Letter of Diego de Valera to Isabel (n.d.), in "Epistolas," epís. 20, pp. 25–27; letter of Isabel to Valera, Tordesillas, May 15, 1476, in BAH 64 (1914) 367. Similarly in 1477 she interceded to free Guanches that Fernando, son of Inés de Peraza, sought to enslave: Luis Suárez Fernández, coord., *Historia general de España y América 5: Los Trastámara y la unidad española (1369–1517)* (Madrid, 1981) 570; Galíndez de Carvajal, *Anales,* 258 (annotation). A royal order of November 8, 1475 from Dueñas grants to Juan de Valladolid, *negro,* the title of judge and chief person of the *"negros and negras, loros y loras* that at present have been brought in great number from Guinea to Seville and live *de asiento* in that city."

23. Palencia, *Crónica,* dec. 3, lib. 26, cap. 6; see Charles Verlinden, "Antonio da Noli and the Colonization of the Cape Verde Islands," in his *The Beginnings of Modern Colonization* (Ithaca, N.Y., 1970) 161ff.

24. Fernando to Diego de Valera. Burgos, May 26, 1476, BAH 64 (1914) 368; and another of September 7, 1476 from Vitoria: Biblioteca Nacional, ms. F.108.

25. Palencia, *Crónica,* déc. 3, lib. 26, caps. 5–6; Pulgar, *Crónica,* pt. 3, cap. 62 (pp. 314–15).

26. Valera, *Crónica* . . . *Reyes,* cap. 22, pp. 81–82; Palencia, op. cit; Antonio Paz y Meliá, ed., *Archivo y biblioteca de la casa de Medinaceli* (2 v., Madrid, 1915, 1922) 1:72–74, 78–79, 82; Torre and Suárez, *Documentos,* doc. 87, 1: 144; Azcona, *Isabel,* 287.

27. Palencia, *Crónica,* déc. 3, lib. 24, cap. 7; dec. 3, lib. 26, caps. 4–5; Paz y Meliá, *Cronista,* doc. 112, p. 234; Ernesto de la Torre, "Unos documentos referentes al vicealmirante francés 'Columbus' (1485–1488)," BAH 104 (1934) 565–80.

28. Palencia, *Crónica,* déc. 3, lib. 27, cap. 5.

29. Valera, *Crónica* . . . *Reyes,* cap. 21; Valera, letter to King Fernando of August 17, 1476, "Epistolas," epís. 7, pp. 12–13.

30. Antonio Rumeu de Armas, "La revindacación por la corona de Castilla de derecho de conquista sobre las Canarías Mayores y la creación del condado de Gomera," *Hidalguía* 7 (1959) 33–60.

31. Alonso de Palencia, *Cuarta Década,* ed. José López de Toro (2 v., Madrid, 1974) lib.31, caps. 8–9; R. Torres Campos, *Carácter de la conquista y colonización de Canarías* (Madrid, 1901) 127, 130, 132; Pulgar, *Crónica,* pt. 2, cap. 76 (p. 330).

32. Pérez-Embid, *Descubrimientos* 211; Miguel Angel Ladero Quesada, *España de los Reyes Catolicos* (Madrid, 1999) 256–70.

33. Luis de la Torre, "Los canarios de Gomera vendidos como esclavos en 1489 [1479?]," *Anuario de Estudios Americanos* 2 (1950) 47–51; Dom J. Wölfel, "La curia romana y la corona de España en defensa de los aborigines canarios: Documentos inéditos y documentos desconocidos," *Anthropos* 25 (1930) 1011–83.

34. Antonio Rumeu de Armas, *Política indigenista de Isabel la Católica* (Valladolid, 1969) 40–44.

35. Palencia, *Crónica,* déc. 3, lib. 27, cap. 1 (2: p. 301).

36. Ibid., and déc. 3, lib. 28, cap. 6 (3:21).

37. Pulgar, *Crónica,* pt. 3, cap. 70; Palencia, *Crónica,* déc. 3, lib. 29, cap. 8 (3: pp. 46–48); Gestoso y Pérez, 9.

38. "*Alla van leyes / donde las mandan los reyes.*" Cf. Pinar, CC 2:559: "Alla van leyes / Do quieren reyes"; in ". . . un juego trobado que hizo a la reyna doña Isabel."

39. Pulgar, *Crónica,* pt. 2, cap. 70.

40. Ibid. Cf. Münzer, 200: "el rey" made Seville safe from malefactors, where before people had not dared walk the streets at night. See also Pulgar, *Letras,* letra 16, pp. 77–83; *Tumbo* 1: 77–83; Ladero Quesada, *Andalucía,* 81; *Siete Partidas* lib. 2, tít. 10, ley 2: clemency should accompany justice so that it is not excessive; Sánchez de Arévalo, "Summa de política," BAE 116:297; Valera, *Doctrinal de principes,* 195. *Ordenanzas Reales de Castilla,* lib. 2, tit. 1, ley 1, institutionalizing the royal *audiencia:* the monarchs are to hear cases two days a week—on Mondays petitions, on Fridays cases of those arrested—according to previous custom. Monarchs emulate God and justice is commended to them by God: they are repeatedly compared to Moses, as in *Partidas* lib. 2, tit. 1, ley 7 and in the Cortes of Burgos in 1453 and of Ocaña in 1469.

41. Pulgar, *Crónica,* pt. 2, cap. 71–72. *Cf.* Palencia, *Crónica,* déc. 3, lib. 29, cap. 9 (3:48–50). Erroneously, Bernáldez, cap. 29, places Fernando there; Vicens Vives, *Historia crítica,* claims Fernando alone received Cádiz's homage and was responsible for an accord between Cádiz and Medina Sidonia of September 13, 1477, and a formal reconciliation of October 1, 1478, formal in that they were still unfriendly.

Chapter 9. Signs and Revelations

1. Pulgar, *Letras,* letra 9.

2. Pulgar, *Crónica,* pt. 2, cap. 73 (p. 328); Palencia, *Crónica,* dec. 3, lib. 29, cap. 10 (3:50–51). Gestoso y Pérez, app. G. Antonio de la Torre, "Un médico de los Reyes Católicos," *Hispania* 4 (1944) 66–72, mentions that Isabel received medical care from a *converso,* Lorenzo Bádoz. Other accounts mention the Palatine physician Juan de Pineda, including as present at the birth.

3. See Juan de Mata Carriazo, *El Alcázar de Sevilla* (Barcelona, 1930); Münzer, 202.

4. Letter appended to Azcona, *Isabel,* and see pp. 289–90: Juan wanted to raise his grandson in Aragón, and advises in no case should he be raised by a *privado.* See also Zurita, *Anales,* lib. 20, cap. 22 (7:336–37); Vicens Vives, *Historia crítica,* 494–95.

5. María de Guzmán was lady of La Algaba, the aunt of Medina Sidonia and wife of Pedro de Ayala of Toledo: Blanca Azquez, "Madre de Sevilla," *Archivo Hispalense,* 2d ser., 14 (1951) 195–210.

6. Bernáldez, cap. 32.

7. Ibid., caps. 32–33. Jacques LeGoff, *Medieval Imagination* (Chicago, 1988) 99, cites advice to husbands concerning "abuse of marriage" in the widely read *Decretum* of Burchard of Worms, a specialist in canon law. It continues: "And if you copulated with her during that time, you shall do penance on bread and water for twenty days."

8. Whatever the cause, Fernando fell gravely ill at the beginning of August, his life in danger, but convalesced quickly: Al[f]onso de Palencia, *Cuarta década,* ed. José López de Toro (2 v., Madrid, 197) lib. 32, cap. 7; Zurita, *Anales,* lib. 20, cap. 25 (8:345).

9. Bernáldez, cap. 33.

10. Vicens Vives, *Historia crítica,* 489.

11. Palma, 73; see also Gómez Manrique, "Regimiento de Principes," in CC 2:111–22: the king is in turn divinely chosen.

12. Pulgar, *Letras*, letra 9. He continues: "God rejected the temple of Enrique and did not choose the tribe of Alfonso: but chose the tribe of Isabel whom he preferred."

13. Palma, 73, 88.

14. CC 2:150–51.

15. Alcántara Suárez, 175.

16. Palencia, *Cuarta Década*, lib. 32, cap. 1.

17. Puyol, in an annotation to Münzer, "Viaje," 114–15. Linda Martz tells me there are two private chapels in Toledo churches dedicated to *los dos Santos Juan*. A praying Isabel and Fernando each have their patron standing behind them on the facade of the monastery of Santa Cruz in Segovia.

18. Pulgar in that letter (above note 12), states that Prince Juan was born to be the terror to those of the mountains, echoing what Luke 1:5–17 says of John the Evangelist. "Those of the mountains" surely alluded to the Moors of mountainous Granada. Moreover, Ezek. 7:17, prophesying an end to come for Israel, except for a remnant, gave a different reading: ". . . they that shall at all escape shall be on the mountains like doves of the valleys, all of them moaning, every one in his iniquity." Thus Pulgar appears to make a compound allusion to the Muslim kingdom and to the unfaithful within: Juan was sent to take both on.

19. Valera, *Doctrinal de principes*, 173.

20. Maravall, *Concepto*, 312.

21. Pulgar, *Letras*, letra 11.

22. Valera, dedication to *Crónica de España* (Zaragoza, 1493). It had at least six Spanish editions between 1482 and 1500.

23. Valera's history began similarly, with the world as divided into Asia, Africa, and Europe, and then moved to Spain and its earliest peoples, descendants of Tubal, a grandson of Noah. Then came Hercules and his nephew Hispan, the Romans, the Goths, and Spain destroyed except for the Christian remnant under Pelayo; and so it proceeded through subsequent rulers, ending with Juan II and Enrique IV. The dedication then indicated all this was but prelude.

24. *Crónica incompleta*, tít. 51, p. 309.

25. Ibid., tít. 52, p. 317.

26. Valera, "Epistolas," epís. 13, p. 17.

27. María Rosa Lida de Malkiel, *Estudios sobre la literatura española del Siglo XV* (Madrid, 1978) 294–95.

28. Cited in Kenneth R. Scholberg, *Satira e invectiva en la España medieval* (Madrid, 1971) 238.

29. Palma, 75–77.

30. "Historia de los hechos de don Rodrigo Ponce de León, marqués de Cadiz," in Codoin 106:148; Joaquín Yarza Luaces, *Los Reyes Católicos* (Madrid, 1993) 22–24. Fernando III's receiving the keys from the *Virgen de las Batallas*, often depicted in paintings, was to be seen in Seville's cathedral.

31. CC 2:150: "Yo soy aquella Maria / del linaje de David."

32. Iñigo de Mendoza, "Dechado," [1475?], in CC 1:72. For women, Eve, and Mary, see William A. Christian Jr., *God and Person in a Spanish Valley* (Princeton, N.J., 1972); Susan Tax Freeman, "Faith and Fashion in Spanish Religion: Notes on the Observation of Observance," *Peasant Studies* 7 (1978) 101–22; and Chapters 1 and 8.

33. Nazario Pérez, *La Inmaculada y España* (Santander, 1954) 77, 80. See Yarza

Luaces, *Reyes Católicos,* 156, on the debate concerning the doctrine of Immaculate Conception.

34. See Carlos G. Villacampa, *Grandezas de Guadalupe* (Madrid, 1924) 32; Pérez, *Inmaculada,* 74, 81. Fraker, *Studies,* 83–86: on poems by Villasandino and others on the Woman, and the Serpent. In Toledo, Beatriz Silva, a lady who had served Isabel's mother, founded the Concepcionistas, an order of nuns that enjoyed Isabel's patronage. See Suzanne Stratton, *The Immaculate Conception in Spanish Art* (Cambridge, 1994) 5–334, particularly pp. 9–10; she and I differ on just how early the image of the Woman of Revelation was associated with the Immaculate Conception in Spain; I gather there is some indication of it being so by the 1490s at the shrine of Guadalupe.

35. Francisco Imperial, in *Cancionero de Baena* (facsimile ed., New York, 1926) no. 226. See also Gimeno Casalduero, 174–77. Imperial relies on Dante's "Purgatory" in the *Divine Comedy,* 20:19–21.

36. Pulgar, *Crónica,* pt. 2, cap. 92.

37. Carriazo, *Alcázar.*

Chapter 10. Inquisition

1. Pulgar, *Crónica,* pt. 2, cap. 96; and see Pulgar, *Reyes,* cap. 24 (1:77).

2. Archivo General de Simancas (AGS), *Estado-Castilla* 1–2, fol. 75; cited in Azcona, *Isabel,* 387.

3. Torquemada, "Las cosas que debian remediar los reyes," cited in Azcona, *Isabel,* 387. Pulgar, *Crónica,* pt. 2, cap. 77 (p. 331): Torquemada was "confesor del rey." Zurita, *Anales,* lib. 20, cap. 49 (8:439): Zurita states that Torquemada was confessor of the king and queen; there is no substantiating evidence and Zurita was not contemporary. Salazar de Mendoza, f. 167–68: Torquemada was (or had been) Mendoza's confessor, and credits Mendoza with requesting he be named *supremo juez* of the tribunal.

4. Julio Caro Baroja, *Los judios en España moderna y contemporanea* (3 v., Madrid, 1961) 126.

5. See Linda Martz, *A Network of Converso Families in Early Modern Toledo* (Ann Arbor, Mich., 2003) 20–29; Nicholas G. Round, "La rebelión toledana de 1449," *Achivium* 16 (1961) 385–446; Albert A. Sicroff, *Los estatutos de Limpieza de Sangre* (Madrid, 1985) 59–61, Suárez Fernández, *Enrique IV,* 81–100; Angus MacKay, "Popular Movements and Pogroms in Fifteenth-Century Castile," *Past and Present* 55 (1972) 33–67; and María del Pilar Rábade Obradó, "Judeoconversos e Inquisición," in Nieto Soria, *Orígenes,* 239–72. Díaz de Toledo, himself a converso, was a high functionary in Juan II's court.

6. Torre and Suárez, *Documentos,* 1: doc. 101, of June 10, 1478.

7. Traveling in Castile in 1484, Nicolas Popielovo wrote in his journal (García Mercadal, 319): "I observed that she [Isabel] had more confidence in the baptized Jews than in the Christians. She puts all her rents in their hands. They are her counselors and secretaries, and also those of the king, and nevertheless, in spite of being respected, they are hated more than anything else."

8. Bernáldez, cap. 43, p. 599; Yitzhak Baer, *A History of the Jews in Christian Spain* (2 v., Philadelphia, 1966) 2:324.

9. Miguel Angel Ladero Quesada, "Judeoconversos andaluces en el siglo XV," in *Actas del III Coloquío de Historia Medieval Andaluza* (Jaén, 1984) 41.

10. Espina's *Fortalitium fidei* was published in 1471 and among the Biblioteca

Nacional *incunabulae* are three more editions by 1494: two of Nuremberg and one of London. Espina was named inquisitor for Barcelona by Torquemada in 1487: Jaime Vicens Vives, *Ferran II i la ciutat de Barcelona* (2 v., Barcelona, 1936–37) 1:411.

11. Escavías, *Repertorio*, cap. 147; Valera, *Memorial*, cap. 83, pp. 240–43.

12. Palencia, *Crónica*, déc. 2, lib. 8, cap. 2 (2:130–34); déc. 2, lib. 9, cap. 8 (2:229–34).

13. Suárez Fernández, *Fundamentos*, 21.

14. Nicolás López Martínez, *Los judaizantes castellanos y la Inquisición en tiempos de Isabel la Católica* (Burgos, 1954) 110; Márquez Villanueva, "Conversos," 323; Américo Castro, *Realidad histórica de España* (Mexico, 1954) 504; *Revue Hispanique* 40 (1917) 233, 235.

15. Papal instructions to Franco, 1475, in Vicente Rodríguez Valencia, *Artículos de Postulador* (Valladolid, 1972) 24.

16. See Fidel Fita, "Fray Felipe de y la Inquisición española," BRAH 16 (1890) 565–70; Juan Antonio Llorente, *Historia crítica de la Inquisición en España* (2^d ed., 4 v., Madrid, 1980–81) 1:125–26; Henry Charles Lea, *A History of the Inquisition in Spain* (4 v.; New York, 1906; rp. 1966, 1988) 1:155n1. Cf. Azcona, *Isabel*, 385–86. Popular fury had been directed against Jews in Sicily in 1474 and hundreds were slaughtered.

17. See Yitzak Baer, *Die Juden im christlichen Spanien* (Berlin, 1970) 344–46; Fidel Fita, "Nuevas fuentes para escribir la historia de los judíos españoles: Bulas inéditas de Sixto IV e Inocencio VIII," BRAH 15 (1889) 449–52. Sixtus IV had put Carrillo in charge of extirpating heresy in Toledo in a bull of June 25, 1478 (Reg. Vat. 587, fol. 235–37; cited in Azcona, *Isabel*, 387), thus possibly spurring *los reyes* to act to outmaneuver that adversary and episcopal control of the Inquisition.

18. Pulgar, *Crónica*, pt. 1, cap. 77 (pp. 331–32); Francisco Cantera Burgos, "Fernando de Pulgar y los conversos," in Roger Highfield, ed., *Spain in the Fifteenth Century, 1369–1516* (New York, 1972) 309–10; Hernando de Talavera, *Católica impugnación del herético libelo que en el año pasado de 1480 fué divulgado en la ciudad de Sevilla*, ed. Francisco Martín (Barcelona, 1961) 186–87. Some biographers of Mendoza claim the Inquisition there and then was Mendoza's idea, but there is no documental evidence.

19. Pulgar, *Letras*, letra 34, p. 110; Cantera Burgos, "Pulgar," 306–8.

20. Bernáldez, cap. 43.

21. The queen's commission reported the measures insufficient: see above, note 17.

22. Pulgar, *Crónica*, pt. 1, cap. 77 (pp. 331–82); Lea, *Inquisition* 1:160–61; Isabel to Seville, October 3, 1480 and November 9, 1480, in Mario Méndez Bejarano, *Histoire de la Juiverie de Séville* (Madrid, 1922) 160–61; see also Jean-Pierre Dedieu, "Les Quatre temps de l'Inquisition," in Bartolomé Bennassar, ed., *L'Inquisition espagnole* (Paris, 1979).

23. "Relación de la junta y conjuración, que hicieron en Sevilla los judíos conversos contra los Inquisidores, que vinieron a fundar y establecer el Santo Oficio de la Inquisición," in Biblioteca Colombina, t. 34 of mss. varios, pp. 207–11; Fidel Fita, "Los conjurados de Sevilla contra la Inquisición," BRAH 16 (1890) 450–56. See also Bernáldez, caps. 43, 44; Azcona, *Isabel*, 412; Márquez Villanueva, "Conversos," 587–88.

24. Bernáldez, cap. 44; Llorente, 1:138; Lea, 1:164.

25. Llorente, 1:136–38. Figures vary. Pulgar, *Reyes*, caps. 96, 120, states that three hundred people burned within the city of Seville in 1481, and reports complaints that the Inquisition abused canon law. See also Ladero Quesado, "Judeoconversos," 34–37; Cantera Burgos, "Pulgar," 338–39. Palencia says five hundred were burned at the stake

in Seville in the first three years. Bernáldez, caps. 43–44: between 1481 and 1488 seven hundred were burned, more than five thousand reconciled, and many others condemned. Cf. Lea 1:165–67. See also Hipólito Sancho de Sopranis, "Historia social de Jerez de la Frontera al fin de la Edad Media," *Anécdota* 3 (1959); Sopranis, "La judería de Puerto de Santa María de 1483 a 1492," *Sefarad* 13 (1953) 309–24; Fidel Fita, "La Inquisición en Jerez de la Frontera," BRAH 15 (1889) 313–46. Perhaps half of those penanced lived within nobles' jurisdictions.

26. Márquez Villanueva, "Conversos," 587.

27. My thanks to Vicente Lleó Cañal for calling this saying to my attention.

28. Azcona, *Isabel,* 412.

29. Pulgar, *Letras,* letra 34; Cantera Burgos, "Pulgar," 309–10.

30. Cited by Carriazo, introduction, Pulgar, *Reyes,* liii–lviii; and see Cantera Burgos, "Pulgar," 316.

31. Pulgar, *Letras,* letra 21. Cantera Burgos, "Pulgar," 317.

32. Montoro, in *Poesía crítica,* ed, Rodríguez Púertolas, 317.

33. Alonso Ortiz, *Los Tratados de* (Seville, 1493), fol. 101.

34. Sigüenza 2:305–6.

35. Talavera, *Católica Impugnación,* 224, 235–36. Talavera is generally presented by scholars as humane and kindly, as he who later insisted Muslims be converted through persuasion, not force. Yet the faith he sought they follow was grim and militant, and he showed no compassion for Jews who would not follow it or had turned away from it.

36. Paul (Hebrews 10), in stating the Mosaic law held a shadow of the awaited good but not its image, supported the stock belief drawn on by Talavera that Christ brought the liberating new law.

37. Fita, "Nuevas fuentes," 459–62; B. Llorca, *Bulario Pontificio de la Inquisición en su periodo constitucional (1478–1525)*(Rome, 1949) 59–63, 73–75; Azcona, *Isabel,* 401, 410; Lea, *Inquisition,* 1:591–92.

38. For the Spanish Inquisition in Aragonese realms, see Torre and Suárez, *Documentos,* doc. 112 (1:204–6); William Monter, *Frontiers of Heresy* (Cambridge, 1990) 3–28; Ricardo García Cárcel, *Orígenes de la Inquisición Española: El Tribunal de Valencia, 1478–1530* (1976) 37–53; Azcona, *Isabel,* 406–8.

39. Archivo Histórico Nacional Madrid, cod. 121, fol. 178r; and in Fita, "Nuevas fuentes," 465–68, 468–71, 475–76; cf. Azcona, *Isabel,* 404. See also Fidel Fita, "Declive y fin," BRAH 15 (1889) 477–89; Llorca, doc. 14, pp. 92–102.

40. Lea, 1:173; Torre, *Documentos,* 2:67–68: On October 17, 1483, Torquemada was named by Sixtus inquisitor of Aragón, Catalonia, and Valencia. In March of 1485 he was referred to as *"juez principal ynquisidor,"* but not yet inquisitor general, in Castile. Luis Suárez Fernández, *La expansión de la fe* (Madrid, 1990) 46, 65–67: In 1487, the monarchs fended off Rome's attack on Torquemada and the arbitrariness and harshness of the Inquisition. The earliest mention of the Holy Tribunal as a royal council is found in a document of October 7, 1488. The 1484 instructions: in Gaspar Isidro de Arguëlles, *Instrucciones del Santo Oficio* (Madrid, 1630).

41. Pulgar, *Crónica,* pt. 2, cap. 79 (pp. 334–36); *cf.* Pulgar, *Letras,* letra 14. See also Palencia, *Guerra de Granada,* lib. 4, in Palencia, *Crónica* 3, 119; Fidel Fita, "La Inquisición de Ciudad Real in 1483–85," BRAH 20 (1892) 462–520; Fita, "Inquisición toledana: Relación de los autos y autillos que celebró desde el año 1485 hasta 1502," BRAH 11 (1887) 289–322; Fita "La Inquisición en Guadalupe," BRAH 23; Suárez Fernández, *Expansión,* 58–65, describes inquisitorial procedures in the tribunal's initial stage.

42. Azcona, *Isabel,* 401, 410.

43. See Fita, "Inquisición toledana"; Lea, 1:166–71; Márquez Villanueva, *Investigaciones,* 295; Márquez Villanueva, "Conversos," 515–16: numerous *conversos* with conciliar positions were sentenced in Toledo. Gómez Manrique's energy and tact ended the plot. He hung the *corregidor'*s lieutenant, Bachiller de la Torre, and five plotters but levied mostly money penalties, "for to bring to justice so many people would have depopulated the city."

44. Sebastián de Horozco, *Relaciones históricos toledanos* (Toledo, 1981) 100.

45. Ibid., 103.

46. Ladero Quesada, *España de los Reyes,* 323. See also Pulgar, *Crónica,* pt. 3, cap. 54 (p. 432).

47. Pulgar, *Crónica,* pt. 3, cap. 95 (pp. 473–74); Zurita, *Anales* 8: lib. 20, cap. 65.

48. Robert B. Tate, *Joan Margarit: Pau. Cardinal-Bishop of Gerona* (Manchester, 1955) 99.

49. Pulgar, *Cronica,* pt. 2, cap. 77 (p. 332).

50. Palencia, *Guerra,* lib. 4 (pp. 119–20).

51. Suárez Fernández, *Expansión,* 64.

52. Pulgar, *Reyes,* cap. 120. Miguel Angel Ladero Quesada, *Hacienda,* 32: "The sums arriving at *la Cámara Regia* would have been considerable but it is very difficult to get at them, for there are only occasional scattered notations." Ladero Quesada, *Reyes Carólicos,* 220, does estimate amounts of confiscations. See also his "La hacienda real de Castilla en 1504: Rentas y gastos de la Corona al morir Isabel I," *Historia, Instituciones, Documentos* 3 (1976) 309–45; and cf. Juan de Mata Carriazo, "La Inquisición y las rentas de Sevilla," in *Homenaje a don Ramón Carande* (2 v., Madrid, 1963) 2:95–112.

53. MacKay, "Popular Movements," 64, concludes: "In the towns, . . . popular unrest came to be used as a weapon against royal government. . . . But it was left to the Catholic Kings to offer the urban populace the spectacle of the Inquisition officially punishing those who, in previous years, had been the victims of popular insurrection. Isabella was a popular monarch and the Inquisition was a popular institution."

54. Suárez Fernández, *Expansión,* 49–50.

55. Pulgar, *Crónica,* pt. 2, cap. 79 (pp. 334–36): in Toledo, testimony, through which the death penalty was given, was accepted from Moors, Jews, servants, and "wicked and vile men." See above, note 41, and below, Chapter 15, on the case of the Infant of La Guardia.

56. *Familias de Toledo,* f. 225v–226, cited in Márquez Villanueva, *Investigaciones,* 94.

Chapter 11. Readying

1. Galíndez de Carvajal, *Anales,* 543.

2. Cited in John H. Elliott, *Richelieu and Olivares* (Cambridge, 1984) 55.

3. Torre and Suárez, *Documentos* 1:179–205.

4. Ibid., 1:209, 215–391. The terms also appear in Azcona, *Isabel,* 299; see pp. 308–31. Pardoned were Portuguese collaborators, notably Beatriz Pacheco and Alonso de Monroy.

5. Clemencín, 599; Valera, *Crónica,* 108; Bernáldez, cap. 35. See also Torre and Suárez, *Documentos* 2: docs. 307, 338, 269, 320.

6. Torre and Suárez, *Documentos,* 1:327–56.

7. Ladero Quesada, *Reyes Católicos,* 34, gives these dates.

8. Convocation had been postponed from the first date chosen, significantly *el día de San Juan* in June of 1479. For the proceedings: *Cortes de León y Castilla* (7 v., Madrid, 1861–1903) 4:109–91; Manuel Colmeiro, *Cortes de los antiguos reinos de León y Castilla* (2 v., Madrid, 1883–84) 2:40–67.

9. The figure of Charlemagne as Christian crusading hero grew in legend (considered history) and had appeared in Alfonso *el Sabio*'s *History of Spain.* See Alfonso X, *Estoria,* 15, 56, 86; Reeves, *The Influence of Prophecy in the Later Middle Ages* (1969; Notre Dame, Ind. 1993) 301–2, and passim; Fraker, *Scope,* 102, 157–58; Barton Sholod, *Charlemagne in Spain: The Cultural Legacy of Roncesvalles* (Geneva, 1966); see also my *Political Power and Religious Language* (forthcoming).

10. Pulgar, *Crónica,* pt. 2, cap. 115 (p. 422).

11. Ibid., lib. 2, cap. 116.

12. Ibid., pt. 2, cap. 95 (p. 352) names them: Burgos, León, Avila, Segovia, Zamora, Toro, Salamanca, Soria, Murcia, Cuenca, Toledo, Sevilla, Córdoba, Jaén, Valladolid, Madrid, and Guadalajara.

13. Juan M. Carretero Zamora, "La consolidación de un modelo representativo: Las Cortes de Castilla en época de los Reyes Católicos," in Valdeón Baruque, *Isabel,* 259–91; see also Carretero Zamora, *Cortes, monarquía, ciudades: Las cortes de Castilla a comienzos de la época moderna (1476–1515)* (Madrid, 1988).

14. Carretero Zamora, "Consolidación," 265–66, 278–79. He lists within this network: "royal councilors, *corregidores,* judges [*oidores*] of the chancery, *contadores mayores* and treasurers, *alcaides,* jurists, and direct servants of the monarchs [*maestresalas, continos, mayordomos, apostadores*], members of the military orders, ambassadors, captains, and so on." Added should be clergy. In effect, "the Castilian monarchy reserved to itself the capacity to name the *procuradores* of the cities" through the established proviso that the king might do so "in special cases complying to my service." Isabel and Fernando interpreted that stipulation as a right to intervene in and even overturn a selection by a council. See also MacKay, *Spain,* 156–57; and Benjamin González Alonso, "La reforma del gobierno de los concejos en el reinado de Isabel," in Valdeón Baruque, 193–312: "The governing style [of the Catholic Kings] was characterized . . . by strict vigilance for the execution of the means they had adopted and the mode in which public officials discharged their posts. . . . A profound renovation of conciliar government" occurred during Isabel's reign (p. 308).

15. Carretero Zamora, "Consolidación," 276–80: Isabel and Fernando exercised "an extraordinarily ironhanded and effective control of each and every decision taken in Cortes." They "defined the modern model." They systematized the function of the Cortes remaining in force through the Habsburg years.

16. The others would be Cortes of 1489 in Toledo, 1499 in Ocaña, and 1502 in Toledo and Madrid. See also, appended to Clemencín, 595–97, "Memoria que dieron los procuradores de Castilla á los Reyes en Toledo año 1480, domingo, seis de febrero."

17. J. Beneyto Perez, "La gestación de la magistratura moderna," *Anuario de la Historia de Derecho de España* 23 (1953) 55–81.

18. Pulgar, *Crónica,* pt. 2, cap. 95; and for an overview of governmental organization, see Ladero Quesada, *España de los Reyes,* 154–244; and Salustiano de Dios, "Las instituciones centrales de gobierno," in Valdeón Baruque, 219-58. A little later another separate council would appear, that of the Inquisition. For the ubiquitous participation of the clergy, seen Nieto Soria, *Iglesia,* 164.

19. See Carretero Zamora, "Consolidación," 280; *Cortes de León y Castilla*

4:111–20; Salustiano de Dios, *El Consejo Real de Castilla (1385–1522)* (Madrid, 1982); Salustiano de Dios, *Gracia, merced, y patronazgo real: La Cámara de Castilla entre 1474–1530* (Madrid, 1973); MacKay, *Spain,* 156–57; Ladero Quesada, *Reyes Católicos,* 117–20.

20. Diego Hurtado de Mendoza, *La Guerra de Granada,* ed. Bernardo Blanco-González (Madrid, 1970) 105; and for Isabel regarding them at Madrigal in 1476: *Cortes de León y Castilla* 4:31.

21. Galíndez de Carvajal, *Anales,* introduction, 533.

22. Alfonso Díaz de Montalvo, *Compilación de leyes del reino* (facsimile ed., Valladolid, 1986). See also Clemencín, 208–14; E. García Vara, "Hijos ilustres de Arévalo, el doctor Alonso Díaz de Montalvo," *Estudios Abulenses* 4 (1955) 39–42. Márquez Villanueva, *Investigaciones,* 86–87: Montalvo worked closely with the other royal secretary, Fernán Alvarez de Toledo Zapata; both were *conversos.* For Alvarez de Toledo and for examples of *converso* networks in royal service, see Rábade Obradó, *Elite.*

23. Fernando de Mexia, *Nobiliario* (Seville, 1492; Madrid, 1974). Valera, *Espejo,* emphasizes the making of nobles by the king rather than by birth. It was written in the 1440s.

24. Pulgar, *Crónica,* pt. 2, cap. 95 (pp. 352–55); Antonio Matilla Tascón, *Documentos de los Reyes Católicos sobre reducción de juros y otras mercedes* (Madrid, 1952). Clemencín, 143, lists who lost what. Isabel alludes to abuses in her will; see Chapter 19. Linda Martz informs me that the issue of whether pious foundations might hold *juros* was never openly decided. See also Stephen Haliczer, "The Castilian Aristocracy and the Mercedes Reform of 1478–1482," *Hispanic American Historical Review* 55 (1975) 449–67; and Alcántara Suárez, 94–96.

25. Azcona, *Isabel,* 344.

26. See Miguel Angel Ladero Quesada, "Economía y poder en la Castilla del siglo XV," in Rucquoi, *Realidad,* 371–88; Ladero Quesada, *Hacienda;* and Ramón Carande, "La economía y la expansión de España bajo el gobierno de los Reyes Católicos," BAH 130 (1952) 213–55; and Carla Rahn Phillips and William D. Phillips Jr., *Spain's Golden Fleece* (Baltimore, 1997) 43–51.

27. In this section I rely principally on Azcona, *Isabel*; Tarsicio de Azcona, *La elección y la reforma del episcopado español en tiempo de los Reyes Católicos* (Madrid, 1960); see also note 28.

28. Codoin 7:544; Tarsicio de Azcona, "Reforma del episcopado y del clero de España en tiempo de los Reyes Católicos y Carlos V (1475–1558)," in Ricardo García-Villaslada, ed., *Historia de la Iglesia en España* (Madrid 1980) v. 3, pt. l, pp. 124–25.

29. See Pulgar, *Crónica,* pt. 2, cap. 95 (pp. 352–55); Azcona, *Isabel,* 344; Fidel Fita, "Concilios españoles inéditos: Provincial de Braga en 1261; y nacional de Sevilla en 1478," BRAH 22 (1893) 209–57.

30. Ladero, "Isabel y los musulmanes," 94.

31. Pulgar, *Crónica,* pt. 2, cap. 96 (pp. 355–56); Palencia, *Crónica,* dec. 3, lib. 28, cap. 8.

32. Bernáldez, cap. 45.

33. Pulgar, *Crónica,* pt. 2, cap. 99 (pp. 358–59); Palencia, *Guerra,* lib. 1; Zurita, *Anales,* 8 lib. 20, cap. 40.

34. Pulgar, *Crónica,* pt. 3, cap. 1 (p. 365).

35. Palencia, *Guerra,* introduction, 77.

36. Suárez Fernández, *Fundamentos,* 22.

37. Fernando's letter patent, given in Calatayud on April 14, 1481. See Antonio de la Torre, "Isabel la Católica, 'coregente' de la corona de Aragón," *Anuario de la Historia de Derecho de España* 13 (1953) 423–28.

38. See Jaime Vicens Vives, *Política del rey católico en Cataluña* (Barcelona, 1940).

39. Palencia, *Guerra* lib. 1 (3:87).

40. Ibid., lib. 2 (3:88–90); Pulgar, *Crónica,* pt. 3, cap. 2 (pp. 355–56); Bernáldez, cap. 53–55 (p. 607–8).

41. Bernáldez, cap. 35 (p. 593); Suárez Fernández, *Conquista,* 128; José Antonio de Bonilla y Mir and Enrique Toral Peñaranda, *El tratado de paz de 1481 entre Castilla y Granada* (Jaén, 1982).

Chapter 12. The Queen's War I

1. Pulgar, *Reyes,* ed., cap. 24, (1:70); the editor brackets this as a later interpolation in the printed text; see his introductory study, p. lxxxii. Pulgar, *Crónica,* pt. 1, ch.4 (p. 256) gives a variant reading.

2. Pulgar, *Reyes,* cap. 134 (2:27).

3. Sevillano Colom, 581.

4. Pulgar, *Crónica,* pt. 3, cap. 4 (p. 369); Pulgar, *Reyes,* cap. 127 (2:10–11).

5. Palencia, *Guerra,* lib. 2, p. 94; see also Ladero Quesada, *Castilla y la conquista;* Washington Irving's sound and readable *The Conquest of Granada* (Boston, 1899); and Leopoldo Eguílaz Yánguas, *Reseña Histórica de la conquista del reino de Granada por los Reyes Católicos según los cronistas árabes* (Granada, 1894).

6. Gerald Brenan, *South from Granada* (Cambridge, 1980) 231.

7. See Miguel Angel Ladero Quesada, *Granada: Historia de un país islámico (1232–1571)* (3d ed., Madrid, 1989); and Salma Khadra Jayyusi, ed., *The Legacy of Muslim Spain* (Leiden, 1992).

8. 'Abd-al Bāsiṭ, "El reino de Granada en 1465–66," in García Mercadal, 252–57.

9. See Angus MacKay, "The Ballad and the Frontier in Late Medieval Spain," *Bulletin of Hispanic Studies* 53 (1976) 15–33; María Soledad Carrasco Urgoit, *El moro de Granada en la literatura: Siglos XV y XVI* (Madrid, 1965) ch. 3; C. Colin Smith, ed., *Spanish Ballads* (Oxford, 1964).

10. See above, Chapter 11, note 41.

11. Pulgar, *Crónica,* pt. 3, cap. 6 (p. 371).

12. Ibid.; Ramón Menéndez Pidal, *Los Reyes Católicos y otros estudios* (Buenos Aires, 1962) 410–12.

13. Bernáldez, cap. 18, p. 608.

14. Palencia, *Guerra,* lib. 2 (p. 97).

15. James Gairdner, ed., *Letters and Papers Illustrative of the Reigns of Richard III and Henry VII* (London, 1861) 1:32.

16. "Un incunable desconocido," ed. Pedro Roca, *RABM* 6 (1902) 162–64; Luis Suárez Fernández, *El tiempo de la Guerra de Granada* (Madrid, 1989) 43.

17. Ladero Quesada, "Isabel y los musulmanes," 102.

18. Bernáldez, cap. 46 (pp. 614–15); Pulgar, *Crónica,* pt. 3, cap. 18 (p. 382).

19. Rodríguez Valencia, *Isabel* 1:249; Luis Suárez Fernández, ed., *Política internacional de Isabel la Católica: Estudio y documentos,* (5 v., Valladolid, 1965–72) 2:219–21.

20. Bernáldez, cap. 60 (p. 609); Palencia, *Crónica,* 3:100–103; Pulgar, *Crónica,* pt. 3, cap. 19 (pp. 382–85); Ladero Quesada, *Castilla y la conquista,* 228ff.

21. Bernáldez, cap. 60 (p. 610).

22. Pulgar, *Crónica,* pt. 3, cap. 19 (pp. 384–85).

23. Bernáldez, cap. 61, (p. 611).

24. Palencia, *Guerra*, lib. 3 (p. 111); Fernando to his sister, Juana, queen of Naples, Córdoba, August 26, 1483, in Antonio de la Torre, *Los Reyes Católicos y Granada* (Madrid, 1946) 156–77; Bernáldez, cap. 61 (pp. 610–11); Pulgar, *Crónica*, pt. 3, cap. 20 (pp. 385–86); cap. 23 (pp. 359–61). See also Suárez Fernández, *Tiempo*, 86–89, 141–46.

25. Palencia, *Guerra*, lib. 3, (p. 116).

26. Paz y Meliá, *Cronista*, 312–15; Ladero Quesada, *Castilla y la conquista*, 40n.; Bernáldez, cap. 63 (p. 612), cap. 68 (p. 616); Palencia, *Guerra*, lib. 3 (pp. 114–15).

27. Pulgar, *Crónica*, pt. 3, cap. 31 (pp. 399–400).

28. Palencia, *Guerra*, lib. 4 (p. 120).

29. Pulgar, *Crónica*, pt. 3, cap. 23 (pp. 390–93); cap. 31 (pp. 400–401).

30. Palencia, *Guerra*, lib. 4 (p. 120).

31. Pulgar, *Crónica*, pt. 3, cap. 31 (pp. 400–1).

32. García Mercadal, 319.

33. Pulgar, *Crónica*, pt. 3, cap. 31 (pp. 400–1); Palencia, *Guerra*, lib. 4 (p. 126).

34. Palencia, *Guerra*, lib. 4 (p. 121); Pulgar, *Crónica*, pt. 3, cap. 32 (pp. 401–2).

35. Pulgar, *Crónica*, pt. 3, cap. 33 (p. 402); Antonio de la Torre and E. A. de la Torre, eds., *Cuentas de Gonzalo de Baeza, tesorero de Isabel la Católica* (2 v., Madrid, 1955–56) (hereinafter *Cuentas de Baeza*) 1:91.

36. Pulgar, *Crónica*, pt. 3, cap. 33 (pp. 402–3); Bernáldez, cap. 71 (p. 617).

37. Fernando to his sister, Juana of Naples, June 2, 1484, cited in Azcona, *Isabel*, 510.

38. Pulgar, *Crónica*, pt. 3, cap. 34 (p. 404); Bernáldez, cap. 74, p. 618; Palencia, *Guerra*, lib. 4, pp. 130–32.

39. Francisco Asenjo Barbieri, ed., *Canción Musical del Palacio* (2d ed., Buenos Aires, 1945) no. 332.

40. Lourie, "Society"; see Chapter 1, note 25.

41. Leopoldo Torres Balbas, "Los Reyes Católicos en la Alhambra," *Al-Andalus* 16 (1951) 197: the Valencian council approved paying them on December 22, 1484.

42. Pulgar, *Crónica*, pt. 3, cap. 41 (pp. 411–12).

43. Fernando to his sister (see above, note 37): ten thousand horse and seventy thousand foot; Palencia, "Guerra," lib. 3 (p. 140): nine thousand horse and twenty thousand foot; Bernáldez, cap. 7 (p. 618), states twelve thousand to thirteen thousand horse, eighty thousand foot, fifteen hundred artillery wagons. Azcona, *Isabel*, 511, cites a letter to Rome listing eleven thousand lances and twenty-five thousand foot; see also Ladero, *Castilla y la conquista*, 117, 120–24, 171, 251.

44. For the shift in military technology from medieval to early modern in the Granada wars, see Weston F. Cook Jr., *The Hundred Years War for Morocco: Gunpowder and the Military Revolution in the Early Modern Muslim World* (Boulder, Colo., 1994) 119–26. "[I]t was the artillery that threw the balance of forces decisively in favor of Spain" (p. 119). "The Granadans were not 'gunless' but they were outgunned"(p. 126). See also Rene Quatrefages, "A la naissance de l'armee moderne," *Mélanges de la Casa de Velázquez* 13 (1979); and his "Etat et armee en Espagne au debut des temps modernes," Ibid., 17 (1981).

45. Pulgar, *Crónica*, pt. 3, cap. 44 (pp. 417–19).

46. Irving, 95. For a fine account of the war: Juan de Mata Carriazo, "Historia de la Guerra de Granada," in Ramón Menéndez Pidal, ed., *Historia de España*, 17: *La España de los Reyes Católicos* (3^d ed., Madrid, 1983) 387–914.

47. Mata and Carande, *Tumbo* 4:826–33.

48. Pulgar, *Crónica*, pt. 3, cap. 44 (pp. 419–20); Bernáldez, cap. 75 (pp. 619–20); Juan de Mata Carriazo, "Asiento de las cosas de Ronda. Conquista y repartimiento de la ciudad por los Reyes Católicos," *Miscelanea de Estudios Arabes y Hebráicos* 3 (1954) anejo 1–139.

49. Pulgar, *Crónica*, pt. 3, cap. 47 (p. 424); *Cuentas de Baeza* 1:92–131.

50. Azcona, *Isabel,* 512; Pulgar, *Crónica,* pt. 3 cap. 48 (p. 425).

51. Pulgar, *Crónica*, pt. 3, cap. 50 (p. 427). Fernando's fever: Torre, *Reyes Católicos y Granada,* 67.

52. *Cuentas de Baeza* 1:82; Antonio de la Torre, "Maestros de los hijos de los Reyes Católicos," *Hispania* 16 (1956) 258.

53. Palencia, *Guerra,* lib.5 (p. 158).

54. "Historia . . . Cádiz," 247–51.

55. Pulgar, *Libro,* 4–5: He would "with the help of God write of the lineages and conditions of those whom one can well believe that in authority over persons and in ornament of virtues and in the abilities they possessed, in science as in arms, were no less excellent than those Greeks and Romans and French whom they so praise in their writings." Pulgar, *Glosa a las Coplas de Mingo Revulgo* is bound with his *Letras* (Madrid, 1929).

56. Bernáldez, cap. 118, p. 357.

Chapter 13. The Queen's War II

1. English version in Mary Purcell, *The Great Captain* (London, 1962) 90.

2. *Cartas autógrafas,* no. 10 (p. 58).

3. Salazar de Mendoza, 194.

4. Münzer, in García Mercadal, 237: there he says he came upon royal servants and royal trunks awaiting the royal party, and he remarks on finding many parrots.

5. *Cartas autógrafas,* no. 9.

6. Ibid., no. 10.

7. Pulgar, *Crónica,* pt. 3, cap. 49 (p. 438).

8. Palencia, *Guerra,* lib. 5, p. 154.

9. Ibid.; Pedro Mártir, *Epistolario* 1: epís. 61, 62; Bernáldez, cap. 79, p. 622; Pulgar, *Crónica,* pt. 3, cap. 6 (p. 433).

10. Bernáldez, cap. 82, p. 624; Pulgar, *Crónica,* pt. 3, cap. 59 (p. 438).

11. Pulgar, *Crónica,* pt. 3, cap. 59, 60 (pp. 437–39).

12. Bernáldez, cap. 79, p. 623; Pulgar, *Crónica,* pt. 3, cap. 60 (p. 439).

13. Pulgar, *Crónica,* pt. 3, cap. 61 (p. 439).

14. Ibid., pt. 3, cap. 55 (p. 432), cap. 66 (pp. 442–44).

15. A. Rodríguez Villa, "Don Francisco de Rojas," *BRAH* 28 (1896) 189. Azcona, *Isabel,* 728, notes a precedent: the naming of Beatriz, Isabel's aunt, master of the Order of Christ.

16. Palencia, *Guerra,* lib. 7, p. 183.

17. Ladero Quesada, *Castilla y la conquista,* 293; Ladero Quesada, *Reyes Católicos,* 258.

18. Letter of April 8, 1487, *Cartas autógrafas,* no. 11.

19. Ladero Quesada, *Reyes Católicos,* 258.

20. Codoin 88:496–98; Torre, *Reyes Católicos y Granada,* 212–13.

21. The elders, *alfaquíes,* come to submit to Fernando, promising to serve the

king and queen loyally, and after their days, the prince don Juan and his descendants, stating that after all, "God is one." Pulgar, *Crónica,* pt. 3, caps. 70–73 (pp. 449–54); Cádiz to Mendoza, April 17, 1487, in Codoin 36:436–38; Suárez Fernández, *Tiempo,* 150.

22. Bernáldez, cap. 88, p. 632: In camp were many priests and friars. The sovereigns and the great nobles had their own chapels; he lists those present.

23. Pulgar, *Crónica,* pt. 3, caps. 75–76 (pp. 455–50). Pulgar was there, as was Diego de Valera, according to Suárez Fernández, *Tiempo,* 150.

24. Bernáldez, cap. 83; Pulgar, *Crónica,* pt. 3, cap. 78, (pp. 459–60).

25. Zurita, *Anales* 8, lib. 20, cap. 70 (p. 525).

26. Pulgar, *Crónica,* pt. 3, cap. 84 (pp. 463–65).

27. Bernáldez, cap. 84, p. 627; Pulgar, *Crónica,* pt. 3, cap. 87 (pp. 465–66).

28. Pulgar, *Cronica,* pt. 3, cap. 76 (p. 458).

29. Francisco Bejarano, "Reanudación del comercio de Málaga con Africa bajo de los Reyes Católicos," separata de *Homenaje a Guillermo Guastavino* (Madrid, 1974) 429–30. The Genoese Centurione were the most active merchants in Málaga. In 1483 Federigo Centurione had negotiated between *los reyes* and the Granadans.

30. Palencia, *Guerra,* lib. 7, p. 190; *capitulación* of Cárdenas with ʿAlī Durdūsh, September 4, 1487, in Codoin 8:399.

31. Bernáldez, cap. 87, pp. 631–32; Pulgar, *Crónica,* pt. 3, cap. 94 (p. 472); and in this section I rely heavily on Miguel Angel Ladero Quesada, "La esclavitud por guerra a fines del siglo XV: El caso de Málaga," *Hispania* 55 (1967) 63–88.

32. Ladero Quesada, *Castilla y la conquista,* 224; Azcona, *Isabel,* 518.

33. Bernáldez, caps. 87–88, pp. 631–34; Palencia, *Guerra,* lib. 7, pp. 196–97: the liberty of one hundred Jewish families of Málaga was negotiated for payment of 170,000 *ducados.* See Suárez Fernández, *Documentos . . . judíos,* 43. Ladero Quesada, "Esclavitud," 77: Isabel on June 6, 1489 declared all Jews free and gave safe conduct to ten Castilian Jews to take them from Carmona across Andalusia, where Jews had been prohibited entry since 1485.

34. Pulgar, *Crónica,* pt. 3, caps. 195–96 (p. 473).

35. "Journals of Roger Machado: Embassy to Spain and Portugal, A.D. 1488," in *Historia regis Henrici Septimi,* ed. James Gairdner (London, 1858), 157–99.

36. Pulgar, *Crónica,* pt. 3, caps. 237–38 (pp. 487–88).

37. Ladero Quesada, *Castilla y la conquista,* 293, for individual loans; Ladero Quesada, *Hacienda,* 221–23; Miguel Angel Ladero Quesada, *Milicia y economía en la guerra de Granada: El cerco de Baza* (Valladolid, 1964) 47–48, 53, 119, 121, 216.

38. Pulgar, *Crónica,* pt. 3, cap. 241 (p. 492); and for Baza: caps. 106–24 (pp. 484–503). See also *Cuentas de Baeza* 1:272, 2:15; Paz y Meliá, *Cronista,* 328–31: copy of letter of Fernando to the king of Naples dated Jaén, September 5, 1489; Münzer, in García Mercadal, 275; Bernáldez, cap. 92, pp. 634–36; Palencia, *Guerra,* lib. 9, pp. 220–28.

39. For the text of seven of his letters to her, and one of hers to him: "Historia . . . Cádiz," 301–11.

40. Ladero Quesada, "Isabel y los musulmanes," 106: "the intervention of the Queen was especially important in diplomatic aspects," in establishing treaties and *capitulaciones.* L. P. Harvey, *Islamic Spain, 1250 to 1500* (Chicago, 1992) 302–4: Sīdī Yahyā became, "safely and profitably," Don Pedro de Granada Venegas.

41. Mártir, *Epistolario* 1, epís. 73; Ladero Quesada, *Milicia,* 52.

42. See Juan de Mata Carriazo, *Los relieves de la Guerra de Granada en la sillería del Coro de la Catédral de Toledo* (Granada, 1985).

43. *Cuentas de Baeza* 1:236–37.

44. Pulgar, *Crónica,* pt. 3, caps. 128, 29 (pp. 505–6).

45. Rodríguez Puértolas, *Poesía,* 325–32; Miguel Angel Ladero Quesada, "Las coplas de Hernando de Vera: Un caso de crítica al gobierno de Isabel la Católica," *Anuario de Estudios Atlánticos* 14 (1968) 365–81. Cf. Pulgar, gloss on *Mingo Revulgo.*

46. Bernáldez, cap. 101, p. 642; Pulgar, *Crónica,* pt. 3, cap. 133 (p. 510).

47. Bernáldez, cap. 104, pp. 645–46.

48. Andrea Navagiero, *Viaggio fatto in Ispagna et Francia,* cited in Otis H. Green, *Spain and the Western Tradition* (4 v., Madison, Wis., 1963–66) 1:92–93.

49. Barkai, 297.

50. Pulgar, *Crónica,* pt. 3, cap. 133 (p. 510); Melchor de Santa Cruz, *Floresta española de apotegemas* (Madrid, 1643) 35; Zurita, *Anales* 8: lib. 20, cap. 39.

51. Miguel Angel Ladero Quesada, *Las Mudéjares de Castilla en tiempos de Isabel I* (Valladolid, 1969) 44–54, 172–82; Codoin 8:411, 421, 439; Torre, *Reyes Católicos y Granada,* 202–13; Miguel Garrido Atienza, *Las capitulaciones para la entrega de Granada* (Granada, 1992).

52. Salazar de Mendoza, *Crónica,* 237; Mártir, *Epistolario* 1, epís. 92 (pp. 171–72); Münzer, 86–101. M. Gaspar y Ramiro, "Entrada de los Reyes Católicos en Granada al tiempo de su rendición," *Revista de Centro de Estudios Históricos Granadinos* 1 (1911) 7–24; María del Carmén Pescador del Hoyo, "Cómo fué de verdad la toma de Granada, a la luz de un documento inédito," *Al-Andalus* 20 (1955) 283–344; Baeza, *Relacion;* Juan de Mata Carriazo, *El "breve parte" de Fernán Pérez del Pulgar* (Seville, 1953).

53. Münzer, 100.

54. Pulgar, *Crónica,* pt. 3, cap. 133 (p. 511). This is Pulgar's penultimate chapter, and his last on the war.

55. Torres Balbas, "Reyes Católicos en la Alhambra," 185–86.

56. Ibid., 191–95.

57. Miguel Angel Ladero Quesada, "La repoblación del reino de Granada anterior al año 1500," *Hispania* no. 110 (1968); no. 112 (1969); Miguel Ángel Ladero Quesada, *Granada después de la conquista: Repobladores y mudéjares* (Granada, 1988) 197–210; Lorenzo de Padilla, "Crónica de Felipe I llamado el Hermoso," Codoin 8:10–12.

58. Ladero Quesada, *Granada después,* 204; Azcona, *Isabel,* 545; C. Villanueva, *Habices de las mezquitas de la ciudad de Granada y sus aquerías* (Madrid, 1961).

59. Hieronymous Münzer, "Viaje por España y Portugal," trans. Julio Puyol, in BRAH 84 (1924) 418; and Bernáldez, cap. 87, p. 632.

60. Ladero Quesada, *Granada después,* 204–5; Azcona, *Isabel,* 548–50; Tarsicio de Azcona, "El tipo ideal de obispo en la iglesia española antes de la rebelión luterana," *Hispania Sacra* 11 (1958) 21–64; Padilla, 9–10. Talavera's archdiocesan church of Nuestra Señora de la Anunciación later became a Franciscan convent and is now the Alhambra parador.

Chapter 14. The View from Granada

1. Juan del Encina, *Poesía lírica y cancionero musical* (Madrid, 1975) no. 30.

2. Garrido Atienza, doc. 67, p. 313.

3. Torre, *Reyes Católicos y Granada,* 304.

4. *Bacon's History of the Reign of King Henry VII* (Cambridge, 1901) 97–98.

5. Padilla, 18.

6. Münzer, 262.

7. Ibid., 130.

8. Mártir, *Epistolario* 1: epís. 6.

9. Ciriaco Pérez Bustamante, "Isabel la Católica y la política internacional," *Curso de Conferencias* 2:35–54; Antonio de la Torre, "La política de los Reyes Católicos en Africa," in ibid. 2:151–72; P. Prieto y Llovera, *Política aragonesa en Africa hasta la muerte de Fernando el Católico* (Madrid, 1952); Rumeu de Armas, *España en el Africa atlántica;* José Antonio Maravall, "El descubrimiento de América en la historia del pensamiento política," *Revista de Estudios Políticos* 63 (1952) 329–48; Pierre Chaunu, *European Expansion in the Later Middle Ages,* trans. Katherine Bartram (Amsterdam, 1979); Pérez-Embid; E. Ybarra y Rodríguez, "Los precedentes de la casa de contratación de Sevilla, 2: Expediciones españolas a la costa africana atlántica durante los siglos XIV y XV," *Revista de Indias* 2 (1941) 5–37; Suárez Fernández, in *Trastámara,* 568–73. See also Chapter 8.

10. Bernáldez, caps. 132–34 (pp. 679–81); Maravall, "Descubrimiento," 329–48; Miguel Angel Ladero Quesada, *Los primeros Europeos en Canarías* (Las Palmas, 1979); Felipe Fernández-Armesto, *The Canary Islands after the Conquest* (Oxford, 1982).

11. Ladero Quesada, *España en 1492,* 98, and see pp. 93–101.

12. Padilla, 16; see also Clemencín, 391–92; Fernando de Zafra, *informe* of April 26, 1493 in Codoin 60:512–17, and see 11:14, and 51:72–74.

13. Münzer, 132.

14. Ibid., 126. See also Ángel Gómez Moreno, "El reflejo literario," in Nieto Soria, dir., *Orígenes,* 315–39.

15. CC 2: no. 922, p. 52.

16. José María Pou y Marti, *Visionarios, Beguinos, y Fraticelos Catalanes (Siglos XIII–XV)* (Vich, 1930) 369–96; and see Chapter 5.

17. Ortíz, *Tratados,* f. 111.

18. See Pedro M. Cátedra, *La historiografía en verso en la época de los Reyes Católicos: Juan Barba y su Consolatoria de Castilla* (Salamanca, 1989) 22–23; and anonymous, *Directorio de príncipes* [1493], ed. R. B. Tate (Exeter, 1977), an updated mirror of princes showing Fernando and Isabel as model rulers.

19. Elio Antonio de Nebrija, *Gramática sobre la lengua castellana* (Salamanca, 1492) prologue; see also Sánchez Cantón, 14–15.

20. Much of the social and economic assessment in this section follows Ladero Quesada, *España en 1492,* 34–70; and his "Economía y poder," 371–88.

21. *Cuentas de Baeza* 2:480–81. The monarchy sends oil to Flanders: Angus MacKay, "Comercio/mercado interior y la expansión económica dei siglo XV," in *Society,* 2:110. Moreover, Sicily under *los reyes* was a center of minting gold coins; it both exported them and re-exported ingots.

22. Ladero Quesada, *España en 1492,* 76–78.

23. Ibid., 34–35.

24. Jacques Heers, "Los genoveses en la sociedad andaluza del siglo XV: Orígenes, grupos, solidaridades," in *Hacienda y Comercio 2: Coloquío de Historia Medieval Andaluza: 1981* (Seville, 1982) 426; Fernand Braudel, *The Mediterranean and the Mediterranean World in the Age of Philip II* (New York, 1972) 1:342–43; Miguel Angel Ladero Quesada, "Almojarifazgo sevillano y comercio exterior de Andalucia en el siglo XV," *Anuario de historia, economía, y sociedad* 2 (1969) 93.

25. M. de Santa Cruz, 2.1 (p. 23).

26. Fernando de Rojas, *La Celestina,* ed. Dorothy S. Severin (Madrid, 1990) 236.

27. Alonso de Santa Cruz, *Crónica de los Reyes Católicos,* ed. Juan de Mata Carriazo (2 v., Seville, 1951) 1:50–51.

28. Münzer, 41–42.

29. Rodríguez Valencia, *Isabel* 1:46.

30. A. de Santa Cruz, 1:69; see also Clemencín, 377–78.

31. Martír, *Epistolario*, epís. 6, March 23, 1488; no. 31, August 1, 1488.

32. Marineo Sículo, *Cosas memorables,* f. 181–82. He came to Spain in 1484, to Salamanca; see Caro Lynn, *A College Professor of the Renaissance: Lucio Marineo Sículo among the Spanish Humanists* (Chicago, 1937).

33. Marineo Sículo, *Cosas memorables,* f. 188, see chapter 7.

34. M. de Santa Cruz, 27.

35. Marineo Sículo, *Cosas memorables,* f. 182, 185; see also Münzer, 36.

36. Pulgar, *Crónica,* pt. 2, cap. 4 (pp. 256–57).

37. Azcona, *Isabel,* 735.

38. Did she use heavy perfume? Isabel possessed civet cats and many bottles, even jugs, of civet oil, a base for strong perfume; but what she did with it and why remains a mystery. It was thought an aphrodisiac; it was also valuable, her supply of it like money in the bank.

39. Norberto Alméndoz, "Retablo musical fernando-isabellino," *Archivo Hispalense* 2d ser. 14 (1951) 351–56; Gonzalo Castrillo Hernández, "La escuela musical castellana en la Corte de Doña Isabel la Católica," *Publicaciones de la Instituto "Tello Téllez de Meneses"* 5 (1951) 219–33.

40. *Carro de las donas* lib. 2, fol. 41r. The author says he saw it with his own eyes, that Fernando and the children were with her, and that she was thus teaching her children how to treat parents.

41. Castrillo Hernández, 221, cites Oviedo: *"Tenía músicos de tamborinos y saltérios e ducaynas e de harpa, e un rrabelico muy precioso. . . . Thenía el Principe muy gentiles menestriles altos de sacabuches e cheremías e cornetas e trompetas bastardas e cinco o seys pares de atabales."*

42. Llanos y Torriglia, *Hogar,* 38.

43. See Clemencín, 221–36, 383–86.

44. Diego López de Toledo, *Los comentarios de Gayo Julio César.* The author was a Mendoza cousin, son of the count of Alba. See also Münzer, 171, 262–64; Clemencín, 397–98; Torre, "Maestros 256.

45. Alonso Ortiz, *Diálogo sobre la educación del Principe Don Juan hijo de los Reyes Católicos,* ed. Giovanni Maria Bertini (Madrid 1983) 160.

46. Gonzalo Fernández de Oviedo, cited in Juan de Mata Carriazo, "Amor y moralidad bajo los reyes católicos," *RABM* 40 (1954) 56–57.

47. Mártir, *Epistolario*, epís. 47.

48. Juan Luis Vives, *De institutione feminae christianae, ch. 3–4.* There is an English edition: *Education of a Christian Woman,* ed. and trans. Charles Fantazzi (Chicago, 2000). See also Clemencín, 166–71, 397; *Carro de las donas;* Torre, "Maestros," 256–66; Münzer, 171.

49. Alejandro had fought in the Portuguese wars and then became her *maestresala.* He had come to Spain with his humanist brother, Antonio, who had also served the court and who had died in 1488.

50. See María Dolores Gómez Molleda, "La cultura feminina en la época de Isabel la Católica," *RABM* 61 (1955) 137–191.

51. Juan de Lucena, "Carta de . . . exhortaría a las letras," in Antonio Paz y Melia, ed., *Opúsculos literarios de los siglos XIV a XVI* (Madrid, 1892) 215–16. See also Antonio de la Torre, "Unas noticias de Beatriz Galindo, 'La Latina,'" *Hispania* 17 (1957) 255–61,

who found no documentary evidence that Beatriz Galindo, mentioned as a Latinist by Pulgar and Marineo Sículo, taught either Isabel or her children, only that she entered court service in 1486 and became a *camarera* of the queen's. *Camarera* is a household position and there is no reason to doubt that she at least helped Isabel with Latin.

52. Sánchez Cantón, 24. He also lists the contents of her library and her tapestries and paintings discussed here.

53. Ibid. That said, most books printed in Spain were religious, and of an approved sort. A papal injunction of 1487 ordered the clergy to keep an eye on what was being printed in theology, and, among events of 1492, it was forbidden to publish entire Bibles in the vernacular. Yet religious books too could support the crown.

54. Juan Bautista Avalle-Arce, ed., *Memorias de Gonzalo Fernández de Oviedo* (2 v., Chapel Hill, N.C., 1974) 1:223. These are excerpts from Oviedo, *Quincuagenas de la nobleza de España* [c. 1554]. Oviedo was a page of Prince Juan's.

55. Sánchez Cantón, 21.

56. Robert Brian Tate, "Nebrija the Historian," *Bulletin of Hispanic Studies* 34 (1957) 127.

57. See R. B. Tate, "Mythology in the Spanish Historiography of the Middle Ages and the Renaissance," *Hispanic Review* 22 (1944) 11–14; Tate, however, discounts the religious component visible here; see also Ramón Menéndez Pidal, "Significance of the Reign of Isabella the Catholic, According to Her Contemporaries," in Highfield, 410–12.

58. Marcelino Menéndez y Pelayo, ed., *Antología de poetas líricos castellanos* (Buenos Aires, 1943) 2:136, 141.

59. I discuss this conjunction in a forthcoming book on political power and religious language in the Western world.

60. Letter to Prince Juan, with presentation copy of *De Hispaniae laudibus,* published in Burgos, 1497: Lynn, 115–16.

61. Pedro Gracia Dei, "Crianza e virtuosa dotrina," in Paz y Melia, *Opúsculos,* 381.

62. Juan Alvarez Gato, "Loor a la Reyna Nuestra Señora [1499]," in *Cancionero de Pero Guillén de Segovia,* Ms. M. 4.114, BN fols. 430–31, cited in Márquez Villanueva, *Investigaciones,* 414–15; Gato also compares Isabel to a noble Amazon.

63. Valera, letter 52; Rodríguez Valencia, *Isabel* 1:369–71.

64. Encina, 57–58.

65. Marineo Sículo, *De Hispaniae laudibus*: Lynn, 115–16.

66. See Chiyo Ishikawa, "*La llave de palo:* Isabel la Católica as Patron of Religious Literature and Painting," in Boruchoff, *Isabel,* 103–19; so her altarpiece "was meant to be a visual summation of her Christological beliefs" (p. 108).

67. Astute foreign observers now saw the iron hand in the velvet glove: see opinions of Isabel cited in Ramón Menéndez Pidal, "The Catholic Kings According to Machiavelli and Castiglione," in Highfield, 505–25; and Boruchoff, "Instructions," 11.

68. Torres Balbas, "Los Reyes Católicos en la Alhambra," 195.

69. For San Juan de los Reyes, see also Chapter 7.

70. See Azcárate, "Sentido," 203–23; Münzer, 251; and Harold E. Wethey, *Gil de Siloé and His School* (Cambridge, Mass., 1936) 10. Siloé, Flemish or German, carried on in the *cartuja* from Juan de Colonia, John of Cologne, who began work on its construction in 1454.

71. Sánchez Canton, 28: Isabel and Fernando in 1494 sponsored the printing of Bartholomaeus Anglicus, the source of Talavera's eagle symbolism. Making much of

the cardinal virtues was Aegidius Romanus, *Regimiento de principes,* as glossed by Castrojeriz on commission of Alfonso XI for Pedro I, and published in Barcelona in 1480 and in Seville in 1482.

72. See note above, and Yarza Luaces, *"Imagen,"* 269–71.

73. Owen Gingerich, "Alfonso X as a Patron of Astronomy," in *Alfonso X of Castile, the Learned King,* ed. Francisco Márquez-Villanueva and Carlos Alberto Vega (Cambridge, Mass., 1990) 32.

74. See Peggy K. Liss, "Isabel, Myth and History," in Boruchoff, *Isabel,* 63.

75. Colbert Nepaulsingh, *Micer Francisco Imperial: "El Dezir a las syete virtudes" y otros poemas* (Madrid, 1977) lcvii.

76. Mena, *Laberinto,* copla 231, p. 161; Yarza Luaces, "Imagen," 270n5.

77. Galíndez de Carvajal, *Anales,* 281. From 1491 Lorenzo Vázquez, probably trained in Italy, transformed the upper part.

78. Richard Bernheimer, *Wild Men in the Middle Ages* (Cambridge, Mass., 1952; New York, 1970) 181. Cf. Azcárate, "Tema," 81–99.

79. I discuss these *rectores* of Gregory's in my forthcoming book on religious language and political power. Ricardo del Arco y Garay, *La idea de imperio en la política y la literatura españolas* (Madrid, 1944) entitles a chapter "España, rectora del mundo"; he deals with Habsburg Spain, but the sentiment was there much earlier.

80. See Tate, "Sanchez de Arevalo," 70, 76: this mythical antiquity and the neo-Gothic thesis had become accepted as accurate history and as legal precedent for Spanish position in Europe and territorial claims. Palencia, Valera, Pulgar, Marineo Sículo pattern history similarly. See Prologue and Chapters 1 and 5.

81. See Santiago López-Ríos, *Salvajes y razas monstruosas en la literatura castellana medieval* (Madrid, 1999); Timothy Husband, *The Wild Man* (New York, 1980), although omitting Spain; Bernheimer; John B. Friedman, *The Monstrous Races in Medieval Art and Thought* (Cambridge, Mass., 1981); Hayden White, "The Forms of Wildness: Archaeology of an Idea," in *Tropics of Discourse: Essays in Cultural Criticism* (Baltimore, 1985) 150–82.

82. Marqués de Lozoya, "La Sala del Solio en el Alcázar de Segovia," *Anuario de Estudios del Arte* (1940) 261; *Memorias de la Academia de la Historia* (1821) 340; anonymous, "Continuación de la crónica de Pulgar," BAE 70, app. 1, p. 522. Juan Alvarez Gato, "Loor a la Reyna Nuestra Señora" [1499], in *Cancionero de Pero Guillén de Segovia,* Ms. M. 4.114, BN fols. 430–31, cited in Márquez Villanueva, *Investigaciones,* 414–15, compares Isabel to a noble Amazon and says that her fame brings all peoples to her: "Vienen tudescos, ingleses, / vienen griegos y romanos, / amazonas y troyanos, / todo gremio de cristianos, / alemanes y franceses. / Vienen de todas naciones / grandes, medianos, ceviles. / Vienen grecianos, bretones, / lombardos y mirmidones, / idolatras y gentiles. / Vienen de todos lenguajes, / . . . los muy robustos salvajes. . . ."—The world, subdued, comes to pay homage to her.

Chapter 15. The Expulsion of the Jews

1. Suárez Fernández, *Documentos . . . judios,* doc. 177, pp. 391–95; see also pp. 378–81, 411–13. Cf. Azcona, *Isabel,* 641–44, who states that the decree offers conversion instead of exile, yet it says nothing explicitly to that effect. Baer, *Historia* 2:435: other royal laws did though, and promised new converts aid, protection, and a period exempt from the Inquisition. Baer, *Juden* 2: doc. 380, a royal decree urges Jews of

Maqueda and Torrijos to convert, but this was in July of 1492, after issuance of the expulsion order. Bernáldez, caps. 110–11, pp. 651–53, says that from Granada *los reyes* decreed all Jews of Spain must hear Christian doctrine, and those that did not wish to convert must leave and not return.

2. *Cortes* 4:101–4, leyes 34–36; Suárez Fernández, *Documentos . . . Judios,* doc. 177, pp. 391–95; see also ibid., pp. 378–81, 411–13.

3. *Siete Partidas,* lib. 7, tit. 24, ley 1.

4. Cf. Dwayne E. Carpenter, *Alfonso X and the Jews: An Edition and Commentary on* Siete Partidas *7:24 "De los judios"* (Berkeley and Los Angeles, 1986); MacKay, "Popular Movements," 33–67; MacKay, "The Jews in Spain during the Middle Ages," in Elie Kedourie, ed., *Spain and the Jews* (London and New York, 1992) 33-50. Carpenter and MacKay see the *Partidas* and the Spanish as more tolerant than the European norm. Cf. Robert I. Burns, "Jews and Moors in the *Siete Partidas* of Alfonso X the Learned: A Background Perspective," in Roger Collins and Anthony Goodman, eds., *Medieval Spain: Culture, Conflict and Coexistence: Studies in Honour of Angus MacKay* (New York, 2002); and Peter Brown, "Religious Coercion in the Later Roman Empire: The Case of North Africa," in his *Religion and Society in the Age of Saint Augustine* (London, 1972) 301–31, who points out the earlier gap between law and practice on the part of political and religious authorities. For a commonplace attitude: Díaz de Games, *Victorial,* 17: "from the death of Alexander on there was no treason in which the Jews or their lineage were not involved."

5. For a case study of Jews and Ferrer's impact: Adeline Rucquoi, *Valladolid en la edad media* (Valladolid, 1987) 2:485–502. See also Chapter 10.

6. Sánchez Cantón, 32: Isabel owned a copy of the Visigothic code, the *Fuero Juzgo.* See also P. D. King, *Law and Society in the Visigothic Kingdom* (Cambridge, 1972).

7. See Chapter 10. For messianism among Jews, see Moshe Idel, "Jewish Apocalypticism 670–1670," in Bernard McGinn, ed., *The Encyclopedia of Apocalypticism* (3 v., New York, 1999) 2:204–37; see also Angus MacKay, "Andalucía y la guerra del fin del mundo," in Emilio Cabrera, coord., *Andalucía entre Oriente y Occidente (1236–1491)* (Córdoba, 1988) 329–42.

8. See chapter 8, note 8.

9. Biblioteca Nacional (Madrid) MS 1.104, f. 46–52.

10. Educated guesses now estimate a population of between 80,000 and 150,000 Jews in Spain in 1492. Baer, *History* 2:510–11n13, cites a letter of Melamed to Señor finding 60,000 Jewish households in Aragón at expulsion, but what is the coefficient? See also Ladero Quesada, *España de los Reyes,* 311; Miguel Angel Ladero Quesada, "Lè nombre des juifs dans la Castille du Xvème siècle," *Proceedings of the Sixth Congress of Jewish Studies* 2 (Jerusalem, 1975) 45–52; Caro Baroja, 1:198. See also below, note 23.

11. Llorca, 106–8; *Cortes* 4:149–51.

12. Azcona, *Isabel,* 635. Azcona is impossible regarding the edict of 1492, as in stating: "*La actitud de los reyes en el mismo no podía haber sido mas positiva e ética*"; see also Lea, *Inquisition,* 1:131–32.

13. Lea *Inquisition,* 1:124. Benzion Netanyahu, *Don Isaac Abravanel* (Philadelphia, 1972) 281n67, sees the expulsion itself as due to pressure exerted by towns and cities; he follows Luis Suárez Fernández, *La expulsión de los judios de Espana* (2d ed., Madrid, 1992), who tends to blame all problems on municipalities; the nobles are his political heroes. Most probably, it was chiefly an interplay of royal and municipal interests that coalesced and culminated in the decree. See also MacKay ("Popular Movements," 33–67, and "The Jews in Spain during the Middle Ages," 33–50), who repeatedly points out the interplay between popular pograms, the economy, and politics.

14. See Suárez Fernández, *Documentos* . . . *judios*, 27–28, 33, 41. Christians on occasion stole Jewish children and baptized them: Lea, *Inquisition* 1:124, cites Luciano Serrano, *Los Reyes Católicos y la ciudded de Borgos (desde 1451 a 1492)* (Madrid, 1943), 187–88; Ladero Quesada, "Esclavitud," 77; Ladero Quesada, *Milicia*, cap. 4; Francisco Cantera Burgos, *Alvar García y su familia de conversos* (Madrid, 1952) 40–46; Haim Beinart, *Trujillo, a Jewish Community in Extremadura on the Eve of Expulsion from Spain* (Jerusalem, 1980) 52–65.

15. Suárez Fernández, *Documentos* . . . *judios*, 344–46; Baer, *Juden* 2: 397–98.

16. Fidel Fita, "La verdad sobre el martirio de Santo Niño de la Guardia o sea el proceso y quema (16 de noviembre 1491) del judio Jucé Franco en Avila," BRAH 11 (1887) 7–134; sentence in Catalan in *Colección de documentos de la Corona de Aragón* 28:68. See also Lea, *Inquisition,* 1:133–34; Henry Charles Lea, *Studies from the Religious History of Spain* (Philadelphia, 1890) 437–68; and Suárez Fernández, *Documentos* . . . *judios,* 44–45.

17. Cf. Baer, *Juden* 2: doc. 372.

18. Fernando's letter of May 12, 1486 to inquisitors of Zaragoza: Arch gen. Aragón, reg. 3684, fol. 96, and Lea, *Inquisition,* 1:132. Inescapable too is the longstanding assumption that the King must be more powerful than the queen.

19. Benzion Netanyahu, *Abravanel,* 38–53, 278n43–45; Baer, *History* 2:387–88n; B. Trend and H. Loewe, *Six Lectures on Isaak Abrabanel* (Cambridge, 1937). Abravanel argued, that is, from the traditional Christian as well as Jewish belief that Jews were to survive until the end of history; Abravanel was also learned in the writings of the church fathers and their commentators.

20. Bernáldez, caps. 110–12, pp. 652–53.

21. See F. Baer, "Ha-tenu'ah ha-masihit bi-tqufat ha-gerus" (The Messianic Movement in Spain at the Time of the Expulsion), *Zion* 5 (1933) 61–77; Enrique Cantera Montenagro, "Judios y conversos de Torrelaguna (Madrid) en tiempos de la expulsión," in *Estudios en memoria del Prof. D. Salvador de Moxó* (Madrid, 1982) 245–55; Eleazer Gutwirth, "Jewish and Christian Messianism in the Fifteenth Century in Spain," in Luç Dequeker and Werner Verbeke, eds., *The Expulsion of the Jews and Their Emigration to the Southern Low Countries (Fifteenth to Sixteenth Centuries)* (Leuven, 1998) 1–22. See also note 7.

22. María Rosa Lida de Malkiel, *Jerusalén: El tema literario de su cerco y destrucción por los romanos* (Buenos Aires, 1973) 28–31.

23. Bernáldez, caps. 110–12. Baer, *History* 2:438, estimates that 100,000 to 120,000 of those who left went to Portugal, and another 50,000 elsewhere. See Münzer, in García Mercadal (1991 ed.), 171–73, on Lisbon's Jews. Haim Beinart, *The Expulsion of the Jews from Spain* (Oxford, 2002) 284–90: Abravanel stated that 300,000 souls departed; Zacut said 270,000, of which 150,000 went to Portugal; Santa Cruz wrote that 123,000 went to Portugal. Beinart estimates that 200,000 left Spain and lists where they went. There is a recent vogue for far lesser figures and no firm evidence. I prefer those of Ladero Quesada, *España en 1492,* 174–75: at most 150,000 emigrated, perhaps 50,000 converted rather than leave. Many thousands more returned and converted by the end of 1494, and others later. "At the turn of the century, perhaps 300,000 Spaniards had some judeo-converso blood" (p. 184). Here he follows Antonio Domínguez Ortiz, *Los judeoconversos* ch. 11, who proposed a figure of 250,000 to 300,000. See also above, n11.

24. Miguel Angel Ladero Quesada, "Las juderias de Castilla segun algunos 'servicios' fiscales del siglo XV," *Sefarad* 31 (1971) 249–64, concludes that royal income from Jews was small and dwindling in 1492; and Ladero Quesada, "Los judios castellanos del

Notes to Pages 312–317

siglo XV en el arrendamiento de impuestos reales," in Salvador Moxó, ed., *Estudios sobre la sociedad hispánica en la Edad Media* (Madrid, 1975) 417–35, finds few Jews involved in treasury activity; most were *gentes modestas,* or poor, living in rural enclaves. The wealthy and tax-farming Abravanel and Señor were marked exceptions. Now see also Mark Meyerson, *A Jewish Renaissance in Fifteenth-Century Spain* (Princeton, N.J., 2004).

25. José Cabezudo Astráin, "La expulsión de los judíos zaragozanos," *Sefarad* 15 (1955) 103–136.

26. Suárez Fernández, "Documentos . . . judíos," 61–63.

27. Pilar León Tello, *Judíos de Toledo* (2 v., Madrid, 1979) doc. 90; Lea, *History* 1:138; Baer, *History* 2:434. Münzer in García Mercadal (1991 ed.), 255, thought the Dominican monastery of Santa Cruz in Avila, and San Juan de los Reyes in Toledo, both built by the monarchs, were built from properties confiscated by the Inquisition. Joseph Pérez, "Isabel la Católica and the Jews," in Boruchoff, *Isabel,* 155–70, argues that profit had nothing to do with instituting the Inquisition and the decision to expel the Jews. I would say *los reyes* did not expect to lose by it, nor did they. At bottom, it provided, as did the Inquisition, various sorts of indirect income—for construction, *mercedes,* war costs, and so on.

28. Sigüenza 2:31–32.

29. Salazar de Mendoza, 192.

30. See Antonio Domínguez Ortiz, "Los conversos de origen judío después de la expulsion," in his *La clase social de los conversos en Castilla en la edad moderna* (facsimile ed., Granada, 1991) 32ff.

31. Pico della Mirandola, *Adversus astrologos,* lib. 5, cap. 1, 12; *Opera* (1504) fol. 158, 164.

32. Machiavelli, *The Prince,* ch. 21.

33. Guicciardini, *Relazione di Spagna* (of 1512–13) in *Opere* (Florence, 1857–67) 6:270ff. The three Italians are cited in Baer, *History* 2:440.

34. See Salomón Ben Verga, *Chébet Jehuda (La Vara de Juda),* ed. Francisco Cantera Burgos (Granada, 1927) 208–9. Cf. Moshe Idel, "Religion, Thought, and Attitudes: The Impact of the Expulsion on the Jews," in Kedourie, 123–39. A messianic streak endured: in exile Abravanel wrote three messianic works, in the first establishing Jewish triumph soon to come, proving Jews the fifth kingdom of Daniel, the people of the saints of the Most High. Nevertheless, says Idel, most Jews did not give themselves up to vituperation or lamentation or mystical messianism but sought to rebuild their lives.

Chapter 16. Christopher Columbus and the Queen

1. Preamble to *The Journal of Christopher Columbus,* trans. Cecil Jane (New York, 1960) 4; Cristobal Colón, *Textos y documentos completos,* ed. Consuela Varela (2d ed., Madrid, 1984) 15–16.

2. Alessandro [Alejandro] Geraldini, *Itinararium ad regiones sub aequinoctiali plagas constitutas . . .* (Rome, 1631) lib. 14, p. 204.

3. *Diary of the First Voyage,* prologue, from a copy made by Bartolomé de Las Casas; and an entry for December 26, 1492 in Colón, *Textos,* 15–16; 101. Cf. Bernáldez, cap. 118, p. 657, stating Columbus's aims, including to circle the globe; pp. 558–60

recount his voyages. See also William D. Phillips Jr. and Carla Rahn Phillips, *The Worlds of Christopher Columbus* (Cambridge, 1992).

4. Antonio Ballesteros, *Cristóbal Colón y el descubrimiento de América* (Barcelona and Buenos Aires, 1945) 2:260.

5. *Colección de los viages y descubrimientos, que hicieron por mar los españoles desde fines del siglo XV,* coord. Martín Fernández de Navarrete (5 v., Madrid, 1825–37) (hereinafter CNavarrete) 2:4, no. 2; Bartolomé de Las Casas, *Historia de las Indias,* Agustín Millares Carlo, ed. (3v., Mexico, 1951) Lib. 1, cap. 80 (1:341–42).

6. Antonio Rumeu de Armas, *Cádiz, metrópoli de comercio con Africa en los siglos XV y XVI* (Cádiz, 1976) 12; Hipólito Sancho de Sopranis, "La genoveses en la región gaditano-xericense de 1460 a 1500," *Hispania* 8 (1948) 355–402; Heers, "Genoveses," 477; Sancho de Sopranis, *El puerto de Santa María en el descubrimiento de América* (Cádiz, 1926) 19–20, 37; Sancho de Sopranis, "Las relaciones entre los marinos de Poniente y del Puerto de Santa María en el decenio, 1482–1492," *Estudios Geográficos* no. 39 (1949) 675–94; Miguel Angel Ladero Quesada, "Palos de la Frontera en vísperas del Descubrimiento," *Revista de Indias* no. 153–54 (1978) 471–506; Ladero Quesada, "Esclavitud," 67; Vicenta Cortés Alonso, "Algunos viajes de las gentes de Huelva al Atlántico," *Anuario de Estudios Americanos* 25 (1968) 565–74.

7. Las Casas, *Historia,* lib. 1, cap. 30 (1:162–63); A. de Santa Cruz, 1: cap. 8.

8. Márquez Villanueva, "Conversos," 307n13.

9. Carl Ortwin Sauer, *The Early Spanish Main* (Berkeley, 1966) 11.

10. Valera, *Epístolas,* epís. 24, p. 31. See also Valera, *Crónica,* lxvi.

11. See Chapter 13.

12. Christopher Columbus, *The "Libro de las Profecías,"* ed. Delno West and August King (Gainesville, Fla., 1991) 9.

13. Medinaceli, "Carta del Duque de Medinaceli al Gran Cardenal Don Pedro González de Mendoza," Cogulludo, March 19, 1493, in *Cartas de particulares a Colón y Relaciones coetanéas,* ed. Juan Gil y Consuela Varela (Madrid, 1984) 144–46.

14. CNavarrete 2:6, no. 4.

15. Las Casas, *Historia,* lib. 1, cap. 178 (2:177–82).

16. Ibid., lib. 1, cap. 29 (1:156).

17. Sánchez Cantón, 28: Isabel owned a manuscript in Castilian and a book in French published in Milan in 1480.

18. John Mandeville, *Mandeville's Travels,* ed. M. C. Seymour (New York, 1968) 225–28. For Prester John: see McGinn, *Visions,* 150.

19. Valera, *Crónica . . . reyes,* cap.3, tells of the Indies and Indians as *salvajes,* men and women armed with silver for they have no iron. He also puts the earthly paradise in the beginning of the East.

20. See Oliveira Martins, 69–108; Rogers; and Elaine Sanceau, *The Land of Prester John* (New York, 1944).

21. *De Orbe Novo: The Eight Decades of Peter Martyr D'Anghera,* trans. and ed. Francis Augustus MacNutt (2 v., New York, 1912); and see below, note 27. Las Casas, *Historia,* lib. 1, cap. 5: "Colón did not call them Indies because others had seen and discovered them, but because they were the Eastern part of India-beyond-the Ganges, which, prolonged eastwards, became Western to us, since the world is round, as is said."

22. Pauline Moffitt Watts, "Prophecy and Discovery: On the Spiritual Origins of Christopher Columbus's 'Enterprise of the Indies,'" *American Historical Review* 90 (1985) 97.

23. Las Casas, *Historia,* lib. 1, cap. 31 (1:165–66).

24. See ibid., lib. 1, caps. 31–32 (1:167); Charles Verlinden and Florentino Pérez-Embid, *Cristóbal Colón y el descubrimiento de América* (Madrid, 1967) 49–51.

25. H[F]ernando Colón, *Historia del Almirante,* ed. Luis Arranz (Madrid, 1984) cap. 12, pp. 87–89; see also Ladero Quesada, *Hacienda,* 84, 216, 223–24.

26. Ladero Quesada, *Castilla y la conquista,* 299.

27. Azcona, *Isabel,* 674.

28. *Capitulaciones del almirante Don Cristóbal Colón y salvoconductos para el descubrimiento del nuevo mundo* (facsimile ed., Granada, 1980) 23, 130, 235; Antonio Rumeu de Armas, *Nueva luz sobre las capitulaciones de Santa Fe de 1492 concertadas entre los Reyes Católicos y Cristóbal Colón* (Madrid, 1985) 130; Samuel Eliot Morison, *Admiral of the Ocean Sea* (2 v., Boston, 1942) 1:103–4; Mártir, *Epistolario,* epís. 130, of May 14, 1493), however, recalled that *los reyes* provided three ships reluctantly, "because they believed the things he said to be chimerical." Isabel, that is, saw Columbus's venture as he stated it, as having only an outside chance of success.

29. CNavarrete 2:11–13, no. 11; Morison, 1:146–47.

30. See above, n. 3.

31. CNavarrete, 2:21–22, no. 15.

32. Las Casas, *Historia,* lib. 1, cap. 94 (1:382–86).

33. *Diary of the First Voyage,* prologue, from a copy made by Las Casas; and entry for December 25, 1492: in Colón, *Textos,* 15–16; 101. He also felt he must beat Antichrist, whose power was to depend on finding hidden treasure, to the gold; see anonymous, *Libro de Anticristo* (Zaragoza, 1496; Burgos 1497); Alain Milhou, *Colón y su mentalidad mesiánica en el ambiente franciscanista español* (Valladolid, 1983) 18, 134, 138. Sabine MacCormack further suggests that Columbus felt he had to prove he was not a instrument of dark forces.

Chapter 17. Isabel and the Indies

1. Colón, *Textos,* 101.

2. Ibid., 264. Las Casas, *Historia,* lib. 1; cap. 176 (2:171–74).

3. Las Casas, *Historia,* lib. 1: cap. 78 (1:332–36); see also Antonio Rumeu de Armas, *Colón en Barcelona* (Seville, 1944) 13–14.

4. Mártir, *Epistolario,* epís. 133, 134.

5. Francisco López de Gomara, *Historia de las Indias,* in BAE 22: 125.

6. Las Casas, *Historia,* lib. 1, cap. 94 (1:382–86).

7. Mártir, *Epistolario,* epís. 133, of September 13, 1493 recalls Columbus at Santa Fe discussing with *los reyes* his plan to travel through the western antipodes to a new hemisphere. Letter 135 of October 1, 1493 indicates a great discovery, but has he reached the coast of India? "Yo no niego por completo, aunque la magnitud de la esfera parece indicar lo contrario. . . ." Letter 142 of October 20, 1494: "they say . . . [Columbus] has nearly arrived at the Golden Cheresonese" (the Malay peninsula).

8. Clemencín 369.

9. Ibid., 372–73.

10. May 2, 1493; CNavarrete 2:22–23, no. 16.

11. Demetrio Ramos Pérez, ed., *La Carta de Colón sobre el descubrimiento* (Granada 1983), facsimile ed., not paginated. Rumeu de Armas, *Nueva luz,* concludes that

letter was registered only in Aragón and only after Columbus's return in 1493, and suggests material was interpolated then.

12. José María Asencio, *Cristóbal Colón* (Barcelona, 1891) 1:466–67.

13. Las Casas, *Historia,* lib. 1, cap. 79 (1:336).

14. See A. de Santa Cruz, 1:108–10; Galíndez de Carvajal, *Anales,* 285.

15. Rumeu de Armas, *Colón en Barcelona,* 39–40.

16. Las Casas, *Historia,* lib. 1, cap. 79 (1:338).

17. Ibid., 1:351. CNavarrete, doc. 45 (2:66–75). That voyage was funded with a sum of fifteen thousand ducats coming through Pinelo, who then worked with Fonseca, whom Isabel and Fernando urged "to put much attention and diligence in securing its prompt departure."

18. Fidel Fita, "Fray Bernal Buyl, o el primer apóstol del Nuevo Mundo," *Boletín Histórico* 1 (1880–81); Fita, "Fray Bernal Buyl y Cristóbal Colón: Nueva colección de cartas reales enriquecida con algunas inéditas," *BRAH* 19 (1891) 185ff; and Fita, "El primer Apostol y el primer Obispo de América," ibid., 20 (1892) 573–615. Vicens Vives, *Historia crítica,* 425: he was wounded while with Fernando fighting in Burgos on September 1, 1475. Gil and Varela, 293–96; and Münzer, 52, 114: Boyl subsequently became a diplomatic emissary of Alexander VI, and prior of three Benedictine monasteries in Málaga.

19. Enrique D. Düssel, *Historia general de la iglesia en Latin América* (Salamanca, 1983) 1:301, 707–8; Ramón Pané, *An Account of the Antiquities of the Indians,* ed. José Juan Arrom (New Haven, Conn., 1999).

20. Rumeu de Armas, *Colón en Barcelona,* 82–83.

21. Colón, *Textos,* 153.

22. Mártir, *Epistolario,* epís. 146, of December 5, 1494.

23. Las Casas, *Historia,* lib. 1, cap. 103 (1:409–13).

24. Mártir, *Epistolario,* epís. 146, 158.

25. CNavarrete, doc. 92 (2:173); Richard Konetzke, ed., *Colección de Documentos para la Historia de la Formación Social de Hispanoamérica* (5 v., Madrid, 1953) 1:2–3.

26. Mártir, *Epistolario,* epís. 164, p. 306.

27. CNavarrete, doc. 33 (3:506).

28. Ibid., doc. 102–3 (2:180–81); John H. Parry and Robert G. Keith, eds., *New Iberian World: A documentary history* (New York, 1984) 2:217–20; Azcona, *Isabel,* 680: Medina, June 22, 1497, and Alcalá, March 7, 1503: *los reyes* ask the audiencia of Valladolid to send prisoners to Cádiz to embark for Española. Las Casas, *Historia,* lib. 1, cap. 112 (1:434–48). F. Colón, cap. 65, p. 234.

29. Colón, *Textos,* doc. 24, p. 213; see also doc. 61, p. 311; Bernáldez, 669–70. On world maps the earthly paradise lay east of Eden, beyond Asia and the known world, in the ocean encircling the globe.

30. See above, note 2.

31. CNavarrete, 2:246: Bobadilla is to return Indians home.

32. Las Casas, *Historia* lib. 1, cap. 78 (1:344–45); Asensio, 2:392ff.; Gil and Varela, 285–90: of the five who came with Bobadilla, one, Francisco Ruiz, Cisneros's *mayordomo,* returned some Indians home; two others, Leudelle and Tisan, were themselves returning. See Azcona, *Isabel,* 702–3, on the thousands baptized by 1500; and n 38.

33. Sauer, 106.

34. Mártir, *Decadas,* lib. 7, cap. 4; Morison, 596.

35. F. Colón, cap. 85, p. 280.

36. Diego Guillén de Avila, *Panegírico de la Reina donã Isabel* (Valladolid, 1509; facsimile ed., Madrid, 1951); cf. chapter 14, note 82; see also Catedra, *Historiografía.*

37. Ovando's instructions: Codoin 31:13ff.; see also Ursula Lamb, *Frey Nicolás de Ovando: Gobernador de las Indias (1501–1509)* (Madrid, 1956) 23–161; Sauer, 147.

38. Las Casas, *Historia,* lib. 1, cap. 78 (1:334); Gil and Varela, 285–86; see also Düssel, 1:301. Cisneros sent his adjutant, Francisco Ruiz, and two other Franciscans close to him. Ruiz returned in six months; he brought with him as prisoner Bobadilla to be tried for peculation and other complaints lodged against him. See also William Eugene Shiels, S.J., *King and Church: The Rise and Fall of the Patronato Real* (Chicago, 1961); and Daniel Olmedo, S.J., "La primera evangelización de América (1492–1504)," *Abside* 17 (1953) 35–67.

39. See Antonio de la Torre, "Los canarios de Gomera vendidos como esclavos en 1489," *AEA* 2 (1950) 47–51; Azcona, *Isabel,* 664; Dom Wölfel, 1077–79; Felipe Fernández-Armesto, *Before Columbus* (London, 1987) 209.

40. See Ladero Quesada, *España de los Reyes,* 401–15, 529.

41. Konetzke, *Coleccion,* 1:5,9.

42. Ibid., 1:9–13.

43. CNavarrete 2, doc. 17, pp. 414–16.

44. Konetzke, *Coleccíon,* 1:16–17.

45. Isabel la Católica, *Testamentaria,* ed. Antonio de la Torre y del Cerro (Valladolid, 1968) 482. Population estimates vary: Sherburne F. Cook and Woodrow Borah, "The Aboriginal Population of Hispaniola," in Cook and Borah, eds., *Essays in Population History* (3 v., Berkeley, 1971) 1:376–41, estimate a drop from 3,770,000 in 1492 to 92,300 in 1508; cf. Sauer, 65–66, 155–56; David Henige, "On the Contact Population of Hispaniola: History as Higher Mathematics," in William F. Keegan, ed., *Earliest Hispanic/Native American Interaction in the Caribbean* (New York, 1991) 291–37; and Kathleen Deagan, "The Archaeology of the Spanish Contact Period in the Caribbean," *Journal of World Prehistory* 2 (1988) 187–233, reprinted in Keegan, 329ff.

46. *Relation of the Fourth Voyage,* July 7, 1503, in Colón, *Textos,* 327.

47. Columbus, prologue to his *"Libro de las Profecias,"*; LeGoff, *Medieval Imagination,* 48: the Woman represented the holy people in the messianic age.

48. Joaquín González Moreno, "El archivo de Medinaceli," *Archivo Hispalense* 34 (1961) 329.

49. Appropriately enough, Fonseca also became bishop of Burgos, for Castile's right to exploring the Atlantic and to claim newly found lands was based on legal arguments put forth by an earlier bishop of Burgos, Alonso de Cartagena.

50. *De Orbe Novo of Peter Martyr D'Anghera,* 66.

Chapter 18. The Catholic Kings

1. Nebrija, preface to *Decadas,* cited in Menéndez Pidal, "Significance," 401–2.

2. Azcona, *Isabel,* 720–21.

3. Mártir, *Epistolario* 1: epís. 125. For a fuller account by a page of Prince Juan's: Gonzalo Fernández de Oviedo, *Batallas y quinquagenas,* ed. Juan Bautista de Avalle-Arce (Salamanca, 1989) 346–48. See for the attending royal physicians and others: Marcelino V. Amasuno Sárraga, in Boruchoff, *Isabel,* 121–53.

4. Mártir, *Epistolario* 1: epís. 126, 127, and see 130.

5. Appendix to Gonzalo Fernández de Oviedo, *Libro de la Cámara del Principe Don Juan* (Madrid, 1870) 195.

6. Clemencín, 355; and see pp. 356–66, for the exchange of letters between Isabel and Talavera cited here.

7. Umberto Eco, in an interview by Clyde Haberman, *N. Y. Times,* December 13, 1988: "In Puritan countries, success shows God's benevolence. In Catholic countries, you're sure God loves you only when you've suffered." Cf. Márquez Villanueva, *In vestigaciones,* 292–93: God sends tribulations as a purge; Christ suffered, *sin lucha no gloria.* This effect of tribulation is in Paul, especially Heb. 12:4; and see above Isabel's letters to Enrique regarding her tribulations.

8. Talavera, "Oficio in deditione urbis Granatae," cited in Rodríguez Valencia, *Isabel* 1:369.

9. Mártir, *Epistolario* 1: epís. 108.

10. Ibid. See also José García Oro, *El Cardenal Cisneros* (2 v., Madrid, 1992) 1:3–47.

11. Mártir, *Epistolario* 1: epís. 150.

12. Rodríguez Valencia, *Isabel* 1:303–4. *Lucero de la vida christiana,* first published in 1493, would, a century later, after the Council of Trent had defined orthodoxy, be expurgated by censors of the Inquisition, if for its theology and not for its view of monarchy. See Yarza Luaces, *Reyes Católicos,* 147–55, on the new Christological emphasis in the 1490s, particularly on the Passion. He also links it "to explaining with clarity to Jews and *conversos* the messianic and redemptive nature of Jesus Christ" (p. 146), the central issue of contention with Jews. See also his discussions of Isabel's taste, books, and art.

13. A. de Santa Cruz, 1:99; Padilla, 21–22.

14. Clemencín, 378.

15. Suárez Fernández, *Trastámara,* 581.

16. Mártir, *Epistolario* 1: epís. 143.

17. Ibid., epís. 24, 29, and elsewhere.

18. Salazar de Mendoza, fols. 358, 362.

19. Ibid., fol. 358; Azcona, *Isabel,* 456, 725–26.

20. Zurita, *Anales* 6, lib. 7, cap. 29.

21. Hurtado de Mendoza, lib. 1.

22. See Azcona, *Isabel,* 576–601; Azcona, *Elección y reforma;* and José García Oro, *La reforma de los religiosos españoles en tiempo de los Reyes Católicos* (Valladolid, 1969) 132: "Toda la historia de la reforma en Castilla lleva muy marcado el sello isabelino."

23. Mártir, *Epistolario* 1: epís. 163.

24. See above, Chapter 15, note 24, and Chapter 10, note 51, concerning the ongoing debate as to whether the Inquisition profited the royal treasury.

25. Sicroff, 122.

26. See above, note 2.

27. Mártir, *Epistolario* 1: epís. 146.

28. Ibid., epís. 171.

29. Ibid., epís. 168.

30. Ibid., epís. 172.

31. Ibid., epís. 174.

32. Ibid., epís. 176.

33. Ibid.

34. Ibid., epís. 179.

35. Ibid., epís. 182.

36. Ibid., epís. 183.

37. Ibid., epís. 192.
38. Ibid., epís. 197.
39. Marineo Sículo, *Cosas memorables,* fol. 186.
40. P. E. Russell, ed., *Spain: A Companion to Spanish Studies* (London and New York, 1985) 268.
41. Linda Martz, in conversation.
42. A. de Santa Cruz, 1:267.
43. See Angus MacKay, "Courtly Love and Lust in Loja," in Alan Deyermond and Ian Macpherson, eds., *The Age of the Catholic Monarchs, 1474–1516* (Liverpool, 1989) 83–94: they had some substantiating data: a case record in Loja of widespread wife-swapping, homosexuality, sexual punning that played on religious language, and assertions of love sickness and diabolic influences indicated something of the turn-of-century social reality.
44. Padilla, 79–80.
45. Pedro M. Cátedra, *La historiografía en verso en la época de los Reyes Católicos: Juan Barba y su* Consolatoria de Castilla (Salamanca, 1989) 46–47, 54–57, 171–370: The poem of 1499 praises Isabel and bundles many themes by then close to standard: The queen was sent by divine providence (54a-d); she is the consolation of Spain, a true intermediary between God and Castile. Her virtues and graces are saintly (prolog, line 4, 6c). God has chosen *los reyes* (32f); they have appeared like a comet. They are *brazos ejecutores* of Providence and also its reflection. They waged civil war as a judgment of God, but especially the Granada war. At Lucena, "Christ fought for his Castilians" (183d). The reader should render thanks. That Isabel is prayerful is a sign of her close relationship with God. Within the royal responsibility for prayer and war, her role is to pray (cf. 276–77); yet the author also connects her role to that of the heavenly cavalry and spiritual combat (c. 309–11). He assumes the devil at work, especially among judaizers, and he displays an apocalyptic cast of mind, providential and messianic.

Chapter 19. The Queen and Her Daughter

1. Bernáldez, cap. 155, pp. 691–92; Galíndez de Carvajal, *Anales,* 295.
2. Ladero Quesada, *Mudéjares,* 77.
3. Mártir, *Epistolario* 1: epís. 212.
4. Ladero Quesada, *Mudéjares,* doc. 85, pp. 262–63.
5. Ibid., doc. 86; see also Ladero Quesada, "Isabel y los musulmanes," 106–10.
6. Bernáldez, 694; Suárez Fernández, *Trastámara,* 566; and see Clemencín, 392–95.
7. Mártir, *Epistolario,* 1: epís. 215; see also Clemencín, 392–95.
8. Márquez Villanueva, *Investigaciones,* 302–3.
9. Güejar: A. de Santa Cruz, 1:193.
10. Azcona, *Isabel,* 554.
11. Ladero Quesada, *Mudéjares,* 370.
12. Mártir, *Epistolario,* 1: epís. 221.
13. Bernáldez, 718; Ladero Quesada, *Mudéjares,* 81n66; Ladero Quesada, "Isabel y los musulmanes," 109.
14. Azcona, *Isabel,* 555.
15. Ladero Quesada, *Mudéjares,* doc.148; Ladero Quesada, *España de los Reyes,* 334–41; Ladero Quesada, *Reyes Católicos,* 269: Castile had no more than twenty-five

thousand *mudéjares*. Ladero Quesada, "Isabel y los musulmanes," 110–12. The royal decree of 1502 gave *mudéjares* the option of baptism or emigration but only to mameluke Egypt and certain other places, and only through Vizcayan ports. Such decrees followed for other kingdoms of Spain, until its *moriscos* were all expelled in 1611.

16. Ladero Quesada, *Mudéjares*, doc. 148. In 1501, Cisneros had the Koran and other books in Arabic confiscated; if scientific, they were sent to the library at Alcalá, and if not, burned in a huge public bonfire. It is estimated that in the sixteenth century there were perhaps one hundred thousand slaves in Spain, most Muslim.

17. Ladero Quesada, "Isabel y los musulmanes," 112–14: the treasurers of her Cámara indicate Isabel and her women wore some *morisca* clothing, especially in daily life, including embroidered shirts in Moorish style, often with arabic letters, and Moorish slippers, narrow and pointed. Royal interiors had Moorish spaces—alcoves, and divans, linens and hangings—and Isabel possessed Granadan jewelry. Knights jousting before her sometimes dressed in Moorish fashion, and rode *a la jineta;* and she had Muslim servants. In art, however, her preference was for things Italian or Flemish. Nor does material taste necessarily signify other sorts of cultural liking.

18. Lynn, 22.

19. Mártir, *Epistolario* 1: epís. 216.

20. See above, note 1.

21. See Torre and Suárez, *Documentos,* 3:64–79.

22. Padilla, 68.

23. Gutierre Gómez de Fuensalida, *Correspondencia de . . . Embajada en Alemania, Flandres, e Inglaterra (1469–1509)* (Madrid, 1907) 113.

24. Azcona, *Isabel,* 718, cites Diego Ramírez de Villaescusa, to Almazán, Antwerp (Amberes), August 12, 1501: in Archivo Histórico, Salazar A 9, fol. 132; see also C. R. Fort, "Juicios de Bergenroth sobre Catalina y Juana de Aragón, hijas de los Reyes Católicos," *BAH* 77 (1920) 319–22.

25. A. de Santa Cruz, 1:245.

26. Mártir, *Epistolario* 1: epís. 222.

27. Fuensalida, 182: March 22, 1501; Mártir, *Epistolario* 1: epís. 222; Padilla, 127–29.

28. Mártir, *Epistolario* 1: epís. 221.

29. Padilla, 80–88.

30. *Cartas autógrafas,* no. 13.

31. Padilla, 84–88.

32. *Cartas autógrafas,* no.14.

33. Mártir, *Epistolario* 2: 249.

34. Torre and Suárez, *Documentos,* 3: doc. 513.

35. Mártir, *Epistolario* 2: epís. 250; A. de Santa Cruz, 1:255–57; Fernando, while agreeing to Philip while he was in France arranging for Charles to marry Claudia, sent along with him Bernardo Boyl, to make certain Spain's interests were represented. Suárez Fernández, *Trastámara,* 599–600; and Padilla, 91–93: Philip was very ill in France, convalesced with his sister, Margaret, who had just married the duke of Savoy.

36. Mata Carriazo, "Tres cortesanos," 9–18; Mártir, *Epistolario,* 2:68–70.

37. Martir, *Epistolario* 2:47.

38. Prudencio de Sandoval, *Historia de Carlos V* (3 v., Madrid, 1955–56) 1:23–24.

39. Mártir, *Epistolario,* epís. 255 (2:48).

40. A. de Santa Cruz,1:301; Padilla, 109–12; Mártir, *Epistolario* 2:63–67.

41. Bernáldez, 695.

42. Mártir, *Epistolario,* 2:86; Nicasio Alonso Cortés, "Dos médicos de los Reyes

Católicos," *Hispania* 11 (1951) 607–57; her physicians during her last years were Nicolás de Soto, Julián Gutiérrez, and Fernán Alvarez de La Reina (or de Guadalupe). She was also attended by one Gracián Mexian Alcaráz, and, from July of 1504, Juan de la Parra, educated at Guadalupe, who had attended Prince Juan and had been sent as the infante Fernando's resident doctor to Arévalo. Llanos y Torriglia, *Hogar*, 75: her travels, her physicians said, caused "that swelling of the legs . . . and those cutaneous exudations that were the first symptoms of her last illness."

43. Mártir, *Epistolario* 2:86; Alonso Cortés, "Dos médicos," 605–57; Azcona, *Isabel*, 733–35.

44. Fuensalida, 196–97.

45. For Isabel's own account: F. Llanos y Torriglia, "Sobre la fuga frustrada de doña Juana la Loca," *BAH* 102 (1933) 97–114; Fuensalida, 196–98, for Juana at La Mota; see also Padilla, 114–16; Mártir, *Epistolario*, 2:74–76.

46. Fuensalida, 210–12, 258; Mártir, *Epistolario* 2:83–84. She had written Philip herself in February, chiding him for having treated Juana badly. Philip responded by agreeing that Juana was hotheaded and was later sorry for things she said, but in what was undoubtedly a misguided effort to be conciliatory, he also said that of course Juana's behavior stemmed from the great love she bore him.

47. *Cronicón de Valladolid*, 219. Cf. Alvarez Gato in Chapter 14, note 82.

48. Sánchez Canton, 95: Isabel's own purchases of tapestries were largely chivalresque in theme, including in 1504 "The History of the Triumph of Love." She had more than ninety of them.

49. Azcárate, "Sentido," 202, 217–20.

50. Pedro de Bejar, who became its prior that year, was a confessor of hers.

51. Now see A. de Santa Cruz, 1:302–4; Azcona, *Isabel*, 721–24; Sandoval, 25; Bernáldez, 721–22.

52. Fuensalida, 286–87.

53. The will itself is transcribed in Antonio de la Torre y del Cerro, ed., *Testamentaría de Isabel la Católica* (Valladolid, 1968) 446–75. The codicil follows on pp. 478–85. All quotations here I have translated from there. Isabel dictated the will to the secretary Gaspar de Gricio, a trusted retainer of Fernando's; it is possible that some tweaking of that testament took place.

54. Alfonso Valdés, *Diálogo de las cosaa ocurridas en Roma*, ed. J. F. Montesinos (Madrid, 1956) 139.

55. She is perhaps more closely following Cardinal Mendoza, who in his own *Testamento* made a very similar statement and invoked as advocates the two Saints John, Christ, and particularly Mary. Mendoza too wanted no serge worn for him and named Cisneros an executor. For the Spanish concept of a good death: Juan Manuel, *Libro de los Estados*, ed. Ian R. MacPherson and Robert Brian Tate (Madrid 1991) cap. 58; Francesc Eixemenis, *Art de buen morir*, published in Castilian in Zaragoza 1479–81, 1481–91, and in Valencia in 1497; and Adeline Rucquoi, "De la resignación al miedo: La muerte en Castilla en el s. XV," in *La idea y el sentimiento de la muerte en la historia y en el arte de la edad media* (Santiago de Compostela, 1988).

56. Pablo de Santa María, in *CC* 2:1565.11: *"aquella serpiente grande Lucifer."*

57. See A. de Santa Cruz, 1:267; Torre, *Documentos* 6:254–55; and Joaquín Yarza Luaces, *Formas artísticas de lo imaginario* (Barcelona, 1987), 126–29, on Saint Michael and the relationship between Virgo in the zodiac and the Virgin Mary and Libra, the scales, identified with justice.

58. Antonio de la Torre, "La colección sigilografía del Archivo de la Catedral de Valencia," *Archivo de Arte Valenciano* 1:4 (1902).

59. Francesc Eixemenis, *Llibre de les dones*, fols. 246ff.: "com en paradis ha jocs, cants, balls e rialles." Cf. *Siete Partidas* pt. 6, ley 1, tit. 1. Alfonso X, "El Fuero Real de España," [1255], in *Los códigos españoles concordados y anotados* (2d ed., Madrid, 1872) 1: lib. 1, tít. 2, pt. 2: God first organized his court in hierarchical order: archangels, angels [and so forth,;] . . . and that ordered extended to human society and politics.

60. LeGoff, *Medieval Imagination,* 75: on the good life and death, and on salvation via a rite of passage. He says prayers were thought more effective than individual alms, and especially to help rescue the soul from purgatory.

61. Azcona, *Isabel,* 743–58, on a 1503 report on sources of income.

62. Fuensalida, 297–304.

63. See Padilla, 119; A. de Santa Cruz, 1:302–4; and Sandoval, 26.

64. Marineo Sículo, *Obra,* (1530) lib. 3, f. 181–87; Padilla, 116; Galíndez de Carvajal, "Adiciones genealógicas" to Pulgar's *Claros varones,* in Codoin 18:438. For extreme unction: José Luis González Novalín, in Ricardo García-Villaslada, ed., *Historia de la Iglesia en España* (Madrid, 1980) 3-1:359.

65. Azcona, *Isabel,* 741.

66. Gracia Dei, 377.

67. Stated in an anonymous short summary of Talavera's life, written three years later: BN Ms. 2878. Original.

Epilogue

1. Alvar Gómez de Castro, *De rebus gestis a Francisco Ximenio Cisnerio, Archiepiscopo Toletano* (Alcalá de Hénares, 1569) lib. 8, f. 52r.

2. Fernando's will; Madrigalejo, January 22, 1516. AGS PR leg. 29, fol. 22. Copy.

3. One Alvaro de Mercado citing the *corregidor* García Sarmiento during an investigation held in 1507 by the royal council; "Informe o Pesquisa contra algunos que hablaron mal de la Reina Católica y su marido," May 17, 1507. AGS. *Estado Castilla*, leg. 1 (2), fol. 192.

4. Rodríguez Valencia, *Isabel,* 1:259–61, includes other encomiums; Mártir, *Epistolario* 2:259; Bernáldez, cap. 202.

5. McGinn, *Visions,* 184–85; Bernáldez, 322–23.

6. Codoin 18:420. Torre, *Documentos* 6:393–94; and Galíndez de Cavajal, app. to *Anales,* 420–21.

7. Fuensalida, 310.

8. Padilla, 120–21, who does not mention Philip, although this is Philip's chronicle. Sandoval, 25, says *pendones* were raised for Juana, "*como proprietaria de estos reinos, y por el rey don Felipe, su legítimo marido*"; this was to follow the Isabelline formula. Cf. Angel de la Plaza Bores, "Exequias por Isabel la Católica y proclamación de Juana la Loca en Valladolid, Noviembre de 1504," *Archivo Ibero-Americana* 30 (1970) 371–77.

9. Suárez Fernández, *Trastámara,* 617.

10. Granada, November 30, 1504. AHN leg. 3466. fol. 89v.; Mártir, *Epistolario* 2:88–89.

11. Rodríguez Valencia, *Isabel* 1:20.

12. A. de Santa Cruz, 306ff.; Azcona, *Isabel,* 423.

13. Mártir, *Epistolario* 2:120ff.; Márquez Villanueva, *Investigaciones,* 132–54; app. 19–20; Azcona, *Isabel,* 423–24; Azcona, *Elección,* 259–65.

14. Gracian: see Suárez Fernández, *Trastámara*, 641. Fernando also annexed Germaine's Navarre to Aragón.

15. Suárez Fernández, *Trastámara*, 652.

16. Galíndez de Carvajal, *Anales*, 562–63.

17. An inscription at their foot, probably reflecting what Fernando wanted remembered as Isabel's and his own greatest achievements, reads: "Destroyers of the Mohammedan sect and the annihilators of insidious heretics, Fernando of Aragón and Isabel of Castile—husband and wife, undivided in opinion—lie enclosed by this tomb." Yarza Luaces, *Reyes Católicos*, 142: In Italy, Iñigo López de Mendoza, count of Tendilla, made the arrangements with the sculptor, Fancelli.

18. Sandoval, 17.

19. William S. Maltby, *Alba* (Berkeley, 1983) 305.

20. Bacon, 197–98.

21. A. de Santa Cruz, 1:303.

22. See Menéndez Pidal, "Catholic Kings," 417–20; Juan de Mata Carriazo, ed., "La política de los reyes católicos explicada al principe Don Carlos," *Archivo Hispalense* no. 13 (1950) 129–62; Francisco Guicciardini, "Relación de España," in Fabie, ed., 193–229.

Index

WITHDRAWN